JENNIFER SERRAVALLO

The Reading Strategies Book

YOUR **EVERYTHING GUIDE** TO DEVELOPING SKILLED READERS

HEINEMANN • Portsmouth, NH

Heinemann
361 Hanover Street
Portsmouth, NH 03801–3912
www.heinemann.com

Offices and agents throughout the world

The author and publisher wish to thank those who have generously given permission to reprint borrowed material:

Figure 2.C: Reading Interest Survey from "'But There's Nothing Good to Read' (In the Library Media Center)" by Denice Hildebrandt, originally appearing in *Media Spectrum: The Journal for Library Media Specialists in Michigan* (vol. 28, no. 3, pp. 34–37, Fall 2001). Reprinted by permission of the author.

"Backyard Digging" from *Playing with Poems: Word Study Lessons for Shared Reading* by Zoë Ryder White. Copyright © 2008 by Zoë Ryder White. Published by Heinemann, Portsmouth, NH. Used by permission of the author.

Figure 11.A: Rubric for Evaluating Responses to Vocabulary and Figurative Language Questions in Fiction from *Independent Reading Assessment: Fiction* by Jennifer Serravallo. Copyright © 2012 by Jennifer Serravallo. Published by Scholastic Inc. Reprinted by permission of the publisher.

Figure 11.B: Rubric for Evaluating Responses to Vocabulary and Figurative Language Questions in Nonfiction from *Independent Reading Assessment: Nonfiction* by Jennifer Serravallo. Copyright © 2013 by Jennifer Serravallo. Published by Scholastic Inc. Reprinted by permission of the publisher.

See page x for image credits.

Cataloging-in-Publication Data is on file at the Library of Congress.
ISBN: 978-0-325-07433-7

Editor: Zoë Ryder White
Production: Victoria Merecki
Cover and interior designs: Suzanne Heiser
Typesetter: Gina Poirier, Gina Poirier Design
Manufacturing: Steve Bernier

Printed in the United States of America on acid-free paper

19 20 21 22 23 WC 24 23 22 21 20
February 2020 printing

Contents

Goal 3 — 76

Supporting Print Work: *Increasing Accuracy and Integrating Sources of Information*

Goal 4 — 104

Teaching Fluency: *Reading with Phrasing, Intonation, and Automaticity*

Goal 5 130 Supporting Comprehension in Fiction: *Understanding Plot and Setting*

Goal 6 162 Supporting Comprehension in Fiction: *Thinking About Characters*

Goal 7 — 190

Supporting Comprehension in Fiction: *Understanding Themes and Ideas*

Goal 8 — 218

Supporting Comprehension in Nonfiction: *Determining Main Topic(s) and Idea(s)*

Goal 9 — 246
Supporting Comprehension in Nonfiction: *Determining Key Details*

Goal 10 — 270
Supporting Comprehension in Nonfiction: *Getting the Most from Text Features*

Goal 11 | 296

Improving Comprehension in Fiction and Nonfiction: *Understanding Vocabulary and Figurative Language*

Goal 12 | 324

Supporting Students' Conversations: *Speaking, Listening, and Deepening Comprehension*

All the strategies in this book are flexible—they can be used in any instructional format, and with most books.

—*Jennifer Serravallo*

Image credits

front cover: ©Mark Airs/Getty Images (target); ©Blinka/Shutterstock (book)

page 11: ©YarKova/Shutterstock

page 24 (left to right): ©iStockphoto.com/HIP; ©Dr. Morley Read/Shutterstock/HIP; ©Sarin Kunthong/Shutterstock

page 25: ©Brand New Images/Lifesize/Getty Images/HIP

page 29: ©Houghton Mifflin Harcourt/HIP

page 31: ©Houghton Mifflin Harcourt/HIP

page 35: ©Jan Hyrman/Shutterstock

page 39: ©Artville/Getty Images/HIP

page 43 (left to right): ©Houghton Mifflin Harcourt/HIP; ©Comstock/Getty Images/HIP

page 56: Michelle Baker and Nick Christoff

page 81: ©Houghton Mifflin Harcourt/HIP

pages 94 and 97: ©dyoma/Shutterstock

page 109: ©Jarvis & Associates LLC/Houghton Mifflin Harcourt/HIP

page 111: ©gst/Shutterstock/HIP

page 120: ©tsnebula23/Shutterstock

page 124: ©Scanty Nebula/iStockphoto.com/HIP

page 127 (left to right): ©Camilla$$/Shutterstock; ©Christine Dodd/Shutterstock; ©Tyler Olson/Shutterstock

page 134: ©Akiko Aoki/Moment/Getty Images/HIP

page 172: ©Park Street Photography/Houghton Mifflin Harcourt/HIP

page 187 (clockwise): ©John F. Kennedy Presidential Library and Museum/HIP; NASA, Alan L. Bean [public domain] via Wikimedia Commons; United Press International, photographer unknown [public domain] via Wikimedia Commons; Phil Stanziola, NYWT&S staff photographer [public domain] via Wikimedia Commons; Abbie Rowe [public domain] via Wikimedia Commons

page 198: ©Houghton Mifflin Harcourt/HIP

pages 223 and 321 (left to right): ©Kevin Schafer/Alamy/HIP; ©Getty Images/HIP

page 237: ©avajjon/Getty Images/iStockphoto.com/HIP (dinosaur); ©Sam D Cruz/Shutterstock/HIP (grassland); ©Robert Marien/Corbis/HIP (fox)

page 259 (left to right): "RIAN archive 612748 Valentina Tereshkova" by RIA Novosti archive, image #612748/Alexander Mokletsov/CC-BY-SA 3.0. Licensed under CC-BY-SA 3.0 via Wikimedia Commons; ©NASA/Harcourt/HIP; NASA on the Commons (Christa McAuliffe and Barbara Morgan) via Wikimedia Commons

page 277: ©foryouinf/Shutterstock/HIP

page 278: ©Han maomin/Shutterstock

page 305: ©Kaphoto/iStockphoto.com/HIP

page 322 (left to right): ©Shutterstock/HIP; ©tsnebula23/Shutterstock

page 328: ©Houghton Mifflin Harcourt/HIP

page 334: Michelle Baker and Nick Christoff

Acknowledgments

Thank you to Gail Ryan, for your wise marching orders.

A heartfelt thanks to the teachers and administrators from far and wide including Tulsa, Oklahoma; New York, New York; Souderton, Pennsylvania; Atlanta, Georgia; Wilton, Connecticut; all over New Jersey; and many many more places, who piloted the lessons, offered feedback, and sent in visuals shown throughout:

Jaclyn Acker
Corey Allen
Elisha Ann
Andrea Batchler
Tricia Buce
Caitlyn Buck
Cheryl Bucko
Jenifer D'Agosta
Laura Dacorte
Amy Darsey
Jamie DeMinco
F. J. DeRobertis
Gina Dignon
Kim Dyer
Irene Fang
Jennifer Felipe
Chelsie Flake
Dawn Glowacki
Merridy Gnagey
Tara Goldsmith
Barbara Golub
Katherine Hale
Kim Johnston
Elisha Li
Diane MacEwen
Rosie Maurantonio
Jessica Mazzone
Jamie Mendolsohn
Faye Odon
Alisa Palazzi
Sari-Lynn Peiser
Heather Pence
Barbara Pine
Lisa Reily
Maggie Beattie Roberts
Patricia Sepessy
Bethany Shellenberger
Lisa Shotts
Laurie Smilak
Meadow Smith
Renee Supple
Cassie Tomsho
Ashley Traino
Cheryl Tyler
Tricia Winkler
Tifanny Robles

Thank you to the wise educators who read early versions of various chapters and offered invaluable feedback:

Kathy Collins
Matthew Glover
Cheryl Tyler
Joseph Yukish

Thank you to my dog walker-slash-copy editor-slash-organizer neighbor David A. M. Wilensky who spent many hours helping me keep all the moving parts in line.

A very hearty thank you to the Heinemann team, from editorial to production to design to marketing, for working tirelessly through all the details from large to teeny tiny to make this book easy to read, easy to use, visually stunning, and available to all:

Cindy Black
Eric Chalek
Suzanne Heiser
Victoria Merecki
Kiele Raymond
Elizabeth Silvis
Denis Skeean
Zoë White
Brett Whitmarsh

Thank you to my mentors and colleagues including Lucy Calkins, Kathleen Tolan, and the staff developers of the past decade and a half from the Teachers College Reading and Writing Project.

And most importantly to my family: Jen, Lola, and Vivie. Thank you for your support, love, encouragement, and laughs.

A Very Brief Introduction to Principles, Research, and Theory, and How to Use This Book

When I showed an early draft of this book to a colleague, she remarked, "It's like you're making a reading teacher's version of Mark Bittman's *How to Cook Everything*!" (2008). I could see the analogy—this *is* a book of "reading recipes" in a way. A clear, concise cookbook is a great model for what on-the-go teachers might need to pick and choose strategies, to target what each reader needs, and to support their differentiated instruction.

You might wonder why I decided to write this book, now. Part of the inspiration came from emails, tweets, and in-person requests from the readers of some of my other Heinemann books. Since *Conferring with Readers* (Serravallo and Goldberg 2007), I've been asked almost daily for "More of what's on page 93," which is essentially a one-page table that includes bunches of strategies that you'd use for readers who read at level L.

And I get it—why create your own recipe for beef bourguignon when one already exists? Wouldn't it be helpful to have a big list of what someone else has already thought up? Not that any cookbook, or this book for that matter, would become a script that you'd follow like a robot—in your kitchen you might swap out the beef stock for chicken stock, or decide you like the meat browned before you

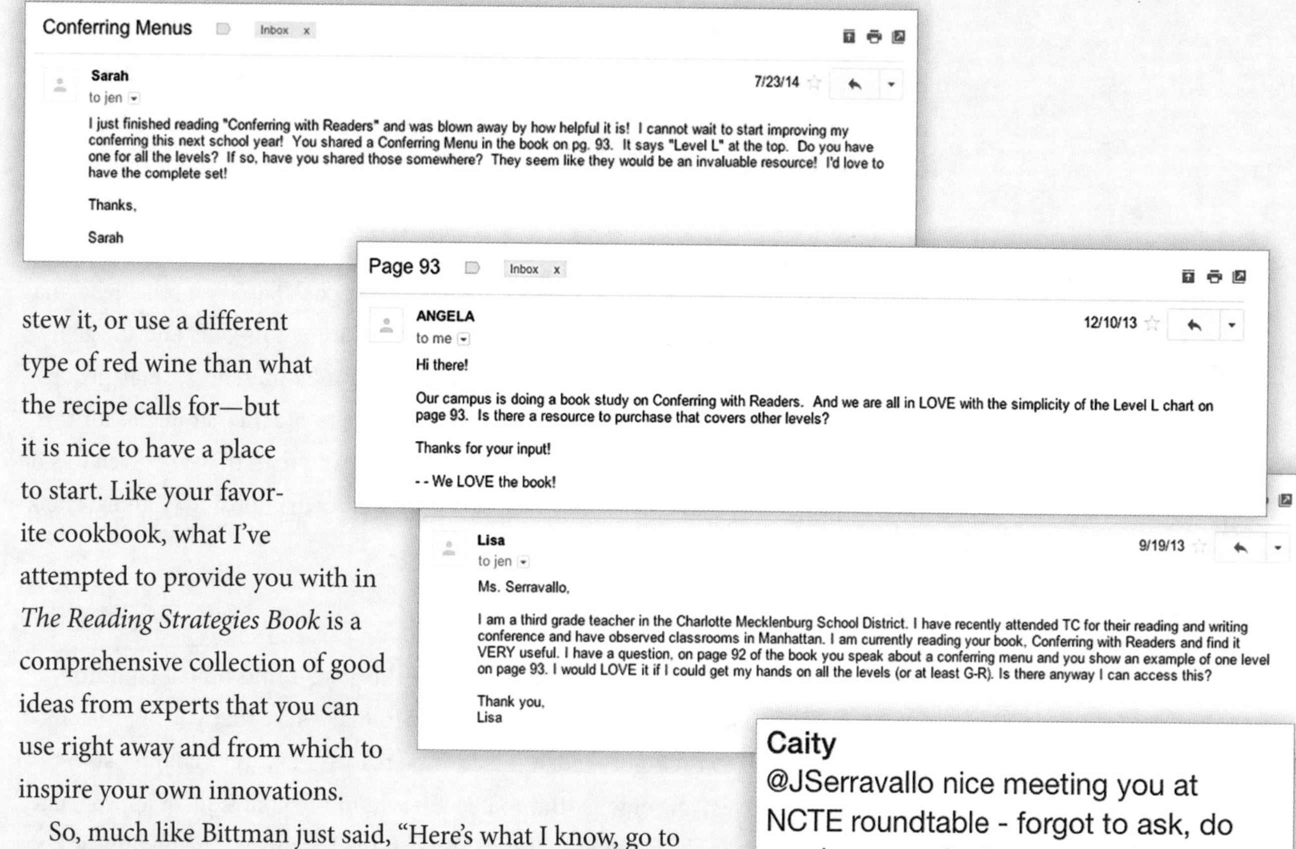
Conferring Menus — Inbox

Sarah — 7/23/14
to jen

I just finished reading "Conferring with Readers" and was blown away by how helpful it is! I cannot wait to start improving my conferring this next school year! You shared a Conferring Menu in the book on pg. 93. It says "Level L" at the top. Do you have one for all the levels? If so, have you shared those somewhere? They seem like they would be an invaluable resource! I'd love to have the complete set!

Thanks,

Sarah

Page 93 — Inbox

ANGELA — 12/10/13
to me

Hi there!

Our campus is doing a book study on Conferring with Readers. And we are all in LOVE with the simplicity of the Level L chart on page 93. Is there a resource to purchase that covers other levels?

Thanks for your input!

- - We LOVE the book!

Lisa — 9/19/13
to jen

Ms. Serravallo,

I am a third grade teacher in the Charlotte Mecklenburg School District. I have recently attended TC for their reading and writing conference and have observed classrooms in Manhattan. I am currently reading your book, Conferring with Readers and find it VERY useful. I have a question, on page 92 of the book you speak about a conferring menu and you show an example of one level on page 93. I would LOVE it if I could get my hands on all the levels (or at least G-R). Is there anyway I can access this?

Thank you,
Lisa

Caity
@JSerravallo nice meeting you at NCTE roundtable - forgot to ask, do you have conferring menus for L-Z to share? conferring book only has L

stew it, or use a different type of red wine than what the recipe calls for—but it is nice to have a place to start. Like your favorite cookbook, what I've attempted to provide you with in *The Reading Strategies Book* is a comprehensive collection of good ideas from experts that you can use right away and from which to inspire your own innovations.

So, much like Bittman just said, "Here's what I know, go to town," I'm trying to give the strategies I rely on most often over to you all. I acknowledge that this book doesn't include literally *everything*, just as Bittman's doesn't, but it does cover a lot of ground. I hope that I've offered a slew of helpful "reading recipes," but also helpful suggestions for how to tweak them to make the teaching your own, so that it best suits the learners in front of you. I hope that this book becomes as dog-eared, sticky-noted, and coffee-stained as your favorite cookbook, but I also hope that by using this book you become ever more confident in your teaching and your ability to coach and prompt readers. I hope that one day you internalize all that's in here and outgrow it.

Just as Bittman includes recipes for stir-fry, though he certainly didn't invent the idea of a stir-fry, the strategies I've crafted in this book stand on the shoulders of decades of research and master teachers from whose work I've been fortunate to learn. I've tried to offer thanks to these greats by "tipping my hat" to them when I could. Although I fear there are places where I've forgotten people, or haven't properly credited the absolute origin of an idea, I feel grateful to be a part of a profession where there is so much sharing and comingling of thinking that one can imagine this would be a hard thing to do.

Navigating the Book

In truth, this book could have been organized any number of ways—by skill, by reading level, by genre. I chose to organize the book into chapters by goal, as I have been very influenced lately by the research of John Hattie (2009). After synthesizing thousands of studies, he concluded that goals coupled with teacher feedback make one of the biggest differences on student achievement and progress. An ideal classroom, I think, is one in which every student has a clear goal, based on reliable formative assessment information. The student would be aware of this goal, and the goal would also guide the teacher's individualized instruction (conferences, small groups). In this ideal reading classroom, students are given time to practice strategies for this goal with the teacher in conferences and small groups, and then they are given lots of time to work independently as they read books of their own choosing (Calkins 2000; Collins 2004; Serafini 2001; Serravallo 2012, 2013a).

How Do I Choose Which Goal to Begin With?

The thirteen chapters that follow are thirteen of the goals I find I most commonly match readers to in grades K–8. The first step is to make sure that you are matching the right goal to the right reader. It is for this reason that every chapter starts off with a brief overview of what the goal is, for whom the goal is most appropriate, and how to assess with that goal in mind. You can read across all the beginning sections of the thirteen chapters that follow to get a crash course in formative assessment and/or pick up a copy of either my Literacy Teacher's Playbook series (2013b, 2014) or Independent Reading Assessment series (2012, 2013a) for more guidance on formative assessment.

After you've done some formative assessments, you may realize that a student could benefit from more than one goal. In fact, this is likely! To know where to start, I will share what I would generally advise, though nothing that follows is a hard-and-fast rule as every reader is unique and reading is a not a perfectly linear process.

The order of the chapters is in a hierarchy of sorts that I use when determining which goal is most important for each reader (see diagram on the next page). For example, the first chapter about emergent reading is often best for those readers who are not yet reading conventionally, typically prekindergarteners and early kindergarteners. Once students begin reading, my first go-to is then engagement, because unless students have strategies for reading with focus and stamina, it's very hard to get them to progress—they have to want to read and have strategies for being successful so that they spend lots of time practicing. Next comes print work—kids need to have strategies to be able to read the words. Then comes fluency, because helping kids to be automatic and read with expression and proper phrasing aids in meaning making. After that, comprehension, divided into seven key areas, in a loose order of importance, with fiction comprehension coming before nonfiction unless you are working in a nonfiction unit or you are a content area teacher in search of strategies to support nonfiction reading specifically. The vocabulary chapter, Goal 11, contains strategies for helping students with vocabulary awareness and determining meaning in both narrative and expository texts. Vocabulary is typically something I would work on with a reader in fiction who has already shown his or her understanding of plot, setting, and characters is strong, and for a nonfiction reader who has main idea and key details down. Writing about reading and strategies for conversation are incredibly important as well, but I place them after the comprehension chapters because it's hard to talk or write well about your reading if you aren't understanding the book. It is important to note that there may be exceptions to this hierarchy. For instance,

Determining Where to Start: A Hierarchy of Possible Reading Goals

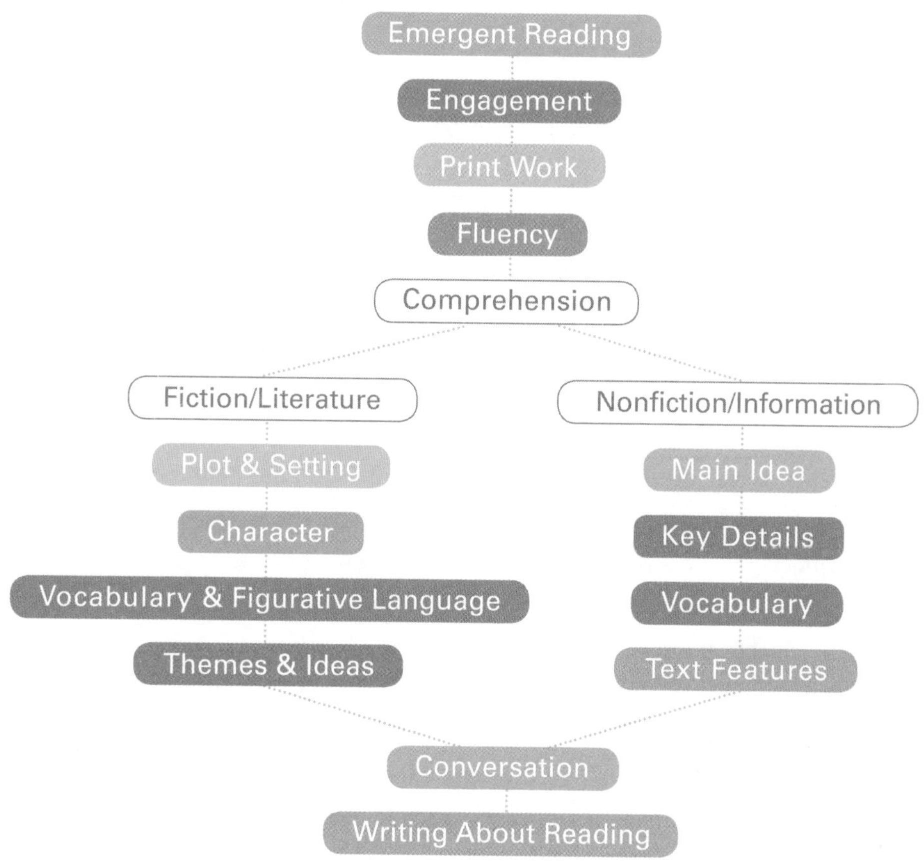

you may have a reader who could work on reading for longer stretches, but that isn't because she needs engagement strategies, it's because she isn't understanding her text, and to support engagement she'd need support with comprehension. Or, after looking at his strengths, you conclude another student could use writing about reading and conversation as tools to deepen comprehension of themes and ideas, in which case you may turn to Chapters 12 and 13 before 7.

How Do I Find the Right Strategy Within the Chapter?

Once you determine a goal for a student, you'll next look for strategies within the chapter. The strategies include support for readers in grades K–8, so there is a range included within every chapter that will match a variety of text levels, skills, and genres.

Levels of text are important to consider when choosing strategies. For example, you wouldn't teach a child who is reading level C books to decode multisyllabic words, just as you wouldn't teach a child reading at level X to check the picture to think about the character's feelings. By scanning any of the "at-a-glance" tables in each chapter (i.e., pages 23, 47, 107), you will notice a column headed "Levels." Each of the strategy pages also includes a margin where the level range is noted. I have chosen to use the Fountas and Pinnell Text Level Gradient™ to give guidance for the level of text complexity that best aligns to each strategy. If you are unfamiliar with this leveling system, you can learn how these alphabetic levels correlate to grade levels and other leveling systems by consulting the chart on page 378.

In addition to considering levels, you'll notice there are also notes on the at-a-glance tables and in the margins about genres that the strategy works best for, as well as the reading skills that the strategies help to support. My hope is that these annotations help you quickly find just-right strategies for your reader!

Navigating Each Page

Each strategy is expanded upon on every page to offer you different ways to quickly understand it so you can use it right away. Take a look at the sample pages that follow with callouts to give you a brief overview of purposes for the parts included on each page. Please consider that depending on how the strategy will be used (in a conference, small-group, or whole-class setting; as a first introduction or a reminder; and so on) you may decide to use only portions of what's offered in connection with a strategy. I also encourage you to give each strategy your own personal touch—change the language, make up new prompts, alter the chart, and so on. In the sections that follow, you can learn more about each of these parts: why I've included them and how you might use them in your own classroom.

Goals, Skills, and Strategies

As I mentioned earlier, this book is organized by goals because I hope that you work to understand each student in your class well enough to be able to articulate a goal for him or her—perhaps one of the thirteen that title the chapters in this book. The goal you chose would then become the focus for your ongoing work with the student in conferences and small groups.

Within each goal, there may be one or more *skills* that a reader would need to work on. For example, if a student is working on a goal of understanding character, that may involve inferring (reading between the lines to name traits and/or feelings) but also synthesis (putting together information across a book to determine how a character changes). Once you've identified the skills, you can find specific strategies to accomplish those skills.

Making Goals Visible

Once you've decided, based on formative assessments, what goal the student is to work on, I recommend having a "goal-setting conference" to discuss this with the student. If at all possible, you may even put the assessment on the table in front of the student and ask the student to reflect on what he or she notices from the assessment. Sometimes a student will know what he or she needs to work on, and when the goal can come from the student, the student will be all the more motivated to work on it (Pink 2009). For more information on goal-setting conferences, see my Literacy Teachers Playbook series (2013b, 2014) or Independent Reading Assessment series (2012, 2013a).

A **strategy** is a step-by-step how-to. This can be used in a conference, strategy lesson, minilesson, or even during another balanced literacy component such as shared reading or interactive read-aloud. It's important that you give children a *how-to* to scaffold their practice until they develop automaticity. To read more about strategies, please see pages 5–10.

4.9 Partners Help to Smooth

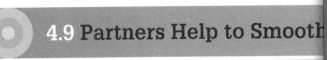

Who is this for?

LEVELS

E–J

XT TYPE

Strategy Partners can help one another read in a smooth voice. When you meet in partner time, put one book between the two of you. Look at the words, listen to yourself, and listen to your partner. Try to read in one voice, pausing at the same places and using the same expression.

Teaching Tip One way to get children to prompt each other in partnerships is to become a "ghost partner." Whisper into children's ears a phrase or sentence starter that you want them to repeat to their partner. In no time at all, they will start taking up the language as their own. So, for this strategy you might whisper, "Let's try that again" or "That sounded choppy, right?" or "Should we try that one more time?" for them to literally repeat to their partner.

Teaching Tips are included with some of the lessons in any instance when I thought that added explanation would help a teacher understand the intention of the lesson, or when I wanted to give other advice, such as how to modify a strategy for students at different reading levels or reading different text types.

Prompts

- What can you tell your partner to help him with his fluency?
- Tell your partner, "Go back and try that again!"
- Tell your partner, "That sounded very smooth."
- Tell your partner, "The way you read that helped me picture it."
- What do you think?
- What will you tell your partner?
- Make sure you're listening carefully and be ready to give your partner advice.

Hat Tips I tried to reference authors and books that the strategy may have been inspired by; sometimes I borrowed a lesson title from another book, other times an idea or concept. Never did I borrow the exact language—that came from thinking about how I would explain it to a student. Just as I used my own natural language and phrasing, I invite you to be inspired by my strategies and make them your own, too!

Partners Help Smooth It Out!

One Book
Two Readers

Listen!

Read Together
Pause Together

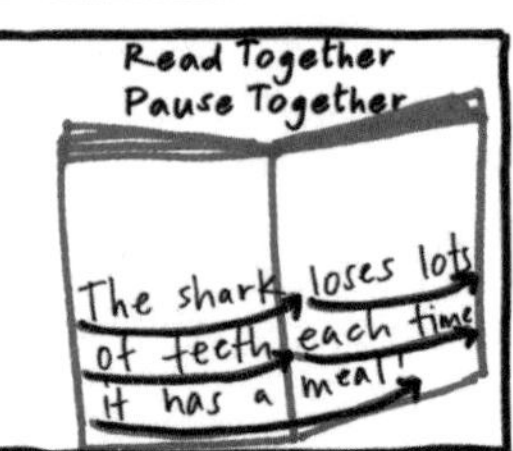

Hat Tip: *A Curricular Plan for the Reading Workshop, Grade 1* (Calkins and colleagues 2011b)

116

THE READING STRATEGIES BOOK

Visuals are included for all lessons. These visuals take many forms such as: a class anchor chart, a tool such as a personalized strategy card or bookmark, student writing, or even photographs of students in action with the strategy. Dozens of teachers from all over this country were involved in piloting the lessons in this book and they have generously shared their work and the work of their students. For more information on creating charts and tools, please see pages 15–18.

The **margins** will guide you to find strategies to fit the appropriate reading level. I indicated the Fountas and Pinnell Text Level Gradient, genre, and skills that will often work best with the strategy. Keep in mind that levels are fluid, so I did my best to guide you toward levels where this would work best, though for certain children the range may be narrower or wider. To learn how these alphabetic levels correlate to grade levels and other leveling systems, please see the chart on page 378.

4.10 Inside Qu... es

Strategy Everything inside of ... the character is talking. The dialog... rator voice when you get to the dialogue tag.

Lesson Language *When I'm reading, I'm always careful to pay close attention to not only the words, but also the marks on the page. The little marks—the punctuation—give us a lot of important information about how to read. They also help us understand what we're reading! For example, it's very important to know when, in a story, the narrator is speaking, and when the character is speaking. But you want to know what? The author helps us! The author uses something called quotation marks—and they look like this* (Show example from a big book and/or hand-drawn large quotation marks.) *Think of it this way—when you first see the mark, you can think of it like the character opening his or her mouth—it's the start of the talking. So when we are reading, the voice we use has to change from a narrator voice to a character voice. Then, when we see the quotes again, like right here* (Point to example.), *that's the closing of the quotation marks, and the closing of the character's mouth. Open quotes, open mouth. Closed quotes, closed mouth. Open quotes, start sounding like the character. Closed quotes, stop sounding like the character. Let's try it together . . .*

Prompts

- Show me where the talking starts.
- There's the quotation mark! Switch your voice.
- I can tell you paid attention to the quotation marks because I hear a difference between the character and narrator.
- That's a tag. Sound like a narrator now.
- The dialogue and narration sounded the same. Go back and try it again.

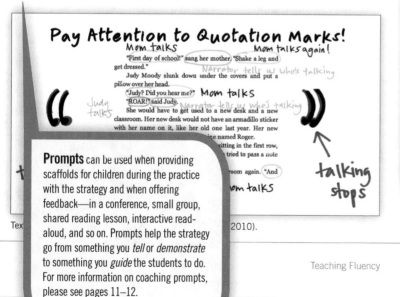

Pay Attention to Quotation Marks!

Mom talks

Mom talks again!

"First day of school!" sang her mother. "Shake a leg and get dressed."

Narrator tells us who's talking

Judy Moody slunk down under the covers and put a pillow over her head.

"Judy? Did you hear me?" Mom talks

"ROAR!" said Judy. Narrator tells us who's talking

Judy talks

She would have to get used to a new desk and a new classroom. Her new desk would not have an armadillo sticker with her name on it, like her old one last year. Her new ...ne named Roger. ...sitting in the first row, ... tried to pass a note

...oom again. "And

...om talks

talking stops

Tex... 2010).

Who is this for?

LEVELS
E–Z+

GENRE / TEXT TYPE
fiction

SKILLS
intonation, expression

Teaching Fluency 117

Lesson Language is included with some of the lessons to show how I might explain or demonstrate a strategy to an individual, small group, or whole class. Keep in mind that you don't always need to use this—some children will be able to get to work after only hearing the strategy, in which case you can follow up with prompts to offer additional support as needed. You should also adapt any and all language to make it your own, use books you know and love in place of those I suggest, and say it in a way that matches the age and experience of the learner(s) you're teaching.

Prompts can be used when providing scaffolds for children during the practice with the strategy and when offering feedback—in a conference, small group, shared reading lesson, interactive read-aloud, and so on. Prompts help the strategy go from something you *tell* or *demonstrate* to something you *guide* the students to do. For more information on coaching prompts, please see pages 11–12.

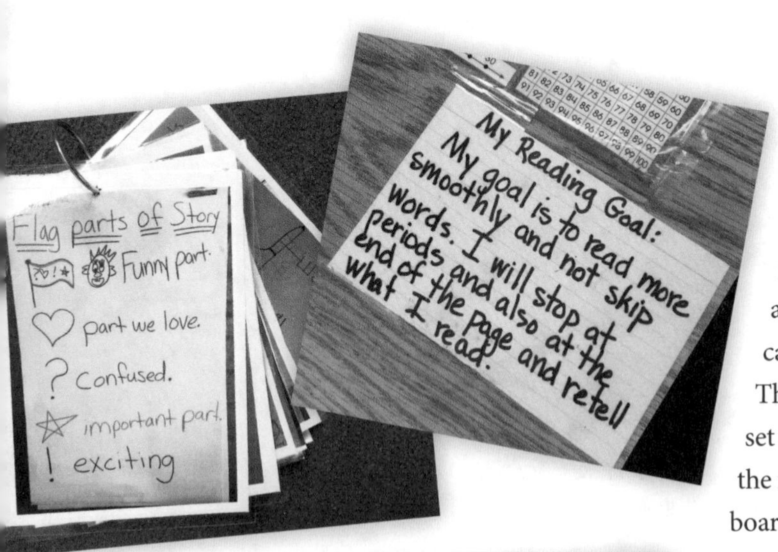

As students begin independent reading, it is unrealistic for the teacher to zoom around the classroom getting each student set up with his or her individual goal. In order to manage the various goals in your classroom, you may consider creating a visual reminder for each individual reader so they can remind themselves what they are working on. This can take the form of a goal card taped to a desk, a set of individual goals on a ring, a bookmark, a page on the inside of their reading notebook, or even a bulletin board that displays each student's goal.

Lilli 's Reading Goals

GOAL: Attack tricky wads		Date: 11/12
Strategies		
Crash into the 1st sound start	chunk it ham blird wall	Make a frame to find chunks hallway
Jump over it, then reread. The monkey was so happy!	Flip the sound! a e i o u	Ask, does it... sound right? look right? make sense?

GOAL: Understanding what I've read		Date: 12/15
Strategies		
Flip back to remember names and important details	At the end of a page, stop and think	Go back and reread if it doesn't make sense
Stop and jot down important parts	Retell the story at the end 1st Next Then After That Finally	

Teachers make goals visible to students as a personal reminder of their work during independent reading.

On Strategies

Effective reading strategies are like my favorite recipes; they teach you how to accomplish something that is not yet automatic in a broken down, step-by-step manner. I wouldn't ever tell a novice cook to just "whip up a soufflé!" without telling her how, just as I wouldn't tell a reader "think beyond the text!" if I saw he wasn't yet able to do it independently.

Researchers, authors, and theorists use the terms *skill* and *strategy* differently (see, for example, Keene and Zimmermann 2007; Afflerbach, Pearson, and Paris 2008; Harvey and Goudvis 2007; Wiggins 2013; Harris and Hodges 1995; Sinatra, Brown, and Reynolds 2002; Taberski 2000; Beers 2002). To me, strategies are "deliberate, effortful, intentional and purposeful actions a reader takes to accomplish a specific task or skill" (Serravallo 2010, 11–12). A reading strategy is step-by-step, a procedure or recipe. Strategies make the often invisible work of reading actionable and visible. Teachers can offer strategies to students to put the work in doable terms for those who are still practicing, so that they may become more comfortable and competent with the new skill.

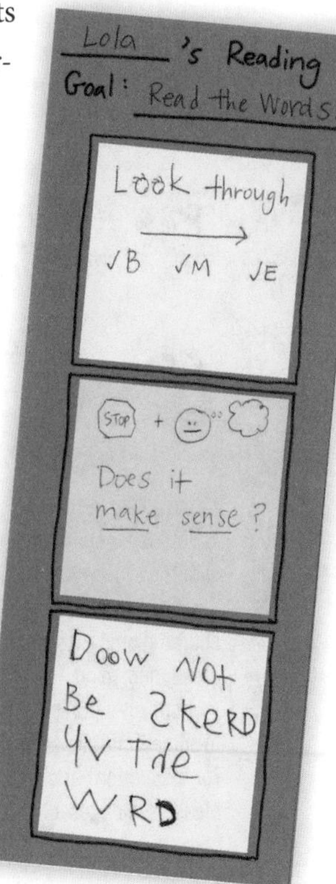

There are *many* strategies for any skill imaginable—three hundred of which are included in this book—though there are others you may make up on your own and still others you'd cull from other professional books and resources you trust.

Just as we offer strategies to students, we want them to eventually outgrow those strategies, too. Once the reader becomes skilled, the *process*, the *strategy*, becomes automatic and something to which the reader no longer needs to give conscious attention. Once the need for conscious use of a strategy fades away it will likely only resurface during times of real difficulty. The objective, therefore, is not that readers can do the steps of the strategy, rather that the strategy helps them be more skilled—to understand the text better, to decode with higher accuracy, to read with greater fluency. Put another way, strategies are a means to an end, not an end unto themselves (Duke 2014; Keene 2008). The strategy is a temporary scaffold, and like any scaffolding it needs to be removed.

Some of the visuals in this book, such as student notebook entries, classroom charts, or even the rare graphic organizer, should also be seen as tools, and as temporary ways for kids to practice something that eventually will become automatic, ingrained, second nature.

I have found the most effective way to work on a goal over time with a student is to introduce one strategy at a time, guide the student in practicing the strategy, and move on to a new strategy when the student appears to be secure with the first one. Over the course of four to six weeks while the student works toward meeting the goal, she may have practiced and developed automaticity with four to eight different strategies. At that point, it is often time to move on to a new goal, or progress to a higher level of text and try to transfer the new learning to the more complex text.

Below is a tree diagram similar to the one on page 5, with a goal, skills, and strategies filled in:

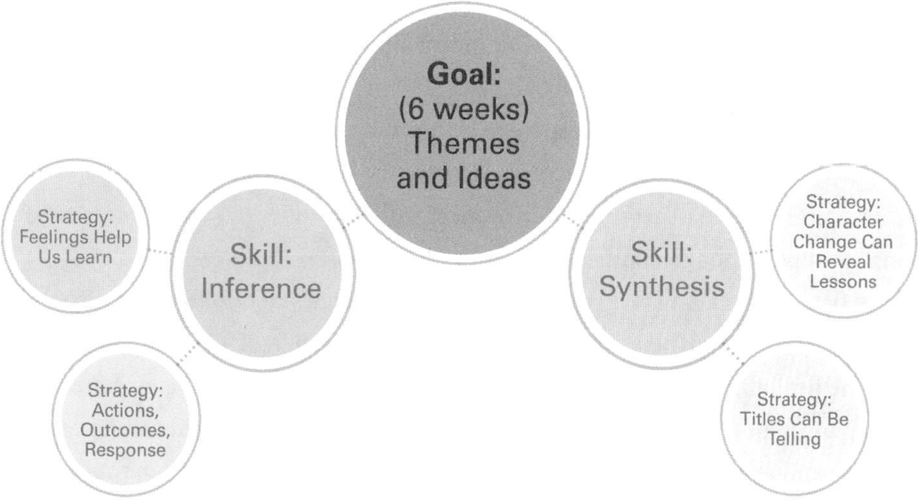

Below is an example of how a goal is taught about and learned during the course of several weeks.

week 1	Teacher (T) taught "Feelings Help Us Learn" in a conference. Student (S) practiced in *Stone Fox* and *The Report Card,* her self-selected books for the week. T checked in at end of week in a small-group strategy lesson.
week 2	T taught "Actions, Outcomes, Response" in a small group. S practiced in *Circle of Gold,* her new self-selected book. S Seemed to struggle. T met with S on Thursday in a conference to repeat lesson, offered a new example. S continued reading *The Whipping Boy,* and practiced some more. T asked student to keep track of thinking in reader's notebook.
week 3	T revisited "Actions, Outcomes, Response" in the first conference of the week. T decided S is doing well. Introduced "Character Change Can Reveal Lessons." S chose *Family Under the Bridge* and *Indian in the Cupboard* this week.
week 4	S practiced last week's strategy in *Rules* and *Hatchet.* At the end of the week, T reviewed the S's work during a conference. T determined she could be more universal in her language and coached the S to rephrase the statements she had recorded.
week 5	T met with S during two strategy lessons this week and helped her to incorporate all three new strategies, when appropriate, in her new books for the week: *Charlotte's Web* and *Stuart Little.*
week 6	T introduced "Titles Can Be Telling" in a conference and student seems able to use the strategy right away. S continued practicing all four strategies during the week in two new books. At end of week, T decided to move to new goal.

You may notice from this six-week detailing of a reader's journey toward meeting a goal that the teacher reflects, assesses, and responds to the student every time she meets with her. In this way, the teacher knows when the student is ready to move on to try out a new strategy and when the student should keep practicing with an already introduced strategy.

Also of note is the fact that the student practices strategies repeatedly, with many books she chooses herself that are at her independent reading level. This high level of readability—where accuracy, fluency, and comprehension are in place—ensures that the child will have the brain space to be practicing working on new skills. Each learned and practiced strategy becomes a part of the student's repertoire.

The teacher in this scenario chose to meet with the student in conferences and small groups, although another teacher may have chosen conferences and book clubs, or shared reading and read-aloud. All the strategies in this book are flexible in this way—they can be used in any instructional format, and with most books. In fact, the flexibility of a strategy is another good test to apply to it. The most helpful strategies are portable, generalizable, transferrable—so that a student can repeatedly practice and apply the strategy, eventually helping the strategy to become automatic.

Prompting and Guiding Readers

What you do not see in the previous six-week story are the details of the interactions between teacher and student.

Within the context of a lesson—either in a small group, in a whole class, or one-on-one—a teacher will offer the strategy to the student, and then make a decision about how much upfront support to provide. He may or may not give a brief explanation, an example, or a demonstration, a decision that is usually based on how much support the teacher feels the student may need to begin practice. A word of caution—many would argue that it's a misconception that everything you might choose to teach would require a lengthy demonstration (Barnhouse and Vinton 2012; Johnston 2004). Many students are ready to get started after just hearing a strategy, and although the student's first attempts are an approximation, the teacher is there to support and guide the student through prompts, coaching, and feedback.

Once students begin to practice, it's important to give the student your utmost attention. This is valuable instructional time in which a two-way feedback loop allows the teacher to learn about how the student is practicing the strategy and what further support she needs, and for the student to receive feedback from her teacher. According to Hattie's (2009) research, this feedback connected to a visible goal has the potential to bring about enormous positive results for the student.

I try to phrase my prompts in as few words as possible. I'm aware that if I'm doing all the talking then I'm probably doing most of the work. I think of prompts instead as gentle nudges, to encourage the child to do the thinking, talking, jotting, and working through the strategy with me as a guide.

I am careful to make sure that the language I use in these prompts is tied to the strategy (perhaps even borrowing some of the same words from the language of the strategy) to make sure my lesson is as focused and clear as possible. I am also careful to avoid using specific words or examples from the book the child is reading whenever possible. For example, to a child practicing a print work strategy of looking at parts of the word to figure out a longer word, I'm more likely to say "What's a part you know?" instead of "You know the word *bear.* That will help you read *t-e-a-r*; give that a try." For a

The feedback that teachers give to students can take many forms. I often find that my prompts fall into one of the following categories:

- compliment (names something the student does well, e.g., "Yes, that's a trait because it describes the character!")
- directive (directs or commands the child to try something, e.g., "Check the picture.")
- redirection (names what the child is currently doing, and redirects the child in a different direction, "That's one way that vowel can sound. Let's try another.")
- question ("What can you try to fix that?")
- sentence starter (gives the child language one might use to respond to a question or prompt, e.g., "In the beginning . . . In the middle . . .").

child practicing inferring about a character's feelings by noticing what the character says and how she says it, I might prompt, "Check the dialogue tag" but not "It says 'She said glumly' so what does *glumly* mean?"

When prompting students, I am also aware of the amount of support I'm giving with the prompts I choose. Prompts where I say more and/or walk the child through steps of the strategy would be *more* supportive. Prompts where I say little (or nothing in the case of nonverbal prompts) would be *less* supportive, requiring the child to do more of the work. I keep in mind Pearson and Gallagher's (1983) often-cited gradual-release model, knowing that for a child to become independent, I need to eventually decrease the amount of support I provide. That said, that doesn't mean I always start with the most supportive prompts and work to the least supportive ones. In fact, quite the opposite. I learned from Marie Clay (1993) that it is often effective to start with a lower level of support and work up to more support as needed, and then within the lesson or across several lessons decrease the amount of support. See the table that follows for examples of more supportive and less supportive prompts.

The prompts that are included with the strategies in this book are a mix of types and a mix of levels of support. My intention is that you use them as examples of how prompts would sound, and then use those exact prompts or ones that come up naturally while you teach to coach the students and provide them with appropriate feedback.

Strategy	More Supportive Prompts	Less Supportive Prompts
	Gradual Release →	
"As you read, put together your own knowledge of places like the one described with the details the author gives you. Tap all of your senses to describe the setting."	• "Think about the places you've been that are like the one described." • "Use all of your senses. What do you see? Hear? Feel? Taste? Smell?"	• "Picture the place." • "Use your senses." • "Say more about the setting." • Teacher points to eyes, ears, and nose to nonverbally prompt.
"When you get information about the character's situation, it should change the picture you have of her in your mind. Think about how her body might look, or what her facial expression is like, based on how she's feeling."	• "Think about what just happened to the character. How might she look?" • "Describe what just happened. Now describe how you would look in that situation. How does the character look?"	• "Describe the character's face." • "Describe the character's body." • "Make your face like the character's."

How the Strategies In this Book Might Fit into Your Current Literacy Instruction

I am a dedicated reading and writing workshop teacher, à la the Teachers College Reading and Writing Project. I believe workshop teaching is most powerful when used as part of a balanced literacy framework. The way I personally would use this book is as an ultimate cheat sheet/guide to fuel all my goal-directed, differentiated instruction in conferences and small groups. I would assign every reader in my class a goal (one of the thirteen chapters that follow), look for patterns to group my students, and then create a schedule for myself that includes groups (when multiple kids would benefit from the same strategy) and conferences (when children had goals that were unique). I'd also use the ideas in this book to inform the kinds of thinking aloud and prompting I did during interactive read-aloud, and the sorts of strategies I taught in minilessons and shared reading. In other words, I'd use it like a big cookbook, each day planning a several course meal. [See Chapter 8 of *Teaching Reading in Small Groups* (Serravallo 2010) or Chapter 4 of either of the Literacy Teacher's Playbooks (Serravallo 2013b, 2014) for examples of what one of my weekly schedules may look like.]

That said, if you or the school in which you teach uses a different approach to reading instruction, you will find that this book offers you support to make your teaching clearer and more focused. In the table that follows, I've brainstormed a short list of ways you might use what's in this book to enhance a variety of different reading instruction frameworks:

Literacy Framework	How You Might Use This Book
Daily 5™ Framework/ Literacy CAFE™ System	The Daily 5™/Literacy CAFE™ approach to independent reading and balanced literacy asks teachers to match students to goals within four categories—comprehension, accuracy, fluency, and expanding vocabulary. Although the CAFE has four, this book has thirteen. "Comprehension" in this book is broken down into three fiction and three nonfiction as well as a chapter on conversation and another on writing about reading. Accuracy, fluency, and vocabulary each have a chapter in my book. If you use the Daily CAFE, you can very easily use this book to find teaching suggestions for your readers in each of the four groups.

continues

Literacy Framework	How You Might Use This Book
Guided Reading and Literacy Centers	Fountas and Pinnell, who many would consider two of today's foremost experts on guided reading, advocate for independent reading to be a part of any guided reading program. Therefore, one of the ways you may use the ideas in this book is to help students have a focus for their independent reading time and to confer with them while they read their independent-level texts. Another way you may use this guide is to think about what your formative assessments tell you about your students as you're planning a guided reading lesson, then scan the overview tables at the start of each chapter to find strategies that both match the level and the goals, and use those to inform your guided reading plans.
Basal Reader/ Anthology	Many basal reader/anthologies include guided instruction time with the teacher in small groups, as well as time when students are independently reading. Based on assessments of your readers (either those included in the basal reader program or some that are mentioned in this book), you can borrow lessons to tweak the existing lessons in the basal, so that you're sure you're teaching the children based on their strengths and needs, not just teaching from the preexisting script. Remember that the writers of the basal reader may have come up with a sensible scope and sequence, but if it doesn't match the learners you have, you won't see maximum progress. You can also use these ideas to focus students' independent reading time and to inform some of the whole-class lessons and read-alouds you may do. You may also find that there is some alignment between what's being taught in the basal (i.e., "compare and contrast") but that the language in this book helps to make the teaching more explicit and specific.
Whole-Class Novels	The suggestions in this book may help you to be explicit with your students about the processes you use as you think aloud about the book. You may offer some strategies to students to use for themselves when they are reading and possibly annotating independently. Although part of your goal is probably to teach aspects of the given work of literature you're studying as a class, children also benefit from clear and explicit how-tos to do the same sorts of thinking in other books they read. Use strategies during your demonstrations, and use the prompts during class discussions. You may consider carving out some time for independent reading in addition to your novel study so that students have time in the classroom, with your support, to apply what you've taught in the whole-class novel to their own reading. This will increase their overall volume of reading and help to make the strategy instruction stick. This independent reading time can be made highly accountable with the inclusion of goals, strategies, and feedback from you.

Supporting Strategies with Visuals

In their Smarter Charts book series (2012, 2014) and Digital Campus course (2014), Kristine Mraz and Marjorie Martinelli offer compelling evidence that when a person provides visuals to accompany any written text or speech, the receiver is more likely to remember it. Inspired by their work, I have included visuals in this book for every strategy, and many of these visuals are classroom charts or student tools. Part of my reason is to help you, *my readers*, remember these strategies so they stick in your minds and you can internalize them and make them your own. The other reason is to encourage you to create visuals whenever you're teaching, to increase the likelihood that your students will remember what *you* say.

Going into great detail about classroom visuals is outside of the scope of this book, so I refer you to the experts, Marjorie and Kristine—their books, their course, and/or their website chartchums.wordpress.com—however, I do want to highlight a few ways that you might create visuals and then incorporate them into your teaching.

What Are the Characteristics of a Helpful Chart or Tool?

Dozens of teachers helped with the creation of the visuals—see the names of these generous educators in the acknowledgments. The ones I chose to use often had a few things in common:

- They are very clear and as simple as possible.
- They are often low on text.
- They have icons, pictures, and/or color-coding.
- They are appropriate for the age and readability level of the students for which they're intended.
- They have clear headings that tell you what the chart's about.

When you are looking to create visuals for your own students to use, consider these principles as some guidelines for creating visuals that will truly support students' independent practice.

Types of Charts and Tools

The charts and tools you'll see in this book fall into a few categories. I've included replicas of some of the charts and tools you'll see throughout the book, with captions explaining what they are and how they may be used. All of these chart and tool types are explained in more detail in any of Martinelli and Mraz's work.

Exemplar Charts. These types of charts often include an annotated piece of text, some student work with callouts, or a chart the class created together that would serve as an explanation for what the reader's own work should look like or what the reader might be looking for in his books when he practices the strategy. These are often crafted with students—the teacher may choose the piece of text ahead of time and then ask students to help her annotate as they work through the strategy.

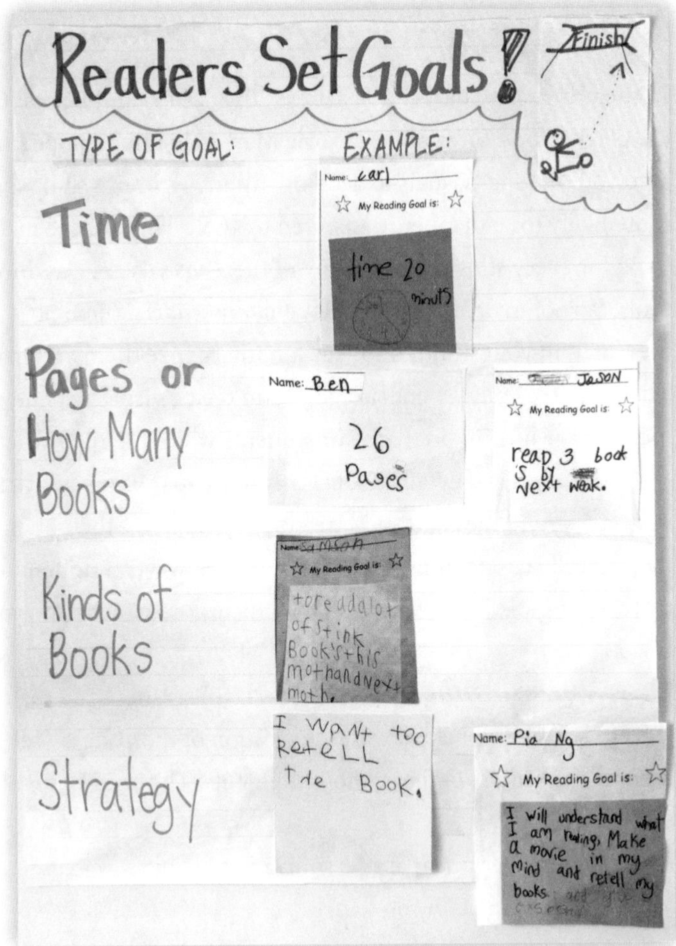

Tools. These visuals are made for individual students to keep in a folder, on a bookmark, in a book baggie, or stuck to a page in a notebook. The intention is that students will have their own, differentiated "chart" to use when they are practicing independently. You may create it with the student, or create it ahead of time, and leave it with the student after a conference or small group.

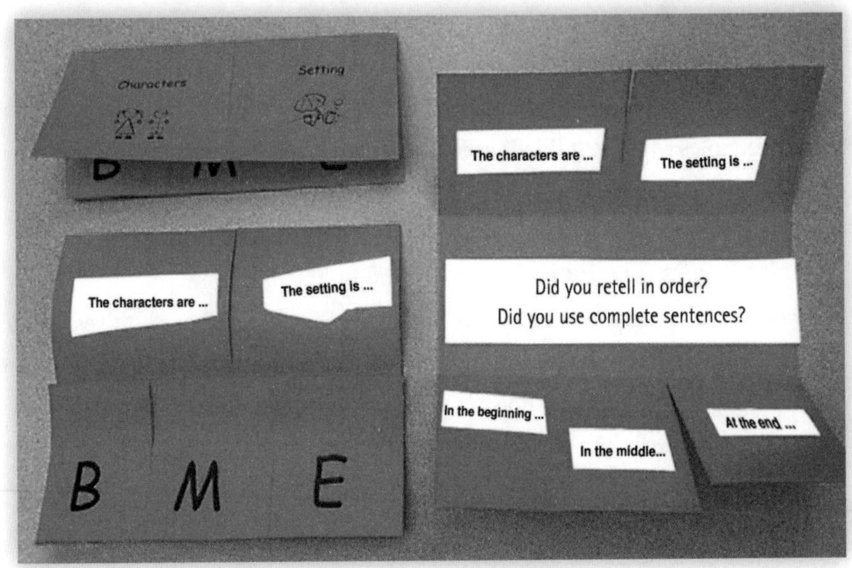

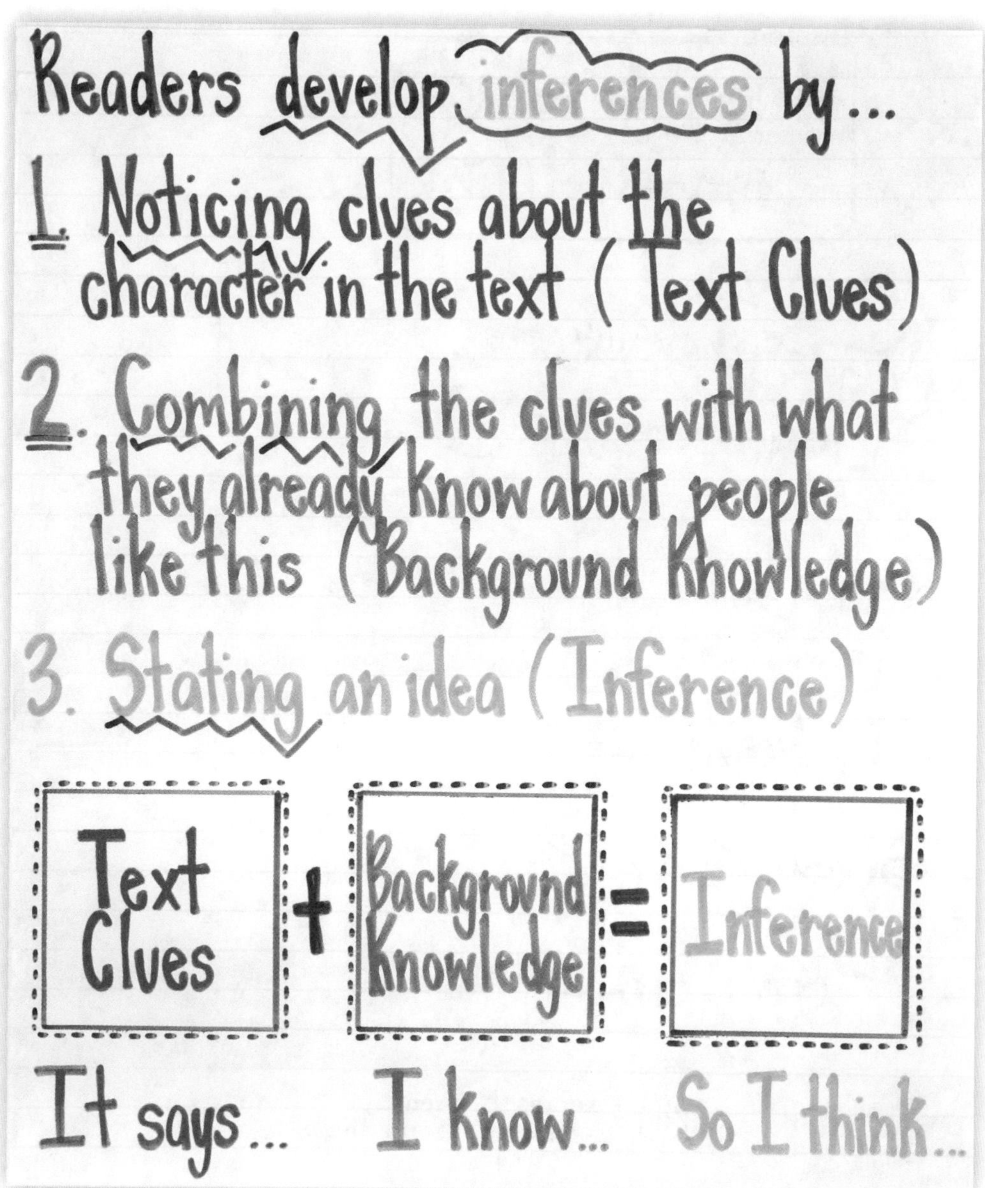

Readers develop inferences by...
1. Noticing clues about the character in the text (Text Clues)
2. Combining the clues with what they already know about people like this (Background Knowledge)
3. Stating an idea (Inference)
Text Clues
+
Background Knowledge
=
Inference
It says...
I know...
So I think...

Process Charts. These charts help to make visual the steps of the strategy, with pictures, icons, and/or key words.

Repertoire Charts. Repertoire charts help remind students of the sorts of strategies they've already been practicing and should be incorporating as part of a regular habit. A collection of individual charts or tools, for instance, four separate process charts, could be combined on one larger chart. Sometimes teachers "retire" the more detailed process chart, and instead rewrite a summary of the strategy on the repertoire chart.

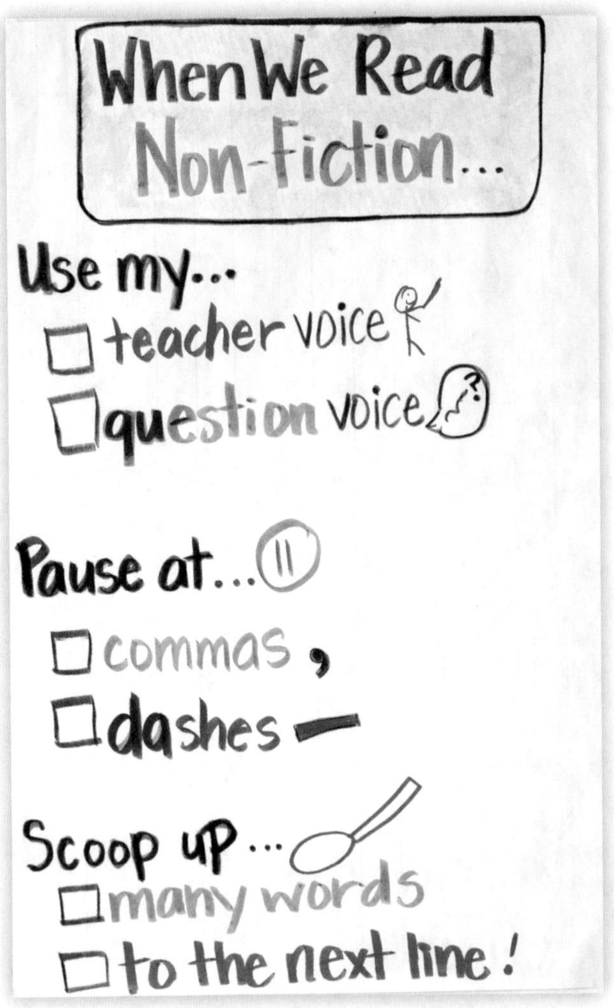

Content Charts. These charts offer students a reference for their work with a strategy, such as a list of character traits or word families.

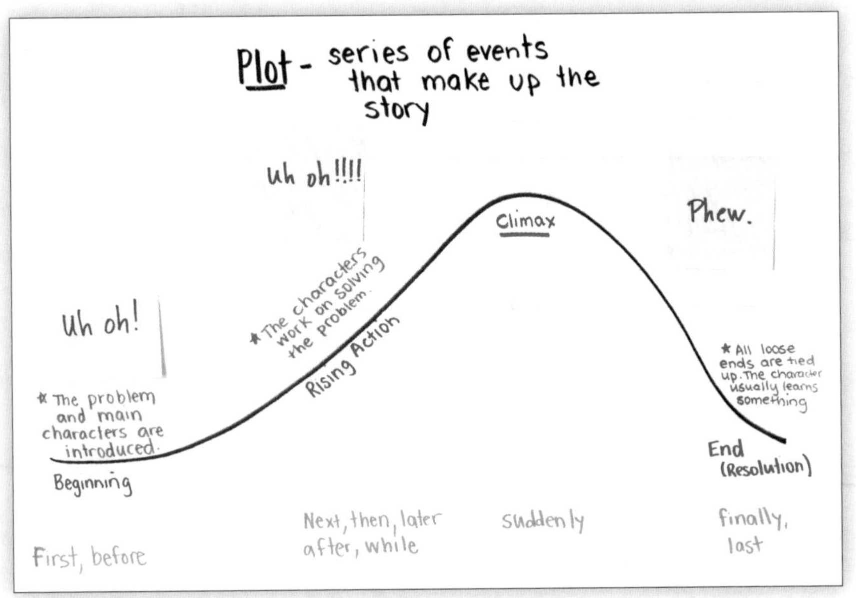

A Note About the Common Core Standards

As this book goes to print, the Common Core is less "common" than it was even a few years ago. Some states are choosing to create their own standards heavily modeled after the CCSS, and others are choosing to create standards that are quite different. Still others are just coming aboard to try to learn about the Common Core. Many, but not all, states are in the nascent stages of using Partnership for Assessment of Readiness for College and Careers (PARCC) or Smarter Balanced Assessment Consortium (SBAC) standardized assessments aligned to the Core.

Whatever state you teach in, and whatever way the political winds are blowing when this book actually reaches your hands, I want us to remember these very important principles of good teaching: We must meet children where they are, we must understand them well to teach them, and we must offer them the right amounts of supports and challenges to grow. I deliberately decided not to include references to standards in this book because I don't believe any standards would change my opinion about these principles. Also, we must remember that standards are a year-end set of outcomes, not a set of prescriptions for how to accomplish them. This book helps you to identify goals for children and gives you the how-to to move them forward. Start from an assessment of what a child can already do, pick one of the thirteen goals, and start teaching. Be secure in the knowledge that your teaching will match your child, and it will inevitably also help the child reach higher standards.

And with that, I'm sure you're ready to get started!

Supporting Pre-Emergent and Emergent Readers

Why is this goal important?

Formal reading programs, intentional phonics instruction, and higher end-of-year benchmark levels have become the norm in most early childhood classrooms across the country. This rush to get children decoding and attending to the print is based on a belief that the sooner they can read the words, the better readers they'll become in the long run (Collins and Glover 2015). However, even though we *may* be able to get children cracking the code earlier and earlier, should we? Or, at least, should that be our priority in prekindergarten and early kindergarten classrooms?

The work of the early childhood researchers Elizabeth Sulzby and William Teale (1991) and well-regarded experts in early childhood literacy such as Kathy Collins and Matt Glover (see, for example, Collins and Glover 2015; Collins 2004, 2008; Ray and Glover 2008) has convinced me that there is an abundance of meaningful work children can do *before* conventional reading—and even in tandem with early conventional reading development. We can meet students where they are and help them engage with and enjoy books, make meaning, acquire vocabulary, use text features to understand, connect the pages, respond to texts by writing and talking, practice their fluency, and perhaps above all, develop identities as confident, engaged, joyful readers (even without decoding).

Think about the last time you watched your own son or daughter, grandchild, or any child you love sitting independently with a book that has been read to her many times. You may have noticed her "reading" the book—perhaps she was saying some of the same words and phrases she's heard you read aloud. Perhaps she was pointing at the pictures. Perhaps she was making facial expressions, or repeating some of the dialogue the character says on each of the pages. In her groundbreaking work on emergent reading, Elizabeth Sulzby found that children's work with familiar texts (texts that had been read aloud to them a handful of times) often fell into some predictable categories—from labeling what they see in the picture, to storytelling with dialogue or narration details, to using story language, to telling of the story using many of the same words as the author, to reading with expression and intonation (Sulzby 1985).

Collins and Glover (2015) expanded on Sulzby's work to study children's reading work with both familiar and unfamiliar texts, in fiction and nonfiction. They found that children's reading often fell into categories as well and that these categories were not fixed. A child may begin to read a book by labeling, for example, and then begin storytelling by the end of the book. Also, a child might storytell in some books, but simply label in others. No matter how children approach a book, we can do a lot to support and nurture them as readers and thinkers during this important stage of reading development.

Sulzby, Collins, and Glover's work can serve as a helpful framework for observing what students do with books, determining ways to support what they are doing, and nudging them ever so slightly forward.

How do I know if this goal is right for my student?

The suggestions for teaching in this chapter are perfect for any young children who are just beginning to read texts independently, though not yet conventionally. They may also be suggestions for readers who are beginning to read conventionally, yet have interests that go beyond the simple patterned texts that beginning readers tend to read. These beginning readers may spend time with books—books some would call "look books"—which are above a student's independent reading level, where the student can learn from pictures and/or practice storytelling (Collins 2004).

To get ready, you'll want to collect some picture books that will support the student's practice. Ideally, they are books that are a blend of information text, list books, alphabet books, and stories. You'll notice along the margins of this chapter that I give some advice about what type of text the strategy works best with. Sometimes I use the word *book* in a strategy and prompts, and other times I may be more specific about the type of book, perhaps using the words *information book* or *story*. This is because some strategies can be flexibly used with different types of texts—stories, information texts, list books—(books), and other strategies are really best only for one type of text (for example, stories). Either way, I encourage you to be mindful of the language you use when teaching strategies and providing prompts. For example, make sure that when you refer to the book as a *story* it really is a narrative—by taking care with your language choices you are teaching your students important lessons about genre!

Books that work best in supporting students in this stage are:

- texts that are visually engaging (If the book is a story, it's helpful if the pictures clearly carry the main events of the story. If the book is nonfiction, the pictures should have detail and a variety of visual elements.)
- stories that have a strong narrative with recognizable dialogue, and some repetition (i.e., *Caps for Sale* [Slobodkina 1987], *The Very Hungry Caterpillar* [Carle 1994], *Knuffle Bunny* [Willems 2004] to name a few)
- informational texts that offer opportunities to learn content from the photographs and other features
- list books with clearly supportive pictures (i.e., *Brown Bear, Brown Bear* [Martin 2010])
- alphabet and number books to help reinforce knowledge of letters and sounds, and numerals connected to a number of objects.

It will be helpful for you to watch your students read books that are familiar and unfamiliar, those that are fiction, nonfiction, or others that don't fall into either category, and notice what they do as they read from the pictures across the pages of the book. Your observations will help you choose from the suggested strategies in this chapter—and will teach you so much about your students as readers.

Strategies for Pre-Emergent and Emergent Readers at a Glance

Strategy	Levels	Genres/ Text Types	Skills
1.1 Be an Explorer Who Finds Treasures in Books	Emergent	Any (with pictures)	Engagement, stamina
1.2 The WHOLE and Teeny-Tiny Details	Emergent	Nonfiction	Summarizing
1.3 Linger Finger	Emergent	Any (with pictures)	Noticing details
1.4 Pictures as Stepping-Stones	Emergent	Narrative	Sequencing, storytelling
1.5 Word Treasure Hunt	Emergent (but beginning to be aware of print)	Any	Sight word automaticity
1.6 Characters Do, Characters Say	Emergent	Narrative (with pictures)	Storytelling, elaborating
1.7 Act It to Storytell It	Emergent	Narrative	Storytelling, dramatic play
1.8 Express the Emotions	Emergent	Narrative (with pictures)	Fluency, expression
1.9 Back Up, Revise	Emergent	Narrative (with pictures)	Monitoring for meaning, inferring
1.10 Use Story Language	Emergent	Narrative	Using transition words and phrases
1.11 Move Your Body, Remember the Words	Emergent	Narrative (familiar, with pictures)	Monitoring for meaning
1.12 Keep in Mind What Repeats	Emergent	Books with repetitive language	Monitoring for meaning
1.13 Talk Like the Character	Emergent	Narrative (familiar)	Fluency, expression
1.14 If You Don't Know, Guess	Emergent	Narrative (unfamiliar)	Inferring, monitoring for meaning
1.15 Readers Explain Their Thinking	Emergent	Any	Inferring, supporting ideas with evidence
1.16 What I See/What I Think	Emergent	Nonfiction or narrative	Monitoring for meaning, inferring
1.17 Talk Like an Expert	Emergent	Nonfiction	Word choice
1.18 Use a Teaching Voice	Emergent	Nonfiction	Fluency
1.19 Connect the Pages	Emergent	Nonfiction or narrative	Synthesizing
1.20 Character Name or Group Name?	Emergent	Nonfiction or narrative	Understanding genre

1.1 Be an Explorer Who Finds Treasures in Books

Who is this for?

LEVEL

emergent

GENRE / TEXT TYPE

any (with pictures)

SKILLS

engagement, stamina

Strategy Find a bin of books in your classroom or a shelf of books in the library. Check out the cover and the inside of the books to see what might be interesting. Take a trip inside the book, like an explorer, and find the treasures such as interesting details or facts you've never known, page by page.

Teaching Tip Across the chapter, you'll find many suggestions for what kids can do with books before they are conventionally reading, but this strategy is a good one for readers who are reluctant to do anything at all. Perhaps because they don't yet see themselves as readers, or perhaps because they don't have experience with books, or maybe even because they realize that they aren't yet reading conventionally, and think that means they can have nothing to do with books. This strategy will encourage kids to stick on a page for longer, aiming to find something new or interesting.

Prompts

- What can you find?
- Do you see anything on this page?
- Look all the way across the page. Tell me what you see.
- Not so fast! Let's stay on the page to see what else we can find.
- That *is* a treasure! You really looked carefully to find that.

This strategy is best introduced in individual conferences with students, followed by a lot of "Wow! Look at that!" and "I didn't know that, did you?" and "What an amazing thing to find!" While coaching students, you may also encourage them to stay on a page for a while, really looking for treasures with "Wait, wait! I think there's more on this page. Don't turn yet!"

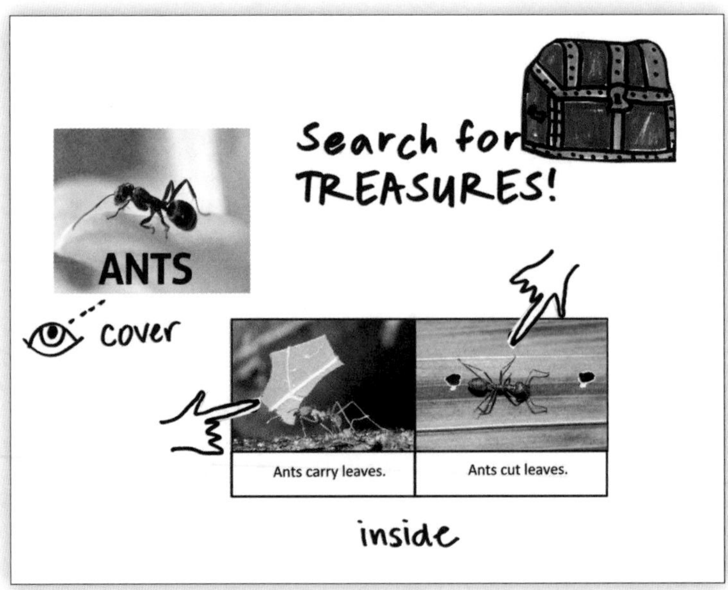

Hat Tip: *A Curricular Plan for the Reading Workshop, Grade K* (Calkins and colleagues 2011a)

1.2 The WHOLE and Teeny-Tiny Details

Strategy Pay attention to the WHOLE and the teeny-tiny details on the page. Sweeping your finger across the whole page, say what the page is mostly about. Then zoom in on small parts, saying one thing for each part you see.

Teaching Tip This strategy will help students internalize an important nonfiction structure of main idea and key details, or "topic sentence" followed by facts.

Prompts

- Use your finger. Sweep it across the whole page.
- Say, "This whole page is about . . ."
- Now zoom in on a small part. Say what you're learning.
- Turn the page and try it again.
- Move your finger to another part. What else did you learn?
- What do all the parts have in common?
- What's the same about all the parts on this page?
- Touch one part. What did you learn? Touch another part. What did you learn?

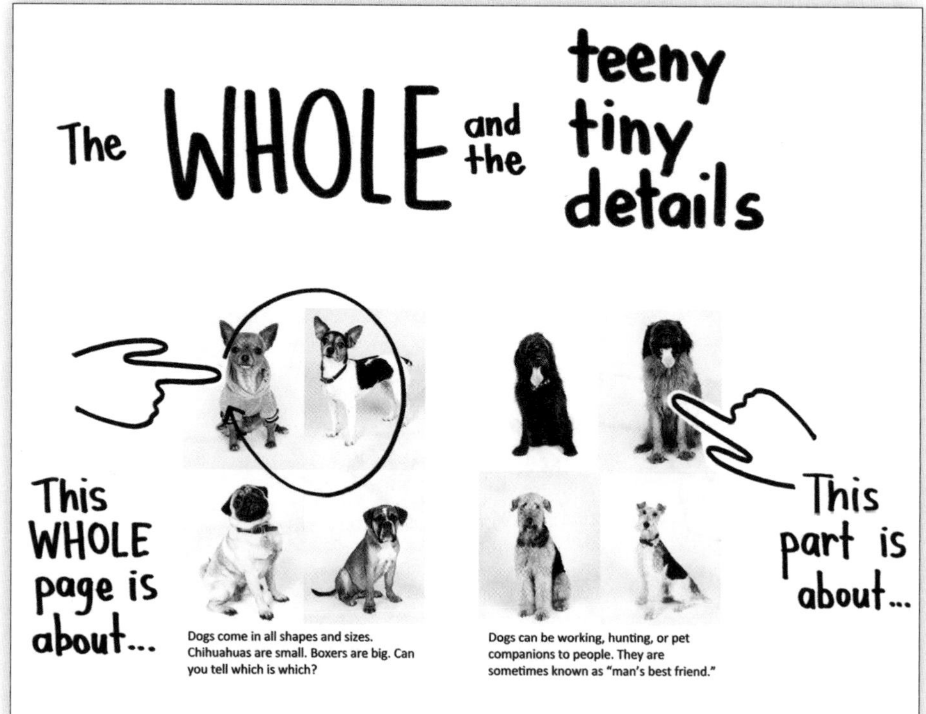

The WHOLE and the teeny tiny details
This WHOLE page is about...
This part is about...
Dogs come in all shapes and sizes. Chihuahuas are small. Boxers are big. Can you tell which is which?
Dogs can be working, hunting, or pet companions to people. They are sometimes known as "man's best friend."

Who is this for?

LEVEL

emergent

GENRE / TEXT TYPE

nonfiction

SKILL

summarizing

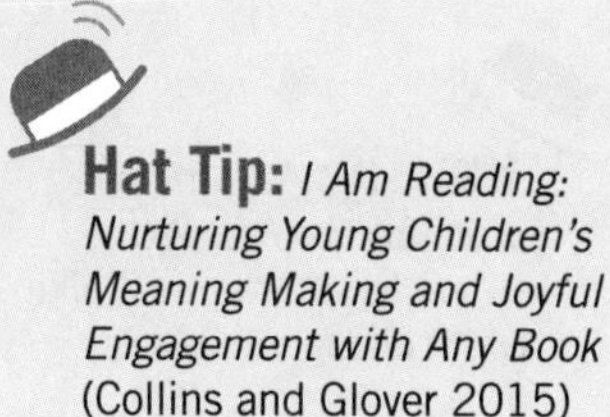

Hat Tip: *I Am Reading: Nurturing Young Children's Meaning Making and Joyful Engagement with Any Book* (Collins and Glover 2015)

1.3 Linger Finger

Who is this for?

LEVEL

emergent

GENRE / TEXT TYPE

any (with pictures)

SKILL

noticing details

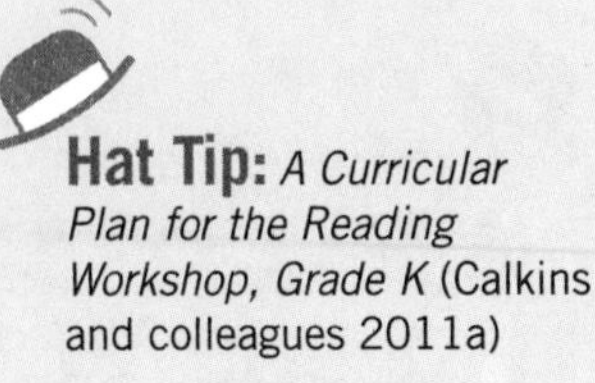

Hat Tip: *A Curricular Plan for the Reading Workshop, Grade K* (Calkins and colleagues 2011a)

Strategy Instead of zooming through your book, pause and stay for a while—linger. Use a linger finger to look across the parts on the page. Say something each time your finger lands in a spot. When you've spent some time lingering on the page, you can turn to the next one.

Lesson Language *When I get to a new book, I know that what's inside is filled with fun, interesting, cool, and beautiful things. I know I need to make sure I don't just rush through the whole thing, getting to the end soon after I've just begun! No, I need to slow down. And one way I slow down is to point with my finger. I like to point all around the page because when I point, it makes my eyes focus and helps me to see something I may have otherwise overlooked. Staying for a while on a page is called* lingering. *So I'm going to try to* linger. *I'm not in a rush! I'm going to use my* linger finger*—hey that rhymes! Say it with me: "linger finger." As I linger, or stay, in one spot, I'm going to say something I see, then I'll move my finger to another spot and say something I see, and so on. I'll only turn the page if I'm sure I've really noticed everything I can.*

Prompts

- Move your finger across the page. Tell me what you see.
- Tell it like a story (*fiction*).
- Tell me what you're learning (*nonfiction*).
- Not so fast! Stay on the page a moment.
- You went across the whole page and said sentences about what you saw!
- Go slow!
- Say something.
- What will you do before you turn the page?

1.4 Pictures as Stepping-Stones

Strategy Every page in the book connects to make one whole story. You can "step" from page to page by using the pictures like stepping-stones. Step on one page's picture to say what happens first, then turn the page to tell what happens next, and so on.

Teaching Tip This strategy will work for students who are returning to a book that was previously read aloud to practice their storytelling, or for those students who are choosing a book that is unfamiliar and are working to storytell from the pictures.

Lesson Language *Watch as I "step" from page to page of* A Visitor for Bear *(Becker 2012), connecting the pages.* (Touch page 1.) *"There was a sign on the door and it says 'NO!' So he doesn't want anyone to come inside."* (Touch the next page.) *"First the bear wanted breakfast so he put on his apron in the kitchen."* (Touch the next page.) *"But a mouse came to his door and he just said 'Get away! Don't you see my sign?' and then he shut the door."* (Touch the next page.) *"And then he went back to his kitchen and put a spoon and a cup on the table."*

Prompts

- Say, "And then . . ."
- Say, "Next . . ."
- Think about how the pages connect.
- So, what happens next? Turn the page and let's see.
- You looked closely at the picture to make sure this page connects to that one.

Who is this for?

LEVEL

emergent

GENRE / TEXT TYPE

narrative

SKILLS

sequencing, storytelling

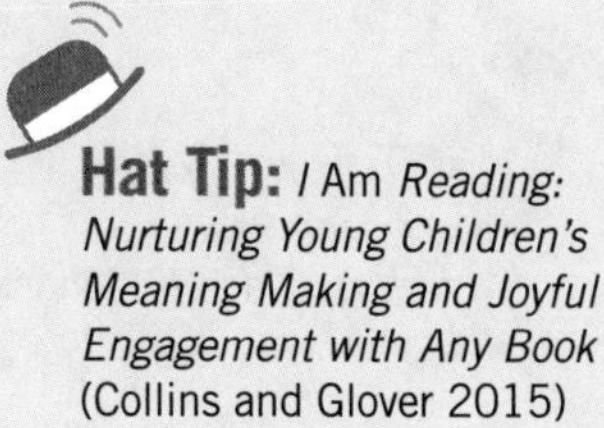

Hat Tip: *I Am Reading: Nurturing Young Children's Meaning Making and Joyful Engagement with Any Book* (Collins and Glover 2015)

1.5 Word Treasure Hunt

Who is this for?

LEVEL

emergent (but beginning to be aware of print)

GENRE / TEXT TYPE

any

SKILL

sight word automaticity

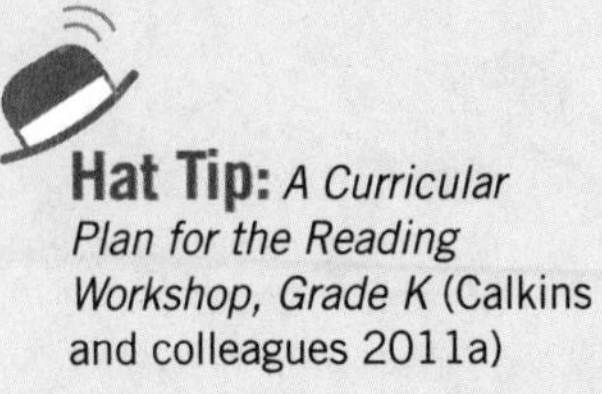

Hat Tip: *A Curricular Plan for the Reading Workshop, Grade K* (Calkins and colleagues 2011a)

Strategy Readers read the pictures and the words. First, read the pictures to understand the story, then go back to hunt for any words or letters you know.

Teaching Tip This strategy, like the others in this chapter, puts precedence on making meaning from texts first for young readers. There will likely come a time, though, as students become more print-aware, know some sight words, learn letters, and realize that the print on the page carries the story/information. This strategy gently directs students back to meaning first, and then gives them the opportunity to practice their newfound skills of finding sight words and letters they may know. The words you would include on a chart such as the one on this page would be the words that the student(s) already know, and they may also appear alphabetized on a word wall.

Prompts

- Let's read the story, first looking at the pictures to understand it.
- Let's check the page. Do you see any letters you know?
- Show me the words you know on this page.
- Shall we hunt for some treasures? Maybe there are words or letters you know on the page.

1.6 Characters Do, Characters Say

Strategy On every page, try to sound like a storyteller. You can look carefully at the picture to say what the character is doing and what the character is saying.

Teaching Tip You can teach this to readers who are reading a familiar story as a way to prime them to try to remember what characters say and do. This also works well in a book that is unfamiliar. In the example that follows, I'm imagining (or inferring) what a character is saying. In the actual story, the character doesn't say anything on the first page.

Lesson Language *On every page, I'm going to try to say two things: what the character does and says. I'll put them together to sound like a storyteller. On the first page of* Harry the Dirty Dog *(Zion 2006), Harry is running down the stairs (that's what he's doing). "No way am I taking a bath!" he said (that's what he's saying).*

Prompts

- What do you think he might be saying?
- Look closely at the picture. What's he doing?
- What's the action on this page?
- Stop here. Say what he does and says.
- You said two things—what he does and what he says!

Who is this for?

LEVEL
emergent

GENRE / TEXT TYPE
narrative (with pictures)

SKILLS
storytelling, elaborating

Hat Tip: *I Am Reading: Nurturing Young Children's Meaning Making and Joyful Engagement with Any Book* (Collins and Glover 2015)

1.7 Act It to Storytell It

Who is this for?

LEVEL

emergent

GENRE / TEXT TYPE

narrative

SKILLS

storytelling, dramatic play

Hat Tip: *A Quick Guide to Boosting English Acquisition in Choice Time, K–2* (Porcelli and Tyler 2008)

Strategy Pause on a page. Use your face, body, and voice to bring the story to life. Add words to explain what you're doing.

Teaching Tip Porcelli and Tyler's phenomenal book *A Quick Guide to Boosting English Acquisition in Choice Time, K–2* (2008) is one I recommend for all pre-K and K teachers who want to help bring story play to their choice time. In their book, the authors suggest ways to have students re-create, play with, and storytell familiar read-alouds when engaged in centers, focused blocks, dramatic play, art, and more. This strategy idea is just one adapted from their book and would work well in choice time or even during partnership time in your regular reading workshop.

Prompts

- Show me with your face and body—what's the character doing now?
- Now storytell that page.
- Imagine the character in this part. Now talk like the character.
- You're really bringing the story to life with your words and with your actions!
- Your acting matches what's happening on the page! Explain what you're doing.

1.8 Express the Emotions

Strategy Think about how the character is feeling on the page. Think about how the character would talk. Use your voice to sound like the character.

Teaching Tip There is a version of this strategy in Chapter 4. The difference here is that although children may not be reading the words, they can still practice reading with expression to match the meaning they are making from the pictures. This strategy can work when children are working with books that are familiar or unfamiliar. To help students tap into their inner actor, you may want to model the way you'd read dialogue from two different parts of a book to show two different emotions. For example, in *Caps for Sale* (Slobodkina 1987), you might model "Caps for sale! Caps for sale! 50 cents a cap!" in an excited, hopeful voice. Then, "You monkeys, you!" in an annoyed, angry tone.

Prompts

- How did the character say that? Show me.
- Say it thinking about how the character is feeling
- I could tell he sounded happy (or mad or sad) because of how you read that.
- Your voice matched the character's feeling on that page.

How is the character feeling?

Say it like that!

Who is this for?

LEVEL

emergent

GENRE / TEXT TYPE

narrative (with pictures)

SKILLS

fluency, expression

1.9 Back Up, Revise

Who is this for?

LEVEL

emergent

GENRE / TEXT TYPE

narrative (with pictures)

SKILLS

monitoring for meaning, inferring

Strategy If you find yourself reading and realize "Wait! That doesn't make sense," you can always fix it. Back up and try to fix what's confusing by changing what you said on an earlier page.

Teaching Tip When readers are working with unfamiliar stories, it's helpful to teach them to use their knowledge of how stories go to read the pictures while storytelling (Collins and Glover 2015). When telling a story, their inference of what is happening on each page may work fine, but in light of new information they might find, it didn't make sense anymore. For example, if a student is reading *Harry the Dirty Dog* (Zion 2006) and starts the reading like this: "There once was a dog who loved to collect things. He collected a brush and put it in a hole in the yard. Then he ran down the street to look for more things to collect." After a few pages the child might start to realize that the dog isn't collecting anything—he's actually getting dirtier and dirtier from visiting a construction site, a playground with dogs, and running through coal. It takes amazing monitoring comprehension and inference skills to say "Wait a second!" and back up to tell the story based on what you see on future pages.

Prompts

- Hmm. Does that go with what you just said? Let's back up and think about what might have happened on this page.
- Oh, so that's what happens next. What do you think happened on the page before?
- Make sure your pages connect.
- I notice you went back to change what happened on that page so it all would make sense.

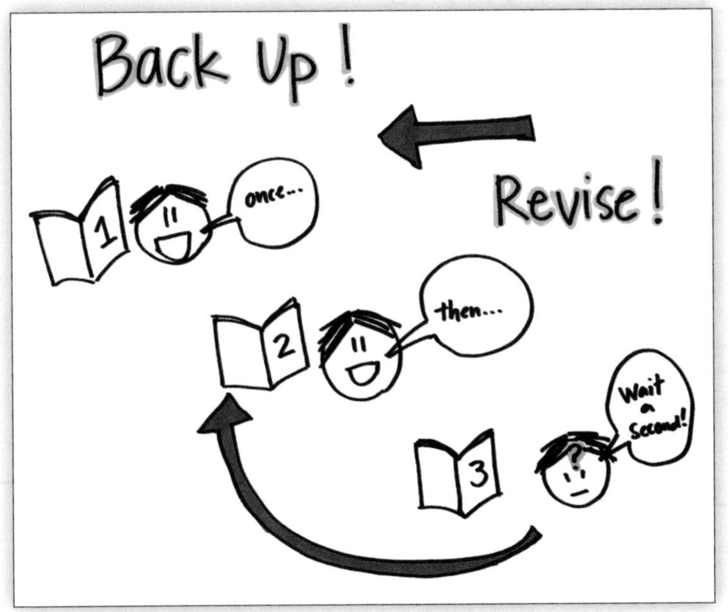

Hat Tip: *I Am Reading: Nurturing Young Children's Meaning Making and Joyful Engagement with Any Book* (Collins and Glover 2015)

1.10 Use Story Language

Strategy Use the words and groups of words we often hear in the stories we read to sound like a storyteller. Some words and word groups you may hear often are: once upon a time, then, happily ever after, after that, later that day, although, now, when.

Teaching Tip This strategy may best be taught in coaching conferences. When sitting with a student who is reading across pages, you might simply offer these phrases, as appropriate, when he or she transitions from part to part or page to page. After hearing you offer them, the reader may begin to incorporate them into his or her own speaking vocabulary. Adapt the words and phrases offered in this strategy based on those that may have come up during read-alouds.

Prompts

- How would the story start?
- What word might you use as you move from page to page?
- We're at the end! What word(s) would you use?
- Let's start the story again. Say, "Once upon a time . . ."

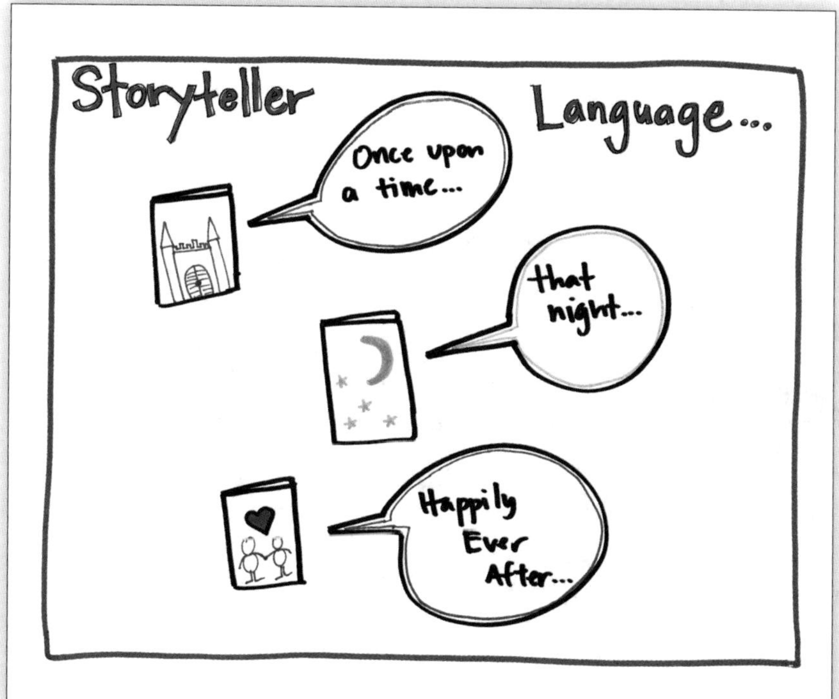

Who is this for?

LEVEL

emergent

GENRE / TEXT TYPE

narrative

SKILL

using transition words and phrases

Hat Tip: *A Curricular Plan for the Reading Workshop, Grade K* (Calkins and colleagues 2011a)

1.11 Move Your Body, Remember the Words

Who is this for?

LEVEL

emergent

GENRE / TEXT TYPE

narrative (familiar, with pictures)

SKILL

monitoring for meaning

Strategy Move your body in the same way you did when the story was being read to you. Think about what the character might be saying or doing, or what the narrator might be telling you. Tell the story that matches the way you're moving your body.

Teaching Tip When reading and rereading some of the "old favorites" that you hope to be part of your "star book" collection (Sulzby 1985), it's helpful to incorporate gestures and body movements to help the story stick. For example, when reading *Caps for Sale* (Slobodkina 1987), you might have all the children shake their finger up at the top of an imaginary tree when saying "You monkeys, you!" Or mime stacking hats on top of their heads while reading "First he had on his own checked cap, then a bunch of gray caps, then a bunch of brown caps," and so on. Children can be encouraged to mimic the gestures you make and also to make their own gestures. The gestures during the read-aloud, when done again as children read independently or with a partner, will help jog their memory of the words of the story that were on that page.

Prompts

- Show me. What did you do with your body when I read this page?
- You remember how you moved your body! Can you remember what the story was on this page?
- Look at the picture closely. Now make your body move.
- That's it (*after the child makes a gesture or action that matches the page*). Now storytell this page.

Hat Tip: *A Curricular Plan for the Reading Workshop, Grade K* (Calkins and colleagues 2011a)

1.12 Keep in Mind What Repeats

Strategy Sometimes books say the same thing over and over again! The repeated pattern can help you remember what's the same on each page, and then you can look at the picture to see what's different. Try to read both parts—the parts that are the same and the parts that are new.

Teaching Tip Books such as *Brown Bear, Brown Bear* (Martin 2010), *Chicka Chicka Boom Boom* (Archambault and Martin 2012), and *We're Going on a Bear Hunt* (Oxenbury and Rosen 1997) are great examples of books where children can lean on the repeated pattern, yet use the picture to say what's new.

Prompts

- What's the same on this page?
- Say what repeats.
- Check the picture to see what's new.
- How is this page different from the last?
- How is this page similar to the last?

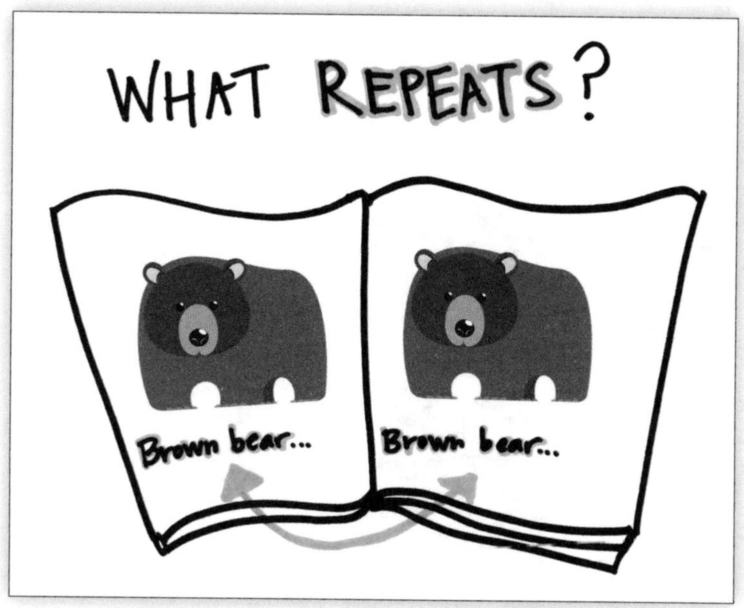

Who is this for?

LEVEL

emergent

GENRE / TEXT TYPE

books with repetitive language

SKILL

monitoring for meaning

1.13 Talk Like the Character

Who is this for?

LEVEL

emergent

GENRE / TEXT TYPE

narrative (familiar)

SKILLS

fluency, expression

Strategy Storytellers make their characters talk. Think about what's happening on the page, and when you open your mouth to speak, pretend you're the character talking. Think about what the character says and how he or she would say it. Say it just like the character

Teaching Tip This would be a great strategy to use when children tend to summarize what is happening on each page, as opposed to using actual story language. You may need to model once or twice the difference between saying, "The family walked by and saw Henry but they thought it wasn't really him" and "Everyone shook his head and said, 'Oh no. It couldn't be Harry.'" You may also want to exaggerate the expression and intonation with your example, showing a reading of a line in a flat, monotone voice and an alternate, preferred reading in an expressive voice.

Prompts

- Say it like the character.
- Pretend you're the character. Say it just like him or her.
- That's what he said. But *how* would he say it?
- You're making your characters talk!
- You're not just telling the story, you're also making your characters talk.
- You said it just how the character probably said it on that page.

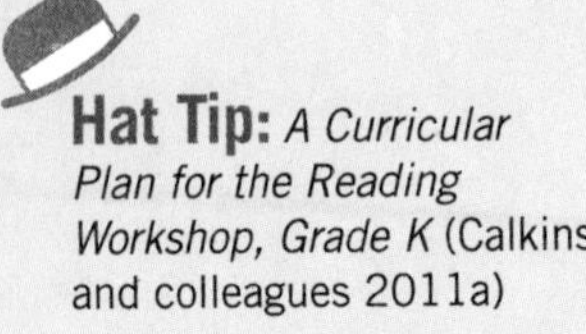

Hat Tip: *A Curricular Plan for the Reading Workshop, Grade K* (Calkins and colleagues 2011a)

1.14 If You Don't Know, Guess

Strategy If you don't know, you can guess (about what's happening, about the feelings, about what someone might be saying). Just make a guess that makes sense with the title, the picture, and what's happened so far.

Lesson Language *I've never read this* Olivia *book before (Falconer 2004), but I can look at the pictures and make a guess about what the story might be. I'm going to look carefully, and make sure my storytelling makes sense. On the first page, I'm going to say, "Olivia likes to sing songs." Then, "She loves to do lots of things like play with balls, and yo-yos and cook, and run and jump and stand on her head!" Do you see how my storytelling matched the pictures and made sense from page to page?*

Prompts

- Look at the picture. Think about what's happened so far. What might be happening on this page?
- I know you don't know, but what might it be?
- Think about what makes sense with what has happened so far.

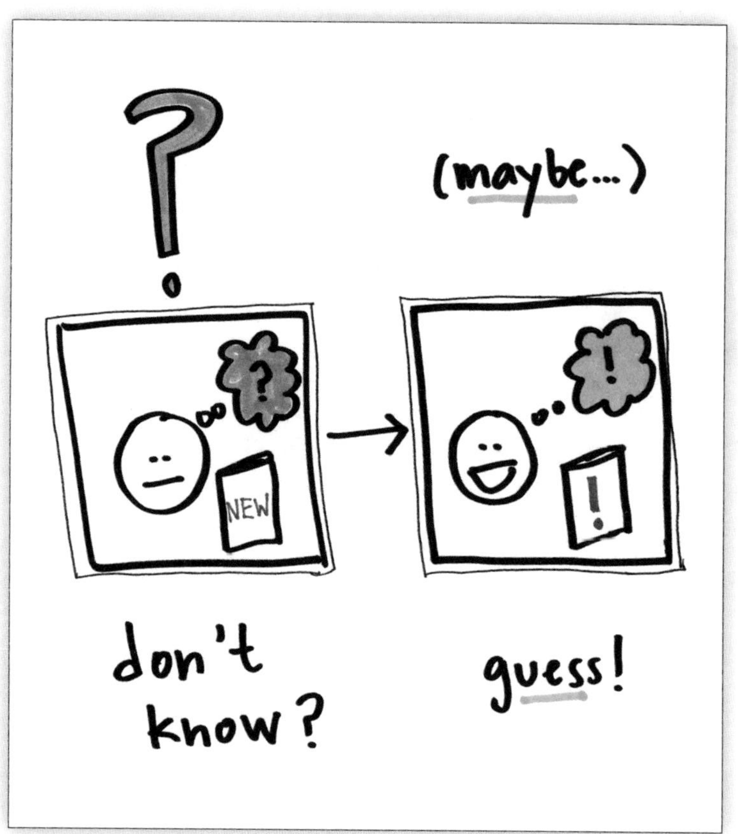

Who is this for?

LEVEL

emergent

GENRE / TEXT TYPE

narrative (unfamiliar)

SKILLS

inferring, monitoring for meaning

Hat Tip: *I Am Reading: Nurturing Young Children's Meaning Making and Joyful Engagement with Any Book* (Collins and Glover 2015)

1.15 Readers Explain Their Thinking

Who is this for?

LEVEL

emergent

GENRE / TEXT TYPE

any

SKILLS

inferring, supporting ideas with evidence

Hat Tip: *I Am Reading: Nurturing Young Children's Meaning Making and Joyful Engagement with Any Book* (Collins and Glover 2015)

Strategy When you turn to a page and have an idea, stop and think, "What makes me think that?" You can look to picture to see what gives you a particular idea. Share your thinking with your partner or a teacher.

Teaching Tip This strategy is best taught in conversation with a reader during a conference, or to a partner engaged in conversation who might be jumping from one part/idea to another.

Prompts

- What makes you think she's sad (or mad or happy)?
- Why do you think they're ____?
- How do you know they're ____?
- Tell me how you got that idea.
- Tell me what made you think that.
- That's a clear explanation! It matches the pictures.

1.16 What I See/What I Think

Strategy Reading is thinking! When you read a page, you can read from the page and say what you see. Then, you can say what's in your mind, or what you think.

Lesson Language *In books there is so much to think about! Watch as I read and think about* We Play Music *(Johnson 2002).* (Model pointing to and around the picture.) *On this first page, I see a drum, a pan, sticks, a bell, and a trumpet. Oh! And a block. I need to look all over the picture to see it all.* (Point to your head.) *I'm thinking that all of these instruments, together, will make up a band. Maybe something with a good beat because there are many percussion instruments.* (Point to the page.) *On the next page, I see a boy with the drum. I notice it's strapped to him, and he's hitting it with his hands. He's smiling and he's on some steps.* (Point to your head.) *I'm thinking that this drum is different than the ones I'm used to, that you play with sticks. He looks happy, like he's enjoying playing! The steps look like the front stoop of a building, maybe in New York City.*

Prompts

- Point to the picture. Say what you see.
- What do you think about on this page?
- Say, "I'm thinking . . ."
- Say, "Maybe . . ."
- Yes, that's a thought because you came up with it on your own!

Who is this for?

LEVEL

emergent

GENRE / TEXT TYPE

nonfiction or narrative

SKILLS

monitoring for meaning, inferring

1.17 Talk Like an Expert

Who is this for?

LEVEL

emergent

GENRE / TEXT TYPE

nonfiction

SKILL

word choice

Strategy Talk like a scientist or expert when you're reading nonfiction. Look carefully at the picture to remember what the author is teaching. Think about the words you'd use to read the page. Use those words when you're reading to yourself or with a partner.

Teaching Tip This strategy will only work if the child knows the vocabulary needed for the book but doesn't use the vocabulary when reading independently or with a partner. For some readers, this strategy might work best when used with books that have already been read to them, or in books that are connected in some way to class studies in science, social studies, or math. If a child has selected an unfamiliar text, you could, in a conference, introduce the vocabulary: "Oh, you notice that drum? That's called a bongo drum. The next time you read this, you can call it that."

Prompts

- I can see you're looking carefully at the details. Can you use a specific word there?
- What exactly is that called?
- What would a scientist call that?
- Try to use the word an expert in ____ would use for that.
- Now you're talking like an expert! The word ____ is one an expert would use when talking about this topic.

1.18 Use a Teaching Voice

Strategy Read the text so it sounds like you're teaching. Think about how it sounds when information books are read aloud to you. Try to make your teaching voice sound the same way.

Lesson Language *Reading information books, books that teach you, sounds different from reading stories. In stories, people talk, and characters do things, and a narrator explains it all. In information books, an author teaches you, and there are lots of facts. Listen to the difference when I read a story with a bear character, and when I read a teaching book, an information book, to learn about bears.* (Model each.)

Prompts

- That sounded like a teaching voice. You told me one fact after another.
- The animals probably wouldn't be talking in a teaching book. Instead, tell me some facts about the animal.
- Look across the picture and tell me what you're learning.

Who is this for?

LEVEL

emergent

GENRE / TEXT TYPE

nonfiction

SKILL

fluency

1.19 Connect the Pages

Who is this for?

LEVEL

emergent

GENRE / TEXT TYPE

nonfiction or narrative

SKILL

synthesizing

Hat Tip: *I Am Reading: Nurturing Young Children's Meaning Making and Joyful Engagement with Any Book* (Collins and Glover 2015)

Strategy The whole book is about one thing, so try to connect the pages. If it's a storybook, it tells one story across the whole book. You can use words like and then . . . and then . . . to make sure the pages connect. If it's an information book, the whole book is about one topic. For information books, you can use another thing . . . or also . . ."

Teaching Tip Modify this lesson based on the type of book the student has chosen. This will help simplify the language of the strategy to make it more memorable.

Prompts

- Think about how these pages connect.
- Say, "And then . . .."
- Say, "Another thing is . . ."
- How does what you learn on this page fit with what you learn on that page?
- How did the character get from here to there?

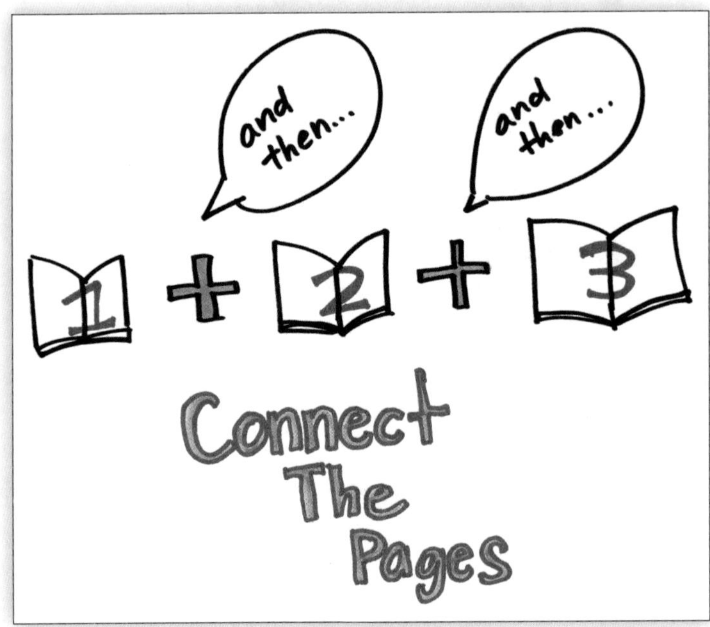

1.20 Character Name or Group Name?

Strategy Think about the kind of book you're reading. Then, think about how the author talks about the *who* in the book. If it's an information book, we should read the *who* as a group word, with an s on the end. If it's a story, we should read the *who* as a single name, without an s on the end.

Lesson Language *When authors teach us about something in an information book, they use the general name of things. For example, in this book* (Hold up the book *Horses and Ponies* by Parragon, 2012.), *where I'm learning about horses, the author uses the word* horses *to teach me about horses in general. Horses* this *and horses* that. *That's because the author is teaching me about what's true about all horses. But, in this story* (Hold up *My Horse* by Karen Hjemboe, 2000.), *the horse is a specific character. So the author doesn't use the word* horses, *the author uses the character name, or* horse. *When I read this story, I say, "My horse ____" and "My horse ____"—there's no s on the end. So when you're reading, try to think about the kind of book you're reading. Is it a teaching book, teaching all about a who, a topic in general? Or is it a story, where the who is a character's name?*

Prompts

- Let's think about what kind of book this is.
- Is this a teaching book or a story?
- How do you know that this is a story?
- How do you know that this is a teaching book?
- So let's think will the *who* have an *s* on the end as you read it?

Stories

Information Books

-S

Who is this for?

LEVEL

emergent

GENRE / TEXT TYPE

nonfiction or narrative

SKILL

understanding genre

Hat Tip: *I Am Reading: Nurturing Young Children's Meaning Making and Joyful Engagement with Any Book* (Collins and Glover 2015)

Teaching Reading Engagement

Focus, Stamina, and Building a Reading Life

Why is this goal important?

You could be the most eloquent teacher, the best strategy group facilitator, the most insightful conferrer. But if you send your kids back for independent reading and they don't read, then they won't make the progress you are hoping and working for (Allington 2011). To put it another way, "Without engagement, we've got nothing" (Serravallo 2010).

Engagement is everything. Research has shown that the amount of time kids spend practicing, on-task, with eyes on print, makes the biggest difference to their success as readers, and across content areas (Allington 2011; Anderson, Wilson, and Fielding 1988; Krashen 2004; Cunningham and Stanovich 1991; Stanovich and Cunningham 1993; Pressley et al. 2000; Taylor, Frye, and Maruyama 1990).

An engaged reader is often one who is "motivated to read, strategic in their approaches to comprehending what they read, knowledgeable in their construction of meaning from text, and socially interactive while reading" (Guthrie, Wigfield, and You 2012, 602). This means that classrooms in which independent reading is not always a solo task and kids interact in partnerships and clubs will likely have more engaged readers (see Chapter 12). It also means that teachers need to work to help readers construct meaning (see Chapters 5 through 11) and that an engagement problem may actually be a symptom of something else—a child who is not understanding, for example. To say it another way, sometimes to help readers with the goal of *engagement*, you actually need to work on *comprehension* (Ivey and Johnston 2013).

When you've ruled out comprehension as the root of an engagement issue and want to focus on engagement itself, you will find that the goal has a few parts. Some may argue that helping children to select books that are a good fit in terms of readability and that will be interesting to them in terms of content should come first (Miller 2009; Von Sprecken, Kim, and Krashen 2000). Kids' attention and their ability to manipulate that focus and bring it back to the task at hand is also important. Stamina also comes into play; the amount of time readers can sustain their reading often requires incremental growth over time and strategies to support that increase. When all of these are in place, readers may attain a condition that Atwell refers to as being "in the reading zone" (2007) or what Csikszentmihalyi calls "flow" (2008).

How do I know if this goal is right for my student?

My favorite tool for figuring out who needs support with engagement is the engagement inventory (Figure 2.A; Serravallo 2010, 2013b, 2014). Essentially a kidwatching tool, it can be used to record student behaviors and signs of engagement and disengagement for one entire reading period, instead of conferring or pulling small groups together. I look for patterns within the class to discover which students need which instruction.

Book logs (Figure 2.B) can also be helpful if they're honestly kept. For kids at level K–Z+, you may use a log that asks a child to record start and end times and start and end pages, and look for a rate of about three-quarters of a page per minute. Much less may mean the child is getting distracted. The book titles over time also tell a story about likes and dislikes.

Interest inventories (Figure 2.C) help to match kids to books when they are having a hard time doing so independently, especially when the inventories ask questions about nonreading things, like hobbies, favorite movies, or TV shows.

Figure 2.A An engagement inventory allows teachers to record reading behaviors to decide on goals relating to engagement.

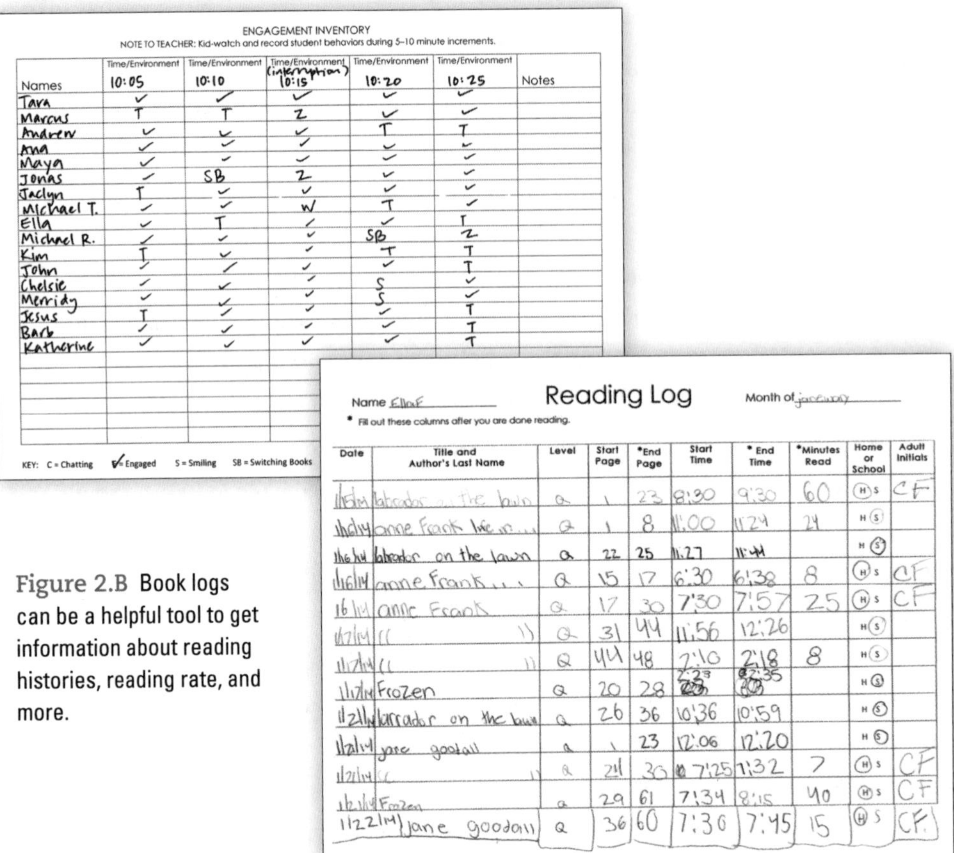

ENGAGEMENT INVENTORY

NOTE TO TEACHER: Kid-watch and record student behaviors during 5–10 minute increments.

Names	Time/Environment 10:05	Time/Environment 10:10	Time/Environment (interruption) 10:15	Time/Environment 10:20	Time/Environment 10:25	Notes
Tara	✓	✓	✓	✓	✓	
Marcus	T	T	Z	✓	✓	
Andrew	✓	✓	✓	T	T	
Ana	✓	✓	✓	✓	✓	
Maya	✓	✓	✓	✓	✓	
Jonas	✓	SB	Z	✓	✓	
Jaclyn	T	✓	✓	✓	✓	
Michael T.	✓	✓	W	T	✓	
Ella	✓	T	✓	✓	T	
Michael R.	✓	✓	✓	SB	Z	
Kim	T	✓	✓	T	T	
John	✓	✓	✓	✓	T	
Chelsie	✓	✓	✓	S	✓	
Merridy	✓	✓	✓	S	✓	
Jesus	T	✓	✓	✓	T	
Barb	✓	✓	✓	✓	T	
Katherine	✓	✓	✓	✓	T	

KEY: C = Chatting ✓ Engaged S = Smiling SB = Switching Books

Reading Log

Name Ella F. Month of January

* Fill out these columns after you are done reading.

Date	Title and Author's Last Name	Level	Start Page	*End Page	Start Time	* End Time	*Minutes Read	Home or School	Adult Initials
1/5/14	labrador on the lawn	Q	1	23	8:30	9:30	60	H	CF
1/6/14	anne Frank life in...	Q	1	8	11:00	11:24	24	S	
1/6/14	labrador on the lawn	Q	22	25	11:27	11:44		S	
1/16/14	anne Frank...	Q	15	17	6:30	6:38	8	H	CF
1/6/14	anne Frank	Q	17	30	7:30	7:57	25	H	CF
1/17/14	" "	Q	31	44	11:56	12:26		S	
1/17/14	" "	Q	44	48	2:10	2:18	8	S	
1/17/14	Frozen	Q	20	28	2:23	2:35		S	
1/21/14	labrador on the lawn	Q	26	36	10:36	10:59		S	
1/21/14	jane goodall	Q	1	23	12:06	12:20		S	
1/21/14	" "	Q	24	36	7:25	7:32	7	H	CF
1/21/14	Frozen	Q	29	61	7:34	8:15	40	H	CF
1/22/14	jane goodall	Q	36	60	7:30	7:45	15	H	CF.

Figure 2.B Book logs can be a helpful tool to get information about reading histories, reading rate, and more.

Figure 2.C Interest inventories are powerful ways to help teachers match kids to books, especially when they ask about more than reading.

Reading Interest Survey

Name: Lola

Do you like to read?

yes

How much time do you spend reading?

30 min /day

What are some of the books you have read lately?

nonfiction about animals, picture books

Do you have a library card? How often do you use it?

yes. I don't usually borrow books

Do you ever get books from the school library?

yes. 2 every Friday

About how many books do you own?

too many to count!

What are some books you would like to own?

joke books, anything with a good story

Put a check mark next to the kinds of reading you like best and topics you might like to read about:

___ history	___ travel	___ plays	___ sports
✓ adventure	___ romance	___ poetry	✓ science fiction
___ biography	___ war stories	___ car stories	___ supernatural stories
___ humor	___ mysteries	✓ folktales	✓ how-to-do-it books
___ art	___ westerns	✓ novels	✓ astrology
___ detective stories			

Reading Interest Survey

Do you like to read the newspaper?

no.

If yes, place a check mark next to the part of the newspaper listed you like to read:

___ headlines	___ editorials	___ sports
___ advertisements	___ columnists	___ entertainment
___ comic strips	___ political stories	___ current events
___ others (please list):		

What are your favorite television programs?

cartoons and some stuff on Disney

How much time do you spend watching television?

only a few shows a week

What is your favorite magazine?

Ranger Rick!

Do you have a hobby? If so, what is it?

I like ballet. I also like arts+crafts and science.

What are the two best movies you have ever seen?

Toy Story, Frozen.

Who are your favorite entertainers and/or movie stars? When you were little, did you enjoy having someone read aloud to you?

yes. I love being read to. I like anybody from Disney movies.

List topics, subjects, et cetera that you might like to read about:

animals, space, folktales

What does the word 'reading' mean to you?

fun!

Say anything else that you would like to say about reading:

I like to read.

Strategies for Engagement at a Glance

Strategy		Levels	Genres/ Text Types	Skills
2.1	A Perfect Reading Spot	A–Z+	Any	Focus
2.2	Vary the Length or Type of Text ("Break Reads")	A–Z+	Any	Focus
2.3	Reread to Get Back in Your Book	A–Z+	Any	Monitoring engagement
2.4	Keep Your Eyes and Mind in the Book	A–Z+	Any	Focus, monitoring for meaning
2.5	Retell and Jump Back In	A–Z+	Any	Retelling, monitoring for meaning
2.6	Fixing the Fuzziness	A–Z+	Any	Monitoring for meaning
2.7	Prime Yourself with Prior Knowledge	A–Z+	Any	Focus, activating prior knowledge
2.8	Set a Timed Goal	A–Z+	Any	Stamina
2.9	Most Desirable/Least Desirable	A–Z+	Any	Focus, stamina
2.10	"Party" Ladder	A–Z+	Any	Stamina, focus
2.11	Purposes for Reading: Go/Stop Mat	A–I	Any	Stamina
2.12	Ask Questions to Engage with the Text	E–Z+	Any	Questioning, focus, stamina
2.13	Mind Over Matter	E–Z+	Any	Attention, focus
2.14	Track Progress on a Stamina Chart	F–Z+	Any	Stamina, focus
2.15	Choose Like Books for a Best Fit	F–Z+	Any	Book choice
2.16	Choose Books with Your Identity in Mind	J–Z+	Any	Book choice
2.17	Visualize to Focus	J–Z+	Any	Visualizing, focus
2.18	Reading Log Rate Reflection	K–Z+	Any	Improving reading rate
2.19	Finding Reading Territories	K–Z+	Any	Book choice, focus
2.20	Reflect on the Past and Plan for the Future	K–Z+	Any	Book choice, stamina
2.21	You've Got to "Get It" to Be Engaged	K–Z+	Any	Monitoring for meaning
2.22	Buzz About Books	K–Z+	Any	Recommending books
2.23	Set Page Goals	L–Z+	Any	Monitoring engagement, focus, stamina
2.24	Read with a Focus to Focus	L–Z+	Any	Focus, stamina
2.25	Monitor Your Stamina and Pace	L–Z+	Any	Stamina, monitoring for meaning
2.26	Does It Engage Me?	L–Z+	Any	Book choice, focus
2.27	Hear the Story	L–Z+	Fiction	Visualizing

2.1 A Perfect Reading Spot

Who is this for?

LEVELS

A–Z+

GENRE / TEXT TYPE

any

SKILL

focus

Strategy Choosing a reading spot is very important. Different people concentrate best in different environments. Think about what you need—bright or dim light? Noisy or quiet? Hard or soft seating? Laying down or sitting upright? Plan out a spot, give it a try, and reflect on how it went for you.

Prompts

- What do you think you need from your environment to get the most reading done?
- Pick a spot that will work for you.
- Tell me why you picked that spot.
- Think about where you've been successful. Pick a spot based on past success.
- Think about what tends to distract you. Choose a different type of spot.
- You considered where you'd do your best reading so thoughtfully. Give it a try and we'll talk in a couple days.

2.2 Vary the Length or Type of Text ("Break Reads")

Strategy Reading longer texts and shorter texts takes a different kind of attention and focus. It may help you to plan stopping places in your longer book and have some texts at the ready for briefer break reads. Articles, short stories, and poems are good texts for this kind of reading.

Teaching Tip This strategy will be particularly helpful for children who struggle with longer, continuous text such as chapter books. However, even readers at lower levels could benefit from a variation on this strategy. Offer children at the lowest levels a "look book" as an occasional break in between the books where they are attending to print (Collins 2004). To change the strategy to be appropriate for lower levels, you'd ask the children to make a pile of the books where they'll be reading the words (instead of marking a stopping place) and then planning to read the look book (instead of reading a short text).

Prompts

- What book(s) have you chosen for your longer reads?
- What book(s) have you chosen for break books?
- Let's plan out how you'll read each.
- Let's set a goal for how much of this book or pile you'll read before you turn to your break book.
- Based on what I've noticed, I think that's a sensible goal for you.

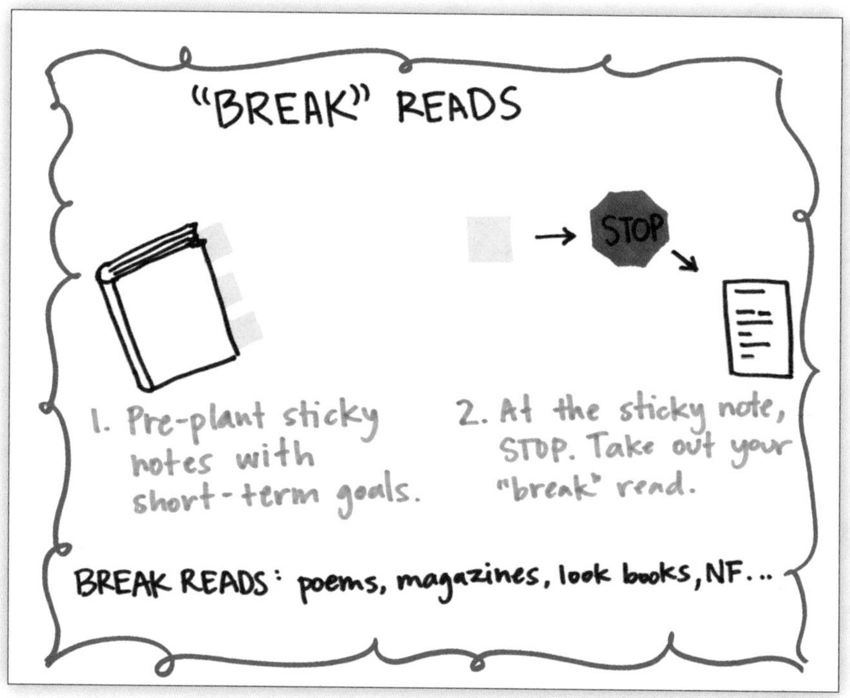

"BREAK" READS
STOP
1. Pre-plant sticky notes with short-term goals.
2. At the sticky note, STOP. Take out your "break" read.
BREAK READS: poems, magazines, look books, NF...

Who is this for?

LEVELS

A–Z+

GENRE / TEXT TYPE

any

SKILL

focus

2.3 Reread to Get Back in Your Book

Who is this for?

LEVELS

A–Z+

GENRE / TEXT TYPE

any

SKILL

monitoring engagement

Strategy When you get distracted, stop and notice where your attention first started to drift. Go back to the last thing you remember not just reading but really understanding. Reread from there to get back into your book.

Prompts

- I see you got distracted there. What's the last thing you remember reading?
- Go back to the last place you remember understanding what you were reading.
- Did you notice yourself getting distracted there?
- What can you do?
- Show me what you'll do now.
- Put your finger on the place you last remember feeling focused.
- I noticed you caught yourself getting distracted. Did rereading help?
- I notice you backed up to reread when you got distracted.

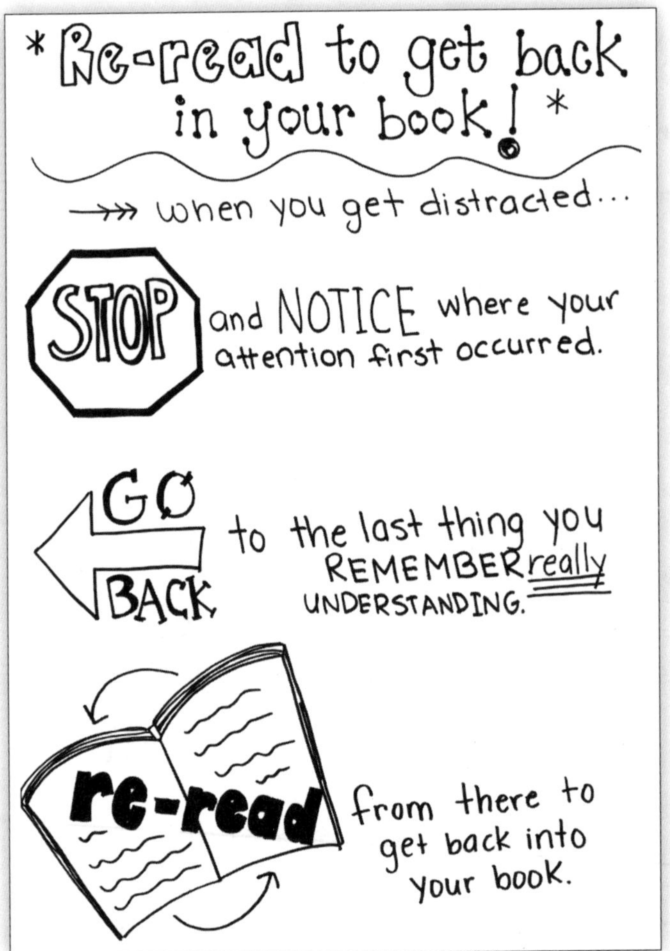

2.4 Keep Your Eyes and Mind in the Book

Strategy Being engaged means keeping not just your eyes but also your mind on the book. As you read, be aware of your attention shifting. When it does, back up and reread. If you notice attention shifting very often, consider if the book isn't a good fit, or if something in your environment is causing you to become distracted.

Prompts

- Can you picture what's happening?
- Are you focused right now?
- Is your mind on the book, or just your eyes?
- What do you notice about your focus?
- I saw you caught yourself getting distracted so you backed up to reread.
- Show me what to do when you get distracted.
- Reread.

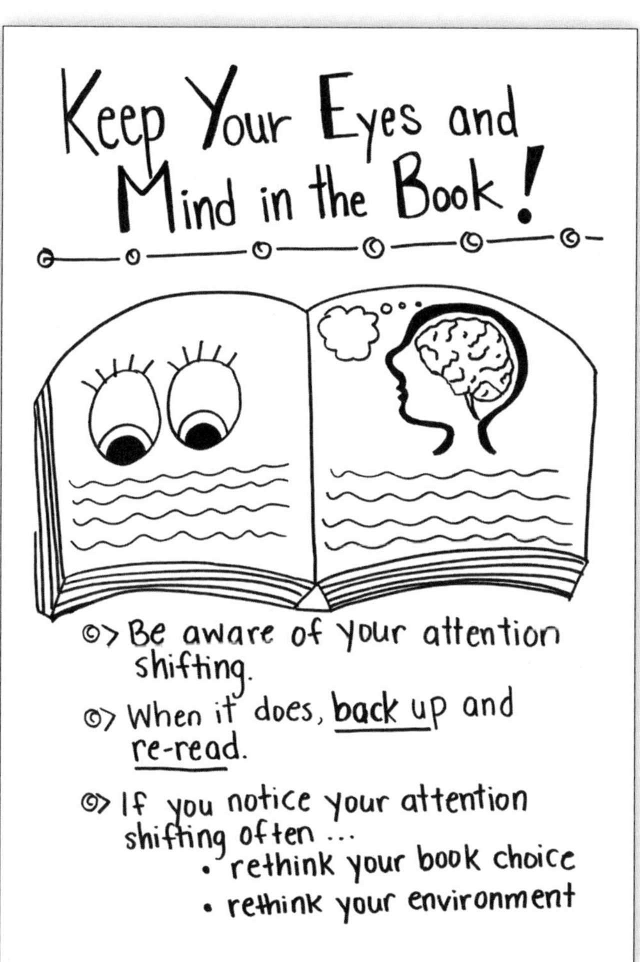

Who is this for?

LEVELS

A–Z+

GENRE / TEXT TYPE

any

SKILLS

focus, monitoring for meaning

2.5 Retell and Jump Back In

Who is this for?

LEVELS

A–Z+

GENRE / TEXT TYPE

any

SKILLS

retelling, monitoring for meaning

Strategy Everyone's mind wanders sometimes; the important thing is that you are able to pull your attention back. Say to yourself, "No. I'm not going to think about that right now." Then, quickly retell what you remember about your book to jump back into it.

Teaching Tip Consider modifying the language of this strategy so it's appropriate for the reading level of the student with whom you're working. For example, children reading at levels A–D most likely won't retell their book sequentially, since the books are often written in a list format. Instead, they may name what the book is mostly about ("This book is about fruit!") or they may repeat the pattern ("I remember! On every page it says, 'I see a _____'").

Prompts

- Retell.
- Say back what you remember.
- What part seems fuzzy? Can you go back and reread to retell?
- When did you find your mind wandering?
- Did your mind wander there? You know what to do. Show me.
- Let me watch you jump back into your book.
- You're retelling before you jump back into the book—that's really going to help you stay focused.

2.6 Fixing the Fuzziness

Strategy It's crucial that you always are sure that you're making sense of what you're reading about. Check in with meaning by asking yourself: What's happening, who is in this scene, and where are they? Can I see what's happening? Am I thinking about, having feelings about, or reacting to what's happening? If you feel like anything is fuzzy, back up and reread to make sure you're understanding.

Prompts

- Stop here to check yourself.
- What's fuzzy? What will you fix?
- Show me how you'll fix the fuzziness.
- Ask yourself, "Who is in this scene?" (*Pause for response.*) Now ask, "What is happening?" (*Pause for response.*) Now ask, "Where are they?" (*Pause for response.*) If you've got all three, read on.
- What can you ask yourself to check your understanding?
- Check in. Are you understanding?

Check in with Meaning!
Make sure it's CLEAR not FUZZY

ASK:

- What's the who? What? Where?

- Can I make a movie in my mind?

- Did I have a feeling/reaction?

Who is this for?

LEVELS

A–Z+

GENRE / TEXT TYPE

any

SKILL

monitoring for meaning

2.7 Prime Yourself with Prior Knowledge

Who is this for?

LEVELS

A–Z+

GENRE / TEXT TYPE

any

SKILLS

focus, activating prior knowledge

Strategy Sometimes setting ourselves up for success helps us to stay focused and engaged. Before beginning to read, think about how your book will go. You can think about its structure, what you know about the topic, what you know about other books by this author, or what you know about others in this series.

Lesson Language *I want to show you how I would set myself up to read two very different books. The first book is a nonfiction book titled* Antarctica *by Mel Friedman (2009). As I look at this book, I'm going to say what I know about the topic, the series, and the genre to get myself ready to read. I know that this is a nonfiction book. I've read other nonfiction books in this series—the True Book series—and I know that they are organized into chapters. In each chapter, I am going to be working to figure out what the chapter is mostly about and what details support it, so that I can summarize each chapter before going on to the next one. That always helps me organize all the facts in my mind. I also know that all the information in this book will be about Antarctica—a topic I know a little about. I know it's extremely cold there, and that there are animals like penguins and seals and whales living there. I also know that there were people who explored the continent and I think some of them died because of the harsh conditions. So, as I read this book I'm going to keep checking in with myself. What are the main ideas of the chapters? How far into the book am I, based on the table of contents? What have I learned?*

Now, let me show you how I get ready to read a very different book. Another book I chose for my reading this week is Granny Torrelli Makes Soup *by Sharon Creech (2005). I've read another book by her, so I can use that to help me. I know that her books always have great lessons, but that it takes some thinking to figure them out. Also, I know that sometimes she uses symbolism in the story, so I'll be sure to think about that when I'm reading. Also, it's fiction and I read a lot of novels. I usually make sure that I'm understanding after each chapter. I also know that usually the story keeps working up to something, and by about three-quarters of the way through there's a big change or turning point in the story. So I can think about that general way stories go to help me.*

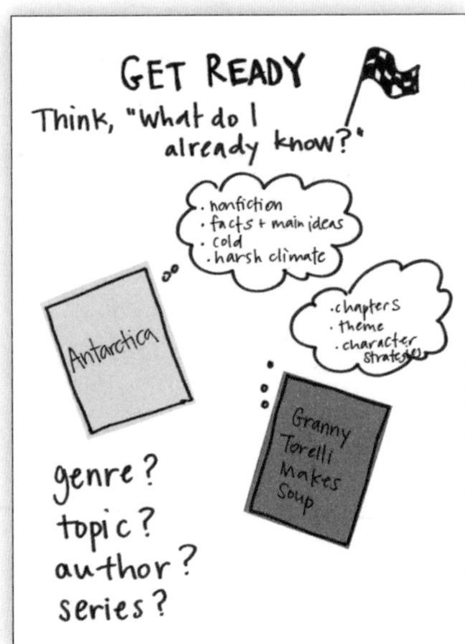

Prompts

- What do you know about this series/author/genre?
- Tell me how you think the book will be structured.
- Based on what you know about this series/author/genre, how will the rest of the book unfold?
- Where are you in the overall story?
- Talk about how you're getting ready to read this book.
- You used what you know about the series to explain the structure!

2.8 Set a Timed Goal

Strategy One way to increase the amount of time you read with focus is to set a time goal for yourself. Use a personal quiet timer and set it for a certain amount of time. When the timer goes off, have the break you need (get up, stretch, let your mind wander for a moment). Then, reset the timer and get back into your reading.

Teaching Tip Teachers often ask me what type of break is appropriate. My suggestion is that the teacher decides on a "break" with the student, or the teacher decides for the student based on what he or she knows about the child. Kids who are very physically active may need a break that involves getting up and moving to help get the wiggles out, such as stretching at their seat. On the opposite end of the continuum are children who may be very sleepy and need a break that will energize them, such as doing quasi-push-ups on their desk, or placing their hands on the seat of their chair to do a quick lift up. A Google search for "movement breaks for the classroom" will yield many specific ideas. Still other students may benefit from taking some time to stop and reflect on what they've read, perhaps even jotting a quick summary or idea. This last idea will help support comprehension, which is linked to level of engagement.

Prompts

- How long do you think you can read before you need a break?
- What's your goal?
- How many minutes will you set the timer for?
- So last time, you thought you'd take a break every __ minutes. How did that work for you?
- So last time you decided to take a break by ____. How did that work for you?
- What do you think you'll try this time?

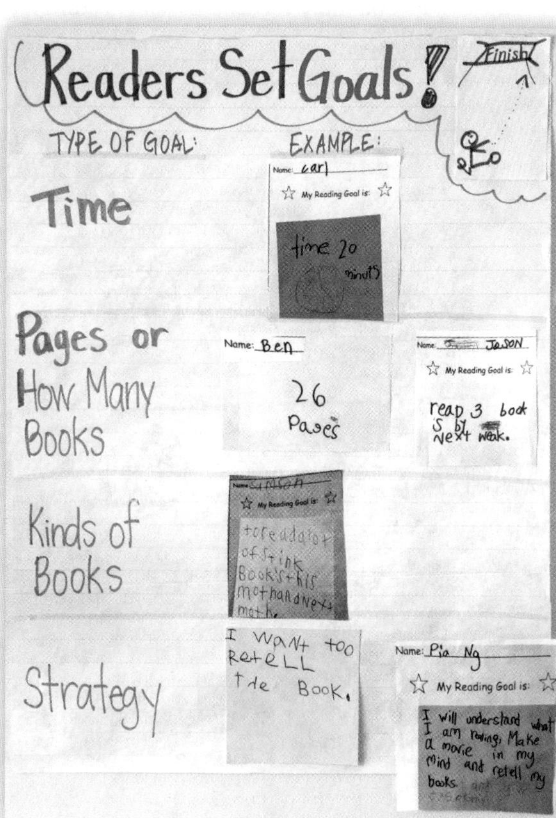

Who is this for?

LEVELS

A–Z+

GENRE / TEXT TYPE

any

SKILL

stamina

2.9 Most Desirable/Least Desirable

Who is this for?

LEVELS

A–Z+

GENRE / TEXT TYPE

any

SKILLS

focus, stamina

Hat Tip: *The Daily 5: Fostering Literacy Independence in the Elementary Grades*, second edition (Boushey and Moser 2014)

Strategy Show what it looks like to be disengaged, distracted, or unfocused with your reading. Name what you did. Now, change your body and mind to show what it looks like to be focused and engaged. Stop and jot—what are the differences between the two? What will you plan to do?

Teaching Tip An easy modification to this lesson for younger students would be to eliminate the stop-and-jot component and instead ask children to talk with a partner or with you in a conference about the differences between the distracted reader stance and the focused reader stance. You may create an anchor chart together, perhaps using photographs of the children from your class, with the heading "Engaged Reading Looks and Sounds Like . . ."

Prompts

- Show me what it would look like if you're reading with focus.
- Can you act like you're pretending to read? Now tell me what's different about real reading.
- Act disengaged, distracted, and unfocused.
- How do the two ways feel different?
- How can you be more focused in your reading? What will you try to do differently?

2.10 "Party" Ladder

Strategy Make very small, short-term goals for yourself (such as jotting on a sticky note or reading a few pages). As you read, and as you accomplish each goal, move your arrow sticky note up the ladder. When you get to the top, you'll "party"—have a short celebration you and I have agreed to.

Teaching Tip The idea behind this strategy is that you'll be breaking down something that feels far away and possibly insurmountable to a student who is currently having little success with reading for a long period of time. The "ladder" makes the longer stretch of reading into a series of short-term goals with a reward. In essence, each move to a new "step" will be a reward in and of itself as it is a visual representation of progress toward a larger goal.

Over time, as a student becomes more capable with the current series of steps, you'll want to help him or her modify the tool to add a new challenge. For instance, if a child first planned to move up the ladder for every three minutes of independent reading, then once the child is able to accomplish that with independence you may decide to increase the short-term goal to five minutes. Or perhaps you'd want to add three more three-minute steps on the ladder to increase the amount of time before the "party."

In any case, the goal is not for the child to become dependent on this ladder to read independently—quite the opposite. You want to increase the amount of time or length of the task until it's just one step: read for the entire independent reading period. At that point, the party ladder can be eliminated as a tool altogether.

Prompts

- How long do you think you can read before we switch the task?
- What sorts of things will you do to help you stay focused—stretch breaks, jot about your reading, retell in your mind?
- Let's make a ladder together.
- Let's practice using it. Place your sticky note on the bottom and let's start.
- Yes! You stayed focused that whole time. Move your sticky note and do what's next.
- What will you do next?

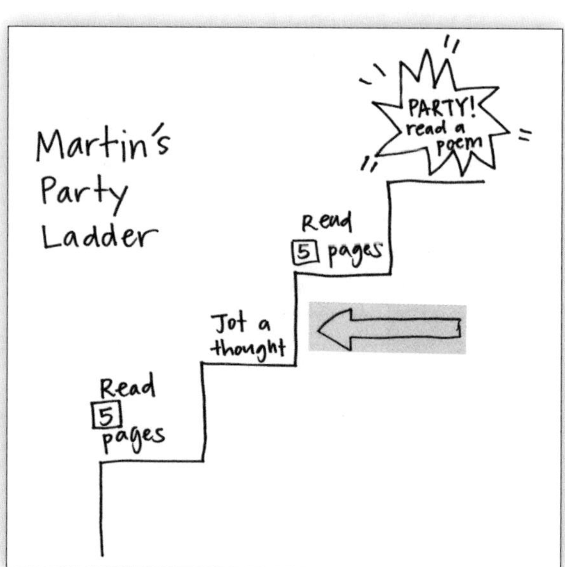

Who is this for?

LEVELS
A–Z+

GENRE / TEXT TYPE
any

SKILLS
stamina, focus

2.11 Purposes for Reading: Go/Stop Mat

Who is this for?

LEVELS

A–I

GENRE / TEXT TYPE

any

SKILL

stamina

Strategy Check your purpose for reading the book. Choose one book from the stack of books on the "go" side of your mat. After you read the book, move it to the "stop" side. Remind yourself of your purpose, pick up your next book, and repeat.

Teaching Tip Be sure to match the rereading "purposes" with what you've taught. Some teachers have a several day cycle for shared reading, for example, where each day students revisit the same text with a new intention. For example, day one might be a picture walk and first read through the text, day two might be a focus on high-frequency sight words, day three may be work on fluency, and so on. Alternatively, you may choose to introduce purposes during small-group time. Vary this strategy for the reading level and other goals you have for the student(s) you're teaching.

Lesson Language *I'm going to give you a mat with two sides, "go" and "stop."* (See figure.) *At the bottom of the mat are some pictures to remind you about things readers do as we read and reread, such as understand the book, smooth out the reading, and make our voice sound like the character. When it's time to start, place all twelve of your books on the go side. Then, look at the picture to see what work you'll do as you read. Next, read one whole book, practicing what the card says to practice. When you finish, move the book to the side that says stop. You can take a quick stretch break if you need it. Then, pick up the next book from the go side and read that, again keeping the purpose in mind. Place it on stop. Take a quick break. Then what comes next? That's right—pick up a book from the start side. If there's still reading time left and you've gotten through your whole stack, you can move the books back over to the start side and begin again, now focusing on the next purpose for reading.*

Prompts

- Looks like you just finished a book. Where does it go?
- Go ahead and put that book on the "stop" side since you just finished it.
- You're getting so much more reading done this way.
- You read them all! Now, go ahead and move the books back to go.
- Check the mat—what are you practicing as you read?

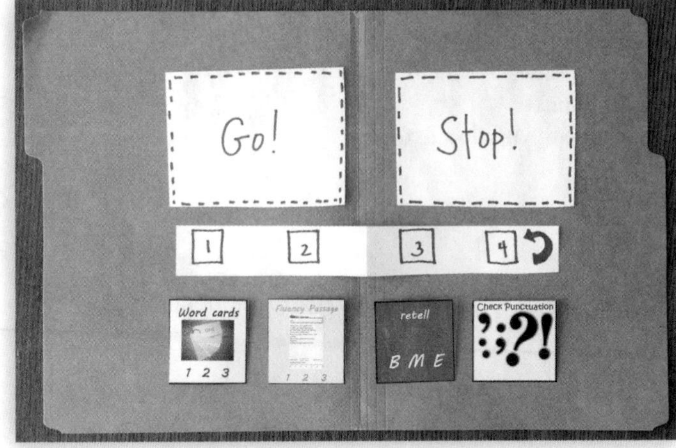

Hat Tip: *A Curricular Plan for the Reading Workshop, Grade K* (Calkins and colleagues 2011a)

2.12 Ask Questions to Engage with the Text

Strategy Engage your mind by asking questions as you read. In fiction you might ask, "What comes next? Why did the character do that?" In nonfiction, you might ask questions about the topic. Read on to answer your questions.

Lesson Language *Part of having your mind turned on to a book, and reading in a wide-awake way, means coming to the text with curiosity. As if you are having a conversation with yourself as you read, you can ask and answer questions to push yourself to want to read on. In a story, you could ask questions about what will come next, why the characters do what they do, or why the author made the choices she or he did. In a nonfiction book, you might wonder about the topic. In both cases, you can read on to discover answers to your questions. If it helps, you could even stop and jot some questions and then answer them as you find out more later in the book.*

Prompts

- What are you wondering?
- What makes you ask that?
- Have you found the answer to your question yet?
- What are you curious about?
- Try starting with who, what, where, when, or why.
- That's what you know. What are you wondering about that?
- That's what happened. What question can you ask about that?
- How much more do you think you'll need to read to answer that?
- Do you think the answer to your question is in this book, or will you need to read another to find that out?
- Tell me about the conversation you're having in your mind.
- What is your guess about the answer to your question?

Who is this for?

LEVELS

E–Z+

GENRE / TEXT TYPE

any

SKILLS

questioning, focus, stamina

Hat Tip: "Engagement with Young Adult Literature: Outcomes and Processes" (Ivey and Johnston 2013)

2.13 Mind Over Matter

Who is this for?

LEVELS

E–Z+

GENRE / TEXT TYPE

any

SKILLS

attention, focus

Strategy Sometimes part of being engaged is just deciding to be. If you approach a book thinking "This isn't for me," then it's like you're switching your brain off from the start. Instead, try to read it like the words are beautiful or what you're learning about is interesting. Notice how your attention changes.

Teaching Tip Ideally you'll work hard to help a child self-reflect on his or her reading interests to choose appropriate materials that will be engaging. This strategy may be best for situations when a child doesn't have choice over the text he or she is reading, such as a testing situation.

Lesson Language *Have you ever heard that when you smile—even if you're not in a good mood—it will actually change your mood from the inside out and it can make you happy? It's true! Sometimes doing something consciously can have an effect on something that we normally think is involuntary or out of our control. For example, when we read, the kind of attitude we approach the reading with can change how much we understand and are able to focus on it. If you approach the book thinking "This isn't for me," then it's like you're switching your brain off before you even start. Instead, try to read like the words are beautiful or what you're learning about is interesting. Notice how your attention changes.*

Prompts

- Get your mind ready.
- Read it out loud like it's the most interesting thing you've ever read.
- Read it out loud like the language is beautiful.
- Now keep reading like that in your mind.
- You've read a bit. Now, tell me what you're noticing about your attention.
- Do you see a difference in your attention?
- What's changed for you as a reader?
- How is this strategy helping you?
- What are you thinking as you read?
- Let me hear how you're reading in your head.
- What are you loving about this book?

Hat Tip: *Building a Reading Life: Stamina, Fluency, and Engagement* (Calkins and Tolan 2010a)

2.14 Track Progress on a Stamina Chart

Strategy Each day, be mindful of when you are focused and engaged in your reading, and when you find you get distracted. The amount of time you can stay on-task is your stamina. Use a chart to keep track of how much you can read and how long you can read. At the start of the reading time, set a goal for your stamina based on how your stamina has been so far, and what you think you can do today.

Teaching Tip This strategy and other similar stamina-tracking strategies in this chapter may help readers visualize the amount of time they spend on-task to set longer time goals. It's important, though, that teachers don't communicate to kids that reading is something that needs to be "muscled through" but is rather something that is enjoyable in its own right. When introducing this strategy, you may compare this type of stamina tracking to something else that is both enjoyable in its own right and that is fun to try to push past your personal best. For example, perhaps an analogy to Olympic athletes who both enjoy their sport and also try to beat their best as part of the fun.

Prompts

- What's your goal for today's stamina, based on what you've done so far?
- Let's take a look at your stamina for the last few days.
- What do you notice from your stamina chart?
- Talk to me about how charting your stamina might be helping you.

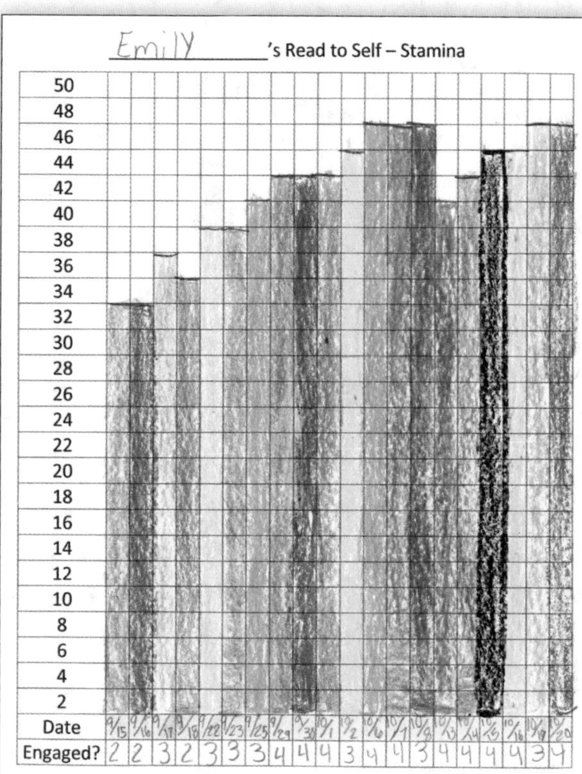

Who is this for?

LEVELS

F–Z+

GENRE / TEXT TYPE

any

SKILLS

stamina, focus

Hat Tip: *The Daily 5: Fostering Literacy Independence in the Elementary Grades*, second edition (Boushey and Moser 2014)

2.15 Choose Like Books for a Best Fit

Who is this for?

LEVELS

F–Z+

GENRE / TEXT TYPE

any

SKILL

book choice

Strategy Readers can turn to resources to help them find the next book they'll be successful with. Browse websites such as Amazon, Goodreads, and BiblioNasium. Type in a book you remember loving and see what recommendations pop up. You can read the reviews and summaries while thinking about what you like about books to see if any of the books suggested would be a good fit for you.

Prompts

- Which book do you most remember loving? Type that one into the website.
- Let's take a look together at some of the other books the website suggests.
- Can you see why this one is suggested to be similar to the one you loved?
- Let's think about which would be a good fit.
- Yes, I think that book is a good choice for you, too, because . . .
- Read the summary before you decide.
- Think about what it is you liked about this book. Which of the suggestions seem to also have that quality?

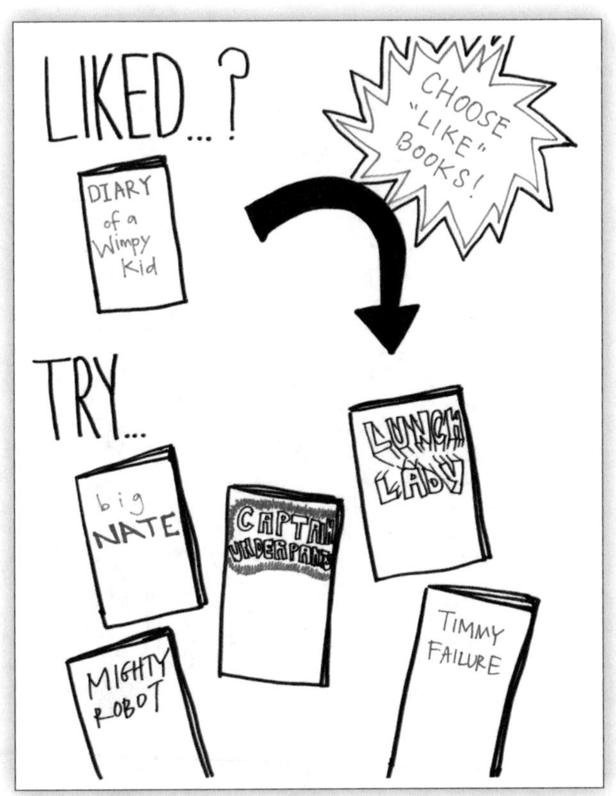

Hat Tip: "Teaching Reading in Small Groups: Matching Methods to Purposes" (Serravallo 2013c)

2.16 Choose Books with Your Identity in Mind

Strategy Choosing a just-right book means more than choosing a book based on level. Instead of going to the library saying, "I'm a ____(level.)," go to the library saying "I'm a reader who enjoys ____ (description of your book interests)." Think, "Where would I find books that fit who I am as a reader?"

Lesson Language *Sometimes in this classroom I hear kids saying "I'm a Q"—that is, they are identifying just by a level of a book that's right for them. Parents do it, too. Sometimes I even hear teachers refer to kids that way. But I have to tell you that books have levels, readers don't have levels. A better way to describe yourself as a reader is based on the kinds of books that interest you—series, genres, authors, topics, themes, characters. Today, instead of saying you're a level ____, I want you to stop and reflect about the kind of books you love using a short questionnaire. Then, declare who you are as a reader. Next, go to the classroom library with that reading identity—not just level—in mind. Think, "Where would I find books that fit who I am as a reader?"*

Teaching Tip You may choose to ask questions in a conference (especially for children at lower reading levels whose writing may not be quick and fluent at this point). For children at higher levels, you can create a questionnaire that they can fill out independently. Following are some suggestions for what you may ask:

- Tell me about the books you've loved. What do they have in common?
- If you were going to ask a friend for a recommendation, what would you tell them to help them suggest the right book?
- A book has a level, what would you say about your interests?
- What do you like outside of reading that you think might help you find a good book?
- Based on what you like to do, what kinds of books do you think you'd want to read?
- Tell me what series, authors, or genres you think you most enjoy.
- Where do you think you could go to find books like that?
- What will you look for within the basket labeled with your reading level?

I'm the kind of reader who likes advencher storys, who likes Character drama, who gets bord of story that don't get to the point, Who dosen't like Si fi.

Who is this for?

LEVELS

J–Z+

GENRE / TEXT TYPE

any

SKILL

book choice

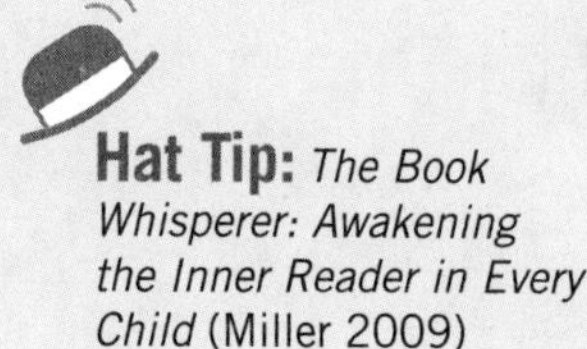

Hat Tip: *The Book Whisperer: Awakening the Inner Reader in Every Child* (Miller 2009)

2.17 Visualize to Focus

Who is this for?

LEVELS

J–Z+

GENRE / TEXT TYPE

any

SKILLS

visualizing, focus

Strategy Creating a picture in your mind that shifts and changes is essential to staying focused. Try to experience all the author is describing by using all of your senses. Read a little, then pause. Think "What do I see? Hear? Feel? Taste? Smell?"

Lesson Language *Much of being an engaged reader means understanding what you read—it's about more than just saying the words you're reading in your head. One of the best ways to make sure you are understanding is to keep a picture in your mind of what the author is describing. You may have heard before that readers "make a movie in their minds"—that means that the pictures you make aren't still, but they move. As the character moves, the picture changes. If you're reading informational texts, you learn about the topic and you can actually see the animal doing the things being described or the plates of the Earth shifting in the book on geology. Read a little. Stop and think about what you read. Use all of your senses to add to your picture. Think, "What do I see? Hear? Feel? Taste? Smell?" You'll find that you'll be as engaged in your book as you would be if you're watching your favorite TV show!*

Prompts

- What do you see? Hear? Taste? Smell?
- Describe your picture.
- How has your picture changed?
- If your picture is fuzzy, go back and reread.
- Make the picture move.
- Describe it.
- (*Nonverbal: gesture to nose, mouth, eyes to prompt for different senses.*)
- Stop here. Use your senses.
- What senses are you using?
- That's what you see—now use the other senses.
- That's what the text says, what are you picturing?

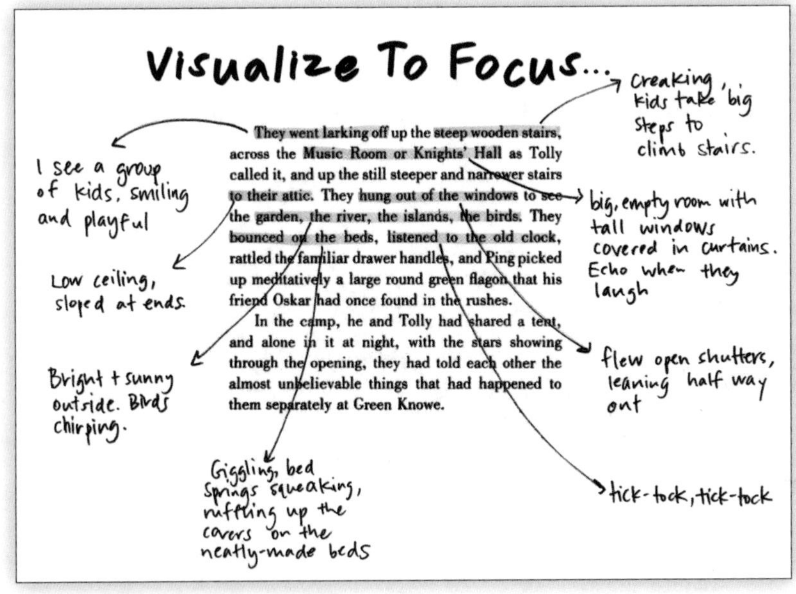

Text excerpt from *An Enemy at Green Knowe* (Boston 2002).

2.18 Reading Log Rate Reflection

Strategy Reading logs are more than paperwork for the student and teacher, they are tools for your own reflection. If you keep your log honestly, you can return to it and ask questions about your reading history. You can ask, "How does my reading rate at school compare to my reading rate at home? How can I bring the conditions of the more successful place to the more unsuccessful place to improve my overall volume?"

Teaching Tip This lesson is currently geared toward students who read at around levels K–Z+, when keeping track of pages and number of minutes reading starts to be appropriate. At lower levels, you may choose to have children keep a very basic log—something like a chart with a place for tally marks to indicate each book read. You could compare total volume at home and in school, and still ask a child to reflect on how he can get his best reading done, and what conditions help him to focus the best. You can find examples of different logs appropriate to different reading levels in *Teaching Reading in Small Groups* or The Literacy Teacher's Playbook series (Serravallo 2010, 2013b, and 2014).

Prompts

- Let's take a look at your log. Tell me what you're noticing about yourself as a reader.
- Look at your reading rate at home. Do you think you're reading books that are a good fit, at a good pace, in a good spot?
- Look at your reading rate at school. Tell me what you notice.
- I agree—the reading rates at home and school look quite different. Let's talk about why that might be.
- So we agreed you get more reading done at ____. How can we work to make sure you're as successful ____?

Reading Log

Name Ella F Month of janewary

* Fill out these columns after you are done reading.

Date	Title and Author's Last Name	Level	Start Page	*End Page	Start Time	* End Time	*Minutes Read	Home or School	Adult Initials
1/23/14	jane goodall				9:34	10:02	22	H S	
1/23/14	Frozen				10:07				
1/23/14	cc				8:15				CF
1/23/14	labrador on the								cf
1/24/14	jane goodall								
1/27/14	Fudge-a-mania		3	30	11:38				
1/28/14	cc	R	31	52	11:38				
1/28/14	cc	R	53	75	6:32	7:19	45	H S	CF
1/28/14	cc	R	75	105	7:20	8:06	45	H S	CF
1/29/14	jane goodall	Q	40	56	10:09	10:24		H S	
1/29/14	Fudge-a-mania	R	106	116	10:25	10:49		H S	

I need to stick to one book.

a little slow. I get distracted

Who is this for?

LEVELS

K–Z+

GENRE / TEXT TYPE

any

SKILL

improving reading rate

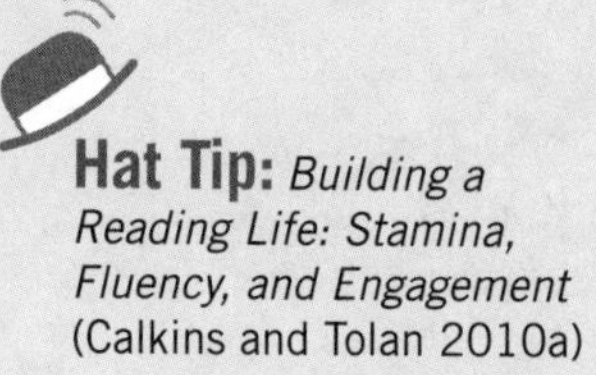

Hat Tip: *Building a Reading Life: Stamina, Fluency, and Engagement* (Calkins and Tolan 2010a)

2.19 Finding Reading Territories

Who is this for?

LEVELS

K–Z+

GENRE / TEXT TYPE

any

SKILLS

book choice, focus

Strategy Readers should be able to answer the question, "Who am I as a reader?" One way to do this is to make a list of books you remember reading and loving. Then, make another list of books you remember disliking. Look across the lists and ask, "What do my favorites have in common? What helps me to love a book?" You might think about types of characters, themes, topics, or the genre.

Prompts

- Make a list of books you've loved the most.
- What patterns do you see?
- Is there anything similar about these books in terms of character? Theme? Topic? Genre?
- So, who do you think you are as a reader?
- What types of books do you think you'll choose?

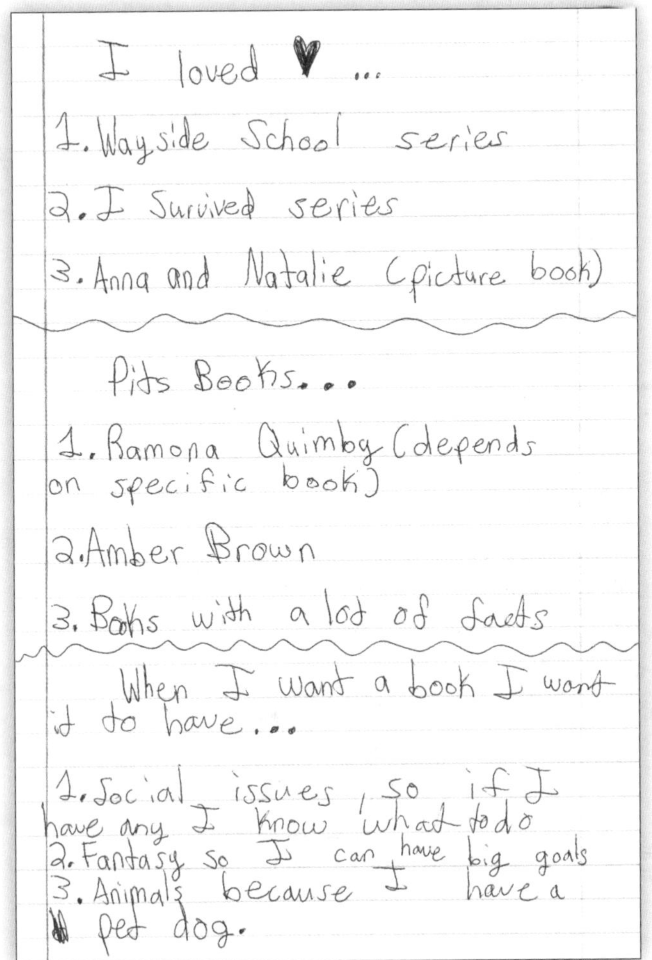

I loved ♥ ...
1. Wayside School series
2. I Survived series
3. Anna and Natalie (picture book)
Pids Books...
1. Ramona Quimby (depends on specific book)
2. Amber Brown
3. Books with a lot of facts
When I want a book I want it do have...
1. Social issues, so if I have any I know what to do
2. Fantasy so I can have big goals
3. Animals because I have a pet dog.

Hat Tip: *The Book Whisperer: Awakening the Inner Reader in Every Child* (Miller 2009)

2.20 Reflect on the Past and Plan for the Future

Strategy Reflect on your reading history to set a better reading future. Look at your reading log to see what books you finished, and read at a good pace. Then think, "What do those good books have in common?" Make some resolutions about the kind of books you'll choose and the kind of reader you want to be.

Lesson Language *It can be hard selecting books from just the cover and the blurb. Chances are good that some books you've picked in the past turned out to be not such great fits for you and that others were fabulous. One way to tell how focused you were while you were reading is to look at your reading rate. When you divide the pages by the minutes you get a page-per-minute (ppm) rate. It should be about .75, or three-quarters of a page per minute. Much slower and it might be showing that you're getting distracted. Look back over your log to see which books you finished and that you read at a good rate while you were reading. See if you can tell what these books have in common—a theme? A character type? A topic? A genre? Then, browse books with that in mind, and/or ask for help from me, or your friends, asking what might fit the same profile. You can also look over your log to notice the patterns around how often you read and where you read. You can use what you notice to make resolutions about future habits.*

Prompts

- Which books did you read at a good pace?
- Divide the pages by the minutes—that's your ppm rate.
- What are you noticing about your ppm rate in these books, versus these?
- Which books do you feel like you read very slowly? Do you remember not being that into them?
- What do all of these books have in common?
- Is there a theme, character, topic, or genre that these books have in common?
- What does it seem like you don't like, based on the books you read slowly?
- What does it seem like you don't like, based on the books you didn't finish?
- What do all the books you finish have in common?
- In what section of the library do you think you'll find other books like this?
- Do you know of any authors or series that might be a good fit?
- I read ____. That might fit with your interests because ____.
- You should talk to ____ (student name). I think he has similar tastes in books.

I want to be the kind of reader who fits in 20 minutes/day, who whants to find more home run books, who wants to find ways to read on the go.

Who is this for?

LEVELS

K–Z+

GENRE / TEXT TYPE

any

SKILLS

book choice, stamina

2.21 You've Got to "Get It" to Be Engaged

Who is this for?

LEVELS

K–Z+

GENRE / TEXT TYPE

any

SKILL

monitoring for meaning

Strategy Part of being an engaged reader is feeling like you're really "getting it." Read a bit. Notice if your mind was wandering or if you could picture what the author was describing and retell what you read. If you felt like you aren't getting it, you may want to try an easier text, or adjust your pace.

Lesson Language *Researchers who study reading have discovered that kids grow the most when they have a healthy diet of texts that are on the easy side. Perhaps that's because it's so important for readers to really "get it" when they read, and because texts on the easier side support readers' stamina so they are able to read more in the same amount of time. Sometimes, although the book may seem interesting or like something you want to read, you aren't quite ready for it. The words might be too hard, or the subject matter might be over your head, or maybe it's just hard to relate to the characters. Other times, you might find that you're rushing to get through the text, and sacrificing the meaning.*

Prompts

- How often do you find yourself pausing?
- When you stop, how do you get yourself back in the book?
- Why do you think you aren't getting it?
- Show me where you first realized you stopped getting it.
- What made this book too hard, do you think?
- What will you look for in your next book?
- Read a bit and I'll stop you to ask you to tell me about how much you understand.
- Read a bit and let's talk.
- Read a bit and stop to notice how focused you were.

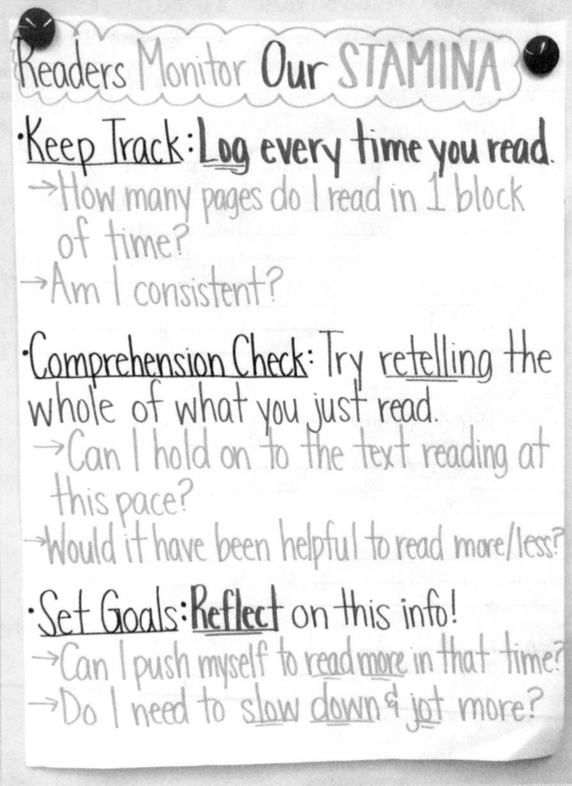

Hat Tip: "Engagement with Young Adult Literature: Outcomes and Processes" (Ivey and Johnston 2013)

2.22 Buzz About Books

Strategy Get to know your peers, and recommend books to them based on who they are as readers. Think about the types of books they enjoy and explain your endorsement using convincing language and mentions of parts (characters, themes, plot points) that will hook them.

Lesson Language *Recommending books well has a few parts to it. First, you need to know who you're recommending to. It's important you know what interests that person has and what his or her reading history is. Second, you have to think about the books you know well that will match with that person's interests. Finally, you need to be persuasive, trying to convince that person by highlighting just the right stuff from the book you're recommending. So, think about the types of books your friend enjoys. When you can think of a book he or she would like, try to explain the parts (such as characters, themes, plot points, or topics) that will hook him or her.*

Prompts

- What do you know about him or her as a reader?
- What books do you know that you could recommend?
- How will you convince him or her that that's the right book?
- Are there any parts from the book you'd want to highlight?
- Tell me why you'd want to highlight that.
- What persuasive language might you use?
- OK, let's practice—convince me to read this book.
- What are a few books you'd consider talking about? Which one is the best?
- How is that book like others your friend has read?

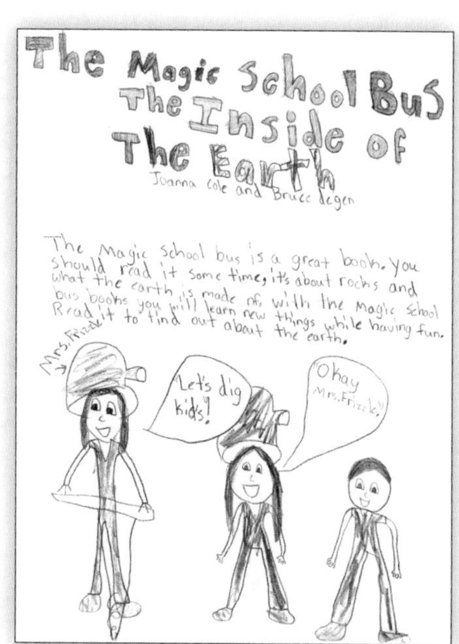

Who is this for?

LEVELS

K–Z+

GENRE / TEXT TYPE

any

SKILL

recommending books

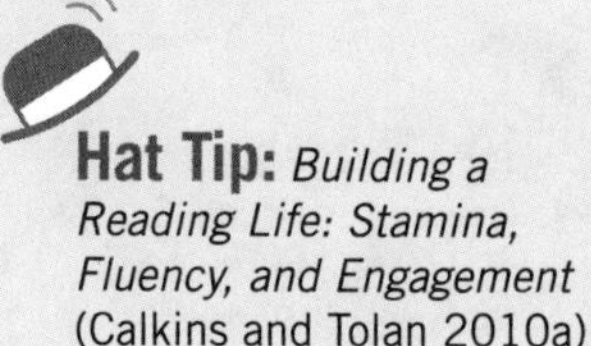

Hat Tip: *Building a Reading Life: Stamina, Fluency, and Engagement* (Calkins and Tolan 2010a)

2.23 Set Page Goals

Who is this for?

LEVELS
L–Z+

GENRE / TEXT TYPE
any

SKILLS
monitoring engagement, focus, stamina

Strategy It helps to set page goals when the time ahead seems too long to maintain focus. Look at your reading log. Think, "How many minutes can I read before getting distracted?" Set a stopping point with a sticky note for each chunk of pages. When you get to the stopping point, reflect on whether you were focused for the whole time.

Lesson Language *Sometimes when you have a whole forty-minute reading period ahead of you, and you're reading a long chapter book, it feels like too long and too much to stay focused. Setting shorter-term goals can help. I like to look at my reading log to see how long I can typically go before getting distracted. Then, I take sticky notes and place them in the book, planning stopping places along the way. When I get to the sticky note, I jot quickly about whether I was focused and engaged. At first, you might stop every two or three pages. But next time, maybe you can make it four or five. Before you know it, you'll be able to read for the whole reading time without taking a break. But it takes time to build up that stamina and focus.*

Prompts

- How many pages do you think you can read before you need a break?
- Do you think that's a good amount for you?
- Let's look at your reading log and check.
- It's OK to take breaks more often—it'll help you get more reading done.
- Put a sticky note where you think you need to stop and take a break.
- What makes you think that's the right number of pages?
- When was the last time you remember reading this many pages without a break?
- Good—keep going, put a sticky note every _____ pages.
- OK, start reading. Let's see if you can stay focused without taking a break.

Hat Tip: "Teaching Reading in Small Groups: Matching Methods to Purposes" (Serravallo 2013c)

2.24 Read with a Focus to Focus

Strategy Not only can you decide what you want to read, but you may also decide what you want to work on and pay attention to as you read. Think about what goal you have for yourself as a reader. Set stopping places in your reading and decide what you'll do when you stop.

Lesson Language *You know what keeps most people focused and working hard? When they are their own boss. And that's what I'd like you to be today—I'd like you to be the boss of your own reading. You all have goals for yourself as readers that we've discussed during conferences. You know what you want to work on to be a better reader. Now, decide how often you'll stop to do some work inside your book. Start by thinking about what your goal is. Think about where, when, or how often you want to stop to jot. Place sticky notes in your book that will serve as a reminder to stop and practice the work you'll do that connects to your goal. Decide what you'll do when you get to those sticky notes.*

Prompts

- What's your goal?
- How often do you think you need to stop?
- What are your plans for when you stop?
- When you stop, what will you do? Jot? Stop and think? Stop and sketch?
- What do you think that will look like?
- Go ahead and read a bit, and I'll watch you stop and do what you planned.
- That seems like a good plan for when you stop.
- If you're not sure what your goal is, let's look back at the work you've been doing.
- Think about how often you'll need to stop to stay focused.
- Think about how stories go. Now think about your goal. Where do you think it makes sense to stop?
- Let's look at how this book is organized. Now think about your goal. Where do you think it makes sense to stop?

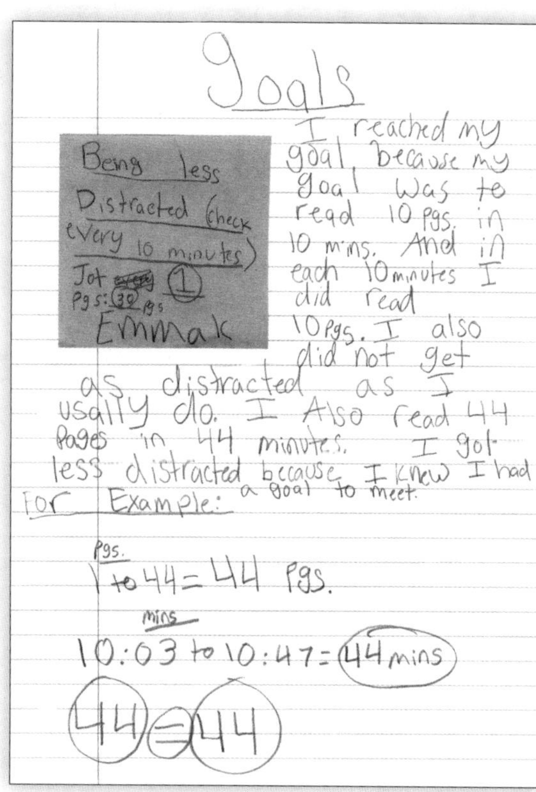

Who is this for?

LEVELS

L–Z+

GENRE / TEXT TYPE

any

SKILLS

focus, stamina

2.25 Monitor Your Stamina and Pace

Who is this for?

LEVELS

L–Z+

GENRE / TEXT TYPE

any

SKILLS

stamina, monitoring for meaning

Strategy Readers need to monitor how fast we read—sometimes we read too fast, sometimes too slow, and sometimes at a perfect pace. We can check this by logging our reading and checking our page per minute (ppm) rate and paying attention to how much we are stopping to check our comprehension (in our minds or on paper). Then, we can set goals: Do we need to read faster or slower? Jot more or less often?

Prompts

- What do you notice about your pace?
- Check your log—what does it tell you?
- How often are you stopping to check in with your comprehension?
- What goal will you make for yourself?
- What goal will you make about your pacing?
- What goals do you have for the frequency of your writing about reading?

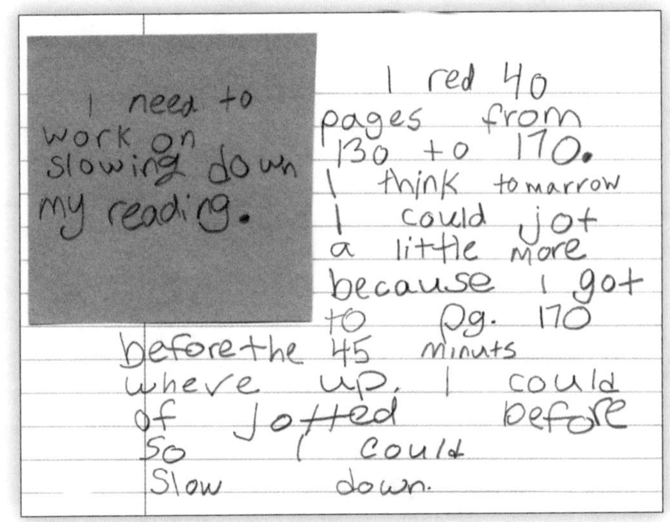

2.26 Does It Engage Me?

Strategy Read the first page of the book. Notice whether you feel like the book grabbed you and if you were eager to read the rest of the book. Ask yourself, "Can I see the story or topic? Do I care to find out what comes next?" If so, the book may be a good fit for you.

Prompts

- How do you feel after the first page?
- What grabs you here?
- Tell me what you picture after reading that first bit.
- Tell me why you'd like to keep reading.
- What makes you want to read on?
- I agree—based on what you've said, it feels like this book might fit you well.
- Do you feel like you were focused on that whole page?

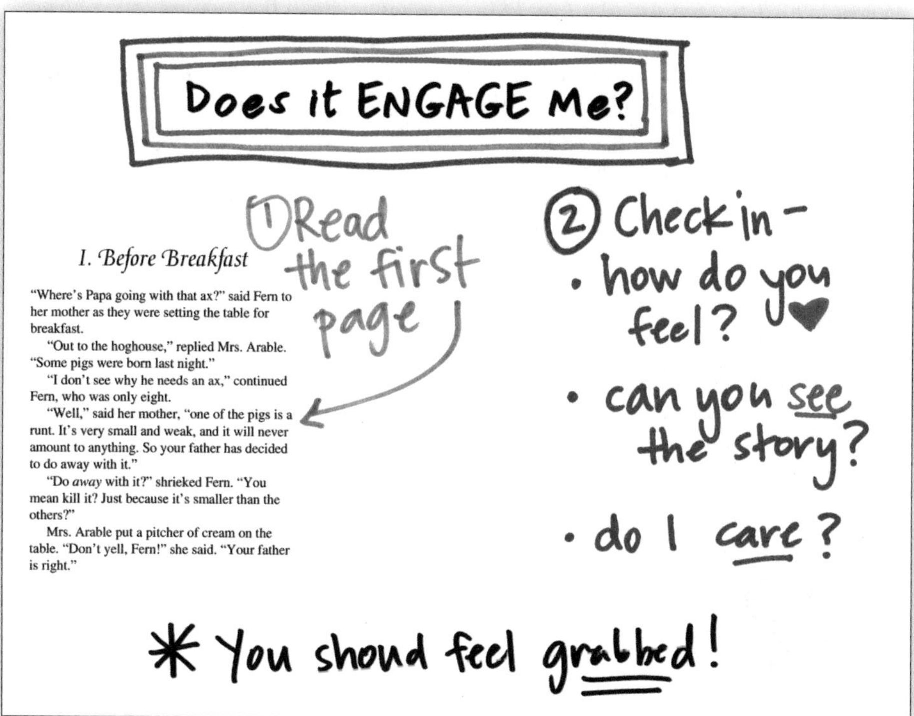

Text excerpt from *Charlotte's Web* (White 1952).

Who is this for?

LEVELS

L–Z+

GENRE / TEXT TYPE

any

SKILLS

book choice, focus

2.27 Hear the Story

Who is this for?

LEVELS

L–Z+

GENRE / TEXT TYPE

fiction

SKILL

visualizing

Hat Tip: *The Art of Slow Reading: Six Time-Honored Practices for Engagement* (Newkirk 2011)

Strategy Even though you're reading silently, try to really hear the story to stay engaged. Read slower than you otherwise might, trying hard to listen for the voice of the author, the voice of the characters. Try to be in the world of the story, not just picturing what you read but really hearing what you read.

Lesson Language *As you all know, we read silently during independent reading. But that doesn't mean that it needs to be quiet in our minds. If you skim through your story, reading very fast, it may be hard to really get a full picture of what you're reading—including the sounds that you might hear in the story. And then you might start to check out of your reading, letting your mind drift. Instead, try to slow down a bit, really working to hear it all. For example, if I started to read* Stone Fox *by John Reynolds Gardiner (2010), I'd want to pay attention to who is telling the story and try to get the voice in my head.* (Read aloud the first two sentences.) *So far I'm not sure. It could be one of the characters—perhaps a younger person because someone else is referred to as "Grandfather." Or, it could be a narrator.* (Read the next sentence.) *Now, I'm noticing that other characters are mentioned and that's usually a sign it's a narrator. So I have to get a narrator voice in my mind. I'm hearing a male voice, sort of deep, reading these words to me. Then, as I get to the first bit of dialogue, here, on page 4, I see little Willy is speaking. The name "little Willy" must mean he's a young boy, so I'm hearing a voice that's a little more high-pitched than the narrator. As you read, be sure to try to get the voice of the characters and the narrator in your mind. Hear it as if it's being read to you, and remember you may need to go a bit slower to do this.*

Prompts

- Go slowly. Really hear it.
- Can you hear the voice of the character? Describe it.
- Describe how the narrator sounds in your head.
- Who is speaking this part—a narrator? A character?
- I can tell you're really picturing—and hearing—what you're reading.
- Read it to me to show me how you're hearing it in your mind.

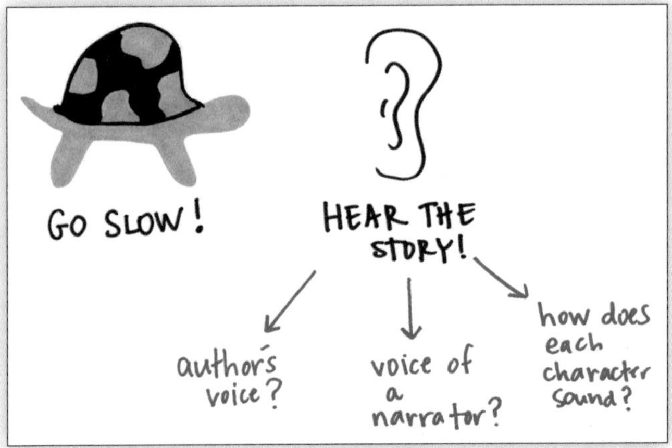

You could be the most eloquent teacher, the best strategy group facilitator, the most insightful conferrer. But if you send your kids back for independent reading and they don't read, then they won't make the progress you are hoping and working for.

—*Jennifer Serravallo*

Supporting Print Work

Increasing Accuracy and Integrating Sources of Information

Why is this goal important?

In order to construct accurate meaning from a text, children need to read words correctly, integrating three sources of information: meaning, syntax, and visual. *Meaning* refers to the reader thinking about what makes sense and reading words that match the picture and/or what's happening so far in the text. *Syntax* means readers use their knowledge of sentence structure, grammar, and parts of speech to read words that agree with the written form of Standard English. *Visual* means that readers look at the letters in the word and use what they know about how words work to read a word that looks like the word in print (Clay 2000, 2001).

Sometimes, as children are learning to read, they overemphasize on one or two of the sources of information or use each inconsistently. This affects their accuracy rate and often ultimately limits their comprehension of the text. Integrating all three sources of information is like being a juggler with three balls in the air. It takes coordination, mental effort, and strategic action. That said, children can be taught to be more aware and to use strategies to help them figure out the print as they read. The ideal is that students learn to search for and use all three sources of information. Students must learn to self-monitor their own reading, and when the word they read doesn't look right, make sense, or sound like it would in text, then they should cross-check. The ultimate goal, writes Clay (1993), is to help foster in children a "self-extending system" whereby children are "independent readers whose reading and writing improve whenever they read and write." By that, she means the strategies we teach one by one, such as those in this chapter, would become secure and habitual so the reader can focus on reading with expression, for example, or deeper inferential comprehension.

The strategies in this chapter are best taught in combination with a systematic word study/phonics program, such as *Words Their Way* (Bear et al. 2015) or the Month-by-Month Phonics series (Cunningham and Hall). Systematic word study will help children learn letter-sound correspondence, as well as some of the rules and patterns to better understand how words work in English. Learning about blends, digraphs, short and long vowel sounds, diphthongs, and so on will help children decode the words in their books. Isolated phonics skill work *without* the application in actual books is shown to be of limited effectiveness, however (Pressley and Allington 2015). There will also be instances where children learn a certain word feature or the sounds a letter combination makes without having ever been taught it during word study—children will pick up all sorts of things about reading just because they are given lots of time to read and write (Taberski 2011).

How do I know if this goal is right for my student?

The best assessment tool you have to determine if this is the right goal is an oral reading record (Fountas and Pinnell 2010a), also known as a "running record" (Clay 2000). Marie Clay (2000, 2001), Irene Fountas and Gay Su Pinnell (2010a), and others have written about and developed resources to make running records a simple yet essential way to record what children read in a short passage and then analyze their reading. Teachers can take a record of a student's reading on any text by recording their reading on a blank sheet of paper, or they can purchase running records such as the Benchmark Assessment System (Fountas and Pinnell 2010a), Developmental Reading Assessment (DRA2) (Beaver and Carter 2015), or Next Step Guided Reading Assessment (Richardson and Walther 2012), which provide more support for those newer to this assessment type. Bear in mind that students' reading is complex, and learning to take a record on a blank sheet of paper may afford the teacher more options without the constraints of a form.

Regardless of what you use, it's important to look at the assessment given and analyze the pattern of errors and self-corrections to learn about which of the three sources of information the student uses sometimes, consistently, or not at all. See the sample in Figure 3.A, along with Clay's *Running Records for Classroom Teachers* (2000), Wilde's *Miscue Analysis Made Easy* (2000), or Goodman, Watson, and Burke's *Reading Miscue Inventory* (2005) for more information about how to take and analyze running records.

Insertions and deletions are always a "no" for "looks right."

At the point of each error, ask three questions: Does it look right? Sound right? Make sense? *Said* makes sense, looks right, and sounds right in place of the word *says*.

For each self-correction, analyze the initial error as well as the self-correction.

For "Syntax/Structure" it's important to ask yourself if the word sounds right in the syntax of the student's language (i.e., English language learners [ELLs]), but not in the way it would sound in a book.

As important as each individual error is, it's also important to notice the overall pattern. What does it seem like the child's strengths are? What does the child tend to do, and what does he or she sometimes do? When making a decision about where to begin instruction, be sure to start from a place of strength.

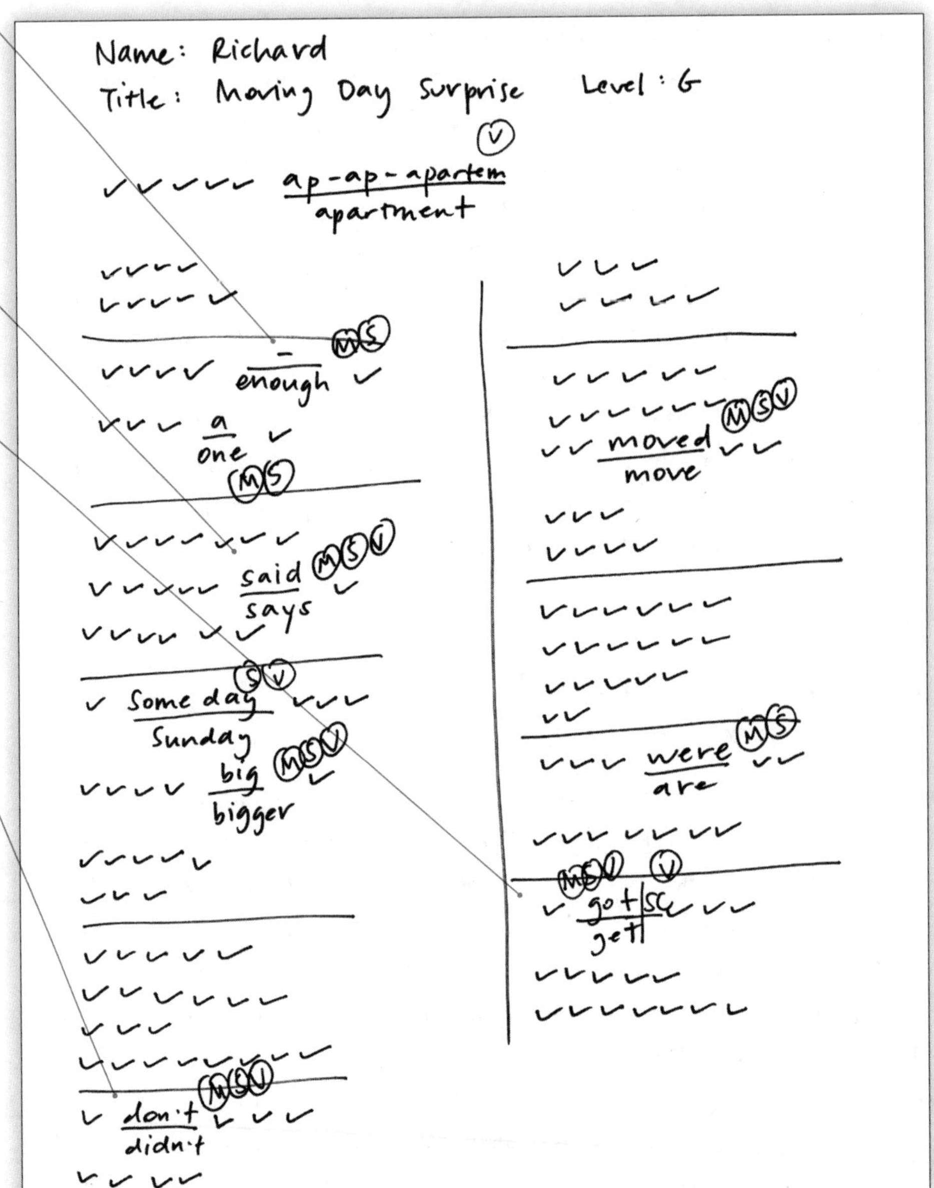

Figure 3.A Analyzed Running Record

Strategies for Print Work at a Glance

Strategy		Levels	Genres/ Text Types	Skills
3.1	Check the Picture for Help	A–K	Any	Integrating sources of information
3.2	Point and Read One for One	A–C	Any	One-to-one matching
3.3	Use a Word You Know	A–Z+	Any	Decoding
3.4	Does That Sound Like a Book?	A–Z+	Any	Integrating sources of information
3.5	Be a Coach to Your Partner	A–Z+ (although prompts you'd coach kids to use vary by level)	Any	Partner reading, decoding, integrating sources of information
3.6	Try, Try, Try Again	A–Z+	Any	Decoding, integrating sources of information
3.7	Slow Down the Zoom, Zoom, Zoom to Make Sense	A–Z+	Any	Decoding, monitoring for meaning
3.8	Think (While You Read the Words)	A–Z+	Any	Decoding, monitoring for meaning
3.9	Make Attempts That Make Sense	A–Z+	Any	Decoding, monitoring for meaning, integrating sources of information
3.10	Juggle All Three Balls	C–Z+	Any	Integrating sources of information
3.11	Apply Your Word Study to Book Reading	C–Z+	Any	Decoding
3.12	Group Letters That Make Sounds Together	D–Z+	Any	Decoding
3.13	Check Beginning and End	D–Z+	Any	Decoding
3.14	Run into the First Part	D–Z+	Any	Decoding, integrating sources of information
3.15	Take the Ending Off	E–Z+	Any	Decoding
3.16	Go Left to Right	E–Z+	Any	Decoding multisyllabic words
3.17	Flexible Sounds	E–Z+	Any	Decoding
3.18	Cover and Slide	E–Z+	Any	Decoding
3.19	Take the Word Apart, Then Put It Back Together	E–Z+	Any	Decoding
3.20	Skip and Return	E–Z+	Any	Decoding
3.21	Look for Vowels That Go Together	G–Z+	Any	Decoding
3.22	Unpacking What It Means to "Sound Right"	J–Z+	Any	Decoding, using structure as a source of information
3.23	Words Across a Line Break	L–Z+	Any	Decoding

3.1 Check the Picture for Help

Who is this for?

LEVELS

A–K

GENRE / TEXT TYPE

any

SKILL

integrating sources of information

Strategy When you get to a tricky word, there's often help in the picture. Make sure you're reading the pictures and the words. You can check the picture and think, "What's happening in the picture? What's happening in the book so far? What word would make sense?"

Teaching Tip This strategy is a go-to essential for children reading at levels A and B, where pictures and following a pattern are the primary ways for them to figure out what the print says. For children reading at level C and beyond, however, this is an important strategy to balance with explicit strategies to decode the print such as 3.13, 3.17, and 3.18 in this chapter (Stahl and Miller 1989).

Lesson Language *This book has pictures and words because the pictures are there to help you understand the story (or information), and to give you help with the words. When you come to a tricky word and you need help, one thing you should do is think about what makes sense. The picture can help. Check the picture and think, "What's happening in the picture? What word would make sense?" For example, when I read this sentence, I might get stuck on this word ____. If I look at the picture, I see ____. So, I think, "What would make sense? I think that what would make sense here is ____. Is that the word?"*

Prompts

- Check the picture.
- Think about what makes sense with the picture.
- I see you checking the picture. What would make sense?
- Tell me what you see in the picture.
- What's in the picture? What did you just read? So what do you think this word could be?
- Now that you checked the picture, and thought about what makes sense, try that word again.
- What's happening?
- What do you see?
- What could that word be, based on what's in the picture?

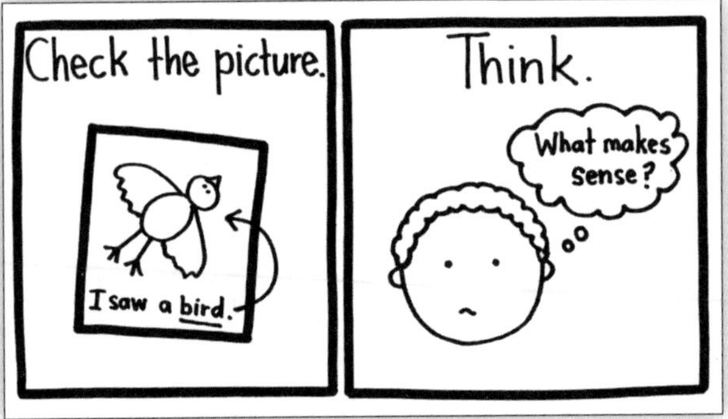

3.2 Point and Read One for One

Strategy Point under each word as you read. Say one word for each word you point under. If you find yourself saying more words than what is on the page, or fewer words than what is on the page, go back to the beginning of the page and start again.

Teaching Tip Emergent readers and beginning readers who are still refining their understanding of a word versus a letter often benefit from tracking the print with their finger. Their pointing should be crisp, and their reading will sound staccato as they read one word for each word on the page. By the time a reader transitions from level C to level D, the need for a finger to track the print should fade away, and the reader should be able to track the print with his eyes. Continuing to point under each word often affects a reader's ability to read with fluency. Like a horse wearing blinders who only sees straight ahead, the finger directs the eye to the word being read. Fluent readers, on the other hand, will need to sweep their eyes under the words instead of pointing one-by-one (see Chapter 4, strategies 4.4, 4.5, and 4.14 for more information and for strategies to support fluency).

Prompts

- Point under each word.
- You're pointing on the word. Try pointing under.
- Pick up your finger after each word, and place it under the next word.
- You ran out of words! What will you do?
- Go back to the beginning of the page and try again.
- You fixed yourself! How did you know that didn't work?

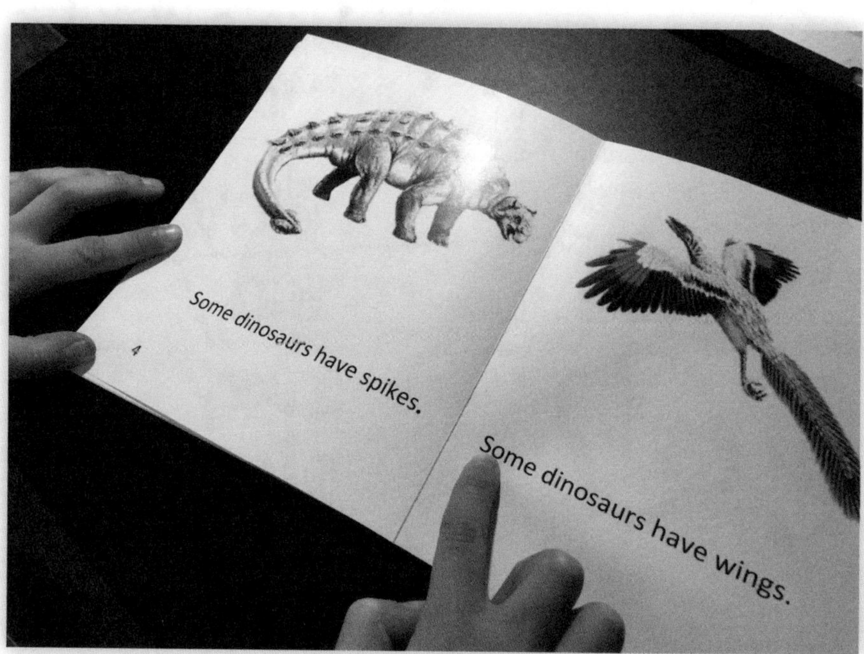

Who is this for?

LEVELS

A–C

GENRE / TEXT TYPE

any

SKILL

one-to-one matching

3.3 Use a Word You Know

Who is this for?

LEVELS

A–Z+

GENRE / TEXT TYPE

any

SKILL

decoding

Strategy You can use a word you know to help you read a word you're having trouble with. Look for a part of the word that's the same as a part in a word you know. Notice what's different. Try to read the word.

Lesson Language *You may find that there is a part in the word you're trying to read that's just like a word you know. Sometimes this part is at the beginning, sometimes in the middle, sometimes at the end. For example, if I'm trying to read the word* grown *I might notice that the* gr *is the beginning of another word I know how to read:* green. *And then I may notice that* ow *is just like in the word* slow. *And I know "n:" /n/. Next, I can think about what is going on in the story. I can think about what kind of word would fit there. Then, I can put together the sounds I know, /gr/-/ow/-/n/, and see if it's a word I recognize that would make sense in the context. The text says, "I'm all grown up."* Grown *makes sense and it matches the letters I see, too!*

Prompts

- (*Nonverbal: tap the word to indicate there was a miscue.*)
- What can you try?
- Is there a part of that word you've seen in other words?
- What part do you know?
- You know that part, it's just like in the word ____.
- What parts do you recognize?
- Read the part you know.
- What part looks tricky? Think of another word
  you can read that has that part.
- I see a part you know.
- You know the word ____. (*Say a word that has the same part.*) Does that help?
- Let me write another word for you. (*Write a word with the same part on whiteboard.*)
  Do you know this word? What part is like the part you're reading?
- Let me show you a word that will help. (*Write a word with the same part on whiteboard and underline the similar part.*) Read this word. Now read the word in your book.

Hat Tip: "A Compare/Contrast Theory of Mediated Word Identification" (Cunningham 1979)

3.4 Does That Sound Like a Book?

Strategy After you read a word, check yourself and think, "Is that how it would sound in a book?" If you don't think it sounds right, go back and try something else.

Teaching Tip Clay (1993) and others might use the prompt, "Can we say it that way?" However, one must be careful with that prompt, especially when working with ELLs or students who speak a different English dialect from what we typically see in books. By saying "That's not how we talk" or "That doesn't sound right" to some children, we may be unintentionally insulting their home dialect and/or culture (Delpit 2006).

Lesson Language *It's important that as you read you are always listening to yourself. A story or article or poem has to make sense, and the words you read have to sound like how books sound. You have to do more than one thing at once! As you already know, you also have to make sure you're paying attention to the letters of the word and it has to make sense! As you're reading, make sure you check and ask yourself, "Is that how it would sound in a book?"*

Prompts

- Did that sound right?
- The word you read looks like that word, but did it sound like how you'd hear it in a book?
- That makes sense, but did it sound right?
- Let's check to see if it sounds right.
- You read ____. (*Reread the way the child read.*) Did that sound right?
- That didn't sound right to me. Try it again.
- I think this is the word that didn't sound right. (*Point to word.*)
- Check yourself, make sure it sounds like a book.

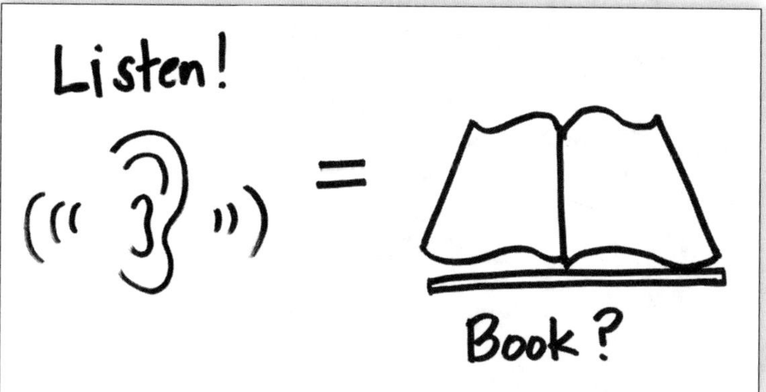

Who is this for?

LEVELS
A–Z+

GENRE / TEXT TYPE
any

SKILL
integrating sources of information

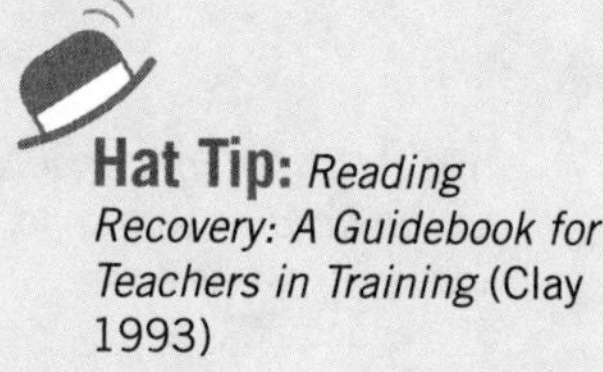

Hat Tip: *Reading Recovery: A Guidebook for Teachers in Training* (Clay 1993)

3.5 Be a Coach to Your Partner

Who is this for?

LEVELS

A–Z+ (although prompts you'd coach kids to use vary by level)

GENRE / TEXT TYPE

any

SKILLS

partner reading, decoding, integrating sources of information

Hat Tip: *A Curricular Plan for the Reading Workshop, Grade 1* (Calkins and colleagues 2011b)

Strategy When you see a mistake, don't just tell your partner the answer, coach him! You can stop your partner and use the words a reading coach would use. Think, "What would my teacher say to me to help me fix up my mistake?"

Lesson Language *Reading with a partner can be fun (and helpful!). You can read together not only to share stories and learn from information books, but also to help each other with the words. When your partner is reading, listen and check what she or he is reading against what's in the book. When you see a mistake, stop and tell your friend to go back and try that again. When your friend is stuck, give your friend a teaching tip like "Check the first letter!" or "Go left to right!" or "Think about what makes sense!"*

Prompts

- What can you tell your partner to do?
- Don't give your partner the word, tell them a tip.
- Tell your partner, "Check the first letter!"
- Tell your partner, "Think about what makes sense!"
- Tell your partner, "Think about what sounds right!"
- Tell your partner, "Something didn't sound right, go back and try it again!"
- What can you say to your partner?
- Act like a teacher, what would I say?
- Looks like your partner is stuck, try to help.
- That was a helpful tip!
- That really helped your partner.

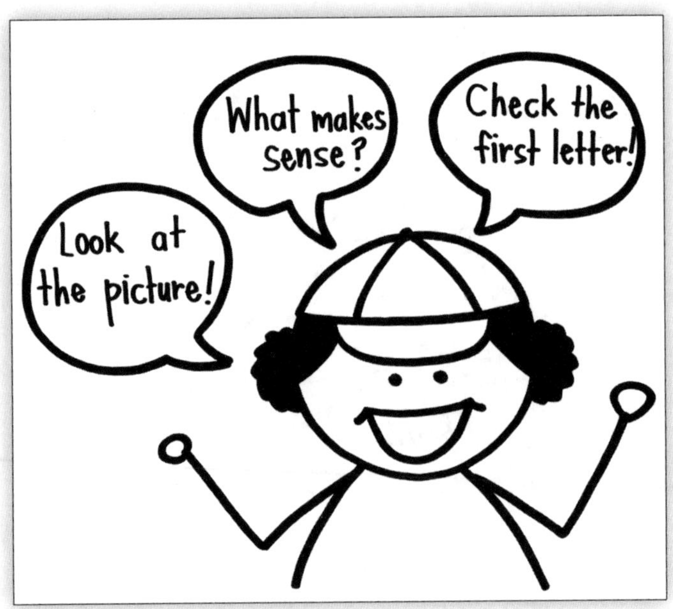

3.6 Try, Try, Try Again

Strategy When you get to a tricky word, don't just try one thing! Sometimes one strategy will work on one word but not another. Make sure you try more than one strategy thinking, "What will help me read this word?"

Teaching Tip You will want to modify the strategy and lesson language to agree with the sorts of strategies you've taught and the sorts of strategies that are appropriate given the level of text that the child is reading. The example visual on this page was a chart used for a small group. After the students in the group practiced the strategy, each child got his or her own mini copy.

Lesson Language *You know so many strategies to help you read tricky words when you come to them. You know how to read the word from left to right. You know how to check the picture and think about what makes sense. You know how to think about what is going on in the story, and how that can help you choose the right word. You know how to look for parts of words you know inside of the larger word. When you come to a new text, you should carry these strategies like a toolbox: using just the right one for just the right job. Just like you wouldn't use a hammer to take out a screw, you shouldn't use the "check the picture" strategy when there aren't pictures! Other times, you'll find that you try one and it won't work; in that case, you should try another one. So, when you get to a tricky word, don't just try one thing! Make sure you think, "What will help me read this word?" and use the strategy or strategies from your toolbox that you think will help the most.*

Prompts

- What strategy do you think you'll try here?
- Let's look at that word. Now pick the strategy you'll use.
- You chose and used a strategy correctly. Did it work? No? Then pick another.
- Think about what other strategies you know.
- What else can you do to help you read that word?
- You gave it a first try. What's the next thing you'll try?
- What do you think will help you read this word?
- What can you do?
- What else do you have in your toolbox?
- What might help you here?

Readers Use More Than 1 Strategy to Figure it Out!

gl→a→d Read left to right.	Can the pictures help me?	? Does it make sense?
Does it look right?	Does it sound right?	swing sw- -ing Do I know any parts?

Who is this for?

LEVELS

A–Z+

GENRE / TEXT TYPE

any

SKILLS

decoding, integrating sources of information

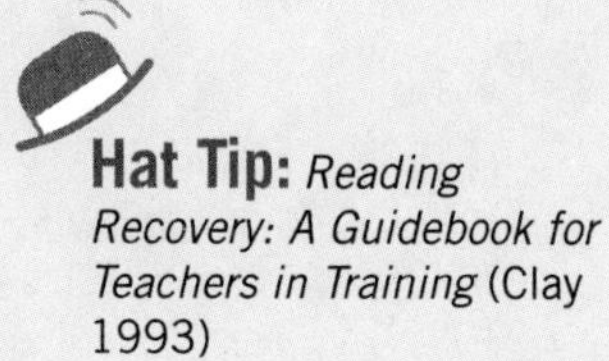

Hat Tip: *Reading Recovery: A Guidebook for Teachers in Training* (Clay 1993)

3.7 Slow Down the Zoom, Zoom, Zoom to Make Sense

Who is this for?

LEVELS

A–Z+

GENRE / TEXT TYPE

any

SKILLS

decoding, monitoring for meaning

Strategy Try not to be a zoom, zoom, zoom reader who keeps breezing through words but not thinking. Always ask yourself, "Is what I'm reading making sense?" and if you answer "No!" go back and fix it up.

Teaching Tip Model reading a few ways: quickly, with and without errors, and slowly, with and without errors. Model pausing to ask yourself, "Did that make sense?" in instances where you can say, "Yes!" and "No! Let me fix it!" As you move to small-group instruction and conferring, be sure to encourage kids to pause and reflect on meaning, both when their reading was accurate and did make sense and when they may have made an error that affects meaning.

Prompts

- Check yourself.
- Did that make sense?
- Slow down, make sure you're thinking about what makes sense.
- I notice you fixed it to make sure it makes sense!
- Yes, you caught yourself there. What made you realize you had to fix that?
- Was that OK?
- Why did you stop? What did you notice?

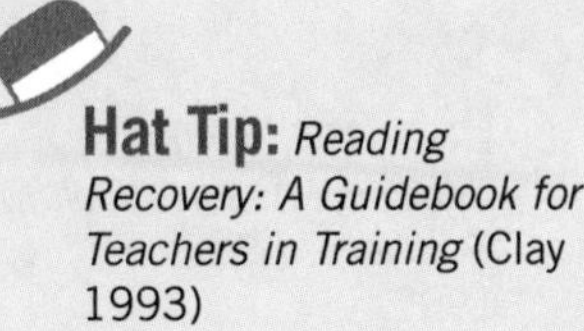

Hat Tip: *Reading Recovery: A Guidebook for Teachers in Training* (Clay 1993)

3.8 Think (While You Read the Words)

Strategy Sometimes you might feel so focused on reading words that you start to think, "Wait. I haven't understood what I just read." When that happens, make sure you go back to reread.

Teaching Tip As you demonstrate monitoring your comprehension as you read, you may choose to assume a "reading pose" and a "thinking pose" that are distinct. Perhaps for the "thinking pose," you put the book down, look up, and point to your forehead. This will help students understand that you aren't *reading* the words, you're thinking aloud.

Prompts

- Check yourself—did you understand what you just read?
- You're reading the words . . . check that you're understanding, too.
- Stop and check to make sure you get it.
- Are you thinking, too, while you're reading?
- Read the words, then tell me what you're thinking.
- Say aloud what you're thinking.
- I can tell you're reading the words *and* thinking while you do it.

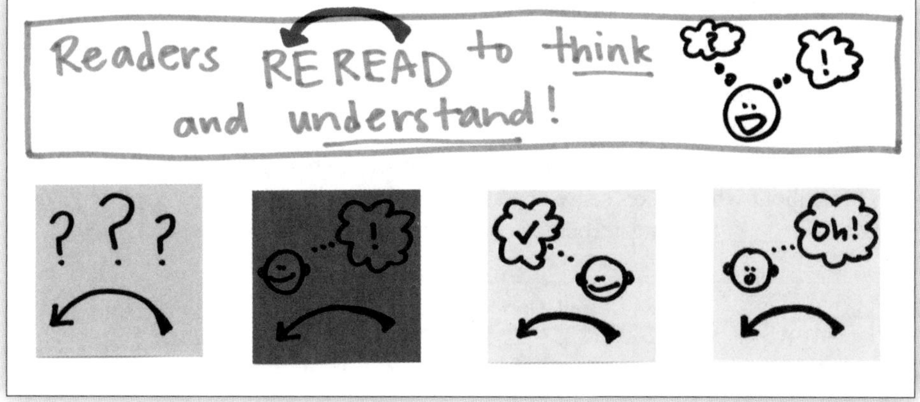

Who is this for?

LEVELS

A–Z+

GENRE / TEXT TYPE

any

SKILLS

decoding, monitoring for meaning

3.9 Make Attempts That Make Sense

Who is this for?

LEVELS

A–Z+

GENRE / TEXT TYPE

any

SKILLS

decoding, monitoring for meaning, integrating sources of information

Strategy When you're sure you know what's happening, but not what the word is, try to come up with a few options that would make sense. Use the information you have so far, and the information in the sentence you're trying to figure out. Say, "It could be ____ or it could be ____ or it could be ____." Then, check the letters of the word to see if it matches any of the words that would also make sense in that spot.

Lesson Language *Let me show you how when I come to a word I don't know, I make some tries at the word, using what makes sense, then check the letters to see what word also looks right* (Reading from *Those Shoes*, page 6 [Boelts 2009]):

> "They have an animal on them from a ____ I don't think any kid ever watched."

I could read up to that word and figure out what kind of word it might be. "Hmm. I think it is going to be a word that is a thing. Let me think about what I know from the whole sentence, and everything so far. It has to be something that has to do with an animal, and it says watched. *Hmm. So it could be* play *or* show *or* TV show*—no that wouldn't work,* TV show *is two words. Hmm. Let me look at some letters.*

I could look at the start of the word: c-a-r. Car. *What word starts like* car *and could make sense there in the sentence? Something you watch. Like a show. Maybe it could be* car . . . cartoon*! That's it.*

Prompts

- What could that word be?
- What else makes sense here?
- Yes, all three of those options make sense. Now let's check the letters.
- Think about what makes sense and see what also *looks* right.
- You said ____. Looking at the letters, could that be right? Why?

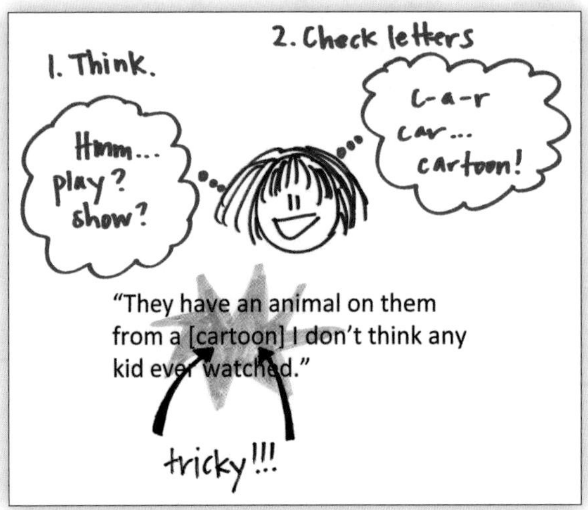

3.10 Juggle All Three Balls

Strategy Readers don't only do one thing when we get to a word. We need to do at least three: (1) think about what makes sense; (2) think about how a book sounds; and (3) think about what looks right.

Lesson Language *When you get to a tricky word you don't know, it's important that you do more than just try to sound the word out. The word you read has to make sense with what's happening in the text so far, and it has to sound like something we'd see in a book. So when you get to a tricky word, think all three—What makes sense? What sounds right? What looks right?*

Prompts

- Does that make sense?
- Does that sound right?
- Does that look right?
- Think about what's happening.
- Look at the letters. What could it be?
- Think about how book language sounds. Would it sound like that in a book?
- Check yourself.
- Yes, that made sense, looked right, and sounded right.
- You caught yourself there! What else could the word be?
- I notice you're thinking about sense (or sound or look), now let's focus on sound (or look or sense).

Who is this for?

LEVELS

C–Z+

GENRE / TEXT TYPE

any

SKILL

integrating sources of information

Hat Tip: "Teaching Reading in Small Groups: Matching Methods to Purposes" (Serravallo 2013c)

3.11 Apply Your Word Study to Book Reading

Who is this for?

LEVELS

C–Z+

GENRE / TEXT TYPE

any

SKILL

decoding

Strategy Connect what you learn during word study and phonics to the words you're trying to read in your books. Make sure you think, "Have I seen a word like this or letter pattern like this during word study?" And if so, use what you know to help you read the word.

Teaching Tip Explicit instruction in word study principles is crucial for many students to become strong decoders. Learning word families, root words, prefixes, suffixes, for example, can be very supportive to developing readers. Research has shown that only those children who already have some knowledge of phonological decoding (that is, understanding that words are made up of parts, hearing the parts in the words, and being able to rhyme words they hear) are able to "decode by analogy"—for instance, "If I know the word trade then I can read the word jade because they both end in –ade" (Ehri and Robbins 1992; Peterson and Haines 1992).

Tweak this lesson to match the features of words the student knows, and the expectations for that level. For example, at level C, you'd focus on initial consonant sounds they may have studied in word study. At level D, you may begin to remind students of blends and digraphs. At level E–Z+, you might focus on word families.

Prompts

- You know ____, ____, and ____ from word study, so use that to help you read this word.
- What word do you know that might help you read this word?
- Think about the words you're studying during word study.
- Yes! You know how to read and write ____ so that will help you read ____.
- Have you seen a word like that before?
- Use what you know to help you read that word.

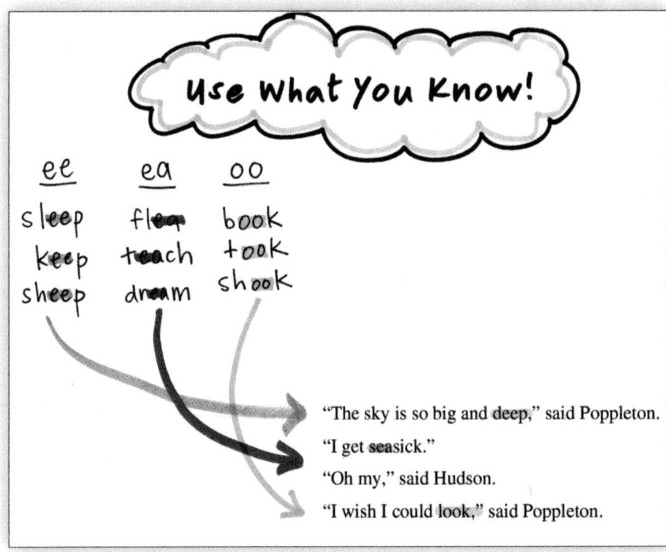

Text excerpt from *Poppleton Everyday* (Rylant 1998).

Hat Tip: "Beginners Need Some Decoding Skills to Read Words by Analogy" (Ehri and Robbins 1992)

"Orthographic Analogy Training with Kindergarten Children" (Peterson and Haines 1992)

3.12 Group Letters That Make Sounds Together

Strategy Look at letters in groups, not just one by one. Many letters make sounds together, and it's important to read them together. Going left to right, look for the letters that go together.

Lesson Language *Lots of times, if you try to sound out a word by reading letter by letter, it won't work. That's because there are letters that go together to make one sound. Here's a list of some of those special combinations.* (Show chart with blends and digraphs.) *Let's say the word we see in the picture, and then say the sound by itself.* (Practice a few or all from the chart you create, reading first the word then isolating the blend or digraph. For example, brown /br/ and glue /gl/ and swing /sw/.) *Then, let's try to read the book and see if we come to some of these combinations. When we do, we'll look at those letter combinations like a group, not just one by one.*

Prompts

- Check the chart.
- Find the blend on the chart. Say it. Now read your word.
- What letters go together?
- Do you see a letter combination?
- You're reading one letter at a time; try reading the letters in a group.
- That's a blend. Read those letters together.
- ____ and ____ (e.g., *c* and *h*) make one sound.
- ____ and ____ sound like ____ (e.g., *c* and *h* sound like /ch/).
- You got the first two letters, now read the whole word.
- This word starts like ____. (*Say another word that starts with the same blend or digraph.*) Does that help?
- That word starts like this word. (*Point to a picture on the blends and digraphs chart.*)

Blends and Digraphs

ch cherry	wh whale	sh sheep	th three	ph phone
bl block	cl cloud	fl flag	gl glue	pl plate
sl slide	br brown	cr crayon	dr dress	fr frown
gr grapes	pr present	tr tree	sc scarf	sk skateboard
sm smile	sn snake	sp spoon	st star	sw swing
ck sock	scr scribble	spr sprout	spl splash	str strawberry

Who is this for?

LEVELS
D–Z+

GENRE / TEXT TYPE
any

SKILL
decoding

3.13 Check Beginning and End

Who is this for?

LEVELS
D–Z+

GENRE / TEXT TYPE
any

SKILL
decoding

Strategy Check the beginning of the word. Now check the end of the word. Think about what word would make sense there. Read the word.

Lesson Language *When you get to a tricky word, it's important that you aren't only checking the start of the word. There are many, many words that start with the same letter! If I read the sentence "This is a ball." And I only looked at the first letter—*b*—and the picture—a boy with a baseball bat and ball—I might say "This is a bat." Both of those would match the picture and the first letter. But, if I also check the end of the word I notice* ll *so I know that bat couldn't work because at the end of bat I hear a /t/ and that means I'd see a* t.

Prompts

- Check the beginning.
- Check the end.
- What makes sense?
- You looked carefully at the beginning to make sure you read it correctly. Now look to the end to make sure you have the ending correct.
- That matches the beginning and the ending. I can tell you looked at both!

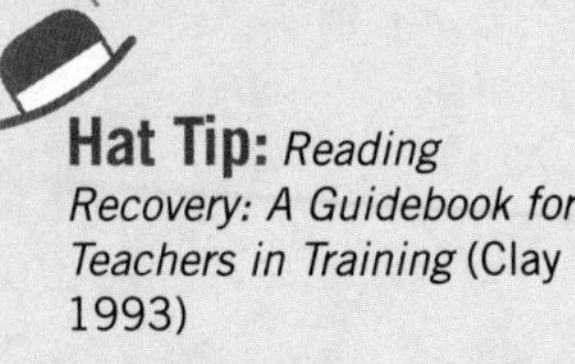

Hat Tip: *Reading Recovery: A Guidebook for Teachers in Training* (Clay 1993)

3.14 Run into the First Part

Strategy Look at the first couple or few letters plus the vowel. When you look at the first few letters together, you're getting a "running start" into the word. Then you can try to read the rest of the word by reading something that makes sense, sounds right, and matches the beginning of the word.

Teaching Tip I use the word "run" as a catchy way to mean "go quickly." I find that sometimes when children approach an unfamiliar word the tendency is to slow down and look only at the first letter. By looking at the first part, or even the word as a whole, some will have a better chance at reading it correctly. Other times, I think that when children slow down to approach an unknown word, they drop the meaning from the entire beginning of the sentence and just start puzzling over the word. Then, as an isolated word, it becomes harder to figure out without the meaning support as well. Overall, this strategy is a way to say "go for it!"

Depending on the level of students you work with, you may want to modify this strategy to be about "running" into the first part that is a blend or digraph (see 3.12, page 91) so that children aren't looking only at the first letter but rather the first couple of letters (level D, E). For children working on decoding multisyllabic words, you would talk to children about "running" into the first syllable, as described in this strategy.

Prompts

- Get a running start into that word.
- You read the first letter. Read the whole first syllable.
- Now that you know how the word starts, run into the whole word.
- Go for it—start at the beginning and let your eyes run all the way through it.
- You went for it! Now check that what you read makes sense.
- You looked at all the letters in the word. Now make sure it sounds right and makes sense. Think about what you've read so far.

Who is this for?

LEVELS

D–Z+

GENRE / TEXT TYPE

any

SKILLS

decoding, integrating sources of information

3.15 Take the Ending Off

Who is this for?

LEVELS

E–Z+

GENRE / TEXT TYPE

any

SKILL

decoding

Strategy Use your finger to cover up the common ending you see (for example, -ing, -ed, -er). Read the first part of the word that's not covered. Then, put the ending back on and read the whole word.

Lesson Language *When you get to a long word, you can sometimes take the word apart. One way to take it apart is to take off an ending. If you see* -ing, -ed, *or* -er, *those are common endings that are added on to a base word. If you cover it with your finger and only pay attention to what's left at the beginning of the word, you may find yourself saying, "Hey! I know that word!" Then, you can add the ending back on and read through the whole word. For example, I recently got to this word in my book* (show, but don't read the word): hurrying. *That's a lot of letters! But I noticed it had an* -ing *at the end. Then I used my finger to cover up the "ing" ending, and what was left is a much shorter word.* Hurry! *I recognized it right away. Then, I added the ending back on to read* hurrying.

Prompts

- Cover the ending.
- Read the part you have uncovered.
- Take your finger off the part of the word. Now say the whole word.
- Look all the way through the word.
- Look at the beginning and ending to read it.
- Cover up the common ending.

3.16 Go Left to Right

Strategy Get your mouth ready to say the first sound(s). Read the first part of the word. Then read the next part. Make sure to go part by part, left to right.

Lesson Language *When you come to a word you don't know, even though the whole word is unfamiliar, there are parts of the word you might know. However, looking at parts of the word randomly won't help. Instead, get a running start into the word and find the parts from left to right. For example, in the word* without *if I saw it had the word* it *inside the word and then went to try to read the word I'd say* w-it-hout *and I wouldn't get the word. Instead, the parts I should put together are* with *and* out. *Another example—in the word* detailed *if I look at the parts I know, left to right, I'd notice* de *and then* tail *and then the -ed ending, which I know can sound like /d/ or /ed/ or /t/. I could try all three and then I could tell the word is* detailed.

Prompts

- What's the first part you see?
- Start at the beginning of the word.
- Work your way across the word, left to right.
- You know that part ____ from the word ____.
- Keep going through the word.
- What are the parts you're looking at?
- I see you split up the word into parts. Did that help?
- I agree, those are the parts of that word.
- Now read it, left to right.

Go Left to Right

Get your mouth ready to say the first sound.

Read the word part-by-part and left to right.

sl → e → d

sled

Who is this for?

LEVELS

E–Z+

GENRE / TEXT TYPE

any

SKILL

decoding multisyllabic words

3.17 Flexible Sounds

Who is this for?

LEVELS

E–Z+

GENRE / TEXT TYPE

any

SKILL

decoding

Strategy Be flexible about vowel sounds—try one, then another—until you read a word that sounds like a word you've heard before and that makes sense in the sentence.

Lesson Language *We know that the English language is a tricky one—there are so many sounds each letter can make. When we come to tricky words, one strategy is to try, try, and try the word again, using different sounds for the vowels in the word. Often when you try different vowel sounds, you'll recognize the word you read as a word you know. Don't forget to always also check to make sure it makes sense in the context of the text and sentence.*

Prompts

- What can you try here?
- Try another sound for that vowel.
- What's another sound that letter can make?
- Try it again, with a different sound for that letter.
- That's one sound that letter can make. What's another?
- Check the alphabet chart.
- Check the vowel chart.
- That was one try! Now try something else.
- That letter can also sound like ____.
- Say all the sounds that letter can make.
- Does that sound like a word you know?

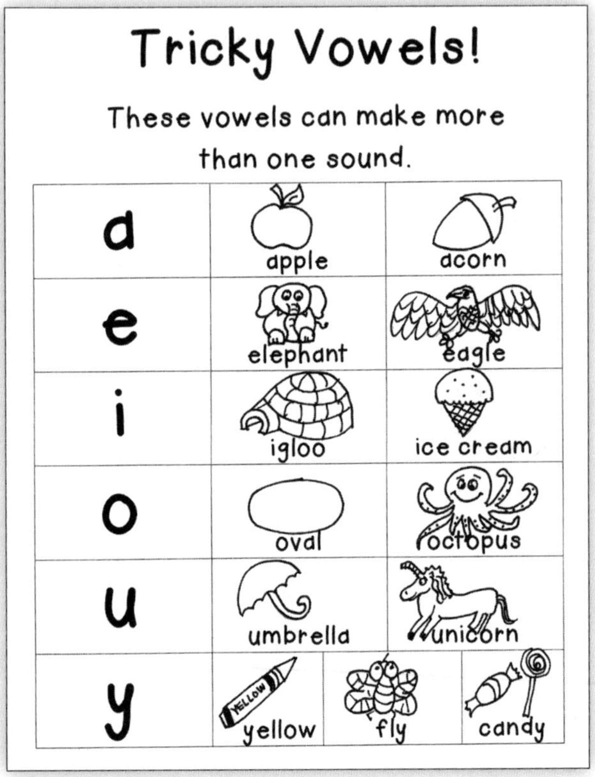

Tricky Vowels!

These vowels can make more than one sound.

a	apple	acorn	
e	elephant	eagle	
i	igloo	ice cream	
o	oval	octopus	
u	umbrella	unicorn	
y	yellow	fly	candy

3.18 Cover and Slide

Strategy When you're trying to read a word part by part, you can cover up the parts you aren't reading now, to focus on the parts you are. Slide your finger across the word left to right to show more and more parts as you read them. Put all the parts together to read the word.

Lesson Language *If at first you don't recognize the word as a whole, a strategy that sometimes helps me is to cover up the word, then slide my finger, hand, or bookmark across the word slowly, revealing one part at a time. For example, if I'm reading the word* underground, *I'd slide my hand across to reveal* un *first. Then* der. *I could put those two parts together:* under. *Then, I'm going to look at the next part. I see the blend* gr *and now when I look at the rest of the word* ound*—that looks like* round *or* hound. *So* gr *and* ound *is* ground. *Let me put it all together now,* underground.

Prompts

- Cover everything but the first part.
- How many parts does this word have?
- Now slide your finger across the word, reading part by part.
- You read the first part. Now read the next part.
- Read the ending.
- Now put it together.
- I notice you read part by part. Did that help you?

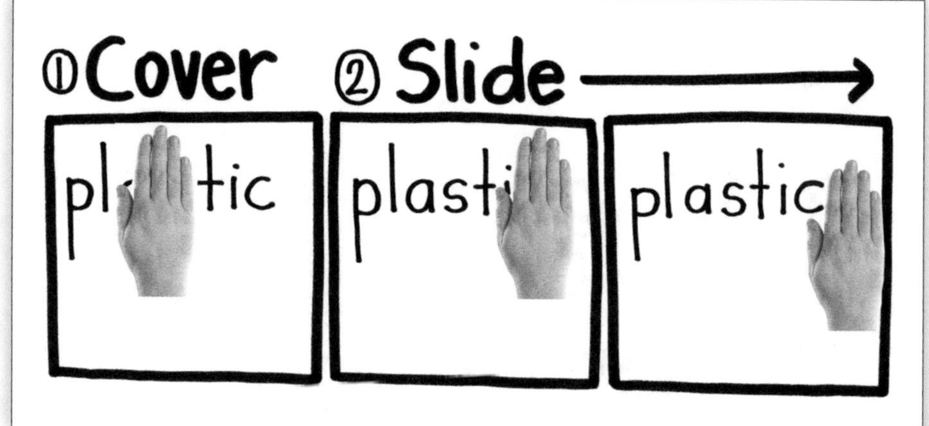

Who is this for?

LEVELS

E–Z+

GENRE / TEXT TYPE

any

SKILL

decoding

3.19 Take the Word Apart, Then Put It Back Together

Who is this for?

LEVELS

E–Z+

GENRE / TEXT TYPE

any

SKILL

decoding

Strategy Readers are like detectives who try to figure out the mystery of a new word. When we get to a word we don't know, we don't just mumble through it. We try to use some strategies to take the word apart, and then put it back together.

Lesson Language *Longer words we find in books are often made up of parts that feel familiar. Some parts are common beginnings:* re-, de-, un-. *Some parts are common endings:* -ing, -ed, -er. *And the middle parts are often parts we see in lots of other words, too, such as the words in word families you've studied during word study. Sometimes you can take apart a longer word, find the smaller parts you recognize because they are like other words you know or parts of other words you know, and then once you know all the parts, put it back together to make a whole. For example, if I come to the word spelled* d-i-s-a-g-r-e-e-d, *I might first think it looks just like a bunch of letters in a too-long, hard word. But then I can look for the parts I know. I know* dis- *and* -ed *and in the middle I see a word I know,* agree. *Now I can put it back together:* dis—agree—ed. Disagreed!

Prompts

- What can you try?
- Let's start trying to take the word apart. What's the first part you see?
- Read the word part by part.
- Try taking off the ending, and let's read the rest first.
- That didn't work! Let's try another strategy.
- You really worked hard at that word, using all the strategies you know, and you got it!

un der gr ou nd

underground

3.20 Skip and Return

Strategy Skip the difficult word. Read on to the end of the sentence or paragraph, thinking about what would make sense in that spot you skipped. Go back to the beginning of the sentence and read it all again, trying to figure out what the word might be.

Teaching Tip This strategy needs to be used in conjunction with level-appropriate strategies for looking at the word—I wouldn't advise teaching children to just skip. As you may notice in the strategy language above and in the lesson language below, I'm advising integrating all three cueing systems and skipping and returning.

Lesson Language *If you use some strategies to try to figure out a word when you get to it, but you find you are still stuck, you might try skipping it, then returning to it once you get more information. Especially when the tricky word is at the start of the sentence, you may not have enough information about what's happening or what would make sense. By reading on, you get more information about what's happening and what would make sense. For example, I'm reading the following sentence.* (Show, don't read: "I want to put pepperoni on my pizza.") *It's easy to see that I would get stuck on the fifth word in that sentence. It's long and tricky! Up to that word, "I want to put"... If I think about what makes sense, it could be anything! I want to put necklaces on. I want to put posters on the wall. I want to put people on stage. It could be anything! But if I skip it and read the rest of the sentence, I get more information: "on my pizza." Now I can think, what would make sense? What would I put on a pizza that starts with* pep? *It could be ...* peppers. *Or* pepperoni. *Let me check the end of the word. I see an* i *so it can't be* peppers*—that would end with an* s. *Let me start at the beginning of the sentence and read the whole thing. "I want to put pepperoni on my pizza." That works! It makes sense, sounds right, and matches the letters in the word.*

Prompts

- Skip it and come back.
- Just say, "Mm" and keep reading to the end of the sentence.
- OK, you skipped it, now let's come back to figure out what the word is.
- Think about what's happening in the sentence. Come back and try to read that word.

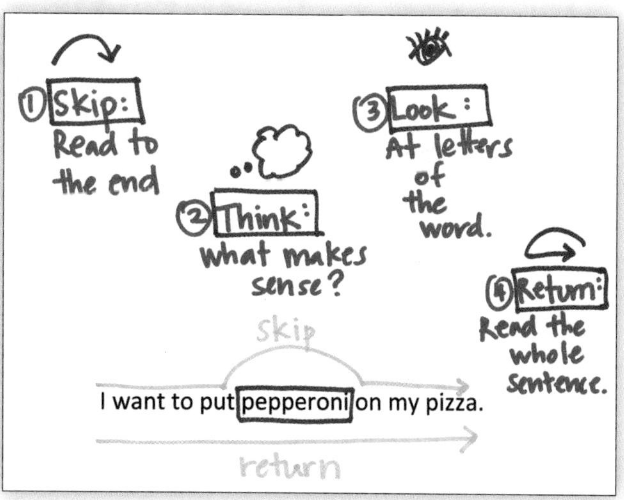

Who is this for?

LEVELS

E–Z+

GENRE / TEXT TYPE

any

SKILL

decoding

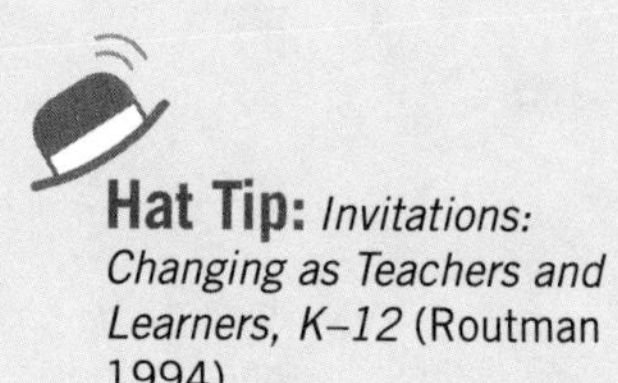

Hat Tip: *Invitations: Changing as Teachers and Learners, K–12* (Routman 1994)

3.21 Look for Vowels That Go Together

Who is this for?

LEVELS

G–Z+

GENRE / TEXT TYPE

any

SKILL

decoding

Strategy As you read through the word part by part, you may see two vowels side by side. Those two vowels need to go together. Think about other words you know that have those same two vowels together to help you read the word.

Teaching Tip This lesson can be adapted to a variety of levels by reminding students of the vowel combinations they've learned during word study. It may be helpful for students to have a content chart, such as the one on page 91 (strategy 3.12, "Group Letters That Make Sounds Together") to remind students of the vowel combinations they have studied.

Prompts

- You read through the word part by part. Show me what the next part is?
- Do you see two letters that go together in this word?
- Those two letters make one sound. Try it.
- What other words do you know that have those two letters?
- Those two letters are also in the word ____. Does that help you read this word?
- You put those two letters together to make one sound and you were able to read the word!

Hat Tip: *The Continuum of Literacy Learning, Grades PreK–8: A Guide to Teaching*, second edition (Fountas and Pinnell 2010b)

3.22 Unpacking What It Means to "Sound Right"

Strategy You can think about the kind of word you're reading to help you read the word. Notice where in the sentence the word appears. Notice what word comes before and after. Thinking about its place in the sentence, think, "What would sound right here?"

Lesson Language *The place a word appears in the sentence can help you understand the kind of word it is that you're trying to figure out. For example, if the word you're trying to figure out comes before a thing, it's probably a describing word (adjective). If it tells what a character is doing, it's an action word (verb). Knowing the kind of word, and then using your other strategies such as breaking the word apart, and thinking about what makes sense, can help you figure it out.*

Teaching Tip This strategy will be most powerful when children have some sense of the different "jobs" that words have in a sentence, something you might have taught during word study or grammar or even embedded into your reading or other writing instruction.

Prompts

- Think about where that word is in the sentence.
- That word comes before a word that is a thing. Does that help?
- What kind of word might that be?
- Do you think that word is a noun, verb, adjective?
- Now that you know what kind of word it is, what do you think that word might be?
- You know the kind of word, now let's use some other strategies.
- Yes! You used where the word appears in the sentence to figure out what that word can be.

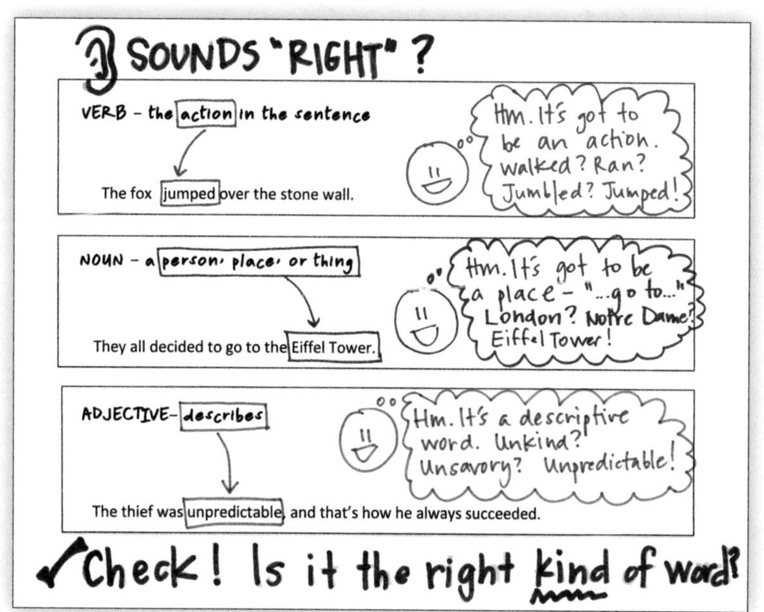

Who is this for?

LEVELS

J–Z+

GENRE / TEXT TYPE

any

SKILLS

decoding, using structure as a source of information

3.23 Words Across a Line Break

Who is this for?

LEVELS

L–Z+

GENRE / TEXT TYPE

any

SKILL

decoding

Strategy When you see a word broken up across two lines and can't figure it out, pause. Write the whole word out on a piece of paper. Look at it as a whole and see if you recognize it. If not, use a strategy you know to figure out multisyllabic words.

Lesson Language *In the book we've been reading as a class, there have been lots of times when I came to a word at the end of the line that was not the whole word. It looks like this* (show an example under a document camera from a recent read-aloud). *At first, it can seem tricky to figure words like this out because our brains are used to seeing words as wholes. If I'm really stuck, I will put the word back together by writing it on a scrap piece of paper. So* doc *and* ument *become* document. *Lots of times after writing it as a whole you'll recognize it right away. If not, you can treat it like you would any other multisyllabic word and use another strategy like cover and slide, or go part by part.*

Prompts

- Having trouble with that word? Let's write it out.
- Look at the word as a whole. What strategy will you try to figure it out?
- Writing it out helped! When you saw it as a whole word you knew it right away.
- Do you see a word broken up on this line?
- That's not a whole word, that's a part of the word—see the hyphen at the end of the line? The word continues on the next line.
- Do you recognize it now that it's a whole?

Hat Tip: "Thinking Intensive Learning: Close Reading Is Strategic Reading" (Harvey 2014)

Integrating all three sources of information takes coordination, mental effort, and strategic action.

—*Jennifer Serravallo*

Teaching Fluency

Reading with Phrasing, Intonation, and Automaticity

Why is this goal important?

Some argue there is a chicken-and-egg relationship between fluency and comprehension. By reading at an appropriate pace, with proper phrasing and with intonation, expression, and emphasis on the correct words, a reader both communicates that the text is making sense and makes sense of the reading (Rasinski 2010, Kuhn 2008). Try to read a text in a staccato, word-by-word, monotone fashion and you will soon discover you understood and remember very few if any of the words you said aloud.

There are exceptions to this rule of fluency and comprehension being inextricably linked. Have you ever met that child who reads a text sounding like he is reading lines for a Broadway audition, only to stop, be asked a simple question about what he just read, and have him tell you he doesn't remember a thing? It's important that in our attempts to teach children to read fluently, we don't send the message that reading is just about performing.

There are a few parts to this goal of reading fluency:

- phrasing or parsing—putting words together into meaningful groups within a sentence
- expression or intonation or prosody—reading to match the feeling of the piece, paying attention to ending punctuation and dialogue marks
- emphasis—emphasizing words in the sentence to match the author's meaning; paying attention to text treatments (for example: bold, italics, or all caps)
- automaticity—reading known words automatically
- pace—reading at a pace that mirrors how we talk, not racing through words or reading at a labored rate.

How do I know if this goal is right for my student?

We wouldn't expect readers at the lowest levels (A, B, C) to read with fluency, as their focus should be on one-to-one matching (reading one word aloud for each word in print) and pointing under the words—reading smoothly and this goal cannot live side by side. However, by level D, we should expect some phrasing, with a couple or a few words in each phrase, and by level E, we should expect some intonation as well. At levels E, F, and G, it's appropriate to help students practice their fluency, though we may not expect perfect fluency as students are still learning to integrate sources of information and work on their print work strategies (see Chapter 3; Joseph Yukish, personal communication, 2014).

I'm not a fan of determining fluency as a goal by holding up a stopwatch as kids read because I believe that children often start to view reading aloud as performance and they stop monitoring for meaning, invalidating the assessment overall, or they feel pressured and the results are skewed by their anxiety. In most cases, if phrasing is appropriate, the pace will be too. So instead of a stopwatch, I think you can listen as students read aloud for a running record, and record their pauses (as slash marks where the pauses occur) and instances of expressive reading (by annotating). You can then go back to evaluate the number of words in a phrase group, where the pauses were and whether they were syntactically appropriate, and how often the reader paid attention to punctuation. See the sample record of oral reading in Figure 4.A. For more information about taking fluency records, see either The Literacy Teacher's Playbook or Independent Reading Assessment series (Serravallo).

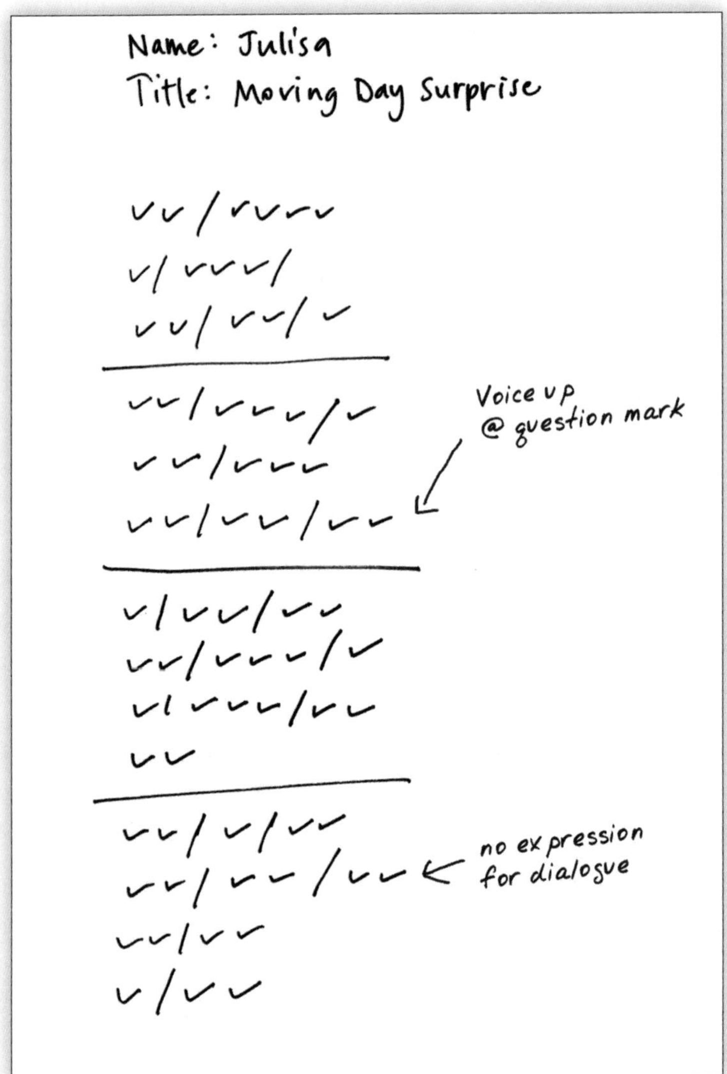

Figure 4.A A record of one student's reading fluency. Pauses are indicated by slashes (/) and notations about expression are in the margins. According to this, I would say the student could work on lengthening her phrases and being more consistent about attending to ending punctuation to inform intonation and expression.

Strategies for Reading with Fluency at a Glance

Strategy	Levels	Genres/ Text Types	Skills
4.1 Read It Like You've Always Known It	A–Z+	Any	Automaticity
4.2 Think, "Have I Seen It on the Word Wall?"	A–Z+ (although words would change based on level)	Any	Automaticity
4.3 Use a "This Is Interesting" Voice	D–Z+	Nonfiction	Intonation, expression
4.4 Make the Bumpy Smooth	D–J	Any	Phrasing
4.5 Say Good-Bye to Robot Reading	D–Z+	Any	Phrasing
4.6 Punctuation at the End of a Sentence	D–Z+	Any	Intonation, expression
4.7 Warm-Up and Transfer	D–Z+	Any	Phrasing and/or intonation
4.8 Punctuation Inside a Sentence	E–Z+	Any	Phrasing
4.9 Partners Help to Smooth It Out	E–J	Any	Phrasing
4.10 Inside Quotes and Outside Quotes	E–Z+	Fiction	Intonation, expression
4.11 Make Your Voice Match the Feeling	E–Z+	Fiction	Intonation, expression
4.12 Fluency Phone for Feedback	E–Z+	Any	Phrasing
4.13 Make Your Voice Match the Meaning	E–Z+	Any	Phrasing, intonation
4.14 Get Your Eyes Ahead of the Words	E–Z+	Any	Phrasing, intonation
4.15 Warm-Up Phrases	F–Z+	Any	Phrasing
4.16 Read Like a Storyteller	F–Z+	Narrative	Intonation, expression
4.17 Push Your Eyes	J/K (or any book where the sentences are broken up across lines)	Fiction (mostly early chapter books)	Phrasing
4.18 Partners Can Be Fluency Teachers	J–Z+	Any	Phrasing, intonation, partnership
4.19 Snap to the Next Line	J–Z+	Any	Phrasing
4.20 Make the Pause Match the Meaning	M–Z+	Any	Phrasing
4.21 Read It How the Author Tells You (Tags)	M–Z+	Fiction	Intonation, expression

4.1 Read It Like You've Always Known It

Who is this for?

LEVELS

A–Z+

GENRE / TEXT TYPE

any

SKILL

automaticity

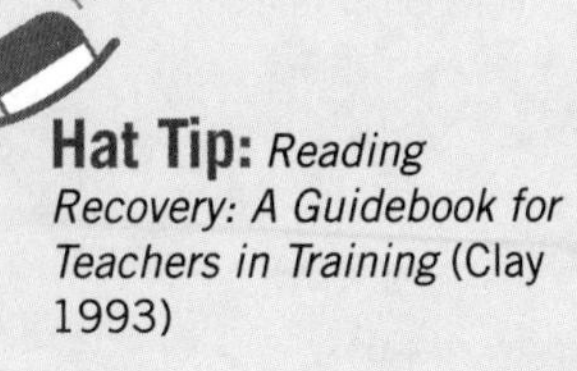

Hat Tip: *Reading Recovery: A Guidebook for Teachers in Training* (Clay 1993)

Strategy When you have to pause to figure out a word, go back to the beginning of the sentence and reread. This time, read the word right away like it's a word you've always known. Reading the sentence as a whole after you've figured out each word will help you hold on to the meaning.

Lesson Language *It's likely that you're going to come to a word or two here or there that you don't know when you first see it. You'll use your strategies to stop and figure those words out—breaking the words into parts, looking for prefixes or suffixes, trying different vowel sounds, or using whatever strategies you know that may work in this instance. Stopping to figure out the word takes a little time, and might take you away from the meaning of the sentence. But you don't want to lose the meaning! So when you take a break to figure out a word, it's important that you reread, reading that new word automatically like it's a word you've always known.*

Prompts

- I notice you're stopping to figure out that word. Make sure you go back and reread the sentence once you figure it out.
- Go back and read the whole sentence.
- Now that you know the word, go back and reread.
- Read it again, with that word you just learned.
- Make sure that's the right word; go back and reread the whole sentence.
- Reread.
- Read it again.

4.2 Think, "Have I Seen It on the Word Wall?"

Strategy Think, "Have I seen this word before on the word wall?" before you stop to try other strategies. The words on the word wall are the ones that show up the most and are the words that should be read automatically.

Teaching Tip Some students seem to know a word wall word in isolation, but not when it's in a book. Others are able to write it using the word wall, but when they come across it in their book, they become stumped. For students to develop automaticity with sight words, it helps to make sure they know them in many ways and across contexts—reading, writing, in isolation, in context and so on. Some students who are good candidates for this strategy can also be taught to "warm up" by reading through the word wall before beginning their independent reading for the day.

Prompts

- Is that a word you know? Check the word wall.
- I think that's on the word wall.
- I see that one on the word wall.
- Look for that word on the word wall first.
- Is that a word you should stop and figure out?
- Is that on the word wall?
- Say that one in a snap!
- Don't try to sound that one out. Check the word wall first.

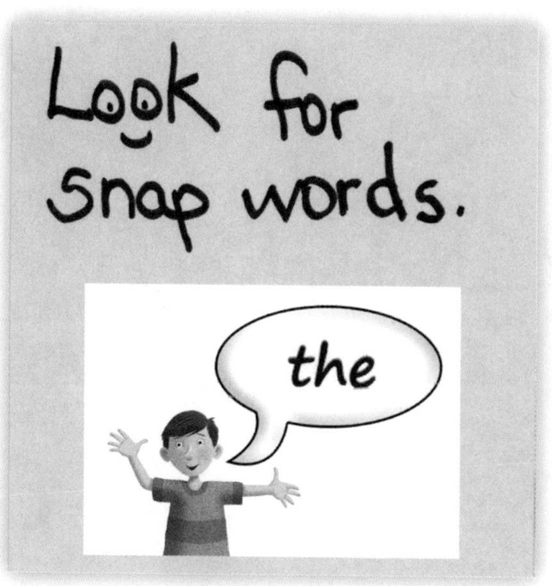

Who is this for?

LEVELS

A–Z+ (although words would change based on level)

GENRE / TEXT TYPE

any

SKILL

automaticity

4.3 Use a "This Is Interesting" Voice

Who is this for?

LEVELS

D–Z+

GENRE / TEXT TYPE

nonfiction

SKILL

intonation, expression

Strategy When reading information texts, you can try sounding like a teacher instead of like a storyteller. Read as if you're teaching interesting facts. Raise your voice at questions.

Lesson Language *When you read nonfiction, it could be easy to read it in a monotone, flat voice, one fact after another. Instead, try to show that the information you're learning is interesting. Look to the ending punctuation to know whether you're going to be giving information (periods, exclamation points) or asking questions (question marks). Since the book is teaching you information, you can read it like you're teaching.* (Model reading something in a flat, monotone voice and model reading with some expression, like a teacher would who thinks the information is interesting.)

Prompts

- Make it sound interesting.
- Your voice was flat there; try to make it sound like the information is amazing!
- You just made that sound interesting!
- I can tell you understood what you just read, based on how you read it.
- Say it like a teacher would.
- I see a question mark. Make your voice match it.

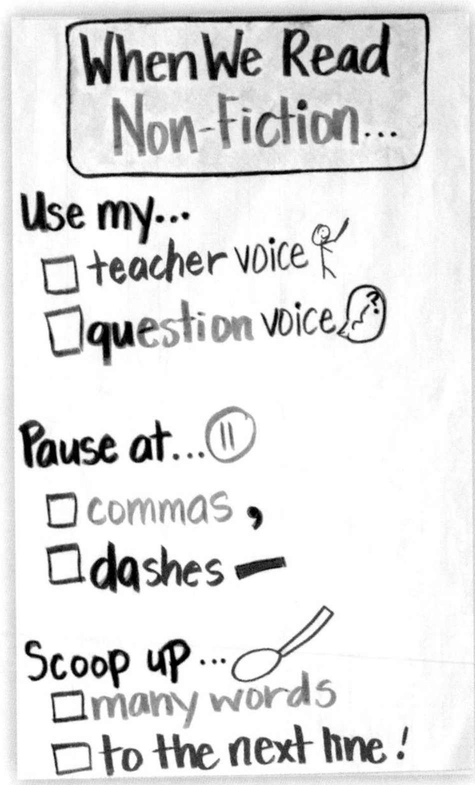

4.4 Make the Bumpy Smooth

Strategy Sometimes it's hard to read smoothly the first time you see something new, when the story or information is new and the words are new, too. Go back after you know the words to try to smooth out the reading. Pause once every few words, instead of after every word.

Teaching Tip Although I would teach this strategy to readers at levels D and E, heed the warning at the beginning of this chapter on page 104 about the extent to which you would expect fluency with readers at these lower levels.

Lesson Language *When you read, your brain is doing so much work, so many things are happening at the same time. One thing your brain has to do is to remember all the letters and the sounds they make. Another thing it has to do is to remember what's going on in the story, and keep track of it all. And then there's reading it smoothly, like how we talk! It's tiring just thinking about it all! For many of us, reading things smoothly when we know all the words and know what the story is about is much easier than doing all those things at the same time.*

Prompts

- Go back and try it one more time.
- Now that you know all the words, smooth it out.
- Do you think you should reread that?
- How did that sound to you?
- Scoop a few words together.
- Smooth it out.
- You read all the words correctly, now reread to make it sound smooth.

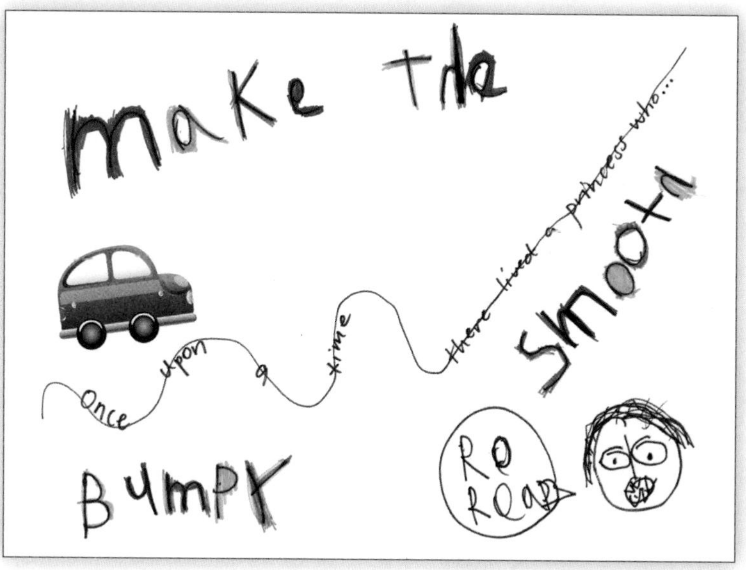

Who is this for?

LEVELS

D–J

GENRE / TEXT TYPE

any

SKILL

phrasing

Hat Tip: *The Fluent Reader: Oral and Silent Reading Strategies for Building Fluency, Word Recognition, and Comprehension*, second edition (Rasinski 2010)

4.5 Say Good-Bye to Robot Reading

Who is this for?

LEVELS

D–Z+

GENRE / TEXT TYPE

any

SKILL

phrasing

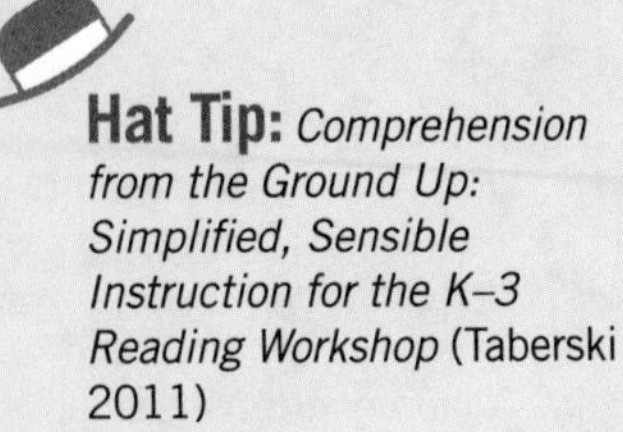

Hat Tip: *Comprehension from the Ground Up: Simplified, Sensible Instruction for the K–3 Reading Workshop* (Taberski 2011)

Strategy Instead of reading word by word, try to scoop up a few words at a time. Read all the words in one scoop together, in one breath, before pausing. Then scoop up the next few words.

Lesson Language *Instead of reading word by word, like a robot, it's important to try to read a few words together. This is called a phrase. To do this, you can try to scoop up a few words at a time. You can slide your finger in a scoop under the few words you're going to read, and then read them all together in one breath. Pause, and then scoop up the next few words. So, instead of sounding like this: "This. Is. A. Dog. He. Likes. To. Play. Ball." It'll sound like this: "This is" . . . "A dog" . . . "He likes" . . . "To play ball."* (Give children a contrastive example by first demonstrating—pointing word by word for the first reading, and then later sliding your finger under the words to scoop a phrase as you read them.)

Prompts

- What words will you scoop up together?
- Scoop under those words.
- Now read those few words all in one breath.
- Try it again; read all of those words without pausing.
- That sounded word by word; try it again by scooping.
- Good, now that you have the words go back and try to read a few together.
- It sounded like all those words were in one scoop, in one breath. Nice job!
- Let me scoop for you, and you read the words.
- Repeat after me. (*Read in phrases and have the student read the same words you just read.*)

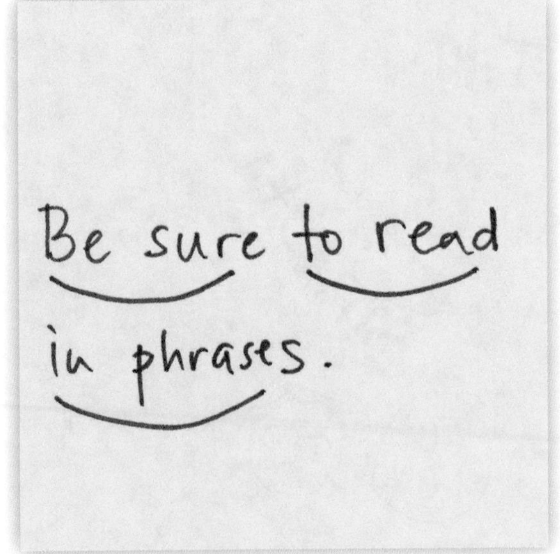

4.6 Punctuation at the End of a Sentence

Strategy Pay attention to ending punctuation. Look ahead to the end of the sentence. Notice if there is an exclamation point, question mark, or period. Make your voice match the punctuation.

Lesson Language *As we've talked about before, readers do more than just read the words—they also read the marks on the page. Ending punctuation gives us a really big clue about how the sentence should be read. It's very important that we pay attention to whether the sentence ends with a question mark, meaning that there is a question and our voice should go up; or an exclamation mark, meaning there is a strong emotion connected to the sentence such as happiness, anger, surprise; or a period, telling us to let our voice go down at the end. If we read a sentence with the wrong ending mark, it may change the meaning of the sentence and confuse us about what's happening in the story, or what the author is teaching in the information book.*

Prompts

- Look ahead to the end of the sentence—what do you see?
- What does that mark tell you to do?
- Make your voice sound like that.
- Good! Your voice matched the punctuation.
- That's a question mark. Make your voice rise.
- That's an exclamation mark. You should read that with expression (*sound excited, shocked, happy, or loud.*).
- That's a period. Pause before going on.

PAY ATTENTION
to ENDING punctuation
How are you?
I went to the park.
Watch out!
* Change your voice.
* Match the meaning.

Who is this for?

LEVELS

D–Z+

GENRE / TEXT TYPE

any

SKILLS

intonation, expression

4.7 Warm-Up and Transfer

Who is this for?

LEVELS

D–Z+

GENRE / TEXT TYPE

any

SKILLS

phrasing and/or intonation

Strategy Warm up on an easier book, getting the feel for fluent reading. When you feel like the reading is easy and smooth, move to a just-right book. Try to make your voice sound just as smooth on the just-right book as it was on the easier book.

Lesson Language *Have you ever watched sports on TV? The Olympics, a basketball game, football? Before athletes go on the field or court or track to do their thing, they need to spend some time warming up. Warming up usually means doing easier exercises to get the muscles ready to do the harder work of the sport. You can think of reading like this. Sometimes when you're working hard at reading, like we are now, practicing reading with fluency, it is a good idea to warm up first. To do this, you take a book that would be considered easy for you—something where you'll know all the words and you can read it smoothly without much effort. As you read it, I want you to be aware of how you let your eyes go ahead of the word you're reading now, how you scoop up many words at a time in a phrase, how you read it based on how the character is thinking. After a minute of that, you should get the feel for it. Then, when you feel like the reading is easy and smooth, move to a just-right book. Now, try to make your voice sound just as smooth in the just-right book.*

Prompts (easy book)

- I can tell you swept your eyes across that line.
- That sounded nice and smooth.
- Your voice matched what was happening.
- You sounded just like the character!
- I noticed you paused when you saw punctuation!

Prompts (just-right book)

- Remember how it felt with the easy book? Do the same with this one.
- You read all the words correctly. Reread and smooth it out.
- Watch the punctuation.
- Scoop under these words.

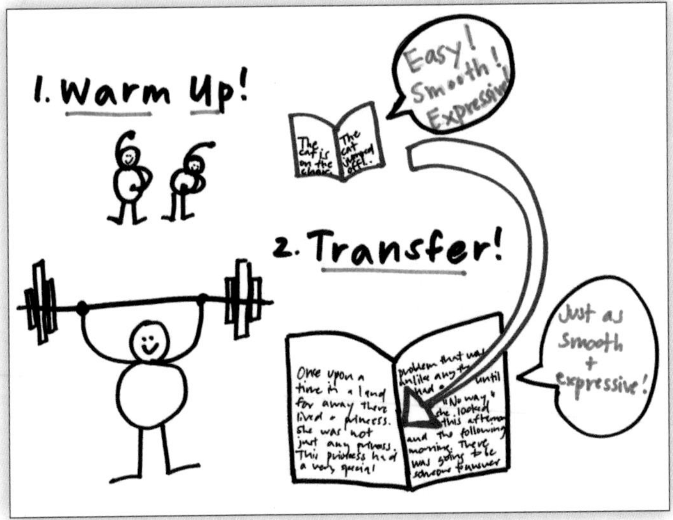

Hat Tip: *Teaching Reading in Small Groups: Differentiated Instruction for Building Strategic, Independent Readers* (Serravallo 2010)

4.8 Punctuation Inside a Sentence

Strategy Look ahead in the sentence for punctuation that tells you when to pause, such as commas, dashes, and semicolons. Read up to the punctuation, take a short break, and then read the next group.

Lesson Language *Now that you're reading harder books with longer, more complicated sentences, chances are good that you'll find some punctuation not just at the end, but also in the middle of a sentence. These commas, dashes, colons, and semicolons* (Show an example of each as you name them.) *are there to help you read the sentences. In between the punctuation marks are phrases, and those words are meant to be read together. To read these longer sentences, look ahead for punctuation. Try to read up to the punctuation in one breath, then take a break. Then, read the next group of words until you see another punctuation mark.*

Prompts

- Read all the words up to this comma (or colon or dash) in one breath.
- Where will you read up to before pausing?
- Do you see any punctuation in the middle of the sentence?
- Try again, but this time don't pause until you get to the comma (or colon or dash).
- That sounded smooth—all the words in this phrase (Point to the phrase.) sounded like they went together.
- The way you read that matched the punctuation on the page.
- I noticed you paid attention to punctuation.
- I noticed you paused at the comma (or colon or dash).
- Look ahead to the next punctuation mark.
- Don't pause until the punctuation mark.

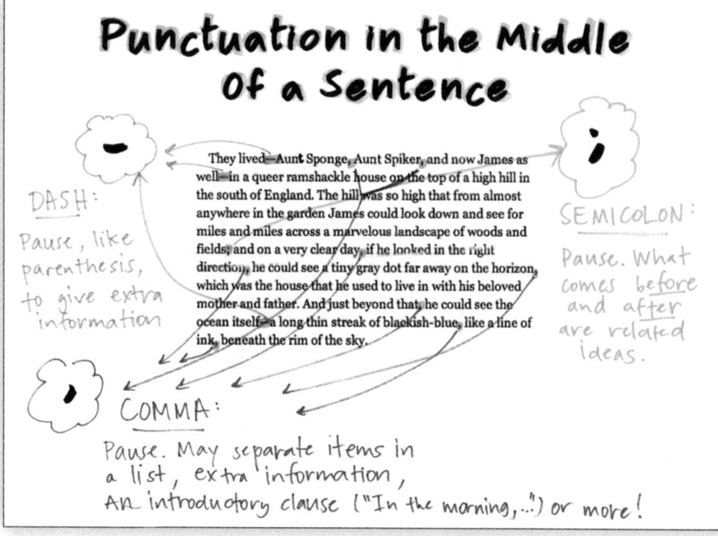

Text excerpt from *James and the Giant Peach* (Dahl 1961).

Who is this for?

LEVELS
E–Z+

GENRE / TEXT TYPE
any

SKILL
phrasing

4.9 Partners Help to Smooth It Out

Who is this for?

LEVELS

E–J

GENRE / TEXT TYPE

any

SKILL

phrasing

Strategy Partners can help one another read in a smooth voice. When you meet in partner time, put one book between the two of you. Look at the words, listen to yourself, and listen to your partner. Try to read in one voice, pausing at the same places and using the same expression.

Teaching Tip One way to get children to prompt each other in partnerships is to become a "ghost partner." Whisper into children's ears a phrase or sentence starter that you want them to repeat to their partner. In no time at all, they will start taking up the language as their own. So, for this strategy you might whisper, "Let's try that again" or "That sounded choppy, right?" or "Should we try that one more time?" for them to literally repeat to their partner.

Prompts

- What can you tell your partner to help him with his fluency?
- Tell your partner, "Go back and try that again!"
- Tell your partner, "That sounded very smooth."
- Tell your partner, "The way you read that helped me picture it."
- What do you think?
- What will you tell your partner?
- Make sure you're listening carefully and be ready to give your partner advice.

Partners Help Smooth It Out!

One Book
Two Readers

Listen!

Read Together
Pause Together

The shark loses lots of teeth each time it has a meal!

Re-Read!

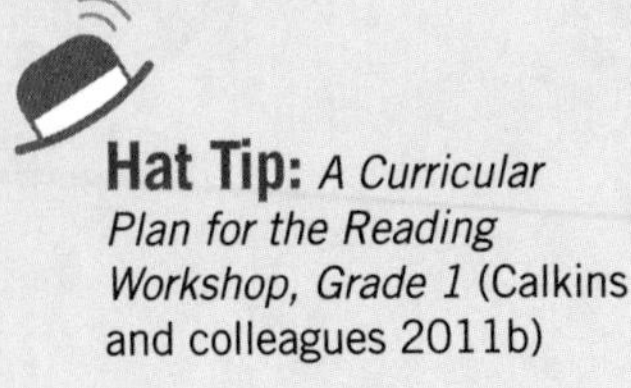

Hat Tip: *A Curricular Plan for the Reading Workshop, Grade 1* (Calkins and colleagues 2011b)

4.10 Inside Quotes and Outside Quotes

Strategy Everything inside of quotation marks is dialogue. Read it so it sounds like the character is talking. The dialogue tag is the narrator talking. Drop back to a narrator voice when you get to the dialogue tag.

Lesson Language *When I'm reading, I'm always careful to pay close attention to not only the words, but also the marks on the page. The little marks—the punctuation—give us a lot of important information about how to read. They also help us understand what we're reading! For example, it's very important to know when, in a story, the narrator is speaking, and when the character is speaking. But you want to know what? The author helps us! The author uses something called quotation marks—and they look like this* (Show example from a big book and/or hand-drawn large quotation marks.) *Think of it this way—when you first see the mark, you can think of it like the character opening his or her mouth—it's the start of the talking. So when we are reading, the voice we use has to change from a narrator voice to a character voice. Then, when we see the quotes again, like right here* (Point to example.)*, that's the closing of the quotation marks, and the closing of the character's mouth. Open quotes, open mouth. Closed quotes, closed mouth. Open quotes, start sounding like the character. Closed quotes, stop sounding like the character. Let's try it together . . .*

Prompts

- Show me where the talking starts.
- There's the quotation mark! Switch your voice.
- I can tell you paid attention to the quotation marks because I hear a difference between the character and narrator.
- That's a tag. Sound like a narrator now.
- The dialogue and narration sounded the same. Go back and try it again.

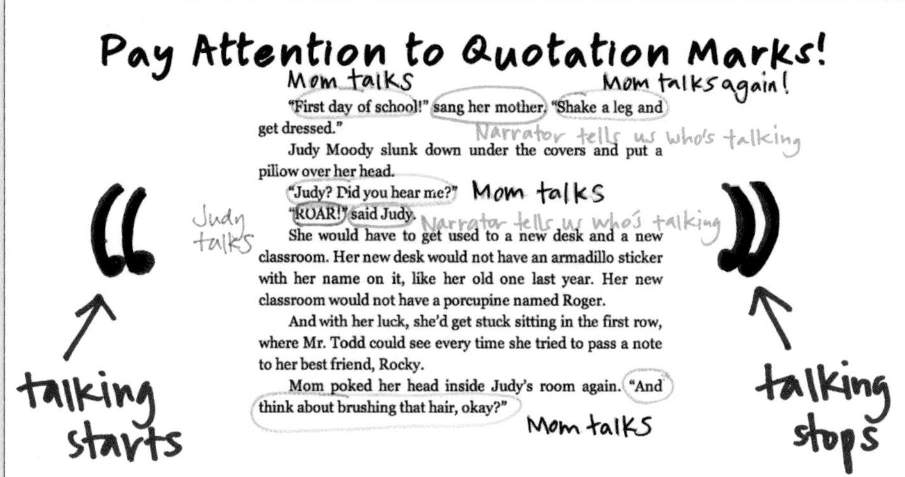

"First day of school!" sang her mother. "Shake a leg and get dressed."

Judy Moody slunk down under the covers and put a pillow over her head.

"Judy? Did you hear me?"

"ROAR!" said Judy.

She would have to get used to a new desk and a new classroom. Her new desk would not have an armadillo sticker with her name on it, like her old one last year. Her new classroom would not have a porcupine named Roger.

And with her luck, she'd get stuck sitting in the first row, where Mr. Todd could see every time she tried to pass a note to her best friend, Rocky.

Mom poked her head inside Judy's room again. "And think about brushing that hair, okay?"

Text excerpt from *Judy Moody Was in a Mood* (McDonald 2010).

Who is this for?

LEVELS

E–Z+

GENRE / TEXT TYPE

fiction

SKILLS

intonation, expression

4.11 Make Your Voice Match the Feeling

Who is this for?

LEVELS

E–Z+

GENRE / TEXT TYPE

fiction

SKILLS

intonation, expression

Hat Tip: *Comprehension from the Ground Up: Simplified, Sensible Instruction for the K–3 Reading Workshop* (Taberski 2011)

Strategy Think about how the character feels. Think about how you sound when you feel like that. Read the dialogue to match the character's feelings.

Teaching Tip This strategy can be modified for readers at different levels. For children in books that have heavy picture support (up to about level J/K), you can cue children to check the picture to see the facial expression of the character, then to make their voice match how the character is feeling. For children at levels where picture support starts to drop off (L–Z+), you might clue children to think about how the character might be feeling based on what he or she said and how he or she said it. Students may therefore look to dialogue tags, and think about the larger context of the story to consider the character's feelings. This is an extra cognitive step, as children will have to first be able to infer, and then they are able to adjust their intonation. For more support with teaching children how to infer character feelings, see strategies 6.1, 6.3, and 6.4 in Chapter 6.

Prompts

- How is the character feeling?
- How would it sound when that character talks?
- Yes! Your voice sounded (sad or happy or mad).
- Go back and read it, thinking about the feeling the character is having.
- Check the picture to help you figure out the feeling.
- Check the dialogue tag. Does that help you think about the feeling? Now make your voice match it.
- Make your voice match the feeling.

Make Your VOICE
Match the FEELING
=
!!! !!!
=
!!!

4.12 Fluency Phone for Feedback

Strategy Listen to yourself read. You can either read with a quiet voice in a spot in the room that won't disturb anyone, or use a "phone." As you listen to yourself, notice how you sound. If you catch yourself sounding flat or choppy, reread to make it sound more like how you'd talk.

Teaching Tip These phones, sometimes called "fluency phones" or "phonics phones," can be purchased or made with a piece of PVC piping. The idea is that the curved tube allows for instant feedback as students read aloud, allowing them to better monitor and adjust their reading. Even when reading at a very low volume, students hears themselves read without disturbing other readers in the classroom.

Prompts

- Let's try reading with the phone. Really try to hear yourself.
- As you listen to yourself read, do you think it sounded smooth or do you want to go back and reread?
- Read this page to yourself, out loud, using the phone. Then let's talk about how it sounded.
- You really listened to yourself there—I noticed you went back to smooth out your reading.
- You're really hearing yourself.

Who is this for?

LEVELS
E–Z+

GENRE / TEXT TYPE
any

SKILL
phrasing

4.13 Make Your Voice Match the Meaning

Who is this for?

LEVELS

E–Z+

GENRE / TEXT TYPE

any

SKILLS

phrasing, intonation

Strategy It's important that when you're practicing reading smoothly, you are focused on what's happening, what you're learning about, or the meaning the author is trying to get across. Depending on the type of text, and the topic, you may change your voice. Have a voice in your head saying, "What's this about?" and make sure your reading matches the meaning.

Teaching Tip The lesson that follows is an example of noticing character emotions to match intonation and expression. This lesson can also be modified to work with other genres. For example, the way it sounds when a person reads nonfiction might be to read it in a, "Whoa! I never knew that!" kind of voice. You could teach a lesson where you show examples of you reading a persuasive piece and a narrative piece and discuss together how your intonation sounds different based on the genre. You will notice that some of the Prompts may work better for narratives, while others will work best for informational texts.

Lesson Language *Remember the other day when we were reading this big book,* The Little Red Hen *(Parkes and Smith 1989), together? We were all reading the page that said, "Then I'll plant it myself, said the Little Red Hen." At first we read it sort of ho-hum. Like, no big deal, I'll just go ahead and plant it. Then we realized—wait. She probably wouldn't be calm about it. She's probably getting really annoyed! All of these people turn her down when she asks for help. Then we went back to read it in an annoyed, frustrated—grrrrrr!—kind of tone. And then instead of reading it like this* (Read in a calm voice.)*, we read it like this* (Read in an annoyed voice.)*. That change in how we read it really matched the meaning. That's what I want you to be thinking about when you're reading your books. Make sure that the way you read it really matches what's happening.*

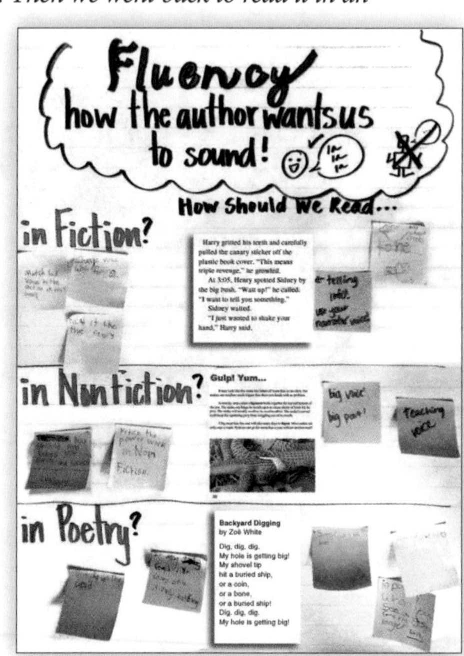

Top text excerpt from *Horrible Harry in Room 2B* (Kline 1997). Bottom text excerpt from *Playing with Poems* (White 2008).

Prompts

- What's happening now?
- What kind of text is this? Show me how you'd read that.
- Does your voice match that?
- Did how you read that make sense with the story?
- Think about what's happening in the story.
- I could tell you were thinking about the kind of text this was.
- I can tell you were thinking about how the character felt here.
- The way you read it matched the story!

4.14 Get Your Eyes Ahead of the Words

Strategy When you are reading smoothly, your eyes should be ahead of the words you are currently reading. That way, your brain starts to preview what's coming next so you'll know where the natural pauses are. Try to let your eyes go ahead as you read the words.

Teaching Tip This is a hard one to model, monitor, or even explain. Research shows, however, that fluent readers actually have their eyes ahead of the word they read. At the very least, I've found this helps to quicken students' pace a bit, which often increases the number of words in the phrase. It's often best to try this strategy on a reread when a student knows and is comfortable with all of the words and can put all the attention into fluency. Be watchful that this strategy doesn't unintentionally communicate that "faster is better," which may cause children to drop their meaning in an attempt to race through words.

Prompts

- Look ahead of where you're reading.
- That sounded smoother. Were you letting your eyes preview what's coming up?
- See if you can read this whole part of the sentence in one breath, and let your eyes move ahead on the line.
- Go back and smooth that out.
- You're looking at each word as you read it. Try reading this group as a phrase and looking ahead at what's to come

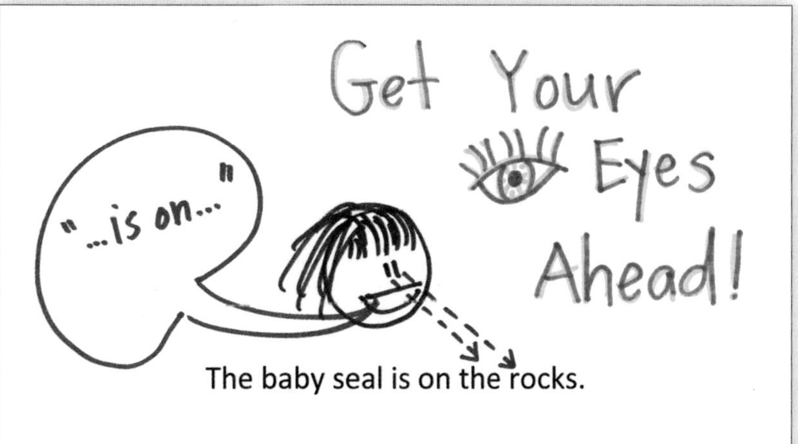

Who is this for?

LEVELS
E–Z+

GENRE / TEXT TYPE
any

SKILLS
phrasing, intonation

4.15 Warm-Up Phrases

Who is this for?

LEVELS

F–Z+

GENRE / TEXT TYPE

any

SKILL

phrasing

Strategy Warm up with phrases that show up often in books. When you see these phrases in your book, read them without pausing.

Teaching Tip When you're working to help kids develop automaticity beyond the word level and into the phrase level, and/or when you're trying to help them see how to group words within a sentence into syntactically appropriate groups, it may help to have them warm up or practice phrases in isolation. Searching for Fry's or Dolch's phrases using Google will help you find long lists (or go to www.timrasinski.com/presentations/fry_600_instant_phrases.pdf for a complete list of Fry's phrases), and you can use ones that are most similar to the phrases students will find in their own books. Choose short and simple phrases for lower levels (i.e., those in the first 100 most common list), and more sophisticated phrases at higher levels (i.e., those in the 300s or 400s groups).

Prompts

- Read this group of words together.
- Warm up with these phrases. Now let's try it in your book.
- You know that phrase. Read it in one breath.
- (*Nonverbal: slide a finger under the phrase to indicate it should be read in one breath.*)
- That word is ____ (e.g., *in, at, with*) so you know the next few words will go together. Read it as a phrase.

at the
for a drive
at the game
in the hall
on the wall
write it down
what did they say?
a long time
have you seen it?
now is the time
this is my cat
two of us
the first word
as big as the first
but not for me
it's about time

Hat Tip: *The Fluent Reader: Oral and Silent Reading Strategies for Building Fluency, Word Recognition, and Comprehension*, second edition (Rasinski 2010)

4.16 Read Like a Storyteller

Strategy When you're reading a story, try to sound like a storyteller. When there is a character talking, make sure you're thinking about what's being said, how the character says it (tone), and what the character's feeling. When the character stops talking, change your voice to sound like a narrator.

Teaching Tip This strategy is an accumulation of a few others. This is a good one to teach once students have already practiced thinking about character feelings and matching their voice (see strategy 4.13, "Make Your Voice Match the Meaning") and when they know the difference between narrator and character talking (see strategy 4.10, "Inside Quotes and Outside Quotes").

Prompts

- Match the character's tone.
- Is that the narrator speaking or the character?
- Read it like a storyteller.
- Yes! I heard the difference between the character and the storyteller.
- Use your narrator voice there.
- Check the punctuation. How do you think the character said that?

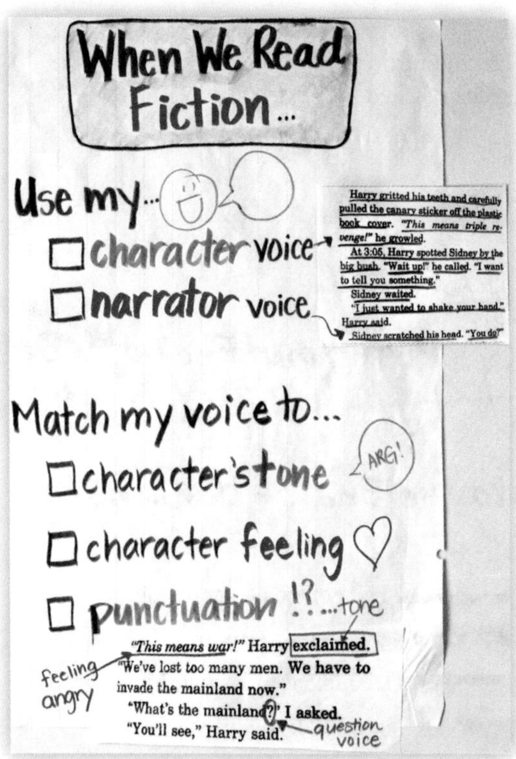

Text excerpts from *Horrible Harry in Room 2B* (Kline 1997).

Who is this for?

LEVELS
F–Z+

GENRE / TEXT TYPE
narrative

SKILLS
intonation, expression

4.17 Push Your Eyes

Who is this for?

LEVELS

J/K (or any book where the sentences are broken up across lines)

GENRE / TEXT TYPE

fiction (mostly early chapter books)

SKILL

phrasing

Strategy Read all the words on one line in one breath. Push your eyes ahead to the end of the line, move them to the next line, then do the same on the next line.

Teaching Tip Not all J/K books will work for this strategy, but those within the Poppleton (Rylant), Henry and Mudge (Rylant), and Frog and Toad (Lobel) series and other similar early chapter books will. Look for books where a longer sentence is broken up across two lines, and where the line break is a natural pause for the reader.

Lesson Language *In the books you used to read, the sentence often went all the way across the bottom of a page. Now that you're reading books with longer sentences, you'll find that the sentence is broken up for you. This is partly because the whole sentence won't fit on one line, but it's also because the authors who wrote the books you're reading now wanted to help you with your phrasing, or knowing when to pause in the middle of a sentence. So when you're reading these books, you should try to read all the words on one line in one breath. Try to push your eyes ahead to the end of the line, move your eyes* to the next line, then do the same.

Prompts

- Read all of this in one breath.
- Push your eyes to the end.
- Try it again, read to the end of the line in one breath.
- Keep going on the next line. You haven't reached the end of the sentence yet.
- Show me where you're going to pause.
- I heard two pauses on that line. Try it once more, but don't stop until the end of the line.
- You read that line in one breath, now go to the next line.
- Say this all together.
- Read it like this. (*Read a line, have the child repeat.*)

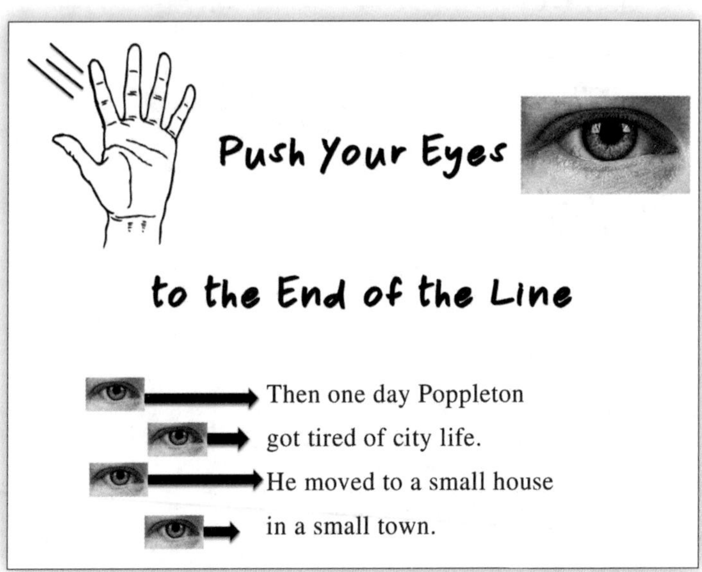

Text excerpt from *Poppleton Everyday* (Rylant 1998).

4.18 Partners Can Be Fluency Teachers

Strategy Partners can help by listening and being a teacher. You can read aloud and your partner can listen to your reading. If there's a spot that sounds choppy or flat, your partner can help you by saying, "Go back and read that again" or "Make your voice match the feeling," just like a teacher would do.

Teaching Tip "Ghost Partner" works well here, too (see "Partners Help to Smooth It Out" on page 116). The prompts included on this page with this strategy would be great to whisper into students' ears to have them practice saying it to their partner. After a few times, they'll get the hang of the language they'd use to "act like a teacher" and they won't need you to whisper in. Added bonus—students doing the coaching or teaching will start to hear the kinds of things they say to their partner while coaching and may even apply it while they are reading their own books.

Prompts

- Go back and read that again.
- Smooth that out.
- Make your voice match the feeling.
- That was smooth reading!
- That sounded just like how you talk.
- I think that was a little choppy. Try it again.

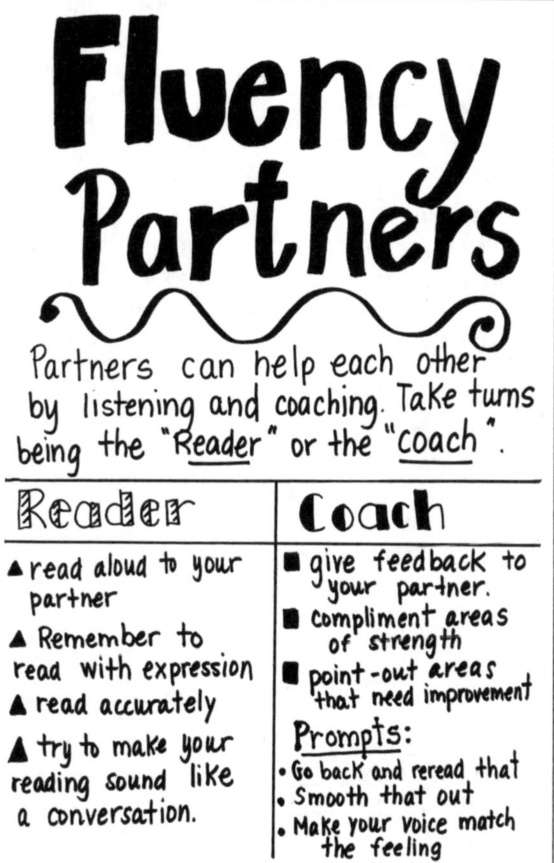

Fluency Partners
Partners can help each other by listening and coaching. Take turns being the "Reader" or the "coach".
Reader
▲ read aloud to your partner
▲ Remember to read with expression
▲ read accurately
▲ try to make your reading sound like a conversation.
Coach
■ give feedback to your partner.
■ compliment areas of strength
■ point-out areas that need improvement
Prompts:
• Go back and reread that
• Smooth that out
• Make your voice match the feeling

Who is this for?

LEVELS

J–Z+

GENRE / TEXT TYPE

any

SKILLS

phrasing, intonation, partnership

4.19 Snap to the Next Line

Who is this for?

LEVELS

J–Z+

GENRE / TEXT TYPE

any

SKILL

phrasing

Strategy Sentences only sometimes end at the end of the line. If you don't see ending punctuation (., !, ?, . . .) at the end of the line, you need to snap to the next line, making your eyes go ahead. Try reading without any pause or break between the end of the line and the next one. Only pause when you see punctuation.

Lesson Language *Now you're reading chapter books where the author fits lots of words onto every page. You won't see a lot of white space, and you also won't often see that the author stops a sentence with a period, exclamation point, or question mark at the end of each line.* (At this point in the lesson, you may show children a book at level G or H, where the end of a line often means the end of a sentence, and a contrasting example at level L, where the end of the line is almost never the end of a sentence.) *Let's look at the end of the lines of the page in this book. Almost no ending punctuation! That means that the sentence starts on a line, and then wraps around to the next line and finishes somewhere in the middle of the next one. That means that you as a reader need to snap around to the next line when you don't see ending punctuation, to try to read that whole sentence together, even when it's broken up across a line. For example, it should sound like this . . .* (Model reading seamlessly one sentence that's broken up across a line.)

Prompts

- Keep going through the line break.
- Did you see ending punctuation there?
- I could tell you snapped your eyes to the next line.
- That entire sentence was in one breath.
- You paused only when you saw punctuation!

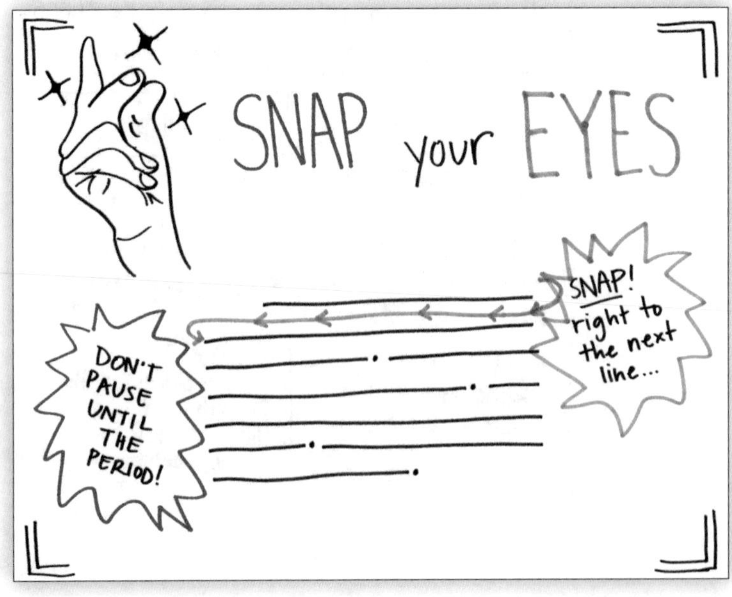

4.20 Make the Pause Match the Meaning

Strategy The place you pause within a sentence can change the meaning of that sentence. If the way you read it doesn't sound right or make sense, go back and try to pause in a different spot until it matches how you think it should sound.

Lesson Language *An author named Lynne Truss wrote a book called* Eat Shoots and Leaves. *It's a book of jokes based on the fact that if you read a sentence with pauses in different places, it changes the meaning of the sentence. For example, let's think about the title. Eats Shoots and Leaves could mean a panda that eats the leaves and shoots of a bamboo plant. Or, it could mean someone or something eats, then shoots (with a gun), and then leaves the place. All based on where the commas are and where you pause. Another example is "Go, get him doctors" versus "Go get him, doctors." With the first example, the illustrator has drawn a picture of a boy who fell off the monkey bars, and the teacher is shouting for others to help him, to get the boy the doctors he needs. In the second example, the illustrator has drawn a boy running away from a hospital, and someone commanding the doctors to chase after him. I want us to think about where we pause in a sentence because it's important that you aren't just reading words in any group you feel like, but rather that you are thinking about what's happening in the story and what the author is trying to teach and that you match your pauses with the meaning. If you read something and it doesn't sound right based on where you paused, go back and try to pause in a different spot. Keep trying that until it matches how you think it should sound.*

Prompts

- You paused here. (*Point.*) Did that sound right?
- Think about where you paused. Did it match what you think that sentence should mean?
- Try the pause in another place. Which one sounded right?
- Where else might you pause?
- Look at the punctuation in the middle of the sentence to help you know where to pause.
- Where's the comma? Read it with a pause in that spot.
- Good job—that matched the meaning of the text so far.

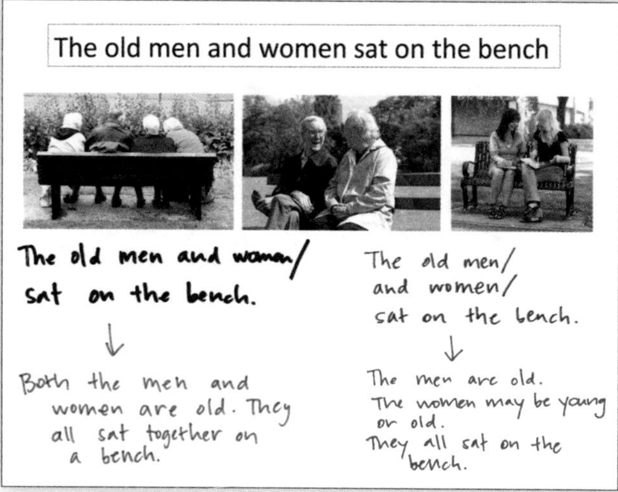

The old men and women sat on the bench
The old men and women/
sat on the bench.
Both the men and women are old. They all sat together on a bench.
The old men/
and women/
sat on the bench.
The men are old.
The women may be young or old.
They all sat on the bench.

Who is this for?

LEVELS
M–Z+

GENRE / TEXT TYPE
any

SKILL
phrasing

4.21 Read It How the Author Tells You (Tags)

Who is this for?

LEVELS

M–Z+

GENRE / TEXT TYPE

fiction

SKILLS

intonation, expression

Strategy When you see dialogue, pay attention to not only what the character says but also how the character says it. Sometimes, the author will just write said. But if the author tells you how the character says it (whispered, shouted, pleaded), you should try to make your voice match it.

Lesson Language *The other day I was reading out loud to my daughter. It was a new book we'd never read before, so I didn't know it. I was reading along and I got to some dialogue. I was thinking, based on what had happened so far, that the character was shouting for help, so I read it like this.* (Read in a shouting voice.) *"But won't you please help?" But then I noticed, right after the dialogue marks ended, the author told me how she meant for me to read it. The dialogue tag said, "whispered Jonas." I apologized to my daughter—"I'm so sorry! I read that wrong!" And I went back and reread like this.* (Reread in a whisper.) *"But won't you please help?" That little change in my tone made me think very differently about the character, what he was feeling, and what was happening right there in the story. It went from being a shout for help—meaning impatience, maybe even annoyance. But a whisper for help is different. It's more pleading, more desperate. Those dialogue tags sure are important in helping us figure out how the character is talking so we can better understand the story.*

Prompts

- Check the tag. Now read it how the author intended.
- Yes—you paid attention to the tag. So what are you thinking about the character now?
- The tag says _____, but you read it like _____. Give that one more try.
- Show me how you'll read it.
- Paying attention to the tag really helps!

It's important that in our attempts to teach children to read fluently, we don't send the message that reading is just about performing.

—*Jennifer Serravallo*

Supporting Comprehension in Fiction

Understanding Plot and Setting

Why is this goal important?

To help students achieve that lost-in-a-book, engaged sort of reading that makes reading enjoyable, they have to understand what's going on. Or, to say it in a way others have, they need to be able to "make a movie in their minds" (e.g., Wilhelm et al. 2001; Harvey and Goudvis 2007; Calkins and Tolan 2010a). To make this mental movie, students need to know what's happening, who's involved in the action, and where the action is taking place. Consequently, checking comprehension by asking a student to retell or summarize the text is a common part of most reading assessments.

Supporting student understanding of plot and setting can have a few parts:

- Understanding problems/conflicts and solutions/resolutions as a way to determine what's most important. As Janet Burroway (2006, 31) puts it, "The features of a story are fewer than those of a face: They are conflict, crisis, and resolution."

- Retelling/summarizing. These terms are often confused, perhaps because some use the terms interchangeably. For instance, Beers (2002, 152) defines retelling as an "oral summary of a text based on a set of story elements." I often think of retelling as sequential, with more detail than a summary, which gives the essential information without too much detail. Regardless of what you call it, students should be able to say back, in sequence, the most important information after reading a section of text.
- Visualizing setting, understanding how setting impacts the events in the story, and tracking when the setting changes.
- Synthesizing cause and effect, so that the reader is clear on what causes certain events to take place, and how all the events in the story connect.

How do I know if this goal is right for my student?

We've probably all heard student retellings of texts that include every single detail, or ones that say too little, or others that mention events without a clear sense of how they are related. For me, understanding plot is the most basic of the comprehension goals for students reading fiction, and I'm sure to include it in any assessments I use to match readers to books, whether running records or a longer whole-book comprehension assessment (Clay 2000; Serravallo 2012, 2013b).

While doing running records, after a student reads a selection of text aloud and you record miscues and self-corrections, ask the student, "What were the most important things that happened? Retell the story for me from the beginning." Transcribe the student's retelling as he or she speaks. When you look back at it, notice if the retelling is in sequence and if it includes the most important information.

Once students are reading chapter books, try planting sticky notes inside a text as they read, and ask them to respond in writing. You may say, "Retell the most important events that happened in this chapter." "Why did that (event) happen?" "Describe the setting. Use as much detail as you can." Or, after several dozen pages, ask, "What is the main problem the character is facing?" (Serravallo 2012).

You can also use conferring opportunities to listen to oral retellings, or to ask questions of the reader. When children talk about their reading, you can listen to their speech for evidence of understanding of key plot events and setting details.

Regardless of whether you look at student writing or listen to them talk, you'll want to evaluate their responses. You can find retelling rubrics, by level, for running records at www.readingandwritingproject.com. The Independent Reading Assessment: Fiction series (Serravallo 2012) also includes rubrics for retelling, problem/solution, cause/effect, and visualizing setting based on level from the Fountas and Pinnell Text Level Gradient™ J–W. Ellin Keene's (2006) *Assessing Comprehension Thinking Strategies* has generic rubrics that can be used on any text. Those using Fountas and Pinnell's Benchmark Assessment System will also find indicators for retelling by level.

To help students achieve that lost-in-a-book, engaged sort of reading that makes reading enjoyable, they have to understand what's going on. Understanding plot is the most basic of the comprehension goals for students reading fiction.

—*Jennifer Serravallo*

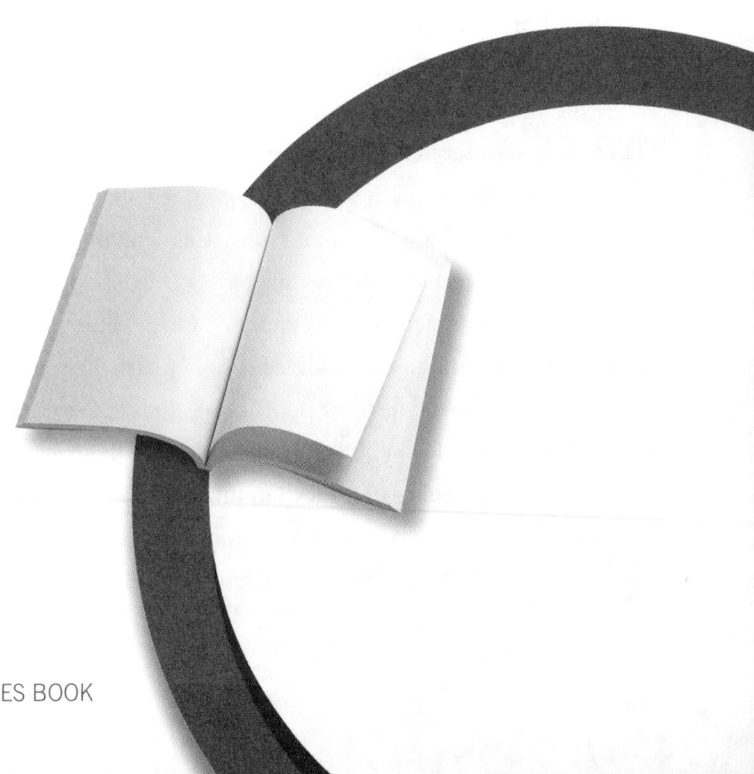

Strategies for Understanding Plot and Setting at a Glance

Strategy	Levels	Genres/ Text Types	Skills
5.1 Lean on the Pictures	A–K	Fiction	Determining importance, retelling
5.2 Title Power	C–M	Fiction	Determining importance
5.3 Summarizing What's Most Essential	E–K	Fiction	Summarizing
5.4 Uh-oh . . . Phew	F–L	Fiction	Determining importance, retelling
5.5 Is This a Multi-Story Book or a Single-Story Book?	J and K, mostly	Fiction	Summarizing, monitoring for meaning
5.6 Reactions Help You Find the Problem	J–R	Fiction	Determining importance
5.7 Series Books Have Predictable Plots	J–Q	Fiction	Retelling, predicting, determining importance
5.8 What's Your Problem?	J–Z+	Fiction	Determining importance
5.9 Who's Speaking?	J–Z+	Fiction	Visualizing, monitoring for meaning
5.10 Let the Blurb Help You	J–Z+	Fiction	Determining importance
5.11 Retell What's Most Important by Making Connections to the Problem	K–Z+	Fiction	Summarizing, retelling, determining importance
5.12 Angled Summaries for Highlighting Deeper Ideas in Plot	L–Z+	Fiction	Summarizing, determining importance, inferring
5.13 Summarize Based on What a Character Wants	L–Z+	Fiction	Summarizing, determining importance
5.14 Chapter-End Stop Signs	L–Z+	Fiction	Determining importance
5.15 Where Am I?	L–Z+	Fiction	Visualizing
5.16 Summarizing with "Somebody . . . Wanted . . . But . . . So . . . "	N–Z+	Fiction	Summarizing
5.17 Two-Sided Problems	N–Z+	Fiction	Determining importance
5.18 Does the Story Have to Be Set There, and Then?	P–Z+	Fiction (especially historical fiction)	Visualizing, determining importance
5.19 Tenses as a Clue to Flashback and Backstory	P–Z+	Fiction	Monitoring for meaning
5.20 Not Just Page Decorations	P–Z+	Fiction	Monitoring for meaning, visualizing
5.21 Plotting Flashback on a Timeline	P–Z+	Fiction	Monitoring for meaning, visualizing
5.22 Vivid Setting Description and Impact on Character	P–Z+	Fiction	Determining importance, visualizing
5.23 Map It	P–Z+	Fiction	Monitoring for meaning, visualizing
5.24 FQR (Facts/Questions/Response) Sheets for Filling in Gaps	Q–Z+	Fiction (historical fiction and fantasy, especially)	Questioning, synthesizing, inferring, monitoring for meaning
5.25 Double Plot Mountain	R–Z+	Fiction	Monitoring for meaning, visualizing
5.26 Historical Notes Prime Prior Knowledge	R–Z+	Fiction	Monitoring for meaning, visualizing
5.27 Analyzing Historical Contexts	R–Z+	Historical fiction	Determining importance, visualizing, inferring
5.28 Micro-/Meso-/Macroenvironment Systems: Levels of Setting	V–Z+	Fiction	Visualizing, determining importance, inferring

5.1 Lean on the Pictures

Who is this for?

LEVELS

A–K

GENRE / TEXT TYPE

fiction

SKILLS

determining importance, retelling

Strategy Touch the page, look at the picture, and say what happened. Turn, look, and touch the next page, say what happened. Keep going through the entire book.

Lesson Language *When you get to the end of a book and want to retell your story to a partner, it might be hard to remember just what happened in each part of your book, and in what order. To help you remember, you can use the pictures. Walking through the pictures as you retell helps you to make sure you're saying the most important parts in the order they happened. Go back to the beginning of the book, touch the page, and briefly say what happened. Then, turn the page and say what happened next, then, and after that.*

Prompts

- What happened first?
- Touch the page.
- Look at the picture to remind you.
- I noticed you said what happened on that page in a brief way.
- Turn to say what happened next. Make sure it connects to what you just said.
- Use "next . . . ," "then . . . ," "and then . . . "
- You can skip a page if nothing major happened.
- What's the next important thing that happened? Turn until you find that page.

5.2 Title Power

Strategy Read the title. Keep the title in mind as you read. Think about what events connect back to the title.

Lesson Language *The title is a carefully chosen part of any book. After all, the author has just a few words (or sometimes just one!) to sum up what's most important in the book. In some chapter books, like those in the Nate the Great series, the title will give away the main problem very clearly. For example,* Nate the Great and the Missing Key *(Sharmat 1982) is about a problem (mystery) of a missing key, and the most important events are when he finds clues that lead him to solve that mystery. The title is one thing to keep in mind as you read, as it may help you figure out the problem or what's most important.*

Prompts

- Check the title. What does the title connect to in the story?
- Think of the title. What's the problem?
- How does the character's problem connect to the title?
- Where in the book did you find the problem? Let's check to see if it matches the title.
- Retell thinking about the title.
- Keep the title in mind. What's the most important part of this chapter?

Book Title	Problem
Nate The Great and the STOLEN BASE	Nate has to figure out who stole the base
WORM BUILDS	worm tries hard to build a tower
HENRY AND MUDGE AND THE BEDTIME THUMPS	Henry is scared of the noises at night

Who is this for?

LEVELS

C–M

GENRE / TEXT TYPE

fiction

SKILL

determining importance

5.3 Summarizing What's Most Essential

Who is this for?

LEVELS

E–K

GENRE / TEXT TYPE

fiction

SKILL

summarizing

Strategy When summarizing, remember to tell what's important. Tell it in the order it happened. Tell it in a way that makes sense. Try not to tell too much.

Lesson Language *A summary is a short recounting of what you just read. When you get ready to summarize, you have to think about what parts of the story you'll tell. Your summary should include enough information to make sense to someone who hasn't read the story before. That means you need to make it clear in your summary how one event led to another. You'll first think about the most important things that happened in the story—probably connecting to the problem in the story, if there is one, or what the character wants the most. Then, you'll tell the most important events in the middle of the story that connect back to the want or the problem. It's important to tell those middle events in order. Then, think about how the whole story ends up, and tell the ending. For each part you tell, try to say it in one short, simple sentence.*

Prompts

- Say the beginning in a shorter way.
- Just tell me the one most important thing that happened in the beginning.
- How does that event connect to the one you just told me?
- Can you say that in a shorter way?
- You told me five things that happened in the middle. Which two or three were most important?
- Turn to the end. What's the most important thing that happened at the end?

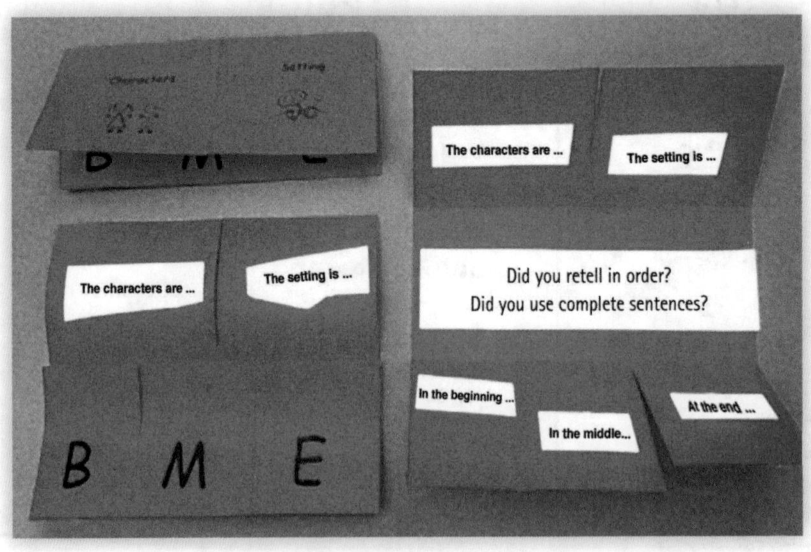

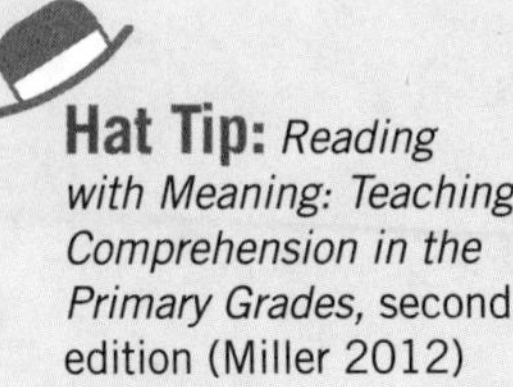

Hat Tip: *Reading with Meaning: Teaching Comprehension in the Primary Grades*, second edition (Miller 2012)

5.4 Uh-oh . . . Phew

Strategy When you retell, think about the problem (uh-oh), how the problem gets worse (UH-OH!) and how the problem gets solved (phew!). Use a story mountain with these parts to retell, touching the parts of the mountain as you go.

Lesson Language *A story goes like this.* (Draw a story mountain.) *Uh-oh (problem), UH-OH (problem worsens), UH-OH! (problem worsens), and the problem gets solved (phew!). If I were going to retell* Cam Jansen and the Mystery of the Stolen Diamonds *(Adler 2004), I would start off with the uh-oh—the problem. In this story, the problem is that someone steals diamonds from the jewelry store at the mall. The problem gets worse and worse—UH-OH and UH-OH!—when Cam and Eric go looking for the thief. They are in a dangerous situation outside the house where the thieves are, and even worse when the baby starts crying and they get pulled inside the house. But then the police show up (phew!), and the criminals are caught and taken away by the police.*

Prompts

- Let's retell. Start with the uh-oh. What's the problem?
- Think about how the problem gets worse.
- Where are you on the story mountain now? Point to it.
- You're giving me a lot of detail. If you had to just tell me the problem using a few words, what would you say?
- Of all the details you told me, what's most important?

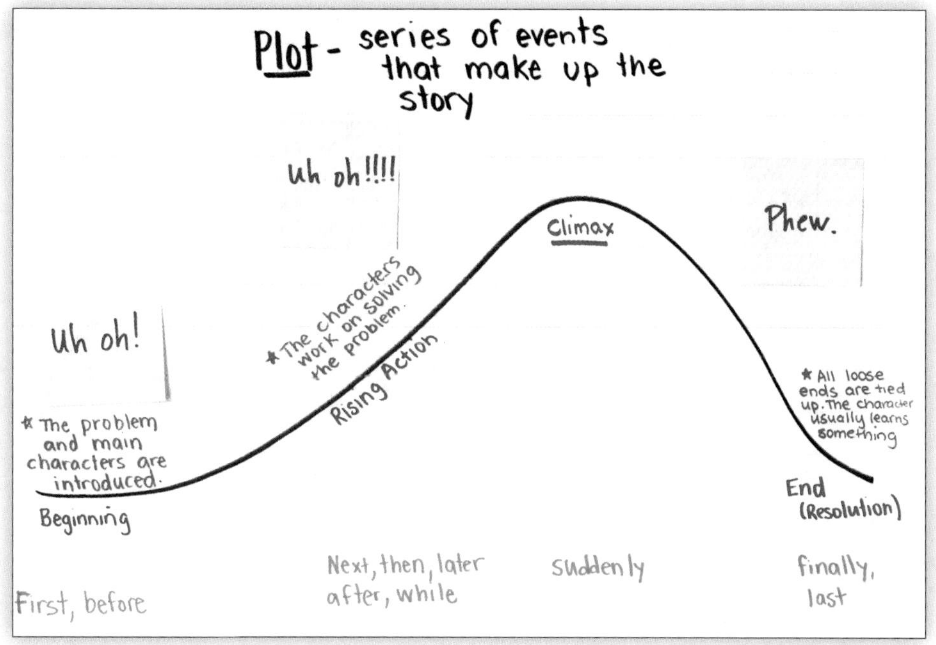

Who is this for?

LEVELS
F–L

GENRE / TEXT TYPE
fiction

SKILLS
determining importance, retelling

5.5 Is This a Multi-Story Book or a Single-Story Book?

Who is this for?

LEVELS

J and K, mostly

GENRE / TEXT TYPE

fiction

SKILLS

summarizing, monitoring for meaning

Strategy After you read the first chapter, think, "Was the problem solved?" If so, then the next chapter will be a new story with the same characters, but a new problem and solution. If the answer is "no," then the story will probably continue into the next chapter, and the problem won't be solved until the end.

Lesson Language *You are reading chapter books! Look at these—Mr. Putter and Tabby (Rylant), Young Cam Jansen (Adler), Frog and Toad (Lobel), Henry and Mudge (Rylant), Minnie and Moo (Cazet)—so many great series to read! As you read these books, I want to talk to you about something that can sometimes be tricky. One thing you need to know as a reader is how your book is set up. Sometimes these chapter books will be a collection of stories. Other times they will be one long story broken up into a few parts.*

Prompts

- What's the problem in this story?
- You got to the end of this chapter. Was the problem solved?
- You're at the start of a new chapter. Is it a new story or the same one?
- Tell me how you know.
- Yes! New problem means new story.

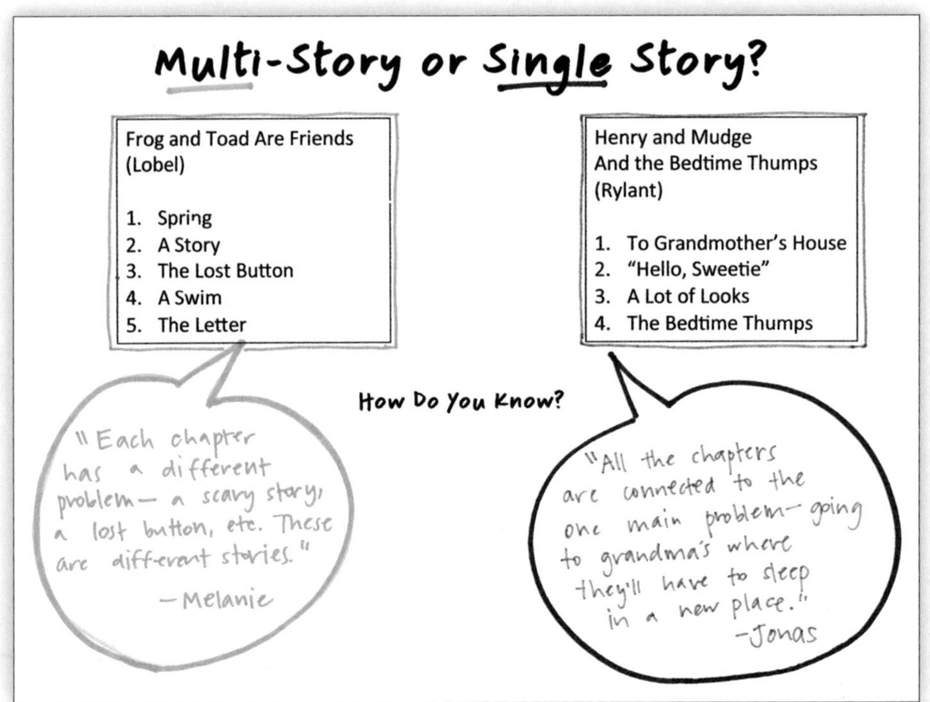

5.6 Reactions Help You Find the Problem

Strategy To find the problem, look at the reactions and feelings of the character. The character might look upset (or sad or worried) in the picture. The author might tell you how he or she is feeling in the words. Or, there may be things the character says, such as "Oh no!" that let you know he or she is having a strong reaction.

Prompts

- How's the character reacting?
- Say what the character might be feeling.
- Check the character's face in the picture.
- Does the character say anything to show his or her feeling?
- Yes, that's something the character says. What does that reaction tell you about what he or she is feeling?

Pay Attention to Character Reactions

DOG AT THE DOOR

James spun around. "Oh, no!" he whispered.
Kimble was scratching at the newspaper in her box, tearing it up, and pawing it into a small mound. As James and Mandy watched, she started panting heavily.

James says "Oh, no!" to tell the reader there's a problem with the dog!

"You're a sissy, Pinky!" the boy shouted. "Get up and fight."
Pinky lay on the sidewalk where the third-grader had knocked him off his bike. His cheeks were fever-hot.

Pinky's cheeks turn red b/c he's embarrassed. This bully is going to cause problems for him!

"Do *away* with it?" shrieked Fern. "You mean kill it? Just because it's smaller than the others?"

Fern shrieks at the news her father plans to kill the pig. She's upset. This is the main problem in the chapter.

Text excerpts (from top to bottom): *Dog at the Door* (Baglio 2002); *Pinky and Rex and the Bully* (Howe 1996); *Charlotte's Web* (White 1952).

Who is this for?

LEVELS
J–R

GENRE / TEXT TYPE
fiction

SKILL
determining importance

5.7 Series Books Have Predictable Plots

Who is this for?

LEVELS

J–Q

GENRE / TEXT TYPE

fiction

SKILLS

retelling, predicting, determining importance

Strategy When you start reading a new book in a series, think, "What do I know about how this story might go from reading other books in this series?" Think about the types of problems and/or how a character solves the problem. Predict how this new book in the series will go.

Teaching Tip Organizing your class into book clubs gives students support for understanding patterns in series books. The chart on this page is the result of one book club's discussion of the patterns they found when studying a series.

Lesson Language *One of the great things about reading in a series is that there is a lot the same from book to book, so a new book can feel as familiar as an old friend. Many of the characters are the same. Many of the plots even follow a similar pattern. When you read a new book in a series, you should use what you already know about series books to help you. For example, if you're reading a Magic Tree House book (Osborne), you should expect that in every book Jack and Annie will start in the tree house reading a book, then they will travel back in time to a new place, and then they will find their way back to the tree house by the end. If you're reading a Cam Jansen book (Adler), you should expect that you'll read a bit about her photographic memory, find out what the mystery is, and then read as she collects clues to eventually solve the mystery. Knowing how the plot will go will help you understand where in the story you are. This will help you to figure out what's most important, to retell what you've read so far, and to predict what might come next.*

Prompts

- What do you know about other books in this series?
- Is there a pattern to how the stories go in other books you've read?
- What might happen based on what you know about how problems were solved in other books in this series?
- What might happen based on what you know about how other stories in this series ended?
- What has happened next in other books in this series? So what do you think will happen next here?
- What's similar about all the books in this series? OK, now just retell the most important parts.

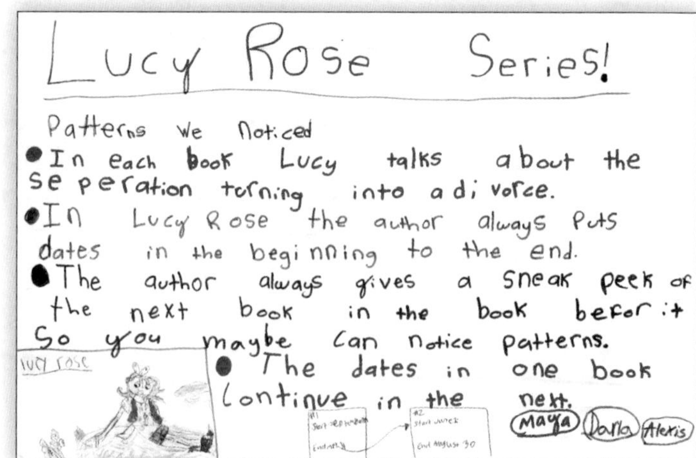

5.8 What's Your Problem?

Strategy One way to find the problem(s) in a story is to think through story elements. Think about a problem a character might have with another character. Think about if the setting is causing the problem. Think about if the problem is based on something the character wants but can't have. Think about if the problem is connected to the overall theme of the story or a social issue within the story.

Teaching Tip This lesson could be modified for those reading at lower levels (J–M) where problems are usually one-dimensional and simple, and for those students reading at higher levels, where problems are often complex and multidimensional. The example in the chart is from Pam Munoz Ryan's (2000) wonderful novel *Esperanza Rising*, which is leveled at V, or end of fifth/beginning of sixth grade.

Prompts

- Where or when does the story take place? Does that seem to be adding to the problem?
- What might a theme in the story be? Is the character's problem connected to that?
- Name a character. Does that person contribute to the problem?
- What problem does the character seem to be dealing with?
- Is there more than one problem? Think about setting, character, theme.
- You told me one problem. Let's think about if there is another.
- That's a problem connected to the setting. Are there any problems with characters?
- Wow, one character with so many problems! You thought about setting, theme, and other characters to learn more about her.

What's Your Problem?

Book:	Problem:	What does it connect to?
Esperanza Rising	Esperanza & mom lose all their riches and need to relocate to CA, deal with a new life.	Character - father dying, uncle taking advantage of the situation Setting - in CA at the time, Mexicans didn't have many opportunities Theme - what you most need is what you have, importance of family. She needs to learn that life can still be good without riches.

Who is this for?

LEVELS

J–Z+

GENRE / TEXT TYPE

fiction

SKILL

determining importance

5.9 Who's Speaking?

Who is this for?

LEVELS

J–Z+

GENRE / TEXT TYPE

fiction

SKILLS

visualizing, monitoring for meaning

Strategy Try to have a mental picture of the people in the scene to keep track of who is speaking. After one person speaks, the other will respond. Notice the new line and the new quotation marks to know the speaker has changed.

Lesson Language *Some of you just started reading chapter books where there are many characters in the same scene, or on the same page. Sometimes, we're going to find a conversation between characters, and when that happens it looks like this* (show page with back and forth dialogue, some untagged). *In the books you're reading now, the author won't always tell you who said it! We aren't used to that. For example, it won't always say, "Said Poppleton" after something he said—as the reader, you need to figure it out yourself. You need to find the last place where the author did tell you who spoke to picture who is in the scene. Then, whenever someone talks you can picture them talking. When you see a new line with new quotation marks, that means a new person speaks. You can picture that new person speaking. Even if the author doesn't say who said it, you can figure it out by keeping track.*

Prompts

- Who said this?
- How do you know who is speaking here?
- Describe what you picture. Can you see the two people talking? Who is talking here?
- Let's backtrack to where we last saw a dialogue tag. Take it from there—who do you think is speaking now?
- It will alternate between the two speakers. So who is this?

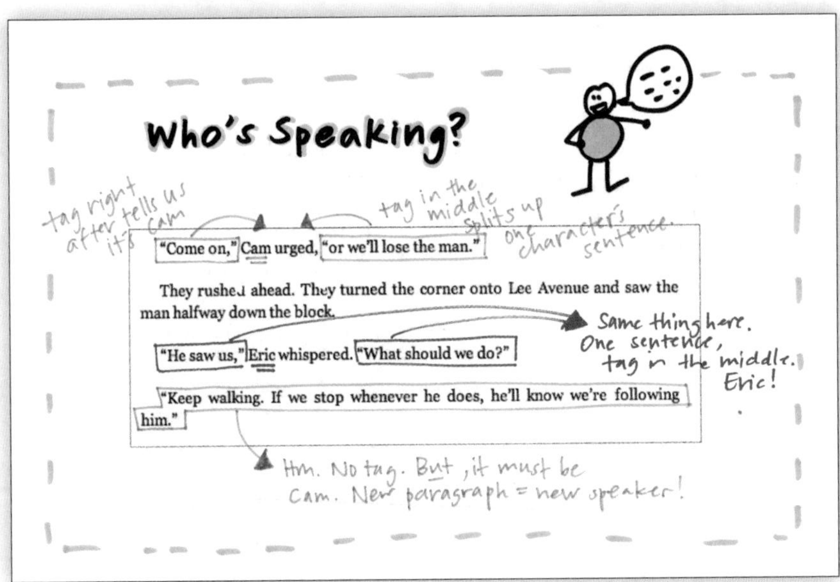

Text excerpt from *Cam Jansen: The Mystery of the Stolen Diamonds* (Adler 2004).

5.10 Let the Blurb Help You

Strategy Read the back cover to orient yourself to the book. Ask yourself, "What's the structure of this text? What will be the most important issues this story deals with? What problems will the main character face?"

Teaching Tip You can modify this lesson to support students with their nonfiction reading by pointing out that the back cover of a nonfiction book may clue the reader in to the sorts of information that will be covered in the book, as well as any perspective the author may have.

Lesson Language

Text Structure	*Figure out what kind of book you're reading. If it says "five wonderful stories . . . ," then you know you're going to read a bunch of different stories in one book. If it's a summary of one story, then you know the whole book will be one story.*
Main Problem	*Look for key phrases like "Find out what happens when (character) has to deal with . . . " or "(Character) has a lot to be unhappy about . . . " that will highlight the problem(s).*
Theme	*Sometimes the book's blurb (or the review quotes) will come right out and tell you what some of the important ideas in the book might be: "A heartwarming story about (theme) and (theme)."*

Prompts

- Read the blurb.
- What information in the blurb will help?
- What will the structure of the book be, based on what you read?
- Do you have any ideas about the main problem the character will face?
- Let's talk about what a theme in this book might be, based on the blurb.
- You got a lot of information from this back cover blurb!

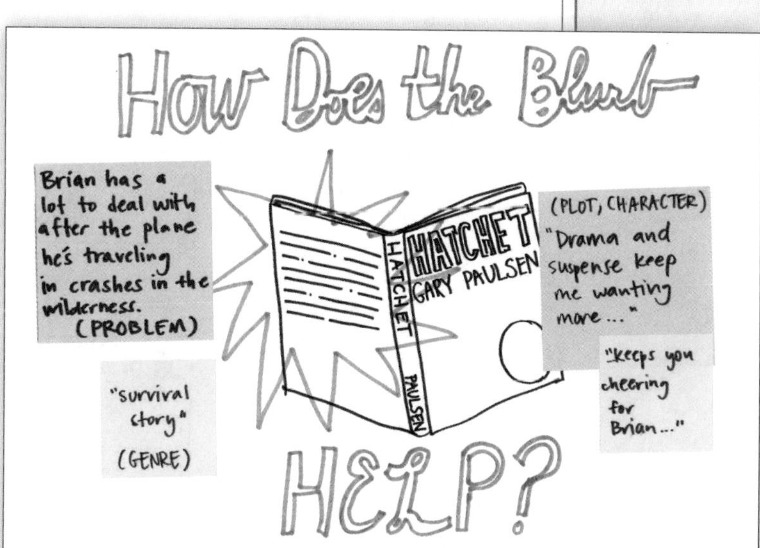

Who is this for?

LEVELS

J–Z+

GENRE / TEXT TYPE

fiction

SKILL

determining importance

5.11 Retell What's Most Important by Making Connections to the Problem

Who is this for?

LEVELS

K–Z+

GENRE / TEXT TYPE

fiction

SKILLS

summarizing, retelling, determining importance

Strategy Find the page or pages with the problem. Explain the character's main problem. Find the page or pages where the character tries to solve the problem. Retell those pages. Find the (re)solution of the problem at the end. Explain how the (re)solution connects back to the problem.

Teaching Tip Up to about level M/N, characters tend to have one main problem and the problem gets solved (i.e., in *Days with Frog and Toad* [Lobel 1979], an example of a level K text, Toad has a kite that won't fly, and after he tries to get it to fly, it flies at the end of the story—problem solved!). At and after levels M/N the characters often have multiple problems, both internal and external, and it's more likely that the problem is *re*solved instead of solved (i.e., in *Amber Brown Is Not a Crayon* [Danziger 1995], Amber is dealing with her best friend moving away, and in the end he does move, but she comes to accept it—this is a resolution). Equipped with this knowledge of text complexity, revise the language in this teaching point to be appropriate for the reader you're working with, and choose the prompts from the list below that also align to the text's complexity.

Prompts

- What's the main problem?
- Find the main problem. Is there another problem?
- Yes! That's got to be the problem. There was a whole chapter about it, and the character has a strong emotion.
- What does the character do in this chapter that connects to the problem?
- Explain how the story ends up. How does the end connect to the problem?
- Does that seem like an internal (inside) or external (outside) problem?
- Is the problem solved or resolved?

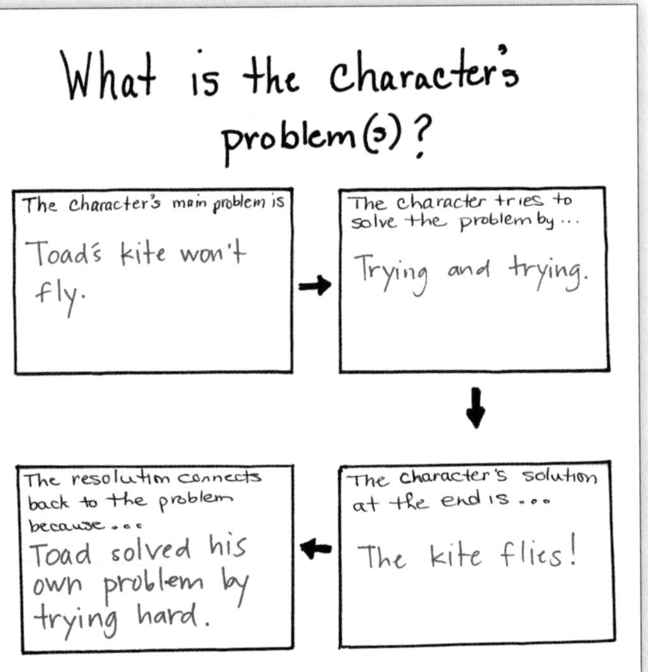

5.12 Angled Summaries for Highlighting Deeper Ideas in Plot

Strategy To summarize only the most important information, it's helpful to stop and say, "What was this story really about?" Whatever your answer to that question is can be your leading statement, a claim. Then, you can tell just the events that best support that deeper idea.

Teaching Tip To write this type of summary, students will need to be able to state a message, lesson, or theme. You can see Chapter 7 for ideas on how to help students with this at various levels of text difficulty.

Prompts

- Start with what the story is *really about.*
- What's the big idea you have from the whole story?
- Say it like a thesis.
- What parts of the story best support that idea? Tell them in order.
- Did anything else happen that you think is important?
- That happened, but does that support your idea?
- Only tell the parts that go with your idea.

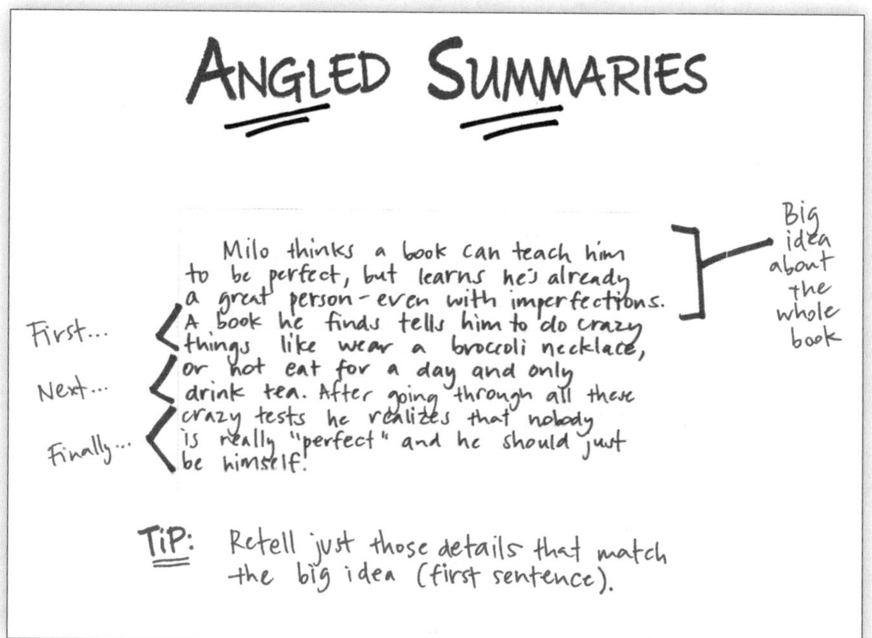

ANGLED SUMMARIES
Milo thinks a book can teach him to be perfect, but learns he's already a great person - even with imperfections.
Big idea about the whole book
First...
A book he finds tells him to do crazy things like wear a broccoli necklace,
Next...
or not eat for a day and only drink tea. After going through all these crazy tests
Finally...
he realizes that nobody is really "perfect" and he should just be himself.
TIP: Retell just those details that match the big idea (first sentence).

Who is this for?

LEVELS

L–Z+

GENRE / TEXT TYPE

fiction

SKILLS

summarizing, determining importance, inferring

Hat Tip: *A Curricular Plan for the Reading Workshop, Grade 4* (Calkins and colleagues 2011c)

5.13 Summarize Based on What a Character Wants

Who is this for?

LEVELS

L–Z+

GENRE / TEXT TYPE

fiction

SKILLS

summarizing, determining importance

Strategy Think about what the character really wants. Then, think about the one, most important event that happened in each chapter that connects back to what the character wants. Summarize by saying the events in the order they happened.

Lesson Language *Sometimes in chapter books, it's hard to summarize just the most important events—there are so many! If you think about what the character wants as the driver of the plot, it can help you to summarize with more focus. For example, in* Pinky and Rex and the Perfect Pumpkin *(Howe 1998), I know after the first chapter that what Rex really wants is to be included with Pinky's grandparents and cousins. In Chapter 2, "The Perfect Day," I could think, "What is the one event that connects to that?" I would say that during the whole car ride, while the grandparents kept saying what a perfect day it was, Rex was totally silent and feeling upset because Pinky was only talking to his cousins and ignoring her. In Chapter 3, "Pumpkin Picking," I might say that every time Rex picked a pumpkin, one of her cousins would say it was too small or skinny or had a bad spot and one time even said it was the "stupidest-looking pumpkin I ever saw" (14). So, in each chapter, I think, of all the events that happen, which is the one that connects back to what the character wants? In this way, I can focus my summary.*

Prompts

- What is the main event of this chapter?
- Can you retell from the beginning?
- What does this character want?
- Tell me one from this chapter.
- Turn back to the beginning—retell.
- Name the main event.
- You are telling me everything; what is most important?
- You are telling me about one chapter—connect all the chapters.
- Yes, that's what the character wants—is it showing up across the book?
- That's the main event that connects with that chapter.
- I like how you read the chapter titles and thought about what was important.

SUMMARIZE...
1 2 3
1.. 2.. 3.. 4.. 5..
① What does the character want?
② Think of one event per chapter that connects back to the want.
③ Summarize by saying events in order.

Hat Tip: Independent Reading Assessment: Fiction series (Serravallo 2012)

5.14 Chapter-End Stop Signs

Strategy Each chapter will have at least one important event. At the end of the chapter, stop and jot about what the most important event is. You can use the chapter title to help. Jot the event on a separate page or on a sticky note. When you pick the book back up to keep reading, you can reread all your jots to remind yourself where you are.

Teaching Tip For this strategy, you can offer students sticky notes, a notebook, or a paper with spots to jot after each chapter, like the student work sample on this page. Some teachers prefer sticky notes because the note stays on the page, next to where the thinking occurred. This helps teachers to quickly re-read the student's writing in the context of the page. Others prefer a paper because it can easily be collected and reviewed by the teacher before tomorrow's lessons. Still others like to use a notebook so students can refer back to their work and it stays neatly in one place. Adapt this lesson to your style!

Prompts

- Check the chapter title.
- What's the most important thing that happened?
- If you had to say the most important thing in one sentence, what would it be?
- Say what's most important in a brief way, short enough to fit on a sticky note.
- Reread your sticky notes to remember the most important event from each chapter.
- Use the sticky notes to help you remember.

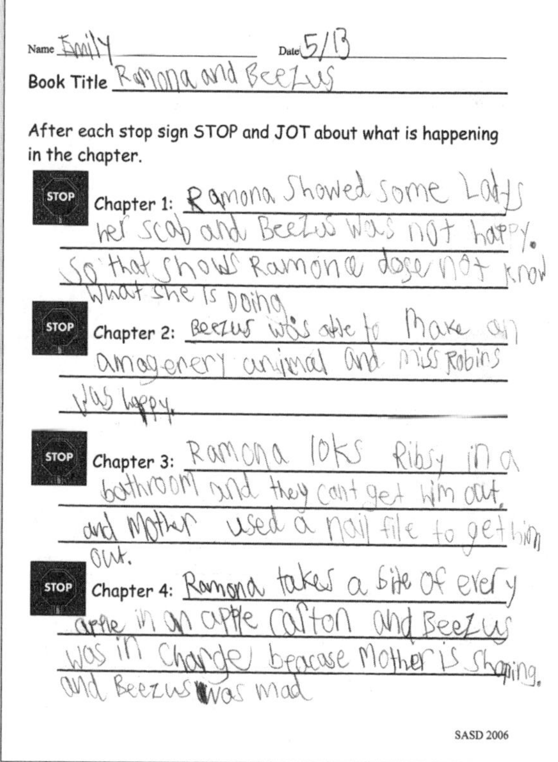

Name Emily Date 5/13

Book Title Ramona and Beezus

After each stop sign STOP and JOT about what is happening in the chapter.

STOP Chapter 1: Ramona Showed some Ladys her scab and Beezus Was not happy. So that shows Ramona dose not know what she is doing

STOP Chapter 2: Beezus Was able to Make an amagenery animal and Miss Robins was happy.

STOP Chapter 3: Ramona loks Ribsy in a bathroom and they cant get him out, and Mother used a nail file to get him out.

STOP Chapter 4: Ramona takes a bite of every apple in an apple carton and Beezus was in charge beacase Mother is shoping. and Beezus was mad

SASD 2006

Who is this for?

LEVELS

L–Z+

GENRE / TEXT TYPE

fiction

SKILL

determining importance

5.15 Where Am I?

Who is this for?

LEVELS

L–Z+

GENRE / TEXT TYPE

fiction

SKILL

visualizing

Strategy Pay close attention to the first words of the chapter, and any picture there may be that tells you the setting. Make sure you're clear on where the chapter is taking place. When you start a new chapter, think about how the character got from the setting in one chapter to the setting in the next.

Lesson Language *In the chapter books you're reading now, you'll notice that the character often moves to a new location between one chapter and the next. To make sure you're clear on where your character is and what's happening, you'll want to slow down your reading at the start of the chapter to check the pictures (if there are any) and the words for clues about where the character is, and how she or he got there. For example, in* The Littles Go Exploring, *the first chapter starts with "Tom and Lucy Little stood on the roof of the Biggs's house" and there is a picture of them standing on the roof (Peterson 1978, 5). You can see where they are, and how the setting shows that they are so much smaller than normal people. When Chapter 2 starts with dialogue, you might wonder, "Where are they?" A quick look at the sketch at the top of the page shows a man next to a fireplace, with a couch on the other side of the room. You might look at that and figure the action is taking place in a living room. Then, in the fourth paragraph, the author tells you, "The Littles were in the living room in their apartment inside the walls." So there, you might say, "Oh! It's not just any living room. They have a whole house inside the walls of a bigger house." Be aware that sometimes the author will explain these changes in setting, and other times you need to infer it—you'll need to figure it out by thinking on your own, based on what makes the most sense from the rest of the story.*

Prompts

- Reread the first page. Are there any details there about where or when this chapter happens?
- How do you think the characters got from there to here?
- Is there a picture on the page to help you?
- Can you find a sentence that tells you about the setting?
- Now you know the setting. What are you picturing it looks like there or then?
- Explain the setting change. What would make sense?
- I noticed you read the clues at the start of the chapter carefully to figure out the new setting!

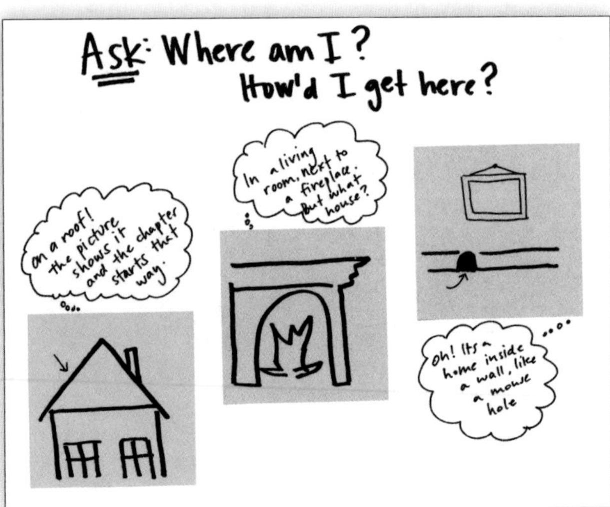

Hat Tip: *Shades of Meaning: Comprehension and Interpretation in Middle School* (Santman 2005)

5.16 Summarizing with "Somebody . . . Wanted . . . But . . . So . . ."

Strategy Think first, "Who is the main character?" Then, "What does the main character want?" Then, "What gets in his or her way?" And finally, "How does it end up?" Be sure the ending connects back in some way to the problem.

Lesson Language *We all read the story* Henry's Freedom Box *by Ellin Levine (2007). Watch me as I summarize this story by thinking, "Somebody wanted . . . but . . . so . . ." Somebody . . . the main character is Henry Brown, a slave. What did he want? He wanted his freedom. But? What was the problem? Well, what stood in his way is that he was a slave in the south. It was very hard to escape, and getting captured would be a dangerous or even fatal mistake. So? How does it end up? Well, I need to make sure I connect back to what he wanted (freedom) and the obstacle (dangers with running away). So, how it ended up is that he was able to mail himself up north and enjoys his first birthday as a free man.*

Prompts

- Who is the character?
- What does the character want?
- What's an obstacle to getting it?
- Name the character.
- Talk about how it ends.
- Connect the ending to what the character wants.
- The part you just told me about was in Chapter 4 of 8, so that can't be the ending; reread the last chapter.
- That sounds like it helped overcome the obstacle.
- That ending clearly connects to what the character wants.

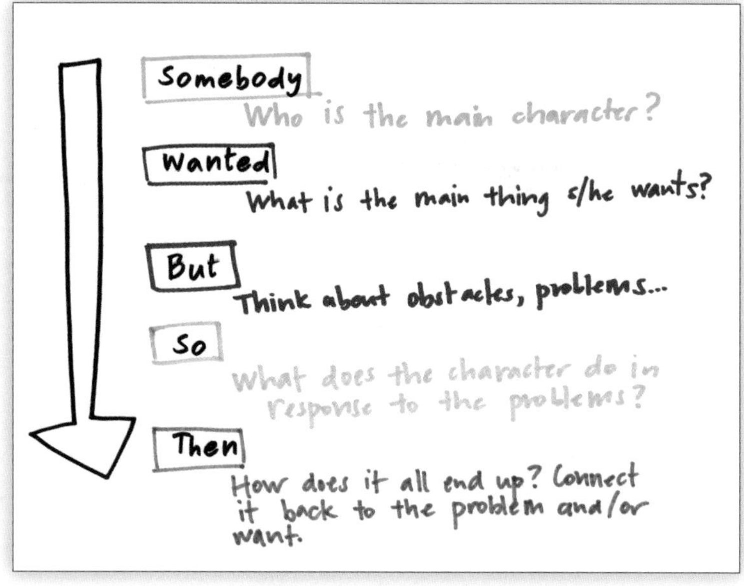

Who is this for?

LEVELS
N–Z+

GENRE / TEXT TYPE
fiction

SKILL
summarizing

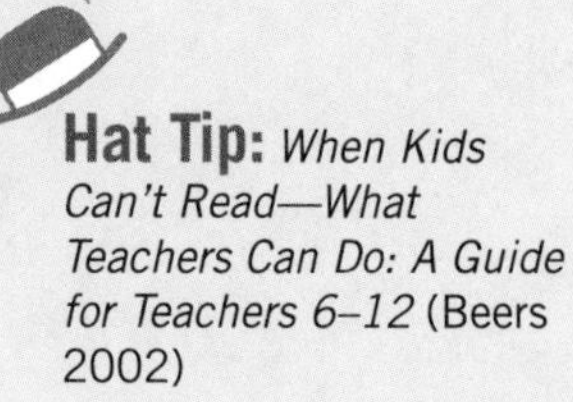

Hat Tip: *When Kids Can't Read—What Teachers Can Do: A Guide for Teachers 6–12* (Beers 2002)

5.17 Two-Sided Problems

Who is this for?

LEVELS

N–Z+

GENRE / TEXT TYPE

fiction

SKILL

determining importance

Strategy Think about the main problem and also how the character feels as a result of the problem. This will help you think about different sides to the main problem. Think, "How do the internal and external problems connect?" and "How do they help the story move forward?"

Lesson Language *In* Amber Brown Is Not a Crayon *(Danziger 1995), the main problem in the story is that her best friend Justin is moving away. We know this is the main problem because of how she acts and thinks. If we were to look at her feelings connected to this main problem, it's clear that this is upsetting her. We know this because she tries to get the family not to buy Justin's house, for example. She wouldn't do that if she didn't care, but she really does. Also, later in the book she talks to her mom about her feelings about all of this and her mom really helps her understand that even if Justin moves away, they can still be friends and they can still talk on the phone. At the end of the story, the main problem isn't solved, exactly. Justin does move away, but she comes to terms with it. Her acceptance—her change in feelings—connects to the resolution in the story.*

Prompts

- What's the main problem?
- Describe the character's reaction to the problem.
- Those are events; what's the character's reaction?
- How do those problems connect?
- What events have happened because of those problems?

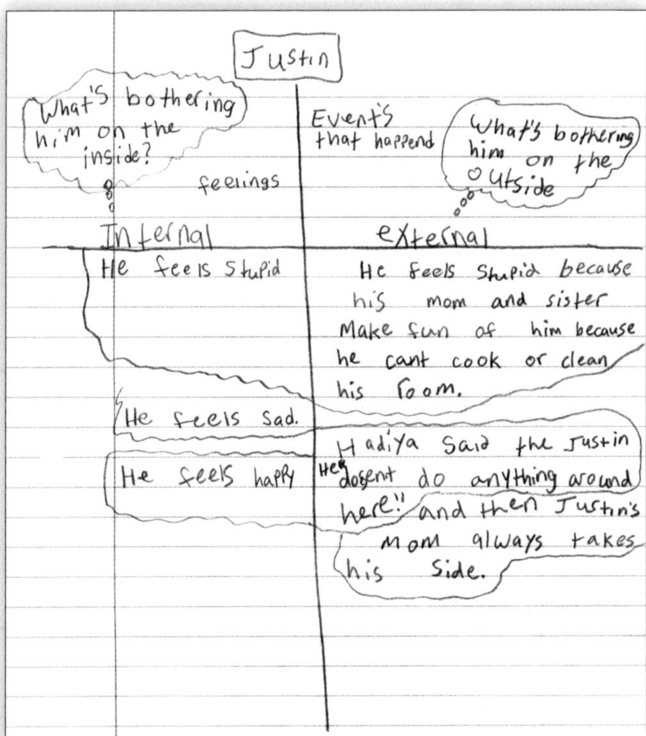

5.18 Does the Story Have to Be Set There, and Then?

Strategy Think about the setting of the story. Consider if the setting is just background, or if it plays an important role in the story. One way to do this is to think, "If the story were set someplace else, or at a different time, how would the story be any different?" Then think, "Based on the setting the author has chosen, what impact does the setting have on the story?"

Lesson Language *Sometimes authors think about the setting of the story almost as a character. By that, I mean that the setting has significance and plays an important role in the story. The setting may affect the characters, or it may even be symbolic in some way. For example, in Eve Bunting's* Fly Away Home *(1993), she chose to set the story in an airport. I could think whether it would matter if the homeless family lived someplace else—a bus station, maybe. Why an airport? Well, much of the day-to-day happenings in a bus station would be the same as an airport, probably, but there's this bird in* Fly Away Home, *and the word* Fly *in the title. So I think that the flying here has to do with freedom, and I think the author wanted all the airplanes to remind us of the bird which has a special significance. By setting the story in the airport, this flying imagery is now in the whole story, not just when we meet the bird. Or for another example, think about the book* The Drinking Gourd *(Monjo 1970), about Harriet Tubman and the Underground Railroad. There's an example of historical fiction, where the story could only happen during the time period. Therefore, details about what it was like then are crucially important to the story.*

Prompts

- Describe the setting.
- Imagine the story in a different place. How would it go?
- Do you think there is any symbolism in the setting?
- Is the setting an historical place and/or time?
- How is the setting important?

Setting...

How important is it?

CONSIDER...

- ➔ the time, place, weather, culture of a story
- ➔ Where does the story take place?
- ➔ When does the story happen?
- ➔ Why is the setting important to the story?
- ➔ Why did the author choose this particular setting?
- ➔ If the setting changed, how would the plot change?

Who is this for?

LEVELS

P–Z+

GENRE / TEXT TYPE

fiction (especially historical fiction)

SKILLS

visualizing, determining importance

5.19 Tenses as a Clue to Flashback and Backstory

Who is this for?

LEVELS

P–Z+

GENRE / TEXT TYPE

fiction

SKILL

monitoring for meaning

Strategy Pay attention to tenses. If the verbs switch from present to past tense, you know the time has changed. Think, "Is the author giving me more information about the characters?" and "Is this scene something that took place in the past? If so, how far back?"

Lesson Language *We've talked about verb tenses in writing and making sure that throughout the whole story we wrote, we use a consistent verb tense. Well, sometimes authors switch verb tense on purpose, and the reason for it is that they are going back in time. Sometimes the author will put a scene right into the middle of another story that is a character's flashback, or memory, of something that happened before. Other times, the narrator might be giving you backstory, or background information, to help you better understand what's happening now. For example, in the book* Home of the Brave *(Applegate 2007), we know that Kek is working on living his new life in Minnesota while also remembering all that happened to him in Africa before coming here. When the narrative is in Minnesota, the narrator Kek uses a present tense: "Dave isn't like my father, / not at all. / But it's been good / to have someone watching over me . . . " (28). However, when Kek is remembering, the author switches to past tense: "At night, before we went to sleep, / my father would make new songs / for my brother Lual and me" (30). As the reader, I need to switch my mental picture and track the plot, realizing that Kek's father isn't there with him in Minnesota—Kek is remembering an event from his past.*

Prompts

- Show me the verbs in this sentence.
- Are these verbs past tense or present?
- Do you think this is a flashback, or something that's happening now?
- Tell me why you think this is a flashback.
- What clues do you have about when this event is taking place?

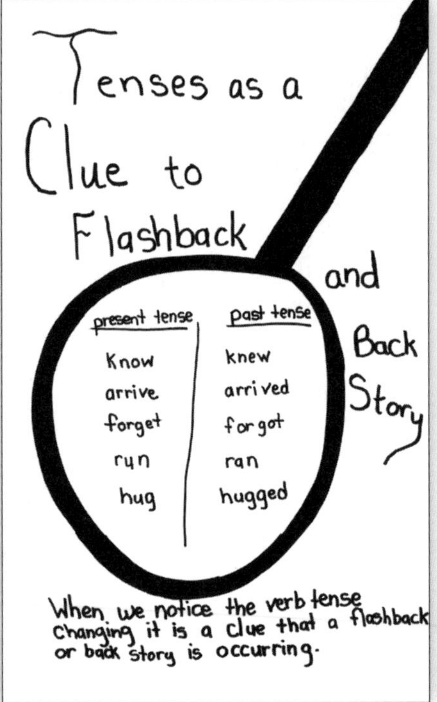

Hat Tip: *What Readers Really Do: Teaching the Process of Meaning Making* (Barnhouse and Vinton 2012)

5.20 Not Just Page Decorations

Strategy Notice white space, dashes, asterisks, and symbols that appear within a page and within a chapter. That is indicating that time is passing or a setting is changing. Be ready to shift your mental picture to the new time or place.

Teaching Tip This strategy could be taught in conjunction with another that helps readers to visualize the setting and/or to infer how characters get from one place in a story to another. See, for example, strategy 5.15, "Where Am I?" in this chapter.

Prompts

- Scan through the chapter to see if the setting will change.
- Read what came right before the asterisks.
- Where are they now?
- How much time has passed? How do you know?
- Is this the same scene or a new one?

Who is this for?

LEVELS

P–Z+

GENRE / TEXT TYPE

fiction

SKILLS

monitoring for meaning, visualizing

5.21 Plotting Flashback on a Timeline

Who is this for?

LEVELS

P–Z+

GENRE / TEXT TYPE

fiction

SKILLS

monitoring for meaning, visualizing

Strategy Flashback gives important info about events that affect characters and who characters are. Notice when time changes to a memory. Think about what the flashback is revealing or teaching about the character(s). Plot the events on a timeline, realizing that even if you come to a scene later in a story, it may have happened in the life of the character before other events.

Teaching Tip This strategy could be taught in combination with strategy 5.19, "Tenses as a Clue to Flashback and Backstory," in this chapter. Readers will need to know when the time and/or place shift and be able to contextualize that shift within the other events in the story.

Prompts

- Show me where the flashback begins.
- Summarize what you learn about the character from the flashback.
- Where will that go on the timeline?
- Is that part of the story moving forward, or a flashback giving you information?
- Think about what you now know about the character from the flashback. How does that make you think about the story in a new way?

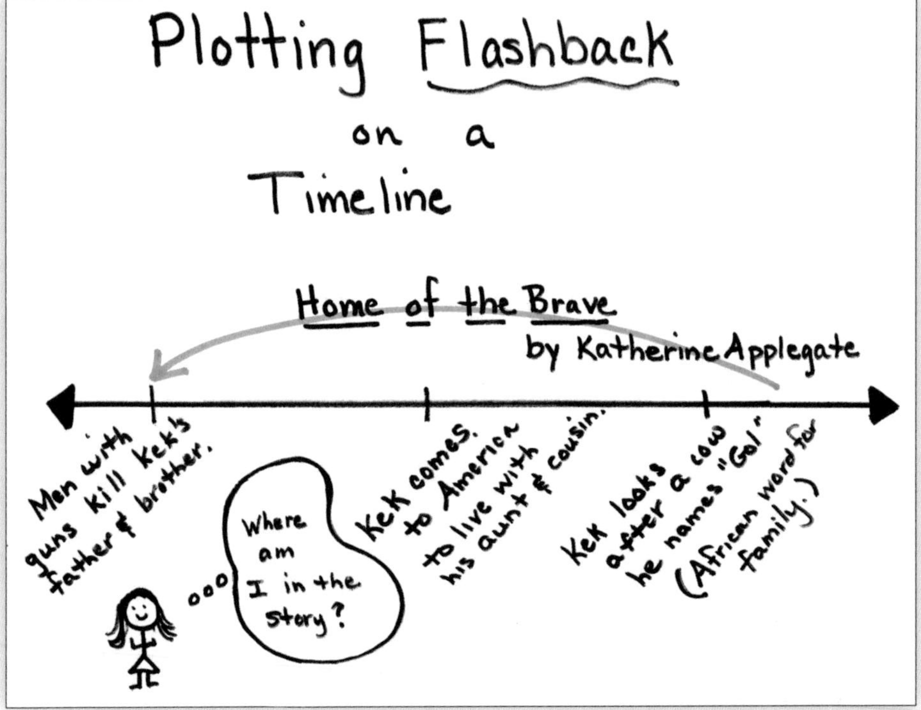

Hat Tip: *Falling in Love with Close Reading: Lessons for Analyzing Texts—and Life* (Lehman and Roberts 2014)

5.22 Vivid Setting Description and Impact on Character

Strategy When the author uses vivid description, slow down. Picture the details the author is giving you about the time and place. Notice what's happening in the time or place alongside what a character thinks or feels. Think, "How does the setting impact the character?"

Teaching Tip Consider using a powerful novel such as Karen Hesse's *Out of the Dust* (2009) to share with children the multiple dimensions of setting. For example, the story begins with Billie Jo, the narrator and main character, recounting her birth. With details such as "born at home, on the kitchen floor . . . over the swept boards" you can learn about the local setting and teach children to infer about the time period (poverty, simple life, no hospital, and so on). The author tells you that it's 1920 in the title of the first poem. You can teach children how to call up what they know about the specific time period—where in history is this, what was happening that year, what is significant, and so on. Later in the story, we learn about the Dust Bowl, and this could be an opportunity to speak with children about how significant events are significant settings to the story as well. And then there is the Great Depression and the effect this time period, and event, in history has on Billie Jo and her family.

Prompts

- Show me where the author describes the setting in detail.
- Say back the details you learned about the setting.
- How does the character act in this setting?
- Why might the setting be important?
- Describe what you picture.

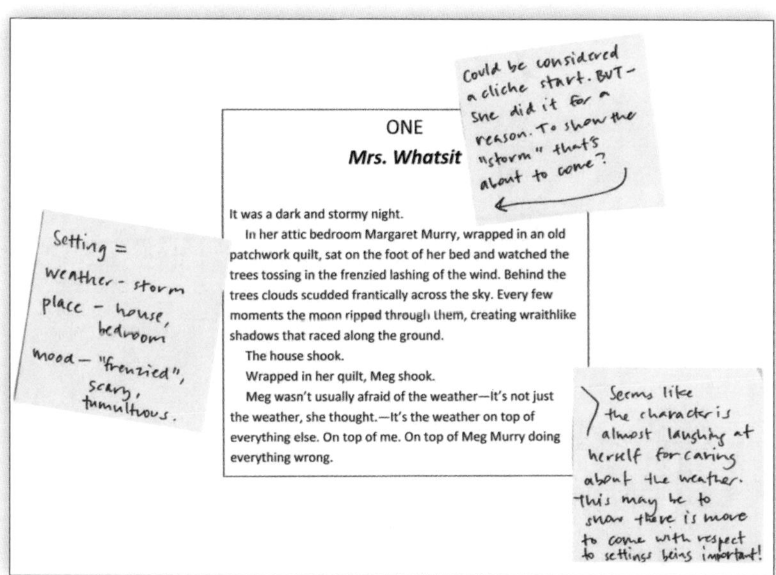
ONE

Mrs. Whatsit

It was a dark and stormy night.

In her attic bedroom Margaret Murry, wrapped in an old patchwork quilt, sat on the foot of her bed and watched the trees tossing in the frenzied lashing of the wind. Behind the trees clouds scudded frantically across the sky. Every few moments the moon ripped through them, creating wraithlike shadows that raced along the ground.

The house shook.

Wrapped in her quilt, Meg shook.

Meg wasn't usually afraid of the weather—It's not just the weather, she thought.—It's the weather on top of everything else. On top of me. On top of Meg Murry doing everything wrong.

Text excerpt from *A Wrinkle in Time* (L'Engle 1962).

Who is this for?

LEVELS

P–Z+

GENRE / TEXT TYPE

fiction

SKILLS

determining importance, visualizing

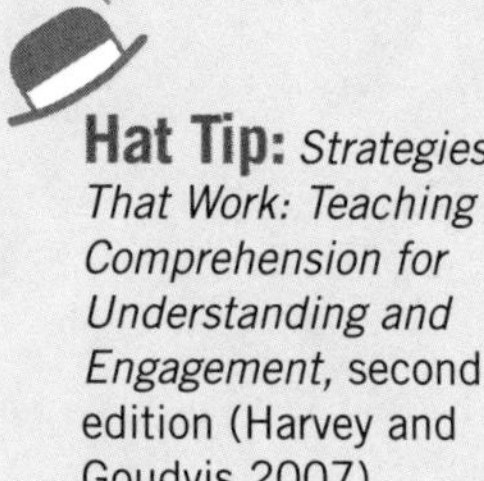

Hat Tip: *Strategies That Work: Teaching Comprehension for Understanding and Engagement*, second edition (Harvey and Goudvis 2007)

5.23 Map It

Who is this for?

LEVELS

P–Z+

GENRE / TEXT TYPE

fiction

SKILLS

monitoring for meaning, visualizing

Strategy When a character travels a lot from place to place, keep a map and track the character's movements. Draw a map based on the details the author gives you about each of the places. Refer to the map as you read, visualizing the character moving from place to place. Think about why the author chose to set the story in those places and how each of the settings impacts the character.

Prompts

- Recall the place(s) you've read about. Draw a map showing all of those places.
- Where is this place compared to that one?
- In this scene, show me on your map where the character is.
- From this chapter to this chapter, show me how the character travels from place to place.
- Looking at the map, describe the significance of the places. What's important about them? How are they impacting the character?

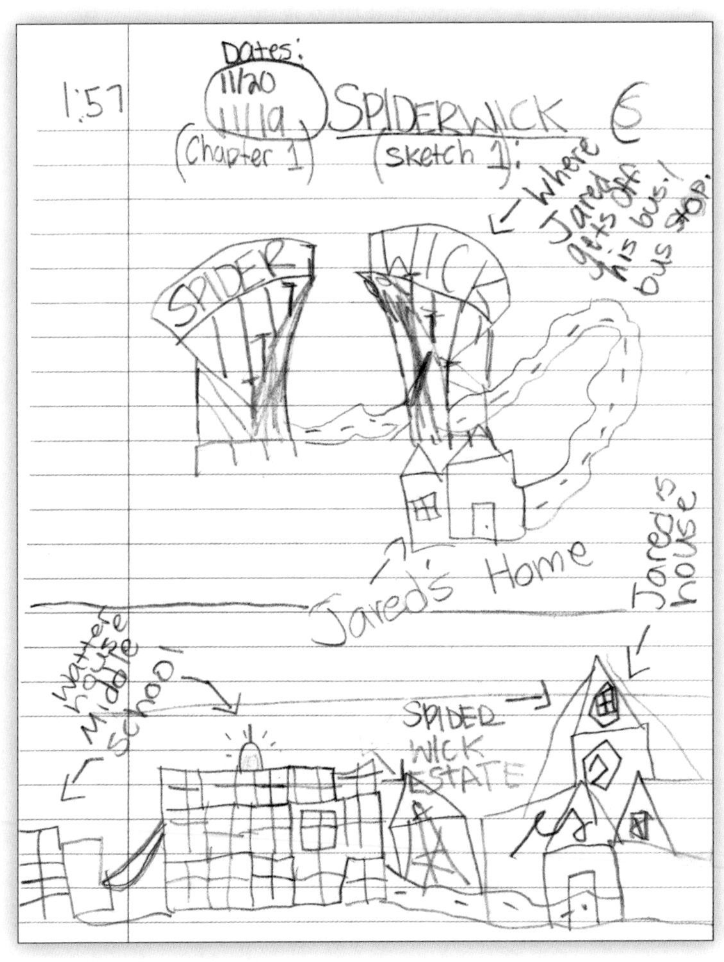

5.24 FQR (Facts/Questions/Response) Sheets for Filling in Gaps

Strategy Sometimes you'll find yourself slightly confused in the story. When you do, think, "What are the facts that I know? What questions do I have?" Then, read on to try to respond to those questions, or offer your own thinking based on what's happening in the text.

Lesson Language *When you read more challenging texts that are set in made-up places (which is often true in fantasy fiction) or in historical times (which is true in historical fiction), you'll find that there are gaps in your understanding. Sometimes, the author will assume you know something or will slowly give you more information as the story goes on. This means you don't have all the information up front, and instead, you need to construct it yourself. Keeping track of what you know, and what questions you have, will help you sort between what's confusing and what's clear in your mind. As you read on in the story, you should be able to respond to or answer the outlying questions based on what you're learning in the text.*

Prompts

- What do you know about the time and place?
- What details did the author give you? What are you still trying to figure out?
- What questions do you have?
- Think about what's important to know, that you haven't learned yet.
- Jot down what's confusing.
- I noticed you followed up on a question. That's going to help you understand!
- Yes, you got more information and were able to answer that.

Title: Home of the Brave   Name: Yesenia

Author: Applegate

Facts:	Questions:	Response:
Father herded cattle	common job?	"my people are herders" yes. p. 29
	Why was Kek's father killed?	war - but why?
Kek is "here" but Lual isn't.	Who is Lual and what happened?	brother. Also died in war?
		→ he was Kek's big brother, a protector + teacher
Cloth is from "the camp"	~~where is the camp?~~ what is the camp?	
	why is Kek not saying ~~the whole truth?~~	? Not answered. Maybe in Africa?
mom, dad, Lual, Ganwar are in his dream	Is his mom dead like Lual and his dad?	Mom's alive!
Mom has been found	Where was she found and how is she getting here?	Another camp?

Who is this for?

LEVELS

Q–Z+

GENRE / TEXT TYPE

fiction (historical fiction and fantasy, especially)

SKILLS

questioning, synthesizing, inferring, monitoring for meaning

Hat Tip: *Strategies That Work: Teaching Comprehension for Understanding and Engagement*, second edition (Harvey and Goudvis 2007)

5.25 Double Plot Mountain

Who is this for?

LEVELS

R–Z+

GENRE / TEXT TYPE

fiction

SKILLS

monitoring for meaning, visualizing

Strategy Keep track of two plots simultaneously. Keep two plot mountain graphic organizers in front of you as you read. As you come to a new, significant event, think about which plot that event aligns to. Add it to that story mountain.

Lesson Language Joey Pigza Swallowed the Key *by Jack Gantos (2014) is a complex novel that explores the journey of the main character, Joey, as he tries to deal with challenges associated with his ADHD. We can look at the many events in the story as falling into a couple of different, yet parallel, story lines. We could follow these different story lines by thinking about Joey's life at school (one setting) and Joey's life at home (a different setting with different characters). Each time I get to a new event in the story, I'll think: "Where did this event happen? With which characters?" Then, I can add the events to that timeline. There may be parts in the story where the two lines intersect—for instance, when Joey's mother goes to school to talk to the counselor. That's an interesting moment to think about from the character's perspective, too, as his two worlds are colliding.*

Prompts

- What seems to be the focus of the main plot?
- Tell me what just happened in your story. Is that part of the main plot or the secondary plot? How do you know?
- Think about what event that new event connects to.
- Add the event to your plot mountain.

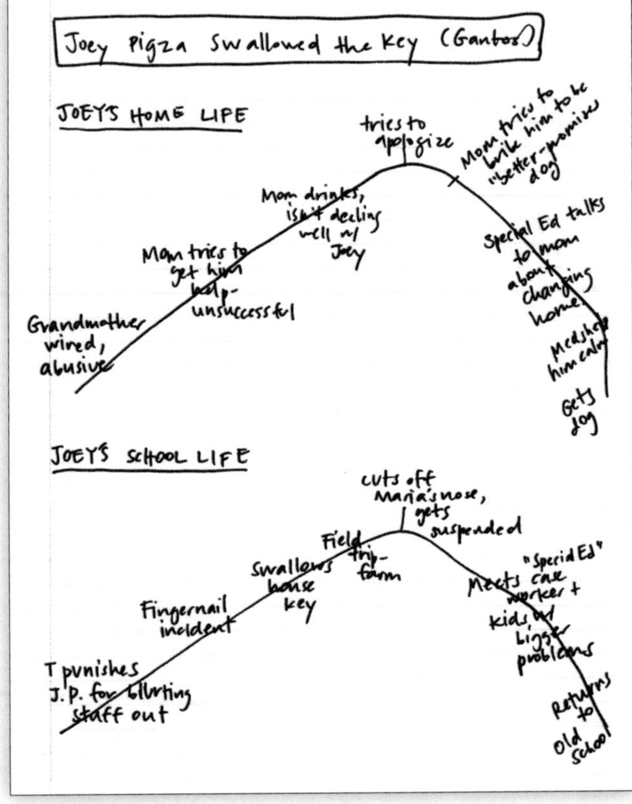

Hat Tip: *Falling in Love with Close Reading: Lessons for Analyzing Texts—and Life* (Lehman and Roberts 2014)

5.26 Historical Notes Prime Prior Knowledge

Strategy Look for the "historical notes" section in an historical fiction novel—sometimes it's in the beginning, sometimes at the end. Read it before you begin reading the story, and again after reading the story, to get more insight into the setting.

Lesson Language *Sometimes when you read a new historical fiction book, you'll find that the story is set during a time period that we haven't studied yet in school. Since it's history, it's set in a time you haven't experienced firsthand. And you may not have even seen a movie or TV show set during that time. When you have little or no background knowledge about the time period, the historical notes can help you to learn a little something. Found either at the start or end of the book, these notes will often give you information about the time period generally, and also information you need to know to understand the story. In* Sadako and the Thousand Paper Cranes *(Coerr 2004), just a few paragraphs tell us so much. We can learn about the larger context (the war), the specific place (a city in Japan), the time (1943–1955) and more. These details help us better understand the story.*

Prompts

- What did you learn from the historical notes that may help you understand the setting of the story?
- After reading the story, what do you wonder about? Check the historical notes to see if your questions might be answered.
- Specifically what did you learn about the time? Place?
- Think back to events in the story. How do details from the notes help you picture it better?
- All of that information you got from the historical notes will surely help you!

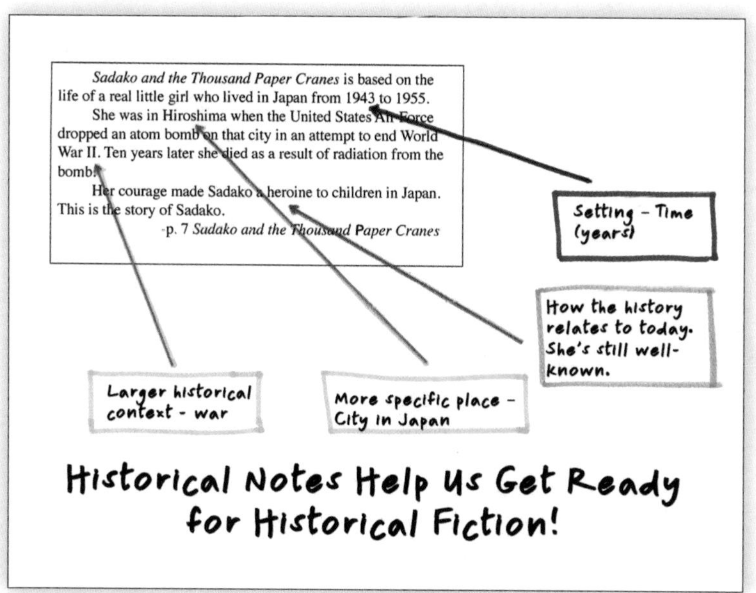

Sadako and the Thousand Paper Cranes is based on the life of a real little girl who lived in Japan from 1943 to 1955.
She was in Hiroshima when the United States Air Force dropped an atom bomb on that city in an attempt to end World War II. Ten years later she died as a result of radiation from the bomb.
Her courage made Sadako a heroine to children in Japan. This is the story of Sadako.
-p. 7 *Sadako and the Thousand Paper Cranes*
Setting - Time (years)
How the history relates to today. She's still well-known.
Larger historical context - war
More specific place - City in Japan
Historical Notes Help Us Get Ready for Historical Fiction!

Who is this for?

LEVELS
R–Z+

GENRE / TEXT TYPE
fiction

SKILLS
monitoring for meaning, visualizing

5.27 Analyzing Historical Contexts

Who is this for?

LEVELS

R–Z+

GENRE / TEXT TYPE

historical fiction

SKILLS

determining importance, visualizing, inferring

Strategy Think about the setting of the story as including both the time and place in history. Consider the details about the social, economic, and political atmosphere of that time and place. Consider what effects the environment has on the character(s).

Lesson Language *When you read historical fiction, it's so important to really understand the historical environment. It's more than just saying "Northeastern United States, 1942." It helps to go a little deeper, thinking about different aspects of what life was like then, to best understand the characters and why they do what they do. You should consider the social environment—think about the kinds of social issues like racism issues, or expectations for gender. Think about the economic environment—what sorts of jobs were available? What did being in different social classes mean at that time? Think also about the politics of the time—who was in power and what were their beliefs about how to lead the place? What laws existed and how might those impact the characters? When an author writes historical fiction, he or she carefully considers all of the aspects of the environment, and it's important that you, as a reader, do as well!*

Prompts

- What do you know about this time and place?
- Can you get information from the text, historical notes, or prologue?
- You may have to research a bit to learn more about this time and place.
- Think about social issues. What's at play here?
- Talk about what you know so far about the economics of this time.
- What details do you know about the politics at this time?

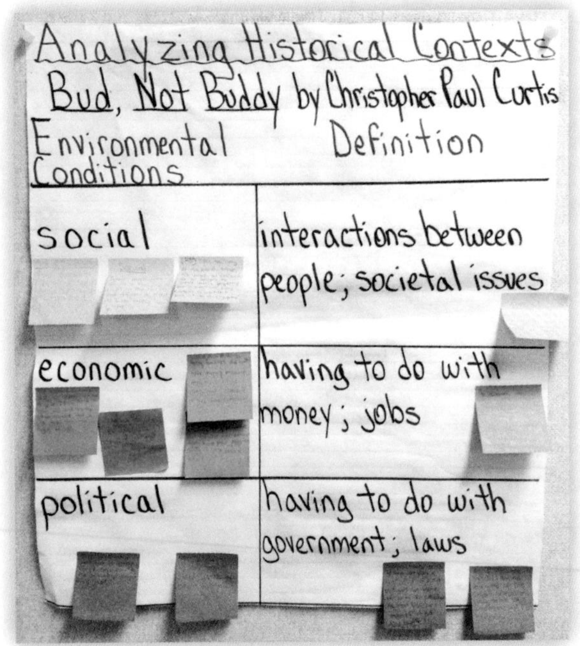

Hat Tip: *Teaching Interpretation: Using Text-Based Evidence to Construct Meaning* (Cherry-Paul and Johansen 2014)

5.28 Micro-/Meso-/Macroenvironment Systems: Levels of Setting

Strategy Notice and name the aspects of a character's environment. This may be based on information the author has given you, or on what you can infer based on text details. Then, think about which of these is important based on the conflicts that the character is experiencing.

Lesson Language *The first level of a character's "setting" that has an impact on the character is known as the* microsystem *and it involves the people and space closest to a character—parents, peer group, local community, school, church. The next level is the less-immediate* mesosystem. *This includes government, news organizations, and geography that is larger than the community. The most global and abstract is the* macrosystem, *which includes, for example, international relations or global climate change. If I were to think about* Home of the Brave *(Applegate 2007), I might consider a few levels of setting for Kek, and how those levels are important to understanding him and the struggles he's facing. His immediate setting, the microsystem, is his new home in Minnesota, the new friends he's making, the volunteer from the church who is helping him. He's adjusting to technologies he's never experienced, and the absence of family. The mesosystem is the geography—cold, harsh northern winter when he's accustomed to a climate in Africa. The macrosystem that affects him is the war-torn country he's left and the family members he is with in the United States, who have changed so significantly because of their experiences with war.*

Prompts

- Describe the character's local setting—home, school, community.
- What are you thinking about the setting?
- Let's think more broadly. Describe the larger setting.
- How is the setting affecting the character?
- What information do you have about the global or political environment?

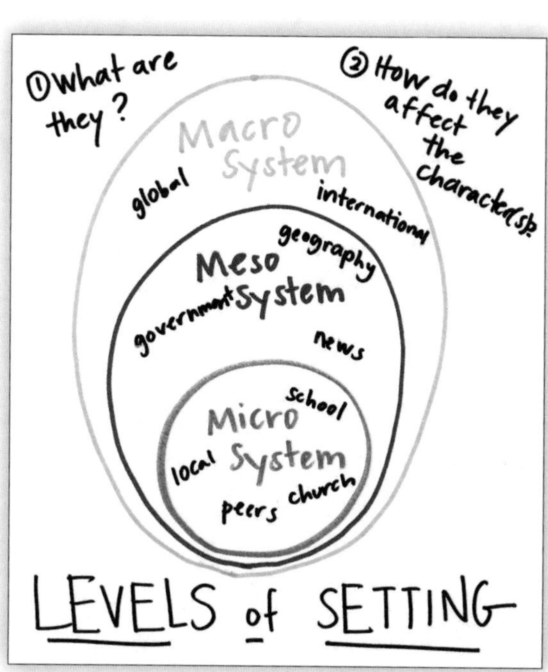

Who is this for?

LEVELS

V–Z+

GENRE / TEXT TYPE

fiction

SKILLS

visualizing, determining importance, inferring

Hat Tip: *Fresh Takes on Teaching Literary Elements: How to Teach What Really Matters About Character, Setting, Point of View, and Theme* (Smith and Wilhelm 2010)

Supporting Comprehension in Fiction

Thinking About Characters

Why is this goal important?

Character development is often intertwined with plot development. Characters are the actors connecting the events of the story and in large part, they help readers to stay engaged while reading. Characters can become our friends, can help us learn about lives outside of our own, and can help us think differently about or better understand people in our own lives.

The challenge to readers' ability to understand characters is that unlike people, literary characters are constructed. Readers need to pay attention to details that the author includes to figure out who the character is. Some of the types of details an author may include are:

- what characters look like, how they dress, what possessions they keep
- what characters say and how they say it

- what is left unsaid
- thoughts the character has that are revealed through the narrator
- the moods and emotions of the character
- a character's actions
- how characters respond to events and other characters
- backstory and beliefs of the character
- the opinions other characters have about the character

(Serravallo 2012).

By pulling all of these details together, readers will need to do the following work to better understand their characters:

- Infer about character feelings, and synthesize change in those feelings.
- Infer about character traits, and synthesize multiple parts of the text to explain a change in traits.
- Synthesize ideas about characters to articulate character theories or interpretations.
- Understand not only the main character but also secondary characters.
- Infer to explain relationships between characters.

How do I know if this goal is right for my student?

Underneath the umbrella of "fiction comprehension," I consider *plot and setting* to be first—knowing what's happening and where it's happening—and *character* to be a very close second. I would assess a reader's ability to understand characters if a student seems to be able to:

- retell the most important events in a story
- understand why events are happening
- determine problem and solution
- visualize the setting.

You could ask a student to read a short text or whole book and jot responses as she reads, or you could read aloud to her and ask her to do the same thing. For younger students whose writing abilities may not give a full picture of how well they understand, it's important to ask questions during conferences and to listen to their conversations about characters with their peers.

Regardless of how you choose to collect samples of your students' thoughts about the characters in their books, you'll need a rubric or continuum against which to judge their responses. I find that understanding expectations for comprehension aligned to complexity of the level is most helpful (Serravallo 2012).

For example, in books most often encountered by first graders (levels E–J), characters tend to be simple, with feelings illustrated and sometimes even stated in the narration. When asked to describe a character, a child should be able to say "He's sad" or "He likes to play baseball."

Around level J/K, a character's feelings may change, but traits stay the same. A reader should be able to say "He's lazy" or "He was upset, but now he's happy because he cleaned up and he can play."

By level N, characters are often multidimensional, with "good" and "bad" traits, and/or we see a new side to the character by the end of the story. A reader should be able to say, "Amber is a good friend to Justin, and is good at spelling, but she can also be jealous and get upset."

By the beginning of grade 4, or around level P, readers should be able to put traits together to name a theory (although it's possible to do this as early as level N). A reader should be able to make a statement about a character, such as, "Koya is very friendly, but when she keeps in her feelings it causes her problems."

Secondary characters become increasingly important, and by around level Q/R those secondary characters tend to be well developed and have major impact on the main character. A reader should be able to articulate that "all the people in India Opal's new town are important to her. Not just as friends, but together they seem to almost add up to have all the qualities of the mom she misses."

All this to say, you have to know about the text level to understand what to expect of a reader's responses. For example, if you have a student who is describing India Opal from *Because of Winn-Dixie* (DiCamillo 2000; a text leveled at R) as a character who is "nice to animals," that would be an indication that the student needs more work on uncovering complexity of character. A student who says this about Mr. Putter from Cynthia Rylant's Mr. Putter and Tabby series would be a reader who is using the depth of thinking I'd expect at that level.

Strategies for Thinking About Characters at a Glance

Strategy		Levels	Genres/ Text Types	Skills
6.1	How's the Character Feeling?	C–Z+	Fiction	Inferring
6.2	What's in the Bubble?	C–M	Fiction	Inferring
6.3	Put On the Character's Face	C–M	Fiction	Visualizing, inferring
6.4	Feelings Change	F–M	Fiction	Inferring, determining importance
6.5	Ready, Set, Action!	F–M	Fiction	Visualizing, inferring, determining importance
6.6	Back Up Ideas About Characters with Evidence	F–Z+	Fiction	Supporting ideas with evidence
6.7	Role-Playing Characters to Understand Them Better	F–N	Fiction	Inferring, visualizing, fluency
6.8	Look for a Pattern	H–M	Fiction	Inferring, synthesizing
6.9	Text Clue/Background Knowledge Addition	H–Z+	Fiction	Inferring
6.10	Who's Telling the Story?	H–Z+	Fiction	Monitoring for meaning
6.11	Character Comparisons	J–Z+	Fiction	Comparing and contrasting, inferring, determining importance
6.12	Empathize to Understand	J–Z+	Fiction	Inferring, determining cause and effect
6.13	Yes, But Why?	L–Z+	Fiction	Inferring, synthesizing
6.14	Interactions Can Lead to Inferences	M–Z+	Fiction	Inferring, determining cause and effect
6.15	Talk and Actions as Windows	M–Z+	Fiction	Inferring
6.16	Out-of-Character Character	N–Z+	Fiction	Inferring, synthesizing
6.17	The Influences on Character	N–Z+	Fiction	Determining cause and effect, inferring
6.18	Complex Characters	N–Z+	Fiction	Inferring, comparing and contrasting
6.19	More Than One Side	N–Z+	Fiction	Inferring
6.20	Conflict Brings Complexity	N–Z+	Fiction	Inferring, synthesizing
6.21	Piling Together Traits to Get Theories	N–Z+	Fiction	Inferring, synthesizing, interpreting
6.22	Consider Character in Context	P–Z+	Historical fiction, biography	Determining importance, inferring
6.23	What's in a Character's Heart?	R–Z+	Fiction	Inferring, synthesizing, determining importance, comparing and contrasting
6.24	Blind Spots	R–Z+	Fiction	Inferring, interpreting, synthesizing

6.1 How's the Character Feeling?

Who is this for?

LEVELS
C–Z+

GENRE / TEXT TYPE
fiction

SKILL
inferring

Strategy One way to get to know our characters well is to make sure we care about how they feel, talk, act, and think. We can imagine ourselves to be in the same situation, or remember a time when we were, and think about how we felt or would feel. Then, we can use a word to describe that feeling, using a chart to help if we need it.

Lesson Language *Characters in our stories have feelings, just like people have feelings. Sometimes those feelings are positive—like happy, excited, amazed. Sometimes those feelings are negative—nervous, sad, worried. It's important to learn about our characters by thinking about how they feel. After noticing the way they act, speak, or think, we can make sure that we use the right word to describe how they feel.*

Prompts

- Check the picture. Do you get any clues about how the character feels?
- How's the character feeling?
- Notice how the character talks. How do you think she or he feels?
- Tell me how the character is speaking. What are you thinking about how she or he is feeling?
- Do you think the feeling is positive or negative?
- Use a word to describe the feeling.

Readers pay attention to the characters in their stories. They notice...
·how they act
·how they speak
·what they say
·what they think
Then, they ask...
"What does this tell me about how the character feels?"
and
"What feeling does this capture?"

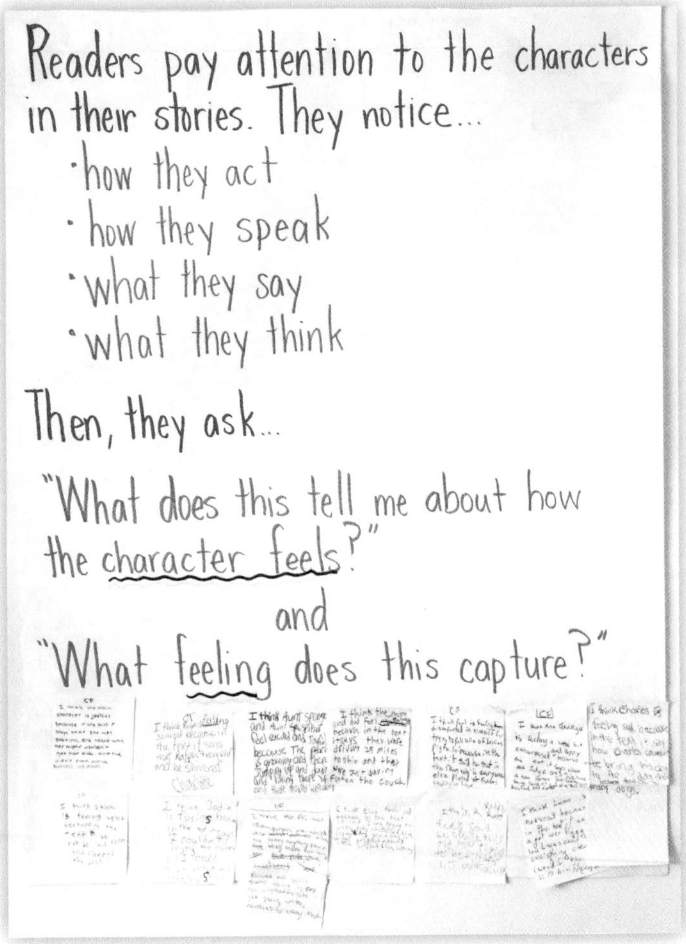

Hat Tip: *Talk About Understanding: Rethinking Classroom Talk to Enhance Comprehension* (Keene 2012)

6.2 What's in the Bubble?

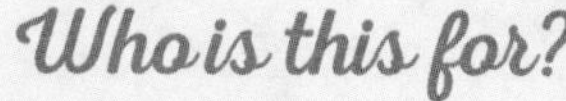

LEVELS

C–M

GENRE / TEXT TYPE

fiction

SKILL

inferring

Strategy We can pause and think, "What's my character thinking here?" or "What might my character be saying here?" Even when the text doesn't tell us, we can imagine, noticing what's happened so far. Pause on the page and put a thought or speech bubble above the character in the picture, point to the bubble, and say what the character might be thinking or saying.

Teaching Tip For children at levels C–H, I try to keep stopping and jotting to a minimum (see chapter 13 for more information about writing about reading), often telling children to simply flag pages with blank sticky notes and/or to use quick symbols to hold on to thinking. You can tweak this strategy for those within that level range and for students at levels I–L who may be able to do more jotting. For lower levels, you can create speech bubbles and thought clouds and affix them to tongue depressors. Children can use these as tools independently and with partnerships. For children who are ready to stop and jot a phrase or sentence, you can give them sticky notes with bubbles and they can affix them to the page and jot what the character might be thinking or saying. In the figures, you can see a variety of variations of this strategy.

Prompts

- What just happened? So, what might your character be thinking?
- What words is your character saying in his or her head?
- Before you turn the page, pause and think about what he or she would be thinking.
- Put your thought bubble on the page.
- That's what's happening. What might she or he be thinking?
- Yes! That thought matches with what's happened so far.
- Pausing there helps you think about what the character's thinking.

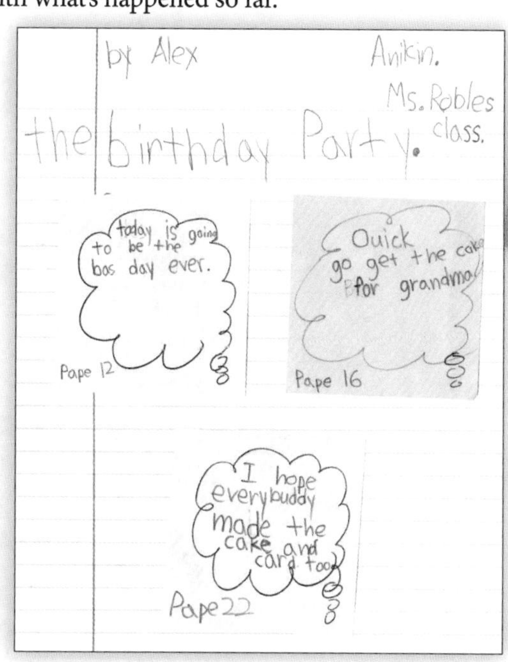

Hat Tip: *A Curricular Plan for the Reading Workshop, Grade 1* (Calkins and colleagues 2011b)

6.3 Put On the Character's Face

Who is this for?

LEVELS

C–M

GENRE / TEXT TYPE

fiction

SKILLS

visualizing, inferring

Strategy Pay close attention to the picture. Look at the expression on the character's face. Make the face yourself. Think, "How's the character feeling?"

Lesson Language *Sometimes you may hear teachers say to "put yourself in the character's shoes" when they want you to try to feel what the character's feeling. But feelings aren't in shoes! Feelings show up on your face and body. When you're happy, you smile—smile with me. When you're sad, you frown—look sad. Well, characters in your books will have feelings, too. When you can't figure out how they are feeling right away, you can make your face match the face of the character. You can think about how you feel when you make that face to better understand how the character must be feeling. You can check the "How Are You Feeling?" chart to see which face most closely matches the one you're making, to know what word to use to describe the feeling.*

Prompts

- Check the face of the character in the picture.
- Make the same face as the face you see here.
- How do you feel when you make that face?
- I see your face changed. What feeling matches that?
- How might your character be feeling?
- Show me on your face.
- Check the feelings chart to find a word that matches that feeling.

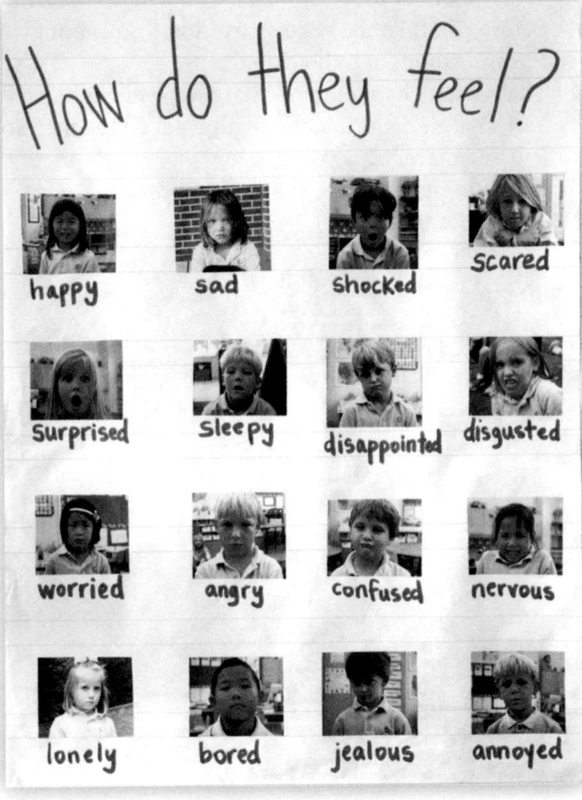

Hat Tip: "Teaching Reading in Small Groups: Matching Methods to Purposes" (Serravallo 2013c)

6.4 Feelings Change

Strategy Notice what happens to the character throughout the book and how what happens causes feelings to change. Think about how the character is feeling at one point of the story. Think, is the feeling a positive one or negative one? Use a word or sketch a picture to describe it. Now, look at how the character feels later. Think, is the feeling a positive one or negative one? Jot the new feeling. Look across the sticky notes to explain how the feelings changed.

Lesson Language *When something happens to you that is fun—you are having a birthday party, your mom buys you an ice-cream cone, or you learn to ride your bike by yourself—chances are you are smiling, saying "Yay!" and feeling happy. But, when something goes wrong—you forget your lunch at home, you get sick, or someone teases you—chances are you feel upset. Good and bad things will happen to your characters in the stories, too. These changes in what happens to them changes their feelings. When you notice a new feeling, you can stop and either jot on a sticky note a word to describe the feeling or sketch a picture of how their face looks. Then, when you meet with me or your partner, you can explain how the feelings changed, and what caused those changes.*

Prompts

- Think about what's happening now. Is it good for the character, or bad?
- How might he or she be feeling here?
- Is this feeling the same or different?
- Explain what caused the change.
- You understand the feeling at the beginning. What is the character feeling at the end?
- You looked closely at the words and pictures to figure out the feeling.
- How has the feeling changed?
- Is the character feeling the same thing here, or something new?

Who is this for?

LEVELS

F–M

GENRE / TEXT TYPE

fiction

SKILLS

inferring, determining importance

6.5 Ready, Set, Action!

Who is this for?

LEVELS

F–M

GENRE / TEXT TYPE

fiction

SKILLS

visualizing, inferring, determining importance

Hat Tip: *A Curricular Plan for the Reading Workshop, Grade 1* (Calkins and colleagues 2011b)

Strategy One person in your partnership is the director and one person is the actor. The director directs the actor while reading by telling the actor how to read or how to behave. Then, the actor and director discuss the character at the end of the scene. You can think about the ideas you have about the character based on how he or she talked and/or acted.

Lesson Language *Acting just like the character acts can help you know him or her as a person. Partners can play actor/director. The actor can say what the character says and do what the character does. The director can tell the actor when she or he needs to go back and replay the scene because it doesn't match what's in the book. After acting, the actor and director can talk about what they learned and how they think about the character now. If you want to re-do the scene, you could try to act differently. Perhaps the character would say certain lines differently, or would move his body in a different way. You can think about not just what the character does and says, but also how he does and says it. Acting it out helps you see this.*

Prompts

- Make sure your voice matches the character.
- Check what's in the book—now act it out that way.
- Think about what the character does, and how he does it.
- Now that you acted like the character, what are you thinking about him or her?
- Do you have any new thoughts about the character?

6.6 Back Up Ideas About Characters with Evidence

Strategy Focus on an idea. Hold the idea on a sticky note in your hand or think of one in your mind. Reread to find a line where the character says or does something that connects to the idea. Explain how that line proves that idea.

Teaching Tip One thing I hear most often in classrooms engaged in character studies is, "Back up your ideas with evidence!" This strategy is a way to help students learn how to do it, instead of just telling them to do it. I agree that teaching children to support their thinking with evidence is important because it's a way to check your thinking with actual facts in the text, it's a way to support your thinking when you're speaking with friends or with a teacher, and it's an all-around important skill for life. However, I always caution teachers to be careful not to overdo it with the evidence. Make sure that there is equal, if not more, attention paid to the actual quality of the idea. See other lessons in this chapter for more support with idea building.

Prompts

- What's the idea?
- What did the character say or do?
- Reread to find the part that gave you that idea.
- Explain how that connects.
- That's what happened, but what's the idea?
- That's what the character did; can you explain how that's proof of your idea?
- That explanation makes sense. You clearly connected proof to an idea.
- That piece of proof really works—I can see how that part gave you the idea.
- That connects to your idea because ____.

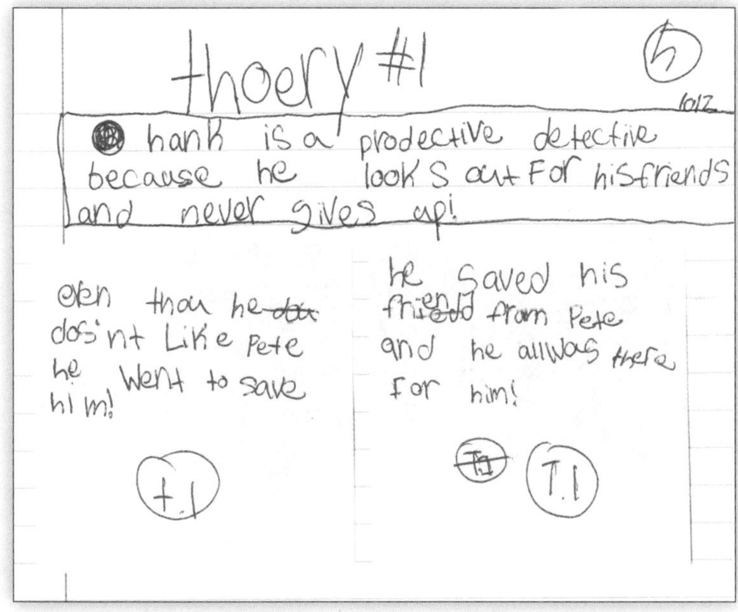

Who is this for?

LEVELS

F–Z+

GENRE / TEXT TYPE

fiction

SKILL

supporting ideas with evidence

Hat Tip: *On Solid Ground: Strategies for Teaching Reading, K–3* (Taberski 2000)

6.7 Role-Playing Characters to Understand Them Better

Who is this for?

LEVELS

F–N

GENRE / TEXT TYPE

fiction

SKILLS

inferring, visualizing, fluency

Hat Tip: *The Common Core Lesson Book, K–5: Working with Increasingly Complex Literature, Informational Text, and Foundational Reading Skills* (Owocki 2012)

Strategy Sometimes the best way to get to know our characters is to stand in their shoes—to do what they do, say what they say, and act how they act. With a partner, choose a scene. Using puppets or props, act out the scene. Try to talk in the voice of the character, and move the puppet just like the character would. When you finish creating the scene, stop and talk about what you think about the characters.

Teaching Tip Many author websites have printable resources of the characters in some of the books you are reading to your children or that they are reading independently (see, for example, www.janbrett.com, www.kevinhenkes.com, www.patriciapolacco.com). These are quick and easy ways to make puppets, but puppets and props could also be made during a choice time or center time. See *A Quick Guide to Boosting English Language Acquisition Through Choice Time, K–2* (Porcelli and Tyler 2008) for more ideas on how to use choice time to support comprehension and enjoyment of stories.

Prompts

- How would your character act?
- Make the puppet talk in the voice of your character.
- Now that the puppet acted like the character, how do you think he or she felt?
- Now that the puppet acted like the character, what kind of person do you think she or he is?
- Based on what the character did or said, what are you thinking now?

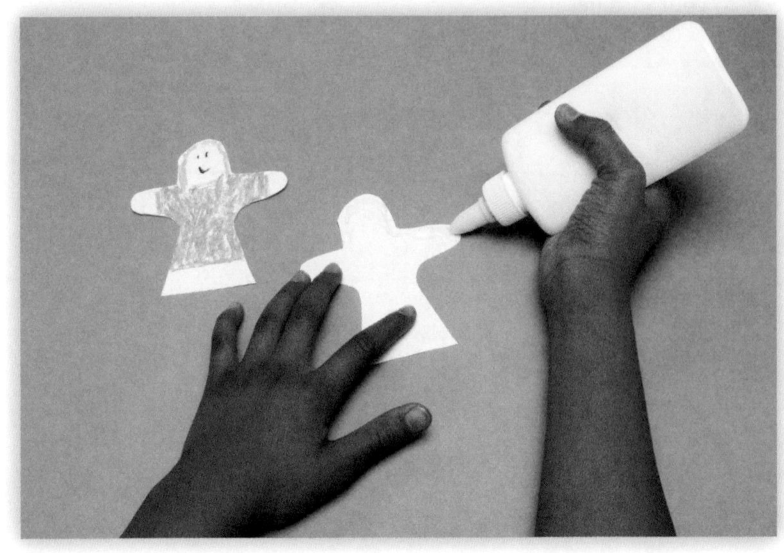

6.8 Look for a Pattern

Strategy Often, traits are revealed through behaviors a character repeats again and again. Try looking at the character in multiple parts of the story. Think to yourself, "What actions, or thoughts, or dialogue repeats? Where is there a pattern?" Use that pattern to name trait(s).

Teaching Tip In texts at the primary elementary levels, it's often the case that to teach children how to distinguish between traits and feelings of a character—two things that are often confused—you can teach children that feelings change while traits stay the same. The challenge is that beginning around level N, we do start to see new traits emerge by the end of the story. For example, in *Jake Drake, Bully Buster* (Clements 2001), the bully acts consistently mean and cruel toward Jake until the end of the story when he's forced to do a project with Jake. Through their time together, Jake starts to realize a few things about him. For one, he has some artistic talent. Also, he is very shy and is scared to speak in front of the class. There is still a pattern of bullying behavior at the beginning, but the new information about him helps us to craft a more complex picture of him. Because of the shift in complexity of characters around level N, I recommend this strategy for readers up to and including level M.

Prompts

- Describe the character in the beginning.
- Describe the character now.
- Check your trait list. What words describe the character?
- Do you see a pattern?
- How is the character behaving again and again?
- What's the same from page to page or part to part?

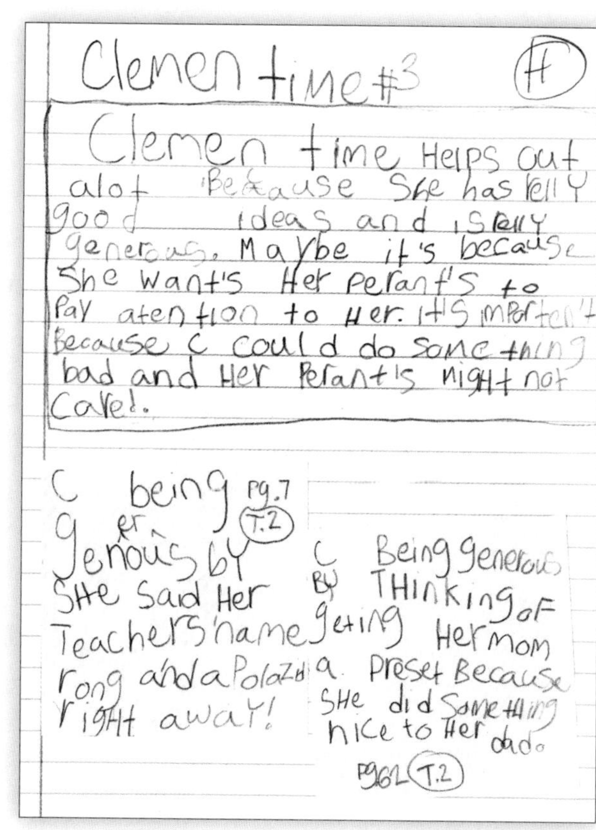

Who is this for?

LEVELS
H–M

GENRE / TEXT TYPE
fiction

SKILLS
inferring, synthesizing

6.9 Text Clue/Background Knowledge Addition

Who is this for?

LEVELS

H–Z+

GENRE / TEXT TYPE

fiction

SKILL

inferring

Hat Tip: *Strategies That Work: Teaching Comprehension for Understanding and Engagement*, second edition (Harvey and Goudvis 2007)

Strategy You can figure out what a character is feeling or learn about the kind of person a character is by relying on what you know about people in real life. First, pay attention to text clues about the character. Then think, "What do I already know about people like this?" This is your background knowledge. Finally, state an inference—something that's not explicitly said but that you can figure out by adding the clues and your background knowledge together.

Lesson Language *When I was reading* Charlie and the Chocolate Factory *(Dahl 1964), I felt like Grandpa Joe was really familiar to me. He reminded me a lot of my own grandfather who perks up and can't stop talking when he's around his grandchildren. In the story, Grandpa Joe tells all these stories—about Willy Wonka, about Prince Pondicherry. He gives Charlie a lot of attention and they seem very close. I know many grandfathers are like that—they care so deeply for their grandchildren and love to tell stories from the old days. It makes me think that Charlie's got the kind of grandfather who loves him very deeply. I think he really enjoys his time with Charlie, and maybe even that Charlie makes him feel kind of young again. You see, it helped me to think about people I know from real life to better understand the characters in the book.*

Prompts

- What do you know about the character?
- What details does the author give you?
- What does this make you think of in your own life?
- Explain how your connection helps you understand the character.
- What ideas are you having?
- That's something the author told you. What do you think about that?

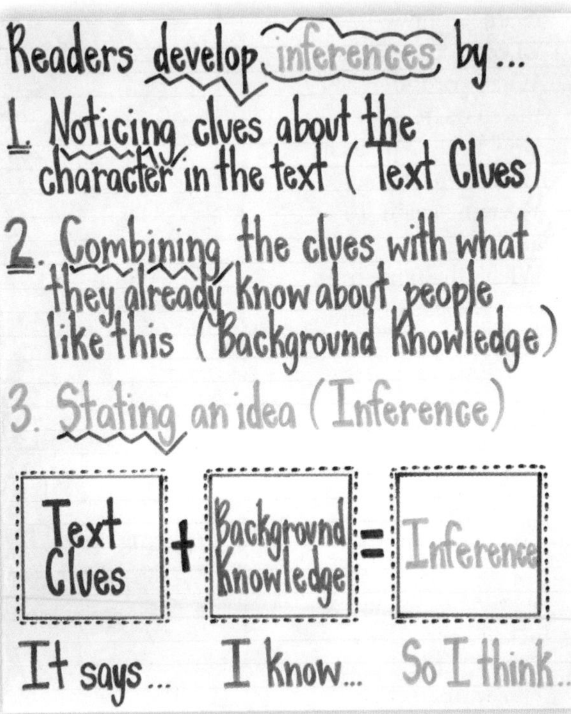

Readers develop inferences by...
1. Noticing clues about the character in the text (Text Clues)
2. Combining the clues with what they already know about people like this (Background Knowledge)
3. Stating an idea (Inference)
Text Clues
+
Background Knowledge
=
Inference
It says...
I know...
So I think...

6.10 Who's Telling the Story?

Strategy Readers ask themselves, "Who is telling this story? Is it a narrator or one of the characters in the story?" Pay close attention to the narration, and the dialogue tags. If a character is telling the story, you'll see I, me, we, my. If a narrator is telling the story you'll see he, she, they and character names. Knowing who is telling the story helps you keep track of what's happening, and helps you better understand the character(s).

Lesson Language *The narrator is a very important part of the story. The narrator can give us information about the characters by describing them. Or, if the narrator is one of the characters, you may also learn about what the character is thinking and feeling. We have to make sure we first know who it is to understand the kind of information we can get. For example, in* Horrible Harry in Room 2B *(Kline 1997) many readers often get confused. The name "Horrible Harry" is in the title—but look at how it starts:*

> Harry sits next to me in Room 2B. He looks like any other second grader except for one thing. Harry loves to do horrible things. When I first met Harry out on the playground, he had a shoebox. I asked him, "What's in there?" "Something. What's your name?" "Doug."

I noticed from the first sentence that the narrator couldn't be Harry—Harry can't sit next to Harry! In the first sentence I also see the word me *so that lets me think one of the other characters is telling the story. Then a few sentences later I see "When I"—I is another clue that it's a character narrating the story. It's not until that last sentence on the page when Harry asks for the name of the narrator that we find out the narrator is Doug. We also learned from this first page a bit about what Doug thinks of Harry—Doug thinks that Harry likes to do horrible things.*

NARRATOR
CHARACTER
"he"
"I"
"she"
"me"
"they"
"we"
names
"my"

Prompts

- Can you tell who the narrator is?
- Look for some pronouns to give you a clue.
- Take a look at dialogue tags. See what the relationship is between the speaker and the narrator.
- The narrator is the one telling the story. Look for a place where there is description.
- Yes, that's right—*he, she, they* means it's not the main character telling the story.

Who is this for?

LEVELS

H–Z+

GENRE / TEXT TYPE

fiction

SKILL

monitoring for meaning

6.11 Character Comparisons

Who is this for?

LEVELS

J–Z+

GENRE / TEXT TYPE

fiction

SKILLS

comparing and contrasting, inferring, determining importance

Strategy Think of two characters. Think of categories you'll use for comparisons (some ideas are: traits, how they handle challenges, likes and dislikes, interests, change, lesson learned). Explain what's similar within each category and/or what's different.

Lesson Language *To compare two characters, it's helpful to think in categories. In most stories, authors develop characters to have traits, they have a challenge or obstacle or problem, they are forced to respond to the problem, and they change over time. Writing about each of these aspects of the characters side by side will help you to understand them each as individuals even better. You can do this with two characters in the same book or two characters from different books. For example, if I wanted to compare Pinky from the Pinky and Rex series (Howe) and Oliver from* Oliver Button Is a Sissy *(dePaola 1979), I may start with a few categories: interests, how other characters treat each of them, their traits, the lesson(s) they learn. I'd say that Pinky and Oliver are both characters who have interests that some may consider outside the norm for boys: the color pink for Pinky and dancing for Oliver. Others treat them very differently, though. In Pinky and Rex, it's not really a big deal for his friend Rex or his parents. It is a problem in the one book in the series about bullying, though, where he gets called a "sissy." And hey—that's just like Oliver. He gets called a sissy, too. They both have similar traits, they are both brave in the face of challenge. And I think by the end they also both learn how important it is to be yourself. So, thinking in categories really helped me to say a lot about the characters, don't you think?*

Prompts

- Think about the words you'd use to describe your character.
- What problem does your character encounter?
- What's similar and different about your character's appearance?
- What interests does each character have?
- Think about the categories you can use to compare.
- Compare each character at the beginning when they come to a problem. How do they respond?
- Look back across your comparisons. Describe the similarities and differences.
- From all you've written, what seems most important when comparing these characters?

CoMPeir & comterast (+) 11/6

Peter!	Clementime!
(S) Peter is Allwys trying to get Attenton	Clementime is Allways trying to get Attention!
(D) Peter has a very uncontrolled temper. He's allways yelling	Clementime has a very controlled temper. She is Allways so calm and Polite
(S) Peter and His relantionship with Fudge is not so good He's always yelling At Him.	Clementime and Her relantionship with Her bother is not so good She's allways calling Him names I think She's Jelous!.

Hat Tip: *The Common Core Lesson Book, K–5: Working with Increasingly Complex Literature, Informational Text, and Foundational Reading Skills* (Owocki 2012)

6.12 Empathize to Understand

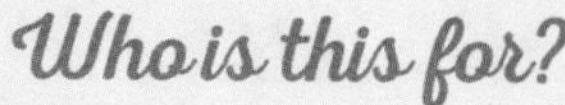

LEVELS

J–Z+

GENRE / TEXT TYPE

fiction

SKILLS

inferring, determining cause and effect

Strategy Notice what's happening to the character. Think about, for example, how other characters are treating him or her, what is going right or wrong for him or her. Imagine yourself to be in the character's position. Try to feel how the character feels, and imagine how you'd react.

Lesson Language *To really understand a character, you can try your very best to experience what the character experiences in the story. You can pay close attention to all that's going on, how people are treating the character, how the character is responding, and you can try to feel what the character might be feeling. Sometimes it helps to draw on your own life experiences that may be similar to the character but even if you don't have a similar experience to draw from, you can try to imagine what the character is going through and what it might be like. In Spinelli's book* Loser *(2002), from the very beginning, the author helps to establish the character as someone who's really out of touch. He wears a giraffe hat to school well past the age when that would be appropriate. People laugh at him and think he's strange, but he's oblivious. If I really were to empathize with him, to try to experience what he experiences, I wouldn't think about what I would do—probably notice when people are laughing and speak up for myself—I have to try to understand what he's going through. It helps me understand that he's really innocent. It makes me think that maybe his parents have been very protective of him for so long that he doesn't even notice cruelty. He has a very positive outlook—and he's happy about it, which I find so strange, but to really empathize, I need to try to understand what he's going through in his situation.*

Prompts

- How are the other characters treating him or her?
- That's what's happening. What's the effect on the character?
- Tell me what the other characters have said or done.
- How is the character feeling?
- How would you feel or react in this situation?
- Say, "In this situation, I'd feel or act _____, so I think my character is or will _____."
- You just told me the character _____. Can you empathize?
- Try to put yourself in the character's position.
- Can you understand how the character is acting? Why the character acts like that?

Hat Tip: *Following Characters into Meaning: Building Theories, Gathering Evidence* (Calkins and Tolan 2010b)

6.13 Yes, But Why?

Who is this for?

LEVELS

L–Z+

GENRE / TEXT TYPE

fiction

SKILLS

inferring, synthesizing

Strategy Understanding a motivation(s)—why it is that the character does what he or she does—helps you understand more about the kind of person he or she is. When talking about the character, don't stop at just saying what she or he does or says or thinks, try to add on your thoughts about why she or he does, says, or thinks that. Sometimes the why comes earlier in the story, other times you need to read on, and still other times you have to infer it.

Lesson Language *Think about yourself. If you went up to your mom and gave her a big hug, there would be a reason for it, right? If you snapped at your little sister—you wouldn't do it out of the blue for no reason. If you study hard for a test in school, and I asked you, "Why?" you could give me an answer, right? Well, characters are just like people in real life—they have reasons for doing the things they do. One of our jobs as readers who are trying to understand our characters is to go a step beyond just saying what they do, and try to say why they do it. Now, the tricky thing is, the character will rarely say, "The reason I'm doing this is . . ." just like we aren't always likely to explain our reasoning in real life without some prompting. So that means as readers we have to piece together the information in the story, make an inference, and try to figure it out.*

Prompts

- Name what the character does or says. Now think, why did she or he do or say that?
- Think about the character's motivation.
- You're telling me what he did, I'm wondering *why*?
- Do you have any clues from earlier that would let you know why?
- Use the words *maybe because* . . . to add on a motivation.
- The motivation you just came up with makes sense based on the story details you told me.

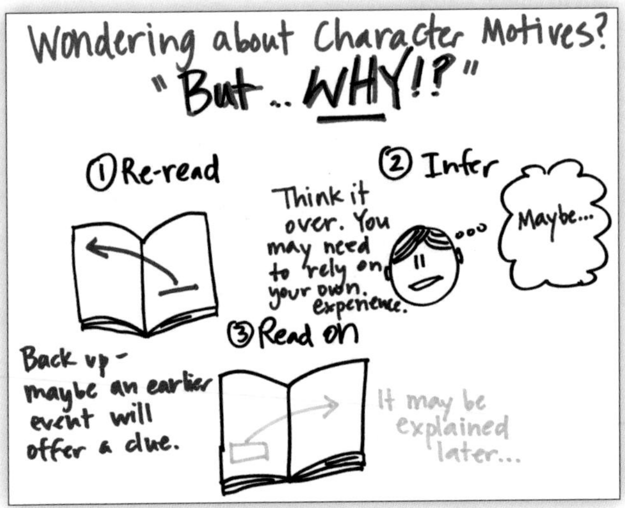

6.14 Interactions Can Lead to Inferences

Strategy Notice a place where a secondary character is interacting with a main character. Think about what a secondary character's actions are making the main character feel, think, act. Shift your perspective. Look at how the main character's actions and words are causing the secondary character to feel, think, and act. What ideas do you have about each of them, and about their relationship?

Lesson Language Because of Winn-Dixie *(DiCamillo 2000) is a great example of a book with many different characters interacting in different situations throughout the book. This would be a great book for thinking about how we can try to understand a character's perspective, and look at the interactions between that character and another one in the story to learn more about each of them. Let's think for a moment about an interaction between India Opal and her father, the night when Opal asks her father to tell her about her mother. If I look at this scene through Opal's eyes, I am thinking that she's feeling excited to learn about her mother. She's probably feeling a little sad, too, because her mother isn't with her and some of the things her father says are hard to hear. Still, the fact that her father trusts her with this information probably makes her feel sort of grown up and mature. Now, if I shift my thinking to the father's perspective, I'd say he's probably feeling nervous, and a little sad too. It's hard to bring up old, painful memories. He's also probably realizing that he can't protect Opal from the truth forever, and that may make him feel a sadness for the end of her childhood. When I think about both characters, I think this scene shows what a strong relationship they are starting to have, and that maybe their relationship is not just one of protector dad and innocent child—instead, she's starting to grow up.*

Character: Iris
Book: Iris and Walter seres
Iris loves her best friend Walter. She wants them to be best friends forever. Iris is happy when Walter is arond. Walters cousin Howie comes to visit. Howie is mean to Iris. Howie said "Does she have to do every thing with us?" Iris is sad. The next day Walter came to Iris's house. He said "Sorry". Iris said "It is ok". Iris and Walter are glad Howie is gone.
Caroline

Prompts

- Find a place where the characters are interacting.
- How is (character name) treating (character name)?
- That's a thought about one character. What do you think about their relationship?
- Explain how (character name) is causing (character name) to feel?

Who is this for?

LEVELS
M–Z+

GENRE / TEXT TYPE
fiction

SKILLS
inferring, determining cause and effect

Hat Tip: *Fresh Takes on Teaching Literary Elements: How to Teach What Really Matters About Character, Setting, Point of View, and Theme* (Smith and Wilhelm 2010)

6.15 Talk and Actions as Windows

Who is this for?

LEVELS

M–Z+

GENRE / TEXT TYPE

fiction

SKILL

inferring

Strategy Notice how the character acts while talking. Pay attention to dialogue, tags, and actions. Draw on a mental list or an actual list of character traits. Ask yourself, what kind of person acts or talks like this?

Lesson Language *When we notice not just what characters say but how they say it, we can think about them more deeply. Let's look at an example from* Circle of Gold *(Boyd 1996, page 37):*

> "Mattie, tell the truth. Your mom would never send you out shopping for clothes with only ten dollars. How much?" Toni repeated patiently.

We can notice that the author decided to tell us how Toni spoke—patiently. We can infer that she's maybe a calm, even-keeled person. She doesn't get frustrated with Mattie, the other character in the scene. A few lines later, Toni acts in a similar way when she responds to her friend with a joke and laughter (38):

> "Then I'll earn some more. Here, now I don't owe you. Thanks for not charging interest." Toni laughed.

Again, she doesn't get frustrated, and she makes jokes to lighten the mood. If the author had written "she said sarcastically" or "she said, rolling her eyes," then we might have a very different picture of who she is as a person.

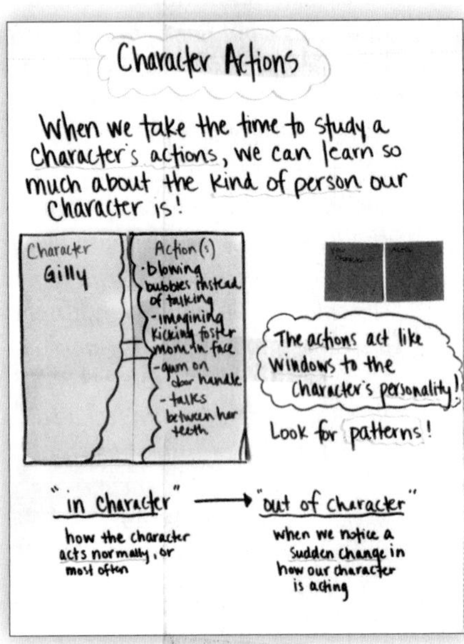

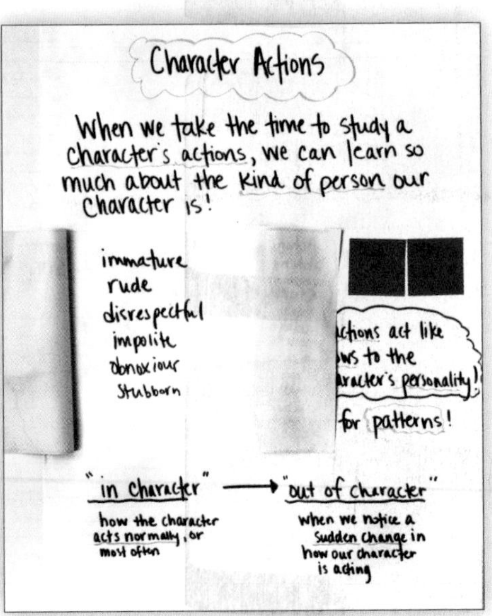

Prompts

- Can you point to a dialogue tag?
- What is the character's action now?
- Name a trait that fits that behavior.
- Look at your list.
- Think about how you would describe her.
- That's what happened; how would you describe that?
- That's a feeling; what's the trait?
- That's a trait of the character across the book.
- That's an important tag to pay attention to—it shows *how* the character said something.

6.16 Out-of-Character Character

Strategy Notice when a character behaves in an unusual way. Compare what the character says and/or does in the present scene to what the character says and/or does in past and future scenes. Figure out if the behavior is temporary or a real change, based on what the character continues to do. Form an idea or theory about the character based on what's surprised you.

Lesson Language *One meaning of the word character is the "distinctive qualities of an individual." In the stories you read, it's likely that a person in the story will display some consistent qualities. But then, you might find yourself in a scene where the character acts differently. You should figure out if that different behavior is just temporary, or if it shows a change. For example, in* Jake Drake, Bully Buster *(Clements 2001), Link is consistently bully-like. He scares Jake. He smiles in a sinister way. He name-calls. But then at the end of the story, when they are working on a project together, we find out that Link is actually afraid of talking in front of the class. We also find out that he is actually quite artistic, something that doesn't quite fit the stereotype of a bully. So if I think about these moments when he acts out of character, does it show that he's changed? No longer a bully? No, I don't think so because later on in the story Jake, the narrator, says "It's not like Link stopped being a bully" (67). So that out-of-character stuff, I think that's just showing a different side to him, a side he probably hides. It doesn't necessarily show he's changed his "character."*

Prompts

- What's unusual about the character's behavior in this part?
- What's different about how the character is acting?
- Do you think the character has changed or is just acting differently right now?
- What's your theory about the character?
- Based on all you know so far, make a theory.
- What's your thinking about why this is happening?

The Rising Tiger
usualy Rob is the type of person that never crys, but now Rob is crying because his dad shot the tiger, his hope. I think that Rob has changed from a solid hearted guy to a sweet heart. JAke S

Who is this for?

LEVELS
N–Z+

GENRE / TEXT TYPE
fiction

SKILLS
inferring, synthesizing

Hat Tip: *Comprehension Through Conversation: The Power of Purposeful Talk in the Reading Workshop* (Nichols 2006)

6.17 The Influences on Character

Who is this for?

LEVELS

N–Z+

GENRE / TEXT TYPE

fiction

SKILLS

determining cause and effect, inferring

Strategy Consider all the influences on the character—the problem(s) the character is facing, the other characters with whom he or she comes in contact, and the setting of the story. Notice how the character interacts and reacts to these different forces. What effect(s) do characters, setting, and problems have on how the character acts earlier and later in the story?

Lesson Language *Studying how a character acts in different situations helps you understand them from different perspectives. This helps you to see them as complete people—with strengths and weaknesses. When I want to think about Rich (also known in the book as "Gabriel") from Sonnenblick's* Are You Experienced? *(2013), I can consider the forces at play—his dad's moods, the problems with feeling like he's overly controlled by both his parents, wanting to impress his girlfriend, and then the setting when he goes back in time and has to acclimate to the new place and time. The way he acts in response to each of these situations helps me understand him as a more complete, nuanced character. I can track these effects in one spot or over the course of the novel.* (Continue modeling by creating a diagram like the one on this page.)

Prompts

- Think about characters first. What effects do other characters have?
- Think about setting. Name the effects.
- Think through story elements to help you consider what's impacting the character.
- Explain how the character reacts.
- I agree that person (or place or event) had an impact—we saw a change in the character.
- You thought about a bunch of different things that influence your character. You are really reading carefully!

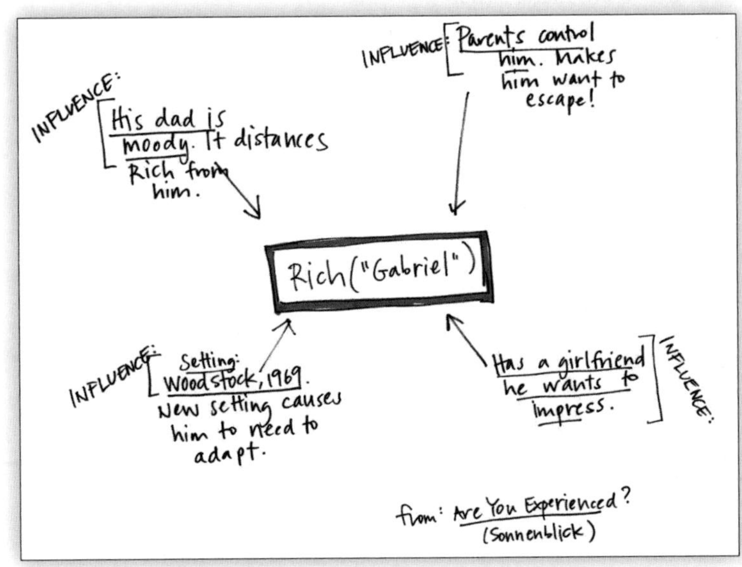
INFLUENCE:
His dad is moody. It distances Rich from him.
INFLUENCE
Parents control him. Makes him want to escape!
Rich ("Gabriel")
INFLUENCE:
Setting: Woodstock, 1969. New setting causes him to need to adapt.
Has a girlfriend he wants to impress.
INFLUENCE:
from: Are You Experienced? (Sonnenblick)

Hat Tip: *Comprehension Through Conversation: The Power of Purposeful Talk in the Reading Workshop* (Nichols 2006)

6.18 Complex Characters

Strategy Characters are not just one way. Notice how a character acts in one situation or scene. Compare it to a time when the character acts or thinks differently. Try to use multiple words that are not synonyms to describe the character.

Teaching Tip To support readers with this strategy, try offering a character trait list that clearly sets up differing character trait types. For example, for younger readers or children reading at lower levels, you could set up a two-sided trait chart with "good" traits and "bad" traits. For children who are ready to use a tool with more vocabulary words, you might organize a list of twenty-five or so words under headings such as "nice" and "mean" and "brave" and provide synonyms beneath those words.

Teaching Tip Consider creating a wall in your classroom where you hang photocopied covers of past read-alouds, with character webs or a list of traits below. Encourage discussion during the read-aloud to help children think about characters in multiple ways, and generate a list of different sides of their character and why and how they act like that. These can serve as not only a reminder that characters are complex, but also a "word wall" of sorts to help them reference vocabulary to describe the characters in books they are reading independently.

Prompts

- What trait are you thinking of?
- What kind of person acts like that?
- Can you find a trait on this list?
- Check the list. What's another word you can use to describe the character?
- Find a spot where you are learning about your character.
- Find a place where the character is talking or doing something.
- Find a different spot. Is there a different trait?
- Name a trait.
- Those traits are pretty similar. Is there a different spot in the book that might show you a different side to your character?
- That's a feeling; what's the trait?
- That's what is happening—what kind of person would do that?
- Yes, that's a trait because it tells me about the kind of person she or he is.

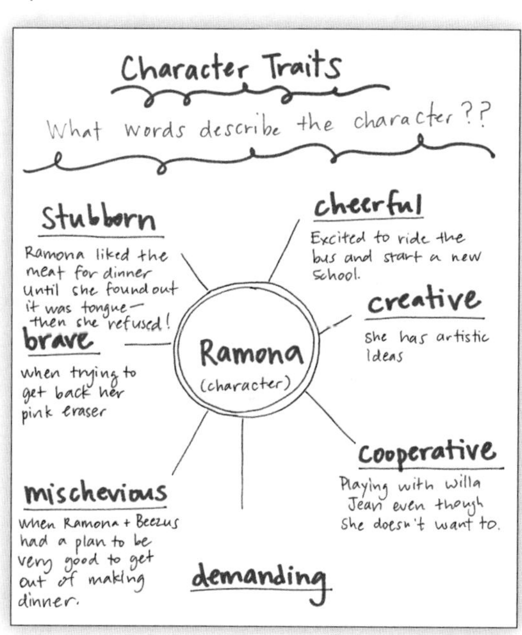

Who is this for?

LEVELS

N–Z+

GENRE / TEXT TYPE

fiction

SKILLS

inferring, comparing and contrasting

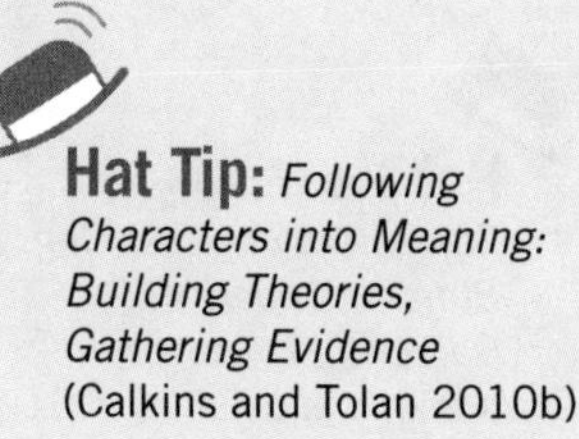

Hat Tip: *Following Characters into Meaning: Building Theories, Gathering Evidence* (Calkins and Tolan 2010b)

6.19 More Than One Side

Who is this for?

LEVELS

N–Z+

GENRE / TEXT TYPE

fiction

SKILL

inferring

Strategy Push yourself to name many traits your character has shown across the story, especially different traits in different situations. Sort a character trait list into two categories—helpful traits and problematic traits. Describe your character in sentences, showing their different sides. Use one of these sentence frames if it's helpful:

- "Sometimes my character _____, but when _____, she or he acts _____."
- "Often my character seems to _____, but sometimes _____."
- "My character is mostly _____. But he or she shows a different side when _____."

Prompts

- Think about your character at the beginning. Describe him or her.
- The trait you just said is _____. Think about if that helps him.
- The trait you just said is _____. Does acting that way cause more problems?
- Try a different part in the book. Maybe you'll find a different trait.
- It does sound like that trait is a problem!
- The trait you just found is definitely different than the other one. Where does it go?
- Do you feel like you're seeing your character from more than one side?
- Explain your character in a whole sentence.

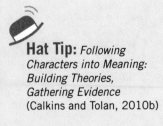

Helpful Traits	Harmful Traits
Cricit is responsible because she was realy for the first day of school.	Cricket was a smarty Pants because because she said "I already read Mr. Popper's Pegins"
Criket and Zoe are besteys.	Kricket was very careless with the book report because she didn't have the book right in front of her. So she was sort of [illegible]sponsible. Helen
Cricket was trying to fit in and not bei[illegible] left out.	Criket and Zoe are both teachers pet because they are both gud eytoshuses.
Cricket was brave because when another teacher got mad at her she said "But I didn't do it" and stood up for herself.	

Hat Tip: *Following Characters into Meaning: Building Theories, Gathering Evidence* (Calkins and Tolan, 2010b)

6.20 Conflict Brings Complexity

Strategy Think about a point of conflict in the story. Notice if the character acts differently before and after the conflict. Describe the character in a way that shows the character's complexity, or different sides of him or her.

Lesson Language *Throughout any story, characters will undoubtedly face obstacles—things that stand in their way of getting what they want, or accomplishing what they set out to do. Also, they'll be faced with conflict, or times when they have issues with another character or another force. How the character stands up to these conflicts, or deals with these obstacles, can help us to learn about them more deeply. For instance, you can think about Harry Potter and all he goes through in just the first book in the series (Rowling 1998). In the beginning of the first book, Harry deals with conflict in his own home—he's mistreated by his aunt and uncle while his cousin Dudley is spoiled. We can look at how he responds to learn something about him. He tends to keep to himself and make the best of his situation (a bedroom under the stairs). Much later at Hogwarts, when he is faced with mysterious happenings that may be dangerous, Harry responds with curiosity and bravery. These are just two small examples in a much longer book, but they both show different sides to his character. Throughout the book, collecting these sorts of character details at points of conflict, obstacle, or challenge can help you to understand the complexities of the character.*

Prompts

- Talk about a point in the story where there's conflict.
- Where does the character encounter a problem?
- What was the character like before this?
- What's the character like after?
- Describe the character to show both sides.
- How does this point of conflict show us a side to the character?

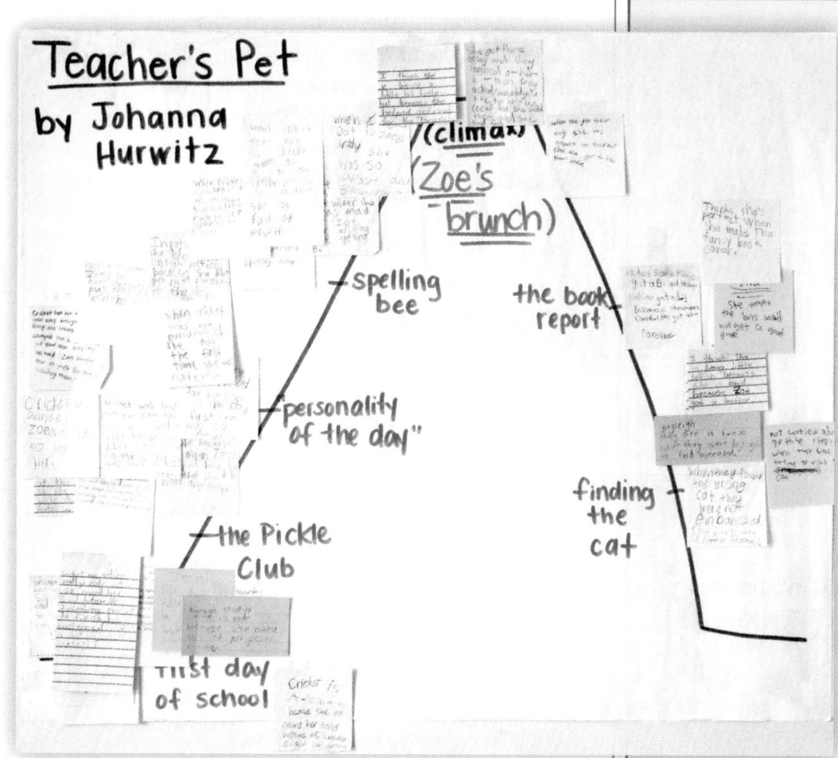

Who is this for?

LEVELS
N–Z+

GENRE / TEXT TYPE
fiction

SKILLS
inferring, synthesizing

6.21 Piling Together Traits to Get Theories

Who is this for?

LEVELS

N–Z+

GENRE / TEXT TYPE

fiction

SKILLS

inferring, synthesizing, interpreting

Hat Tip: Independent Reading Assessment: Fiction series (Serravallo 2012)

Strategy Craft a theory about your character by compiling all the smaller ideas you have. Look across character's traits, wants, desires. Pile them up. State a bigger theory about who the character really is or what she or he really wants, not just in one spot but as a pattern across the text.

Lesson Language *In more complex books, characters also get more complex. In one scene or one place in the book, the character may show one side of his or her personality. You may have an idea in that spot about who that character is. A little while later, the character may act another way. It's the pile of all these thoughts you have here and there that will give you a bigger theory. For example, in* The Great Gilly Hopkins *(Paterson 1978), we first meet Gilly, who is brash, rude, and really hard to handle. She talks back to adults and frightens some people. Later in the book, we notice how she longs for her mother, and she acts desperate, and much more mild. Toward the end of the book, we see her as a caretaker when Trotter and William Earnest are sick with the flu. We may start to pile these details about her together to get a theory. When does she act one way? When does she act another? It seems like she's rude, you might say, to keep people at arm's length. She wants to protect herself, so she'd rather people leave her alone than try to love them and get hurt. She's already been abandoned by her mom, and she can't take that kind of heartache again, you might theorize. She acts tough to protect herself, although she's really soft on the inside.*

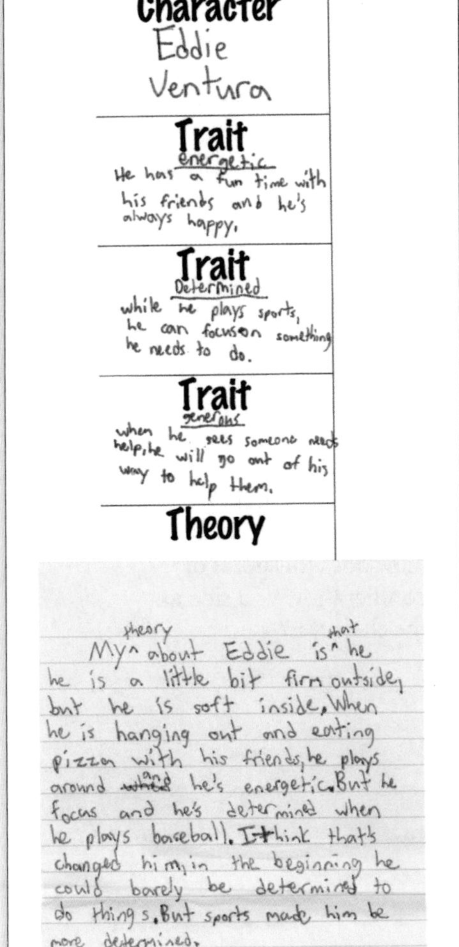

Prompts

- Name a few traits of your character, from different spots in the book.
- That's a feeling; name a trait.
- Those two traits are very similar. What's another trait?
- Yes—I think those traits show different sides to the character.
- What's a theory you have?
- Put all the traits together. Look across them. What theory do you have?
- Pile all the traits together. What are you thinking now?

6.22 Consider Character in Context

Strategy When you read about people in history, you need to think about them in the context of that time. As you read, think about who the character was, where the character was, what was happening to your character, and why. As you read, collect the clues that you think matter most and be prepared to discuss them with your book club. Through your discussion, you'll come to those details and ideas that are most important to understanding your character.

Lesson Language *When reading* The Watsons Go to Birmingham—1963 *(Curtis 1995), you could collect many clues about any of the characters and think about what's important in the context of that time. Let's try it with the big brother, Byron. We have clues about him: for one, he thought he was really cool. His younger brother calls him a "juvenile delinquent" because he's always getting into trouble. Also, he sticks up for his brother when he's being teased about his eyes. A lot of these details about who he was could work for a character who is thirteen in a novel set in present day. But then we get some details about him that clearly place him in the time period. Like when he refers to other kids as "squares" (91), when he uses a hair relaxer on his hair, or how he responds to the very significant historical event of the church bombing—in a way, the event brings out a kinder, more caring side of him. If I were going to meet with my book club, I'd bring all of these clues so that together we could work to form a theory about who he is as a person, both with the details from the historical time period and other details about him that might be true of a thirteen-year-old today.*

Prompts

- What did you learn about your character in this part?
- What details did you notice about what was happening to your character because of the time period?
- What seems unique about your character because of the time period?
- How does your character seem to fit with the time period? What does she or he do or say, how does she or he act?
- What clues about your character would help your club best get to know him or her?
- What seems most important about your character?

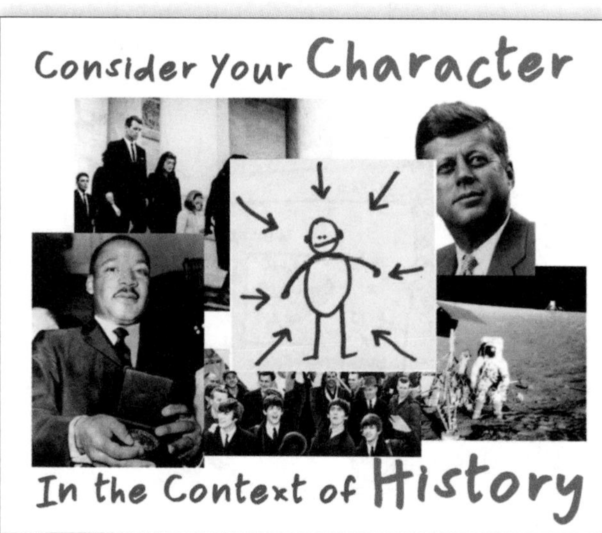
Consider Your Character
In the Context of History

Who is this for?

LEVELS

P–Z+

GENRES / TEXT TYPES

historical fiction, biography

SKILLS

determining importance, inferring

Hat Tip: *Strategies That Work: Teaching Comprehension for Understanding and Engagement*, second edition (Harvey and Goudvis 2007)

6.23 What's in a Character's Heart?

Who is this for?

LEVELS

R–Z+

GENRE / TEXT TYPE

fiction

SKILLS

inferring, synthesizing, determining importance, comparing and contrasting

Strategy Notice if the character's external actions are in or out of sync with the character's internal thinking. Consider what this says about the kind of person the character is, and what the character is really thinking or feeling. Ask yourself, "Who is this character, to others? Who does this character want to be?"

Lesson Language *Crash Coogan in* Crash *by Jerry Spinelli (2004) is a case study in conflicted actions and thoughts. As he changes, grows, and develops across the story, what's in his heart becomes more and more clear to the reader. You can get insights about him through the contradictions between how he appears to others and how he thinks and feels without showing it to others. Take the scene on page 126 where he's with his friend Mike, his partner in crime. Mike shows him a water gun he intends to use and Crash responds cautiously with, "You're gonna get suspended." For the first time, he appears to have a conscience! Mike teases him, and Crash starts to blush and then acts defensive and tough again. Then he grabs Mike's shirt, pushes it up to his chin and forces his head back. Mike backs down and admits he's "Not a dud" (127). Right after the scene, we learn what's going on in Crash's head. He says "Was Mike right? Was I a dud? . . . . Crash Coogan. The Crash Man. Suddenly the name didn't seem to fit exactly." This conflict helps us understand how he's changing, maturing, learning from his past mistakes. Though Mike still sees Crash as the tough bully he always was, Crash starts to sense something else in his heart. He wants to be different.*

Prompts

- Where is a spot where what the character says conflicts with what the character does?
- Point to a scene where you learn about the character's internal thinking.
- Look at the internal thinking alongside the action.
- Look at the dialogue alongside how it's being said.
- Who do you think the character really wants to be and be seen as?
- I can tell you picked up on the differences between thoughts and actions.
- Yes, that's a part that really shows the character's true intentions.

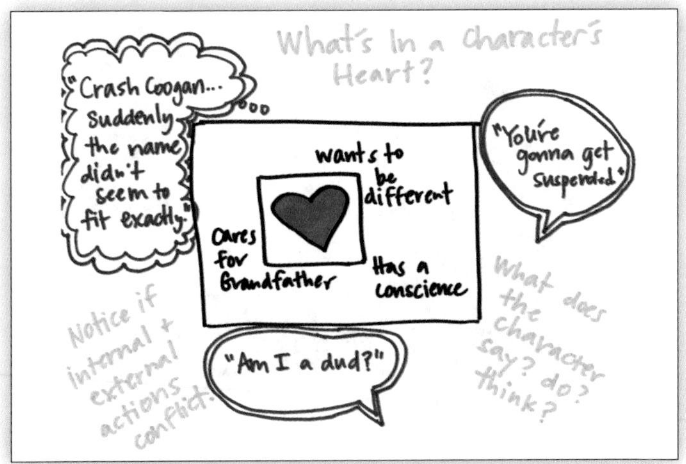

6.24 Blind Spots

Strategy Sometimes a story is told from a narrator other than the main character who lets us in on what the main character knows and doesn't. What the main character doesn't know, his or her blind spots, can teach us about the character, help us to understand other characters, and help us better understand the decisions each character makes. Ask yourself, "What are the character's blind spots? What impact do those blind spots seem to have?" Use those blind spots as a way to interpret what the character is really about.

Lesson Language *In* Loser *by Jerry Spinelli (2002), there is a great example of a character whose blind spots reveal a lot about who he is as a character. From the very beginning of the story when he arrives for his first day of school wearing a large giraffe hat, the other characters react to the absurdness of it, yet he is both unaware and unfazed. This blind spot, this lack of awareness of others' reactions about him, makes us perhaps, at first, feel sorry for him. But as we see this lack of awareness continue, we may start to envy Zinkoff. We may think how nice it is to not have to be aware of others' perceptions of you all the time. We may think about how he seems like such an innocent person, and we may start to question whether that's a good thing or not—to be more innocent than peers and to keep that innocence well past when one should. Is it a good thing that he doesn't seem to grow up? As his life in elementary school progresses, others' reaction to him goes from that of shock to merely ignoring him, yet he stays the same. At the end of the book, we see another instance of a blind spot—the fact that he goes looking for a girl who has already been found and misinterprets the search parties as looking for her when they are really looking for him. He maintains his innocent aloofness through all of this as well, searching for her in freezing cold and on the edge of death. Through this, it is actually the other characters who change in response to him—he's not quite a hero, but he does begin to be noticed in a positive way for the first time ever, changing from "loser" to "nobody" to "somebody."*

Prompts

- What does the character seem to be aware of?
- What does the character seem to be missing?
- What do the character's blind spots tell you?
- Yes—that's a blind spot. Now talk about what ideas you have about the character.
- What is that making you think?

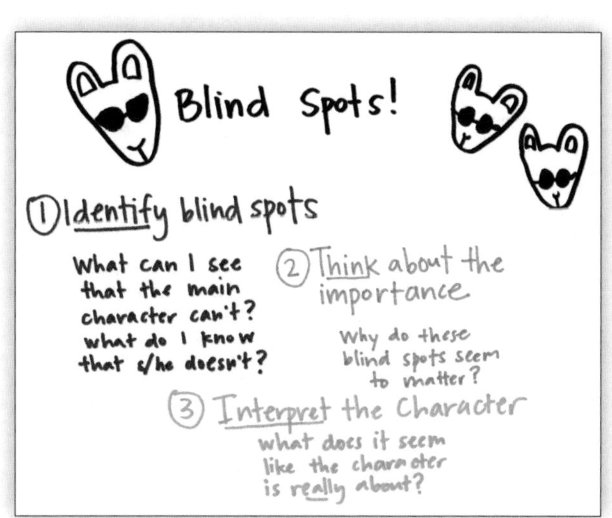

Who is this for?

LEVELS

R–Z+

GENRE / TEXT TYPE

fiction

SKILLS

inferring, interpreting, synthesizing

Supporting Comprehension in Fiction

Understanding Themes and Ideas

Why is this goal important?

Stories are rich with issues and ideas, many of which don't always jump off the page at you. It takes imagination, inference, determining importance, and ability to synthesize all that happens in a story to try to understand the ideas that are hiding. As Stephanie Harvey and Anne Goudvis (2000) explain, "Themes in books are the underlying ideas, morals, or lessons that give the story its texture, depth, and meaning. The themes are rarely written out in the story. We infer themes. Themes often make us feel angry, sad, guilty, joyful, frightened. We tell kids that we are likely to feel themes in our gut" (109).

Although some may argue that the text has a theme, which the author intended, and it's the reader's job to figure it out, I'm a bit more in literary theorist Rosenblatt's (1978) camp when it comes to interpreting themes. I think that interpretation needs to be rooted in the details of the text, but that it's really also about the interaction the reader has with the text. This means that two different readers reading the same story may interpret theme differently, because the prior knowledge and experiences that each of them has is unique.

Why is it important to teach children to think about themes and ideas and symbolism? When children are taught to think with more depth about the reading, that's when the reading really begins to matter. It's no longer about noticing the next event on the plot line, it becomes about letting stories help us see our world, feel something, question our own beliefs.

Although at early elementary levels, themes are often easily accessible ("Friends are important"), as students progress through more challenging texts, the themes often get to be more and more like life itself—multidimensional, contradictory, messy. Symbolism starts to appear in some stories around levels P/Q, and at these levels students can understand more of the text when they consider how the people, places, or objects represent something beyond their physical description.

Put simply, although thinking deeply about text may be an enjoyable part of reading literature, it's also fair to say that without understanding themes, ideas, symbolism, or social issues that show up in the text, it could be that you misunderstand or at the very least *miss* a lot of what the story is about.

How do I know if this goal is right for my student?

As with the other comprehension goals, it's important that you keep in mind the intersection between the task (determining theme or interpreting symbols) and the text (reading level) in mind when you're assessing your students.

For example, in many primary-level texts, or up until about level K/L, a lesson is clearly connected to what the character learns and it is sometimes even explicitly stated in the text. Teachers can look to see if children know where to look, and if they can repeat the theme in the same language the author uses.

By levels children typically read in late second and throughout third grade (M–P), it's more likely that the theme isn't explicit, and readers would need to infer to figure it out. In these more challenging texts, I look to see if students can name a theme as a sentence (i.e., "You can create your own family by surrounding yourself with people who love you") rather than just a single word (i.e., "Family").

Beginning around levels R/S, texts often have multiple themes, and I might ask a student "What else?" or "Do you have any other ideas?" to see if they are picking up on more than just the most dominant theme.

At all levels, I think it's important to consider whether the child's interpretation encompasses all or most of the story, or if the student is just picking up on something that happened on one page or in one scene (themes that take into account the whole book show deeper understanding). With children reading at early fourth-grade levels (P/Q), I would also ask about symbolism and look to see whether they are able to articulate how a concrete object represents an abstract idea (Fountas and Pinnell 2010b; Serravallo 2012).

To assess how students understand themes and ideas, I find it helpful to ask students to answer questions in an independent-level text, either during conferences, in a read-aloud, or in a text they read silently. Some questions that I tend to use include:

- What do you think this story is *really about*?
- What is a message/lesson/theme you take away from this story?
- What did you learn about from reading this story?
- What might the ____ symbolize?

It is likely that you aren't assessing just themes and ideas, but rather that this is part of a more holistic assessment of fiction comprehension. Therefore, I would choose this goal for a student once the student has demonstrated an ability to understand plot and setting, character, and vocabulary with relative consistency and when the student is ready to do more deep, critical thinking about his or her stories.

Strategies for Understanding Themes and Ideas at a Glance

Strategy		Levels	Genres/ Text Types	Skills
7.1	Notice a Pattern and Give Advice	D–K	Patterned book with characters	Inferring, synthesizing
7.2	The Difference Between Plot and Theme	G–Z+	Fiction	Inferring, determining importance
7.3	We Can Learn (and Give Advice) Based on How Characters Treat Each Other	I–Z+	Fiction	Inferring, determining importance
7.4	What Can Characters Teach Us?	J–Z+	Fiction	Inferring, determining importance
7.5	Look Out for What Characters Teach Each Other	J–Z+	Fiction	Inferring, determining importance
7.6	What Are You Left With?	J–Z+	Fiction	Inferring, determining importance
7.7	Mistakes Can Lead to Lessons	J–Z+	Fiction	Inferring, determining importance
7.8	Feelings Help Us Learn	J–Z+	Fiction	Inferring, determining Importance
7.9	Compare Lessons Across Books in a Series	J–Z+	Fiction	Inferring, determining importance, comparing and contrasting
7.10	Actions, Outcomes, Response	J–Z+	Fiction	Inferring, determining importance, synthesizing
7.11	Book-to-Book Connections	K–Z+	Fiction	Inferring, synthesizing
7.12	Dig Deeper to Find a Story's Topics	K–Z+	Fiction	Inferring, determining importance, synthesizing
7.13	From Seed to Theme	K–Z+	Fiction	Inferring, interpreting
7.14	Find Clues About Theme in the Blurb	K–Z+	Fiction	Inferring, determining importance, synthesizing
7.15	The Real World in My Book	N–Z+	Fiction	Inferring, determining importance
7.16	Stories Teach Us About Life Issues	N–Z+	Fiction	Inferring, determining importance
7.17	Readers Ask Themselves Questions	N–Z+	Fiction	Inferring, determining importance
7.18	Character Change Can Reveal Lessons	N–Z+	Fiction	Inferring, determining importance
7.19	Symbols Repeat	N–Z+	Fiction	Inferring, determining importance
7.20	Respond to Issues That Repeat	N–Z+	Fiction	Inferring, determining importance
7.21	Aha Moment	N–Z+	Fiction	Inferring, synthesizing, determining importance
7.22	Identifiers, Identity, and Ideas	Q–Z+	Fiction	Inferring, determining importance
7.23	Secondary Sages	Q–Z+	Fiction	Inferring, determining importance
7.24	Titles Can Be Telling	R–Z+	Fiction	Inferring, determining importance

7.1 Notice a Pattern and Give Advice

Who is this for?

LEVELS

D–K

GENRE / TEXT TYPE

patterned book with characters

SKILLS

inferring, synthesizing

Strategy Notice what the character does over and over. Think, "Should he or she be doing that?" Give advice to the character. Think about if that advice is helpful for your life, too.

Lesson Language *In this book* Bedtime Fun *(Newkirk 2000), a little girl starts out by saying she doesn't want to go to bed, and does all she can to avoid it. Remember? She tries to stand on her head, she jumps on her bed and plays with her bear. Over and over, she keeps pretending like it's playtime, not bedtime! If I gave her advice I'd say, "You shouldn't be playing, you should be going to bed! It's important to go to bed at bedtime." That's good advice for this character, but it's also good advice in my life for my five-year-old who always tries to get out of bedtime, but then is so tired in the morning. In fact, I'm going to read her this story so maybe she'll learn it!*

Prompts

- What does the character do over and over?
- What's the pattern here?
- What would you tell the character?
- Give advice.
- Start with, "You should ____."

Hat Tip: *What Readers Really Do: Teaching the Process of Meaning Making* (Barnhouse and Vinton 2012)

7.2 The Difference Between Plot and Theme

Strategy When we want to figure out a theme in a story, we can stop and jot an important note about what's happening in the plot, and then we can infer by asking ourselves, "What's the big idea about what's happening in this story?"

Lesson Language *Plot is what happens in the story, and theme represents the bigger ideas of the story. The plot carries the big ideas. Plot is made up of events you can track. Themes are rarely stated and must be inferred. In* Moving Day Surprise *(Stolberg 2003), you might say that the story is mostly about a boy who is nervous to move to a new apartment because he'd miss his friends and his school. But at the end of the story he finds out that he's moving to a large apartment in the same building so it's not as much change as he thought. What the story is about—the important events—is the plot. But to say a big idea or a theme, it's important to think beyond just what happens. I might say it's about how it's hard to change. Or maybe I could say, "Sometimes we worry when we don't need to." Or even, "It's great to get a pleasant surprise!" These are all ideas—they came from my head—and they are not the actual things that happen in the story, although I have to think about what happens to get my idea.*

Prompts

- What's happening?
- What's most important in all you just told me?
- What is your idea about what's happening?
- What else do you think is a possible big idea from the story?

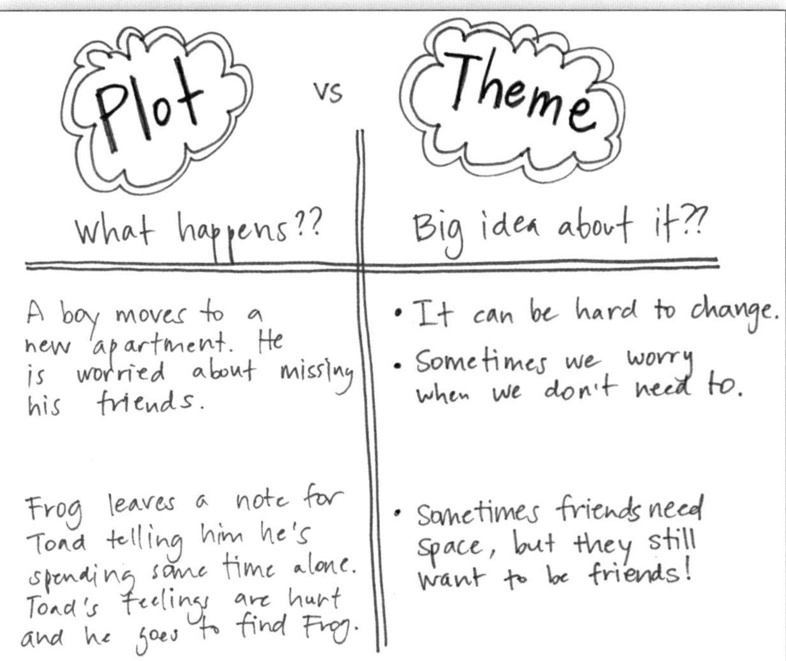

Who is this for?

LEVELS

G–Z+

GENRE / TEXT TYPE

fiction

SKILLS

inferring, determining importance

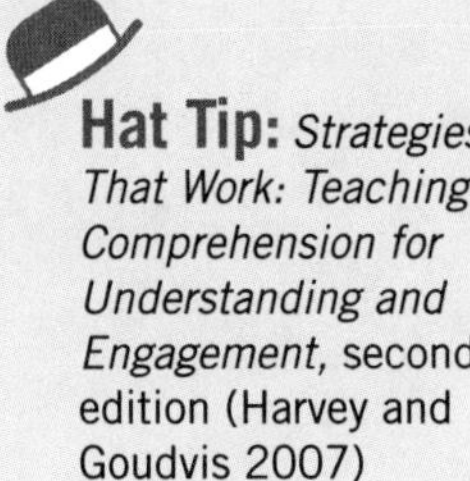

Hat Tip: *Strategies That Work: Teaching Comprehension for Understanding and Engagement*, second edition (Harvey and Goudvis 2007)

7.3 We Can Learn (and Give Advice) Based on How Characters Treat Each Other

Who is this for?

LEVELS

I–Z+

GENRE / TEXT TYPE

fiction

SKILLS

inferring, determining importance

Strategy Notice how the characters treat each other, especially in spots where their behavior is surprising. What would you tell the character to do? Give advice by saying, "You should . . ." The advice you give can be a lesson you take away from the story.

Lesson Language *Sometimes characters in books treat other characters in ways that surprise us, perhaps because it's not how we would have treated someone in real life. This surprise might be a good thing (because the character acted with kindness or bravery or thoughtfulness) or a bad thing (because the character was selfish or mean or rude). For example, think about Sharon in* Freckle Juice *(Blume 2014). Perhaps you were surprised when Sharon lied to Nicky to get him to buy a disgusting juice that was supposed to help him grow freckles. She deceived him during his most hopeful moments! I can imagine myself jumping right in the story and giving her some advice. I might say, "Sharon, try to think about how others are going to feel based on your actions." Or "Sharon, sometimes people need a friend to talk to, not someone to trick and lie to them" or "Sharon, you should help Nicky see that he's great just the way he is—he doesn't need freckles." The advice you'd give a character could be a lesson that you could take away from the story, too.*

Prompts

- Find a spot where the character surprises you.
- Notice how the character is treating another character.
- What would you tell that character?
- Say the advice you'd give.
- So, based on that advice, what might *you* learn from this story?

Essence

IF I could talk to Edward I Would Say "your team did good you tried your best And you Practisted A lot. You did not want to let your teacher down And he was happy because you tried your best And did All that you Could do And Im very very happy For you. You could OF Practisted A little harder. You could have gave up And let the other team win but iF you would have done that you would not have made your teacher happy And you did make him happy And I think that mr. Lester is happy For you And even the team.

7.4 What Can Characters Teach Us?

Strategy List out some of the positive traits of a character in your book. Think about when your character acts that way, and why. Then think, "What can this character teach me about living, to be a better person?"

Lesson Language *Sometimes you find people in your life who you look up to. Perhaps the person shows courage, even when something is scary. Perhaps the person is generous, even when she doesn't have much to give. Perhaps he is patient, even during times when you'd be easily frustrated. These people we look up to like role models can inspire us to be better, and do better. Characters in our books can do the same. Like people, they have traits. We can look at the situations where certain traits show up and think about what those traits can teach us. For example, in the story "Neighbors"* (Poppleton, *Rylant 1997), Poppleton gets so frustrated by Cherry Sue that he soaks her with a hose! Not nice. But, we might notice what Poppleton does right away—he feels awful and apologizes to Cherry Sue. We might notice that that takes courage to do that—to admit when you've made a mistake. We might think, "Poppleton taught me that if you are getting frustrated with someone, it's better to talk about it than to do something you might regret" or "Poppleton taught me that everybody makes mistakes sometimes, and when you make a mistake you should apologize." Or if I were to think about his trait, I might say, "Sometimes you have to have courage to speak up and fix a problem between your friend and yourself."*

Prompts

- Find a spot where the character shows a good trait.
- How would you describe how the character is acting here?
- What can the character teach you?
- What are you learning from this character?
- You can try, "____ taught me that if ____, you should ____."
- You can try, "____ is acting like ____, so I'm learning ____."
- Think about that trait. What can you learn?

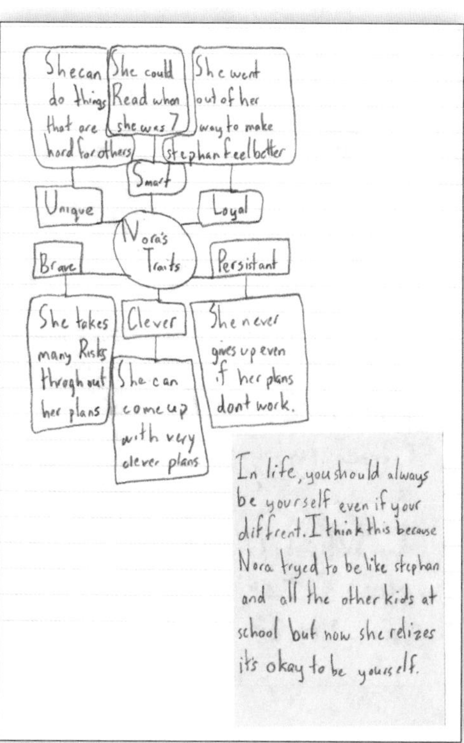

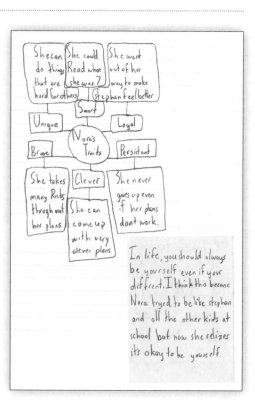

Who is this for?

LEVELS

J–Z+

GENRE / TEXT TYPE

fiction

SKILLS

inferring, determining importance

Hat Tip: *Reading with Meaning: Teaching Comprehension in the Primary Grades*, second edition (Miller 2012)

7.5 Look Out for What Characters Teach Each Other

Who is this for?

LEVELS

J–Z+

GENRE / TEXT TYPE

fiction

SKILLS

inferring, determining importance

Strategy Other characters can help teach the main character a lesson. Notice a place where the character slows down to explain something to another character. Then think, "What does the main character learn?" Try to put the lesson in your own words.

Lesson Language *In beginning chapter books, the character will often come out and teach another character something. In the final story in Lobel's* Days with Frog and Toad *(1979), Toad gets upset when Frog goes off to be by himself. When Frog realizes he upset Toad, he explains, "This morning when I woke up I felt good because I have you for a friend. I wanted to be alone. I wanted to think about how fine everything is." And then Toad replies, "Oh. I guess that is a very good reason for wanting to be alone." Right there on the page, the character teaches another character something, and the character says what he learns. I could learn something from that, too. I might say, "Just because a friend wants to be alone, it doesn't mean he doesn't want to be your friend anymore." Or, "All friends need space from each other, sometimes."*

Prompts

- Can you find a spot where one character explains something to another character?
- Check the end of the story.
- Now say it in your own words—what did you learn?
- That's what the character said. What did you learn?

7.6 What Are You Left With?

Strategy Reread the last paragraph or page. Think about what the author leaves you to think about by studying the narrator's or a character's final words. Say it like a lesson.

Lesson Language *The end of the book is often where the author wraps it all up. All the problems get resolved, we find out what happens with the character, and we can also, if we're really, really paying attention, find the lesson in the last words. Sometimes it's the narrator, sometimes it's the character, but often somebody says something that helps us think about what the whole story is about. For example, in* Ivy and Bean *(Barrows 2007), the story ends with the two friends, who resisted playing with each other in the beginning of the book, saying this:*

> "See you tomorrow."
>
> "See you tomorrow."
>
> And the day after that, and the day after that, Bean added in her mind.
>
> Ivy, holding her mother's hand in the middle of the street, turned around to look at Bean. "And the day after that," she said. (113)

I can be the kind of reader who doesn't just breeze past the last words, but stops to think about if they are holding a lesson. What's happening here is that the friends are promising to see each other tomorrow and the next day and the next day. These same two people who didn't want to play together earlier in the book. What this teaches me is that people who are really different can end up being really good friends.

Prompts

- Reread the ending.
- Look again at the last paragraph (or page). Does the narrator lead you to a lesson?
- That's what it says at the end. Try to say the lesson in your own words.
- What's the last thought you have after reading the end of the book?
- Explain how the whole story ends up. So what's the lesson?
- Explain how the problem was solved. So what's the lesson?

Who is this for?

LEVELS
J–Z+

GENRE / TEXT TYPE
fiction

SKILLS
inferring, determining importance

7.7 Mistakes Can Lead to Lessons

Who is this for?

LEVELS

J–Z+

GENRE / TEXT TYPE

fiction

SKILLS

inferring, determining importance

Strategy Think about what mistakes the character made. Then, think about what he or she learned from that. You can use the sentence starters:

- "When you (or people) ____, you (or they) should or shouldn't learn ____."
- "You don't have to ____ to ____."
- "It takes ____ to ____."
- "Try to (or not to) ____ when you ____."

Prompts

- What mistake did the character make?
- Look for a place where the character feels badly about what he or she did—that might clue you in to the mistake.
- Let's think about how the character acted right after.
- Do you think the character learned?
- Try to say it like a lesson.
- Try to say it like a lesson that's not just about this book, but that's about life in general.

Mistakes Can Lead to Lessons

Title	Character's Mistake	Possible Lessons
The Meanest Thing to Say (Cosby)	Little Bill thinks he needs to be mean to a new boy to win a game.	• "You don't have to be mean to fit in." • "It takes courage to stand up to your friends."
Pinky + Rex and the Perfect Pumpkin (Howe)	Rex smashed the pumpkin because she felt left out and jealous.	• "When you feel upset, try to talk to people you trust."
Stuart Goes to School (Pennypacker)	Stuart tries to throw away his lucky magical cape.	• "Try not to give up too quickly when things don't go your way."

7.8 Feelings Help Us Learn

Strategy Pause in a place where the character's feelings change. Notice what causes the character's feelings to change. What did she or he learn in that moment of the story?

Lesson Language *When a character's feelings change—from bad to better, or from good to worse, often the thing that made the feelings change can teach a lesson. Usually, the character learned something and perhaps you, the reader, can learn too. In* Kenny and the Little Kickers *(Marzollo 1992), Kenny is a kid who would rather sit on the couch and watch TV than try something new—especially something like soccer, which he doesn't feel like he'd be good at. He's mopey and wants to say no to his father and coach, but he doesn't. But at the end, when he makes the winning goal and feels successful, he learns something. We might say he learned that trying new things can be rewarding. That's something we, the readers, can learn too.*

Prompts

- What's the character feeling at the beginning? When does it change?
- Find a place where the character's feelings change for better. For worse.
- Let's reread that spot with the change in feelings.
- What do you think the character learned?
- What could you learn?
- What does the change in feelings teach you?

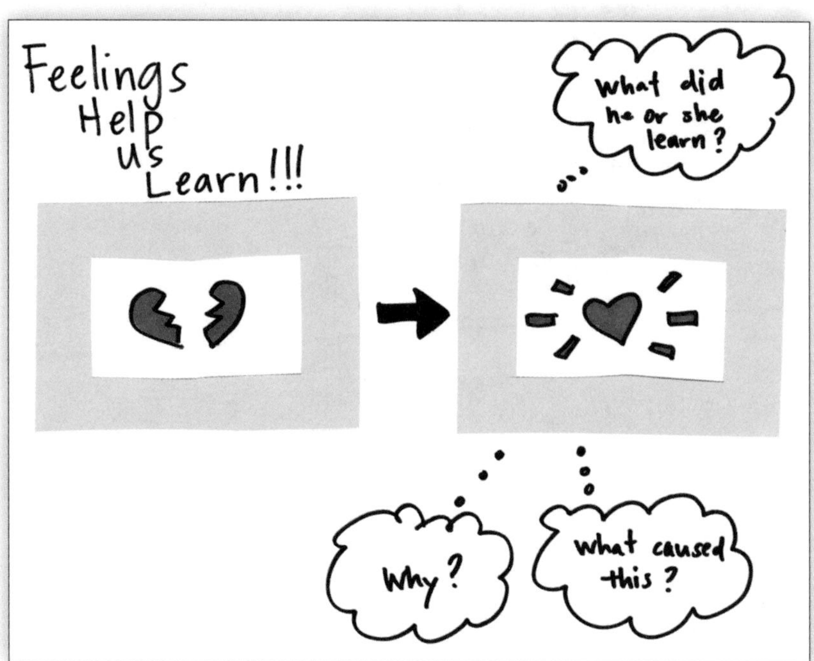

Who is this for?

LEVELS

J–Z+

GENRE / TEXT TYPE

fiction

SKILLS

inferring, determining importance

7.9 Compare Lessons Across Books in a Series

Who is this for?

LEVELS

J–Z+

GENRE / TEXT TYPE

fiction

SKILLS

inferring, determining importance, comparing and contrasting

Strategy In a series, characters are the same but lessons learned often vary. Compare what the character learned in one book in the series to what the character learned in another book in the series.

Lesson Language *We already know that books in the same series have a lot of things in common—the main characters and sometimes even the secondary characters are the same, and sometimes the plots follow a common pattern. Usually, though, the character learns different lessons. One way to figure out the lesson in one book is to compare it to books across a series. Howe's Pinky and Rex series is one great example. Across the series, you might learn about how to deal with being jealous of a new baby sibling, what to do when confronted with a bully, or even how to handle jealousy when your best friend stops giving you attention.*

Prompts

- Put two books in the same series side by side.
- What's different in the lessons that the character learns in each of these books?
- What did the character seem to learn in this one? How about this one?
- Talk about what each book is mostly about. Now what does the character learn in each?

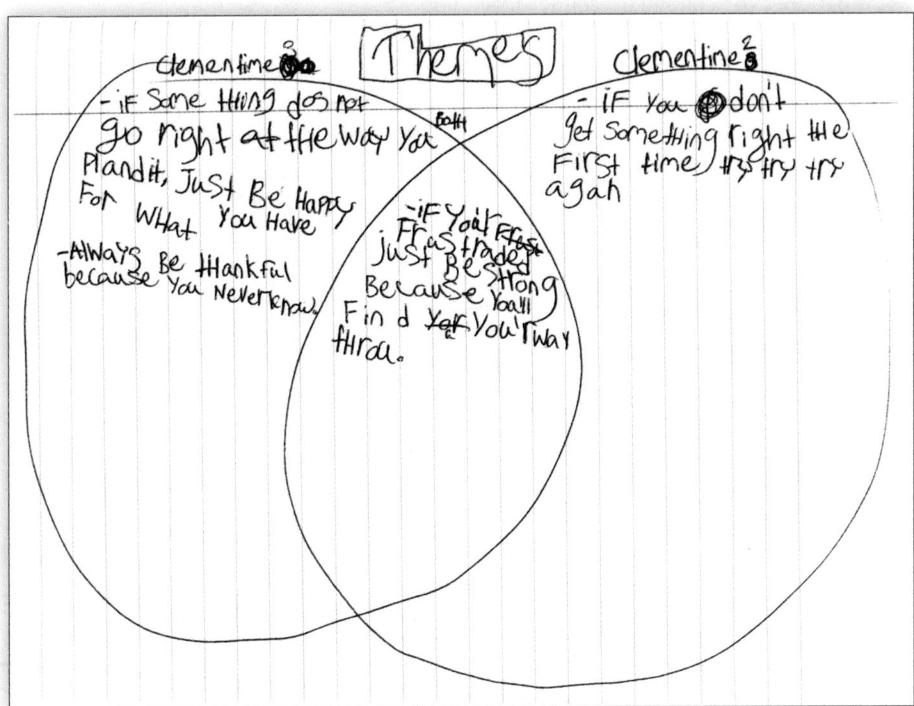

Themes
Clementine
-if Same thing dos not go right at the way You Pland it, Just Be Happy For What You Have
-Always Be thankful because You Never know
Clementine
-if You don't get Something right the First time try try try agah
Both
-if You're Frustrated Just Be strong Because You'll Find Your way thru.

7.10 Actions, Outcomes, Response

Strategy Understand that the actions of one character can have effects on other characters. Consider the character's actions and the outcome. Think, "How do other characters respond? What can we learn from their response?"

Lesson Language *When I read* Poppleton *(Rylant 1997)—you know, the one where Cherry Sue keeps inviting Poppleton over to eat toasted cheese and spaghetti—I noticed an action that seems important. Poppleton takes the hose and sprays Cherry Sue with water! Remember that part? So Poppleton (that's the character) sprays or hoses (that's the action) Cherry Sue (that's the other character). Now, I'm going to turn to the page where Cherry Sue responds. Responds just means—what does she do afterward because of the action? I notice that she acted surprised and asks him why he did it, and then that starts a conversation between them. This makes me think that a lesson in this story might be, "You should talk to your friends when you have a problem." That's what Cherry Sue did and it seemed to help. So I think that's something I can learn from the story, too.*

Prompts

- How does this character affect that one?
- Name two characters who interact often. What can you say about how one affects the other?
- Name the character's actions.
- Name the effect on the other character.
- What lesson are you learning based on how one treats the other?
- Try, "(Character) acts (describe behavior) toward (character), and that's teaching me . . ."

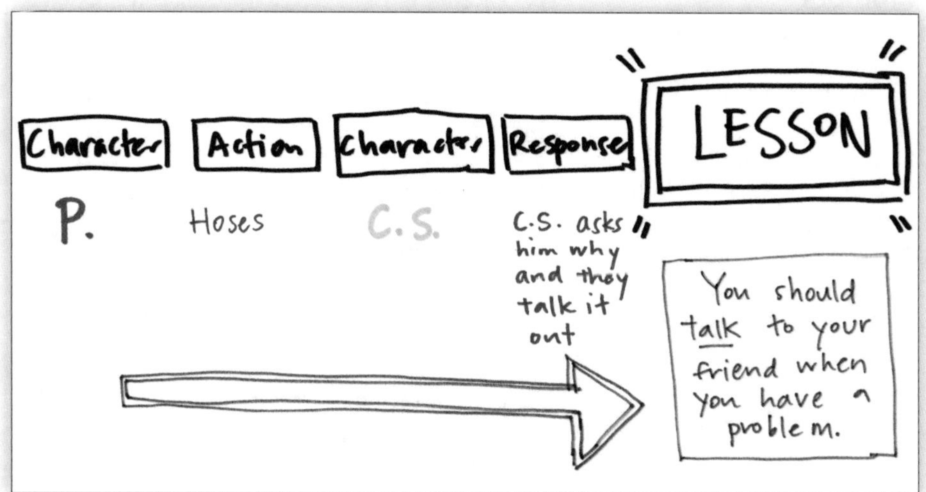

Who is this for?

LEVELS

J–Z+

GENRE / TEXT TYPE

fiction

SKILLS

inferring, determining importance, synthesizing

7.11 Book-to-Book Connections

Who is this for?

LEVELS

K–Z+

GENRE / TEXT TYPE

fiction

SKILLS

inferring, synthesizing

Hat Tip: Independent Reading Assessment: Fiction series (Serravallo 2012)

Strategy Think about other books that remind you of a book you're reading. Remind yourself of what you learned from those other books. Think about whether any of the lessons from other books you've read apply to the book you're currently reading.

Lesson Language *When I finish a book, the whole story is sometimes swirling in my mind. I'm thinking about characters, changes, problems and solutions, all the events that happened. I usually want to also think about what I learned. I do this to try to carry a message or lesson from the book into my life. When I try to do this, thinking about other books it reminds me of sometimes helps. For example, when I finished reading* Baseball Ballerina *(Cristaldi 1992), a story about a girl who loves baseball but whose mom wants her to do ballet, I made an instant connection to another story—* Oliver Button Is a Sissy *(dePaola 1979). Even though Baseball Ballerina is a girl, and Oliver is a boy, they both had parents who wanted them to be something and do something different than what they wanted. I already jotted down a message about Oliver Button in my notebook. I wrote, "This story is really about how you should be who you really are, and not worry about what others think." So, when I think about Baseball Ballerina, do I think that would work as a lesson for this story, too? I actually do. At the end of the story, she uses her baseball talents—being able to catch something that flies high in the air—and it's what everyone celebrates about her. She was also worried that her baseball teammates would make fun of her for doing ballet, but they were supportive after all. I do really think that just like Oliver, Baseball Ballerina learns how important it is to be herself.*

Read Aloud Titles	THEMES	
CRASH	Friends can come from unexpected places.	Find something to respect + appreciate in everyone.
THOSE SHOES	what you need is more important than what you want.	You should put friends ahead of "stuff!"
Days With Frog + Toad	Even though you're different you can still be friends.	It's important to communicate.
PINKY and REX and the BULLY	Stand up for yourself.	Be true to who you are.

Prompts

- Check the chart—what are some other books we've read that are similar to this one?
- What other books does this one remind you of? Why?
- Look at the lessons we learned from those.
- What lessons from that book apply to this one as well?
- Can you make a connection with lessons?

7.12 Dig Deeper to Find a Story's Topics

Strategy To determine a story's theme, it helps to first name some topics—one-word issues, ideas, or concepts. It is likely that any one story will connect to more than one topic. You can think about the struggles that character is going through, the way the story ends up, and/or the title to help you figure out what those words might be.

Teaching Tip This is a great strategy to introduce during whole-class read-aloud, and then to build a chart like the one pictured on this page for students to use as a reference. Although some may refer to these one-word topics as themes, I prefer to teach children that a theme is something stated as a sentence, like a claim or thesis statement. You may see strategy 7.13 for an idea of how to build upon this naming of a single word, to a complete idea about the book.

This strategy, as with others, can be adapted for different levels. The words you would include on a chart for second graders reading at K–M might be *friendship* and *loneliness*, whereas for eighth graders it might be more like *innocence* or *authority*.

Prompts

- Can you think of one word that fits with this story?
- Think about the character's problem. If you said it in one word, what would it be?
- Check the chart of words that are common topics in books. Do any fit with this one?
- Explain your thinking.
- You might say, "I think it could be ____ (topic) because ____."
- Think about how the story ends. What's the last thing you're left thinking about?

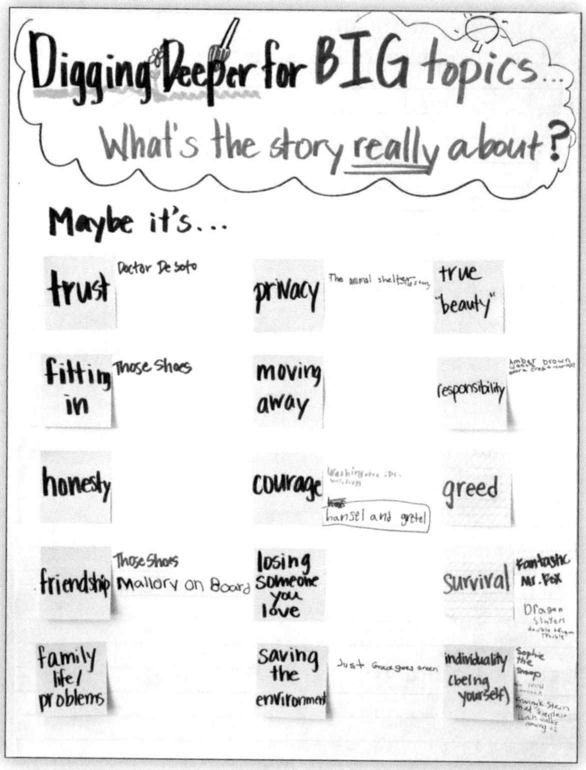

Who is this for?

LEVELS

K–Z+

GENRE / TEXT TYPE

fiction

SKILLS

inferring, determining importance, synthesizing

7.13 From Seed to Theme

Who is this for?

LEVELS

K–Z+

GENRE / TEXT TYPE

fiction

SKILLS

inferring, interpreting

Strategy As you read, think about the topics that are showing up in your book. Say it first as one word (a seed). Next, ask yourself, "What's the author saying about this big idea?" and use that word in a sentence. Use the theme board as help for how it sounds to say a theme.

Teaching Tip If students struggle with the first part of this strategy, see strategy 7.12.

Lesson Language *Any one book can be about many things. To name a theme, it sometimes helps to start with a single word that is like the seed of that theme. For example, I could talk about* Are You There, God? It's Me Margaret *(Blume 1970) with the following seeds (and many more!): change, growing up, moving, friendship, fitting in, religion, jealousy. But those one- or two-word phrases are just the seeds of the theme. I have to ask, "What' the author saying about this?" and say the theme as a sentence. So it might be: "Many girls feel pressure to fit in with their peers."*

Prompts

- List some topics that are showing up in your book.
- Let's check the chart of the topics that typically show up in books. Which apply to your book?
- Let's think about what the author says about this topic.
- What do you think the lesson might be?
- Use the topic word in your lesson.

Theme: message or lesson you can learn from a story.

Common topics:

- courage
- dreams
- kindness
- fears
- being yourself
- equality
- hope
- differences
- friendship
- hard work
- honesty
- love
- family
- jealousy
- not giving up
- doing the right thing
- acceptance
- peace

Ask yourself:

- What did the character(s) learn?
- How did the character(s) grow or change?
- Why did the character(s) act this way?

State the THEME as a sentence:

- Think: So WHAT about the topic?

Hat Tip: *Strategies That Work: Teaching Comprehension for Understanding and Engagement*, second edition (Harvey and Goudvis 2007)

7.14 Find Clues About Theme in the Blurb

Strategy Read the back cover blurb. If you read it before reading the story, you might have a hunch about what theme or two might be in the story. If you read it after or while reading, you can think about what happens in the story and how the blurb connects. Then ask yourself, "What does this story teach me?"

Lesson Language *Back cover blurbs often give the reader a gist of the story—just enough to entice us to really want to read it and find out what will happen. Listen to this blurb from the back of* Julian's Glorious Summer *(Cameron 1987):*

> Bicycles—shiny, whizzing, wobbly bicycles—scare Julian more than lions or tigers. But how can he tell that to his best friend, Gloria? She can already ride with no hands. So instead of telling the truth, Julian makes up a little fib. And he almost gets away with it—until his little fib backfires and Julian finds himself in the biggest, most confounding fix ever.

Doesn't that sound like a great story? It makes me want to read it to find out what the biggest fix ever is going to be. But even before reading, I have a hunch that something about the importance of being honest with your friends might come up in this story. I got that hint because I know that he's struggling with telling Gloria a fib that ends up backfiring, which means it's going to be a problem for him—and we know that problems are often also clues to the lessons characters learn.

Prompts

- Read the blurb
- What do you think the character might learn?
- What might a problem in the story be?
- Based on the problem, what might the lesson be?
- Think about how the blurb connects to the whole story you read. What's most important?

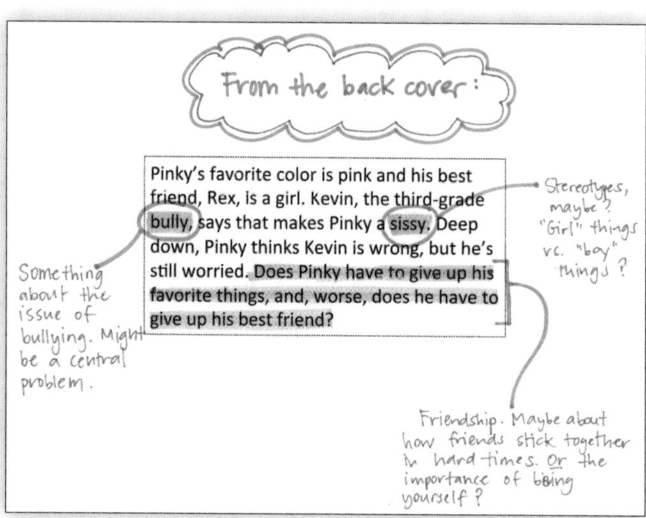

From the back cover:
Pinky's favorite color is pink and his best friend, Rex, is a girl. Kevin, the third-grade bully, says that makes Pinky a sissy. Deep down, Pinky thinks Kevin is wrong, but he's still worried. Does Pinky have to give up his favorite things, and, worse, does he have to give up his best friend?
Stereotypes, maybe? "Girl" things vs. "boy" things?
Something about the issue of bullying. Might be a central problem.
Friendship. Maybe about how friends stick together in hard times. Or the importance of being yourself?

Text excerpt from *Pinky and Rex and the Bully* (Howe 1996).

Who is this for?

LEVELS

K–Z+

GENRE / TEXT TYPE

fiction

SKILLS

inferring, determining importance, synthesizing

7.15 The Real World in My Book

Who is this for?

LEVELS

N–Z+

GENRE / TEXT TYPE

fiction

SKILLS

inferring, determining importance

Strategy We can uncover the real-world issues in the stories we're reading and use what we read in books to think more deeply about our lives. We can think about what aspect of our world the author might want us to think about, what the author might be trying to say, and then consider what's important.

Lesson Language *Writers of stories are often writing about the world, and the real-world social issues that real people grapple with each day—issues such as homelessness, race, class, gender stereotypes, and more. When we find these sorts of issues in our books, we can think about how the author writes about it, and what ideas the story is giving us. For example, in* Fourth Grade Rats *(Spinelli 1993) we might notice that the main character Suds keeps talking about the kinds of things he should do to "be a man" and what is acceptable behavior for boys versus girls. We might say, "Oh! The author is writing about gender issues." But it's important to go beyond just naming the real-world issue in your book and to begin to say something about it. In this book, you might say "Suds learns by the end of the book to stop worrying so much about 'being a man' and accepts himself for who he is, so maybe what the author is saying is that gender is just one part of who you are, or that it's a mistake to think you need to act a certain way just because you're a boy or a girl."*

Prompts

- What real-world issues are you finding in your book?
- Based on what happens in the story, what might the author be saying?
- What ideas are you having based on what happens with this issue in the book?
- Name another issue. Let's think about it together.
- That's something that happens. Think about how it connects to the issue.

Title	Real World Issue?	So What About It?
Fourth Grade Rats	Gender Issues	Stop worrying so much about boy vs. girl stuff—accept who you are.
One Green Apple	Difference/ Outsider	Everyone has something unique and special to contribute. Differences make our world a better place.

Hat Tip: *Comprehension Through Conversation: The Power of Purposeful Talk in the Reading Workshop* (Nichols 2006)

7.16 Stories Teach Us About Life Issues

Strategy Think about what issue or issues (race, class, gender) are in the text. Then think, "What is the character learning that connects to the issue? What might I learn?"

Lesson Language *When characters learn lessons, it's often an important time in the book to really pay attention. When the character learns something, we can learn something, too. For example, in* The Great Gilly Hopkins *(Paterson 1978), one big change in Gilly from the beginning to the end is that she starts out with very negative attitudes toward people who are not white (such as her neighbor and teacher) and people who have learning differences (such as her foster brother or the other children in her class). By the end of the book, she realizes that all of these people in her life are caring, kind, and nothing to be afraid of. She softens up and ends up loving many of them. We might say, "Based on what Gilly learned, I can think about times when I prejudge people based on some characteristic or trait, and how important it is to really get to know a person before making a judgment."*

Prompts

- What issue is showing up in your book?
- What are you learning?
- What is your character learning?
- Reread the last page.
- Find the part where the character has a major problem.
- Turn to where the character learns something.
- That's what happens; I want to know what she or he learned.
- That's the issue; what's your idea about issue?
- I agree, that's a lesson for the character.
- I like how you phrased the lesson in a way that can apply to other books.

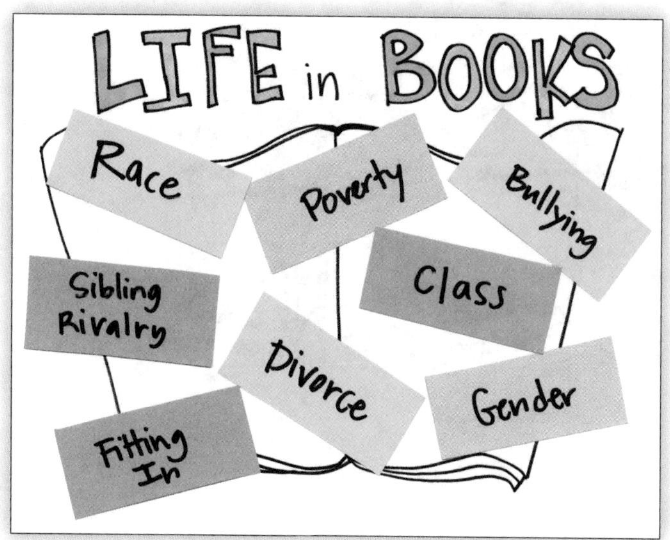

Who is this for?

LEVELS

N–Z+

GENRE / TEXT TYPE

fiction

SKILLS

inferring, determining importance

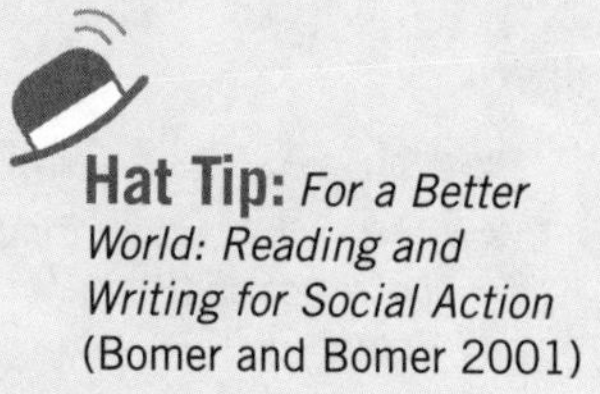

Hat Tip: *For a Better World: Reading and Writing for Social Action* (Bomer and Bomer 2001)

7.17 Readers Ask Themselves Questions

Who is this for?

LEVELS

N–Z+

GENRE / TEXT TYPE

fiction

SKILLS

inferring, determining importance

Strategy To think beyond the surface of the story, into deeper meanings and ideas, it's helpful to ask yourself questions (and then try to answer those questions!). You can pause before, during, and after reading to ask:

- Is what's happening in this story fair?
- From whose perspective is this story being told?
- Whose perspective is absent from this story? What would that person say or do or think about this situation?
- Who in this story seems to have "power"? What impact does that power have?
- Who am I upset with in this story? What's the root of the issue?

Prompts

- What are you wondering about?
- What question can you ask of the text to think about it more deeply?
- Check the chart. What question would apply here?
- Ask yourself a question.
- Try asking and answering a question about fairness.
- Try asking and answering a question about power.
- Don't worry if it's the "right" answer—your inference just needs to be based in details of the story.

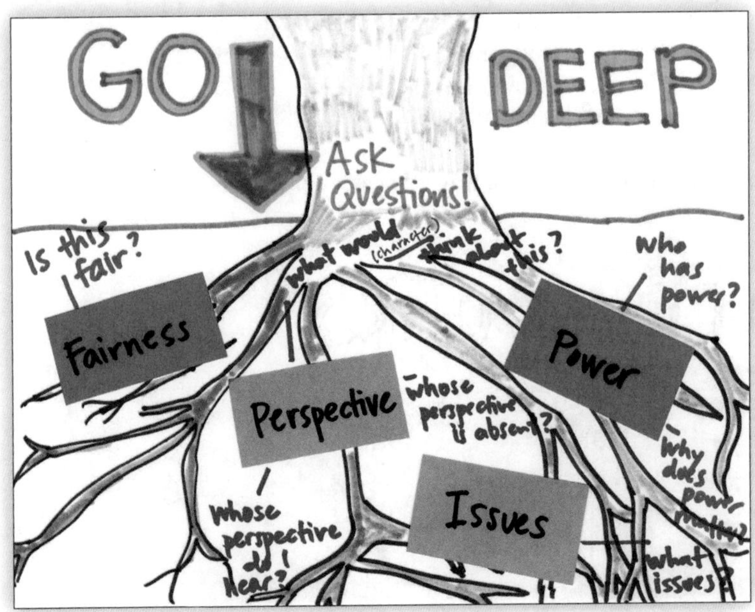

Hat Tip: *For a Better World: Reading and Writing for Social Action* (Bomer and Bomer 2001)

7.18 Character Change Can Reveal Lessons

Strategy Think of the character and his or her traits at the beginning of the story. Think of the character at the end of the story. Ask yourself, "How has the character changed? What made that change happen? What am I learning (about a theme, idea, or message) based on how he or she has changed?"

Lesson Language *When characters change, they often reveal something new about themselves through their actions, speech, or thoughts, or they come to some realization about themselves. When we pay attention to that change, it can reveal deeper meanings in the whole story. For example, take the main character in Spinelli's book* Crash *(2004). Crash changes from a bully at the beginning of the story to someone who can empathize with his pacifist Quaker next-door neighbor, Penn Webb. He stands up to Mike (who was his partner in bullying earlier in the book) and even thinks aloud about whether the name "Crash" fits him anymore, since he's started to be much kinder. This is a remarkable change, and one that can teach us something. We could think about what we learn from this change—that being kind is more fulfilling than being cruel, perhaps. Or that the best way to undo a bully is to show him kindness.*

Prompts

- What were you thinking about in the beginning of the book?
- What were you thinking about at the end of the book?
- Who is this character as a person?
- What did the character learn?
- Think about what has happened.
- When I am trying to look for bigger ideas, I try this: Even though _____, you should _____.
- Are you saying _____, what kind of person would do that?
- Yes, that is an idea about you, not from the book.

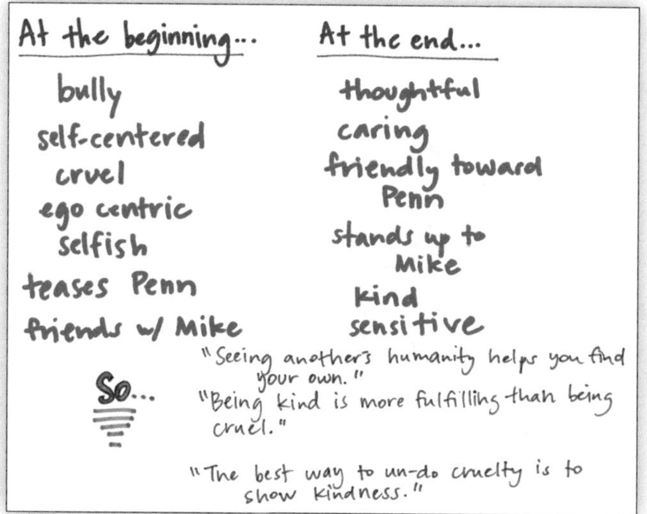

At the beginning...
bully
self-centered
cruel
ego centric
selfish
teases Penn
friends w/ Mike
At the end...
thoughtful
caring
friendly toward Penn
stands up to Mike
kind
sensitive
So...
"Seeing another's humanity helps you find your own."
"Being kind is more fulfilling than being cruel."
"The best way to un-do cruelty is to show kindness."

Who is this for?

LEVELS

N–Z+

GENRE / TEXT TYPE

fiction

SKILLS

inferring, determining importance

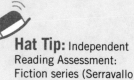

Hat Tip: Independent Reading Assessment: Fiction series (Serravallo 2012)

7.19 Symbols Repeat

Who is this for?

LEVELS

N–Z+

GENRE / TEXT TYPE

fiction

SKILLS

inferring, determining importance

Strategy Notice something that repeats—an object, a person, the setting. Ask yourself what idea or concept that physical thing might symbolize or represent.

Lesson Language *During a read-aloud of the picture book by Maribeth Boelts,* Those Shoes *(2009), you might stop to think aloud about the repetition of the shoes and what the shoes might symbolize. You might say, "Hmm. These shoes keep coming up again and again. The author titled the book* Those Shoes, *and the main character is acting like the shoes are the center of everything. Maybe I can think of them as more than just physical shoes. Maybe I can think about what they represent. Maybe they represent money—they are expensive, and since he is poor, they are out of reach the same way wealth is. Or maybe they represent peer pressure—it's like when he sees them on everyone's feet he feels like he needs to have them too. I know that sometimes there is pressure to look like peers, as in this case, but maybe the shoes could represent all kinds of pressure to fit in and conform." Even though the shoes are a physical thing, and are really important in the story as that physical thing, I can think about the ideas that connect to them to get ideas about what they might symbolize or represent.*

Prompts

- What repeats?
- What are you wondering about that?
- What is the question you have?
- What could that object mean?
- Notice what repeats.
- Tell me your question.
- Craft a question of what you have been wondering about.
- That's what happened; what is a question about it?
- That's a question; try to answer it.
- I liked how you noticed something that repeats.
- That question is great; there isn't a clear answer in the text so far.

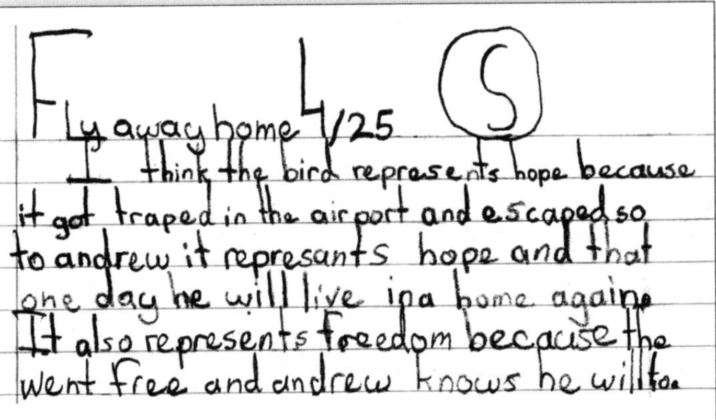

Fly away home 4/25 (S)
I think the bird represents hope because it got traped in the airport and escaped so to andrew it represants hope and that one day he will live ina home again. It also represents freedom because the went free and andrew knows he will to.

Hat Tip: *Falling in Love with Close Reading: Lessons for Analyzing Texts—and Life* (Lehman and Roberts 2014)

7.20 Respond to Issues That Repeat

Strategy Think about an issue that keeps showing up in the book from chapter to chapter (race, class, gender, bullying, fairness). Think about what characters and the narrator say about it. Think, "What does the author seem to be saying about this issue?"

Lesson Language *In Eve Bunting's book* One Green Apple *(2006), the story of a Muslim immigrant's field trip to an apple orchard with her class, I notice the idea of difference keeps repeating. At the start of the book, the main character and narrator Farah thinks, "It was not like this in my village" (5) remarking on how it's strange that in her new country boys and girls sit together. Then later, everyone can speak English and Farah is upset when she can't communicate like they can. She doesn't want to be seen as stupid. Then later in the book, Farah chooses a green apple when everyone else chooses one that's red—that's different, too. Some of her classmates try to stop the different, green apple from being juiced with their red ones to make apple cider, but it goes in anyway. Then later, at the end, she thinks, "Laughs sound the same as at home. Just the same. So do sneezes and belches and lots of things. It is the words that are strange. But soon I will know their words. I will blend with the others the way my apple blended with the cider" (28). At this spot, I'm noticing a change in the ideas around difference as she starts to think about what she has in common with this new place and new people. If I collect all of the details that have to do with this issue of being different, I think the author might be saying that although there may be differences today, soon she will blend with others. Or to say it another way, although people are different, there are still ways we can find things in common because we are all people.*

Prompts

- What issue are you noticing repeat?
- What is the author saying about it?
- Name an issue.
- State your response.
- Jot that down.
- That's what the character does; I am asking what issue that deals with.
- That's an important idea about the story.
- I agree that is an issue—the proof you just offered supports it.
- That makes sense the author is saying that about an issue based on how the character is acting here.

Issue	What the author seems to be saying	My response
Gender	Some of the characters think girls should stay quiet (like Crash's sister) and ~~to~~ women shouldn't work (Crash's mom).	I disagree! Crash is stuck in the olden days.
Stereotypes about "jocks"	The stereotypes are that jocks are bullies which he is at first—but then he becomes kinder.	Sometimes people act how they think they are supposed to act, and then they finally learn who they want to be.
peace/war	Penn Webb is a pacifist and he sort of triumph in the end, so peace = good!	I agree and I like how P.W. showed C. to be peaceful.

Who is this for?

LEVELS

N–Z+

GENRE / TEXT TYPE

fiction

SKILLS

inferring, determining importance

Hat Tip: *Shades of Meaning: Comprehension and Interpretation in Middle School* (Santman 2005)

7.21 Aha Moment

Who is this for?

LEVELS

N–Z+

GENRE / TEXT TYPE

fiction

SKILLS

inferring, synthesizing, determining importance

Strategy Look for a passage, often toward the end of the book, where the character reflects. Reread it. Ask yourself, "What's a message from this passage? How does the message relate to a theme of the book?"

Lesson Language *Sometimes the author will let us into the mind of the character. Often when the story is told in first person—When we see a lot of I, we, me, my in the narration—we get extra insight into the character's thoughts. In books like this, the author will sometimes include a part where the character says what he or she thinks about the events of the story; this part is usually toward the end of the book, perhaps after a problem is resolved or we see a character change. During those reflective moments, we get extra help with finding out what one of the lessons might be.*

Prompts

- Can you find a spot where the character reflects?
- Reread the spot where the character reflects.
- What is the character reflecting about?
- Based on the reflection, what message(s) are you thinking about?
- Connect that to what the whole book is mostly about.
- What does the character's reflection make you think?

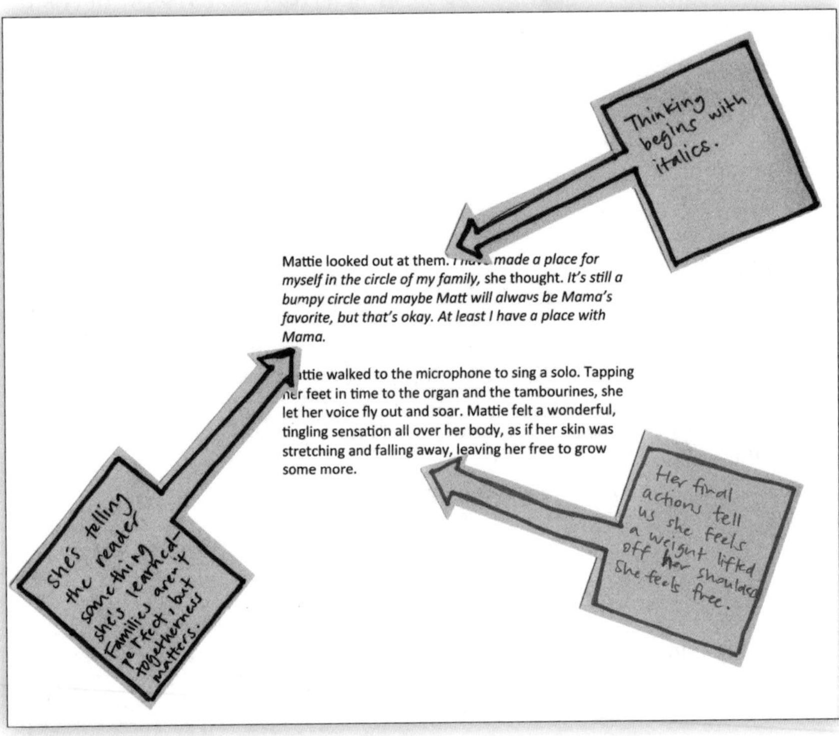

Text excerpt from *Circle of Gold* (Boyd 1996).

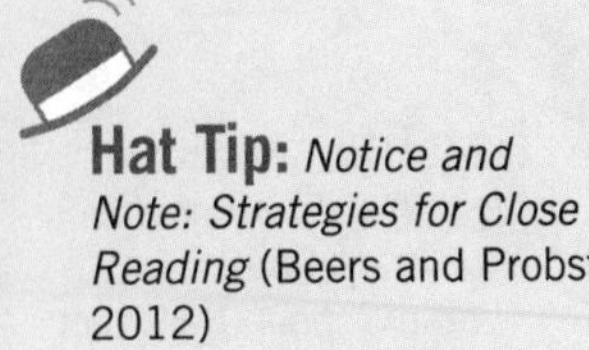

Hat Tip: *Notice and Note: Strategies for Close Reading* (Beers and Probst 2012)

7.22 Identifiers, Identity, and Ideas

Strategy Consider the identities of any one character. Think about how their identity relates to their problem(s) or what they learn in the story. State a theme in universal language.

Lesson Language *Any one character—or person in your life—belongs to a series of groups and can be identified along a number of dimensions. In our world, these different identity markers help make our world diverse and people unique. When you're reading a story, keep in mind that the author purposefully created a character who belongs to certain groups and who can identify in different ways. Knowing this can help us tap into some of the possible messages or lessons in the story. Let's consider a character from our recent read-aloud. Let's think about the main character, Auggie from R. J. Palacio's book* Wonder *(2012). What do we know about him? Let's think through these categories:*

- *ability*
- *age*
- *ethnicity*
- *gender*
- *race*
- *religion*
- *sexual orientation*
- *socioeconomic status (class)*
- *body image ("lookism")*
- *educational background*
- *academic/social achievement*
- *family of origin, family makeup*
- *geographic/regional background*
- *language*
- *learning style*
- *beliefs (political, social, religious)*
- *globalism/internationalism*

(Continue discussion and think aloud to show the point that there is more than one dimension to consider when we think of a character's, or person's, identity. Yes, for Auggie there is the salient feature of his facial disfiguration, an important part of the story, but there is so much more to Auggie that matters. It matters, for example, that he's a middle school student and an important theme in this story is how middle school–aged children treat one another. It's also important that he's really bright—he outgrows the ability to be homeschooled by his mom, he picks up on social cues very easily from others. As you lead the discussion, you may think aloud about any aspects that students don't immediately pick up on and/or prompt the students to think through each item on the list saying something like, "How about age? Does age matter at all in this story? What do we know about the main character's age?")

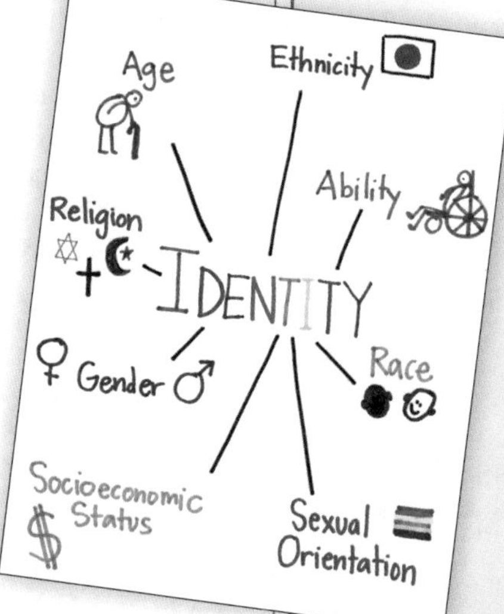

Prompts

- Let's think about the character's identity.
- How does that aspect of the character's identity matter to the story?
- Can you think of a theme that emerges because of that aspect of the character's identity?
- Can you think of another?
- What else do we know about the character? Why might that matter?
- That's one theme based on the character's identity. Can you think of another?

Who is this for?

LEVELS

Q–Z+

GENRE / TEXT TYPE

fiction

SKILLS

inferring, determining importance

Hat Tip: "Sample Cultural Identifiers" (National Association of Independent Schools 2010)

7.23 Secondary Sages

Who is this for?

LEVELS

Q–Z+

GENRE / TEXT TYPE

fiction

SKILLS

inferring, determining importance

Strategy Look for a place where a secondary character who is older or wiser speaks to a main character. Think to yourself, "What is the older character teaching the younger one?" Then, try to put the lesson in your own words, stating what it is that you, the reader, should learn.

Lesson Language *You may have a person in your life who is older and offers you advice—maybe it's a parent, a grandparent, or a teacher. Many child characters in children's literature also have people who offer them advice, and when we read and notice such advice is being given, we can read with extra alertness to learn from them, too. For example, in* The Tiger Rising *(DiCamillo 2002), the hotel housekeeper Willie May tells a long story about her pet bird who daddy warned would just get eaten by a snake by suppertime. When an author spends that much time in such a small book having a minor character speak, you should think, "This must be important." By connecting it to what's happening in the book you might think, "Willie May is trying to warn them that you have to think about what freedom might bring" or even that the story she's telling is foreshadowing what's to come with the fate of the tiger.*

Prompts

- Who in this story is an older and wiser character?
- Does anyone in this story give advice to another character?
- Think about a spot where you remember them interacting.
- What can you learn from the interaction?
- Put that character's advice in your own words.
- What's the lesson that you think you might learn from that?
- Yes, that's a way to say it that is universal, not book-specific.

GLORIA DUMP

She showed Opal that people can change and don't judge people by what they did in the past find out what type of person they are now. Also, don't judge people too quickly just because they've been mean (or wrong) in the past.

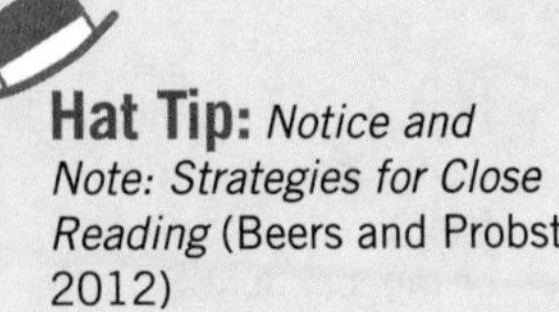

Hat Tip: *Notice and Note: Strategies for Close Reading* (Beers and Probst 2012)

7.24 Titles Can Be Telling

Strategy Reread the title of the book. Think about what's included in the title. Think about how that title connects to multiple aspects of the book—its characters, setting, and/or theme. State an idea that seems to be a thread throughout the book and that is also reflected in the title.

Lesson Language *After finishing the book* Crow Call *(Lowry 2009), I went back to the title of the book. My first thought was, "Well, that makes sense that she titled it that. There was a scene in the book where they used a crow call." But I know that titles often have deeper meanings, or if the author didn't actually intend something deeper they can certainly help me to think about the book more deeply. For example, if I just said, "Oh, that's why it's called that, it was in the book" she could have just as easily called it "flannel shirt" or "cherry pie." Why* Crow Call*? Well, I can think about how it connects the parts of the book. The story shows a girl trying to connect to her father who has been away at war. He takes her crow hunting and they use the crow call to draw the birds near. I could think that maybe the girl is like a crow call, trying to get closer to her father. Or I can look at the scene when the crow call is used. The daughter convinces her father not to shoot any crows. In fact, after using the crow call she whispers, "Look, Daddy. Do you see them? They think I'm a crow!" We could look at the crow call as something symbolizing what her father is doing to call her back after being away so long. So perhaps what the story is about is the idea of getting back together after being away, or a story about what brings people together, how you can call them home.*

Prompts

- What's a thread throughout the book?
- What connects to the title?
- That's how the title connects to one story element; how does it connect with another?
- That idea fits with the story! What's another idea you have?
- Try adding, "Or maybe . . ."
- Try saying, "It could also be . . ."

Life after Winn Dixie
The author may have chosen this title because It has a very Strong meaning behind it. It only takes one Person to Change a relationship, or make a really big impact. When People meet other People one Person could Change others lives so their life is more Sucsesful. Because of Winn-Dixie the characters lives Chenged. Like the preacher, Otis, OPAl, Gloria Dump!

Who is this for?

LEVELS

R–Z+

GENRE / TEXT TYPE

fiction

SKILLS

inferring, determining importance

Supporting Comprehension in Nonfiction

Determining Main Topic(s) and Idea(s)

Why is this goal important?

Craftily written, engaging nonfiction for children often includes zinger, wow-worthy facts. Some readers, when asked to talk about what they learned in a whole book, will say back only these sorts of facts: "Did you know that the hippo population in the Congo decreased from 22,000 to 400 in less than twenty years?!" When pressed to say more, many can't. The thing is, as cool as it is to know some stand-out facts, children are more likely to learn and remember the information when they can create mental files, storing and organizing the information inside larger categories (Calkins and Tolan 2010c). These categories may be the topics, subtopics, and/or main ideas of the text. Learning how to understand what a section of a text or whole text is *mostly about* is critical to comprehension.

This task of understanding the most important content varies depending on the complexity of the text. Texts at levels typically read by first and second graders (levels C–L) are more likely to be a collection of information about a topic (e.g., African animals) or subtopic (e.g., elephants). By the time we get to third-grade levels (levels M–P), the text usually has a main idea (e.g., elephants are interesting creatures) with a lot of support for the reader to figure it out—an introduction highlighting the main idea and/or headings and topic sentences that spell it out clearly. By late fourth to early fifth grade (levels Q/R–Z+), texts often have multiple main ideas contained in the same text. These multiple ideas may show more than one perspective or point of view on a topic or may explore different aspects of the topic (e.g., people both are a cause of and offer solutions for the problem of animal poaching in Africa). The ideas in the texts at this level often need to be inferred.

The work of the reader becomes more complex as texts get more complex, and the task of determining importance becomes more challenging when the topic is not aligned to a student's prior knowledge. Students at any grade level often need support in the form of strategies. One study found that although readers are sometimes able to automatically determine the main idea, expert readers often need to think through a process and apply strategies in order to construct a main idea (Afflerbach 1990).

How do I know if this goal is right for my student?

A short-text or whole-book comprehension assessment can help you determine your students' abilities when it comes to determining importance in nonfiction texts. After students read a portion of a text or a whole text, you can ask them to respond to questions in writing or aloud. Some of the questions or prompts you may consider using are:

- What is this text (or chapter or book) mostly about?
- What is the main idea?
- Please summarize what you've read so far. Be sure to include the main idea and supporting details.

For younger students, it's usually more accurate to get information about comprehension in a conference, by asking a child to state the main topic and/or idea aloud. By around second grade, or when children are reading at about level J/K, you may choose to select a short text, such as a *Time for Kids* article, and prompt students to write a main idea or a summary with a main idea and key details. To see how students accumulate all the facts within longer stretches of text, you could choose a nonfiction book and plant sticky notes inside it asking students about the main idea of a section and/or the whole book (Serravallo 2013a). In addition to these more informal assessments, you can find more formal standards-aligned performance tasks available online (see, for example, www.readingandwritingproject.com), which ask students to determine main idea and/or to summarize.

Regardless of how you chose to collect samples of your students' thinking to determine how well they are able to state topics, subtopics, and/or main idea(s), you'll need a rubric or continuum against which to judge their responses. A good rule of thumb is that a main topic(s)/idea(s) should take *most* if not all of the text into account and should be aligned to the level of complexity of the text. In other words, a fifth grader reading on grade level should be able to name multiple main ideas in a text, and a second grader should be able to name the main topic (Serravallo 2013a).

Strategies for Determining Main Topic(s) and Idea(s) at a Glance

Strategy	Levels	Genres/ Text Types	Skills
8.1 One Text, Multiple Ideas (or Topics)	A–Z+	Nonfiction	Synthesizing, determining importance
8.2 Notice What Repeats	A–I	Nonfiction	Determining importance
8.3 Topic/Subtopic/Details	J–Z+	Expository nonfiction	Summarizing, retelling
8.4 Ask Questions, Form Ideas	J–Z+	Nonfiction	Determining importance, questioning
8.5 Boxes and Bullets	J–Z+	Expository nonfiction	Synthesizing, determining importance
8.6 Survey the Text	J–Z+	Expository nonfiction	Synthesizing, determining importance
8.7 Paraphrase Chunks, Then Put It Together	L–Z+	Nonfiction (article)	Determining importance, paraphrasing, synthesizing
8.8 Sketch in Chunks	L–Z+	Nonfiction (article)	Synthesizing, determining importance, visualizing
8.9 Most Important . . . to Whom?	M–Z+	Expository or narrative nonfiction	Determining importance, summarizing
8.10 What Does the Author Say? What Do I Say?	M–Z+	Expository or narrative nonfiction	Comparing and contrasting, synthesizing, inferring, determining importance
8.11 Add Up Facts to Determine Main Idea	M–Z+	Expository nonfiction	Determining importance, summarizing
8.12 Track Down Opinion Clues in Solutions	M–Z+	Expository nonfiction	Determining importance, synthesizing
8.13 Opinion–Reasons–Evidence	M–Z+	Expository nonfiction	Determining importance, synthesizing
8.14 Time = Parts	M–Z+	Narrative nonfiction	Summarizing, determining importance
8.15 Why Does the Story Matter?	M–Z+	Narrative nonfiction	Determining importance, synthesizing
8.16 What? and So What?	M–Z+	Nonfiction	Determining importance, synthesizing
8.17 Clue In to Topic Sentences	M–Z+	Expository nonfiction	Determining importance
8.18 Shrink-a-Text with a Partner	M–Z+	Nonfiction	Summarizing, determining importance
8.19 Consider Structure	M–Z+	Nonfiction	Synthesizing
8.20 Determining Author's Purpose, Point of View	O–Z+	Nonfiction	Determining importance
8.21 What's the Perspective on the Topic?	O–Z+	Nonfiction	Determining importance
8.22 Tricks of Persuasion	P–Z+	Nonfiction	Determining importance, inferring
8.23 Perspective, Position, Power	P–Z+	Nonfiction	Determining importance, inferring, critiquing

8.1 One Text, Multiple Ideas (or Topics)

Who is this for?

LEVELS

A–Z+

GENRE / TEXT TYPE

nonfiction

SKILLS

synthesizing, determining importance

Hat Tip: *Navigating Nonfiction in Expository Text: Determining Importance and Synthesizing* (Calkins and Tolan 2010c)

Strategy When you read the first section, chunk, or chapter, state what it's mostly about (so far) in one sentence (or one word, for readers up to level M). As you read on, notice whether the next part offers more information about the same idea, or if the author has moved on to a new idea. Collect each new main idea (or main topic for readers up to level M) as you go. For levels R–Z+, at the end of the reading, you may be able to put the separate main idea statements together into one, more complex statement.

Teaching Tip This strategy can be used for any text level with some slight tweaking of the language. For children at lower levels (up to level M), their books are typically about one topic, and may contain subtopics. For readers at levels M to R, the whole book will likely be about one main idea. At around levels R and higher, you'd want to include the last sentence in the strategy, offering the option to synthesize multiple ideas into one complex idea. Keep this language tweaking based on complexity in mind as you read all the lessons in this chapter.

Lesson Language *We are all familiar with this class favorite,* Bugs! Bugs! Bugs! *(Dussling 2011). When we first started reading it, remember how we noticed that the author comes right out and tells us a main idea on the first page? She tells us that even though bugs look scary, they are really just dangerous to other insects, not people. I might think, "Oh. That must be what the whole book is about, since that's what she wrote in the introduction." Sometimes that's true—what's stated in the introduction is what the whole book will be about. But I also know I need to be aware, always thinking, always paying attention. I can think about each page as I read and consider if it fits with that same first idea, or if the author has gone on to a new one. We learned about the praying mantis and the dragonfly and how they hunt and eat other bugs. Yes, those still go with the first main idea. But about halfway through, listen to this: "Some bugs hunt other bugs. Not to eat themselves, but to feed their babies." She seems to switch gears a bit. Let's see if the next page is still about how we don't need to worry about bugs, or if there is a new idea, that bugs hunt to feed their young. I see the fact that the hunting wasp feeding its babies is on this page. So it seems like this book is really about more than one main idea: That we don't need to be afraid of bugs, and that bugs hunt to feed themselves and their young.*

8.2 Notice What Repeats

Who is this for?

LEVELS

A–I

GENRE / TEXT TYPE

nonfiction

SKILL

determining importance

Strategy To figure out what a book is mostly about, it's helpful to pay attention to the word or words you see again and again. On each page, notice what repeats. Think, "Does this word tell me what the book is mostly about?"

Teaching Tip Up until about level J, books often don't have a main "idea" but rather a "main topic"—it's the difference between saying the book is about "baseball" (topic) and the book is about how "baseball is an important part of American culture" (topic + idea). For younger readers, or children reading at lower levels, asking them to determine a main idea may be too challenging of a task considering the complexity of the text.

Prompts

- What repeats on each page in the words?
- What repeats on each page in the pictures?
- What is this book mostly about?
- State the main topic.
- Look for what's the same.
- Put a finger on any words that are the same on these couple of pages.
- You found a repeating word! Now, what's the topic?

8.3 Topic/Subtopic/Details

Who is this for?

LEVELS

J–Z+

GENRE / TEXT TYPE

expository nonfiction

SKILLS

summarizing, retelling

Strategy First, find the topic—what the whole section or chapter is mostly about. Next, find a subtopic or a smaller part of the topic. Finally, list details that you learned that connect to the topic and subtopic.

Lesson Language *In nonfiction texts, it's important to have an idea of the overall structure and to know which information supports which topics. Topics are sometimes even broken up into subtopics, with information supporting those smaller pieces. Sometimes these topics and subtopics are separated with headings and subheadings. Keep a chart or outline to help you keep track of the information the author is presenting.*

Prompts

- Check the headings or subheadings.
- What's the *topic* of this section?
- What's the *subtopic* on this page?
- Tell me what it's mostly about.
- What details support that subtopic?
- Headings will have a larger font than subheadings.

Topic	Subtopic	Details
cactus	Animals like to live in cacti.	• Every year animals come and makes new homes. • Different animals like rats, birds and bats live in the cactus.
cactus	cacti are really big	cacti can grow to 108 feet tall. more than 50 animals can live in the cacti.

Hat Tip: *Strategies That Work: Teaching Comprehension for Understanding and Engagement*, second edition (Harvey and Goudvis 2007)

8.4 Ask Questions, Form Ideas

Strategy Wonder and question as you read, and work to actively answer your questions. Collect all the questions and answers as you go. Based on all of the questions and answers, think "What does it seem like the text is mostly about?"

Lesson Language *Before reading the first page of* The Titanic *by Deborah Kent (1993), I wondered what it was like on the Titanic in the beginning. After reading, I could tell that it was calm and almost regal. I was also wondering what happened to cause the ship to sink. As I read, I learned that there were many more safety features than on any other ship, but they only had room for 1,200 in lifeboats even though there were 2,200 passengers and crew. The ship makers thought the ship was "unsinkable." When the ship was warned about icebergs, the radio operator never delivered the message. The ship collided with an iceberg, which tore a huge hole in the ship and the people in charge soon realized the ship would float for only another two minutes at most. If I look back at all the questions and answers from this first chapter, I can find some patterns that will help me think about what the chapter is mostly about. The very beginning aside, it seems most of what I learned was about the overconfidence of the ship makers, and the disaster that resulted from not being prepared.*

Prompts

- Jot what you're wondering.
- Look back at all of your questions.
- Reread your questions. Is there a pattern? What is the text mostly about?
- Make sure to answer your questions, if you can.
- Look at all you've written down. What's the main idea?

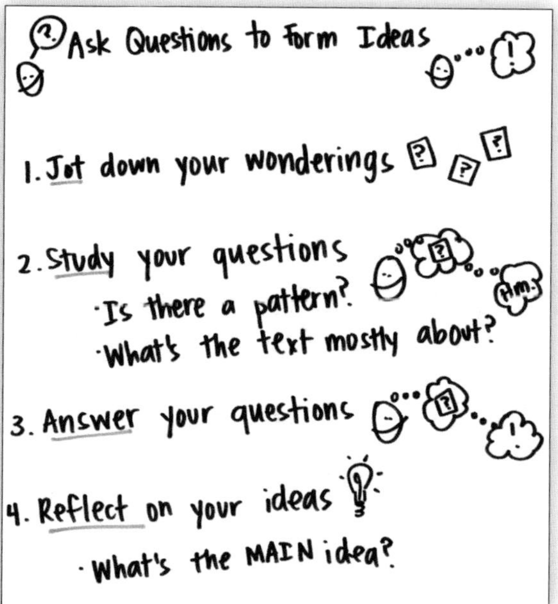

Who is this for?

LEVELS

J–Z+

GENRE / TEXT TYPE

nonfiction

SKILLS

determining importance, questioning

Hat Tip: *Comprehension Through Conversation: The Power of Purposeful Talk in the Reading Workshop* (Nichols 2006)

8.5 Boxes and Bullets

Who is this for?

LEVELS

J–Z+

GENRE / TEXT TYPE

expository nonfiction

SKILLS

synthesizing, determining importance

Hat Tip: *Navigating Nonfiction in Expository Text: Determining Importance and Synthesizing* (Calkins and Tolan 2010c)

Strategy Draw a box and several bullets beneath it on a sticky note or in a notebook. As you read, think about the information you just read. Ask yourself, "Does this sentence say what this part is mostly about (box), or is this a detail (bullet)?" Write or mentally place the information you read on the graphic organizer as you learn it.

Teaching Tip This is another strategy that you can modify the language to be about topics and details (below level M) or about main idea and details (at around level M–Z+).

Lesson Language *Nonfiction expository texts have an architecture—a way they are built. When authors are trying to teach you something new, it's common that they will have big topics and ideas, and then give you more information by giving you details that fit with those big topics and ideas. Sometimes the main idea comes first, and then they follow it with the details. Other times, you'll need to read all the details and then you'll come to the main idea in the conclusion. Sometimes the main idea is stuck somewhere in the middle. As you read, it helps your understanding if you can organize the information, figuring out which of the sentences are "bullets"—or supporting details or facts—and which of the sentences are "boxes"—or main ideas or topics.*

Prompts

- Say back the information you just read.
- Do you think that information is the main idea, or a detail?
- How do you know if it's a main idea or detail?
- Check to see if the other information on the page is a part of that sentence.
- Check to see if that sentence supports the other information on the page.

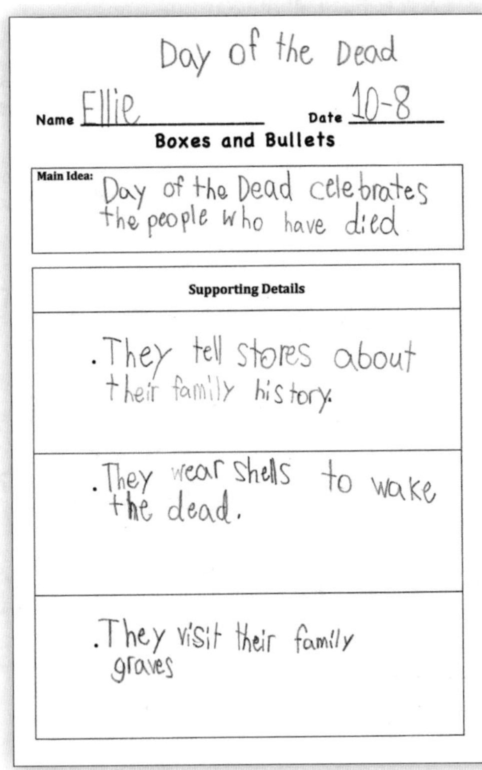

Day of the Dead

Name Ellie Date 10-8

Boxes and Bullets

Main Idea: Day of the Dead celebrates the people who have died

Supporting Details
. They tell stores about their family history.
. They wear shells to wake the dead.
. They visit their family graves

8.6 Survey the Text

Strategy Survey the text by glancing at the big things that jump out at you visually—the heading(s), title(s), and visual(s). Ask yourself, "What does it seem like this text is mostly about?" Then, go back and read the text with that main idea in mind. Check the facts you learn to see if they really do fit with the main idea statement you've already made. When you finish reading, revise the main idea statement based on the new information you have.

Teaching Tip You can help students synthesize a larger section of text—a whole book—by teaching them to survey the table of contents before beginning to read. You can also tweak this to focus on either main idea or main topic depending on text level.

Prompts

- Look across the page. Tell me what you see.
- If you put all the visuals together, what do you think it's mostly about?
- What do most of the features have in common (topic or idea)?
- Check the facts to make sure that's the main idea.
- Do you have any changes to make to your main idea statement, after reading the facts?
- Hmm. It seems like that doesn't quite fit. Revise your thinking.
- You put all the visuals together to figure out what it's mostly about!

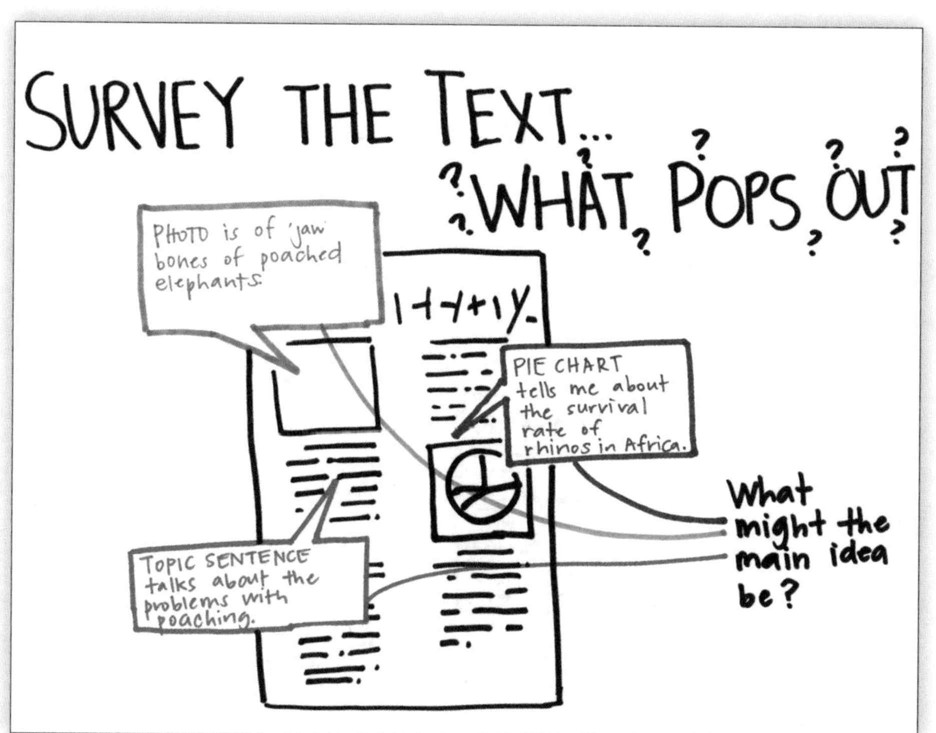

Who is this for?

LEVELS
J–Z+

GENRE / TEXT TYPE
expository nonfiction

SKILLS
synthesizing, determining importance

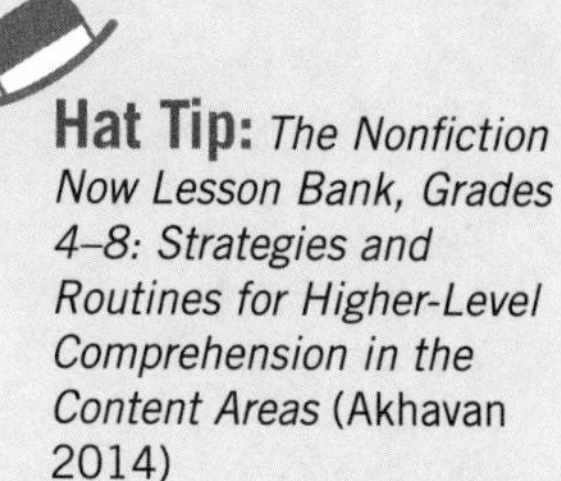

Hat Tip: *The Nonfiction Now Lesson Bank, Grades 4–8: Strategies and Routines for Higher-Level Comprehension in the Content Areas* (Akhavan 2014)

8.7 Paraphrase Chunks, Then Put It Together

Who is this for?

LEVELS

L–Z+

GENRE / TEXT TYPE

nonfiction (article)

SKILLS

determining importance, paraphrasing, synthesizing

Strategy Stop after every paragraph or short section. Think, "How can I say what I learned in my own words?" Jot a note in the margin. At the end of the article, read back over your margin notes and think, "So, what's this whole article mostly about?"

Teaching Tip Part of the challenge for many readers as they move to expository nonfiction from reading stories is that the pace of their reading needs to slow down. Strategies like this one that ask readers to stop and chunk the information as they go helps to slow them down and monitor their comprehension before moving on. It also supports their ability to synthesize the information, as they are stopping throughout the text to pull together smaller amounts of information rather than reading the entire text before stopping to think about main ideas.

Prompts

- Stop there. Jot a note.
- What's most important in what you just read?
- Say it in your own words.
- Don't write the same thing the author wrote; think and try to say it on your own.
- Look back across your notes.
- What is the *whole* article about?
- That main idea statement takes into account most of the information you just read!
- It seems like slowing down to think is helping you to think about main ideas as you go.

Hat Tip: *Strategies That Work: Teaching Comprehension for Understanding and Engagement*, second edition (Harvey and Goudvis 2007)

8.8 Sketch in Chunks

Strategy Stop after every paragraph or short section. Think, "What am I picturing?" Draw a quick sketch. At the end of the article, look back over your sketches and ask yourself, "So, what's this whole article mostly about?"

Lesson Language (Read aloud the first paragraph of "Coral Reefs in Trouble" [*Time for Kids* 2012].) *I'm picturing a collection of coral reefs and maybe a speech bubble that says "Oh no!" I'm going to draw a line and read the next paragraph and sketch.* (Read next paragraph aloud.) *I'm going to draw some coral and black out or scribble most of it to show that just 8 percent is healthy and the rest is dead. Then I'm going to draw a line and read the next paragraph to see what I picture.* (Read aloud next paragraph.) *I learned that pollution, overfishing, and higher temperatures are harming the reefs. So I'm going to sketch an old plastic bottle, a fishing pole, and a thermometer with a high temperature. Now, as I look back across my sketches, I might say, "This whole article is about the causes and crisis of endangered coral reefs."*

Prompts

- Stop there.
- What are you picturing?
- Stop and sketch what you see in your mind.
- Look back at your sketches—what's the article mostly about?
- Decide how much you'll read next before sketching again.
- I can see why you drew that sketch—it matches the information on the page.

Who is this for?

LEVELS

L–Z+

GENRE / TEXT TYPE

nonfiction (article)

SKILLS

synthesizing, determining importance, visualizing

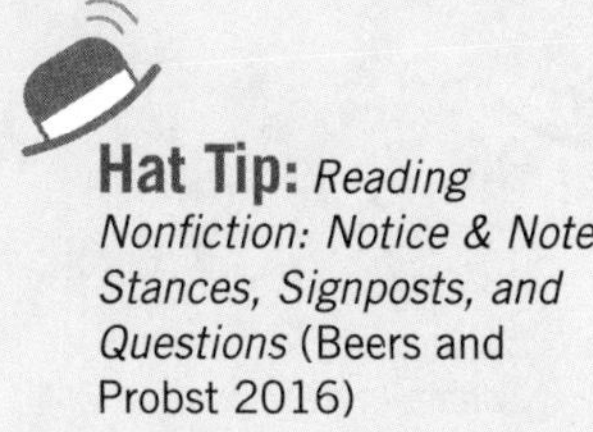

Hat Tip: *Reading Nonfiction: Notice & Note Stances, Signposts, and Questions* (Beers and Probst 2016)

8.9 Most Important . . . to Whom?

Who is this for?

LEVELS

M–Z+

GENRE / TEXT TYPE

expository or narrative nonfiction

SKILLS

determining importance, summarizing

Strategy What the reader thinks is the most important idea and what the author thinks is the most important idea may not always be in agreement. First, write down what you think is most important. Then, write down what you think the author thinks is the most important idea. Look back to the text to see which of those is supported by more of the details from the text.

Prompts

- What do you think is the main idea? What facts support that?
- Does the author state (in a heading, topic sentence, introduction) the main idea? List the facts that support it.
- What details fit with that idea?
- Let's check to see if that's what it's *mostly* about. Do *most* of the details support it?
- What's different about your idea and what you think the author's idea might be? How can you check to see which one is what the section or page or book is mostly about?

I think the most important idea is water is one of the most precious resouces on Earth.
the author thinks we need to use it wisely.

Details
1. Two thirds of our bodies are made up of water.
2. useses for cooking, cleaning, gardening, Making electricity, moving objects, brushing our teeth, and washing our bodies.
3. All the way to dinosaur they all needed water.
4. water is decreasing.

Hat Tip: *Strategies That Work: Teaching Comprehension for Understanding and Engagement*, second edition (Harvey and Goudvis 2007)

8.10 What Does the Author Say? What Do I Say?

Strategy Collect a couple of books on the same topic, in which authors have different perspectives. Organize the different authors' thinking. Then form your own response by thinking, "What do I think about the ideas presented?" You may decide one of the arguments is most compelling, persuasive, or logical, or you may decide that what you believe is some combination of the two.

Lesson Language *I just read these two books—*Sharks *by Seymour Simon (2006) and* Shark Attack! *by Cathy East Dubowski (2009). From the two covers, you're probably thinking, "Yikes! Sharks are scary." I thought the same thing at first. But then when I read, I noticed that the authors had slightly different ways of getting across the information. Simon starts out by telling the reader that although people often think of sharks as menacing creatures, the truth is that there are few shark attacks on people each year, and most people survive them. He puts aside your fears right away and says that we should actually be fascinated because they are really quite amazing creatures. Dubowski's book, on the other hand, begins with a true story of Rodney Fox and the account of his gruesome attack by a shark. It's not until page 14 that we start to learn that attacks are quite rare. It's almost like she's trying to feed into our fears, but wants to present both sides of the story—the scary parts about sharks, and then the truth about the rarity of attacks. If I examine these two different spins on the same topic, I can reflect on my own thinking about sharks. What do I think? From all the information I learned about sharks from both of the books, I'm more likely to agree with Simon—they're fascinating. I think he did a better job at convincing me because of details such as . . .* (Go on to list specific details to show how ideas need to be supported with text evidence.)

Prompts

- What's the perspective on the topic in this book? How about in that one?
- What's different about the ideas the author is presenting in each?
- What's your response to each of the ideas?
- Which idea do you think is more logical, persuasive, or compelling?
- Which idea can you back up with the most detail?

for Volcanoes	Against Volcanoes	My opinion
• Magma helps form the earth • errupting in the sea to form islands • Volcanic Soil helps plants. • Hiking can be Scenic	• Damages towns • Consumes lives • hurts animals • Aftershocks • lava flows burn eco • lava burns ecosystems which means you must restart the ecosystem, consuming soil and oxygen for humans. • Animals die and they cannot reproduce • Smoke pollutes the air	• Volcanoes can be scenic and calm but sometimes dangerous • Peoples lives are lost! • the soil helps the environment grow faster • The old crust will crumble and the hot magma will melt it into magma.

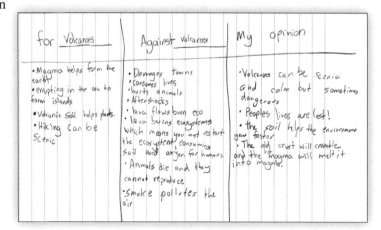

Who is this for?

LEVELS

M–Z+

GENRE / TEXT TYPE

expository or narrative nonfiction

SKILLS

comparing and contrasting, synthesizing, inferring, determining importance

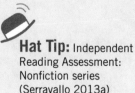

Hat Tip: Independent Reading Assessment: Nonfiction series (Serravallo 2013a)

8.11 Add Up Facts to Determine Main Idea

Who is this for?

LEVELS

M–Z+

GENRE / TEXT TYPE

expository nonfiction

SKILLS

determining importance, summarizing

Strategy Focus on one section. Read several paragraphs. List several facts that seem to connect. In your own words, what is this section mostly about? As you read on to collect more facts, you may need to revise your main idea.

Lesson Language *In the book* Jungles *by Illa Podendorf (1982), the section is titled "What Kinds of Plants Make a Jungle" goes on for several pages and contains many facts. After reading the section, the facts that seem to go together are: most grow tall and straight; most have flowers near the top; some spread low; many strangler trees grow on other trees; there are many vines that climb to the tops of trees; orchids grow high up, fastened to other plants; the jungle is always green. If I looked at all of those facts, I could say, "There are many different kinds of plants in the jungle" or even "Plants will do whatever they need to survive in the jungle."*

Prompts

- What did you learn after reading those paragraphs?
- What are three facts that fit together?
- How do they fit?
- What is your thinking about the main idea?
- What do all of those facts have in common?
- Go back and reread.
- List three facts that fit together.
- Put that into your own words.
- That's the topic; what's the main idea?
- That's a fact; can you put a few together?
- I like that main idea statement—you told me the "what" and the "so what."
- Yes, those three facts fit together; that word is repeated in all three.

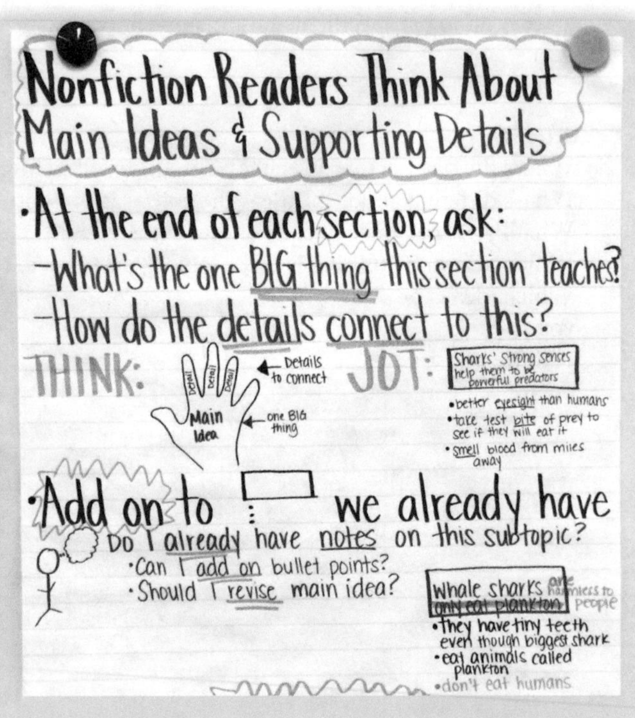

Hat Tip: *Talk About Understanding: Rethinking Classroom Talk to Enhance Comprehension* (Keene 2012)

8.12 Track Down Opinion Clues in Solutions

Strategy If the text is written in a problem-solution structure, first identify the problem the author presents. Then, notice what solution the author offers. Think, "How is this solution different from other possible solutions? What does it seem the author is arguing for?"

Lesson Language *In the* Time for Kids *article "Cleaning Up After Isaac" (2012), the author first presents the problem: Hurricane Isaac left a big mess in the gulf region and caused an estimated $1.5 million in damages. The solutions he presents are that both presidential candidates visited the area and offered help, utility crews worked over labor day weekend to fix power lines, and work crews worked to clean up the mess and get rid of large dead rodents that washed up during the storm. He concludes the article saying that life was pretty much back to normal by September 1. If I look at the solutions presented, I might say the main idea is, "In times of trouble, others should come to offer help." Looking for the solution might help you find the author's argument, too. I think in this example the author believes that help is important in disasters like Hurricane Isaac.*

Prompts

- Identify the problem.
- Where will you look to read about the solution the author proposes?
- Now that you know the solution, say what this section is mostly about.
- Think about what the author is arguing for.

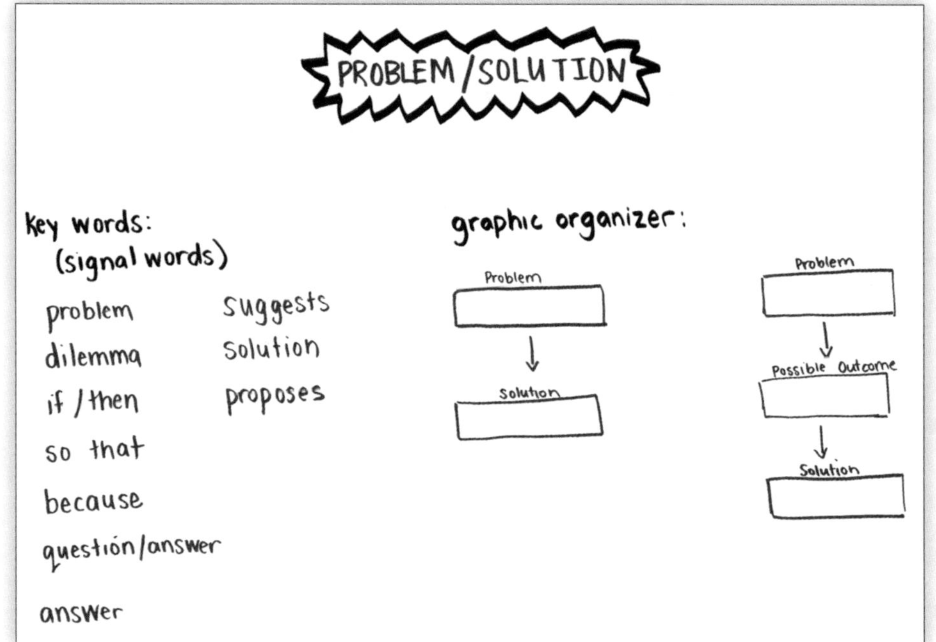

Who is this for?

LEVELS

M–Z+

GENRE / TEXT TYPE

expository nonfiction

SKILLS

determining importance, synthesizing

Hat Tip: *Inside Information: Developing Powerful Readers and Writers of Informational Text Through Project-Based Instruction* (Duke 2014)

8.13 Opinion–Reasons–Evidence

Who is this for?

LEVELS

M–Z+

GENRE / TEXT TYPE

expository nonfiction

SKILLS

determining importance, synthesizing

Hat Tip: *Inside Information: Developing Powerful Readers and Writers of Informational Text Through Project-Based Instruction* (Duke 2014)

Strategy Notice how the text is organized. Think, "Does the author state an opinion then back it up, or does the author give details then conclude with an opinion?" Knowing the structure will help you find the main idea.

Lesson Language *Pay attention to the three levels or layers of information that are presented. By working up from evidence to reasons to opinion, you can figure out the main idea. Or, if the opinion is clear, you can find the reasons that support the opinion, and the evidence that backs up the reasons. Depending on how the text is organized, it may make sense to build up to an idea or opinion, or to back up the opinion with the information.*

Prompts

- What's the author's opinion?
- What reasons support the opinion?
- What evidence backs up the reasons?
- Summarize the information you learned in this section.
- Now that you know all the facts, add them up to conclude the reason.
- That opinion is backed up by the facts.

8.14 Time = Parts

Strategy In narrative nonfiction such as biographies, the piece will still have an overall topic (such as a person) with subtopics (such as their childhood, early adult life, and end-of-life successes). You can think of each major time period as a part of the whole, and ask yourself, "What's this part mostly about?" You can often state an idea about that portion of the story. Then, you can put each part together to come up with an idea about the whole.

Teaching Tip Most of the strategies in this chapter help readers with comprehension of expository nonfiction texts, but this strategy is an exception. Part of the reason for the absence of many narrative nonfiction strategies is that I often employ strategies from literature to help readers with narrative nonfiction. For example, in biographies people can be seen like characters in fiction, with traits, motivations, and obstacles. In that case, I'd apply strategies from Chapter 6. I also might support readers of biography by helping them to retell the significant events in a person's life, borrowing retelling strategies like those that appear in Chapter 5. If you're looking for more narrative nonfiction strategies, try the chapters geared toward reading fiction.

Prompts

- What's the first part?
- Use the chapters to help you figure out the parts.
- Thinking about just this part of the person's life, what seems to be the main idea?
- What does it seem like the main idea of this part of the person's life is?
- Put all the main ideas together. What's the main idea of the whole biography?

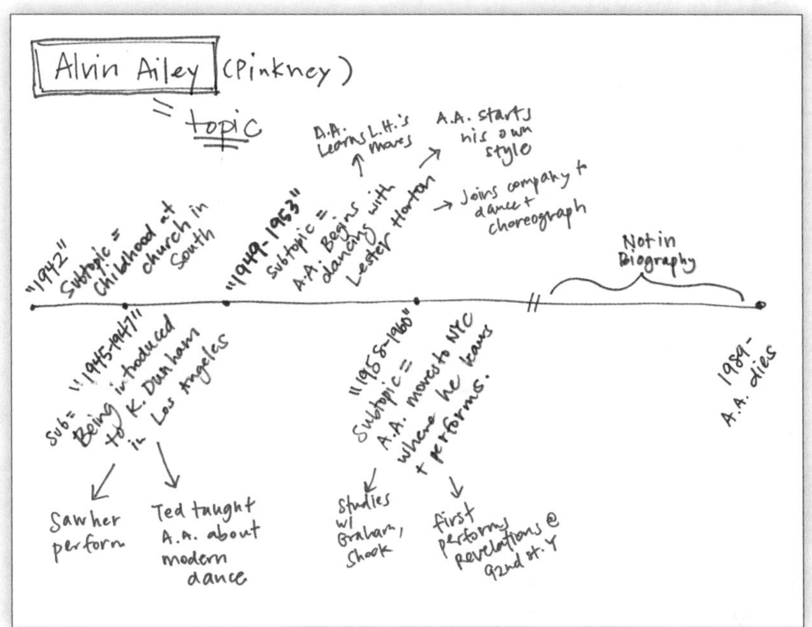

Who is this for?

LEVELS

M–Z+

GENRE / TEXT TYPE

narrative nonfiction

SKILLS

summarizing, determining importance

8.15 Why Does the Story Matter?

Who is this for?

LEVELS

M–Z+

GENRE / TEXT TYPE

narrative nonfiction

SKILLS

determining importance, synthesizing

Hat Tip: *The Rhetoric of Teaching: Understanding the Dynamics of Holocaust Narratives in an English Classroom* (Juzwik 2009)

Strategy In narrative nonfiction, true information told in stories, the main idea may be a question of what's most important about the story as a whole. After reading a true story we can ask ourselves, "What are the lessons this person has learned as a result of his or her victory or struggle?" or "What traits am I learning about this person?" or "Why does the author think the experiences of this person matter enough to write a story about him or her? What should we take away?"

Lesson Language *In* Boycott Blues *(Pinkney 2008), the author tells the story of Rosa Parks and other civil rights leaders. Based on all the details of the hardships that the leaders faced and how they kept persevering, as well as some of the final lines: "Now you see the power of the won't-stop shoes / Now you know the story of the boycott blues . . . Bye-bye boycott blues" (34), I think one possible thing the author might think is important about this story is that it was because of the ongoing efforts of a few that many today enjoy greater freedoms. I think the author feels gratitude toward those who came before her.*

Prompts

- What's important about this story?
- Think about why the author told the story.
- Look for a theme at the end, like you would in a fictional story.
- What seems to matter about this person or story?
- State what you're going to take away from this story.

As Readers Of Biography, We...

Preview The Text
- Think, "What do I already know about this person?"
- Think, "What details should I focus on? What relates to their big victory or big struggle?"

Read Closely
- Follow our "tracking a theory" steps
- Use traits that precisely match evidence!

Find the Hidden Meaning
- Ask, "What was my subject's big decision?"
- Ask, "What did my character choose NOT to do?"
- Ask, "What can I learn from their choice?"

8.16 What? and So What?

Strategy A main idea is more than a topic. To state the main idea, it's important to know what the text is about (the topic) and then to be able to say so what about it. The "so what" can be the angle, idea, or perspective that the author brings to the topic.

Lesson Language *The main idea of a text is more than just what the text is about (the topic). You can say this book is about whales. Or this one is about animals adapting. Or that this one is about celebrations in Central America. You would probably be able to say that without even reading the book! The title gives you that. Figuring out the main idea often requires a little thinking and a little work. The work you do as a reader to figure out the main idea is to collect all the information, notice what the author writes about and how he or she writes about it. And then, to step back from the text to ask yourself, "So what?" Your answer to "so what" might be about why the author wrote it. Or what unique perspective the author is bringing to the topic. Or, about how of all the books out there in the world on this topic, what makes this one unique? For example, in the book* Exploding Ants: Amazing Facts about How Animals Adapt *(Settel 1999), each section tells about a different animal and something interesting about how it's adapted. So, I could say the topic is "animal adaptation." But so what? So what about that topic? What's the author's angle? What does the author think about animal adaptation? Well, the author seems to be sharing not just any kind of adaptation, but gross ones. Ones that have to do with things like bloodsucking or swollen body parts or making homes in disgusting places such as dung. The author is not including, for example, facts about how a polar bear is white to blend in with the snow—something with no gross-out value. Still, I think the author is saying that it's kind of amazing and cool, even though it's also gross. So if I put all that together I'd say, "Although some animal behaviors are gross to humans, they are critical to their life on earth."*

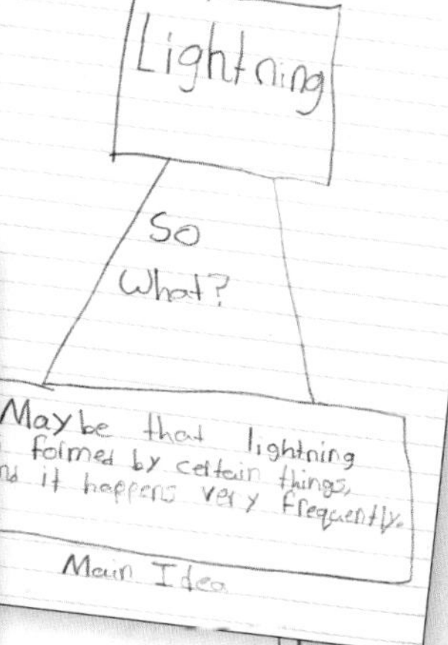

Prompts

- What's the topic of the book? Check the title.
- What's this section mostly about?
- That's the topic. What's the main idea?
- What's the author's angle or slant?
- What do you think the author is trying to say about that topic?

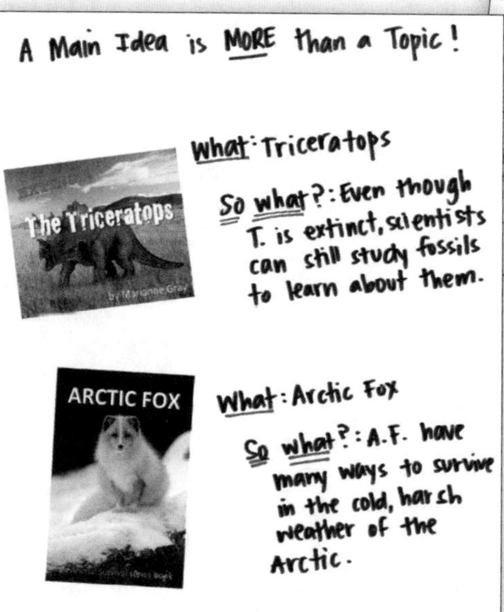

Who is this for?

LEVELS

M–Z+

GENRE / TEXT TYPE

nonfiction

SKILLS

determining importance, synthesizing

Hat Tip: Independent Reading Assessment: Nonfiction series (Serravallo 2013a)

8.17 Clue In to Topic Sentences

Who is this for?

LEVELS

M–Z+

GENRE / TEXT TYPE

expository nonfiction

SKILL

determining importance

Strategy Find a sentence that seems to sum up what the whole page (or part or section) is mostly about. This may be at the beginning, end, or even hidden somewhere in the middle. When you think you've found it, check the other facts to make sure those facts support the main idea. They don't all have to, but they mostly have to. If you find that most facts don't support that sentence, try a different one.

Lesson Language *There is a sentence hidden in most sections of nonfiction books and in most articles that tells you straight out what the main idea of the text is. The weird thing is that it's called a topic sentence even though it tells you way more than the topic alone—it also tells you an idea about the topic. For example, in* Jungles *(Podendorf 1982), the section called "What Kinds of Animals Live in a Jungle?" starts with this topic sentence: "A jungle is a home for many kinds of animals." Then, every sentence after gives numerous examples of different animals who live in the jungle. Not all authors come right out and tell you at the beginning, but there is often a topic sentence somewhere in each section to help you out.*

Prompts

- Find the sentence that tells you what this section is mostly about.
- I agree—all the details connect back to this one sentence. You found the topic sentence!
- Which sentence seems like a main idea?
- Now read on, and check each sentence to make sure it connects with the main idea.

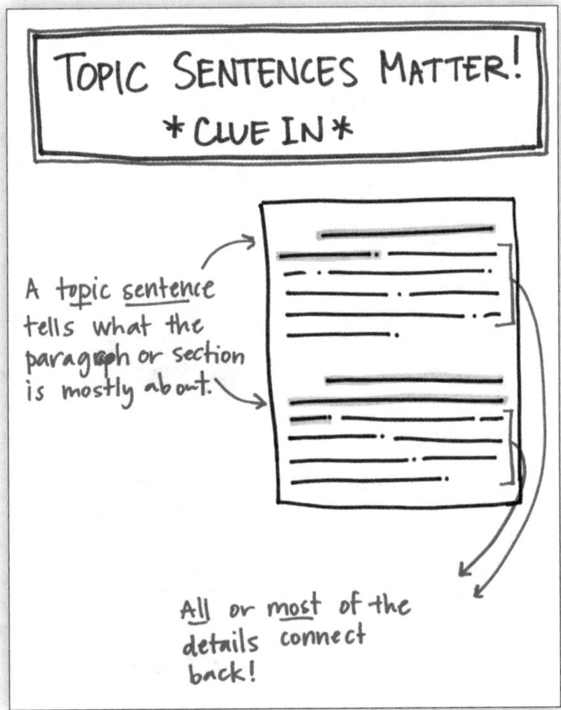

Hat Tip: Independent Reading Assessment: Nonfiction series (Serravallo 2013a)

8.18 Shrink-a-Text with a Partner

Strategy Read a chunk of text with your partner. Decide together what the main idea of the text is—try to shrink everything you just read into one sentence. Be sure not to just agree with the first thing your partner says—think critically and be sure you can back up your idea with details from the text. Read on and repeat.

Teaching Tip After students practice doing this a few times with a partner, you can gradually release responsibility and have them practice the strategy independently, encouraging them to have that same pattern of pausing after a chunk, discussing it (this time with themselves!), and backing it up before moving on.

Prompts

- Read a chunk.
- Decide what the main idea is.
- Try to say it using fewer words. Use just a sentence.
- You're listing facts; try to just say the main idea.
- Do you agree with your partner? How would you rephrase it?
- You worked together to come up with a main idea that's clear and concise.

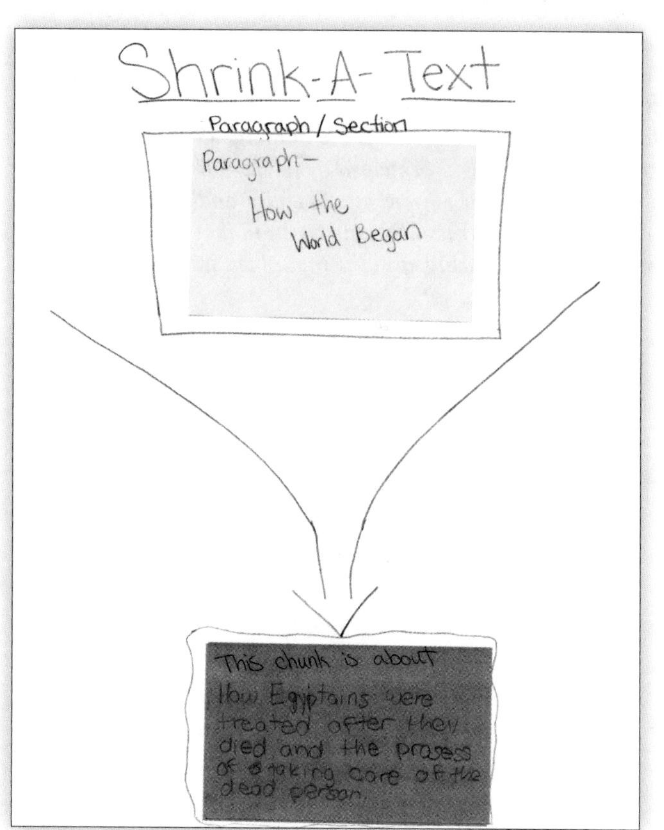

Who is this for?

LEVELS
M–Z+

GENRE / TEXT TYPE
nonfiction

SKILLS
summarizing, determining importance

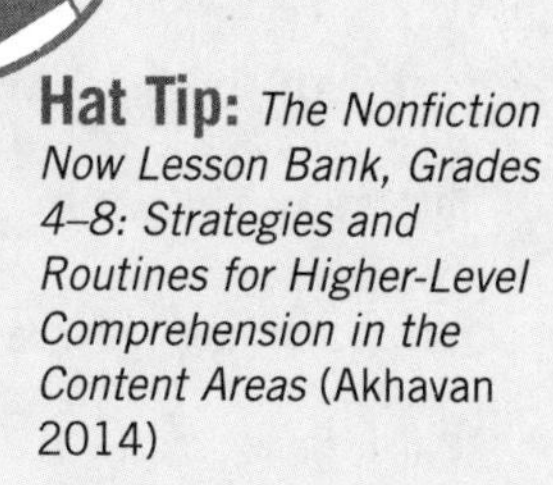

Hat Tip: *The Nonfiction Now Lesson Bank, Grades 4–8: Strategies and Routines for Higher-Level Comprehension in the Content Areas* (Akhavan 2014)

8.19 Consider Structure

Who is this for?

LEVELS

M–Z+

GENRE / TEXT TYPE

nonfiction

SKILL

synthesizing

Strategy Read the text through once. Think, "How is the information being presented? What's the overall structure?" Then, think back to the information you learned. Make a main idea statement that takes the whole text—and its structure—into account.

Teaching Tip This lesson is one to teach after each text structure has been introduced in a series of separate lessons. To introduce each structure, you may point out key words within a text. You might also introduce some kind of graphic organizer to show children how to graphically represent the structure. See the charts that are included with these two pages as examples of the key words and graphic organizers you might use. Keep in mind that a graphic organizer in and of itself is not a strategy. You would need to give students a "how-to" to unpack the information and include it in the graphic organizer. So, for example, a strategy to help children navigate a problem-solution structured text might sound something like strategy 8.12, "Track Down Opinion Clues in Solutions."

Lesson Language *It's often easier to work to figure out the main idea of a text when you can be sure about the text structure the author is using. For example, if the text is organized into a compare-and-contrast structure, the main idea should take into account both topics or ideas being compared. Let's say the book is comparing whales and dolphins. If I only talked about an idea about whales, then I'd only be giving a part of the idea, not the main idea. Instead, my statement might be something like, "Whales and dolphins share similar characteristics because they are both mammals, but their feeding and size cause some differences." If the text structure is narrative, the main idea could be more like a theme or lesson learned, and the reader might be helped by relying on strategies from the chapter about theme. If the book or article is written in a cause-and-effect structure—say, exploring the reasons why hurricanes form and the destruction they leave behind—both the cause and effect would need to be included in the main idea statement.*

Hat Tip: *Navigating Nonfiction in Expository Text* (Calkins and Tolan 2010c)

Navigating Nonfiction in Narrative and Hybrid Text (Calkins and Tolan 2010d)

Prompts

- You said "cause and effect"—make sure your main idea statement tells why and also what happened.
- You said "narrative"—think back to what you know about determining a theme or lesson.
- What's the relationship between the information being presented?
- How is the information organized?
- Take a look at these graphics. Which represents the way the information is organized?

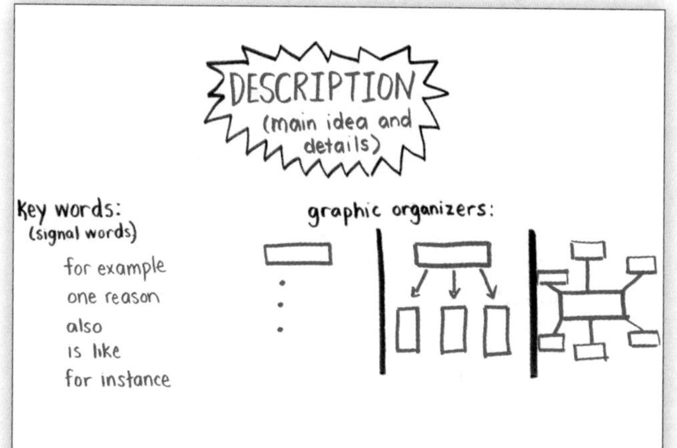

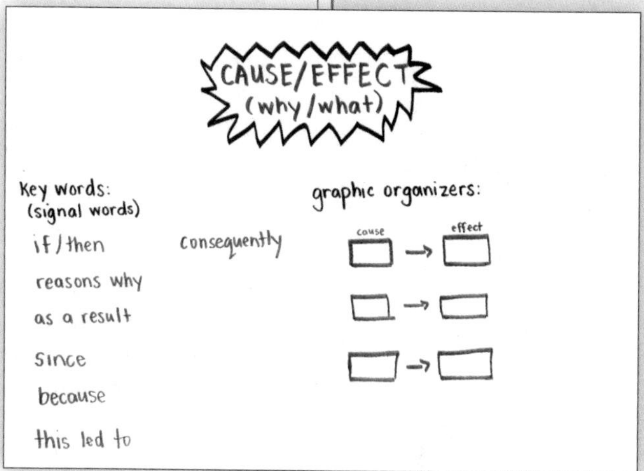

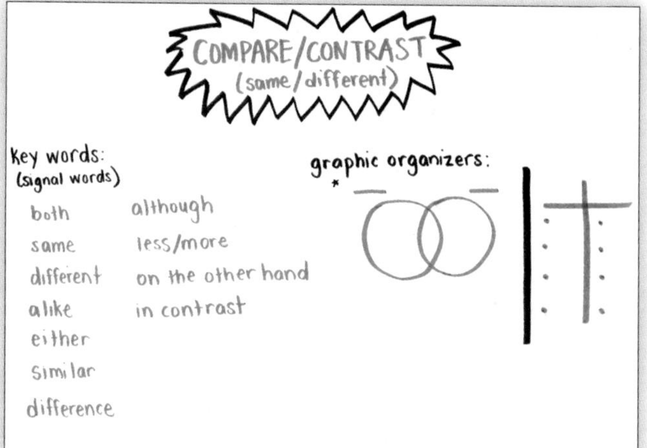

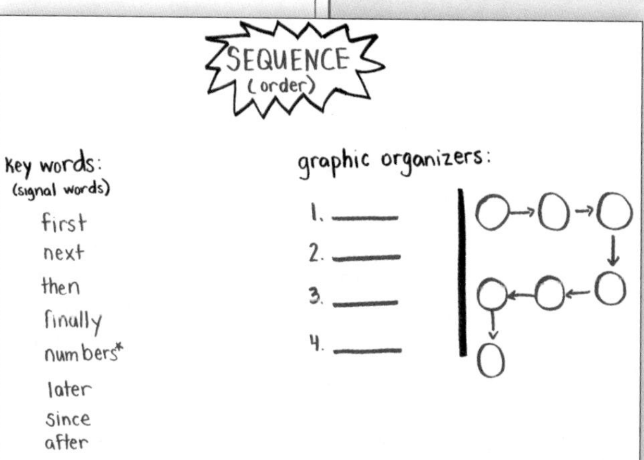

8.20 Determining Author's Purpose, Point of View

Who is this for?

LEVELS

O–Z+

GENRE / TEXT TYPE

nonfiction

SKILL

determining importance

Hat Tip: *Comprehension Through Conversation: The Power of Purposeful Talk in the Reading Workshop* (Nichols 2006)

Strategy Be aware of the author's reason for writing and any potential bias that comes from that. First, learn about who the author is (from an author bio included in the book). Then, consider what stake the author has in the topic based on his or her background. As you read, consider what facts are being included and what is being excluded. Consider if there are any "opinion words" being used alongside the factual information.

Lesson Language *The book* Face to Face with Whales *by Flip and Linda Nicklin (2008) at first glance looks to be a straightforward book about whales—there are photographs, lots of facts. But I wonder if the authors have a certain perspective on the issue that will shape the kinds of information they include? One look at their bio tells us that they live in Alaska and Hawaii, two places good for viewing whales. OK, good, that helps to make them experts on the topic. I also see they've written four other books about the subject. Again, all signs point to expert. At the end of the bio, it says, "He is active with Whale Trust, a conservation and research organization." If I thought about that, what kind of person would join the Whale Trust and what kind of slant might they have on the topic? I think someone who loves the creatures and wants to do all they can to protect them. Let's look inside to see if there are any opinion words that go along with that idea. I see on page 5: "I've been lucky to spend my life with whales" and excited on the next page: "They are* better *swimmers than we are" and* thrilling. *The author is clearly excluding any details that would make you feel terrified of these large creatures and is including details and opinion words to lead you to believe they are beautiful, fascinating creatures, a perspective that goes along with his bio!*

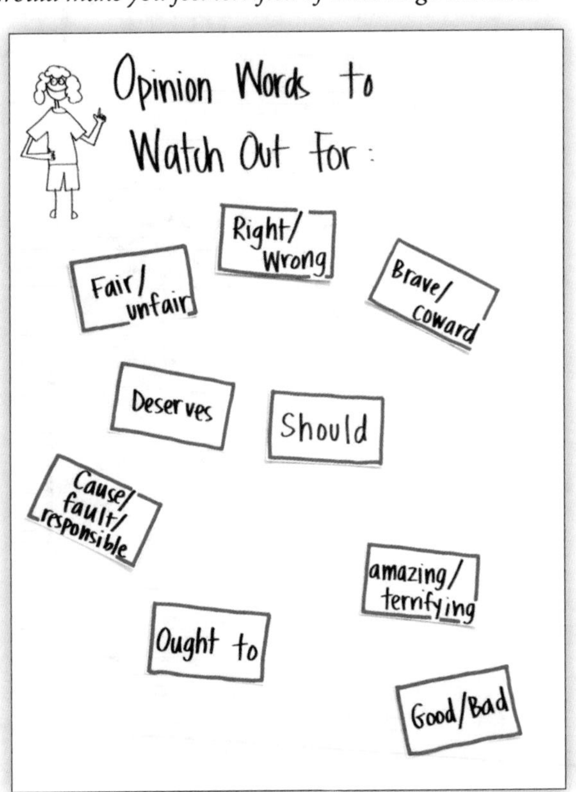

Prompts

- What do you know about the author?
- What does the author's background tell you about any potential bias?
- Think about the facts in the book. Why do you think the author included what he or she did?
- Do you see any opinion word?
- What's the slant?
- Which facts go with that slant?

8.21 What's the Perspective on the Topic?

Strategy Read the title and identify the topic. Read the first and last paragraph. Think: What is the author's perspective? What is the author saying? Read the entire article (or book), collecting facts and details that connect with the main idea. Revise your main idea statement if needed.

Prompts

- What do you think the author's perspective on the topic is?
- How do you know?
- What words give you a hint about the perspective?
- Read the first paragraph.
- Think about all of the details so far.
- That's the topic, tell an idea about topic.
- I like how you revised the main idea when you jotted new information.
- Yes, that detail fits with the main idea.

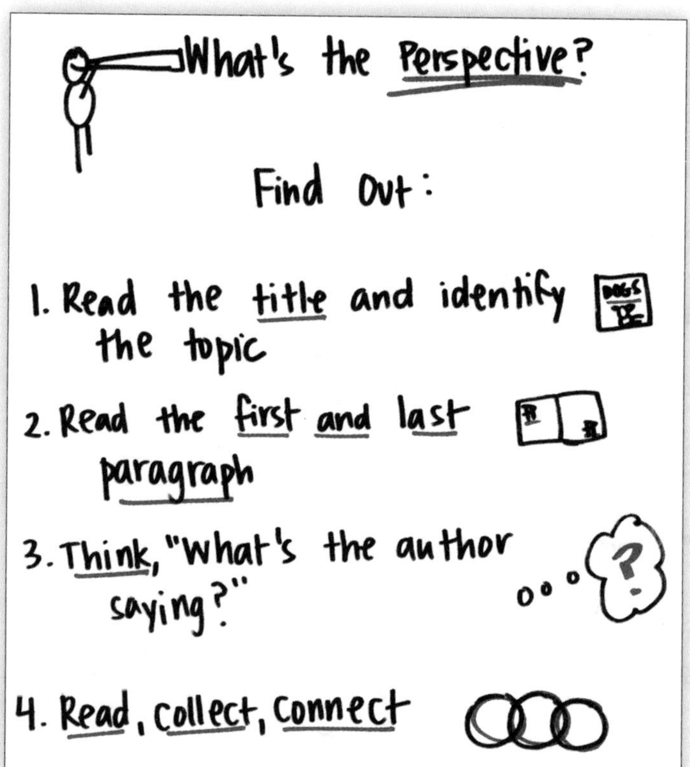

Who is this for?

LEVELS

O–Z+

GENRE / TEXT TYPE

nonfiction

SKILL

determining importance

8.22 Tricks of Persuasion

Who is this for?

LEVELS

P–Z+

GENRE / TEXT TYPE

nonfiction

SKILLS

determining importance, inferring

Strategy Nonfiction isn't always just straight-up facts. Sometimes, the author is trying to convince you of an idea as well. To figure out the idea, pay close attention to the tricks of persuasion (see chart). Look not just at the information being presented, but also at how it's being presented, especially with the choice of words and voice the author uses.

Prompts

- When do you see something that doesn't seem like a fact?
- How is this information being presented?
- Look at the choice of words.
- That's the fact. Name the opinion words.
- Notice who it seems like the author is siding with.
- The author won't always come right out and say their idea, you may have to infer it.

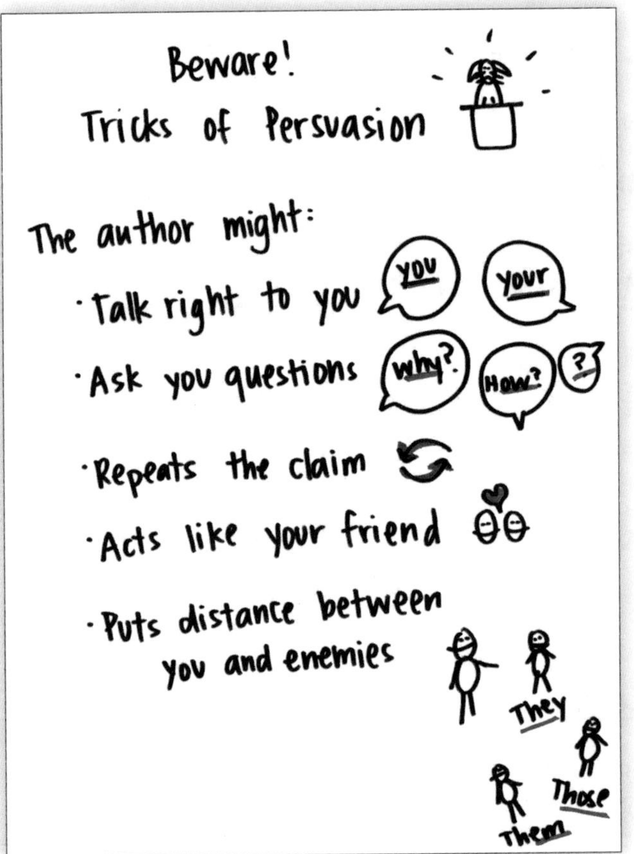

Hat Tip: *Inside Information: Developing Powerful Readers and Writers of Informational Text Through Project-Based Instruction* (Duke 2014)

8.23 Perspective, Position, Power

Strategy Once you understand a main idea of the text, consider the perspective of the author in crafting a text with that main idea. Then, think about our position to that idea (agreement or disagreement; insider or outsider) and the power inherent in the text (whose perspective is represented and whose is omitted?).

Teaching Tip This strategy brings critical reading to nonfiction. Choosing this strategy means a decision to teach children that as readers, they have the power to not simply believe everything they read—they can consider the author's choices in the information that was included and omitted, the group(s) to which the author belongs, and what that author's stake in the topic is and to think about where they, as readers, stand in relation to the information presented. They may be considered an "outsider" or "insider," or someone who agrees or disagrees with what's included. This strategy would work especially well in critiquing nonfiction articles and news.

Prompts

- What do you know about the author? Why does that matter to this topic?
- Think about whose perspective this is being told from.
- Where do you stand on this topic?
- Do you consider yourself an insider or outsider in relation to the information in this text? What does that make you think about this text?
- Who seems to have power here? What does that make you think about the topic?

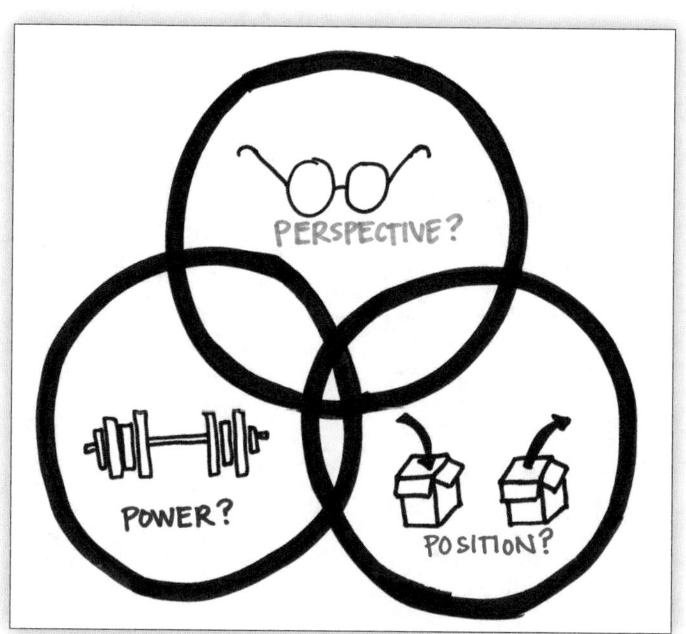

Who is this for?

LEVELS

P–Z+

GENRE / TEXT TYPE

nonfiction

SKILLS

determining importance, inferring, critiquing

Hat Tip: *Girls, Social Class, and Literacy: What Teachers Can Do to Make a Difference* (Jones 2006)

Supporting Comprehension in Nonfiction

Determining Key Details

Why is this goal important?

There is a difference between reading for *details* and reading for *key details*. That difference is in the reader's ability to determine importance. In doing so, he or she will find the details that support or connect with the main topic/ideas.

In their book *Strategies That Work,* Harvey and Goudvis (2000) write, "Determining importance means picking out the most important information when you read, to highlight essential ideas, to isolate supporting details, and to read for specific information. Teachers need to help readers sift and sort information, and make decisions about what information they need to remember and what information they can disregard" (117). As important as it is for readers to understand what the text is *mostly about* (see pages 218–245), readers also need to sort through all the information and identify which facts align to the main idea. Or, as Harvey and Goudvis declare:

"Readers of nonfiction have to decide and remember what is important in the texts they read if they are going to learn anything from them" (118).

Determining key details is the difference between taking a highlighter to every single word in a textbook, and highlighting just those facts that align to your purpose for reading, or that align to what the author is trying to say.

Bear in mind that as texts get more complex, this task of supporting an idea (or topic) with related details becomes more challenging. In first- and second-grade-level books, the text is often very cohesive and it would be hard to find a detail that strays from the main topic of the book. As texts get more complex, the density of information increases, meaning there is more information on every page. In books at these levels, not all of the details align to the main idea. And by fourth- or fifth-grade-level texts, the texts are often complex enough to have multiple main ideas, a greater increase in words on each page, and even text features that add extra information to complement the information in the main text, meaning the reader needs to sort through even more facts from a variety of locations within the book.

How do I know if this goal is right for my student?

Some students are whole-to-part thinkers, and others are part-to-whole thinkers. That is, some are able to step away from the reading of a text or text selection and distill its essence, or main idea, down to a sentence. When prompted, these readers may be able to back up the ideas with "evidence," "support," or "proof" of why that main idea fits the selection. Others may begin telling you about a selection by repeating a list of information, until they finally conclude with, "So I guess it's about . . ." and then state a main idea only after reviewing all the details first. In either case, you'll want to pay attention to the connectedness between the main idea (or topic) and the details that the student recounts. Students who will benefit from this goal are those who:

- support a main idea statement (or main topic) with just one detail, and need prompting to list more than one
- support a main idea (or topic) with just one portion of the text (for example, by looking only at a photograph)
- list seemingly random facts to support a main idea (or topic)—some may fit with the idea/topic and others may not

- can state a main idea or "gist" of a text after having read it, but need prompting to support the idea/topic with specific information.
- need support understanding which details in the text are most important.

You'll need some form of evaluating a student's ability to determine key details aligned to a main topic or idea. You could ask a child to read a book or short text, such as an article. Then, ask the student to tell you (during a conference) or write down what the text is mostly about and what details support it. Evaluate the *quantity* of details the student can provide as well as the *quality*—the student will ideally provide multiple details, from across many sections/portions of the text, that strongly relate to the main idea/topic. For a level-by-level rubric for what to expect at levels J–W, see the Independent Reading Assessment: Nonfiction series (Serravallo 2013a).

Strategies for Determining Key Details at a Glance

Strategy		Levels	Genres/ Text Types	Skills
9.1	Compare New to Known	A–Z+	Nonfiction	Activating prior knowledge, visualizing
9.2	Reading with a Sense of "Wow"	A–Z+	Nonfiction	Monitoring for meaning
9.3	A Spin on KWL	A–Z+	Nonfiction	Activating prior knowledge
9.4	Check Yourself	A–Z+	Nonfiction	Monitoring for meaning
9.5	Gather Up Facts	A–Z+	Nonfiction	Synthesizing, monitoring for meaning
9.6	Consistently Ask, "How Do I Know?"	A–Z+	Expository nonfiction	Determining importance, summarizing
9.7	Click and Clunk	A–Z+	Nonfiction	Monitoring for meaning
9.8	Read, Cover, Remember, Retell	A–Z+	Nonfiction	Summarizing/ retelling, monitoring for meaning
9.9	Generic, Not Specific	A–J	Nonfiction	Monitoring for meaning
9.10	Scan and Plan	J–Z+	Expository nonfiction	Sequencing, planning, reading process
9.11	Code a Text	L–Z+	Nonfiction	Monitoring for meaning
9.12	Translate a Text	L–Z+	Nonfiction	Determining importance, summarizing
9.13	Important Versus Interesting	L–Z+	Nonfiction	Determining importance
9.14	Slow Down for Numbers	M–Z+	Nonfiction	Visualizing, monitoring for meaning
9.15	Using Analogies	M–Z+	Nonfiction	Monitoring for meaning, visualizing
9.16	Keying In to What's Important (Biographies)	M–Z+	Biography	Determining importance, summarizing
9.17	Following Procedures	M–Z+	Procedural nonfiction	Monitoring for meaning, determining importance
9.18	Answering Questions	M–Z+	Nonfiction	Questioning, inferring
9.19	Event Connections	P–Z+	Narrative nonfiction	Understanding cause and effect, sequencing, summarizing
9.20	Statistics and Stance	P–Z+	Nonfiction	Determining importance, critiquing, inferring

9.1 Compare New to Known

Who is this for?

LEVELS

A–Z+

GENRE / TEXT TYPE

nonfiction

SKILLS

activating prior knowledge, visualizing

Hat Tip: *Comprehension Through Conversation: The Power of Purposeful Talk in the Reading Workshop* (Nichols 2006)

Strategy As you read, try to do more than just collect the facts as they come. Try instead to create an understanding. To do this, compare and/or connect the information the author is giving with what you already know. Create a mental picture of the new information you're learning.

Lesson Language *Some may think that reading nonfiction is just about collecting and memorizing lots of facts. I've seen children reading nonfiction books with a pen in hand, copying each new fact they learn onto their sticky notes. But collecting all the facts doesn't mean you actually understand what you've read. Instead of trying to memorize or list it all, try to really "get" what the author is saying. Sometimes this means that you have to connect to information you already know to help you understand something new, and try to picture what you've learned. For example, as I was reading about sharks, I came to a fact that sharks have many rows of teeth. I didn't have any information about that before, so it's a new fact. I connected it to what I know about a human's mouth—I've seen a bite mark before and I know we have one row of teeth on top and one below. So then I could picture what a bite mark would look like that had a few rows on top and on the bottom. I could picture the jaws of a shark to see the rows of teeth on top and on the bottom. Because I connected to what I knew, and because I could picture what I've learned, I'm sure that I'm understanding this new information.*

Prompts

- Think about what you already know.
- Think about what you're learning.
- What's the same?
- What's different?
- Picture what you're learning.

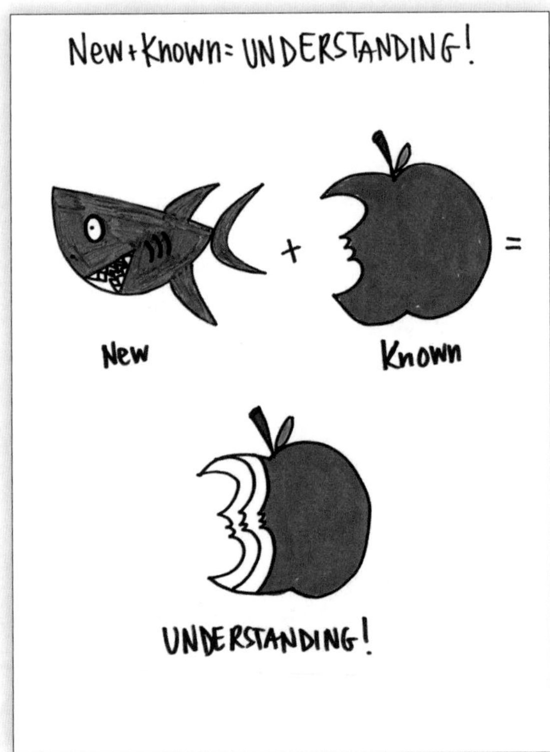

9.2 Reading with a Sense of "Wow"

Strategy Approach the text expecting to learn. As you read new information (facts, figures), or see something new (photographs, diagrams), pause and let the information sink it. React and respond with "Wow, I never knew . . ."

Lesson Language *When you read with curiosity and interest, you're more likely to learn and remember the new information you encounter. The stance you take as a nonfiction reader may be slightly different than that of a fiction reader, because when you read nonfiction you read to understand facts, numbers, visual information, and more. As you read, try to let the information "sink in," thinking about how it answers questions or satiates your curiosity. You may even react to new information as you come across it, by saying "wow" and adding on to what's so interesting about what you just read.*

Prompts

- What did you learn that's new to you?
- Say back what you learned. Start with, "Wow, I never knew . . ."
- What's sinking in?
- What did you feel like you missed?
- If you can't say it back, try to reread.

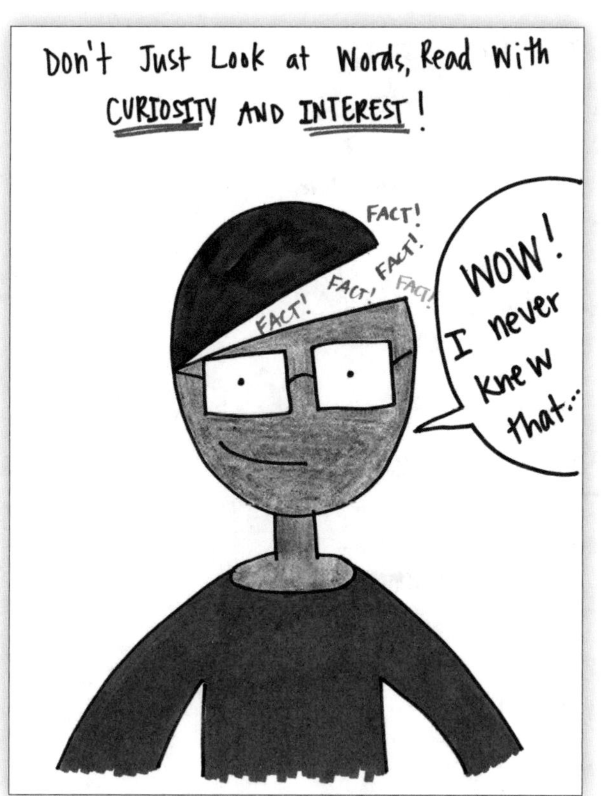

Who is this for?

LEVELS

A–Z+

GENRE / TEXT TYPE

nonfiction

SKILL

monitoring for meaning

Hat Tip: *Comprehension Through Conversation: The Power of Purposeful Talk in the Reading Workshop* (Nichols 2006)

9.3 A Spin on KWL

Who is this for?

LEVELS

A–Z+

GENRE / TEXT TYPE

nonfiction

SKILL

activating prior knowledge

Hat Tip: *Reading for Real: Teach Students to Read with Power, Intention, and Joy in K–3 Classrooms* (Collins 2008)

Strategy Before reading, talk or write about what you know for sure, what you think you know, and what you wonder. Then, read getting ready to learn new information.

Lesson Language *To be sure you're picking up on the key details an author is teaching you, it's important not to let preconceptions or misconceptions get in the way. Before reading, you can jot or talk about what you know for sure about a topic, what you think you know about a topic, and what you wonder about your topic. Sometimes if you approach a book thinking you know something—say, that all spiders have six legs—and then you read a fact that says, "Spiders have eight legs" you might not even let it sink in that what you said you knew at first was actually wrong.*

Prompts

- You can start with, "I'm not sure, but I think . . ."
- What's something you're sure you know? How are you sure?
- What are you wondering about your topic?
- What do you know a little about? What do you want to learn about more deeply?
- What are you learning, now that you've read this part?

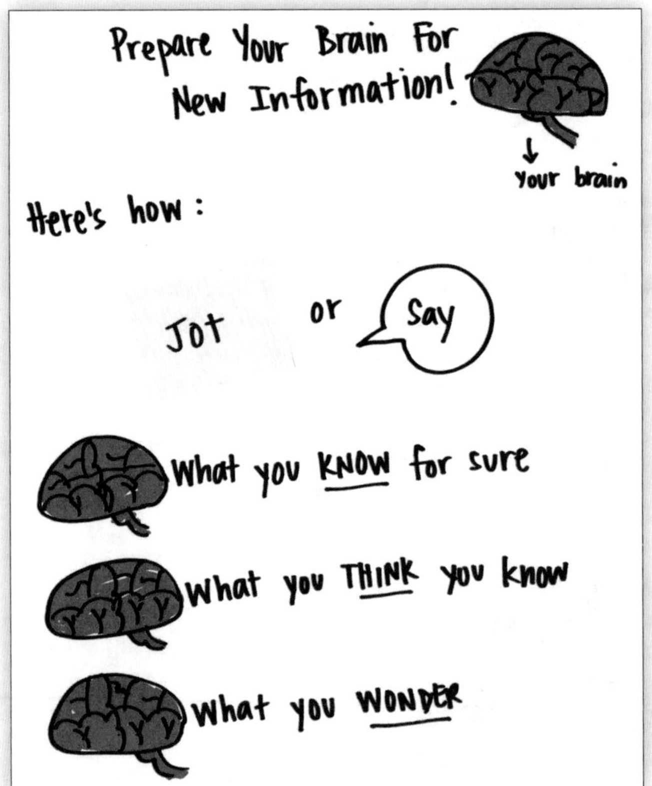

Prepare Your Brain For New Information!
your brain
Here's how :
Jot
or
Say
What you KNOW for sure
What you THINK you know
What you WONDER

9.4 Check Yourself

Strategy When the information you read feels confusing, stop and say, "Huh?" Then go back and reread, considering why it's confusing. Did you misread the fact? Did the fact contradict something you thought you already knew about the topic? As you reread, be prepared to revise your thinking.

Lesson Language *Expect that when you read nonfiction, you are going to get a lot of information presented to you all at once. Many readers will slow down when reading nonfiction as a way to give their brains time to process the new learning, and also to monitor their own understanding. Read knowing that it's not really reading you're doing unless it's making sense! If anything feels confusing or unclear, it's important to reread. Try to figure out why you were confused and try to fix up the confusion before reading on.*

Prompts

- What was confusing here?
- What made that fact confusing?
- Go back and reread.
- Based on what you just read, what are you thinking about what you knew before?
- Based on what you just read, do you think you read it incorrectly the first time?

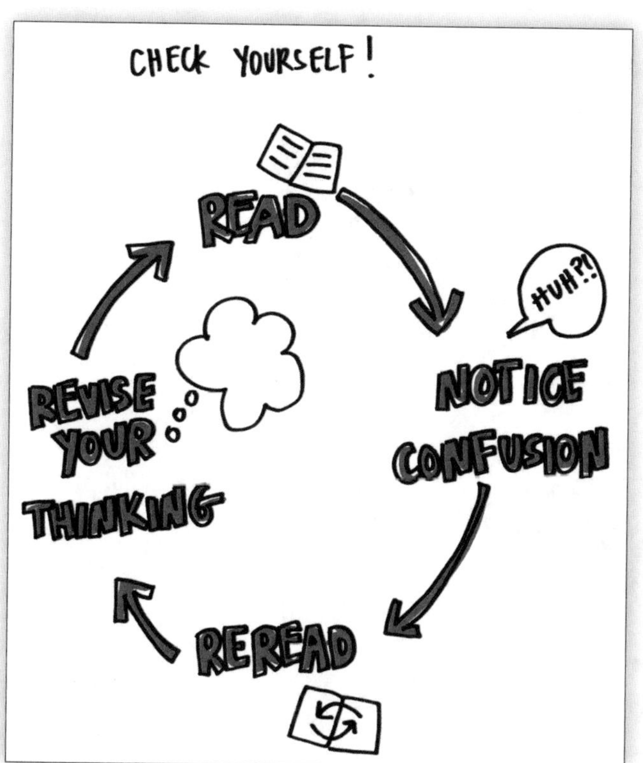

Who is this for?

LEVELS

A–Z+

GENRE / TEXT TYPE

nonfiction

SKILL

monitoring for meaning

Hat Tip: *Reading for Real: Teach Students to Read with Power, Intention, and Joy in K–3 Classrooms* (Collins 2008)

9.5 Gather Up Facts

Who is this for?

LEVELS

A–Z+

GENRE / TEXT TYPE

nonfiction

SKILLS

synthesizing, monitoring for meaning

Strategy After reading a part of a book (or, a whole book or article if it's short), it's important to go back to recall what you read. Gather up facts by listing them. You can start with, "In this page (or part or book), I learned that . . ."

Lesson Language *In a nonfiction book, facts come at you fast and furious like raindrops in a thunderstorm! It's important to make sure you're keeping track of all you learned. One way to do that is to stop often and gather up what you know. Watch me as I read this section and then stop, not just zooming along to the next part of the book but rather stopping to see if I can say back all I read, fact by fact. I might put some of the facts in my own words to check that I really understood. Other facts I might repeat using the same language the author used.*

Prompts

- List the facts you remember.
- What did you learn in this part?
- List what you remember.
- That's one fact. Let's try to list a few.
- Yes! All the facts you listed are from this part.

Hat Tip: *Reading for Real: Teach Students to Read with Power, Intention, and Joy in K–3 Classrooms* (Collins 2008)

9.6 Consistently Ask, "How Do I Know?"

Strategy To find the details in the text that match with the most important ideas being presented, you'll have to sort through them all. After reading a section or whole book, you can start by saying what the whole book is mostly about and touching your palm. Then, ask yourself, "How do I know?" and see if you can go back to the text to say back the facts that are most connected to the idea, listing them across your fingers.

Teaching Tip This lesson can be modified to be about the "topic" with supporting details instead of "main idea" with supporting details, for those students who are reading books at levels A–L.

Lesson Language *I think this first chapter in* Ancient Greece *(Newman 2010) is mostly about* (Touch palm.) *how even though ancient Greeks lived thousands of years ago, we can still feel their influence today. How do I know? Well, I know because* (Touch one finger.) *it says in the book that our laws and government are rooted in what the Greeks did. It also said that* (Touch another finger.) *math and science, subjects we study in school, came from the Greeks. Also* (Touch a third finger.), *many building designs that we still use today started in ancient Greece. All of these facts connect to that one main idea.*

Prompts

- State your idea.
- Name detail(s) that match that idea.
- Explain how you know.
- How does that detail connect to the main idea? Explain the connection.

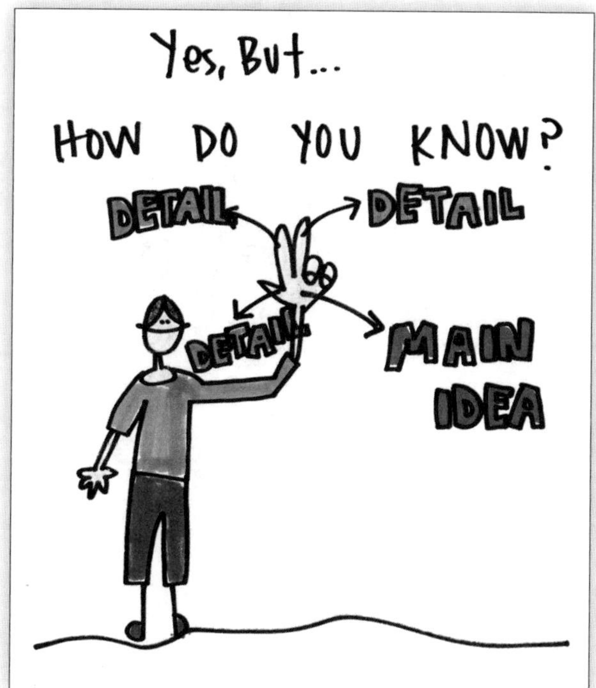

Who is this for?

LEVELS

A–Z+

GENRE / TEXT TYPE

expository nonfiction

SKILLS

determining importance, summarizing

Hat Tip: *Inside Information: Developing Powerful Readers and Writers of Informational Text Through Project-Based Instruction* (Duke 2014)

9.7 Click and Clunk

Who is this for?

LEVELS

A–Z+

GENRE / TEXT TYPE

nonfiction

SKILL

monitoring for meaning

Hat Tip: *Reading & Writing Informational Text in the Primary Grades* (Duke and Bennett-Armistead 2003)

Strategy After reading each sentence, think about whether you get it ("click!") or it's confusing ("clunk!"). As you read it should feel like "Click, click, click." When you hit a "clunk," go back and reread to be sure you understand.

Prompts

- Did you understand that?
- Check yourself before moving on.
- Did it make sense? Did it "click?"
- You didn't understand? Go back and reread.
- Make sure you're understanding!
- Think to yourself as you're reading.

Read, Stop, Think:
Is It a CLICK?
(keep reading)
Is It a CLUNK?
(Reread)
Do You Get It?

9.8 Read, Cover, Remember, Retell

Strategy Read as much as you can cover with your hand or a sticky note. Cover the text you just read. Focus on remembering what you read (it's OK to be quiet!). Say back what you remember (it's OK to peek back!). Repeat.

Teaching Tip This strategy is one of my favorite strategies to teach when students are beginning to research, although it works any time you want to slow children down to monitor their comprehension. When researching, what often happens is that students copy down information without really understanding it. Covering up the information before retelling (or taking notes) forces the reader to understand it well enough to put it into his or her own words. I also find that students read with a different level of attention and concentration knowing that they have to say back what they learned without reading it from the text.

Prompts

- Read. Now cover.
- Say back what you read.
- You can peek!
- Not sure? Uncover the text and reread. When you think you have it, cover it again.
- Make sure you think as you read, to make sure you "get" it.
- Retell it.

Know What You're Reading!

Here's how:

step 1: READ!

step 2: COVER!

step 3: REMEMBER!

step 4: RETELL!

Who is this for?

LEVELS

A–Z+

GENRE / TEXT TYPE

nonfiction

SKILLS

summarizing/retelling, monitoring for meaning

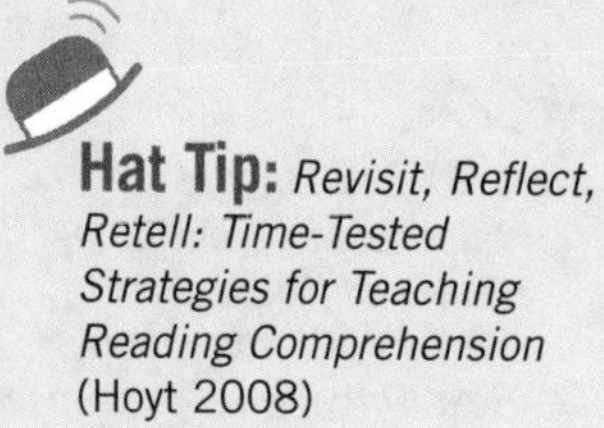

Hat Tip: *Revisit, Reflect, Retell: Time-Tested Strategies for Teaching Reading Comprehension* (Hoyt 2008)

9.9 Generic, Not Specific

Who is this for?

LEVELS

A–J

GENRE / TEXT TYPE

nonfiction

SKILL

monitoring for meaning

Strategy In nonfiction texts, when a thing is mentioned, it's often meant to describe the whole group of things, not one specific thing. Read to make sure you understand how nouns are used to describe the broader fact or information being explained.

Lesson Language *In a storybook, when you see the word* Lion, *it's usually meant to refer to one specific lion, whose name in the story might even be* Lion, *like in the fable "The Lion and the Mouse." However, when you read a nonfiction book and see the same word—a lion or lions—the author doesn't mean one specific lion, but rather lions in general. For example, "Lions often hunt together with other members of their pride" doesn't refer to one specific group of lions, but rather describes any group of lions, or lions in general.*

Prompts

- Explain what this fact is teaching you.
- What is the thing or animal being taught about in this fact?
- Which thing(s) does this fact apply to?
- Is that word meant to mean one thing specifically or a group in general?
- When that word (*Point to a noun.*) is used, what do you picture?

UNDERSTAND NOUNS IN NONFICTION:

SPECIFIC

GENERIC

Hat Tip: *Inside Information: Developing Powerful Readers and Writers of Informational Text Through Project-Based Instruction* (Duke 2014)

9.10 Scan and Plan

Strategy First, scan the page or section to see how the information is organized and laid out. Then, make a plan for how you'll read the information. Finally, read it according to your plan. Decide if your plan helped you understand, and then plan for the next section or book accordingly.

Lesson Language *Sometimes the pages in the nonfiction books we read are busy and filled with stuff! There may be words in one place, pictures in another, a diagram over here, a map over there. It could start to feel like you're inside a corn maze, trying to find your way through, unless you have some plan for how you'll read. It helps to step back from a page and figure out how you'll read it first. Some people like to start with the visual information, and then start in on the words. Other people like to read the headings and decide which section or sections they'll read because those sections fit with what they are hoping to learn about. Others are words-first people, who check the pictures as they read. No matter what, it helps to have a plan to find your way across the page. Once you've followed your plan, you can think about how it worked for you and plan the next part or book you read based on how the first plan went.*

Prompts

- What's first? Why?
- You planned to look at all the visuals first. Now, as you read the words, check back with the visuals.
- Read this first part. Let's see how your plan works out for you.
- Now that you've finished this section, will you read the next section the same way?

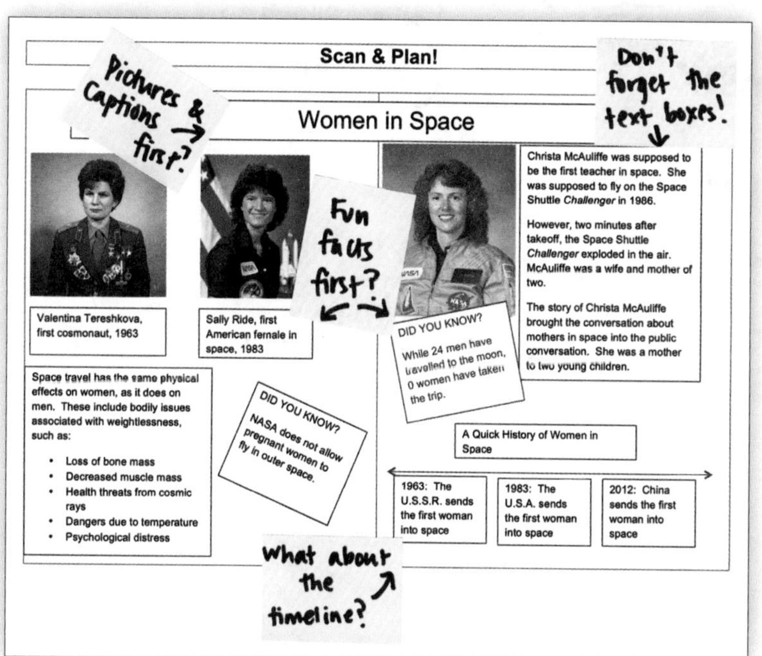

Who is this for?

LEVELS

J–Z+

GENRE / TEXT TYPE

expository nonfiction

SKILLS

sequencing, planning, reading process

Hat Tip: *Reading for Real: Teach Students to Read with Power, Intention, and Joy in K–3 Classrooms* (Collins 2008)

9.11 Code a Text

Who is this for?

LEVELS

L–Z+

GENRE / TEXT TYPE

nonfiction

SKILL

monitoring for meaning

Hat Tip: *Comprehension Intervention: Small-Group Lessons for the Comprehension Toolkit* (Harvey, Goudvis, and Wallis 2010)

Strategy Read a chunk. Think, "What did I just read? What should I jot to help me remember?" Then, translate the author's words into a symbol system to help you remember. These symbols will help you go back and quickly skim the information, which is important in nonfiction texts when there is often so much information packed together.

Teaching Tip You may decide to introduce a certain symbol system to students, or let them invent it on the run. Your decision may be based on the age level of the students you teach and the familiarity the students have with annotating texts.

Prompts

- Think about what you just read. What symbol would you use to remind yourself?
- Check the chart of symbols. How would you respond to this part?
- Make sure you're reading just a chunk! Stop and jot.
- Think of the words the author wrote. What is your response?
- Go back and skim the symbols. Remind yourself of what you read.
- Make sure you know what you read before you move on.

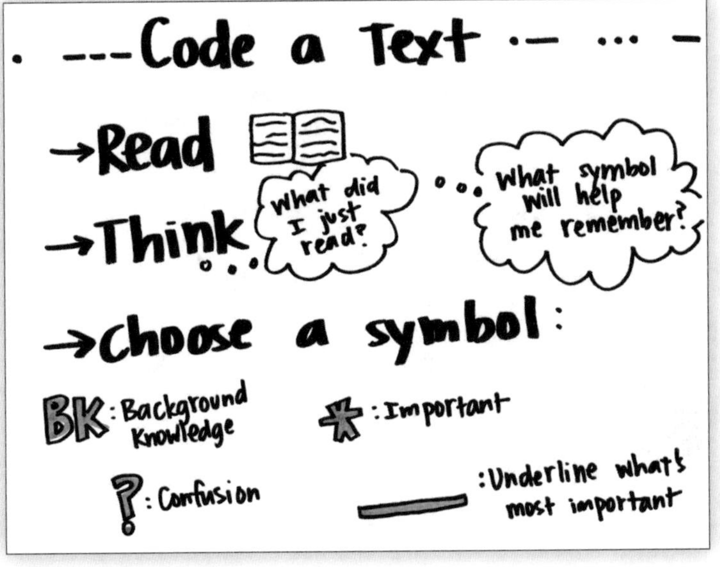

9.12 Translate a Text

Strategy Go back to a text you've coded. (See strategy 9.11, "Code a Text," page 260) to use the symbols as a springboard for more writing. Think back to what prompted you to write the code or symbol in the first place. Then, think about a quick word or phrase you'd write to hold on to your thinking.

Lesson Language (Show the students how you go back to a symbol such as an asterisk and think out loud.) *Hmm. Why did I think this part was important?* (Jot down a quick phrase to hold on to what's important. Then, find another symbol, perhaps a question mark.) *I had a question here. As I read on, I was able to answer it. Let me just jot the important information I got because I asked this question.*

Prompts

- Look back at your symbols. What would you jot?
- Take the symbol and turn it into a phrase.
- Don't write everything the author wrote, just the most important information.
- What's the important information you'd jot here?
- Nicely done—you got your thoughts down to just one phrase.

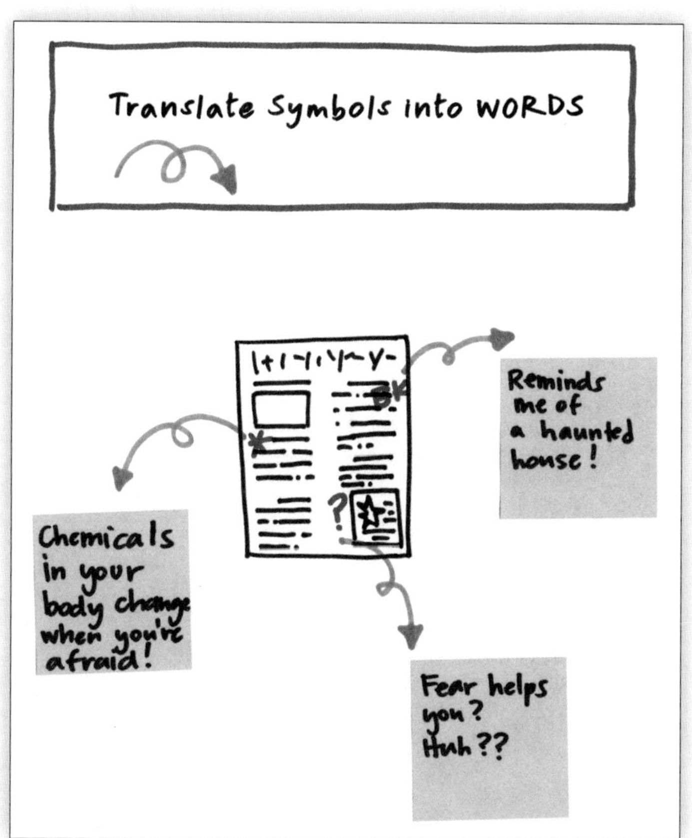

Who is this for?

LEVELS

L–Z+

GENRE / TEXT TYPE

nonfiction

SKILLS

determining importance, summarizing

Hat Tip: *Comprehension Intervention: Small-Group Lessons for the Comprehension Toolkit* (Harvey, Goudvis, and Wallis 2010)

9.13 Important Versus Interesting

Who is this for?

LEVELS

L–Z+

GENRE / TEXT TYPE

nonfiction

SKILL

determining importance

Strategy After reading a fact, stop and think: "Does this fact support the main idea of this page (or section or book)?" If it doesn't, it may be that the author included something interesting, but that isn't necessarily important to understanding the main point of the page (or book).

Lesson Language *For information to be considered a key detail, it has to be a detail that connects to the main idea that the author is presenting. In most nonfiction books, though, the author fills the pages with information that is important (or key) and also information that is meant to wow, amaze, gross out, or otherwise keep the reader reading. It's all great information because it keeps us reading and engaged. However, when we go to summarize a text, we need to sort through all the information and just present what's most connected to the main idea. For example, if I'm reading the section "Harsh or Heroic?" in a book about the Middle Ages and I read "Joan of Arc was accused of witchcraft and burned at the stake" I might think, "Whoa! I can't believe that. Things were crazy back then" (Kenney 2007). Though I'm interested in that fact, I also have to figure out if the detail is also important, so I have to check to see if it connects to the main idea. The main idea of the page is that although the times of castles and knights seems exciting, few had power and many lived harsh lives. The fact about Joan of Arc is certainly loosely related, but I think there are other facts in this section that better connect to the main idea. I'd file this one away as interesting, but not important to the main idea.*

Prompts

- Interesting or important? How do you know?
- Explain how it connects to the main idea.
- Does it connect to the main idea? If not, file it away as interesting, but not necessarily important.
- Yes, you're right that's an interesting side fact because it doesn't connect to the main idea.
- Check the fact.
- What are your thoughts about that fact?

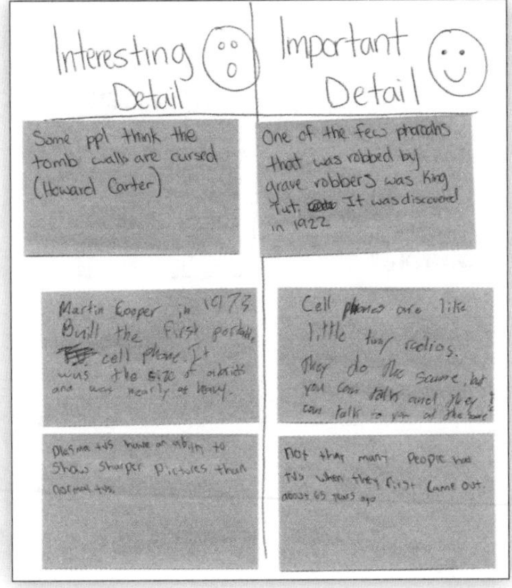

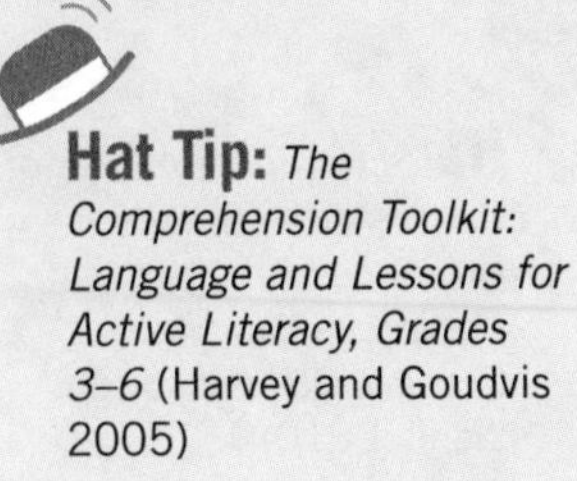

Hat Tip: *The Comprehension Toolkit: Language and Lessons for Active Literacy, Grades 3–6* (Harvey and Goudvis 2005)

9.14 Slow Down for Numbers

Strategy When you see numbers in a book, the author is giving specific information. Sometimes it takes a minute to understand the numbers. It's helpful to stop and think, "How is this number being used?" and then try to see what the fact with the number is trying to teach you. You can stop and think, "How would I picture this?" You can take a moment to make the picture in your head, or even draw it quickly as a sketch.

Lesson Language *Sometimes when we read nonfiction we will need to switch our thinking from our reading brain to our math brain! Nonfiction authors include numbers to teach us about all kinds of things including size, scale, distance, quantity, age, dates, and more. While it may seem easy to just breeze past the information, the author put it there for an important reason so we should slow down to try to understand it. For example, in Seymour Simon's book* The Moon *(2003), we learn on the first page that "The moon is Earth's closest neighbor in space. It is about one quarter of a million miles away" (1). As a reader, I need to stop and think about how the number is being used—to teach about a distance. Then, to try to get some picture of it. I know, for instance, that I live ten miles from school. So a quarter of a million miles is 250,000 miles which is such a big number and such a hard thing to imagine. Even if I can't exactly picture how far that is, I can imagine it and understand it's a great, great distance. Later on that page Simon uses more numbers with this fact, "The moon takes about twenty-seven days and eight hours to go around the Earth once" (1). That's three numbers in one sentence! So again, I'd slow down to think how each number is being used and to try to visualize what the numbers are teaching me.*

Prompts

- How is the number being used (length, weight, size, number of years, etc.)?
- What do you picture in your mind?
- Draw a sketch.
- How does that number help you understand the fact?
- What other thing you know uses that same number for size (or weight or length)?

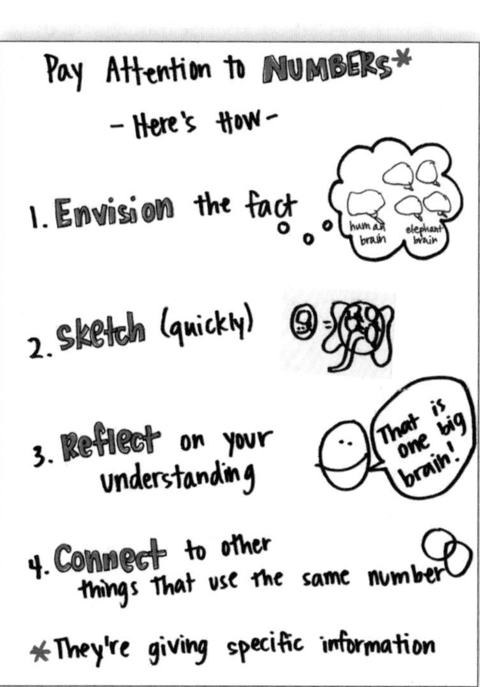

Who is this for?

LEVELS

M–Z+

GENRE / TEXT TYPE

nonfiction

SKILLS

visualizing, monitoring for meaning

Hat Tip: *Inside Information: Developing Powerful Readers and Writers of Informational Text Through Project-Based Instruction* (Duke 2014)

9.15 Using Analogies

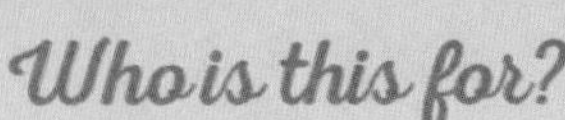

LEVELS

M–Z+

GENRE / TEXT TYPE

nonfiction

SKILLS

monitoring for meaning, visualizing

Strategy Sometimes the author will compare information to something else, to help you better understand the fact. Be on the lookout for words like like, as, or than. Then create a picture in your mind of the two things being compared. Think about what aspect of those two things is similar, and why the author would be comparing them.

Lesson Language *The introduction in Seymour Simon's* Sharks *(2006) includes this sentence: "You have a better chance of being hit by lightning than of being attacked by a shark" (7). The book is not about weather or lightning, so why would he be talking about it when presenting this fact? I see the word "than" in this sentence, so the author must be comparing two things—the chances of being hit by lightning and being attacked by a shark. I can picture the two, and the information I think he's trying to teach is that being struck by lightning is rare, and therefore being attacked by a shark is even rarer. Here's another sentence from the same page for you and your partner to think about: "Sharks have killed fewer people in the United States in the past one hundred years than are killed in automobile accidents over a single holiday weekend" (7). What is being compared here?*

Prompts

- What's being compared?
- Say what's the same about the two things.
- What do you picture in your mind for each thing?
- Think about why the author made that comparison.
- What conclusion can you draw based on that comparison?
- How does that comparison help you understand the topic?
- That explanation makes sense with the rest of the information on this page.

9.16 Keying In to What's Important (Biographies)

Strategy Think first, "What are the major obstacles or problems the person needs to overcome?" Then, think, "What are the ways the person overcame those obstacles?" Finally, think, "What is this person famous for because of how he or she lived his or her life?"

Lesson Language *In expository nonfiction, the most important details are ones that connect to the main ideas. In biographies, it's often helpful to use what we know from reading stories to understand what's most important. In David A. Adler's* A Picture Book of Jackie Robinson *(1997), the author starts the story of his life sharing some of Robinson's challenges early in life: his father worked for extremely low wages on a plantation and was so frustrated that he left the family in search of better work and never came back. Once he was gone, the plantation owner told Robinson's mother that she and her children had to leave as well. In the south in the 1920s, an African American family didn't have too many options and were often treated poorly by their white neighbors. But soon after learning of these hardships and obstacles, we learn that Jackie had an interest—playing sports. And this interest helped him to stay focused and go to college and become a star in several sports. The story then shares some new obstacles about his efforts to play on a team and being told he couldn't because he was black, and then some of the ways he overcame those challenges. At the end, this is what the author wants us to understand about Jackie—that he was not only a gifted athlete, but also a courageous man who fought for equal rights. This is often a pattern in biographies—the author shares the obstacles, and then we learn about the efforts to overcome them.*

Prompts

- Find an obstacle in the story.
- What is the most important obstacle this character faced?
- How did the person overcome the obstacle?
- Why is the obstacle important to understanding this person's story?
- Retell what's most important.
- State the obstacles the character overcame, and how it connects to what he or she is famous for.

Benjamin Franklin

Obstacle:	Solution:
The Penns won't pay the tax for Pennsilvania.	Ben talks to the king to take control of Pensilvania, and persuaded the english government.
Important because:	**Why it connects:**
Ben showed that he won't give up and that he showed effort to help Pensilvania	Ben invented a lot of things to help the people

Inventors don't give up.

Who is this for?

LEVELS

M–Z+

GENRE / TEXT TYPE

biography

SKILLS

determining importance, summarizing

9.17 Following Procedures

Who is this for?

LEVELS

M–Z+

GENRE / TEXT TYPE

procedural nonfiction

SKILLS

monitoring for meaning, determining importance

Hat Tip: *Inside Information: Developing Powerful Readers and Writers of Informational Text Through Project-Based Instruction* (Duke 2014)

Strategy To understand a procedural text, such as a recipe or set of directions, it's important to check your understanding with four questions:

- *When* would this procedure be useful?
- *Why* does the author think this is useful?
- *What* materials do I need to complete the procedure?
- *How* do I complete it?

Be sure to read the entire piece—introduction, materials, and steps—to be able to answer these questions.

Lesson Language *Some of you have decided to read this series of books that often includes a set of directions within them at some point. When you come to the procedure, you may find it helpful to pause for a moment and switch gears. You're no longer collecting information under a main idea. Now, you're collecting information as a series of steps. For example, in* Getting Physical: The Science of Sports *(Parks 2003), I came to a procedure in chapter eight under the heading "Ollie Physics." If I thought about why the procedure is useful, I would imagine that anyone interested in the science of sports might be interested in not only learning about it passively but also learning how to actually do some of the sports that are explained in the book. It would be useful when the reader has a skateboard and is interested in trying it. What would I need? Looks like just a skateboard. How do I do it? I see there is a series of five steps to follow. On page 46 there is a series of pictures, but across pages 45–48 there are actual explanations for how to do it, so I'll need to read each step and then look at the picture to help me visualize it.*

Prompts

- Check your understanding before you move on.
- Say back what's most important in this procedure. Let's start with materials.
- Can you repeat the steps back in the order they happened?
- Look across the page to see if there is anything you didn't read yet.
- Make sure you've read it all.

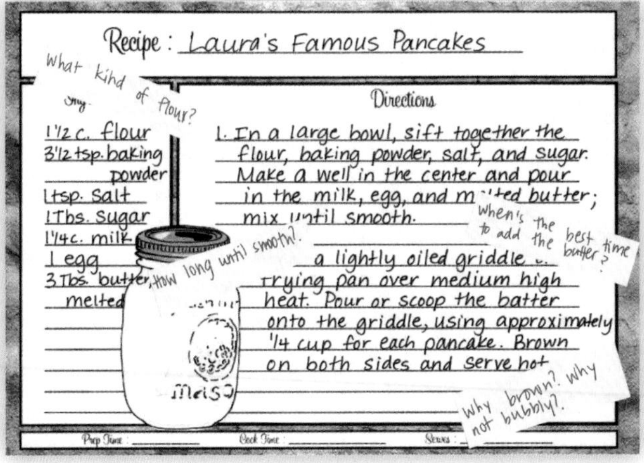

9.18 Answering Questions

Strategy Keep track of questions as you read. When you finish reading a section, pause to think about whether your question was answered based on what you just read.

Lesson Language *Asking questions is an important part of reading information texts. It helps you to stay focused on the reading you're doing, and it helps to engage you in doing the reading well. It also helps you to monitor what you're understanding, and what you still are wanting to know. But it's equally important to not just let those questions float away at the end of the reading—we should seek to answer them, or make a plan for getting them answered. You can keep track of what your questions are, how they can be answered, and what the answer is.*

Prompts

- What questions do you have?
- How will you answer those questions?
- What are you wondering?
- Think about what your plan is to get that question answered.
- Keep track of questions *and* answers.

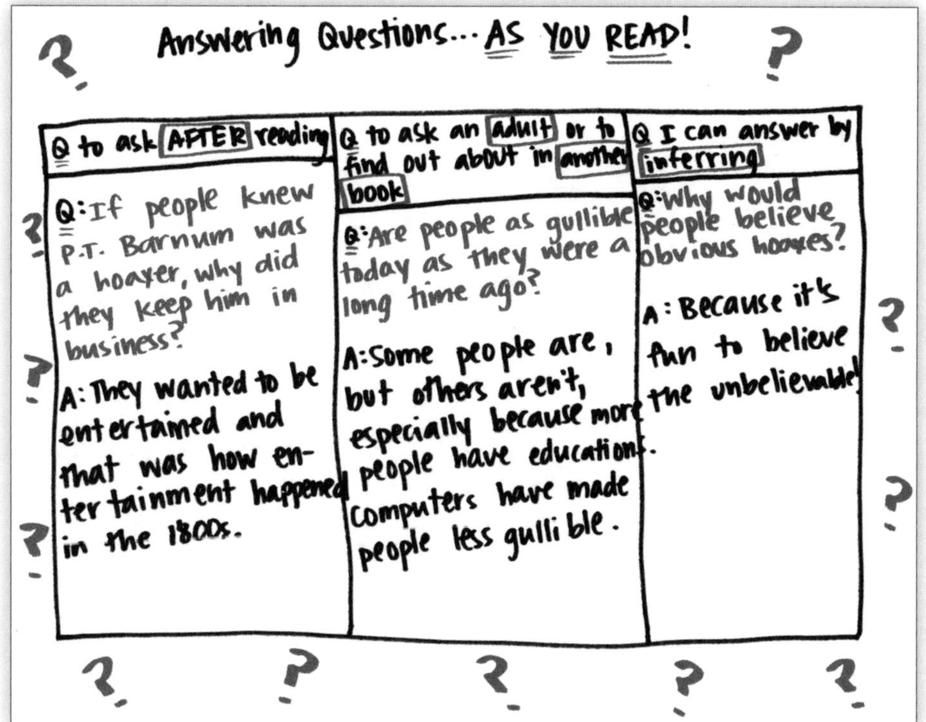

Who is this for?

LEVELS

M–Z+

GENRE / TEXT TYPE

nonfiction

SKILLS

questioning, inferring

Hat Tip: *Do I Really Have to Teach Reading? Content Comprehension, Grades 6–12* (Tovani 2004)

9.19 Event Connections

Who is this for?

LEVELS

P–Z+

GENRE / TEXT TYPE

narrative nonfiction

SKILLS

understanding cause and effect, sequencing, summarizing

Strategy Historical accounts that contain lots of information can be hard to track. After each event you read about, jot down a few key words and use an arrow to show what event led up to this event, and what event followed from the event. The flowchart you create will help you show the relationship between events. Go back and use the flowchart to remind yourself of the important events and the relationships between them.

Teaching Tip For readers who could use more support with sequencing, you may look for some ideas contained within chapter five. That chapter includes strategies that could be easily tweaked to work with narrative nonfiction. For example, keeping track of flashbacks is one lesson that is included in Chapter 5 that can be tweaked to help readers of historical narratives. Sometimes in historical accounts the entire text is not organized in sequential order, but rather the author collects related information together and each section repeats the timeline. For example, a text about immigration may include a section on immigration from Italy and then another section on immigration from Ireland, where the two stories actually overlap and share time on a timeline. A reader would need to be prepared that in the second section they may be learning about events that happened during the earlier part of the timeline they established from the first section, in the same way a reader of narratives would have to be prepared for flashbacks or foreshadowing.

Prompts

- What seems important here?
- Jot down that event.
- Think about how it connects to the other event you jotted.
- Which event led to which event? Draw an arrow connecting them.
- Yes, I agree. The book does say this event came before this one. Show that on your flowchart.
- Use your flowchart to remember what you read.

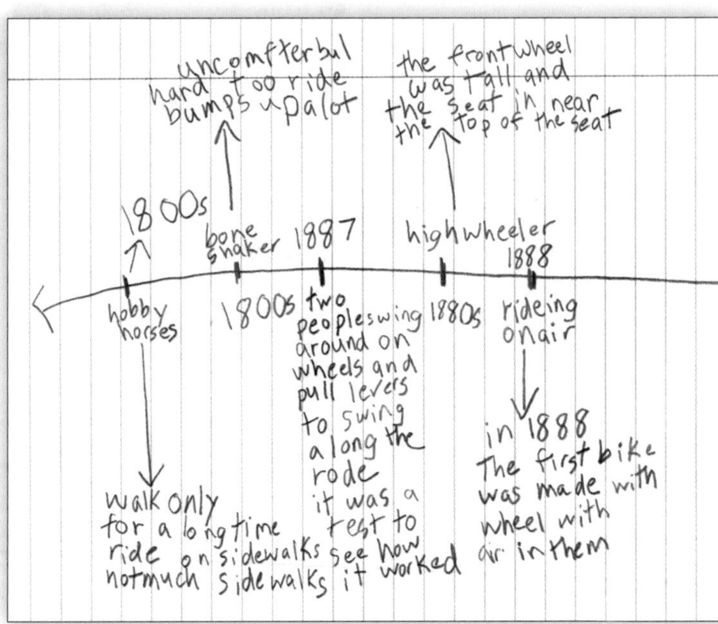

9.20 Statistics and Stance

Strategy Notice the statistics an author includes and those the author chooses not to include. Think about what the inclusion of those statistics tells you about what "side" the text is on. Think about what the author is choosing to inform you about and what the author is purposefully leaving out.

Teaching Tip The Teachers College Reading and Writing Project has done some very influential work on teaching children to craft arguments, debate aloud with their peers, and craft writing that argues for a certain point of view. This strategy helps readers to pick apart another writer's arguments and could also be used to help children craft their own arguments with a slight tweak in the language. For example, in one of the argument writing tasks, readers are asked to view a short video clip showing a dietician arguing for the inclusion of chocolate milk on school menus. She cites statistics about the numbers of vitamins and other nutrients in milk and how without the chocolate, most children choose not to drink it at all. Another clip children in the unit watch is one by popular chef Jamie Oliver, who fills a school bus with white sugar to show how much sugar is consumed because of chocolate milk. He then cites statistics to show the rates of childhood obesity. Statistics can be very convincing, and the ones the author chooses to use—and to omit—can tell us about what the author is trying to get us to believe. Childhood obesity rates? Chocolate milk is bad. A missed chance for a long list of nutrients? Chocolate milk is good.

Prompts

- What statistics do you notice?
- Look at the pattern. Think about what these statistics tell you.
- Consider why the author included the ones he or she did.
- Which "side" is this text on?
- What is the argument here?
- Think about what statistics were left out.

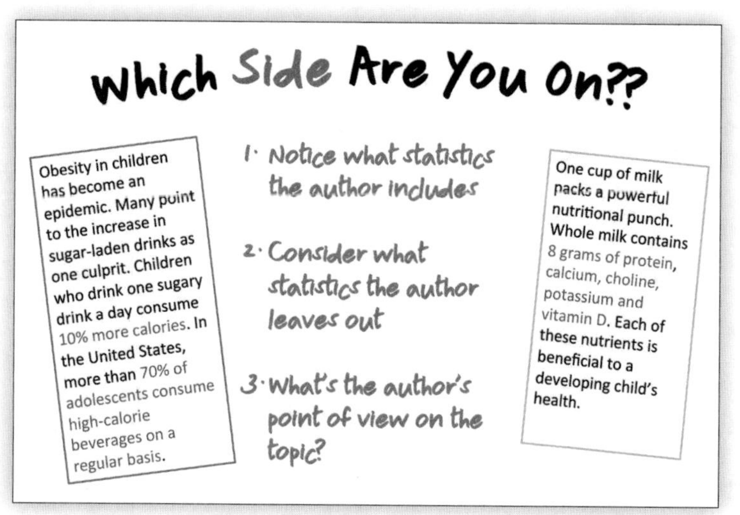

Who is this for?

LEVELS
P–Z+

GENRE / TEXT TYPE
nonfiction

SKILLS
determining importance, critiquing, inferring

Hat Tip: "Teaching Beyond the Main Idea: Nonfiction and Point of View (Part I)" (Roberts and Roberts 2014)

Supporting Comprehension in Nonfiction

Getting the Most from Text Features

Why is this goal important?

If I were to play a word association game with a group of elementary teachers, the kind where I say a word and they tell me the first word that pops into their minds, I would bet that a large majority of them would answer my "nonfiction" with "text features." It's true—text features are a really large part of reading, navigating, and understanding nonfiction text. They help to support the main information in the text, add to it, and/or help us navigate it. The types of features are limitless: photographs, illustrations, maps, charts, graphs, sidebars, tables of contents, indexes, and so on.

Despite their central role in nonfiction texts, researchers have found that teaching text features in isolation may not be effective (Duke 2014; Purcell-Gates, Duke, and Martineau 2007). To really treat these features as the information-rich resources they are, we need to shift our thinking about them. Instruction needs to be more than about *identifying the* features; rather we need to help students *use* these features to get more information from a text. We also need to show students how to synthesize the visual and textual information in features with the information presented in the main text. We need to help them understand the purpose and function of the features, and then move beyond simply naming them. We should teach children how to explain what information the features provide.

How do I know if this goal is right for my student?

It's helpful to have some knowledge about the role that nonfiction features play at varying text levels and then to assess your students' ability to demonstrate understanding that matches the text's complexity.

At the lowest levels where the text is very spare, the photographs and illustrations may actually carry more facts or details than the text itself. Up to around level N, text features are often used to illustrate and/or support the main text. Authors often use pictures, illustrations, or other features that are highly visual to reiterate the key information presented in the text. Beginning around level O, text features may give extra information, going beyond what the text says. For example, we may find a diagram of germs that shows the specific shapes that bacteria and viruses can take, when the text simply teaches how germs come in different shapes. Readers will need to gather information from both the pictures and the text, and the job of synthesizing the information in the feature with the text becomes more challenging. By the time a reader is navigating books and articles at around level Q, text features become more text-heavy—almost like sections with their own main ideas and details. By around level U, pages become even denser and more feature-filled. Readers must be able to explain how features relate to one another as well as to the main text across a section or chapter.

Armed with this information about the changes in how features are used across levels, you'll want to decide on a way to assess your student's ability to handle the features at whatever level he or she is currently reading. You can assess this in ways similar to how you'd assess any other area of comprehension: ask the student questions in a conference, have the student stop and jot during a read-aloud, ask the child to read a text independently and respond to questions or prompts you've preplanted, look at the child's writing about reading, and/or listen to a child talking with a peer.

In general, here's a list of what you might notice. I've listed these potential findings in order from least comprehension demonstrated to most comprehension demonstrated:

- ignores the text features
- can name what the text feature is ("That's a map.")
- can name what the text feature is and its purpose ("That's a map. It shows where something is.")
- can explain what the text feature is teaching, in isolation of the main text ("That's a map. It shows where earthquakes are most likely to occur.")
- can explain what the text feature is teaching by combining information from the main text and the feature ("That's a map. It shows where earthquakes are most likely to occur. The red lines must be the fault lines because I notice that the earthquakes are right next to them.")
- can connect the meaning of the text feature to the main text and other features ("That's a map. It shows the locations of fault lines and the places where earthquakes are most common. I notice that in the west coast and along different islands in Asia there are both the most frequent and strongest earthquakes. If I compare it to the other map with the edges of the plates, it seems like the edges of the plates are where the earthquakes happen most.").

Obviously, you'd have different expectations for a kindergartener reading at level C and a fifth grader reading at level S. We wouldn't want any reader to ignore the features, but although we may expect a reader at level C to only give a simple statement about the feature ("That's a kitten, a baby cat."), we may expect more of a child reading at a fifth-grade level. At level S, a reader should be able to do the most sophisticated work on this list (connecting all the features with the main text). When you feel as though children could use more support in this area, consider making this a primary goal. They can practice during nonfiction studies during reading, and also during content area times (science, social studies) when engaged in reading.

Strategies for Understanding Text Features at a Glance

Strategy	Levels	Genres/ Text Types	Skills
10.1 Make the 2-D into 3-D	A–Z+	Nonfiction	Visualizing, determining importance
10.2 Cover Up Then Zoom In	A–Z+	Nonfiction	Questioning, determining importance
10.3 Reread and Sketch with More Detail	A–Z+	Nonfiction	Visualizing, monitoring for meaning
10.4 Caption It!	A–Z+	Nonfiction	Summarizing
10.5 Get More from Pictures	A–I	Nonfiction	Visualizing, inferring
10.6 Labels Teach	C–J	Expository nonfiction	Synthesizing
10.7 Bold Words Signal Importance	F–Z+	Nonfiction	Synthesizing, monitoring for meaning
10.8 Fast Facts Stats	G–Z+	Expository nonfiction	Synthesizing, monitoring for meaning
10.9 Diagrams Show and Tell	G–Z+	Nonfiction	Synthesizing
10.10 Why a Visual?	G–Z+	Nonfiction	Synthesizing
10.11 Glossary Warm-Up	I–Z+	Expository nonfiction	Monitoring for meaning, synthesizing
10.12 Don't Skip It!	J–Z+	Expository nonfiction	Making a reading plan
10.13 Integrate Features and Running Text	J–Z+	Expository nonfiction	Synthesizing
10.14 Hop In and Out Using the Table of Contents	J–Z+	Nonfiction	Determining importance
10.15 Maps	M–Z+	Nonfiction	Synthesizing, summarizing
10.16 Old Information, New Look	N–Z+	Expository nonfiction	Determining importance, synthesizing
10.17 Go with the Flow (Chart)	N–Z+	Expository nonfiction	Summarizing
10.18 Cracking Open Headings	P–Z+	Expository nonfiction	Inferring
10.19 Sidebar as Section	Q–Z+	Expository nonfiction	Summarizing, synthesizing, determining importance
10.20 Primary Sources	R–Z+	Expository nonfiction	Synthesizing, determining importance, summarizing
10.21 Take Your Time (Line)	R–Z+	Nonfiction	Synthesizing, monitoring for meaning, summarizing
10.22 Graphic Graphs	R–Z+	Expository nonfiction	Synthesizing, monitoring for meaning

10.1 Make the 2-D into 3-D

Who is this for?

LEVELS

A–Z+

GENRE / TEXT TYPE

nonfiction

SKILLS

visualizing, determining importance

Strategy Photographs, illustrations, and diagrams in books are meant to represent real things. Try to take the 2-D, or flat image and imagine it to be 3-D, like it is in real life. You can make it seem more real by adding in details from other senses (smell, touch, and so on). Read the words in the caption and in the surrounding text to help your imagination.

Teaching Tip Modify the language in the strategy for younger readers, English language learners, or readers reading at a lower level. Instead of saying two dimensional and three dimensional, you could just say "flat" and "like in real life."

Lesson Language *In* Amazing Salamanders *(Shanahan 2012a), this picture of a salamander on a leaf is captioned with this fact: "Salamanders have soft, moist skin" (11). If I use my imagination to make the flat picture seem more real, I can imagine picking the salamander up in my hand. I think it would feel very light and I can imagine the soft skin as it slithers on my hand. It's also kind of slimy, I think, because the caption says "moist" and it looks shiny, too. I think its body would feel kind of round, like a worm, and the toes on its feet would be tiny and sticky, since it's holding onto a leaf.*

Prompts

- Read the caption. Now look at the picture. Describe what you see.
- Make it seem more real. Say what you see.
- What do you imagine, beyond just the flat picture?
- Use your senses.
- What else do you see?
- Use the caption and the rest of the page to say more.

Hat Tip: "Teaching Reading in Small Groups: Matching Methods to Purposes" (Serravallo 2013c)

10.2 Cover Up Then Zoom In

Strategy Use a sticky note to cover an image on the page. Read the text on the page and think, "What is this teaching me so far?" Then, uncover the image and zoom in on it, asking, "What new information am I getting from this image?" or "What parts of what I just read also show up in this image?"

Teaching Tip Depending on the age and reading level of the student, you may also choose to flip the directions in this strategy, having the child first look at the picture or other visual on the page, and second look at the words. Bear in mind that at the lowest levels (A, B, C, D) children must rely on pictures to read the words, and this strategy would only be appropriate once the child has read the book successfully several times and is revisiting the text as a reread.

Prompts

- Cover it up first. Now zoom in.
- Remember what you just read? Now tell me what you see.
- Can you add more facts by looking at the picture?
- What else are you learning from the picture?
- Really look closely, part by part. Try to say more.
- You learned something from the picture because you looked closely.

Who is this for?

LEVELS

A–Z+

GENRE / TEXT TYPE

nonfiction

SKILLS

questioning, determining importance

Hat Tip: *Inside Information: Developing Powerful Readers and Writers of Informational Text Through Project-Based Instruction* (Duke 2014)

10.3 Reread and Sketch with More Detail

Who is this for?

LEVELS

A–Z+

GENRE / TEXT TYPE

nonfiction

SKILLS

visualizing, monitoring for meaning

Strategy Read the text. Sketch a picture based on the information you remember. Go back and reread the text. Try to add more detail to your picture based on the detail you read in the text. Repeat until you think you have all the important information represented in your drawing.

Lesson Language *Every time I read and reread some facts, I get more information to help me picture what I'm learning about with even more detail. For example, the first time I read the section "Bees" in* Animals that Store Food *(Shanahan 2012b), I stopped and sketched—you guessed it, a bee. I also remembered that bees collect nectar from flowers, so I drew the bee on the flower. But I guess the first time I read I didn't completely understand the next part—that when it turns to honey it puts the honey in a honeycomb. So when I read it again, I pictured the nectar turning to honey in a bee's stomach. So I drew a little close-up of a stomach and added in the honey, with the label "Honey." And then I drew an arrow to a honeycomb to show that's where the honey goes. So, each time I read, I understood more of the whole section and could add more to my drawing.*

Prompts

- Stop and picture what you just learned.
- Jot down some details in a sketch.
- Now, as you reread, see if you can gather up more information.
- Look at your sketch. Can you add more detail based on what you've learned on the second reading?
- Try to get more details based on what you learned.
- I think your sketch captures all the important information!

10.4 Caption It!

Strategy: Read the text. Look at the picture. Think, "If I had to write one sentence explaining this picture, what would I say?" Use the information in the main text to help you.

Lesson Language *Sometimes photographs and illustrations in nonfiction books don't have captions. When this is the case, it's usually because the information from the main text gives you enough to be able to understand it. To check your own understanding, you can try writing a caption (actually writing it on a sticky note, or just "writing it" in your head). For example, when I was reading Seymour Simon's book* The Moon *(2003), I came to this picture of the surface of the moon. I learned on the page that there are craters on the moon, so I could write a caption saying, "The surface of the moon isn't flat, but is instead covered with craters and mountains."*

Prompts

- Think about the main text when you're trying to caption the picture.
- Use your own words in the caption, not just a fact you read.
- Good information, now say it in a shorter way. Make a one-sentence caption.
- What information from the text could help you?
- Retell what you read. Now say what fact(s) relate to the picture.

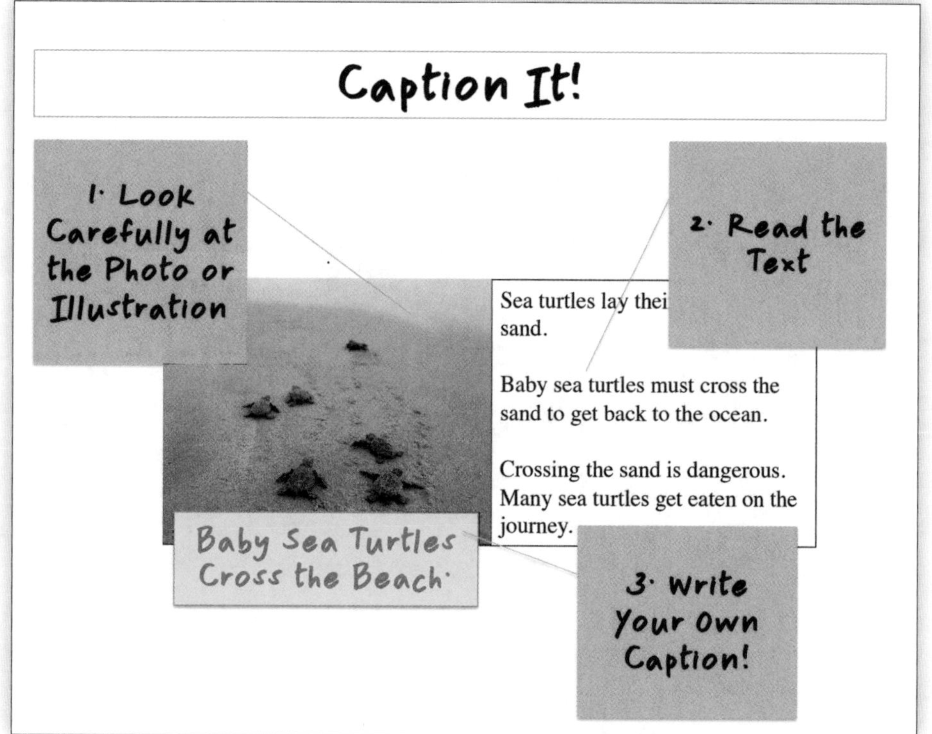

Caption It!
1. Look Carefully at the Photo or Illustration
2. Read the Text
Sea turtles lay thei
sand.
Baby sea turtles must cross the sand to get back to the ocean.
Crossing the sand is dangerous. Many sea turtles get eaten on the journey.
Baby Sea Turtles Cross the Beach.
3. Write Your Own Caption!

Who is this for?

LEVELS

A–Z+

GENRE / TEXT TYPE

nonfiction

SKILL

summarizing

Hat Tip: *Navigating Nonfiction, Grade 3* (Boynton and Blevins 2007)

10.5 Get More from Pictures

Who is this for?

LEVELS

A–I

GENRE / TEXT TYPE

nonfiction

SKILLS

visualizing, inferring

Hat Tip: *Read It Again! Revisiting Shared Reading* (Parkes 2000)

Strategy Look at the picture. Read the words. Think, "What in the picture is the same as what's in the words? What's new?" Try to "write" extra facts out loud.

Lesson Language *When there are very few words, you can look to the picture to get more facts. For example in* Life Cycles: Worms *(Nelson 2009), I read this fact: "Worms eat plants." Then, when I look at the picture, I see the tip of a worm up against a leaf. I could point to that and say more facts I learned, "Worms can eat a leaf, even one that's bigger than it is! It uses its mouth to eat. It eats things that have fallen on the ground."*

Prompts

- What do the words say?
- Look at the picture. Say more.
- Point with your finger. Say a fact based on where you're pointing.
- What can you learn from the picture that's not in the words?
- That's something you learned from the words. What can you learn from the picture?

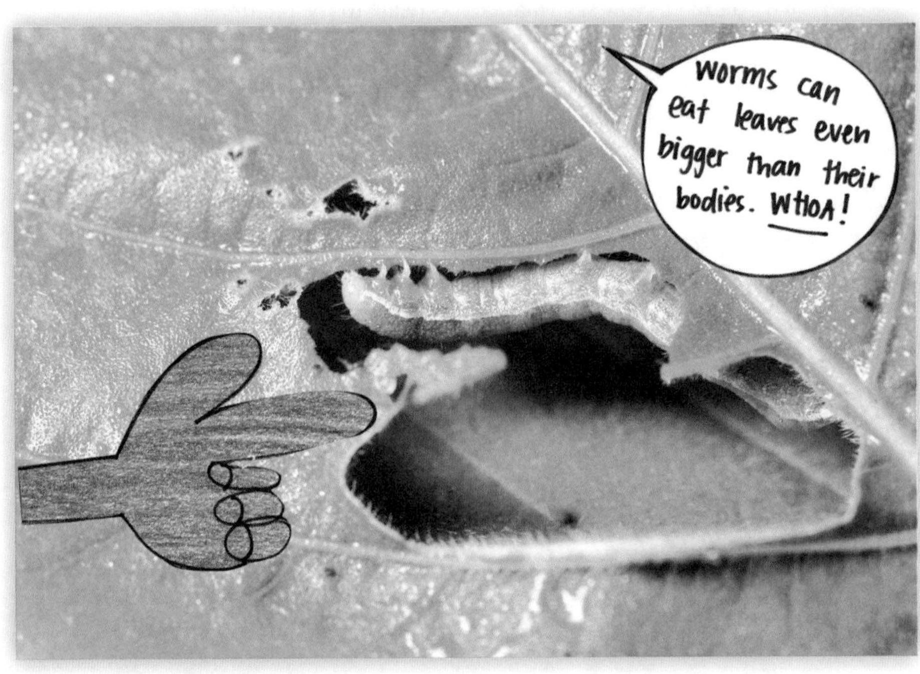

10.6 Labels Teach

Strategy Read the text. Look at the picture. See what the label is labeling. Think about how the picture, text, and label all fit together.

Lesson Language *In the book* See Me Grow *(Arlon and Gordon-Harris 2012c), the author uses a lot of labels. On the pages with the heading "In a Pouch," we learn about kangaroos and koalas. The facts the author teaches us are that a baby kangaroo is called a joey. Then, in the picture we see a big kangaroo and a smaller one in the pocket. There is also a close-up of a kangaroo's head. "Joey" is labeled so we can connect the fact—baby kangaroo—to the picture of what it looks like. Then, there is a caption that says, "A joey sometimes sticks its head out of the pouch" (12). The caption helps me to know that the close-up is of the same thing as the smaller photo, and I learned something else about baby kangaroos.*

Prompts

- Where do you see a label?
- Tell me how the facts you learned and the label connect.
- How does the label help you?
- Put together all the information on the page.
- Now that you read the label and saw the picture, go back and read the rest of the page.
- Think about how it connects.

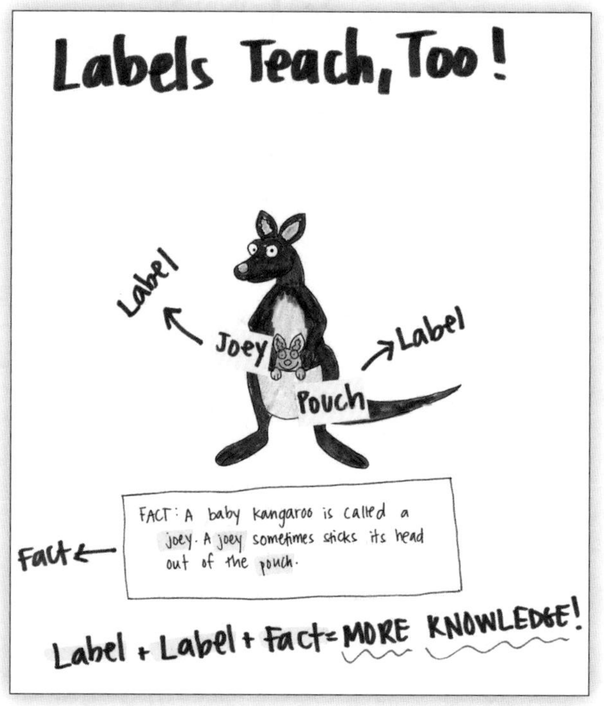

Who is this for?

LEVELS
C–J

GENRE / TEXT TYPE
expository nonfiction

SKILL
synthesizing

10.7 Bold Words Signal Importance

Who is this for?

LEVELS

F–Z+

GENRE / TEXT TYPE

nonfiction

SKILLS

synthesizing, monitoring for meaning

Strategy Read a sentence with a bold word. Think, "Do I already know what this word means?" or "Can I figure it out based on how it's used here?" If yes, keep reading. If not, stop and flip to the glossary. Read the definition. Come back to the sentence and explain the fact with a new understanding of that word.

Lesson Language *Sometimes the author will bold words that are important to understanding the topic. Sometimes you'll know what these words are. Other times, the bolded text is a feature that tells you, "Stop! Flip to the glossary." For example, when I was reading* Bighorn Sheep *by JoAnn Macken (2005), I came across this sentence: "A baby, or lamb, can walk in a few hours" (4). The author bolded the word lamb but honestly, I already know what that word means. And even if I didn't, the author just told me that the lamb is a baby sheep right there in the sentence. I'm going to decide not to turn to the glossary. But later I see this: "If a ram sees danger, he snorts" (10). Snorts. I've heard it before but I'm not exactly sure what it means. Someone said something about snorting when someone was laughing once in class, but that doesn't make sense here. So now I'd better check a glossary. Let's see* (Flip to back.). *The definition says, "Make a sound by blowing air out through the nose" (22). So if I go back to the fact, I can figure out that the ram is making a noise to communicate to the others in the herd.*

Prompts

- Do you see any bold words?
- What does that word mean? Not sure? Check the glossary.
- Can you figure it out based on the context on this page?
- Now that you've read the definition in the glossary, can you put the information together with what you read on this page?
- Based on everything you've read about this word, what does it mean?
- Yes! That definition includes information from the glossary and the text.

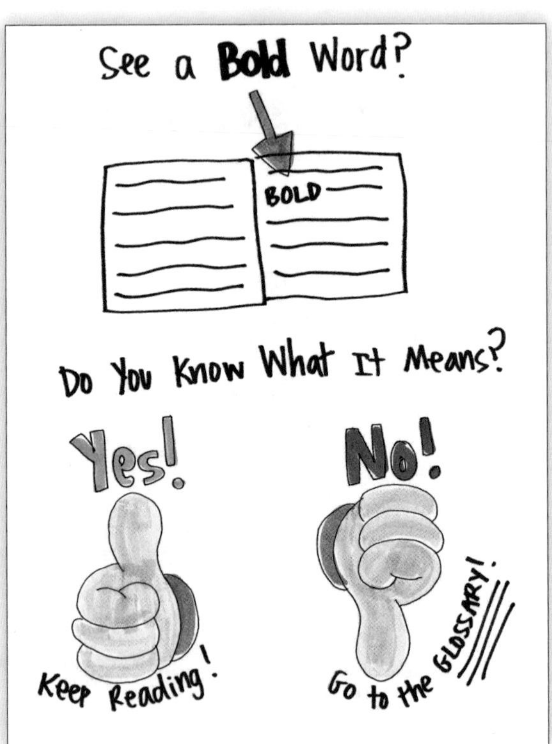

10.8 Fast Facts Stats

Strategy Read the fast facts after you have read the rest of the book. Think about what you already read (and saw in features) that connects to each fact. Think, "How do these facts help me know more about what I just read?"

Lesson Language *Often the fast facts are harder to understand than the rest of the book, so it's helpful if you first read all the other information, and then turn to the fast facts. Sometimes the fast facts will give you statistics—numbers—that will make much more sense once you have some prior knowledge about the topic. The fast facts are usually on a page by themselves without any pictures to help you. For example, in the book* Bighorn Sheep *(Macken 2005), the fast facts page gives information about diet, average weight, life span, height, and length. Many of these words would be hard to read by themselves. However, after reading the whole book, and reading that the bighorn sheep eats grass (an easy to understand fact and supported by a picture), reading "Diet: grasses and leaves" would help a reader to understand, "Oh, diet must mean what they eat. Because I just read that they eat grass. Now I know they also eat leaves."*

Prompts

- What did you learn from the "fast facts" page?
- How does the information fit with the rest of the page or book?
- Think about what you already know about the topic before you read it.
- Even if you can't read that word, can you figure out what it might mean based on what you've read so far in the rest of the book?
- Think about what you know.
- Keep the information from the rest of the book in your mind.
- Good! You figured out what that means because you thought about what you know.

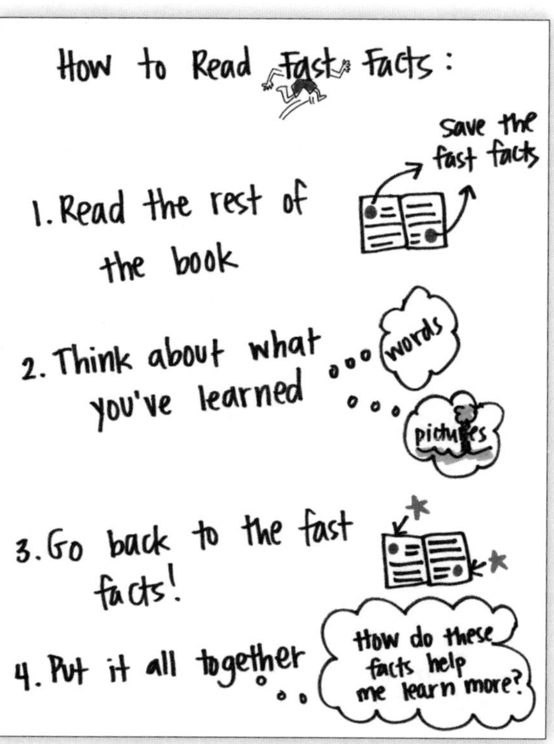

How to Read Fast Facts:
Save the fast facts
1. Read the rest of the book
2. Think about what you've learned
words
pictures
3. Go back to the fast facts!
4. Put it all together
How do these facts help me learn more?

Who is this for?

LEVELS
G–Z+

GENRE / TEXT TYPE
expository nonfiction

SKILLS
synthesizing, monitoring for meaning

10.9 Diagrams Show and Tell

Who is this for?

LEVELS

G–Z+

GENRE / TEXT TYPE

nonfiction

SKILL

synthesizing

Hat Tip: *Navigating Nonfiction, Grade 3* (Boynton and Blevins 2007)

Strategy Read the title to find out what the diagram is showing you. Read the labels to understand the important parts of the diagram. Finally, think about how the diagram connects to the information in the text.

Lesson Language *In* Penguins: Meet the Heroes of a Frozen World *(Arlon and Gordon-Harris 2012b), there is a diagram that I found a little hard to understand when I first came to it. It's this one here—three egg shapes in black and white next to a photograph of an actual egg. I know it has something to do with eggs, since it's in the section "Penguin Eggs," but I'm going to slow down and look more closely to see if I can figure it out. When I read the labels, I see that the light-brown egg says "Life-size emperor penguin egg," and the black one says, "Life-size African penguin egg," and the white one says, "Life-size fairy penguin egg." After reading the labels, I see that it has nothing do to with colors of eggs—this diagram is trying to teach me about sizes, and comparing the sizes of eggs from different penguins. Now, I'm going to put together what I learned with the rest of the text. Across the rest of the book I learned about these different types of penguins and I know that the emperor penguin is the biggest and the fairy penguin is much smaller. So when I put that information together with the diagram, it's making me think that the size of the egg depends on the size of the fully-grown penguin! Which makes sense because I also learned on this page that the egg must be kept warm. A tiny penguin couldn't keep an enormous egg warm.*

Prompts

- What's this diagram teaching you?
- Read all the parts of the diagram, including the labels.
- Now that you've read the labels, explain what you're learning.
- How does this diagram help you learn what you just read?
- Now that you're seeing it in a diagram, what else are you learning?

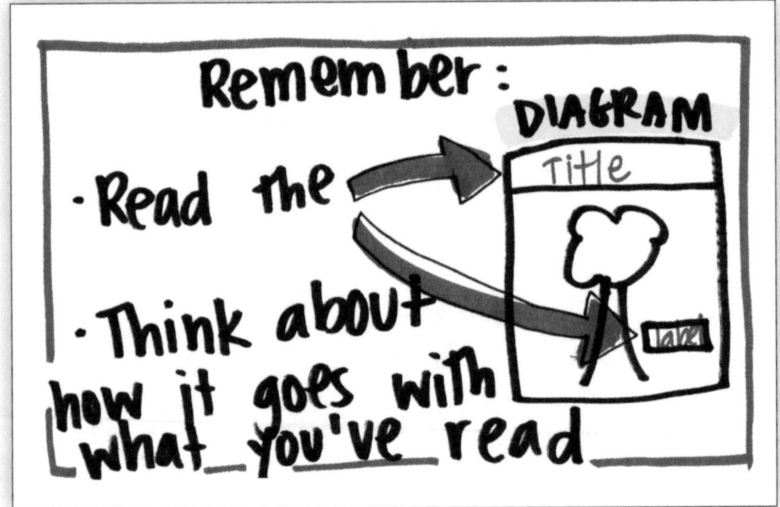

Remember:
DIAGRAM
Title
· Read the
· Think about
how it goes with
what you've read
label

10.10 Why a Visual?

Strategy When you see a visual (graph, chart, picture, diagram, and so on) on the page, stop and think: "What information is this visual giving me? Why is it important to the information in this section?"

Lesson Language *In the book* Amazing Sea Lizards *(Woolley 2012), the author usually has a few sentences on each two-page spread, and three or four pictures. I know when I read this book that I can't just skip past the pictures. I have to stop and think, "What information is this visual giving me? Why is it important?" In the beginning of the book, I learn that the lizards live only on the Galapagos Islands and they spend a lot of time in the sea, which is unique because no other lizard does this. As I look across the pictures, I see some islands in a sea, a lizard crawling out of water, and a lizard sitting in some water. So, let me think about what I'm learning from the pictures and why the pictures are important. Well, I'm used to seeing pictures of lizards on trees or in a desert, so it's strange to see a lizard sitting in water. This picture helps me better see what that would look like. I also notice that the islands are very natural—no buildings or cars or anything that we have where we live. So that makes me think that the Galapagos Islands, where this lizard lives, may not have people who live there. The pictures are important because they helped me better picture this place that I've never been to, and which is so unlike what I'm used to.*

Prompts

- What did you learn from this picture?
- Why is this picture important?
- Read the text first. Now look at the pictures. What more are you learning?
- Why did the author choose this picture to put on this page?
- What can you learn from this?
- You told me more details than what the author wrote because you looked closely at the picture.

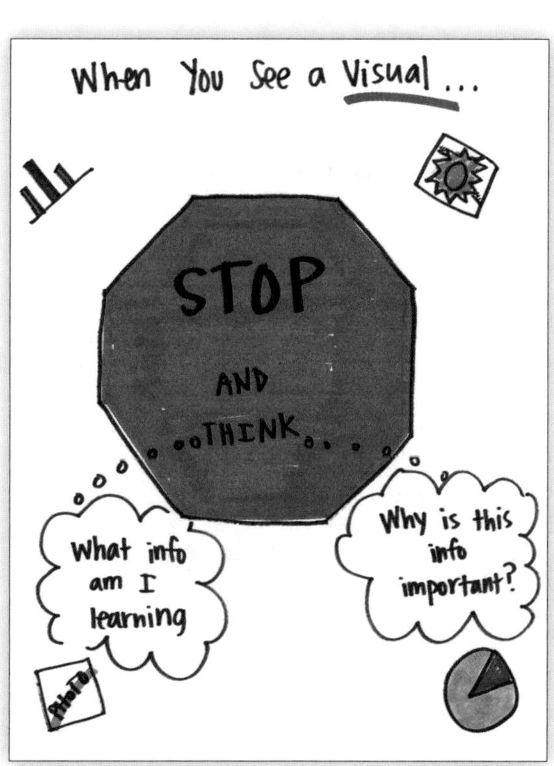

Who is this for?

LEVELS
G–Z+

GENRE / TEXT TYPE
nonfiction

SKILL
synthesizing

Hat Tip: *Inside Information: Developing Powerful Readers and Writers of Informational Text Through Project-Based Instruction* (Duke 2014)

10.11 Glossary Warm-Up

Who is this for?

LEVELS

I–Z+

GENRE / TEXT TYPE

expository nonfiction

SKILLS

monitoring for meaning, synthesizing

Hat Tip: Independent Reading Assessment: Nonfiction series (Serravallo 2013a)

Strategy Preview the words and definitions that you'll come across in the chapter (or book or article). Get a basic understanding of the words. Read the text, keeping the words in mind. When you come to a word that you remember from the glossary, try to learn its meaning in more detail by getting information from the text.

Teaching Tip For more lessons to support students' vocabulary knowledge, see Chapter 11.

Prompts

- Let's read through the glossary first, to get a heads-up on the words you'll see.
- What word are you trying to figure out?
- Do you remember seeing it in the glossary?
- Check it in the glossary.
- Referencing the glossary seemed to help you.

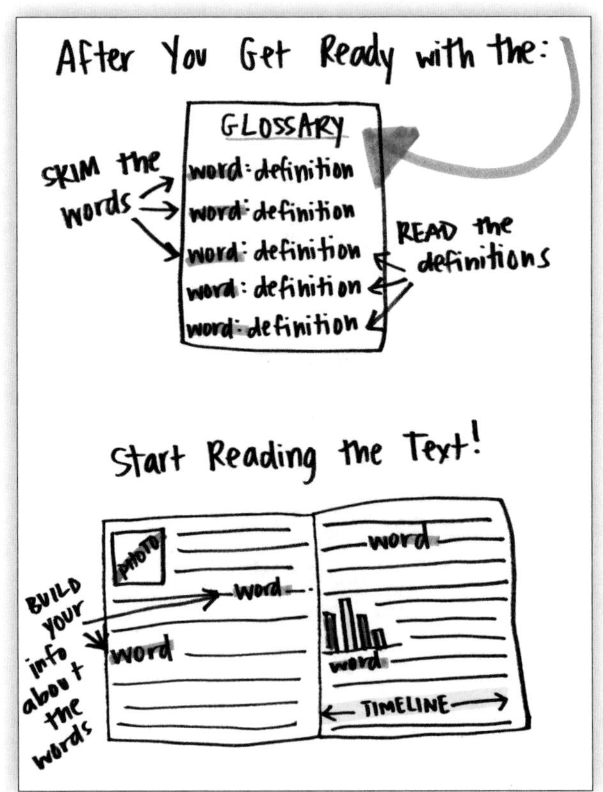

10.12 Don't Skip It!

Strategy Reading a page in nonfiction texts means understanding both the words and the graphics. Read in an order that makes sense to you (words first, graphics first, or going back and forth between the two). Before turning the page, make sure you've read it all—both the graphics and the words.

Teaching Tip I find that many students are text-feature readers who tend to ignore the main text on the page, and others are text readers who slip right past the text features. Looking at everything on the page will often slow a reader's pace down, and also requires more synthesis and mental effort as the reader puts together all the information on the page or in the section. Teaching them to make a plan before reading a page with a variety of information (visual and text) and then asking them to check that they got it all before they turn the page will hold readers accountable for understanding how information fits together.

Prompts

- Where will you start?
- Show me with your finger what your plan is for reading the whole page.
- How will you make sure you read and look at everything?
- OK, now that you have a plan, let's start reading.

Who is this for?

LEVELS

J–Z+

GENRE / TEXT TYPE

expository nonfiction

SKILL

making a reading plan

Hat Tip: *Inside Information: Developing Powerful Readers and Writers of Informational Text Through Project-Based Instruction* (Duke 2014)

10.13 Integrate Features and Running Text

Who is this for?

LEVELS

J–Z+

GENRE / TEXT TYPE

expository nonfiction

SKILL

synthesizing

Strategy Put the information from the running text together with the information from the various features you encounter—photographs, captions, diagrams, and so on. First, scan the text to see what's included. Then, read and study all the features. Read the text, pausing frequently to refer back to other sources of related information.

Lesson Language *The book* Farm *(Arlon and Gordon-Harris 2012a) is a text-feature bonanza! On just a two-page spread titled "Dairy Farm" there is a heading, several diagrams, a flowchart, captions, an inset box, and a few sentences of running text. It's hard to know where to look first. So, before I read the main text, I'm going to read the section heading. Then, I'm going to go left to right, studying all the features to make sure I understand what they're showing. I see the farm and the names of all the parts of the farm from this one. Across the top, I see a sequenced flowchart of how milk becomes cheese. Below that on the right I see a diagram of a cow with "udder" labeled. Now, I'm going to go back to the main text. As I read the first few facts about dairy farms, I'm going to look to the picture of the farm itself to better understand the facts. When I read "The milk is taken away every day to be processed," I can connect that to one of the steps on the flowchart. And of course I'd keep going to make sure I read the whole page. But the point is that I use the features with the text as I go to better understand.*

Prompts

- Stop there. Which text feature should you look at to go with this text?
- Scan the page first.
- Show me what you're scanning.
- Read a little more slowly. Connect the features as you go.
- Make sure you take a look at all the features before you start reading.

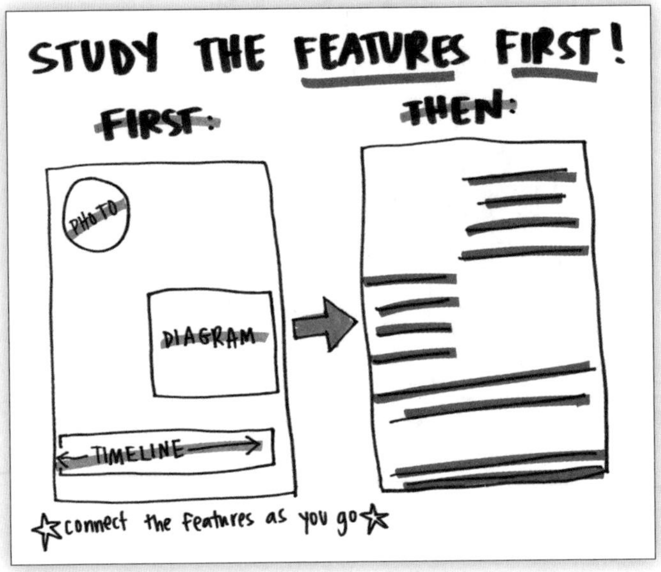

Hat Tip: *Comprehension Through Conversation: The Power of Purposeful Talk in the Reading Workshop* (Nichols 2006)

10.14 Hop In and Out Using the Table of Contents

Strategy Have your research question in mind. Scan through the table of contents thinking, "Which chapter(s) might contain the information I'm looking for?" Keep in mind that the titles of the chapters might be in slightly different words than the name of the topic you have in mind.

Teaching Tip You could teach a very similar lesson using the index. Teach children to have their topic in mind, and look for related key words in an index to help them find what they're looking for. I want to note here, though, that my belief about nonfiction reading is that most of the reading students do should be of whole, continuous texts. I would use a strategy like this one only when I'm involved in a research project, or I'm teaching children how to seek out specific sorts of information for other reasons, such as to answer a question or confirm a piece of information they are reading in their whole-book nonfiction reading.

Prompts

- What are you hoping to learn?
- Look at the table of contents with your question in mind.
- What made you pick that chapter?
- You might need to think of other words that mean something similar to the topic you have in mind to find the right chapter.
- Scan the table of contents.
- Which chapter will you read first?

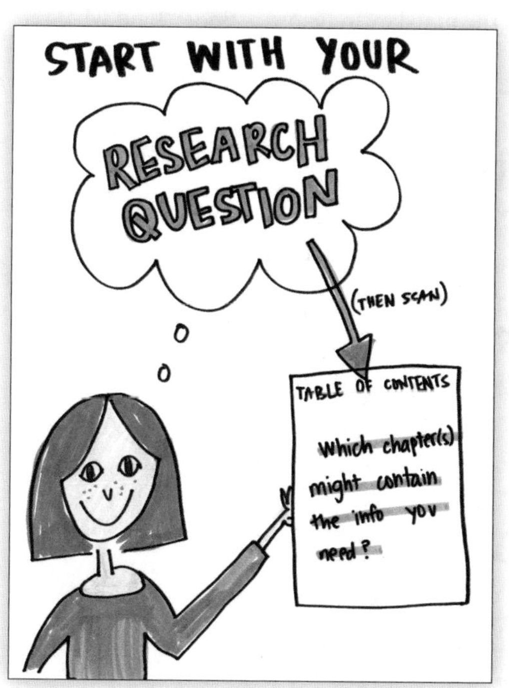

Who is this for?

LEVELS

J–Z+

GENRE / TEXT TYPE

nonfiction

SKILL

determining importance

Hat Tip: Independent Reading Assessment: Nonfiction series (Serravallo 2013a)

10.15 Maps

Who is this for?

LEVELS

M–Z+

GENRE / TEXT TYPE

nonfiction

SKILLS

synthesizing, summarizing

Strategy Read the map's title. Find any symbols, key, scale, or legend that helps you understand the codes on the map. Read all the labels to understand what each part of the map is. Think about any special colors that may be used and what those colors are trying to show. Summarize what you learn, and consider how the map is helping you learn more about the section's or book's topic.

Lesson Language *As I turned to page 12 in* The Weather Today *(Feely 2012), I noticed that most of the page is taken up by a map. I'm going to first orient myself by reading the title: "What's Happening Outside? What's the Weather Like Today?" Let me think about that—this map will probably show me different weather around the world on one day. I see there is a big box filled with symbols, and the title of the box says "International weather symbols." Each symbol correlates to a kind of weather such as rain, snow, sleet, and so on. As I look down at the map, I see a dot pointing to a spot in the world, and a callout box telling the name of the city, the temperature, and the type of weather. And oh! There are the symbols again. So in Johannesburg, for example, it looks like an overcast sky because there is a big circle filled in black. It's so interesting how on one day there is different weather all over the world.*

Prompts

- Check the title first.
- What do the symbols mean?
- Connect the symbols to what you see in the rest of the map.
- Explain what you're learning from the map.
- Nice job using the information from the map key to help you understand what the author is teaching with this map.
- How does this map help you learn about the other information in the section?

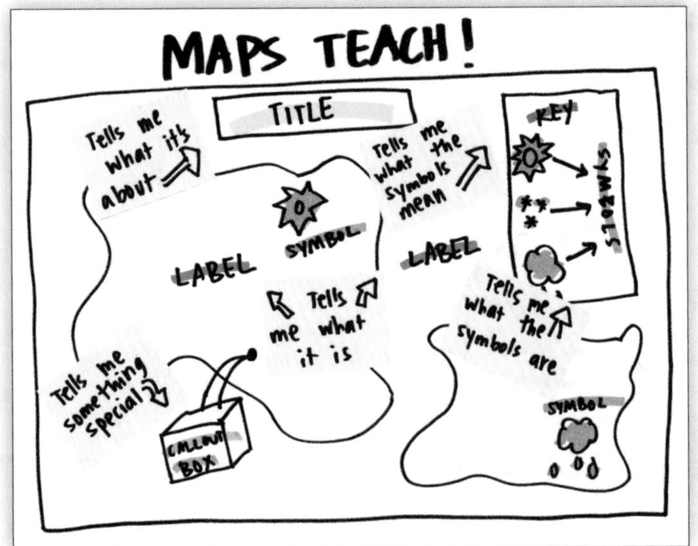

Hat Tip: *Navigating Nonfiction, Grade 3* (Boynton and Blevins 2007)

10.16 Old Information, New Look

Strategy Look at the graph, especially the key, to figure out what the graph is showing. Think about how the information in the graph connects to the information in the article (or section or book or text). Think, "How is the information in the graph a new look at the information I already learned?"

Lesson Language *In the article "White House Turned 200!"* (Scholastic News 2000)*, I see a huge photo of a model of the White House. Each room shows how all the furniture is set up, almost like a dollhouse. The graph shows the types of rooms (bedrooms, kitchens, and so on) and a symbol to represent one room. In the main part of the page I can see the rooms and I could count up the bedrooms myself, or in the graph I could look and see that there are sixteen symbols in that row, so therefore there are sixteen bedrooms. It's the same information, but shown in a new way. Seeing the information twice, presented differently, helps me better understand.*

Prompts

- Check the key.
- Explain what you see in the graph.
- To understand it, let's think about what you learned on the rest of the page.
- Connect the information here (*point to graph*) to the information here (*point to main text*).
- Is the information extra or showing the information in a new way?
- What's it teaching you?

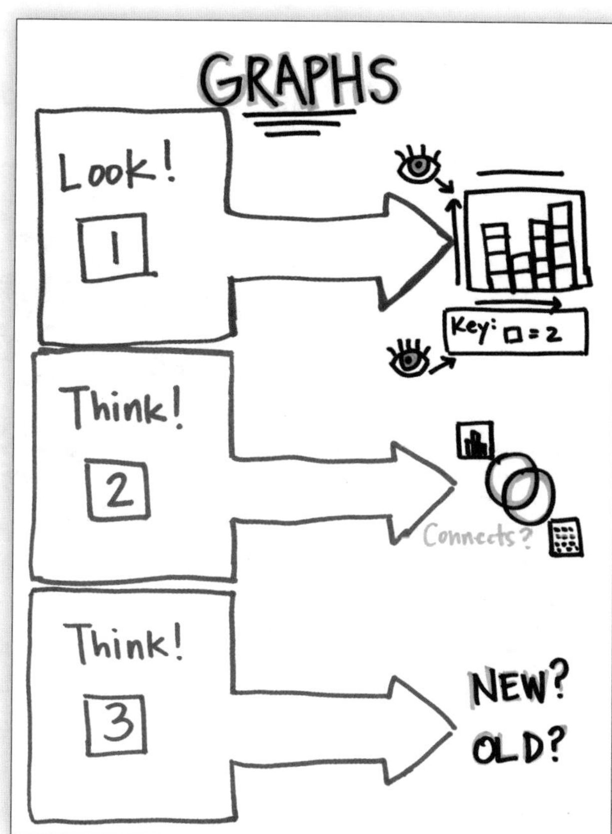

Who is this for?

LEVELS

N–Z+

GENRE / TEXT TYPE

expository nonfiction

SKILLS

determining importance, synthesizing

10.17 Go with the Flow (Chart)

Who is this for?

LEVELS

N–Z+

GENRE / TEXT TYPE

expository nonfiction

SKILL

summarizing

Hat Tip: *Navigating Nonfiction, Grade 3* (Boynton and Blevins 2007)

Strategy Read the title to understand what the diagram is teaching you. Then, look at each illustration or photo along with its caption in the order it appears in the flowchart. Follow the arrows and numbers to read each step in sequence. Make sure you understand one before you move on to a new one.

Teaching Tip This strategy will be particularly helpful for those students who need support understanding sequence, narrative, and/or procedures. See, also, strategy 9.17 for help with teaching students how to follow procedures. Written procedures are sometimes coupled with flow charts.

Prompts

- Show me what you'll read first.
- What will you read next?
- Make sure you go in order—left to right or top to bottom.
- Did you understand what you learned from that step? Retell the most important information.
- Summarize what you learned from this whole flowchart.

10.18 Cracking Open Headings

Strategy Read the heading or subheading that's causing confusion. Back up to a title or heading from earlier in the section. Think, "What can I infer this section might be about, based on what the whole book or section is about?" Read on to gather information from that section. Go back and reword the confusing heading in a way that is clearer.

Lesson Language *Some headings and subheadings are like the boldest, clearest traffic signs: They tell us exactly what's to come and help us navigate the text. Other headings and subheadings, however, are worded in a less clear way. The author may have been clever or creative, but it's leaving us a bit confused! When you notice that the heading or subheading is written in a way that can't literally mean what it says, you'll have to infer the meaning. Often, you won't be able to fully infer the meaning until you read the whole section and then go back to the heading to think about it. For example, in Bobbie Kalman's* What Is a Primate? *(1999), I came to the section called "Thumbs Up!" and thought, "What could this section be about?" I backed up to the larger section that this smaller section was in—the title was "A Primate's Body." So then, I started thinking that "Thumbs Up!" must be about how thumbs are important to primates. I then read the section to check to see if the details matched.*

Prompts

- Read the heading. What do you think it means?
- Based on what you read in this section, try renaming the heading.
- Use the information in the section to say the heading in a less clever way than the author did.
- Go back to the heading.
- What's this section mostly about?
- List back what you learned. Now can you explain the heading?
- The way you just said that heading was simple and clear!

CLEVER HEADING:	SECTION IS ABOUT:	MY NEW HEADING
Ready for Action	moving... how our bodies move when we play sports	MUSCLES
Power Up	how we get more energy or more power when we play sports	STRENGTH, POWER, ENDURANCE, SPEED
Dressed for Success	clothing, or... uniforms that people wear when playing sports	INCREASING SPEED, PREVENTING AIR RESISTANCE

From: Spring Into Action

Who is this for?

LEVELS
P–Z+

GENRE / TEXT TYPE
expository nonfiction

SKILL
inferring

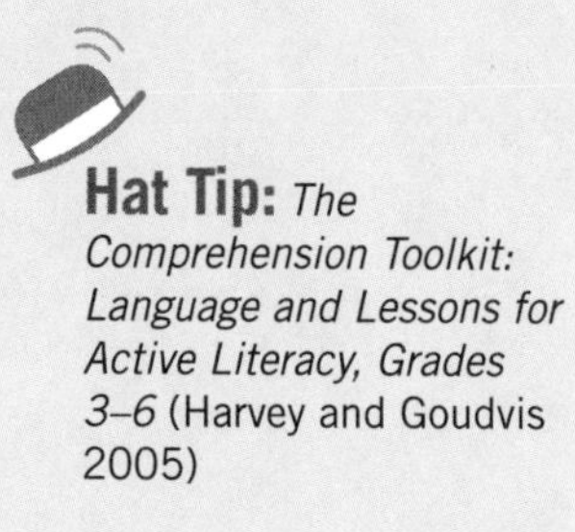

Hat Tip: *The Comprehension Toolkit: Language and Lessons for Active Literacy, Grades 3–6* (Harvey and Goudvis 2005)

10.19 Sidebar as Section

Who is this for?

LEVELS

Q–Z+

GENRE / TEXT TYPE

expository nonfiction

SKILLS

summarizing, synthesizing, determining importance

Strategy Read the sidebar. Think of it like a section. Ask first, "What's the main idea?" and second "What details support it?" Summarize the key information you learn in a few sentences.

Lesson Language *In more complex texts, the text features often have a lot of text, or words, in them. They are self-contained, in a box off to the side, and need to be read. Often, it's helpful to read the main text on the page first and then read the sidebar or other text-heavy text feature, thinking about its own main idea and details. You can use any strategies you know to help you do this (heading, topic sentence, adding up details, and so on). For example, in Barbara Brenner's book* If You Were There in 1492: Everyday Life in the Time of Columbus *(1998), almost every chapter has a sidebar of information included at some point. Each chapter talks about life in general, and then there is a sidebar with information about Columbus specifically. For example, in the chapter "In Sickness and in Health" the reader learns all about the most common diseases of the time period and the medicines and medical techniques that were used to try to cure people of those diseases. When I come to the sidebar about Columbus, I read facts about how Columbus and the other Spaniards he traveled with were often the cause of disease, and that they contracted diseases as well. The information in this sidebar is related to health, but it is its own section with its own main idea.*

Prompts

- Think about what strategy you'll use to help you find the main idea.
- What's the purpose of this sidebar? What's it mostly about?
- How would you summarize what you read?
- Give just the main idea and key details.

Sidebar	Main Text
What the food chain is. □→○→△→◊ □ gives energy to ○ which gives energy to △ which gives energy to ◊.	Producers provide many things 1. Food for 2. Shelter
Brackish zone organisms do not like to live in the ~~Bra~~ brackish zone. The brackish zone is ~~where~~ the point where freshwater meets saltwater.	Garbage can kill wildlife, but animals adapt to these things. Garbage with organisms living in them

10.20 Primary Sources

Strategy Read the title of the primary source and think, "How is this document connected to the main text?" Then, read trying to figure out the main idea and key details from the primary source. Finally, ask yourself, "How did what I just learn give me extra information that connects to the main text?"

Lesson Language *In Benoit's interesting book,* The Hindenburg Disaster *(2011), a reader can learn so much technical information about the airship, how it was made, the physics of the gases used to make it fly, and more. When you read the section "Filming the Disaster," you can learn the details of the timeline on the fated day when the airship crashed. But when I read the section "Oh, the Humanity!" I learned about the firsthand account of Herbert Morrison, a radio announcer who was on the scene that day and who witnessed the horrible event. He describes what happened in such detail with such emotion that the details of the event make it come to life.*

Prompts

- Explain what you learned from the primary source by itself.
- How does the primary source help you understand the rest of the text?
- Talk to me about the perspective of the person in the primary source.
- What's the new information?
- You can say, "In the text I learned . . . and when I read the primary source I learned . . ."

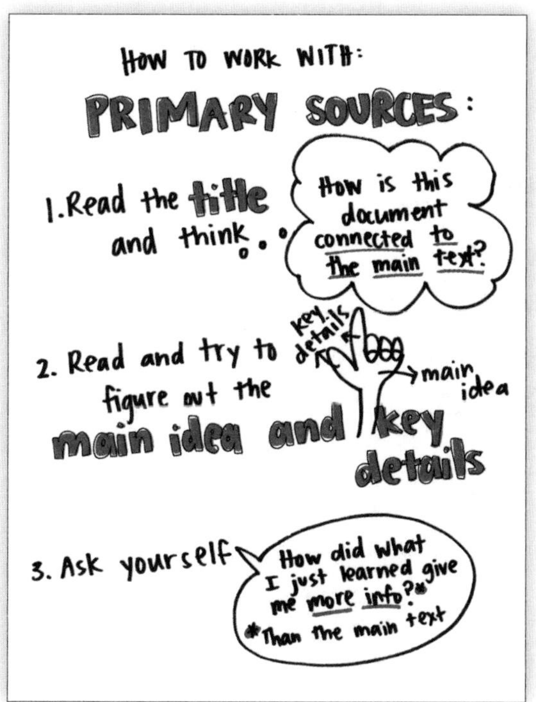

HOW TO WORK WITH:
PRIMARY SOURCES:
1. Read the title and think...
How is this document connected to the main text?
2. Read and try to figure out the main idea and key details
key details
main idea
3. Ask yourself
How did what I just learned give me more info?*
*Than the main text

Who is this for?

LEVELS
R–Z+

GENRE / TEXT TYPE
expository nonfiction

SKILLS
synthesizing, determining importance, summarizing

10.21 Take Your Time (Line)

Who is this for?

LEVELS

R–Z+

GENRE / TEXT TYPE

nonfiction

SKILLS

synthesizing, monitoring for meaning, summarizing

Strategy Read the title of the timeline, if there is one, to learn what the timeline is going to show. Look at the dates included and match up the dates in the timeline to the dates in the rest of the text. Read the labels that describe the event connected to each date, and think about any information you learned from the rest of the book that would help you understand that event better. Summarize what you learned by telling the key events in order.

Lesson Language *In* The Civil Rights Movement in America, *Elaine Landau (2003) includes a large two-page timeline at the back of the book. To understand it, I'll first read the title: it just says "Timeline: The Civil Rights Movement," so I think I'm going to learn all the key dates about the civil rights movement. Below, I notice there are dates—just the years—along the top, and then key information and sometimes photographs with that information. I'll read left to right, each event first, and then at the end summarize what I learned overall from this timeline. When I read a certain fact, such as: "1955: The Montgomery bus boycott begins and lasts for nearly thirteen months," then I can also think about the information from pages 17–20 where I learned about this event in more detail. This timeline helps me see where that event occurred in relation to the others I read about throughout the book.*

Prompts

- What do you remember reading about that connects to this event?
- Show me how you're going to study this timeline.
- Yes, you start with the title. What's next?
- I like how you're thinking about the information from the book to help you understand each event on the timeline.
- Try to summarize what you learned.

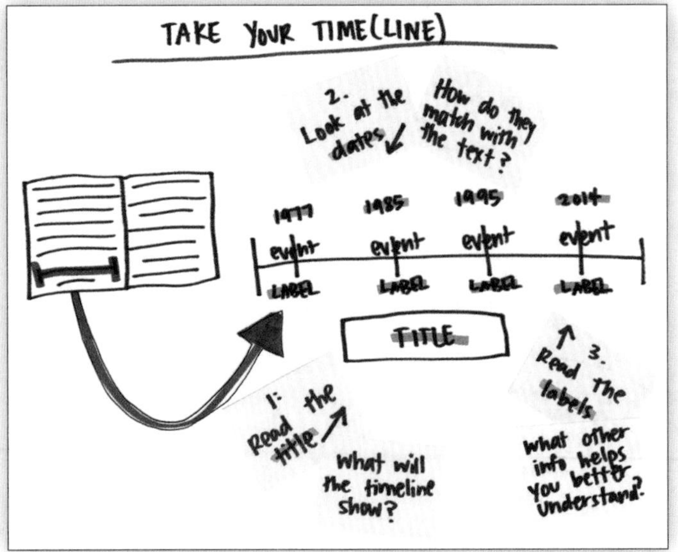

10.22 Graphic Graphs

Strategy Graphs—line, pie, or bar—pack a lot of information into a visual. Read the title of the graph first to be sure you understand what it's about. Then, read the labels to understand what each dot or bar or pie slice or line represents. Say back what you learned.

Teaching Tip I find that graphs are much more common in periodicals such as *Time For Kids* or *Scholastic News* than in most nonfiction books. This strategy might work best in a lesson where you supply the text so that you're sure the student will be able to practice and apply the strategy right away.

Prompts

- What will you look at first?
- Don't skip the labels—they're important.
- Say back what you learned from this.
- After reading the title, what do you think this graph will teach?
- Explain how what you read here fits with the rest of the section.

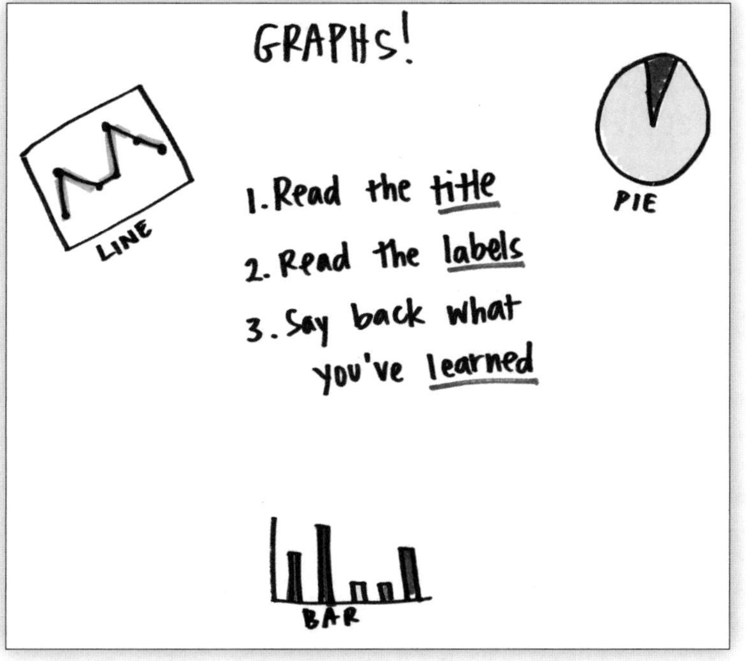

Who is this for?

LEVELS
R–Z+

GENRE / TEXT TYPE
expository nonfiction

SKILLS
synthesizing, monitoring for meaning

Hat Tip: *Navigating Nonfiction, Grade 3* (Boynton and Blevins 2007)

Improving Comprehension in Fiction and Nonfiction

Understanding Vocabulary and Figurative Language

Why is this goal important?

A reader's ability to understand vocabulary and language in a text has been empirically linked to reading comprehension, which is why instruction around words and language deserves such a prominent place in our classrooms (Baumann and Kame'enui 1991; Becker 1977; Stanovich 1986; Beck, McKeown, and Kucan 2013). Vocabulary is one of five core components of reading instruction that are essential for successfully teaching children how to read (National Reading Panel 2000). Vocabulary knowledge helps students access background knowledge, express ideas, communicate effectively, and learn about new concepts. "Vocabulary is the glue that holds stories, ideas, and content together . . . making comprehension accessible for children" (Rupley, Logan, and

Nichols 1998/99). In fact, research shows that if students are truly to understand what they read, they must be able to understand, not only decode, upward of 95 percent of the words (Betts 1946; Carver 1994; Hsueh-chao and Nation 2000; Laufer 1988).

Given the research on the link between comprehension and vocabulary knowledge, many schools have rushed to implement vocabulary programs. Although some students learn words this way, research actually suggests that most word learning occurs unconsciously and through normal reading, writing, speaking, and listening (Miller 1999; Nagy, Anderson, and Herman 1987; Krashen 2004; Baumann, Kame'enui, and Ash 2003). Therefore, teachers can do a lot to support their students' vocabulary goals by creating a classroom in which children read a lot, are encouraged to notice when words are new, learn strategies for figuring out what those words may mean, and are encouraged to use those words when they write and speak.

In their new book, Cobb and Blachowicz (2014) note that there are multiple aspects of comprehensive vocabulary instruction—fostering word consciousness, teaching individual words, providing rich and varied language experiences, and teaching word-learning strategies. Most of the strategies in this chapter will help students with the first and final aspects—fostering consciousness (or monitoring for meaning as they read to notice when a word or phrase the author uses is new) and learning new words and phrases by figuring them out when they encounter them in their reading. Some strategies in this chapter are also to help encourage students to use the word(s) once they figure out their meanings, as research has shown that this is an important part of getting the words to "stick" and become a part of the child's own vocabulary.

How do I know if this goal is right for my student?

There are a few ways you can determine that a focus on vocabulary and figurative language would best benefit a given student. One is to assess a student's overall word knowledge. You can use a standardized word knowledge assessment to gather whether the student's word knowledge is appropriate for his or her age or grade.

What's also important in determining this to be a worthy goal is to ask a child to *define* and/or *explain* the meaning of a previously unknown word that you highlight in a longer text passage. You'll want to choose to ask about words and/or phrases with appropriate contextual support—words that are defined within the text or words whose meaning can be figured out by looking closely at or reading an illustration or text feature. The intention here is not to assess a child's existing vocabulary knowledge, but rather his or her ability to read for clues and details, and to infer or deduce the meaning of the word. A student whose general vocabulary knowledge isn't great, but who can figure out meanings on the run through use of context will develop a richer vocabulary by continuing to do what he or she does and by increasing his or her overall volume of reading.

Evaluate what the student tells you or writes about when asked to explain the meaning of a word or phrase. A student who has a misunderstanding, or one who gives a simple yet accurate "gist" of a definition, may benefit from this goal. Students who are able to describe or explain the meaning of a word or phrase with detail from the text are usually solid in this area. See the sample rubrics for level O (Figures 11.A and 11.B); level-specific rubrics can be found in the Independent Reading Assessment series (Serravallo 2012, 2013a). Keep in mind that the depth of student responses should vary depending on the level of the text, the complexity of the words, and the amount of contextual support provided.

	Exceptional	Proficient	Approaching
What does it mean in this scene when the nurse is "cool as a cantaloupe"? (from *Chocolate Fever* by Robert Smith [2006]—Level O)	She stays calm and tells everyone what to do and where to go when the others are panicking. *(Synthesizes the larger context to explain the meaning of a word or phrase)*	All calm, relaxed. *(Uses immediate context to accurately define the word or phrase)*	She's really cool; like, kids like her. *(Demonstrates a partial understanding; may borrow language directly from the text)*

Figure 11.A Rubric for Evaluating Responses to Vocabulary and Figurative Language Questions in Fiction (Independent Reading Assessment: Fiction series [Serravallo 2012])

	Exceptional	Proficient	Approaching
Explain what antibodies are. (from *Germs Make Me Sick!* by Melvin Berger [1995]—Level O)	Antibodies are something that are in your body all the time. They look like plants. They attack germs so you don't get sick. *(Demonstrates deep understanding of the term using information from across multiple parts of the text; explains and/or describes the meaning)*	A special protein that protects you from germs. *(A precise, accurate definition using information from one portion of the text)*	Antibodies don't always get rid of the germs. *(Shows a partial understanding and/ or language borrowed directly from the text)*

Figure 11.B Rubric for Evaluating Responses to Vocabulary and Figurative Language Questions in Nonfiction (Independent Reading Assessment: Nonfiction series [Serravallo 2013a])

Strategies for Understanding Vocabulary and Figurative Language at a Glance

Strategy		Levels	Genres/ Text Types	Skills
11.1	Retire Overworked Words	E–Z+	Any	Word choice, inferring, using words in a correct context
11.2	Say It Out Loud	E–Z+	Any	Decoding, word recognition
11.3	Insert a Synonym	H–Z+	Any	Activating prior knowledge, monitoring for meaning
11.4	Categorize Context with Connectors	J–Z+	Any	Inferring, synthesizing
11.5	Multiple Meaning Words	J–Z+	Any	Monitoring for meaning, inferring
11.6	Look to Text Features	J–Z+	Nonfiction	Synthesizing, inferring, monitoring for meaning
11.7	Picture It	J–Z+	Fiction, poetry, narrative nonfiction	Inferring, visualizing
11.8	Word Part Clues—Prefixes and Suffixes	K–Z+	Any	Understanding how words work
11.9	Stick to Your Story	K–Z+	Fiction	Inferring, monitoring for meaning
11.10	Use Part of Speech as a Clue	L–Z+	Any	Inferring
11.11	Infer to Figure It Out	L–Z+	Any	Inferring
11.12	Mood as a Clue to Meaning	L–Z+	Fiction (mostly)	Inferring
11.13	Use the Just-Right Word (Trait Word Sort)	M–Z+	Fiction (mostly)	Inferring
11.14	Know the Word, Use the Word	M–Z+	Any	Using words in a correct context, word choice.
11.15	Context + Clues = Clarity	M–Z+	Any	Inferring, synthesizing
11.16	Be Word Conscious	M–Z+	Any	Monitoring for meaning
11.17	Word Relationships in a Phrase	M–Z+	Poetry, fiction (mostly)	Inferring
11.18	Help from Cognates	M–Z+	Any	Inferring
11.19	It's Right There in the Sentence!	M–Z+	Nonfiction (mostly)	Synthesizing
11.20	Use a Reference and Explain It	O–Z+	Any	Using references, inferring based on context
11.21	Find Similarities (and Differences) Within Groups	P–Z+	Any	Inferring
11.22	Read Up a Ladder	P–Z+	Nonfiction (mostly)	Synthesizing, inferring
11.23	Be Alert for Word Choice	R–Z+	Fiction, poetry	Inferring
11.24	Get to the Root	R–Z+	Any	Understanding how words work, inferring

11.1 Retire Overworked Words

Who is this for?

LEVELS

E–Z+

GENRE / TEXT TYPE

any

SKILLS

word choice, inferring, using words in a correct context

Strategy Notice when you choose an overworked word to describe a character, theme, or topic—nice, mean, stuff, thing. Stop and say, "What do I really mean here?" Revise your language to be more specific.

Teaching Tip Reading–writing connections benefit students because they can practice the same way of thinking across the day and across contexts. For ideas of a writing spin on this strategy, see Georgia Heard's *Revision Toolbox* (2014).

Lesson Language *Mark Twain once said, "The difference between the right word and the almost-right word is the difference between lightning and a lightning bug." When we work to talk about the characters in the books we read, the ideas that the author is presenting in the text, or the topics that we read about, it's important to check our language and use the right word. When you find yourself using a word that can mean so many things—nice, mean, stuff, thing—stop yourself and say, "What do I really mean here?" Try to revise your comment by picking a precise word.*

Prompts

- What word would you use?
- Let's brainstorm another word that is closer to what you're trying to say.
- Check the character trait list. Is there a better one?

Checking In... Am I Being as Precise As Possible?
We use the precise, exact word that fits the character perfectly at that part of the story. We ask ourselves:
→ What is my character's pattern of behavior?
→ What clues does the author give with body language or tone of voice?
→ How are the secondary characters reacting to him/her?
We use our precise traits with evidence to build a theory
We ask ourselves:
→ WHY is the character this way?
→ What has happened in his or her life to make them this way?
→ Who has hurt or helped them along the way?

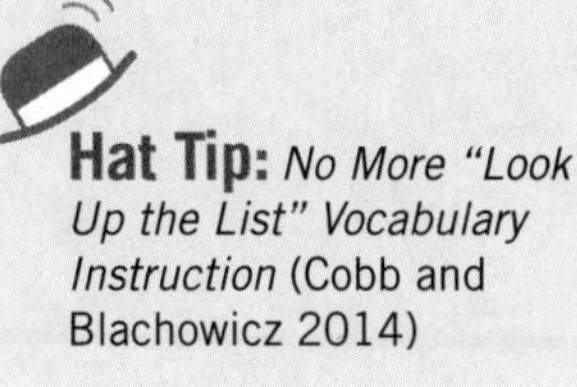

Hat Tip: *No More "Look Up the List" Vocabulary Instruction* (Cobb and Blachowicz 2014)

11.2 Say It Out Loud

Strategy When you come to an unfamiliar word, try to say it out loud. It may be the case that you are seeing a word in print for the first time that is actually a word you have heard or have said; a word you already know!

Lesson Language *English is a funny language, with words spelled in ways that might make it challenging to automatically recognize them. Sometimes, if there's a word for which you think you don't know the meaning, it could actually be just a case of you not knowing how to pronounce it right away. You can stop and try to say the word one way then another, changing the sounds of the vowels or breaking up the syllables in different places. You may surprise yourself and say it in a way that makes you think, "Oh, I know that word!"*

Prompts

- Let me hear you try it.
- Try to say it in a different way.
- Try a different vowel sound here and here.
- Try to break up the syllables in a different way.
- Put an emphasis on the first part of the word instead of the last.
- Does that sound like a word you've heard?

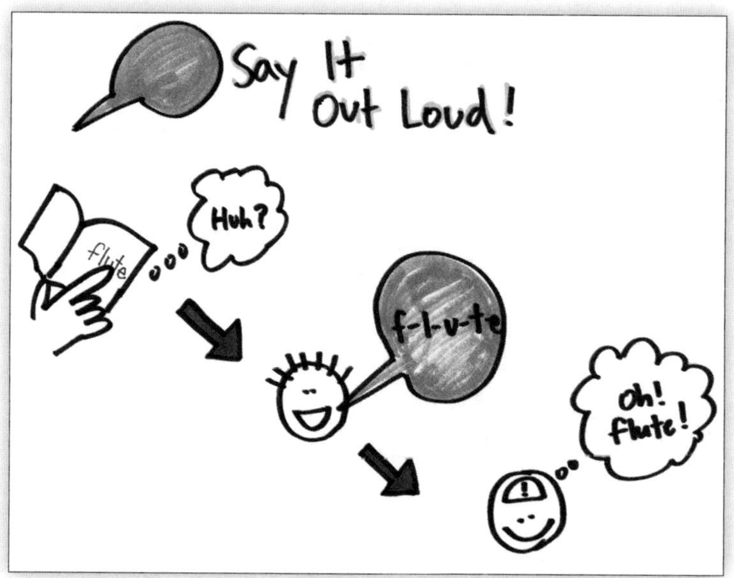

Who is this for?

LEVELS

E–Z+

GENRE / TEXT TYPE

any

SKILLS

decoding, word recognition

Hat Tip: Independent Reading Assessment: Fiction series (Serravallo 2012)

11.3 Insert a Synonym

Who is this for?

LEVELS

H–Z+

GENRE / TEXT TYPE

any

SKILLS

activating prior knowledge, monitoring for meaning

Strategy When you come across an unfamiliar word, insert a word you know that would fit the sentence and the larger context. Read on to check that it still makes sense.

Lesson Language *I was reading this section, "Get My Message?" from Bobbie Kalman's book* What Is a Primate? *(1999). When I came to this sentence, I had to stick in a synonym that made sense. Here's the sentence: "Gorillas use many sounds to 'talk' to one another. Female gorillas grunt to scold their young" (10). That word—*g-r-u-n-t. *I don't know what it means, even though I can pronounce it. But based on what I'm learning about in the sentence, I can put in a synonym, something to do with talking or communicating. I think* grunt *means "Makes a sound" so that it still makes sense. Once I stuck in a synonym, I would read it like this, "Female gorillas make a sound to scold their young."*

Prompts

- What's going on so far? So what might this word mean?
- Try a word. Does that make sense?
- Stick in a word that would make sense here.
- Would that word keep the meaning of the sentence?
- What's another word the author might have used that would still make sense?
- Say a word you know. Keep reading.

Insert a SYNONYM
(a word that means the same/similar thing)
angry? mad?
When her best friend grabbed her toy, she was furious with him.
by? next to? near?
He placed the glass of orange juice alongside his plate.

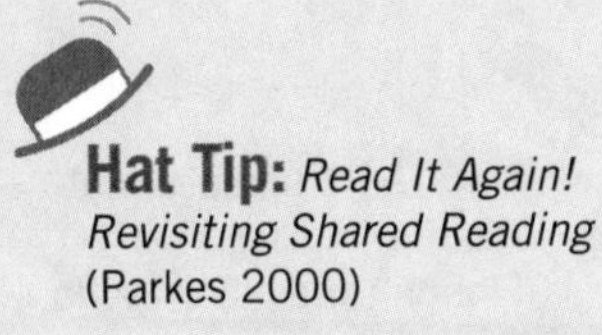

Hat Tip: *Read It Again! Revisiting Shared Reading* (Parkes 2000)

11.4 Categorize Context with Connectors

Strategy Notice words that connect things like *and* or *but*. Think, "Is the word being used here linking to a word that means the same thing or something different than the rest of the sentence?"

Teaching Tip The language in the above strategy is intentionally simplified so that it will work with even a first grader reading a book at level J. As texts get more complex, so do the "linking words," or conjunctions. Modify this lesson by giving level-appropriate examples in the strategy and by providing a chart that supports understanding the meaning of those words. For a slight spin on this strategy, see the strategy on page 320, "Find Similarities (and Differences) Within Groups" in this chapter.

Prompts

- Do you see any connector words in this sentence?
- Are there any other words in this same sentence that might mean the same as this word?
- Because the linking word is ______, you should think that this word is opposite (or same) as what's in the rest of the sentence.
- The author gave you a clue about this word right in the sentence. Check the linking words.

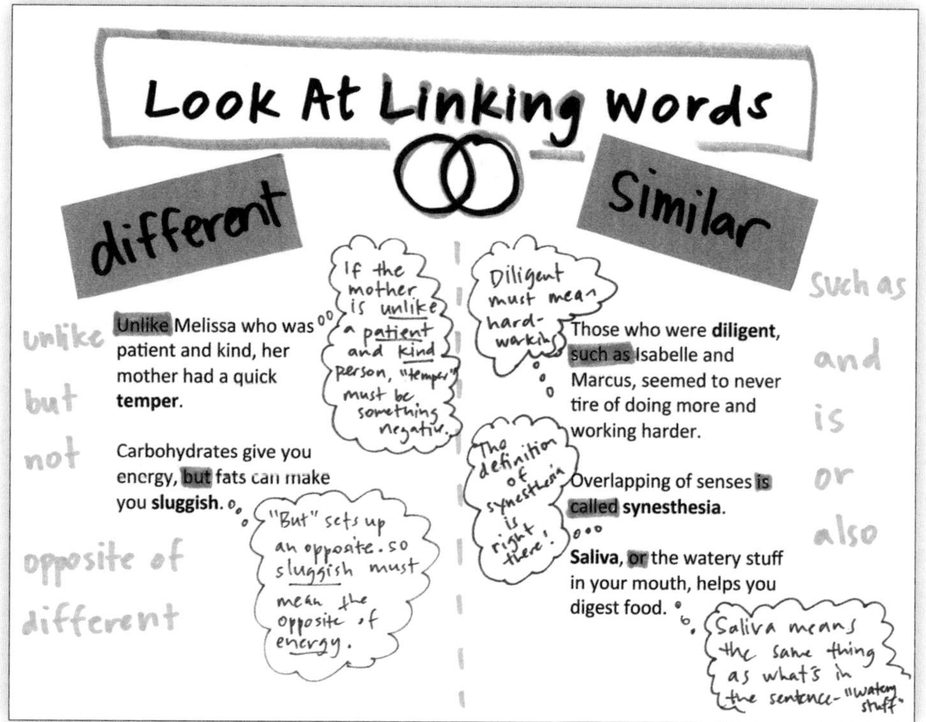

Who is this for?

LEVELS

J–Z+

GENRE / TEXT TYPE

any

SKILLS

inferring, synthesizing

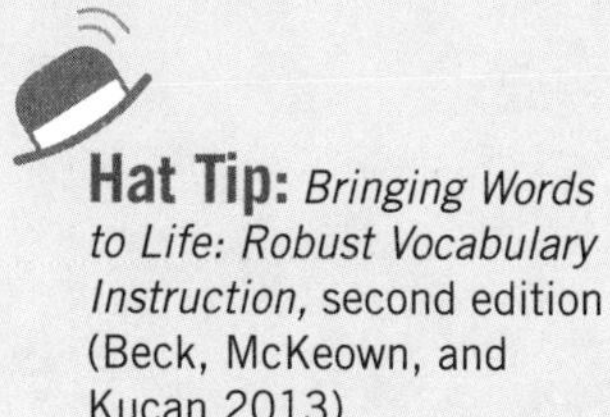

Hat Tip: *Bringing Words to Life: Robust Vocabulary Instruction*, second edition (Beck, McKeown, and Kucan 2013)

11.5 Multiple Meaning Words

Who is this for?

LEVELS

J–Z+

GENRE / TEXT TYPE

any

SKILLS

monitoring for meaning, inferring

Strategy When a word isn't making sense within the context, it might be a multiple meaning word. Read the context before and after. Think about how the word is being used. Choose a definition that makes sense in the context of where you came across the word.

Lesson Language *The same one word can have different meanings depending on how, when, and where it's used. For example, the word force might mean to make someone do something. But, if you're reading a science text, it could mean a pressure, or something that causes an object to move or change, such as the force of gravity. When you realize the word is being used to mean something different from how you know it, you'll want to apply strategies as if the word is brand new to you (even though you know one meaning). Using any of the other strategies you've learned, such as using context, thinking about the "job" the word has, or even thinking about words it sounds similar to in other languages, might all be helpful ways to figure it out.*

Prompts

- How's the word being used?
- What is a meaning you know for that word?
- How do you know it can't be that meaning?
- What's another meaning that might make sense here?
- That's one meaning of the word, but does that make sense here?
- What other strategy could you use to figure it out?

Words can have Multiple Meanings!
She made me
Force of gravity.
She forced me to do it. I didn't want to!

11.6 Look to Text Features

Strategy Check the features on the page, in the section, and across the book (for example, the glossary). Find information that teaches you about the word. Use the sentences around the word. Go back to the sentence and try to use the definition in the context.

Lesson Language *When you're learning about a new topic, you'll likely also be learning new words that are specific to the topic. In many cases, the author won't leave you high and dry, grasping at the meaning of those words. It's likely that the author will help you. One place the author might give some help is in the text features. You can look on the same page, within the same section, or even in a glossary (when the word is bolded) to get information about the word's meaning. Check those in addition to the sentences surrounding the sentence in which the word appears. Then, it's a good idea to go back to the sentence where the word first appears to try to apply the definition to how it's being used. For example, if you come across the word habitat in* No Animals, No Plants *(Irvine 2007), you might notice that the word is bolded—then you can look in the glossary and find a quick definition. You could also notice that the photographs show a man using a chainsaw to cut down a tree in a jungle, a panda eating bamboo in a jungle, and a jeep driving over a plain. You might think, "It might have to do with the place" or "It's what the jungle can also be called for endangered animals." Then, you'd want to go back into the text and use the new understanding of the word to say, "One of the most important reasons why species become endangered is because people are destroying the place where the animals live."*

Prompts

- Are there any features here that would help?
- Based on this picture (or sidebar or map or so on), what might the word mean?
- Is it bold? If so, check the glossary.
- Look across the entire page or section.
- Go back and use the definition in the sentence.
- You used the picture *and* the glossary—I think you understand the word now!

Who is this for?

LEVELS

J–Z+

GENRE / TEXT TYPE

nonfiction

SKILLS

synthesizing, inferring, monitoring for meaning

Hat Tip: Independent Reading Assessment: Nonfiction series (Serravallo 2013a)

11.7 Picture It

Who is this for?

LEVELS

J–Z+

GENRES / TEXT TYPES

fiction, poetry, narrative nonfiction

SKILLS

inferring, visualizing

Strategy When you think a writer may be using a phrase in a figurative way, not a literal way, stop and picture it. Get an image in your mind of what each separate word means, then what the words mean together. Take a guess at what the phrase means, keeping in mind what's happening in the rest of the text.

Lesson Language *We're going to read the book* The Book Report from the Black Lagoon *together (Thaler 2010). I picked it because it's a book packed with figurative language. That means that the author uses words figuratively and you have to think about how it means something different than if the author were to mean it literally. For example, early on in the story, one of the characters says, "read my lips." Now, if the character meant that literally there would be words printed on your lips that you'd read. But that's not what she means. She means to watch her lips move and figure out what she's saying. Let's try another one. The character says it takes him three minutes to read a stop sign. Literally three minutes? No, he means it figuratively. What do you think he actually means? That he's a very slow reader.*

Prompts

- What do you see?
- Tell me what you picture—for just this word.
- Tell me what you picture—for this whole phrase.
- That may be what it means. Explain how it would fit with the rest of the story (or poem or text).
- I can tell you pictured it to see that it can't literally mean that. What do you think the author is trying to say?

Hat Tip: *Reading with Meaning: Teaching Comprehension in the Primary Grades*, second edition (Miller 2012)

11.8 Word Part Clues—Prefixes and Suffixes

Strategy Some longer words are actually made of parts—prefixes, suffixes, and base words. When you know what each of the parts means, then you can put the parts together to figure out what the word means. Separate the parts of the word, think about what each part means, and then put the word back together.

Teaching Tip Create word family charts with the students and have them up and in the classroom to serve as a resource as children read and come to unfamiliar words. Try to think aloud during read-alouds or minilessons when you come to complex, long words that have familiar word parts. Part of the usefulness of this strategy is in knowing what the word parts mean, the other is in actually going through the steps of deconstructing and reconstructing the word. This strategy can be modified depending on the reading level and grade level—choose those prefixes and suffixes your students are most likely to encounter based on the level(s) of texts they're reading.

Family	Prefix	Examples	Meanings
"Not"	dis-	Disobedient Disagree	Not obedient, misbehaved Don't agree, different opinions
	un-	Unhelpful Unlock	Not helpful Not locked
	in-	Incomplete Independent	Not complete/finished Don't depend on others, can do it by yourself
	im-	Imperfect Immature	Not perfect, have flaws Not mature, juvenile
	non-	Nonfiction Nonliving	Not fiction, real Not alive
	ir-	Irresponsible Irregular	Not responsible Not regular
	il-	Illegal Illiterate	Not legal Not literate, can't read or write

Prompts

- What part do you see?
- What does that part mean?
- Put that together with the rest of the word. What does the entire word mean?
- You know that part.
- Check the chart.
- What other words do you know with that same prefix (or suffix)?

Who is this for?

LEVELS

K–Z+

GENRE / TEXT TYPE

any

SKILL

understanding how words work

Hat Tip: *Spelling K–8: Planning and Teaching* (Snowball and Bolton 1999)

11.9 Stick to Your Story

Who is this for?

LEVELS

K–Z+

GENRE / TEXT TYPE

fiction

SKILLS

inferring, monitoring for meaning

Strategy Think about what's happening. Come up with a definition. Use the context in the story to explain why that meaning works. Try not to make up a scenario that doesn't really exist to come up with an explanation.

Lesson Language *It's important that you don't invent details to explain or rationalize a definition of a word or phrase that is unfamiliar. Instead, try to stay within the limits of what's actually happening in the story. For example, let's say you come across the following sentence in* A Series of Unfortunate Events, Book 1: The Bad Beginning *(Snicket 1999):*

> So unless you have been very, very lucky, you know that a good, long session of weeping can often make you feel better, even if your circumstances have not changed one bit. (57)

You might say, "I think the word means friends *because friends can make you cry if they're mean to you and they'd need to change so that you can feel better." Meanwhile, in the story, there wasn't anything that happened with friends making another character cry. This is an example of making up the details to explain a definition. The meaning may fit with the sentence, but because it doesn't fit with the larger context of the story, that can't be the correct definition. What's actually happening is that the siblings in the story are in a terrible situation where everything is going wrong around them. So I think a better definition of the word that would make sense with what's actually happening would be "your experiences" or "your environment" or "your situation."*

Prompts

- Think about the whole context, not just the sentence.
- Explain why you think that's the meaning.
- Does the way you explained it fit with the details of the whole story.
- You mentioned ______. Did that happen in the story, or are you saying it *might* have happened?
- I notice you thought about what was happening in the story to figure out what that word means.

STICK TO THE STORY!
(make sure you're not making it up)
hurricane: a Severe storm that begins...
1: THINK: what's happening?
2: DEFINE: "It means..."
3: GO BACK: Use context to explain

Hat Tip: *Bringing Words to Life: Robust Vocabulary Instruction*, second edition (Beck, McKeown, and Kucan 2013)

11.10 Use Part of Speech as a Clue

Strategy When you come to an unfamiliar word, think about the "job" the word has in a sentence. Is it a noun, verb, adjective, adverb? Use your knowledge of the job of the word to help you figure out what the word might mean.

Teaching Tip Understanding parts of speech can help with both understanding the meaning of a word and also with reading the word. For a print work example of a similar strategy, see "Unpacking What It Means to 'Sound Right,'" page 101.

Prompts

- What job does that word have in this sentence?
- Think about what kind of word it comes after (or before). Does that help figure out the job it has?
- What's the part of speech?
- Is it a person, place, thing?
- Is it an action?
- Is it a describing word?
- Now that you know the job of the word, what might it mean?

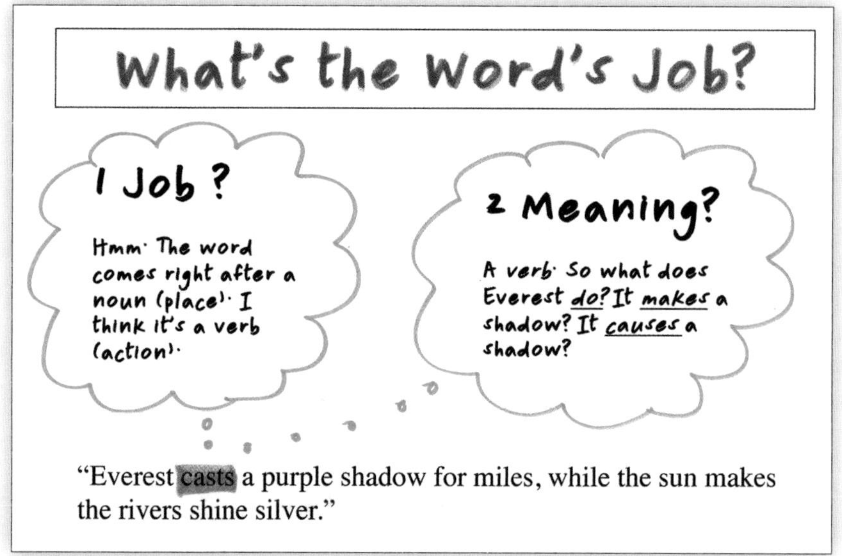
What's the Word's Job?
1 Job?
Hmm. The word comes right after a noun (place). I think it's a verb (action).
2 Meaning?
A verb. So what does Everest do? It makes a shadow? It causes a shadow?
"Everest casts a purple shadow for miles, while the sun makes the rivers shine silver."

Text excerpt from *To the Top!* (Kramer 1993).

Who is this for?

LEVELS

L–Z+

GENRE / TEXT TYPE

any

SKILL

inferring

11.11 Infer to Figure It Out

Who is this for?

LEVELS

L–Z+

GENRE / TEXT TYPE

any

SKILL

inferring

Hat Tip: *Strategies that Work: Teaching Comprehension for Understanding and Engagement*, second edition (Harvey and Goudvis 2007)

Strategy Stop when you come to a word you haven't heard before or for which you don't know the meaning. Pick up on clues in the text or from a picture that might help you guess at what the word means. Think about how it fits with the title or what's happening, and what kind of word it is (positive or negative). Put all of that together to infer its meaning!

Teaching Tip You may notice that the language in this strategy includes the language you've seen in other strategies in this chapter (for example, strategy 11.10 which is about using mood to figure out the meaning of unknown words). The point of this lesson is that readers need to be resilient and, at times, need to apply more than one strategy to figure out the word. It's a good idea to occasionally teach a repertoire strategy like this one no matter what goal you're working on with a student so that you are encouraging children to try another strategy if the first one doesn't work.

Prompts

- Stop when you come to a word you don't know.
- You said you know all these words . . . what about this one?
- Check the picture. What might it mean?
- Reread what comes before. Does that help?
- Keep reading past the word. Can you figure out what it means now?
- Say back what you think the clues are.
- Yes, I think that meaning makes sense with the clues you collected.

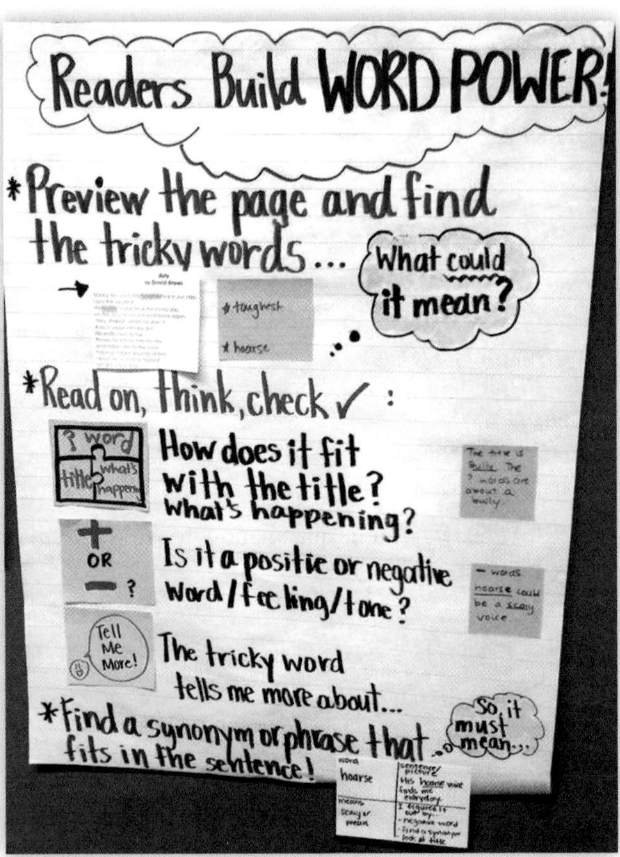

Readers Build WORD POWER!
*Preview the page and find the tricky words...
What could it mean?
*toughest
*hoarse
*Read on, think, check ✓:
How does it fit with the title? What's happening?
Is it a positive or negative word/feeling/tone?
Tell Me More!
The tricky word tells me more about...
*Find a synonym or phrase that fits in the sentence!
So, it must mean...
hoarse

11.12 Mood as a Clue to Meaning

Strategy Think about the general mood or feeling in the sentence or paragraph. Is it positive or negative? Based on the overall mood, what's a word or phrase that would fit in place of this word? Try to explain or define the word, keeping the context in mind.

Lesson Language *When we read the book* Sylvester and the Magic Pebble *(Steig 1969) as a class, we realized that the author uses such rich language and to really understand the story, we should pause to figure it out. One place where we can think about mood to help us is midway through the story when the parents are crying because they miss their son. We found a couple of words in this part. One was in this sentence: "They concluded that something dreadful must have happened . . ." and another on the next page: "They were miserable. Life had no meaning for them anymore." The mood in this scene is definitely negative, sad. So the words mean things that are connected to that mood. Dreadful means horrible, awful, terrible. Miserable means depressed, devastated, sad. Then, later in the story when Sylvester comes back to life as a donkey and the family is happy, we see this: "You can imagine the scene that followed—the embraces, the kisses, the questions, the answers, the loving looks, and the fond exclamations!" Here, they are so happy, so overjoyed, that fond exclamations must mean something having to do with celebrating or saying things aloud in a happy voice.*

Prompts

- What word are you trying to figure out?
- What is one word you are focused on?
- What do you think it might mean?
- Can you explain it?
- What's the mood?
- Name the feeling you get here.
- Explain it.
- That's what's happening; what's the feeling?
- That's what the text says; what's the definition?
- Great explanation; you gave me a couple examples to show you understand.
- You figured out a feeling from the sentence by paying attention to word choice.

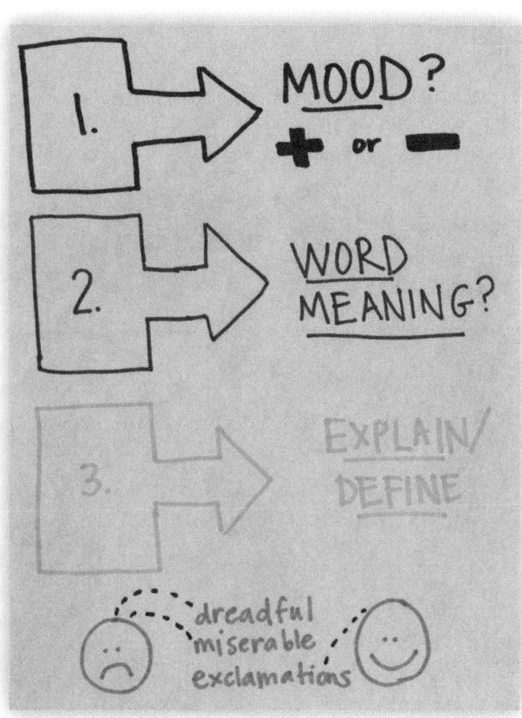

Who is this for?

LEVELS
L–Z+

GENRE / TEXT TYPE
fiction (mostly)

SKILL
inferring

11.13 Use the Just-Right Word (Trait Word Sort)

Who is this for?

LEVELS

M–Z+

GENRE / TEXT TYPE

fiction (mostly)

SKILL

inferring

Strategy Decide first if the word describes something positive or negative. Then, think about what words the word is most similar to. Sort the word into a category with other synonyms. Think (and talk with others) about what makes the words in the same category similar and what the subtle differences are between each of the words.

Teaching Tip Research shows children need to use words to know them (Cobb and Blachowicz 2014). During character studies, or when children are working on a character inference goal, helping them not only to think about character but also to use appropriate words to describe characters can offer an opportunity to help them improve their vocabulary. To use this strategy, think about the words you want your students to know for describing character traits and/or feelings and preprint them on slips of paper. Have students work in collaborative groups to sort the words, thinking about whether the words have a positive or negative connotation. Then, ask them to categorize the words under a more common heading (e.g., "nice," "bad," etc.). After they've worked with the words they can then reuse the chart they've made as a resource during their character inference work. The strategy and prompts here are to support children with the work of understanding and classifying the words. You may offer strategies to help children put this chart into action, such as the first strategy in this chapter ("Retire Overworked Words"), or strategies from Chapter 6 such as "Role-Playing Characters to Understand Them Better" (page 172) or "Interactions Can Lead to Inferences" (page 179) that ask students to use trait words to describe character.

Prompts

- Is it positive or negative?
- What's a word that means something similar?
- What kind of word is this?

11.14 Know the Word, Use the Word

Strategy Find a word from your reading that you want to learn. Try to figure it out from the context and/or look up the meaning of the word using an outside source. Save the word somewhere (perhaps in your reader's notebook). When you write and when you talk in partners or book clubs, try to use the word.

Lesson Language *Learning a word is about doing more than just figuring out a word and moving on in your reading. When you want to learn a word, you'll need to read it, understand it, and then use it—when you write and when you talk. When you first see the word, you might kind of know what it means. Then, if you work to give a definition, you understand it even more. But when you use it in writing or talking, then it becomes part of your vocabulary.*

Prompts

- Think about how it was used in the book you read. How could you use it when you write or talk?
- Reread the definition. Remind yourself what the word means. Try to use it.
- Try to use it in a sentence.
- What word fits with the topic of what you're trying to say or write?

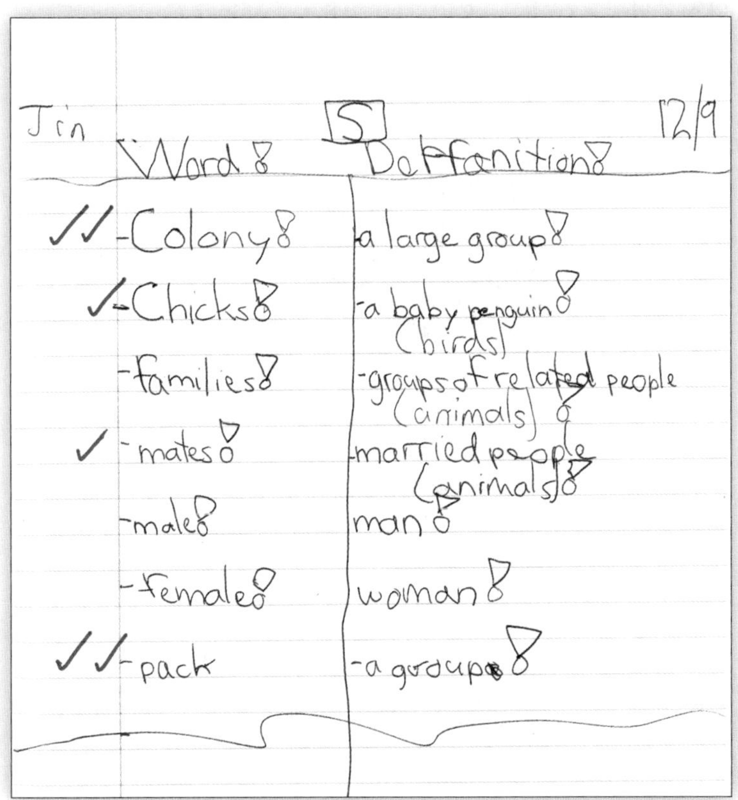

Jin — S — 12/9

Words:	Definitions:
✓✓ -Colony:	a large group:
✓ -Chicks:	-a baby penguin: (birds)
-families:	-groups of related people (animals):
✓ -mates:	married people (animals):
-male:	man:
-female:	woman:
✓✓ -pack	-a group:

Who is this for?

LEVELS

M–Z+

GENRE / TEXT TYPE

any

SKILL

using words in a correct context, word choice

Hat Tip: *No More "Look Up the List" Vocabulary Instruction* (Cobb and Blachowicz 2014)

11.15 Context + Clues = Clarity

Who is this for?

LEVELS

M–Z+

GENRE / TEXT TYPE

any

SKILLS

inferring, synthesizing

Strategy Stop and say back what's happening. Think, "How is the word being used?" List out all the clues that you have that relate to the word. Think, "What might this word mean?"

Lesson Language *Sometimes the word won't make sense right away. If that happens, you can use four steps to figure it out. For example, if you get to the word bejeweled in* Judy Moody Gets Famous! *(McDonald 2001), you might first say what's happening. "Judy is in class with her friend Jessica. She's kind of annoyed by her for some reason. She's talking about her as a 'Queen Bee' and they said she has a crown on that has rubylike gems." You could think, "How is the word being used?" and realize that it's being used to describe the crown. Then, you can think about the details you know that connect to the crown—that she's pretending to be a queen and it has rubies. Then, you can think that bejeweled means that it's fancy, or with lots of jewels, or with rubies in it. Any of those would be a close enough meaning to keep track of what's happening and to keep reading.*

Prompts

- What's going on in the story right now?
- What have you learned so far in this text?
- From all you told me, what do you think is a clue to the meaning?
- What details from the text do you think go with this word?
- How is the word used?
- Try a definition.

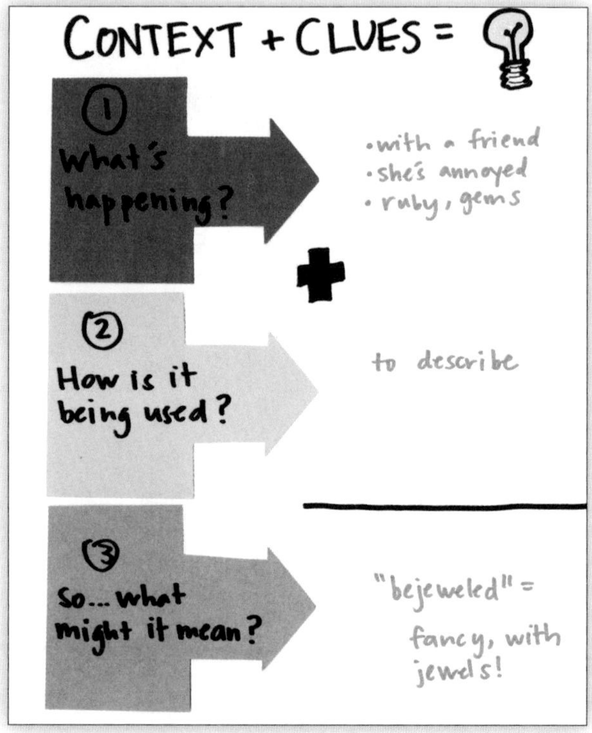

Hat Tip: *Bringing Words to Life: Robust Vocabulary Instruction*, second edition (Beck, McKeown, and Kucan 2013)

11.16 Be Word Conscious

Strategy Make sure you're keeping track of your understanding. Always ask yourself, "Do I know this word? Do I know how this word is being used?" If you answer "No," then use a strategy (or strategies) of your choice to figure the word out.

Lesson Language *Before you can stop to use one of your strategies to figure out a new word, you need to know what you know (and what you don't). Savvy readers are word conscious;, they are aware of the words they read. They recognize when they know the word and when they know the word in the particular context in which it appears. Sometimes you may see a word that you recognize immediately, but the way the word is being used in the sentence is different from how you usually see it being used. Other times, you may be reading a sentence, aware of what's happening, and then see a word you've never seen before. In either instance, it's important to stop and ask yourself, "Do I know this word? Do I know how the word is being used?" Whenever your understanding gets interrupted by a word you don't know, or when a word is used in a way that's unfamiliar to you, it's important to stop and apply a strategy to figure it out.*

Prompts

- What strategy will you try here?
- Do you think you are reading too fast to catch the words you don't know?
- You said you know all these words? Tell me about this one.
- Think about how the word is being used. Do you know the word in this context?
- You realized you didn't know that word. That's a first step!
- Now that you figured out that word is being used in a different way than you usually see it, what will you do now?

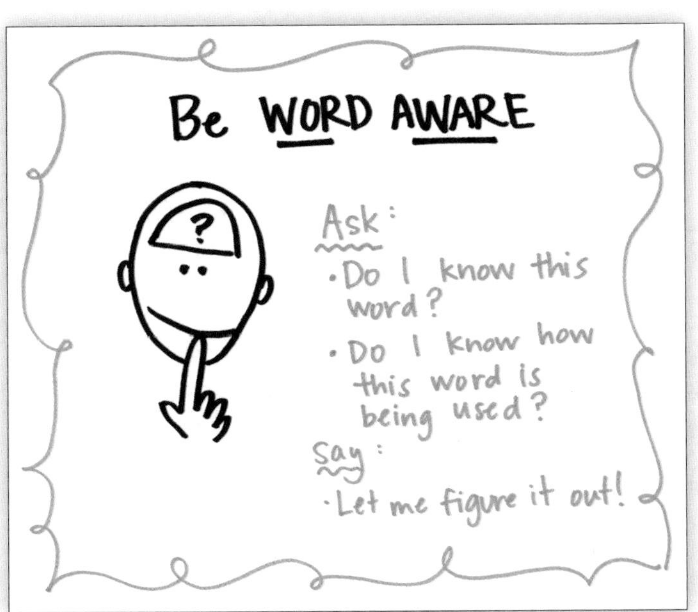

Who is this for?

LEVELS

M–Z+

GENRE / TEXT TYPE

any

SKILL

monitoring for meaning

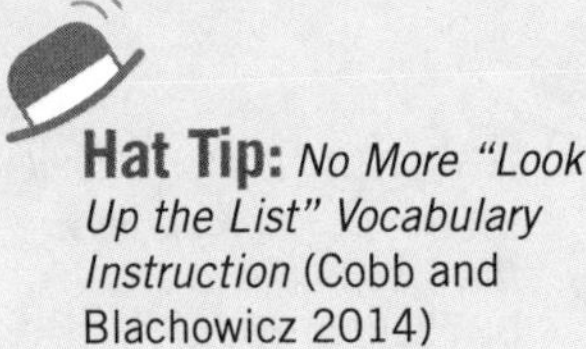

Hat Tip: *No More "Look Up the List" Vocabulary Instruction* (Cobb and Blachowicz 2014)

11.17 Word Relationships in a Phrase

Who is this for?

LEVELS

M–Z+

GENRES / TEXT TYPES

poetry, fiction (mostly)

SKILL

inferring

Strategy It's not always the words alone that are tricky, but sometimes it's words together—in relationship to other words—that become confusing. Think about how the words are working together. Use the chart as a reference. Think, "What does the phrase mean here, based on the relationship between the words?"

Teaching Tip The chart provided on this page is an example of what you might create with your children. Of course, charts that are created with the children, using examples they provide, will hold much greater meaning for them and will be more likely to be referenced during their practice.

Relationship	What Is It?	Example
Oxymoron	Words that are put together that have very different, sometimes opposite, meanings	Sound of silence Living dead
Pun	Humorous use of words because at least one word in the phrase sounds like another word but has a different meaning	A chicken crossing the road is poultry in motion.
Metaphor	Comparing two words without using like or as	That desk is such a pig sty.
Hyperbole	Exaggeration	I've been waiting in line forever.
Idiom	A saying that doesn't mean what the words in the phrase literally mean	Let's hit the road.

Other word relationships to define: synonym, antonym, homonym, homophone, homograph, detonation, connotation, alliteration, simile, slang, onomatopoeia, spoonerism, palindrome, collective noun, anagram, riddle.

Prompts

- Think about the words as a group.
- How are the words being used together?
- What does each word mean separately? What might they mean together?
- Check the chart. What type of phrase is it?
- Instead of taking it literally, think what else the author might mean here.

Hat Tip: *No More "Look Up the List" Vocabulary Instruction* (Cobb and Blachowicz 2014)

11.18 Help from Cognates

Strategy Many English words have their roots in other languages, so knowing another language can help you figure out some of the most tricky vocabulary you'll come across in English. Think of a word in the other language you know that looks like or sounds like the English word. Think about what the word means in the other language and see if a similar meaning would fit in the context in which you encountered the English word.

Teaching Tip This strategy would be best for a student who knows another language or is an English language learner.

Prompts

- Do you know a word in another language that looks like this?
- Can you think of a word that sounds like this?
- Think about what the word means in the other language.
- Think about what this word might mean in English.
- Think about how it's used here—it might not mean the exact same thing, more likely something similar.

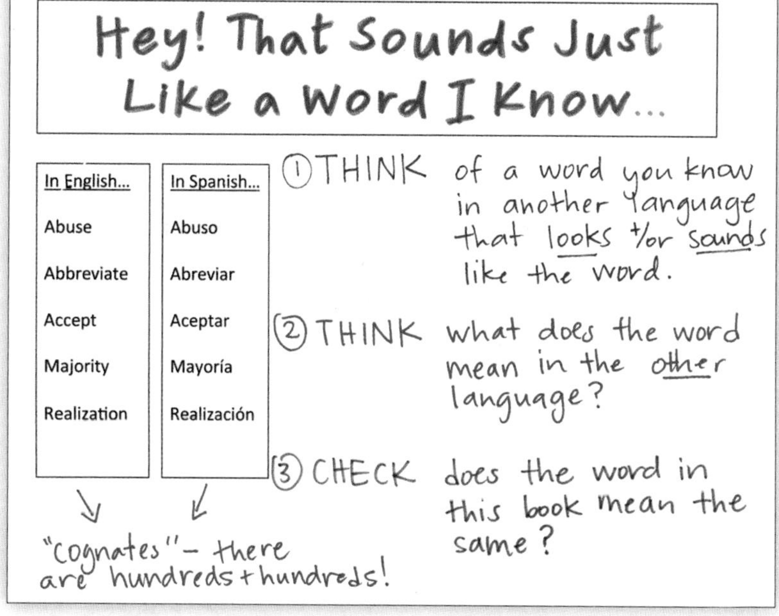

Who is this for?

LEVELS

M–Z+

GENRE / TEXT TYPE

any

SKILL

inferring

Hat Tip: *No More "Look Up the List" Vocabulary Instruction* (Cobb and Blachowicz 2014)

11.19 It's Right There in the Sentence!

Who is this for?

LEVELS
M–Z+

GENRE / TEXT TYPE
nonfiction (mostly)

SKILL
synthesizing

Strategy Authors of nonfiction will often stick the definition of a challenging word right in the same sentence as the word itself appears. After finding a challenging word, look before the word and after the word to see if the word is defined. Seeing words like *also*, *or*, and *this is called*, or punctuation like commas or dashes, gives you a clue that the definition is right there!

Lesson Language *Let's look at a few examples of sentences from a book we know—* Penguins *by Arlon and Gordon-Harris (2012b)—where the authors used a word that is important for learning about the content, and then gave us the definition right in the same sentence. Let's think about how we know the definition is there, too.*

> "So each year penguins molt—their feathers fall out" (21).
>
> "Krill are like tiny shrimps" (22).
>
> "These penguins used to make their nests out of their own poop, called guano!" (41).

In the first example, we can figure out the word molt *because the definition follows a dash. Dashes and commas are commonly used when an author will stick a definition right there in the sentence, so make sure you watch out for that. The second sentence has the word* krill *which we can figure out because we see the words* are like. *And the last sentence has the word* guano. *How can we figure that one out? There's that key word,* called!

Prompts

- Reread the whole sentence.
- Do you see any key words that tell you the definition is in the sentence?
- Does the author explain the word?
- Look at the punctuation. I think I see something that clues me in to a definition.
- Yes, the definition is right there. You saw the commas and knew that.
- Yes, the definition is right there. You used keywords to help you find it.
- You're right, there's no definition. For this one, you'll need to use a different strategy. What else can you try?

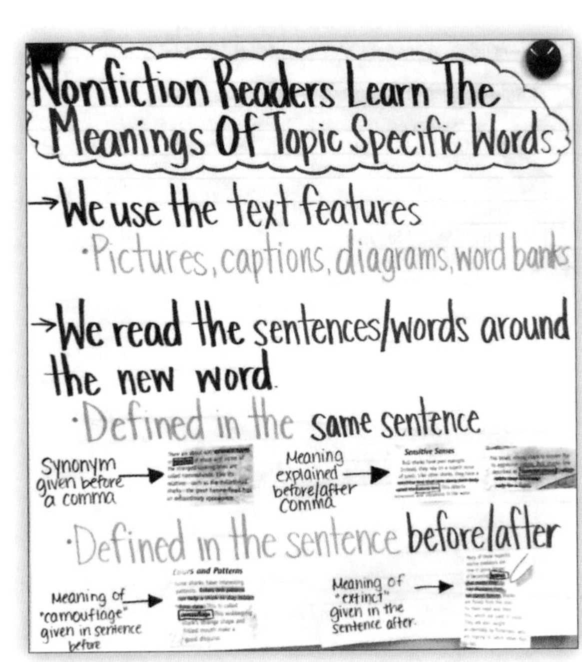

11.20 Use a Reference and Explain It

Strategy Find a definition (or definitions) by consulting a reference or knowledgeable source. Go back to the text to see how the word is being used to choose the correct definition or to consider whether the word is being used literally or figuratively. Explain what the word means in your own words based on how it's being used.

Lesson Language *When you've found that you've tried every strategy you can and you still can't figure out the word, you may choose to look it up. You don't want to be interrupting your reading on every page to run to a reference, but if you find that not knowing the word interferes with understanding what you're reading, or if you are just really curious about what the word might mean, you may choose to seek an outside source. Whether you use dictionary.com, an actual physical dictionary, or a knowledgeable person, the important thing to remember is that a simple definition is rarely enough to really help you understand the word. You'll want to always think about the context in which the word appears to make sure you're choosing the right definition (as we know many words have multiple meanings!). Also, be aware that sometimes a word will be used as part of a larger phrase, which can skew the usage of the word from literal to figurative.* (See "Word Relationships in a Phrase," page 316.) *Consider what the author means to say and why the author chose the word, and try to explain the meaning in your own words based on how it's being used.*

Prompts

- What can you check to help you?
- You found a few definitions. How can you figure out which is correct in this context?
- Let's reread to check what's happening right now in the text.
- Which definition applies in this case?
- You figured out that it was the second definition, not the first, that works in this context. You're really thinking about the meaning!

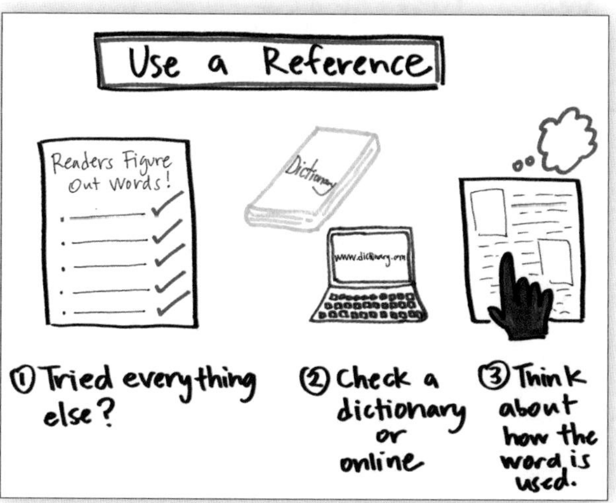

Who is this for?

LEVELS

O–Z+

GENRE / TEXT TYPE

any

SKILLS

using references, inferring based on context

11.21 Find Similarities (and Differences) Within Groups

Who is this for?

LEVELS

P–Z+

GENRE / TEXT TYPE

any

SKILL

inferring

Hat Tip: *Learning to Learn in a Second Language* (Gibbons 1993)

Strategy When you see the author using a series of descriptive words within one sentence, that group of words may be similar. If there is a group of words that are similar, you might use the ones you know to figure out the ones you don't. In other cases, if the group of words contains words that show opposition, such as: *not*, *unlike*, *other*, *while*, or *whereas*, you can figure out that the unfamiliar word likely means something different than the others in the group.

Teaching Tip It seems common that students get thrown off by these tiny conjunctions within a sentence if they aren't reading carefully, aware of the function they serve in the sentence. It's crucial to bring these words to students' attention once they reach books with longer, more complex sentence structures and a higher incidence of these words. It may be interesting for you to scan the books you're offering to your students with this in mind: How often do you see words like this used? Generally, the more they are used the more challenging the books tend to be overall.

For a slight spin on this strategy, see the strategy on page 303, "Categorize Context with Connectors," in this chapter.

Prompts

- Check the conjunction—will this group of words mean the same thing or will there be an opposite thrown in?
- What do the other two words mean? So what might this one mean?
- Think about how it's being used. What might it mean?
- As a group, what's the overall meaning? So what might this one word mean?
- You said what these two words mean. And if you see *whereas* you need to think *opposite*. So, what might this one mean?

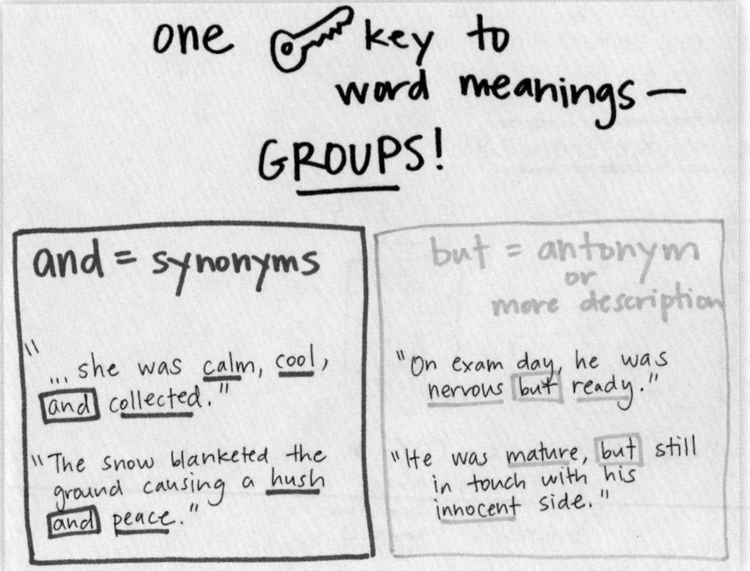

11.22 Read Up a Ladder

Strategy Collect several books on the same topic. Read the easiest of the books first, collecting words and definitions in your notebook that are important to the topic. Read the next most challenging book, using the prior book and your notebook as help. Collect new words and meanings as you read. Continue until you can read the most challenging book you chose.

Teaching Tip This strategy will work very well for nonfiction, where most of the vocabulary students will encounter will be content-specific and will likely overlap with other books at various levels. It also helps children reading "up ladders" to have prior knowledge so they can better use the context when they get to a more challenging text. You may find that there are some types of fiction as well where familiarizing yourself with the setting or time period (such as historical fiction) helps you to read other books set in a similar time or place. Still, most of the challenging vocabulary in fiction will be what Beck, McKeown, and Kucan (2013) term "tier 2" vocabulary—words that occur across a variety of domains in mature language situations, such as *bewildered*, *ceased*, or *embraces*. In nonfiction we often find "tier 3" vocabulary—words that are context-specific, such as *pharaoh*, *tomb*, *sarcophagus*, or *hieroglyphics*.

Prompts

- Which books can you find that deal with the same topic?
- Those are all broadly connected by topic, but you'll want to be a little more focused for this strategy to work.
- You collected several books about ____. Which looks easiest?
- What words did you learn from this first book that might help you as you read the next one?

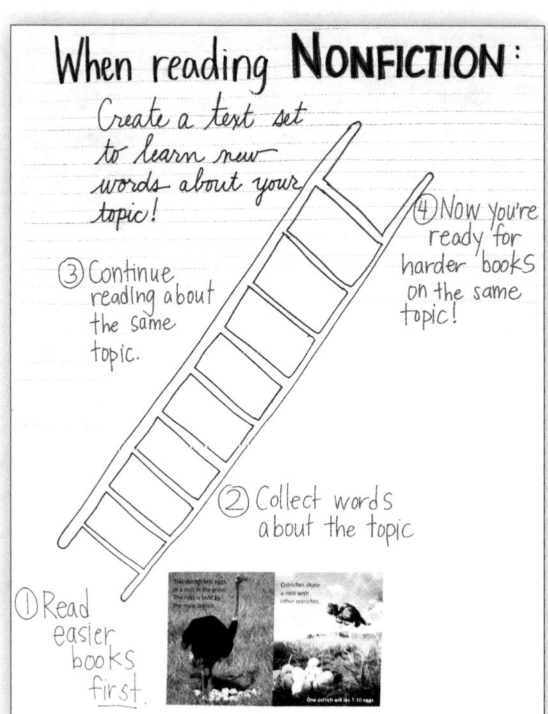

Who is this for?

LEVELS
P–Z+

GENRE / TEXT TYPE
nonfiction, mostly

SKILLS
synthesizing, inferring

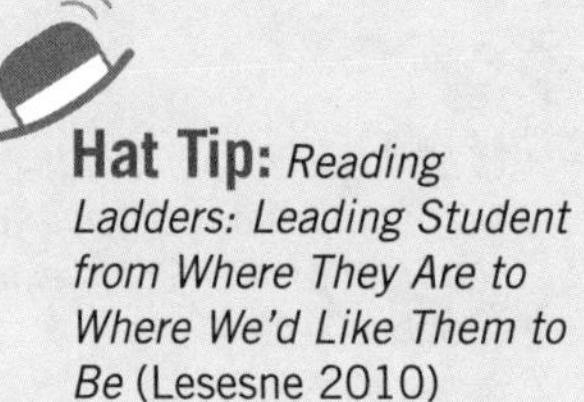

Hat Tip: *Reading Ladders: Leading Student from Where They Are to Where We'd Like Them to Be* (Lesesne 2010)

11.23 Be Alert for Word Choice

Who is this for?

LEVELS

R–Z+

GENRES / TEXT TYPES

fiction, poetry

SKILL

inferring

Strategy Find or figure out the definition of the word. Think about the context. Ask yourself, "What's the feeling, mood, tone, or connotation of the word, based on how it's used?"

Lesson Language *Words that authors use may have a denotative meaning and a connotative meaning. That is, when we look up a word in a dictionary we can find the technical definition of the word, but the word may also carry some unofficial meanings, or layers of meaning, as well. We can read alert to descriptive language that might communicate something deeper than what the word literally means. For example, the words youthful or juvenile both mean young, but carry different layered meanings. Youthful is often positive, and communicates a "full of life" kind of feeling. On the other hand, juvenile usually is used in a negative way to communicate someone who acts young and immature when they should act more mature. You can stop to think about why the author chose the precise word she or he did, and what that word choice is helping you to understand about what's being described.*

Prompts

- Based on how the word is used, do you feel like it's got a positive or negative connotation?
- Why do you think the author chose this word?
- What other words would work here? Think about why the author chose this one instead.
- That's what it literally means. What other layers of meaning are in this word?

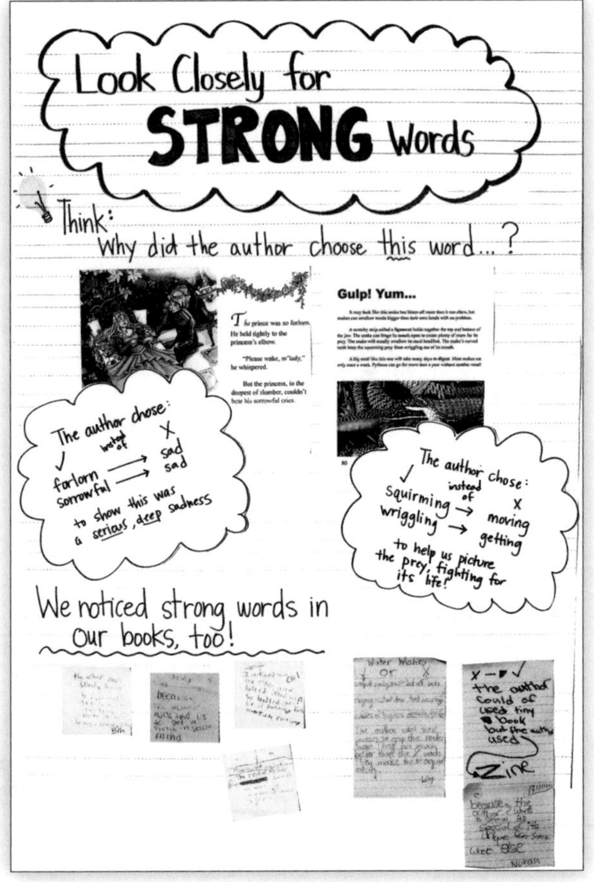

Hat Tip: *Vocabulary Is Comprehension: Getting to the Root of Text Complexity* (Robb 2014)

11.24 Get to the Root

Strategy Readers look for roots they know within a longer word. Notice the beginning and end to see if it changes the meaning of the root at all. Then, think about how the word is being used. Ask yourself, "What does this word mean?"

Teaching Tip For more information on prefixes and suffixes, see strategy 11.8 in this chapter, "Word Part Clues—Prefixes and Suffixes."

Prompts

- Name a prefix.
- Is there a suffix? Name it.
- Look at what's left—that's the root.
- Is there a root you know?
- Where else have you seen that root?
- What might that word mean, because you know the root?
- Check the beginning and ending of the word, too.
- Based on the other parts that are combined with the word, what might it mean?

Roots We Know	Words with that Root	What the Whole Word Means
acu (sharp)	acute acupuncture accurate	→ short-term → procedures using needles → correct, to the point
ann/annu (yearly)	annual annuity anniversary	→ each year → fixed & paid each year → yearly celebration (ex. marriage)
flu/flux (flow)	fluid flush fluxuate reflux	→ flows easily, like water → clean, wash away → change back + forth → boil so water is vaporized then returned to stock
jac/ject (throw)	eject project dejected	→ force something out → extend outward, protrude → sad, depressed

Who is this for?

LEVELS

R–Z+

GENRE / TEXT TYPE

any

SKILLS

understanding how words work, inferring

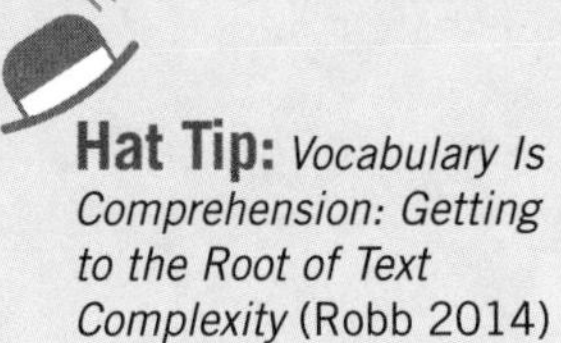

Hat Tip: *Vocabulary Is Comprehension: Getting to the Root of Text Complexity* (Robb 2014)

Supporting Students' Conversations

Speaking, Listening, and Deepening Comprehension

◎ Why is this goal important?

Book clubs and partnerships play a crucial role in supporting student comprehension and also in making the reading process a social one (Nichols 2006). When kids talk well about books, the conversations can be invigorating, engaging, and enlightening. When they don't go well, kids get bored and off task and time is wasted. What most kids often need is instruction into how to talk well, period, and also how to talk well about *books*.

There are two sides to the productive conversation coin. First, students need to have a hearty repertoire of conversational skills. Second, they need good stuff to talk about, meaning that their comprehension of the text and the depth of their thinking can impact the conversation.

Some of the conversational skills that students will need to practice, in a loose order from those that are most basic, beginner, and crucial to those that are for more experienced conversationalists:

- Active listening—when students hear a thought, they need to understand it and process it. Then, they need to reflect and respond to what they just heard.
- Body language—it's respectful to show you're listening and that you care, with your eyes on the speaker and body oriented toward the others in the conversation.
- Staying on topic—instead of just waiting your turn to share what was already in your mind, it's important to listen and say something relevant to the topic "on the table."
- Conversation-worthy topics—students need to consider what is worth talking about because it's interesting or important, and what might be less conversation-worthy because it's obvious or off topic.
- Elaborating—strong conversation needs to be about more than just reading off of a sticky note. Children can learn to add on, defend, and explain their thinking.
- Respectful language—people want to feel heard, so even when a child wants to disagree, there is a way to do it that values what the person before them said, and a way that shuts down conversation or makes people feel hurt.
- Accountability—good conversation is accountable to both the book (citing places or parts that fit with your thinking) and the group (referencing what others before you have said).
- Balance—we want to be sure the overtalkers are aware that sometimes their voices need to fade out, just as much as the quieter students need to chime in.
- Keeping conversation moving—although we want kids to stick to the topic, we don't want the conversation to become redundant. Knowing when we've said all there is to say and having the knowledge to move things along is important.
- Questioning—questions can help to invite elaboration from a speaker, clarify someone's points, or even invite in a quieter voice.
- Stamina—it takes time to build up to having a long, meaningful conversation. Often it's a culmination of mastering many of the other skills on this list that provides that stamina.
- Flexible thinking—children should come to a partnership or club expecting (or hoping!) that their minds will be changed or they'll think something different by the end of the conversation. This requires them to be flexible, ready to accept new ideas and try them on for size.

- Debate—when everyone agrees about everything, it's hard to get the conversation to a new place or to bring about new ideas. A little healthy disagreement or proposing a "devil's advocate" idea can spice things up.
- Empathy—it takes a certain maturity to consider someone else's ideas, especially when that person comes at something from a different perspective. Students need to learn to put themselves in the shoes of another reader to consider their ideas seriously.

How do I know if this goal is right for my student?

Listen to your students' conversations about books—whether in a whole-class conversation, literature circles, or with a partner (Daniels 1994; Calkins 2000). I find my listening is most focused when I take notes. For me, it's most helpful to transcribe what I hear and to analyze each turn kids take in light of both conversation and comprehension skills (see Figures 12.A and 12.B). When you determine that the content of the conversation seems to be causing the conversation to fall flat—most likely this will be the case if the students are overly literal and are only retelling the story—then you may find help in Chapters 5 and 6, which focus on strategies to support comprehension. If you feel like conversational strategies would be the best help, you'll find plenty of ideas within this chapter.

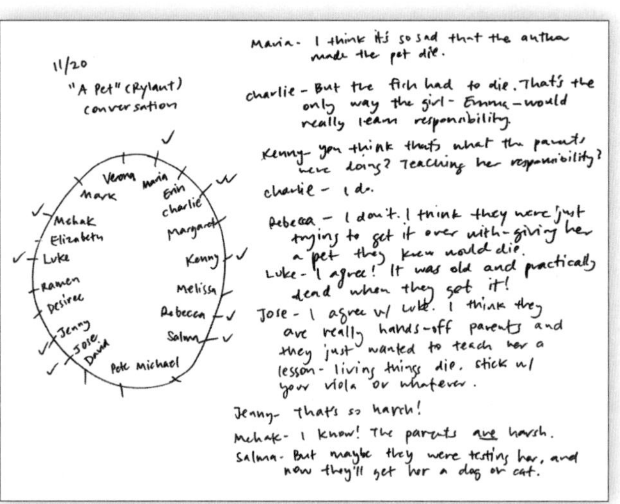

Figure 12.A One way to take notes during conversation is to have an identified spot on your note page for each speaker and keep track of who is speaking. On the other side of the page, write shorthand notes to capture the essence of what each student said.

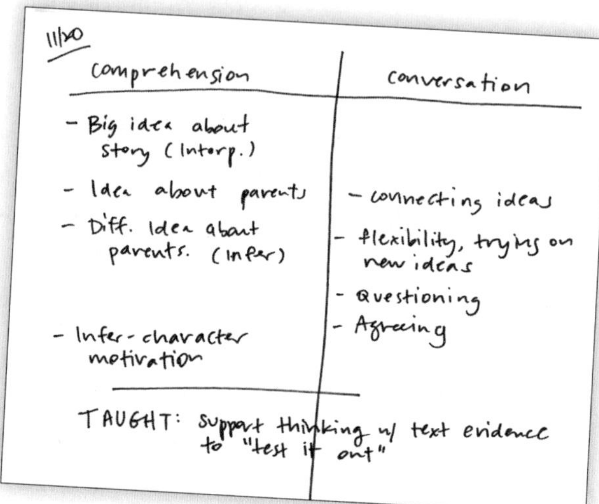

Figure 12.B Some teachers prefer to take notes during conversation by dividing a page in half—one side for notes about conversational skills (strengths and needs) and the other side for comprehension skills (strengths and needs). This type of note taking requires more in-the-moment processing on the part of the teacher to translate what students say and how they say it into skill names you'd write down on the page.

Strategies for Supporting Conversations at a Glance

Strategy	Levels	Genres/ Text Types	Skills
12.1 Listen with Your Whole Body	A–Z+	Any	Active listening, body language
12.2 Listen and Respond	A–Z+	Any	Active listening
12.3 Invite Quieter Voices	A–Z+	Any	Balancing conversation
12.4 Say Back What You Heard	A–Z+	Any	Active listening
12.5 Taking Turns Without Raising Hands	A–Z+	Any	Body language
12.6 Level-Specific Partner Menus	A–Z+	Any	Varies
12.7 Keep the Book in the Book Talk	F–Z+	Any	Staying accountable to the text, staying on topic
12.8 Super STARter Jots	J–Z+	Any	Determining importance, conversation-worthy topics
12.9 Conversation Playing Board	J–Z+	Any	Talk stamina, staying on topic
12.10 Sentence Starter Sticks	J–Z+	Any	Talk stamina
12.11 Keep the Line Alive	J–Z+	Any	Elaborating, staying on topic
12.12 Taking Risks with Gentler Language	J–Z+	Any	Offering new perspectives
12.13 Talk Between and Across	A–Z+, but probably best for J–Z+	Any	Talk stamina, comparing and contrasting
12.14 Conversation Cooperation	L–Z+	Any	Cooperating, collaborating
12.15 Say Something Meaningful	M–Z+	Any	Active listening, staying on topic
12.16 Try an Idea on for Size	M–Z+	Any	Thinking flexibly, empathizing
12.17 Challenge Questions	M–Z+	Any	Questioning, debating
12.18 Moving On to a New Idea	M–Z+	Any	Keeping conversation moving
12.19 Determining the Importance in Another's Ideas	M–Z+	Any	Determining importance, staying on topic
12.20 Power Questions	M–Z+	Any	Questioning
12.21 Bring on the Debate	O–Z+	Any	Disagreeing respectfully

12.1 Listen with Your Whole Body

Who is this for?

LEVELS

A–Z+

GENRE / TEXT TYPE

any

SKILLS

active listening, body language

Strategy Turn your hips, shoulders, and head toward the speaker. Make sure your hands are still. Lean in. Nod as you listen.

Lesson Language *You might think that listening begins with your ears, but it actually begins with your whole body. You can face the speaker with your shoulders, hips, and head so that your ears will catch what your friend is saying. If your hands are still (and maybe even empty), that will help you to have your attention on the words your friends are saying, instead of the objects in your hands.*

Teaching Tip There may be some children who can actually concentrate best when they have something in their hands to work with (such as a squeeze ball) and other children for whom eye contact is challenging. Use your judgment and your knowledge of your children's needs when deciding whether to use this strategy, particularly if you work with children who have sensory issues or ADHD or are on the autism spectrum. Modify what "listening" looks like for your students.

Prompts

- Turn to face who's speaking.
- Make sure you're listening with your whole body.
- Nod as you listen to show you are paying attention.
- Check your body.
- How can you change your body to show you're listening?

12.2 Listen and Respond

Strategy Listen to what the person before you said. Think, "What do I think about that?" Then, share your thoughts that connect to the other person's idea. This will not necessarily be what you already wrote down or already had planned to say.

Lesson Language *Sometimes when you come to a club or partnership conversation, you get so excited to talk about what you were thinking when reading independently that you don't listen well enough to the other people in your group. Or sometimes you might find that you're rehearsing what you want to say over and over in your mind that you can't actually hear what others say. When that happens, you miss out. When you listen carefully to others, the new thoughts your friends offer might help you revise your own thinking, come to new conclusions, or even get a whole new idea. A good practice is to make sure you're really taking in what the other person said, and then responding in a way that connects to what he or she said. To do this, you might listen, then think, "What do I think about that?" and then share your own thought in response to what you heard. This is different from just sharing something you already had written down or something you planned to say.*

Prompts

- Stop and think about your response before you speak.
- Does that connect to what the person before you said?
- Make sure your thought connects.
- Think, "What do I think about that?"
- You have a thought that connects? Good, go ahead and share it.

Who is this for?

LEVELS

A–Z+

GENRE / TEXT TYPE

any

SKILL

active listening

Hat Tip: *Comprehension Through Conversation: The Power of Purposeful Talk in the Reading Workshop* (Nichols 2006)

12.3 Invite Quieter Voices

Who is this for?

LEVELS

A–Z+

GENRE / TEXT TYPE

any

SKILL

balancing conversation

Strategy Pay attention to who is talking a lot and who is not talking. Be prepared to invite quieter voices in the conversation with a question. The more specific the question is, the better. "What do you think about ____?"

Lesson Language *Part of your responsibility as a club member is making sure that there is a balance of talk. That doesn't mean that everyone needs to take the exact same number of turns talking—that would feel fake. Instead, we want to make sure that there aren't people who seem to talk constantly and there aren't any people whose thoughts go unheard. Be aware, and if you see someone who could use an invitation, try to ask a specific question to draw out their thinking. You might say, "What do you think about ____" and pose a specific question. Sometimes very general questions like "What do you think?" are harder to answer and may make the quieter person feel put on the spot.*

Teaching Tip Sometimes students can benefit from having some visuals to help them to "see" who is talking a lot. Some teachers like to use talking tickets or coins. For example, everyone in the group would get a predetermined number of coins (or tickets). Then, every time students add their "two cents," they put their coin (or ticket) into the center pile. At a glance, children can see who is talking and who has a lot of coins remaining. This will help them self-monitor. See the photograph below for an example.

Prompts

- Pay attention to who talks.
- Pay attention to who doesn't speak much.
- How can you invite someone in?
- Say, "(Name), what are you thinking about this?"
- Try to ask a question to invite someone to share.
- Let's take a break, think a moment. Now, who hasn't spoken in a while? Can someone invite him or her to speak?

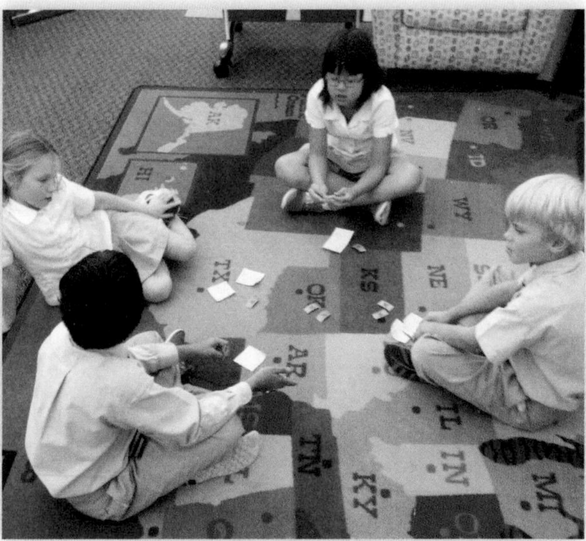

Hat Tip: *Scaffolding Language, Scaffolding Learning: Teaching English Language Learners in the Mainstream Classroom*, second edition (Gibbons 2014)

12.4 Say Back What You Heard

Strategy Listen to what the person before you said. Paraphrase, and then add your own thought. Say, "I heard you say ____. What I think is ____."

Lesson Language *Active listening is an important part of being a helpful book club member or partner in a partnership. Good conversation is more than just saying what you already have in your mind or what you've written down in your notes. It's important that you listen, take in what the person before you said, and respond in a way that connects to their idea. To force yourself to not just listen, but really hear the other person you're talking to, you can try to paraphrase what they said before you say something new. Paraphrase means saying the gist of what they said. To do this, you'll need to listen carefully and process what the other person is saying. Then, you'll say back what you thought you heard. You might use the words "I heard you say . . . " or "Are you saying . . . " or "So what I think I heard is . . . " Then, continue with your own thought. This might be something additional, in support of your classmate's comments, or it could be something in disagreement. Either way, it needs to somehow connect to what the person before you said, and it needs to stick to the same topic.*

Prompts

- Say back what you heard.
- Try to say it in your own words.
- Say, "I think you said . . ."
- Now that you paraphrased the person before you, try to add your own thoughts.
- If you're not sure, you can ask the person to repeat him- or herself.
- Does that thought connect to what the person before you said?

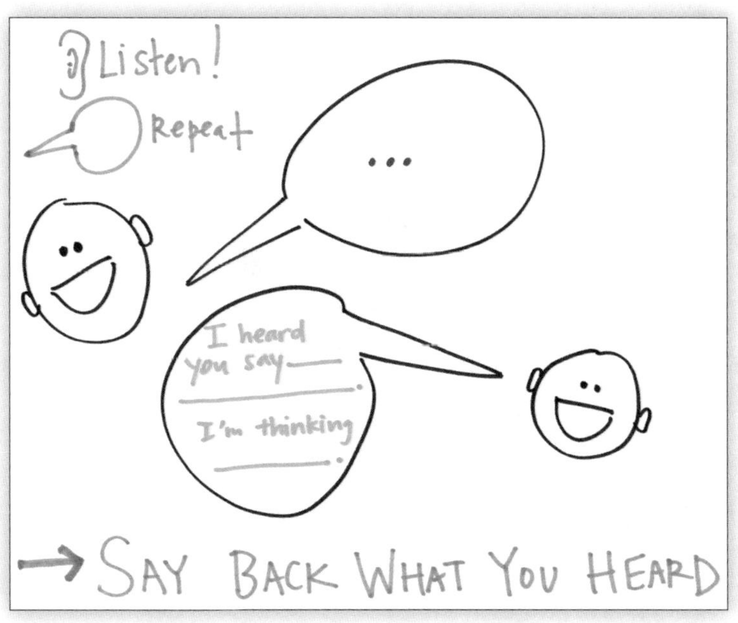

Who is this for?

LEVELS
A–Z+

GENRE / TEXT TYPE
any

SKILL
active listening

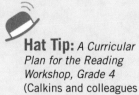

Hat Tip: *A Curricular Plan for the Reading Workshop, Grade 4* (Calkins and colleagues 2011c)

12.5 Taking Turns Without Raising Hands

Who is this for?

LEVELS

A–Z+

GENRE / TEXT TYPE

any

SKILL

body language

Hat Tip: Donna Santman, personal communication

Strategy Know when it is time for your voice to be heard. It is not about just sharing around a circle. Instead, try to make eye contact with the others in the group. Notice when a voice fades—that quiet space is time for you to speak up. At other times, you should let yours fade out when someone else starts talking and let him finish his thought.

Lesson Language *When adults are in a conversation, it's unusual to have people raising hands before they speak. Everyone in the group has an equal responsibility to be a part of the conversation. Everyone in the group has an equal responsibility to listen. It's also unusual that the conversation would go in a circle—one person to the next to the next. What usually happens is that someone has an idea and they listen for the quiet to know it's their turn to talk. I think everyone in this class or group is ready to try this kind of communicating that involves our eyes* (Point to your eyes.) *and our bodies* (Point to your shoulders.) *and our ears* (Point to your ears.). *Let's listen for the quiet, make eye contact to know when it's our turn, and be ready with good ideas in our minds. And if it happens that more than one person has an idea at the same time and more than one person talks at once, one voice should get quieter. You might say, "You go ahead" or "I'll go after you" or "You first."*

Prompts

- Make eye contact.
- You'll know it's your turn when you hear quiet.
- Right there—did you notice how someone paused and looked your way? That's your cue to start talking.
- It sounds like there are a few people trying to talk at once. Let's hear one voice, then move to another.

12.6 Level-Specific Partner Menus

Strategy Take a look at your partner menu to set yourself up to work together. Decide what you'll do as you read your book. Read and then do as the menu says. When you've finished, pick a new purpose and read again.

Teaching Tip The lesson language on this page would work well for readers at levels A/B, and the visual (partnership strategy card) would work better for readers around levels L–Z+. You can adapt the menu for any reading levels. See a source such as Fountas and Pinnell's *Continuum of Literacy Learning* (2010b) for advice on what types of reading behaviors would be most helpful for each level.

Lesson Language *I'm going to give you a card to share that is going to be your "partnership menu." Like a menu at a restaurant, you're going to pick something off of it. All of the options on this menu are things that will help you practice reading together as partners. The first couple of things on this menu are options that we've already talked about in your individual conferences and small group lessons. The first option is this one.* (Point to the first sticker with a book cover.) *We always talk about how important it is to get ready to read by reading the front cover. As partners, you can talk about what you see on the front cover before you start reading. The second sticker* (Point to the next one.) *has a finger pointing under a word. This is to remind you that one thing you can do together as partners is to make sure you point under each word as you read it. The third sticker reminds you to talk about the book when you finish reading it by sharing your favorite part and saying why that part is your favorite. Again, these are all things I've taught you to do independently but now I want you to practice them with your partner. So let's start. Take a look at your menu and let me hear you decide what one thing you'll do with your first book. Now, let me watch you read and work together.*

Partner Routine
1-Prepare for partner time with post-its in your book.
2-Retell what you've read so far-your partner will rate it!
3-Choose from your Reading Menu
4-Write a B♥B entry or add to one!

Act Out a Part That's:
-Dramatic
-Important
-Well-written
Then, talk back and forth

Talk About **Confusing Parts:**
-Was it a **tricky word**? Use all your strategies together!
-Did your **mental movie get blurry**? Reread it together and talk about it!

Share your **Post-its** or **B♥B entries!**
-Talk long back and forth about one idea
-Use the "Talking Map" to make a plan!

Prompts

- Pick one purpose.
- Make sure you're practicing what you picked from your menu.
- You did a nice job working together with one focus. What will you do next?
- How can your partner help you with that?

Who is this for?

LEVELS
A–Z+

GENRE / TEXT TYPE
any

SKILL
varies

Hat Tip: *Teaching Reading in Small Groups: Differentiated Instruction for Building Strategic, Independent Readers* (Serravallo 2010)

12.7 Keep the Book in the Book Talk

Who is this for?

LEVELS

F–Z+

GENRE / TEXT TYPE

any

SKILLS

staying accountable to the text, staying on topic

Strategy State a connection to yourself, the world, or another text. Bring it back to the book you are discussing and explain how the connection you made helps you understand this book. "This reminds me of ____ and that helps me understand ____ in this book."

Teaching Tip There has been a lot of criticism recently about "text-to-self" connections, and how too often children's discussions of literature have started to become more about the children themselves than it is about the book they are supposed to be discussing. With that in mind, some places have banned "text-to-self" connections altogether, and have said that all discussions about texts must stay "within the four corners" of the text. While some may think this is a wise course of action, I believe that a reader's reactions, responses, and transaction with the text are all crucial to their construction of meaning (Rosenblatt 1978). The strategy on this page honors the natural outside-of-the-text connections children make based on their own prior experiences (life, other books, the world) and also encourages them to bring the conversation back to the text under discussion.

Prompts

- What connection can you make?
- Explain how that connection helps you understand this book.
- Bring the connection back to the book.
- And that helps me understand . . .
- So in this book . . .
- You connected that in a way that helped you better understand!

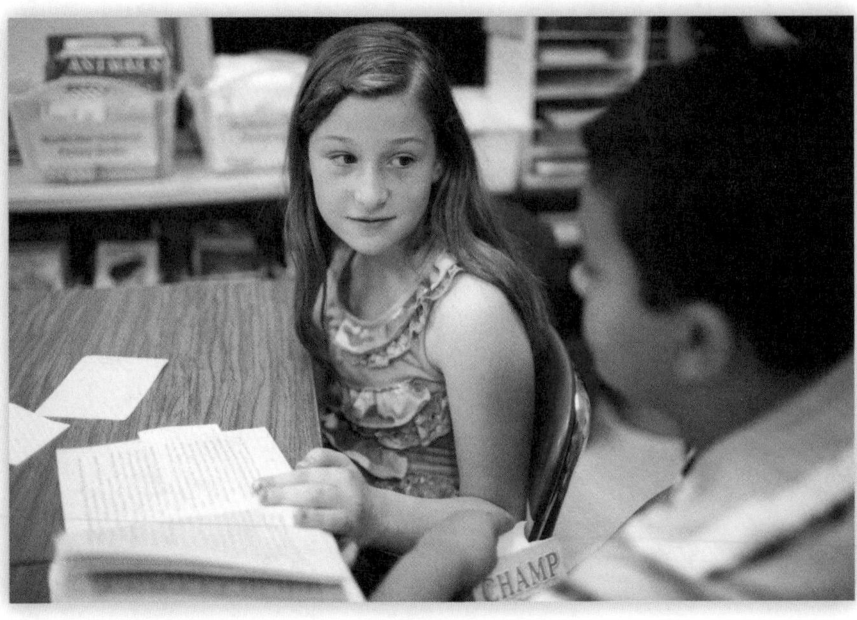

12.8 Super STARter Jots

Strategy Read through your jots. Put a star next to the jot(s) that you believe will spark a great conversation in your partnership.

Lesson Language *When you stop to jot during your independent reading, you might have a number of reasons for stopping. You might jot to help yourself remember something that happened so that when you go back to the book you can jump back in. You might stop to jot an idea that you want to think about more. Sometimes you jot a question, and then later find the answer to the question. Not all of these jots will make the best conversation starters. The ones that are best to get a conversation going are ones that are ideas, not something that's literally in the book. Ideas that you're really curious about, or ones where you want to get other perspectives, might get things going. Also, ideas that are unique or even controversial might bring on debate or encourage your friends to think about things in a different way. So before you start talking, read through your jots to see which ones are really going to work for the purpose of conversation.*

Prompts

- Read over your jots. Which one might work for conversation?
- Why do you think that one will work?
- You said you are curious about your friends' responses to this one. I think that will be a good conversation starter, then.
- Choose one, checking the chart to see which might be conversation-worthy.
- Go ahead and put stars next to those you chose to begin the conversation today.

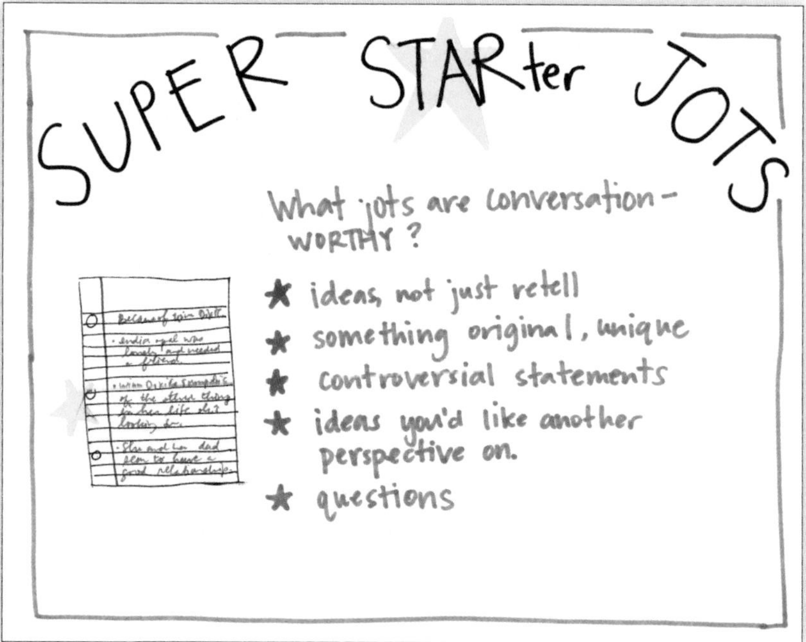

SUPER STARter JOTS
What jots are conversation-WORTHY?
★ ideas, not just retell
★ something original, unique
★ controversial statements
★ ideas you'd like another perspective on.
★ questions

Who is this for?

LEVELS

J–Z+

GENRE / TEXT TYPE

any

SKILLS

determining importance, conversation-worthy topics

12.9 Conversation Playing Board

Who is this for?

LEVELS

J–Z+

GENRE / TEXT TYPE

any

SKILLS

talk stamina, staying on topic

Strategy Each member chooses her or his best thoughts on sticky notes and stacks them in a pile on an individual square of the playing board. One member selects an idea and places it in the center. All members of the club think about, focus on, and talk about the idea in the center. Move on to a new idea when there is nothing left to say about the one in the center.

Lesson Language *Create a playing board with a spot for each club members' stack of sticky notes and a square in the center. The first person takes his or her best sticky note, reads it, and moves it to the center square. The idea in the center is now "in play." All club members try to focus on talking about the one idea that is "in play" for as long as possible. When it feels like the idea is talked out, then a different club member takes a new idea from his or her pile, reads it, and moves that one to the center so that it becomes "in play." If at any time someone forgets about what the focus of the conversation is, you can look back at the center of the playing board for help.*

Prompts

- Check the center of the board.
- (*Tap or point to sticky note in center.*) Does what you just said match this?
- Good job sticking to the topic.
- Do you think we can keep going with this topic or is it time to switch to another one?

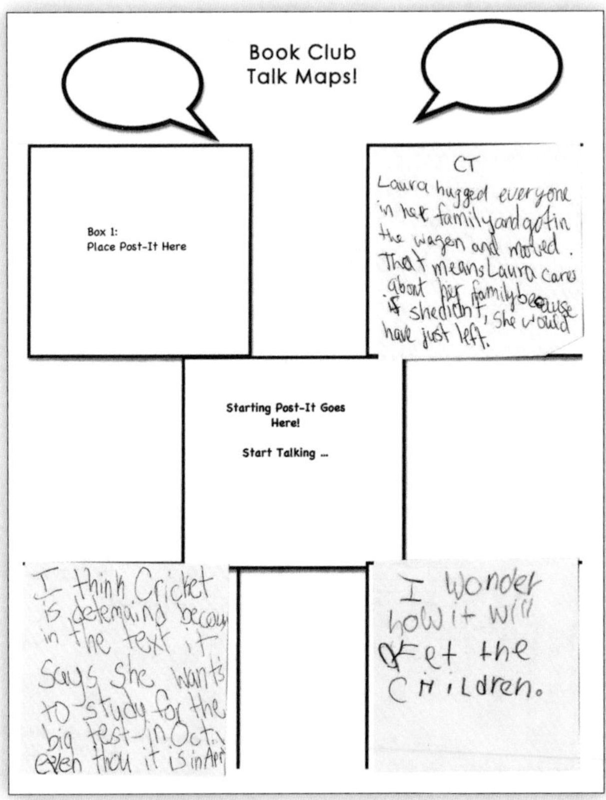

Hat Tip: Donna Santman, personal communication

12.10 Sentence Starter Sticks

Strategy Select a stick from the pile. Use the sentence starter on that stick to start talking. Make sure what you say connects to what the person before you said.

Lesson Language *To keep the conversation moving in a way that builds on past ideas and furthers the thinking in a new direction, it is helpful to use sentence starters that can act as transitions. These sentence starters can prompt you to move from one thought to the next. Some sentence starters you might use are:*

- In addition . . .
- On the other hand . . .
- I agree with you because . . .
- I disagree because . . .
- I'd like to add on to what _____ said . . .
- This might not be right, but maybe . . .
- Why do you think . . . ?
- What do you think about . . . ?

I've put these sentence starters on popsicle sticks in a cup. When you feel like your conversation is stuck, try pulling a sentence starter stick and use that starting phrase to get the conversation going again.

Prompts

- Pick a sentence starter from the can. Read what it says. Use it to start talking.
- Read the prompt. Think about what you can say that completes the sentence.
- Think what you can say that connects to what the person before you said.
- What is the prompt asking you to do?
- Should you be saying something similar to what the person before you said or something different, based on that sentence starter?

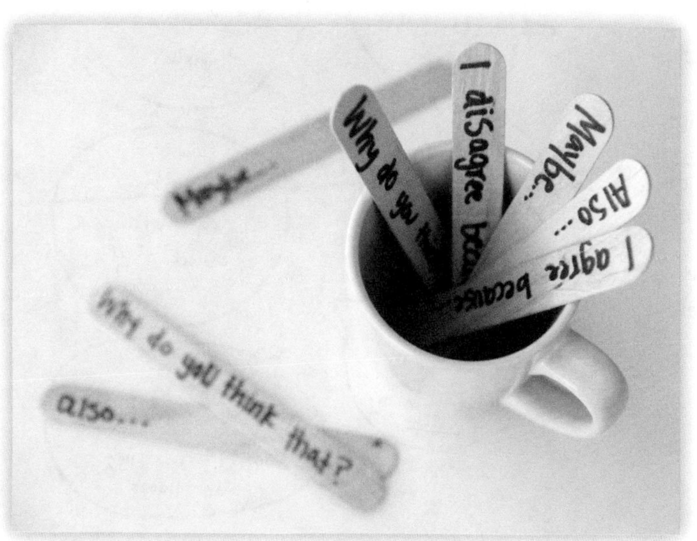

Who is this for?

LEVELS

J–Z+

GENRE / TEXT TYPE

any

SKILL

talk stamina

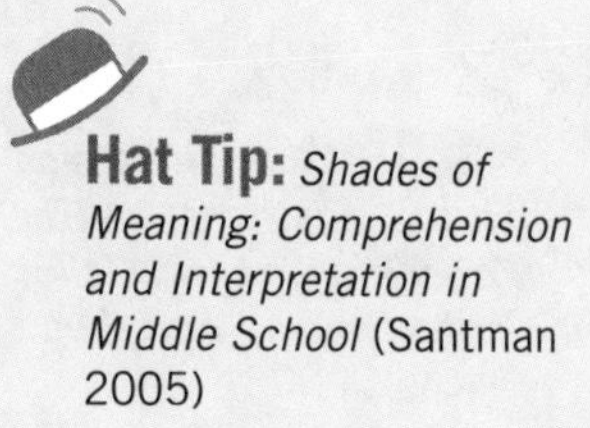

Hat Tip: *Shades of Meaning: Comprehension and Interpretation in Middle School* (Santman 2005)

12.11 Keep the Line Alive

Who is this for?

LEVELS

J–Z+

GENRE / TEXT TYPE

any

SKILLS

elaborating, staying on topic

Hat Tip: *Comprehension Through Conversation: The Power of Purposeful Talk in the Reading Workshop* (Nichols 2006)

Strategy Think about the topic that the person is talking about. Consider how you can respond—by adding on, agreeing, disagreeing, providing support, or asking a question. Then, say something that keeps the same line of conversation, or topic, alive. Use a sentence starter if you need help.

Lesson Language *When we have a conversation, we have to make sure we're always connecting what we say to what the person before us said. When someone starts on a topic, that's the beginning of the line of thinking. When we add on, we want to keep that line alive instead of moving on to a new topic. We want to hear what the person before us said, then consider if we are adding on, agreeing, disagreeing, supporting the idea, or even asking a question about it. Then we add in our idea, making sure we're still sticking to the topic. We build and add and grow and deepen until it feels like there is nothing left to say about the topic. Then we know it's time to start in on a new line of thinking.*

Teaching Tip Some children benefit from being able to see this visually. You could get Unifix cubes—commonplace math manipulatives—to use as a temporary scaffold. When someone begins to talk about a topic or "line of thinking" you can start a new tower. Each time someone adds a related thought, you can add another cube to that same tower. When the topic shifts to a new line of thinking, start a new tower. Before you know it, children will be working to build a higher tower by sticking to one line of thinking.

Prompts

- Make sure you heard what the person said.
- Think about the topic we're talking about.
- What can you add on that keeps the line of thinking alive?
- Does that fit with the topic or is that a new topic?

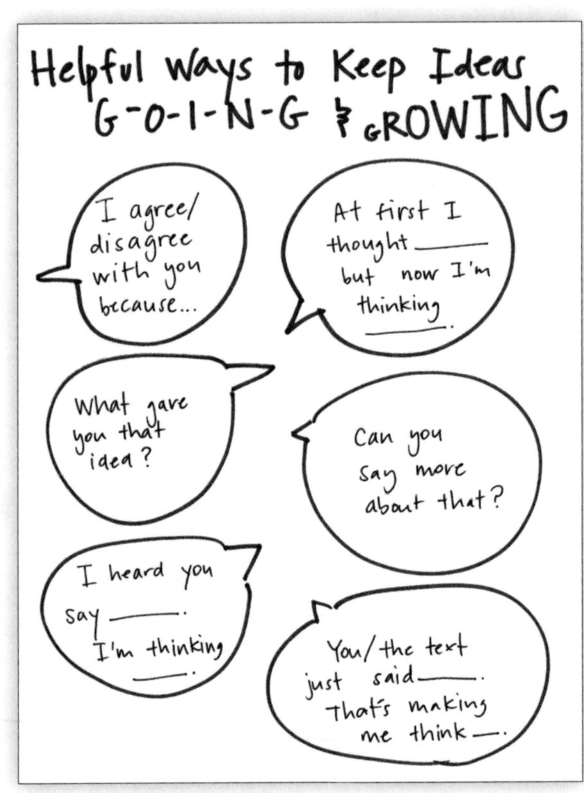

12.12 Taking Risks with Gentler Language

Strategy If you feel like what you want to say is a little risky, and you don't necessarily want to commit to it, you could use softer language to share your idea. Starting with "I am not sure I think this, but ____" makes the risk feel less risky!

Lesson Language *Conversation can start to feel boring if everyone is saying the same thing, over and over, and is always agreeing all the time. Sometimes there needs to be a voice who can speak up, offering a different perspective on a topic. Even if it's not an idea you're fully committed to, it's still something you can offer to the group to discuss, debate, and decide about. You can separate yourself a bit from the comment by using gentler language that shows you aren't 100% behind the idea, but you think it's one about which you're interested in hearing from others.*

Prompts

- Can you think of an idea that you might be reluctant to share?
- What do you want to say, but you're afraid to?
- You can just put it out there with, "Maybe . . . "
- If you're not sure, you can get your friends' thoughts about the idea.
- Be brave! Share what you're thinking.

Who is this for?

LEVELS

J–Z+

GENRE / TEXT TYPE

any

SKILL

offering new perspectives

12.13 Talk Between and Across

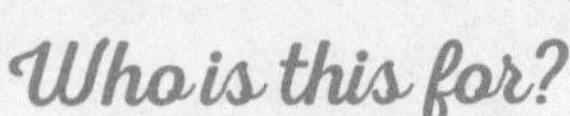

LEVELS

A–Z+, but probably best for J–Z+

GENRE / TEXT TYPE

any

SKILLS

talk stamina, comparing and contrasting

Strategy Put multiple texts together with a common topic, theme, character, or setting. Think about how the information in the texts can be compared and contrasted. Next, compare and contrast your own thinking with that in the text(s).

Lesson Language *Sometimes gathering up a text set of related books will help us to think more deeply than looking at any one by itself. In fiction, we could talk across books that have a common theme, characters who are similar, or books that are set in the same time period. In nonfiction, we could gather up a set of books that explore the same topic, perhaps with different angles or slants or perspectives on the information. Or, we could put together a hybrid of genres. For example, we could read a few books that have a main character who is a bully, and then also read some articles about bullying. The different texts in our set helps us to have ready-made perspectives on a topic. We can then think about how our own thinking juxtaposes with the ideas in the text(s). We can also put together, or synthesize, the different ideas. Also, we can compare and contrast the different perspectives of the different authors.*

Prompts

- Compare how this author and this author view the same topic or theme.
- How does your thinking compare or contrast with the author(s)?
- Say, "This author thinks _____, but this one thinks _____."
- Say, "This author thinks _____, but I think _____."
- What do all of the texts have in common?
- How does what author A wrote help you think differently about what author B wrote?

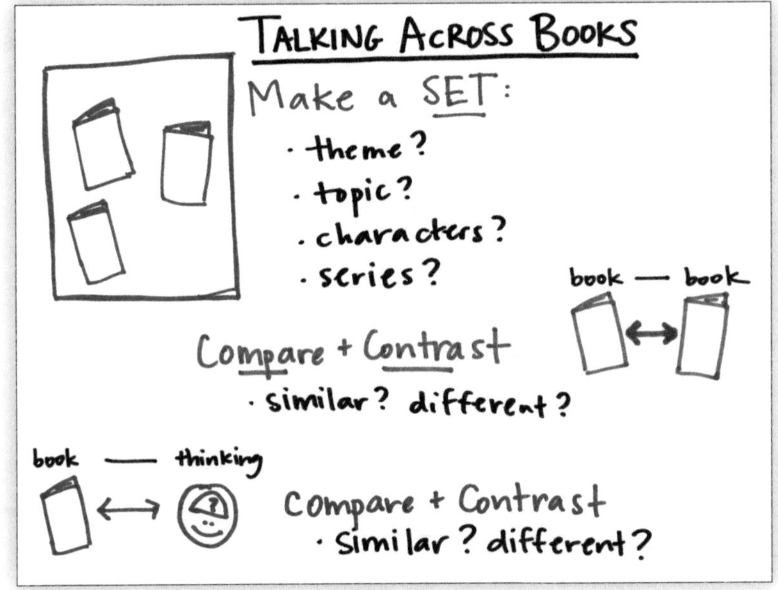

Hat Tip: *Comprehension Through Conversation: The Power of Purposeful Talk in the Reading Workshop* (Nichols 2006)

12.14 Conversation Cooperation

Strategy Being part of a book club means knowing how to cooperate and be part of a team. To have a good conversation, it's important that everyone has read the same pages, that you talk together, and that you set helpful goals. At the end of a conversation, you can check with your club by saying, "How did we do this time?" If you feel like there is room for improvement, you can make a promise to do something better or different for next time.

Teaching Tip I'm imagining the prompts that go with this strategy might be used to facilitate a conversation with a club that needs some support cooperating. Guiding the children to self-reflect and make their own promises for improvement may be more effective than telling them what you want them to do differently (especially if you've already tried that and it didn't work!).

Prompts

- Talk about how your conversation went today.
- Look at these four categories. (*Point to chart: "Play Your Part"; "Set a Page Goal Together"; "Talk Together"; "Help Each Other."*) How do you think you did?
- If you were to change one thing about your conversation today, what would it be?
- Let's all name some promises for how we'll plan for next time.
- Let's all name some promises for how we'll participate next time.

Who is this for?

LEVELS

L–Z+

GENRE / TEXT TYPE

any

SKILLS

cooperating, collaborating

12.15 Say Something Meaningful

Who is this for?

LEVELS

M–Z+

GENRE / TEXT TYPE

any

SKILLS

active listening, staying on topic

Strategy Think about what you want to share. Ask yourself, "Is what I have to say relevant to the book and to what's being discussed?" If so, share it. If not, park the thought on the side of your mind or jot it down so you can come back to it another time.

Lesson Language *Make sure that what you share is grounded in either the text and/or your thinking about the world informed by the text you just read. It should also connect to what you and your partner or club or class are discussing. Sometimes when we are talking, things pop into our minds and we have to carefully consider whether sharing it is going to help us to think more deeply about the book or if it's going to take us off on a tangent. When we realize the idea we have is off track, we need to park it on the side of our brain and get back into focus on the story and/or on the conversation.*

Prompts

- How does that fit with the topic that's being discussed?
- How does that fit with the book?
- Explain how your comment adds to the conversation.
- Should that be shared or parked?
- I think that idea takes us off on a tangent. Please park it for now.
- That comment seems relevant to the book we're discussing!

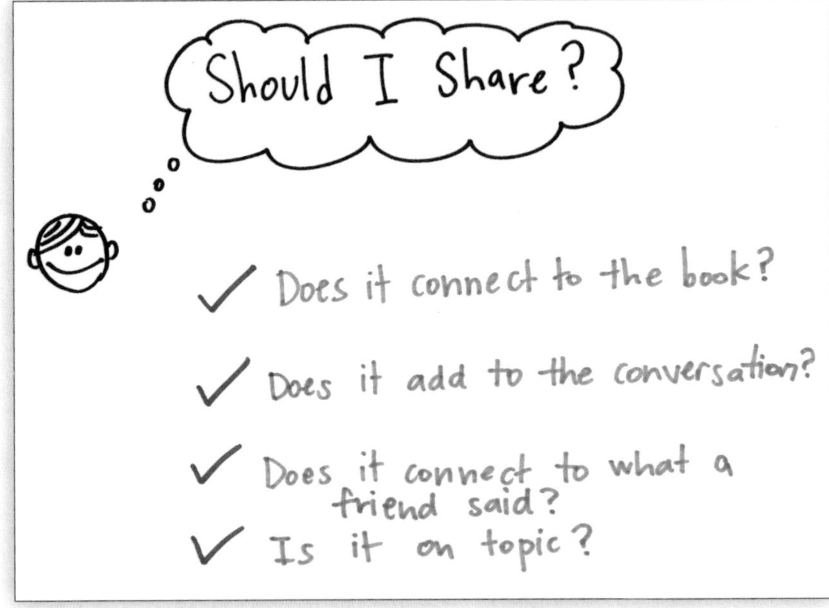

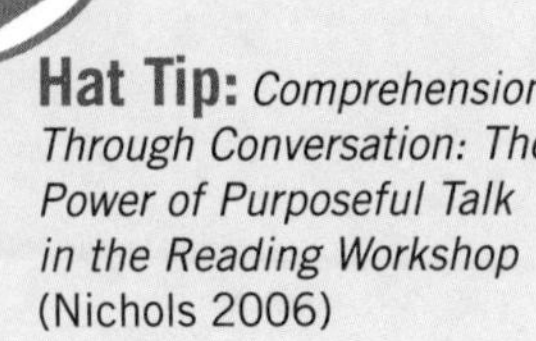

Hat Tip: *Comprehension Through Conversation: The Power of Purposeful Talk in the Reading Workshop* (Nichols 2006)

12.16 Try an Idea on for Size

Strategy When you listen carefully, you may hear another person's idea that is very different from a thought you had. Stop and consider, "What evidence is there in the text to support that idea?" Try the idea on and see if you can back it up. Doing so may give you a new perspective and may help you outgrow your original thinking.

Lesson Language *When we were talking about "A Pet," (in* Every Living Thing *1988) Cynthia Rylant's story about a young girl who wanted a dog or cat but whose parents got her a goldfish instead, I notice we had some differing opinions about the parents. Some of you said, "The parents are just teaching her responsibility by getting her a goldfish, a pet they knew would die." Others of you said, "The parents are too self-involved. They don't even care about her and just got her something cheap and easy that they knew would die so she'd stop bothering them." Let's take one of those ideas and even if it's one you can't possibly believe right now, let's try it on for size. We're going to go back into the text and see if there is any evidence we can pull that would support the idea—even if it's not an idea we originally thought up.*

Prompts

- Go back into your book and see if you can find some proof.
- Think about how it goes with the idea you just said.
- Say, "One place in the book that goes with that idea is . . . "
- Say, "That idea is similar to mine because . . . "
- Say, "What do you mean by that?"

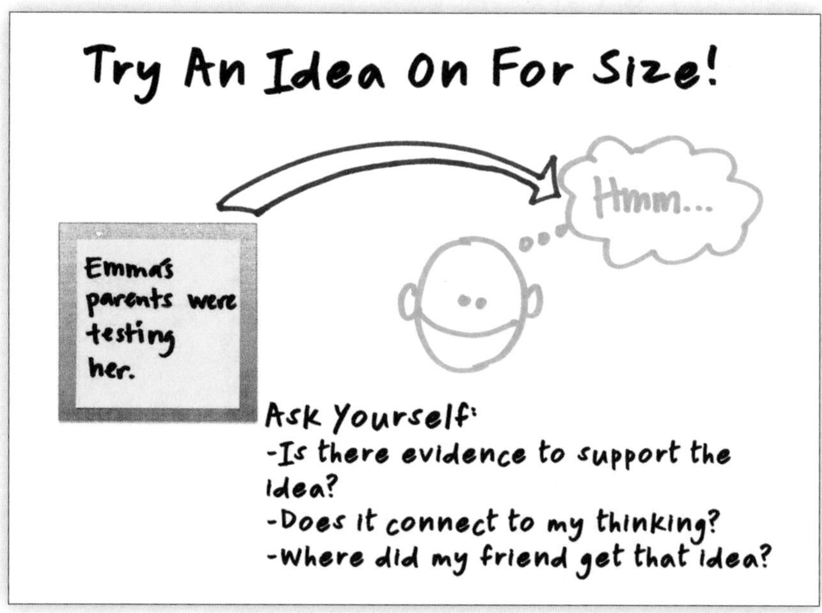

Who is this for?

LEVELS

M–Z+

GENRE / TEXT TYPE

any

SKILLS

thinking flexibly, empathizing

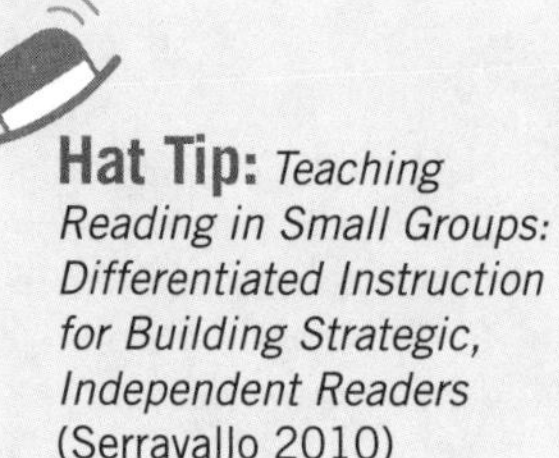

Hat Tip: *Teaching Reading in Small Groups: Differentiated Instruction for Building Strategic, Independent Readers* (Serravallo 2010)

12.17 Challenge Questions

Who is this for?

LEVELS

M–Z+

GENRE / TEXT TYPE

any

SKILLS

questioning, debating

Strategy Asking questions of each other and of the characters in the book is a great way to get conversation going stronger. You can think about things you don't agree with—something that the character did or something that a friend in your group said—and begin a challenge. Think of a question you can ask to get your partner or club to say more about their idea and/or to defend their thinking.

Lesson Language *Questions can keep a conversation going and growing, or they can stop it dead in its tracks. The difference is whether the question that is asked actually pushes people to think more deeply about the stories and their ideas, or whether it's something that can be answered with a simple response or a yes or no answer. For example, if we are thinking about our recent read-aloud* Sylvester and the Magic Pebble *(Steig 1969), a question that would stop our conversation is something like, "What did Sylvester find?" A complete answer is "A pebble that turned him to stone." And then we're done. But a question that asks us to think deeply about the text is one without a quick response, a question that can't be answered by just flipping to a page in the book. A question such as, "You told us what happened at the end, but I'm wondering what you think the author is trying to teach us in this story?" That kind of question requires all involved in the conversation to really think deeply.*

Prompts

- Think about something the character did that you didn't like.
- Think about something a club member or partner said that you disagree with.
- Say, "I disagree because . . . "
- Say, "I wouldn't have done what ____ did when . . . "
- Say, "Why do you think the character acted that way?"

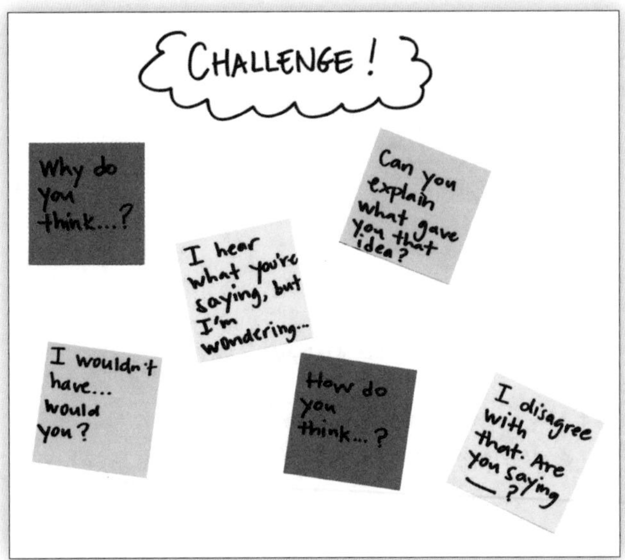

Hat Tip: *Teaching Reading in Small Groups: Differentiated Instruction for Building Strategic, Independent Readers* (Serravallo 2010)

12.18 Moving On to a New Idea

Strategy It's good to stick to one topic, but when you notice you're all repeating the same idea about the topic, it's time to move on. You might begin by saying, "It seems like we're all saying the same thing. Who has a new idea?"

Lesson Language *We have to make sure we are moving the conversation forward. That means we are adding on to an idea, challenging an idea, or reconsidering something. If we aren't going deeper with the topic we're talking about, it's time to shift gears to another topic. When it seems like people keep saying the same thing in new words, then someone should speak up to switch topics. For example, if we're talking about India Opal from* Because of Winn-Dixie *(DiCamillo 2000) and someone says, "It seems like she's very lonely because she wants to make friends with the dog." And then another person says, "I agree. She acts lonely being by herself." And then a third person says, "Yes, if she wasn't so lonely she wouldn't have wanted to keep the dog." And then a fourth person chimes in, "Dogs do help when you're lonely." You might notice that it sounds like we're sort of saying the same thing in different words. We need to move past that idea and into new territory—another character, the idea of loneliness, the importance of the dog, or something else.*

Prompts

- Think about if you're adding on to the idea or if you're repeating.
- Do you feel like you have more to say about the topic?
- Think of something related to this idea that can help us move past this point.
- Let's think of what else we could talk about.
- It seems like we're repeating.
- Let's move off this topic. Who's got a new one?

Who is this for?

LEVELS

M–Z+

GENRE / TEXT TYPE

any

SKILL

keeping conversation moving

12.19 Determining the Importance in Another's Ideas

Who is this for?

LEVELS

M–Z+

GENRE / TEXT TYPE

any

SKILLS

determining importance, staying on topic

Strategy When you try to connect your ideas meaningfully to what the person before you said, you can try first to listen carefully to someone's thought. Next, think about what was most important about what was said. One way to do this is to listen for key words that rang true or lingered in your mind. You can then say, "When you said ____, it made me think ____."

Lesson Language *Sometimes when a friend of yours is talking, he or she will elaborate on their thinking for a few sentences. It then becomes hard to know what to latch your next comments on to from all that person said. I'm going to show you one student's comments and I'm going to think aloud about the different points I might consider important, and how I might connect my thinking to what I heard.*

Here is what my friend said: "I think the author is trying to say that even when you spend a long time apart from someone else, there is a way you can have a relationship. I mean, the girl in the book hadn't seen her dad in a long time but since they went out together to call crows, they found something they can do together. And also when they got the flannel shirt. And the pie. So I think there is some way they can still be together after all this time."

After listening to my friend talk, there are a few key words and ideas that linger:

- *Relationships*
- *Effects of time*
- *Finding ways to connect*
- *Symbolism of things in the story: crow call, flannel, pie.*

If I were to speak up next, in order to stay "on topic" I don't have only one option. In fact, there are a number of different topics I can pick up on that would all connect to what my friend was talking about.

Prompts

- What did you hear the other person say?
- Think about what was important to you.
- Can you say back what you heard? Start with, "When you said . . . "
- Can you say back what you're thinking about that idea?
- Give your response.
- Yes—your response connected to ____'s ideas.

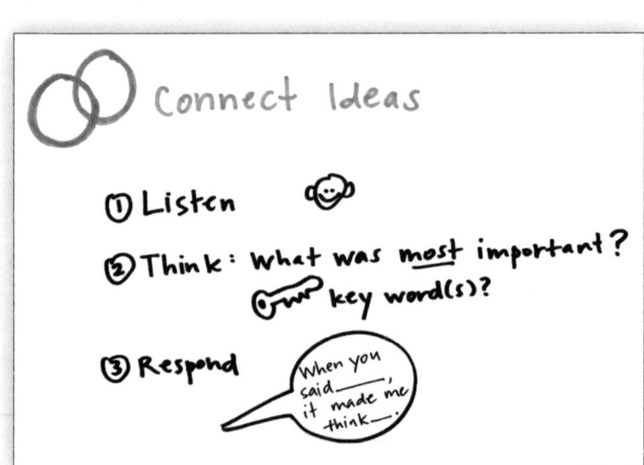

12.20 Power Questions

Strategy Questions can keep the conversation going strong by exploring new aspects of ideas that individuals hadn't explored alone. Powerful questions are often ones that begin with why and how and won't have a simple yes-or-no answer. Think about what you wonder—about the book or about another person's ideas—and consider sharing your question, not just a statement.

Teaching Tip As the chart on this page suggests, you may extend this strategy to be a series of four or more lessons where you introduce to children different types of question stems, and the different sorts of information that those questions might get at. The point is not for students to check off each type of question each time they talk, but rather to be aware of how their questions can keep the ideas in the conversation growing.

Prompts

- Think about what you're wondering.
- Think about what she just said. What can you ask to keep the conversation going?
- Start with "Why . . . ?"
- Start with "How . . . ?"
- That's a statement. If you were to ask a question, what would it be?

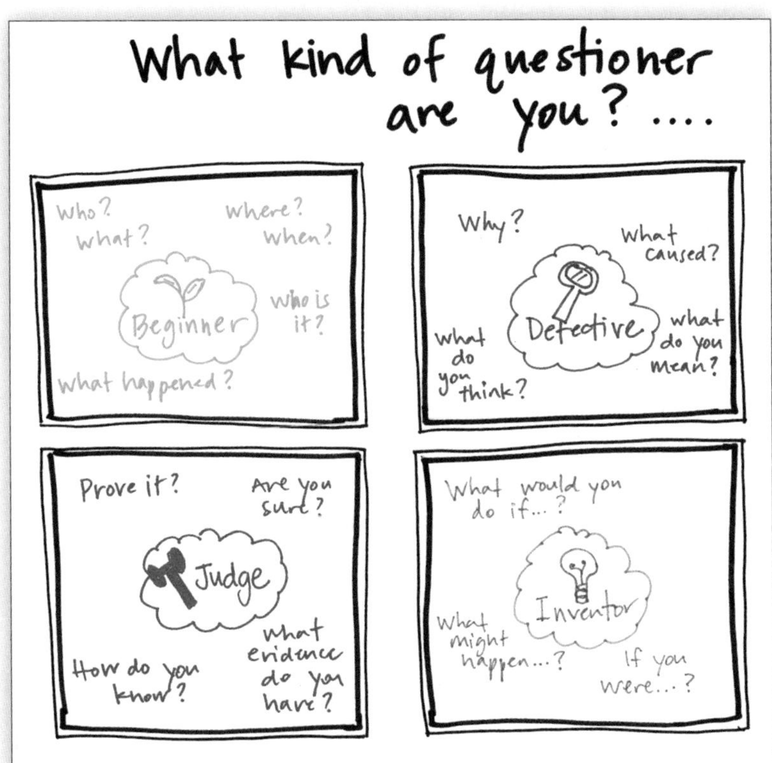

Who is this for?

LEVELS
M–Z+

GENRE / TEXT TYPE
any

SKILL
questioning

12.21 Bring on the Debate

Who is this for?

LEVELS
O–Z+

GENRE / TEXT TYPE
any

SKILL
disagreeing respectfully

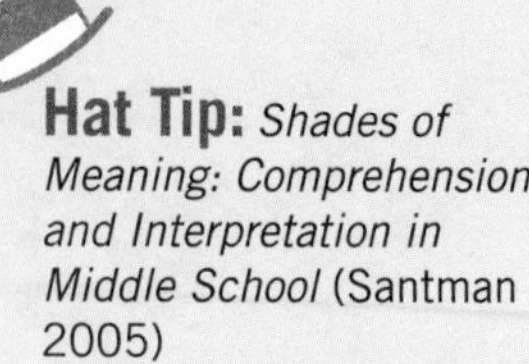

Hat Tip: *Shades of Meaning: Comprehension and Interpretation in Middle School* (Santman 2005)

Strategy Debate can sometimes make conversation seem more interesting and can open up our thinking. Even if you aren't sure you think about things differently, you could offer a different perspective for the sake of debate. You can say, "I am not sure, but have you considered ____?" or "On the other and ____" or "Or could it be ____?"

Teaching Tip If you're interested in developing debate skills with your students, I highly recommend taking a look at some of the argument and debate work that Teachers College Reading and Writing Project has been developing over the last year or two. They have crafted curriculum (published as the Units of Study in Opinion/ Argument, Information, and Narrative Writing series by Calkins and colleagues [2013]), have materials available on their website, and offer mini-institutes for further professional study.

Prompts

- What idea can you offer that's different?
- Think about what your partner just said. If you want to debate the idea, what can you offer?
- Start with, "On the other hand . . . "
- Start with, "Or . . . "
- It sounds like that idea is very similar. Try a different idea.
- Yes, that idea feels quite different. It should make the conversation interesting!

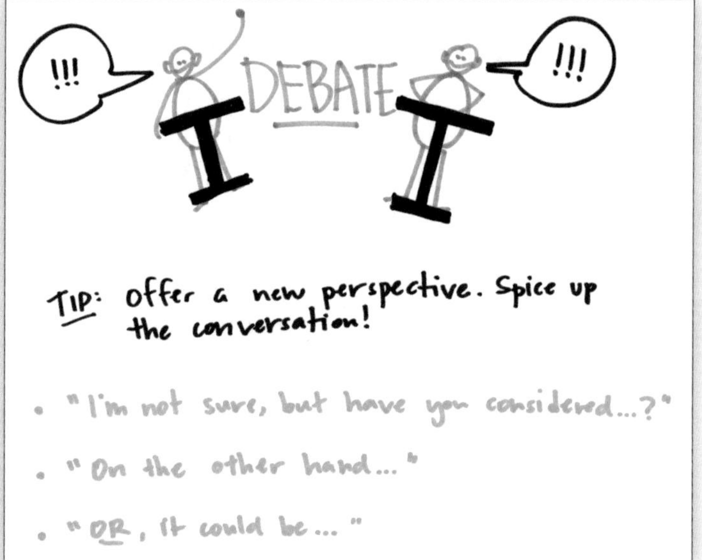

What most kids often need is instruction into how to talk well, period, and also how to talk well about *books*.

—*Jennifer Serravallo*

Improving Writing About Reading

◎ Why is this goal important?

Writing well about reading isn't a simple goal. It incorporates both the thinking readers do as they read and the ability to compose text in a way that both captures and furthers that thinking. For many children, the concept that readers need to think deeply—and sometimes even to write about those thoughts—is a foreign one; many are happy with just following the gist of the plot, putting the book back in the classroom library, and moving on their merry way. Teaching children to write well about their reading is about teaching them that their thinking about books matters. It matters enough to take the time to write it down. Still, a teacher needs to be careful that the writing doesn't overtake the aesthetic experience we strive for to maximize engagement and joy with reading (Rosenblatt 1978; Ivey and Johnston 2013). One way to balance this is to allow writing about reading to be the choice of the reader, and to offer that reader choice of when to respond and even how to respond (Atwell 2014).

Many children you've identified as having a goal involving writing about their reading may need a comprehension goal as well. That is, not only do they need to practice writing, but they'll also need to know what it is they are writing about. Most of the strategies included in Chapters 5 through 11 would support deeper thinking about fiction and nonfiction, and therefore many of them could be easily turned into writing about reading strategies as well.

This chapter contains teaching ideas for strategies in support of the goal of writing about reading, including:

- strategies for writing to reflect about yourself as a reader and your reading identity (to support engagement, described in Chapter 2)
- strategies for writing short, in-the-moment sticky notes to hold onto ideas while in the midst of reading
- strategies for composing longer, more elaborate writing to expand on thinking
- strategies for improving how to articulate ideas, whether in short or long form.

How do I know if this goal is right for my student?

You'll notice that many of the ideas are marked as goals for readers in upper elementary and middle school grades, and there are not so many for primary-aged children. This is not because younger children cannot write about their reading, but rather because I believe that the writing about reading takes so much time for younger readers that I question whether it is worth the time. What kindergarten and first-grade students need most is to read a lot, to practice strengthening their print work, fluency, and comprehension. Toward the end of the first-grade year, you may decide to turn to some strategies in this chapter for occasional writing about reading practice with most of your class. It's the rare first-grade student for whom writing about reading will be the most important goal at any point in the year.

I often find that I choose to support a child with writing about reading in a few instances:

- when the child's oral expression of their comprehension (what they say when talking with peers or with a teacher in a conference) far outpaces their ability to articulate their ideas in writing

- when writing could be used as a tool to support their comprehension, because without writing they have a hard time remembering what they were thinking as they read or tracking the literal information from the book
- when their other writing abilities are strong (as evidenced by their story writing, essay writing, or information writing), but their thinking during reading seems superficial.

Take a look at a variety of your students' work—the short jots they write in the margins of articles they read or on sticky notes stuck inside the books. Look at longer responses to reading they may keep in a reading notebook or journal.

For support with more formal structured writing about reading, such as literary essays or book reviews, you may check out Angelillo's *Writing About Reading* (2003), Calkins and McEvoy's *Literary Essays: Writing About Reading* (2006), or Roberts and Wischow's *The Literary Essay: Analyzing Craft and Theme* (2014).

Strategies for Improving Writing About Reading at a Glance

Strategy		Levels	Genres/ Text Types	Skills
13.1	Sketch a Memory	E–Z+	Not applicable	Reading-history reflection
13.2	Quick Stops Using Symbols	E–Z+	Any	Varied
13.3	Transitioning from Sentence to Sentence	G–Z+	Any	Connecting Ideas
13.4	Buying Stock in Sticky Notes	G–Z+	Any	Quick jotting
13.5	Nonfiction Readers Stop and Jot	J–Z+	Nonfiction	Quick jotting
13.6	What Can I Do with a Sticky Note?	J–Z+	Any	Considering purpose for writing about reading
13.7	What's Worth Keeping?	L–Z+	Any	Determining importance
13.8	Five-Sentence Summary	M–Z+	Fiction, Narrative nonfiction	Summarizing, determining importance
13.9	My Reading Timeline	M–Z+	Any	Reading-history reflection
13.10	Note Taking Helps to Understand Nonfiction	M–Z+	Nonfiction	Determining importance, synthesizing
13.11	The Best of Times, the Worst of Times	M–Z+	Any	Reading-history reflection
13.12	What Happened/What It Makes Me Think T-Chart	N–Z+	Fiction	Determining importance, inferring
13.13	Lifting a Line	N–Z+	Any	Inference, questioning, interpreting
13.14	Writing Long	N–Z+	Any	Elaborating, inferring, interpreting
13.15	Write, Talk, Write	N–Z+	Any	Considering new points of view, revising ideas
13.16	Character Connections Web	P–Z+	Fiction	Inferring, synthesizing
13.17	Compare Books for New Ideas	P–Z+	Any	Synthesizing, interpreting
13.18	Reacting, Responding	P–Z+	Any	Making connections, reacting
13.19	Flash Essay	P–Z+	Any	Supporting ideas with reasons and text evidence
13.20	Writing to Question and Critique	P–Z+	Any	Questioning, critiquing
13.21	Write from Inside the Story	R–Z+	Fiction	Visualizing, inferring
13.22	Idea Connections	R–Z+	Any	Synthesizing, interpreting, comparing and contrasting
13.23	Pile It On	R–Z+	Fiction	Synthesizing, interpreting, inferring

13.1 Sketch a Memory

Who is this for?

LEVELS

E–Z+

GENRE / TEXT TYPE

not applicable

SKILL

reading-history reflection

Strategy Think of a positive reading memory you have. Draw a sketch of all the details you can remember including where you were, who was with you, and what were you reading. Think about what made that experience so positive. Finally, write a plan for how you can create more positive reading memories like that one!

Teaching Tip Writing about reading encompasses not only writing about what you've read (comprehension) but also reflections about who you are as a reader. It's likely that across the course of the year, students will grow and change. Plan to use some of the writing about reading strategies on these pages as well as some ideas for reflecting on reading identity in Chapter 2 ("*Focus, Stamina, Engagement, and Building a Reading Life*") at multiple points across the year.

Prompts

- Imagine the place in your mind.
- Think about where you were. What details do you remember?
- Think about what you were reading.
- Was anyone with you?
- What is it about this spot that helped you read?
- Let's make a plan.
- How will you create this same experience this year?

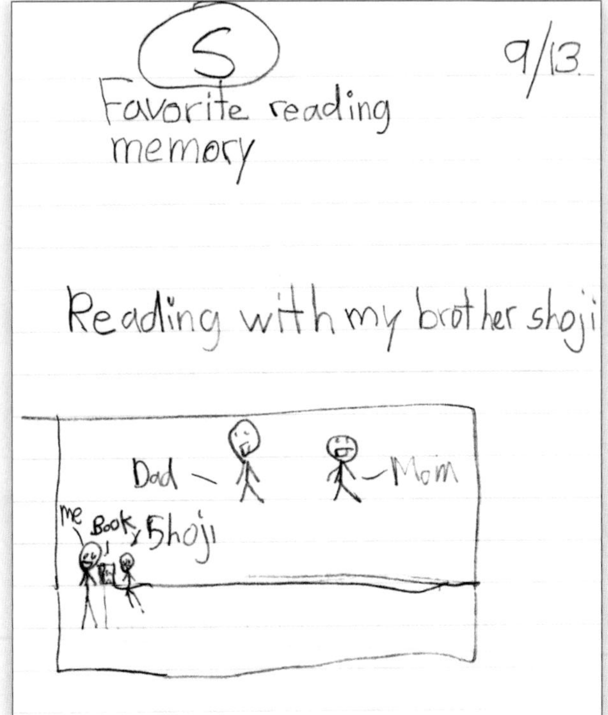

Hat Tip: *Building a Reading Life: Stamina, Fluency, and Engagement* (Calkins and Tolan 2010a)

13.2 Quick Stops Using Symbols

Strategy When you find yourself reacting in a moment of the text, but don't want to take long to stop and jot, you can hold onto your thought with a symbol. Write quickly, then keep reading. Later, when you want to revisit your thinking you can look at the symbol and think, "What was the thought I was having on this page?"

Teaching Tip This strategy is an age-appropriate way to teach young readers to plan for conversation or reading time with a partner. It takes just a moment to quickly jot a symbol on a sticky note. I have seen some kindergarten teachers use a variation of this strategy by making sticky notes with symbols ahead of time, or paper bookmarks with different symbols, and giving them out to children to place in their books (some get nervous with writing implements out at the same time as books—understandably!). For older readers, this strategy might be a way for them to remember a spot where they had a thought or reaction, but where they don't want to stop to write a few sentences. They can quickly flag the spot with a symbol and return to it later at the end of reading time. This will help them maintain their engaged reading state.

Prompts

- What are you thinking here?
- What symbol could you use? Check the chart.
- Jot a quick symbol and keep going.
- Let's go back to your jots. Use them to explain what you're thinking.

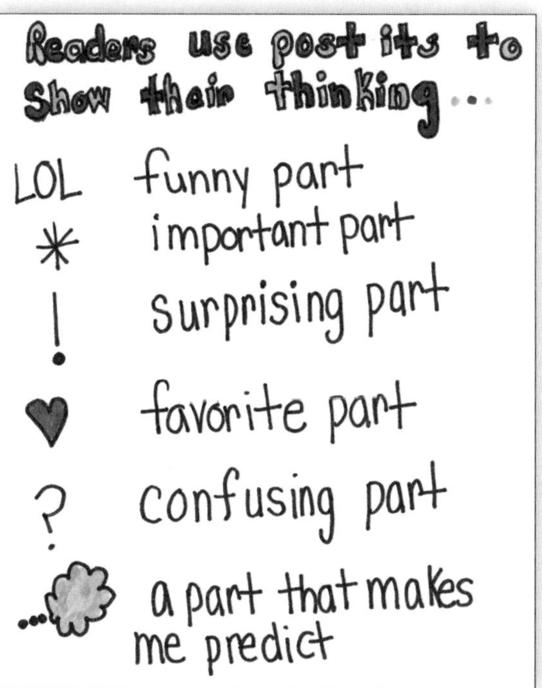

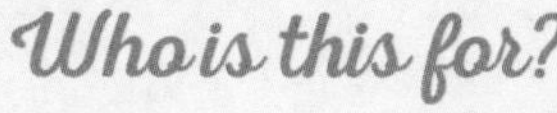

LEVELS

E–Z+

GENRE / TEXT TYPE

any

SKILLS

varied

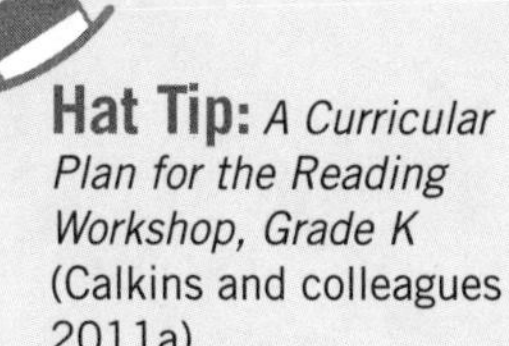

Hat Tip: *A Curricular Plan for the Reading Workshop, Grade K* (Calkins and colleagues 2011a)

13.3 Transitioning from Sentence to Sentence

Who is this for?

LEVELS

G–Z+

GENRE / TEXT TYPE

any

SKILL

connecting ideas

Strategy Think about the connection between two sentences you want to write. Think, "What word or phrase can I use to start the second of these two sentences?" Reference the chart for help if you can't think of one on your own.

Teaching Tip This strategy is to help children with elaborating beyond a first in-the-moment idea to doing some longer-form writing to explore their thinking. Younger readers may be writing just a couple of sentences, while older readers may be filling notebook pages. Adapt the language in the strategy and the sorts of transition words and phrases you choose to introduce to the age level and ability level of the readers you're teaching.

Lesson Language *When writing long about a text, sometimes you'll find that you have many ideas, with lots of evidence to site, that lead you to new ideas, new evidence, and so on. To be clear on how one sentence connects to the next, you'll need to carefully consider the transition words and phrases you use. Just listing one idea after another, or one detail from the text after another muddies your overall meaning. Then, when you or a teacher goes back to the writing, it becomes hard to understand what you really wanted to say.*

At first, you may find that you need to go back to what you've written to reread and revise. When you do this, you'll be thinking, "What is the connection between these two sentences?" and then you'll choose a transition word or phrase that captures that connection. Eventually, I hope you'll be able to use these transition words and phrases comfortably, as you write.

Purpose/ Meaning	Examples
Agreement Similarity	Not only . . . but also In addition First, second, third Equally important And Also As well as
Opposition Contradiction	In contrast Despite/in spite of Even so/though Then again But And yet/still Besides Although
Cause Purpose	With this in mind In order to If/then Whenever Because of Given that
Examples Support	In other words To put it differently Another thing to realize Including Surely Especially Surprisingly In fact

Purpose/ Meaning	Examples
Effect Consequence	As a result In that case For Thus Then Hence Therefore
Conclusion Summary Restatement	Generally speaking Given these points After all In summary In conclusion In brief To sum it up
Time Sequence	To begin with After Later Then Eventually Meanwhile Until now

13.4 Buying Stock in Sticky Notes

Who is this for?

LEVELS

G–Z+

GENRE / TEXT TYPE

any

SKILL

quick jotting

Strategy When I realize I'm having a thought, I stop and think, "Will writing this thought down help me read better? Help me talk to my partner or club about my reading? Help me talk to my teacher about my reading?" If I want to hold onto the thought, I jot my thought quickly on a sticky note, stick the note on the page where I had the thought, and keep reading.

Teaching Tip The point of the sticky note is to emulate the marginal note taking that you can do when the book belongs to you—the idea is written right alongside the text that sparked the thinking. This has a number of benefits. For one, when you confer with the student about his or her thinking, the text evidence for the idea is right there. Second, when children reference their sticky notes in conversation, they can easily reference the text, too. Sometimes people ask, "But does it have to be sticky notes?" because they are feeling challenged with the management of all of the small yellow squares. Where do students put them when they finish the book? How do I keep them organized? How do I monitor what kids have written? I often offer the following solution: Have each student keep a two-pocket folder with one page per week for first- and second-grade readers, or a notebook with one page per book for grades 3 and above. Teach children what ideas are worth writing down and which sticky notes are worth keeping (see strategy 13.7, "What's Worth Keeping?" or 12.8, "Super STARter Jots") and, once a week, let them select which to keep as a portfolio of sorts and which to let go of. The goal is that these sticky notes help the reader in the midst of reading to track their thinking and hold onto the story, they help to make thinking visible for the purpose of your conferring and assessment, and they help the student to prepare for conversation with their friends. The intent is for them not to become a nuisance! If they really are unmanageable, you could have children keep running notes in a notebook, though I don't recommend this in the primary elementary grades as the notebook and pencil often become a distraction to reading.

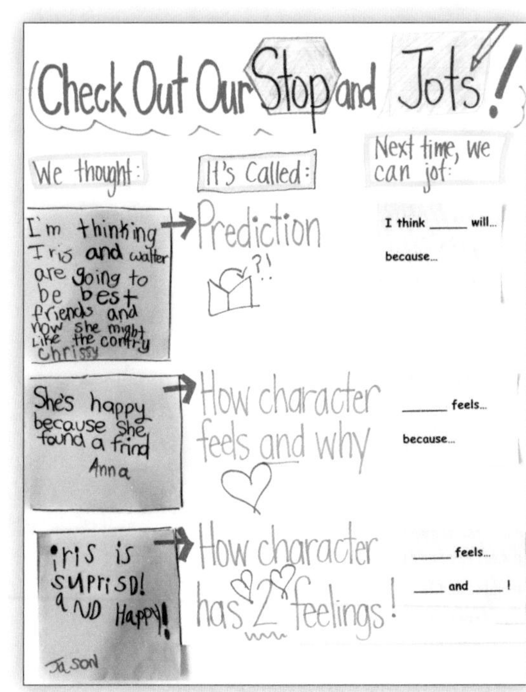

Prompts

- Stop when you have a thought.
- Jot what's on your mind.
- Jot quickly so you can get back to reading.
- Is it a thought you want to hold on to? If so, jot it quickly.
- I see you jotted just a few times today, in spots that really matter to you.

13.5 Nonfiction Readers Stop and Jot

Strategy Writing about nonfiction will help you hold onto important information and ideas as you read. When you read and find your mind click on—perhaps because you learn something new (information, words), see a strong image, feel curious, or want to hold on to the main information in a section—it's a good idea to stop and jot.

Lesson Language *As I read, I'm going to think about the ways that nonfiction readers hold onto ideas and information.* (Read from first page of *Sea Otters* by Bobbie Kalman, 1996.) *Hmm. This word marine is a new one for me, and I think it might be important to understanding sea otters. So that I don't forget, I'm going to jot down the word and a quick definition.* (Jot: Marine: animals that live in saltwater.) *Let me read on.* (Read aloud the next two pages.) *Whoa. That was a lot of information in that section. Before I move on, I'm going to jot a quick boxes-and-bullets summary.* (Jot in a box: Many animals are related to otters. Jot in bullets beneath the box: Weasels, badgers, and skunks are in the same family; North American, Asian, Brazilian are different types of sea otters.) *Let me show you as I read one more page.* (Read the section "A Sea Otter's Body.") *Well this page was just fascinating. You know what I'm thinking? It seems like the sea otter is designed for seawater. I am thinking it probably evolved to be that way. I'm going to jot that thought down.* (Model jotting.)

Prompts

- After reading that section, are you thinking anything?
- What do you think you can jot that will help you hold on to the information?
- Let's stop and jot.
- Show me what you'll write after that part.
- Let's check the chart. What kind of writing will help you?
- I noticed you thought about what would help you when you stopped to jot that.

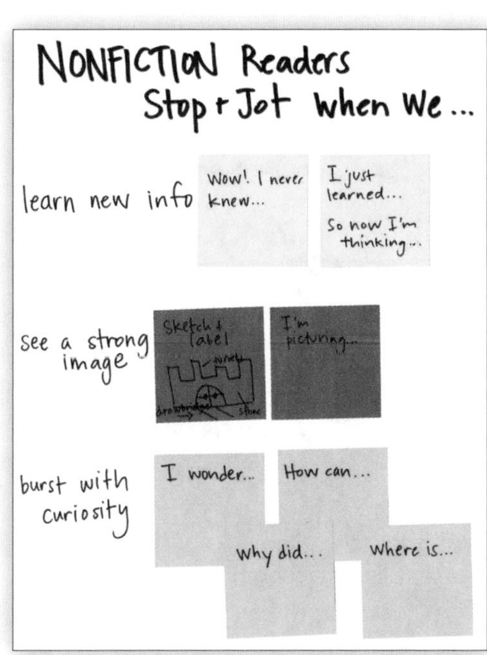

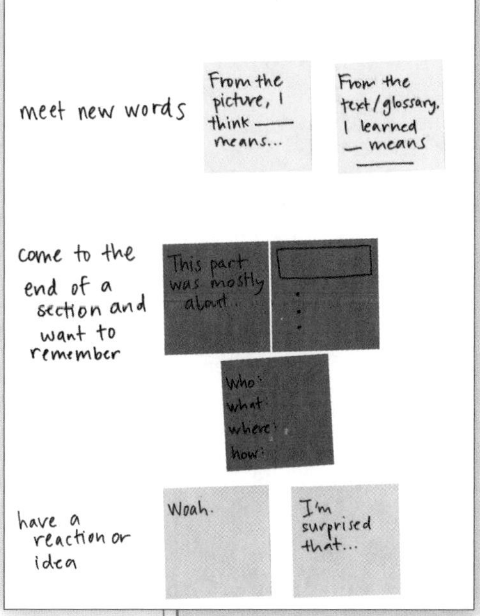

Who is this for?

LEVELS
J–Z+

GENRE / TEXT TYPE
nonfiction

SKILL
quick jotting

13.6 What Can I Do with a Sticky Note?

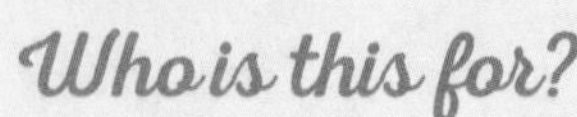

LEVELS

J–Z+

GENRE / TEXT TYPE

any

SKILL

considering purpose for writing about reading

Strategy Sticky notes are tools that help you think as you read, remember what you've read, and/or talk and write in more detail later about what you were thinking. It's important that you think, "What's my purpose for writing this?" and/or "How will I use this?"

Teaching Tip This lesson might be a good one if you have a student who is over-jotting so much that it's interfering with his reading and/or overall stamina. It also might help a child who is reluctant to use sticky notes because he or she doesn't see the point. Showing students that sticky notes aren't just meant to be discarded at the end of reading, but rather should be used to talk or write about ideas in more depth and that they are tools for holding on to thinking on the run and reflecting or revising thinking, helps to connect a purpose to the action. Without the purpose, many students will jot on sticky notes because they think that's what they are supposed to do or because they are aiming to fulfill a task set out by the teacher.

Prompts

- What do you want to write on that sticky note?
- Let's think about your purpose.
- How will keeping that written down help?
- Who do you plan to share that thought with?
- Is that jot to help you? Explain how it'll help.

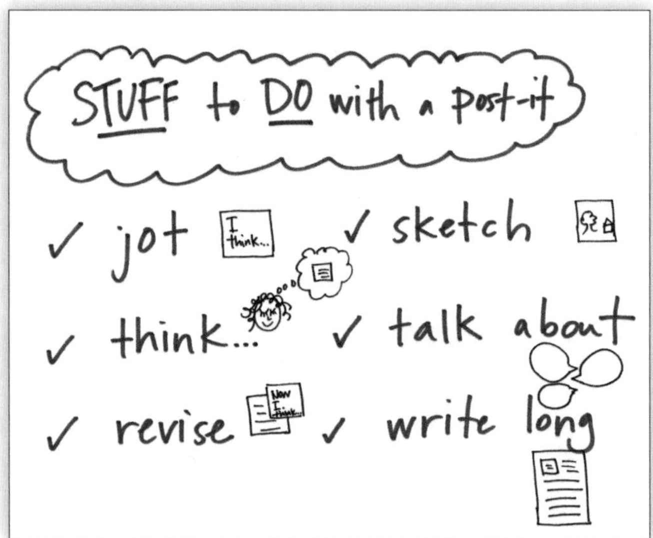

STUFF to DO with a post-it
✓ jot
I think...
✓ sketch
✓ think...
✓ talk about
✓ revise
Now I think...
✓ write long

13.7 What's Worth Keeping?

Strategy Reread your sticky notes. Do they pass the "worth keeping test"? (See figure below.) If they do, save them with the book title as a heading on the page.

Lesson Language *At the end of the week when it's time to put your independent reading books back, you may find that you have amassed a collection of sticky notes. The question is, what's worth keeping? Use the following questions* (see figure on this page) *to guide your reflection. Once you've selected the ideas you want to keep, you'll organize them into your reading notebook with a title on the top of the page, and the sticky notes that go with that book on the bottom of the page.*

Prompts

- Reread what you have.
- What seems worth keeping?
- What's going to help you?
- How do you plan to use those sticky notes?
- I can tell you really considered which sticky notes were going to help you.

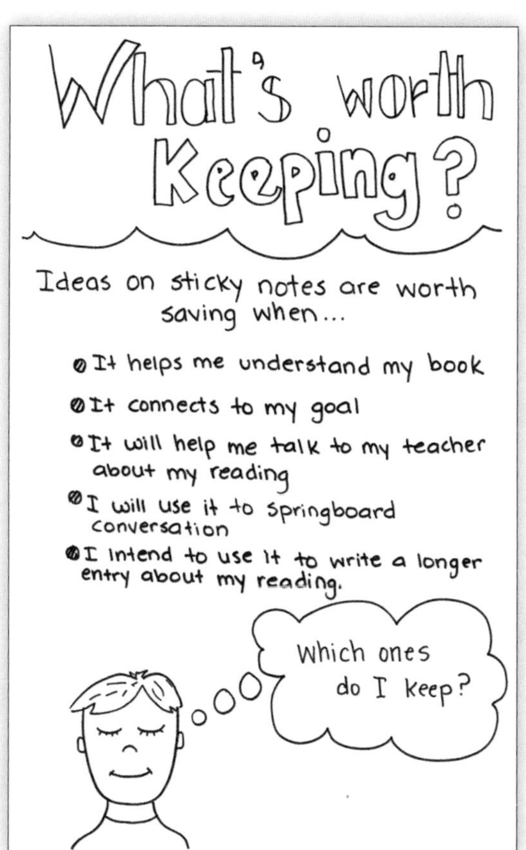

What's worth Keeping?
Ideas on sticky notes are worth saving when...
It helps me understand my book
It connects to my goal
It will help me talk to my teacher about my reading
I will use it to springboard conversation
I intend to use it to write a longer entry about my reading.
Which ones do I keep?

Who is this for?

LEVELS

L–Z+

GENRE / TEXT TYPE

any

SKILL

determining importance

Hat Tip: *Writing About Reading: From Book Talk to Literary Essays, Grades 3–8* (Angelillo 2003)

13.8 Five-Sentence Summary

Who is this for?

LEVELS

M–Z+

GENRE / TEXT TYPE

fiction, narrative nonfiction

SKILLS

summarizing, determining importance

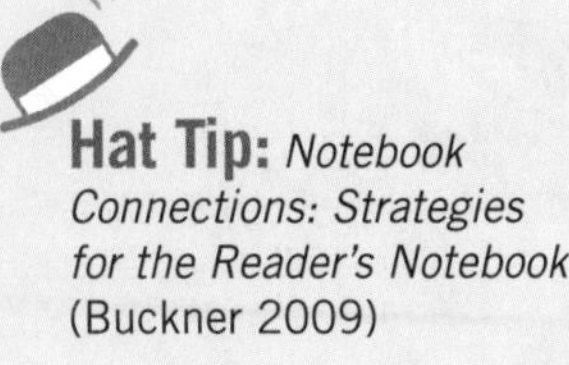

Hat Tip: *Notebook Connections: Strategies for the Reader's Notebook* (Buckner 2009)

Strategy Think about the text you just read. What are the five most important events, in the order they happened? Tell them out loud to yourself, across your five fingers. Write them on the page, one sentence per event.

Lesson Language *Research has shown that one of the best ways to understand what you read is to practice summarizing it. Summarizing is a skill in and of itself, as well as a strategy to help you understand. When you are forced to say just what is most important about a selection of text that you read, you have to sort through all the details and just pick the most essential ones. For example, if I was going to give a five-sentence summary of* Sylvester and the Magic Pebble *(Steig 1969), I would include these sentences:*

- *Sylvester found a magic pebble that made his wishes come true.*
- *When faced by a lion, he accidentally wished to become a rock.*
- *His parents tried everything to find him and were incredibly unhappy.*
- *His parents went on a picnic and happened to find the same magic pebble.*
- *His parents wished him back again, and he became himself.*

Notice that I didn't include every single detail, just the big events that move the story along. I told them in a way that would make sense even to someone who hadn't ever read the story like we had.

Prompts

- What happened first?
- Was that the most important event that happened next?
- You're at the middle finger, that should be about the middle of the book.
- One finger left—what's the conclusion of the story that connects back to the initial problem or what the character wanted?

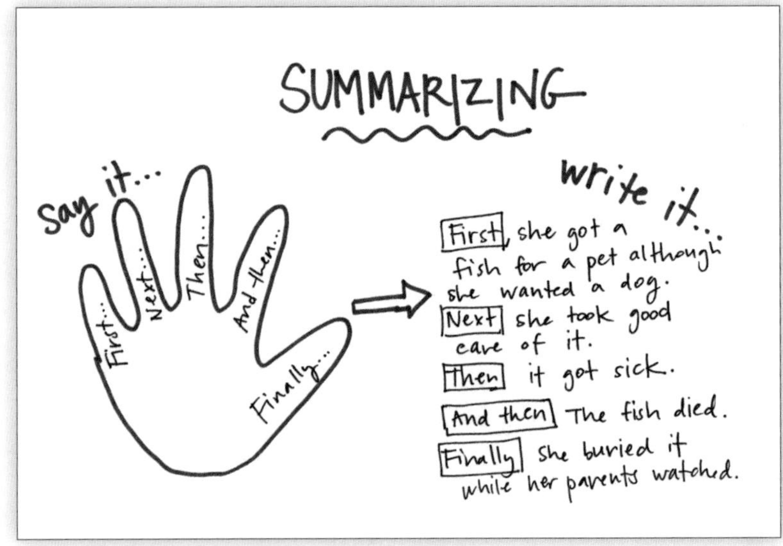

SUMMARIZING
Say it...
First...
Next...
Then...
And then...
Finally...
write it...
First, she got a fish for a pet although she wanted a dog.
Next she took good care of it.
Then it got sick.
And then The fish died.
Finally she buried it while her parents watched.

13.9 My Reading Timeline

Strategy Think about your history as a reader and create a timeline that shows a journey of big events from birth until now. After creating your timeline, you can reflect on how your history is informing your present.

Lesson Language *Just as you grow and change as a person, you may grow and change as a reader. Who you were as a first-grade reader—what you read, who you shared your reading with, where you liked to read, how you read—is probably different than who you are today. By reflecting on your history, you can better understand the reader you are today. We'll do this activity again in a few months, to see if even within one school year you find yourself becoming a different type of reader.*

Prompts

- Think of the W's to prompt your thinking—What did you like? Where did you read? When did you read? And so on.
- Include events from your home reading life and school reading life.
- What were events that really stand out?
- You included events from your whole life. That will really help you think about the reader you are today!

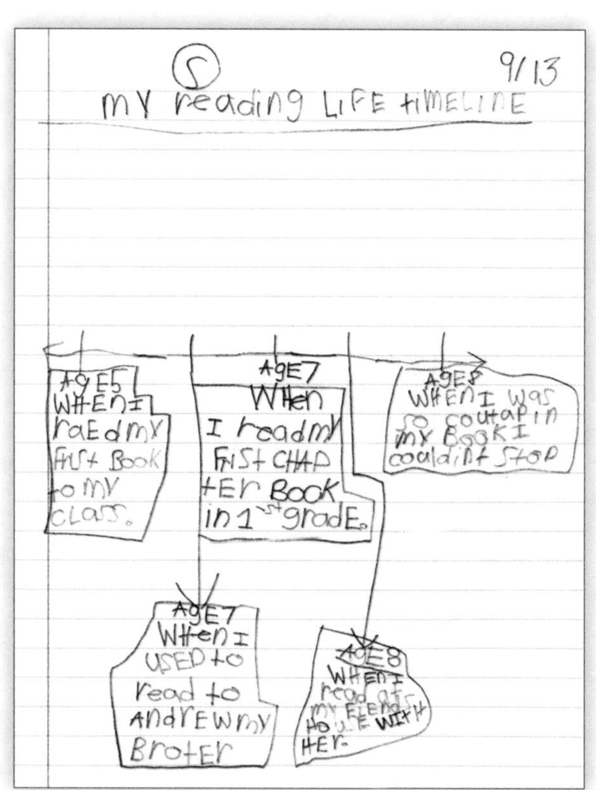

Who is this for?

LEVELS

M–Z+

GENRE / TEXT TYPE

any

SKILL

reading-history reflection

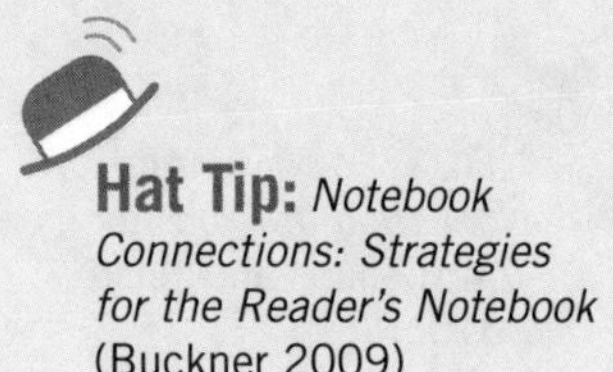

Hat Tip: *Notebook Connections: Strategies for the Reader's Notebook* (Buckner 2009)

13.10 Note Taking Helps to Understand Nonfiction

Who is this for?

LEVELS

M–Z+

GENRE / TEXT TYPE

nonfiction

SKILLS

determining importance, synthesizing

Strategy Read the entire page or section. Think about the graphic organizer you may want to use to represent the information, based on the structure of the text. Reread the page or section and fill in the information.

Teaching Tip Before students will be able to use this strategy, they will need to have been taught about different text structures and how graphic organizers can help. (See, for example, strategy 8.19, "Consider Structure.") It's also important to note that this is a strategy to support students with note taking when their goal is to research and record what they've read for a purpose—either because they are doing writing about the topic or plan to talk with/teach a partner about the topic. Not all nonfiction reading should result in writing, and not all nonfiction reading should be connected to research. Children should have plenty of experience reading whole, continuous texts and applying comprehension strategies while reading, without necessarily recording their learning down on paper.

Prompts

- How do you think you'll take notes?
- Think about the structure of the text.
- How do you know what the text structure is?
- Now that you know the structure and how you'll take notes, reread.

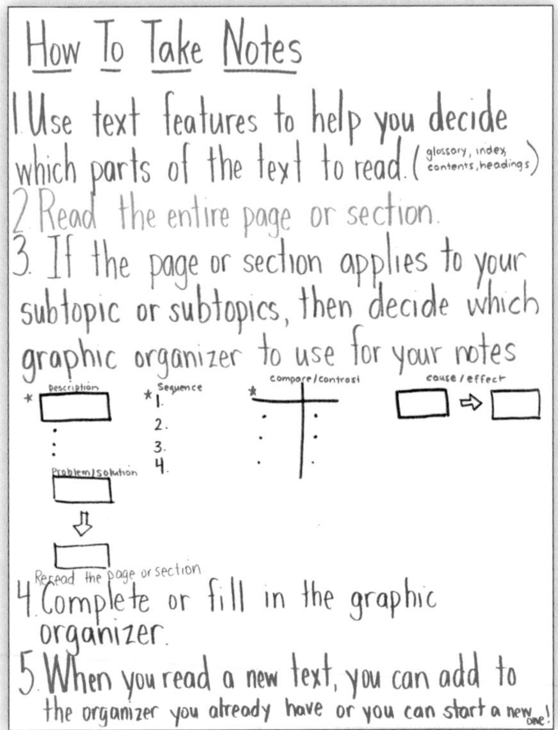

How To Take Notes
1. Use text features to help you decide which parts of the text to read. (glossary, index, contents, headings)
2. Read the entire page or section.
3. If the page or section applies to your subtopic or subtopics, then decide which graphic organizer to use for your notes
description
sequence
1.
2.
3.
4.
compare/contrast
cause/effect
problem/solution
Reread the page or section
4. Complete or fill in the graphic organizer.
5. When you read a new text, you can add to the organizer you already have or you can start a new one!

Hat Tip: *Navigating Nonfiction in Expository Text* (Calkins and Tolan 2010c)

Navigating Nonfiction in Narrative and Hybrid Text (Calkins and Tolan 2010d)

13.11 The Best of Times, the Worst of Times

Strategy Think back in your memory to times when reading felt positive, powerful, joyful. Write about those times and what helped to create that feeling. Think about the opposite—times when reading felt hard, disappointing, boring. Write about those times and what happened. Look back across what you've written and make resolutions: "I think I will need to . . ."

Lesson Language *My goal is that each and every one of you feels like you have a reading life that matters. That you couldn't imagine life without books. That you see yourself in the books you choose to read. That you are curious and seek out the answers to those questions in your books. But if we were being honest, for all of us there are probably times when reading was wonderful—those are the best of times. And times when reading was terrible—the worst of times. When we are honest about these different sides to our reading histories, we can think about what we need to do to create a reading life for ourselves going forward that really matters.*

Prompts

- When did reading feel positive for you?
- Close your eyes and think of a positive memory.
- Think about the opposite. When was reading less enjoyable?
- When you look at your list, what patterns do you see?
- What do you want to do for this year?

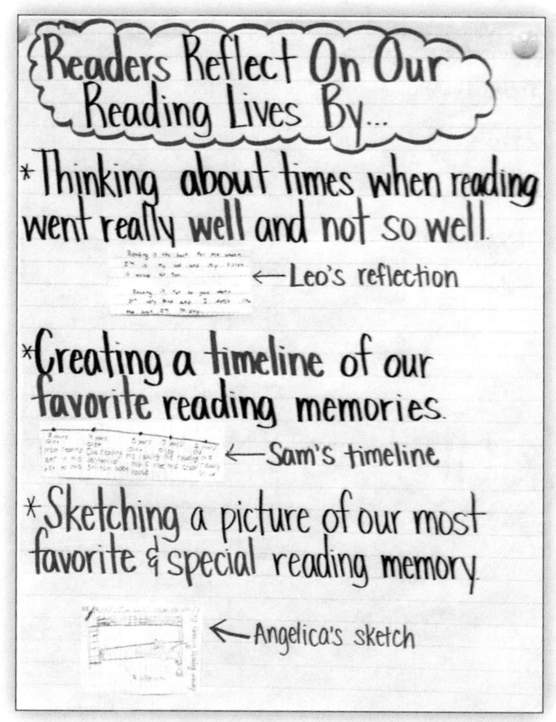

Who is this for?

LEVELS

M–Z+

GENRE / TEXT TYPE

any

SKILL

reading-history reflection

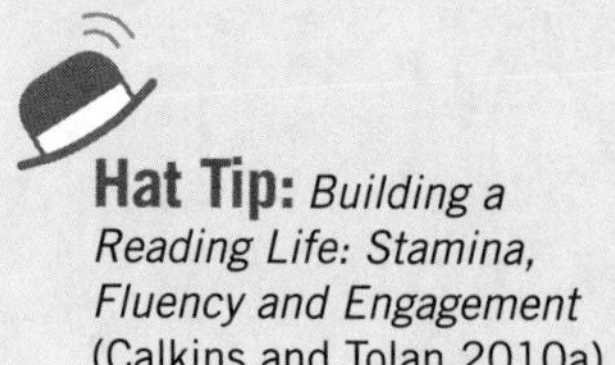

Hat Tip: *Building a Reading Life: Stamina, Fluency and Engagement* (Calkins and Tolan 2010a)

13.12 What Happened/What It Makes Me Think T-Chart

Who is this for?

LEVELS

N–Z+

GENRE / TEXT TYPE

fiction

SKILLS

determining importance, inferring

Strategy To keep track of the important moments in your story and the responses you have to those moments, you can keep a two-column T-chart. Stop and jot the important event on the left. On the right, write your thoughts, reactions, questions, or ideas.

Lesson Language *The meaning you make in a text is like a conversation between what's in the book and what's in your mind. Your reactions, thoughts, and questions to the story matter. As you read, you can keep track of not only the important events but also what you think about those events. When you do this, you'll have an ongoing log of your thinking across the text.*

Prompts

- What is most important to remember here?
- Think about an event that was important to the character.
- What made you write that down? What's your response?
- Why do you think that was important?
- What are your thoughts about what happened?

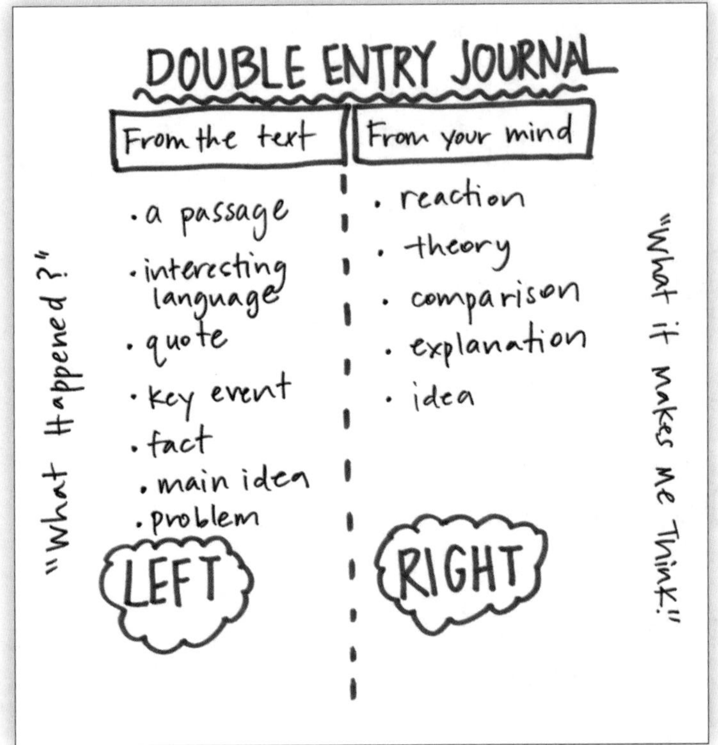

13.13 Lifting a Line

Strategy Find a powerful line from the text you're reading. It may be something beautifully crafted, something a character says that is profound, or something the narrator says that reveals something about the plot, characters, or theme. Copy the line into your notebook and write your thoughts, comments, and reactions that spring from that line. Try not to censor your thinking; write fast and without a filter.

Lesson Language *Part of what makes reading literature so enjoyable to me is that authors sometimes have this way of capturing so much in so few lines. These lines—you know them when you come across them—just tug at your heart or make you pause and think or say something so common in such original language that it's worth taking some pause. It's also true that while I often have an initial emotional reaction, these one-liners sometimes hold deeper ideas that when I write about them help me better understand the story—or life! I wanted to just share one of these with you from our recent read-aloud,* Amos and Boris *(Steig 1971). Toward the end of the book, the whale says, "You have to be out of the sea really to know how good it is to be in it." When I first read that, I thought, that's true in life—sometimes we don't know how good we have it until we experience something else. And then I took that idea and wrote about it, which brought me to writing about times in my life when I take things for granted. And then I found myself writing about how we have this saying "the grass is always greener" and how not appreciating the things of our own lives leads to jealousy. And then finally I wrote concluding that while I've been guilty of this in my life, I'm making a promise to myself to start being more grateful for what I have.*

Great Gilly Hopkins (K. Paterson) October 23

Quote: "That all that stuff about happy endings is lies. The only ending in this world is death."

I think this is about promises. There is a difference between what people promise you and what promises you make for yourself. Some people go around expecting everything to be handed to them. They want stuff to just fall in their laps and if they don't get their way they don't work for it. Other people are different: they want something? They go for it. The difference is whether you believe in fate or hard work!

It's true, though, that some are dealt a bad hand like Gilly. It's not easy to start off your childhood being shuffled around from place to peace. I guess it is a bit of luck that brings her to Trotter. That experience helped her to see what happens when people care for her. It showed her what's possible.

Prompts

- Find a line that stuck with you.
- In this chapter, what line seems to still be in your mind?
- Start writing your thoughts.
- Try to keep going, write more. Try a prompt like, "In addition . . ." or "On the other hand . . ." or "For example . . ." or "This makes me think . . ."

Who is this for?

LEVELS

N–Z+

GENRE / TEXT TYPE

any

SKILLS

inferring, questioning, interpreting

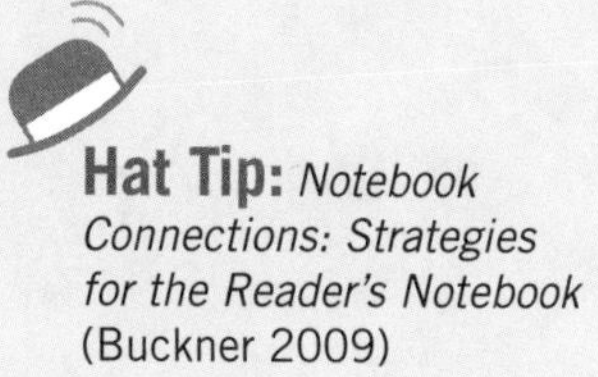

Hat Tip: *Notebook Connections: Strategies for the Reader's Notebook* (Buckner 2009)

13.14 Writing Long

Who is this for?

LEVELS

N–Z+

GENRE / TEXT TYPE

any

SKILLS

elaborating, inferring, interpreting

Strategy Take a sticky note that you think has a strong starting idea written on it. Place it on the corner of your page. Use the prompts we use for keeping conversation going to have a conversation with yourself on paper. When you feel stuck, pick a new prompt and keep going.

Teaching Tip Check out the talk prompts in Chapter 12 and specifically "Sentence Starter Sticks" (page 337) and "Listen and Respond" (page 329) strategies for ideas of the types of prompts that fuel conversation.

Lesson Language *Just as we hold on to our ideas as we read by stopping and jotting quickly on a sticky note, we can also nurture these ideas so they grow into something bigger and deeper. The in-the-moment thought you have may be just the tip of the iceberg for something hidden below. One way to get at what's below is to take the same prompts we use when we talk to our friends in book clubs, in whole-class conversations, or in partnerships, and use them to have a conversation with ourselves—on paper. You can start with the first idea on the sticky note, then set your pen free, writing and adding on, and growing your first thought. When you feel like you're stuck for what to write next, look back at the list of sentence prompts, pick another, and try to keep going. I bet you'll find something coming from your pen that surprises you!*

Prompts

- Just a sentence starter to get you going.
- What's your starting idea? Keep writing long.
- Don't let your pencil stop moving.
- Don't worry about perfection. Write to get your ideas down.

I'm wondering if the turtle will make Leo happy. Will he be a true friend?

10-16

"Slower Than the Rest"
Cynthia Rylant

At first I was wondering if the turtle would become a friend when on page 2 Leo believed he would never feel happiness again. This made me so sad! Charlie seems like he's going to help. For example, Charlie could "listen" to all of Leo's stories. When Leo brings him to school, it shows how Charlie is an important part of his life. He seems to put himself in Charlie's position and really understands him.

The thing that's still a little sad to me, though, is that his family seems so separate from him. Although Charlie may make a good friend, he won't ever be a substitute for a mother and father who love and take care of him. He's always in the position of taking care of a pet.

Hat Tip: *Writing About Reading: From Book Talk to Literary Essays, Grades 3–8* (Angelillo 2003)

13.15 Write, Talk, Write

Strategy Take an idea you have about a character, theme, or something else in the book. Write a half page or more to elaborate on your thinking. Then, get together with your book club, partnership, or class to discuss your thinking. After discussion, come back to your notebook and write about what you're thinking now. In particular, think about how your ideas have changed or shifted, or how you've gotten a new perspective because of the conversation.

Prompts

- How has your thinking changed?
- What did you think before, and what are you thinking now?
- You can say, "Before, I thought . . . but after talking I'm thinking . . ."
- Think about ideas your partner or club members shared. What's new from what you had written down before?
- What are you thinking now?

The Library Card

Originaly I thoght Mongoose was the type of person who acted sneaky because he was loyal to weasel but now, I'm thinking He only Does so if he wants to. If he feels it's safe

Writing Long

On the one hand Mongoose is loyal to weasel because he dosenot want to have fights with weasel and he wants to keep his freind but on the other hand he is stubborn and he will only do things if he wants to and if he thinks it's the right thing to do. I'm relizing that mongoose thinks before he does something unlike weasel who does what ever his dreams tell him to do. The important thing about this is it causes them to fight alot it also causes disagrements. For example, They always fight about the cars they will get when they grow up.

After talking with my Partner Now I'm thinking that Mongoose has a struggle he wants to stay close to weasel but since they are diffrent it is hard be cause they want diffrent things. I'm also relizing Weasel acts like a trouble maker because he wants to be famous among the students and students that will be students when he grows up. I'm relizing the root is where they go to talk. The root could symbolize Dreams and Freedom because it's so high above the ground. A lesson weasel could learn is you should not be a trouble maker just because you could be famous and you should try to acomplish your dreams in a better way.

Who is this for?

LEVELS

N–Z+

GENRE / TEXT TYPE

any

SKILLS

considering new points of view, revising ideas

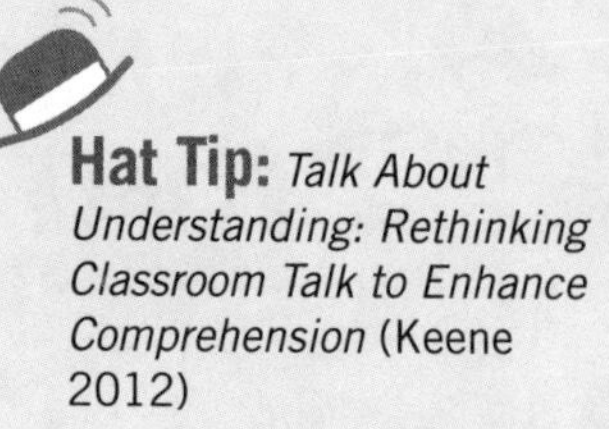

Hat Tip: *Talk About Understanding: Rethinking Classroom Talk to Enhance Comprehension* (Keene 2012)

13.16 Character Connections Web

Who is this for?

LEVELS

P–Z+

GENRE / TEXT TYPE

fiction

SKILLS

inferring, synthesizing

Hat Tip: *Notebook Connections: Strategies for the Reader's Notebook* (Buckner 2009)

Strategy Write the names of each of the main and secondary characters spread out on a notebook page. Draw arrows or lines between them. On those lines, write about how each character affects another or ideas that you have that come from their interactions.

Lesson Language *In stories with multiple, well-developed characters, the connections between the characters are almost as interesting to study as the characters themselves. By studying character interactions and the ways characters affect one another, we can develop deeper ideas about the characters and possibly even uncover some of the themes in the story.*

Prompts

- How does this character affect this one?
- Think about an important interaction between these characters. What ideas do you have about them?
- How does this character seem different with this one, rather than this one?
- Write what you're thinking on the line.
- What new ideas do you have?
- Good—that's an idea, not just a fact about the characters.

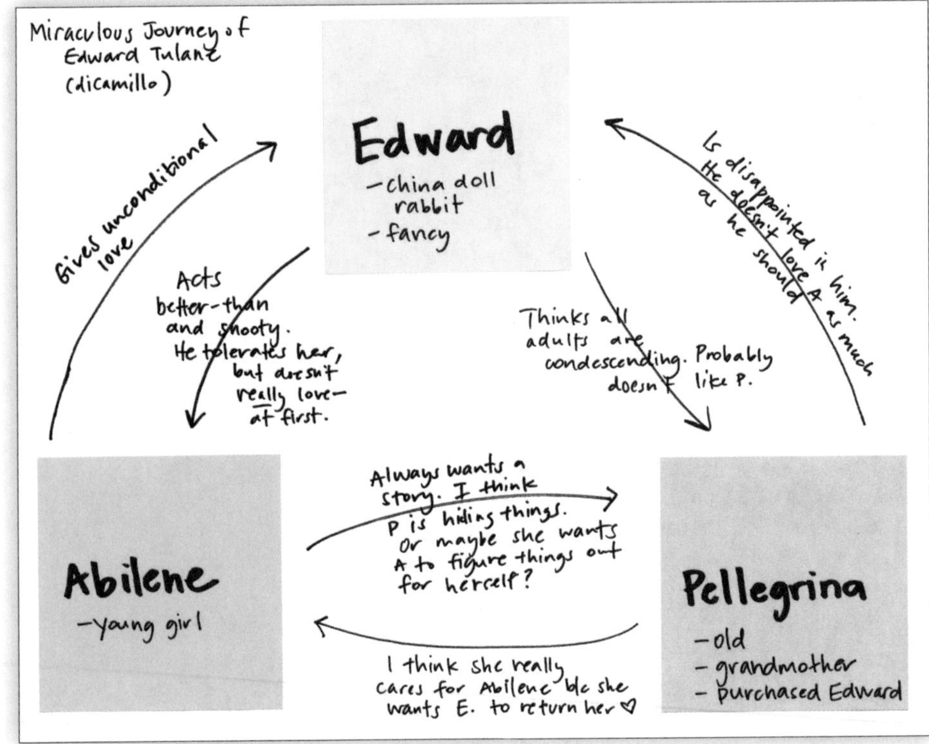

13.17 Compare Books for New Ideas

Strategy Take two books with something in common (same setting, similar themes, characters that remind you of each other). In a Venn diagram or three-column chart, begin to think in categories to expand on the similarities and differences. Some categories you might use are: characters (main, secondary), settings, themes, ideas, symbols. Notice how in comparing and contrasting you have new thoughts about either or both books.

Prompts

- What category are you using to compare?
- Let's think first about characters. What's the same, what's different?
- I notice many differences listed here. Let's think about similarities.
- If you look back across what you've written, what categories do you think you've used to compare? What else could you use?
- How does comparing help you think about new ideas?
- How does contrasting help you think of new ideas?

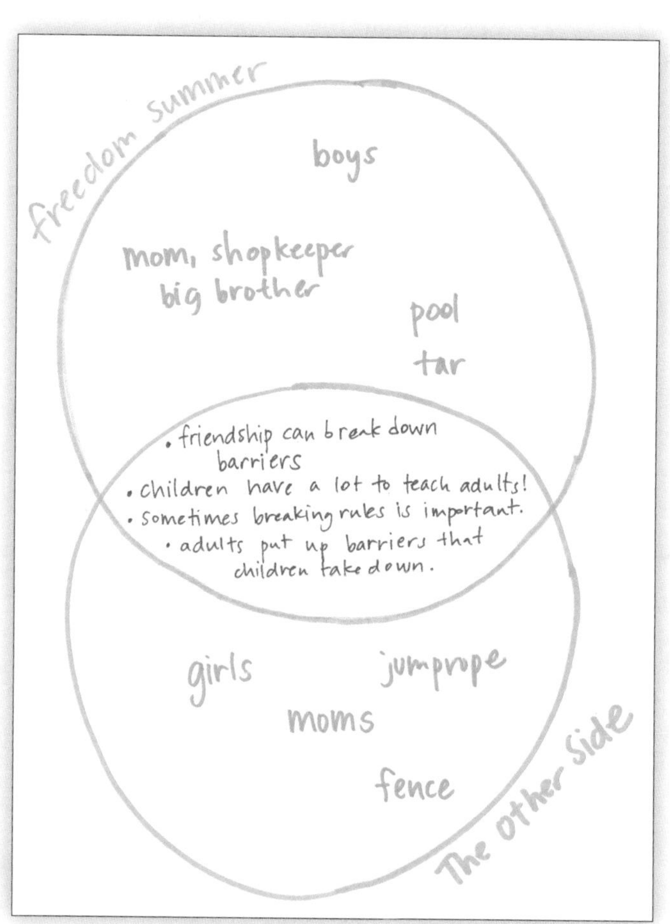

Who is this for?

LEVELS

P–Z+

GENRE / TEXT TYPE

any

SKILLS

synthesizing, interpreting

13.18 Reacting, Responding

Who is this for?

LEVELS

P–Z+

GENRE / TEXT TYPE

any

SKILLS

making connections, reacting

Hat Tip: *Writing About Reading: From Book Talk to Literary Essays, Grades 3–8* (Angelillo 2003)

Strategy When you find you have a strong emotional response to a book, stop to react and respond. Write about your feelings, what gave you those feelings, and how you plan to read or live differently because of the book.

Lesson Language *Sometimes when you finish a book, you find that it just stays with you. It sticks in your heart: you can't stop thinking about it and it's hard to even move on to a new book. This emotional response to the story is a powerful one, and it's the kind of thing many choose to either talk or write about. Some of the ways you know you had a strong reaction to a book:*

- *The book upset you, or made you cry.*
- *The book made you laugh and feel joy.*
- *As soon as you finished reading it, you wanted to reread all or parts of it.*
- *There were lines from the book that stuck in your head, and you wanted to write them down and/or remember them.*
- *You saw something from a whole new perspective because of what's in the book.*
- *The book was enjoyable to read, but you felt upset that it's over, like you wish there was a sequel or one hundred more pages in the book.*
- *The characters were so real to you that they felt like friends, and you miss them now that the book is over.*

When you have any or all of these emotional connections to the book, you can hold on to them by writing about them, almost like a journal, in your reading notebook. You can describe the feelings you had, and what parts made you feel that way. You could talk about how you feel your life would be different because you've read the book. You can write about how the book has changed you or what you plan to read or do next.

Teaching Tip The point of this lesson is not to kill the aesthetic experience of reading with an assignment (Rosenblatt 1978). Instead, it's an invitation to children to use writing as a tool to hold on to their most powerful feelings in response to something they've read. Some children will reject the idea of writing about their responses, and others will enjoy it. I think this, and the other strategies in this chapter, should be options, invitations.

13.19 Flash Essay

Strategy Think about your thesis, supporting points, and evidence. Talk through the essay first, with a partner, as if you're writing your paragraphs aloud. In one sitting, and without stopping, try to write the entire essay.

Teaching Tip This strategy will work best if a student has some prior knowledge and experience about literary essays, or at least essay structure in general. There are innumerable ways to structure an essay, but a simple intro–three body paragraphs–conclusion structure is a simple way to get kids writing these flash essays. A visual tool, like the one on this page, is also very helpful. You may even consider providing students with sentence starters for each part of the paragraph to further scaffold the quickness and automaticity that this type of flash drafting requires.

Prompts

- Start with your thesis—what's the whole essay about?
- Now, give your three main reasons that will become your body paragraphs.
- Time for the next paragraph—what's this paragraph mostly about? Say it as one sentence.
- Give example(s) from the text to prove that reason.
- Next body paragraph—same as the last.
- Conclusion—wrap up by saying in a new way.
- Say that paragraph again.
- How does that detail from the story support that reason? Explain it.

S Fourth grade rats

I think suds was treated unfairly. I know this because when joey got the beestinng Judy billings payed attention only to joey and it felt like suds wasnt there. Also even when suds said he liftted his fathers weights Judybillings thought joey said that.

Also, when they went to Joeys house Joey forced him to help mess up the room and to not crie when it dies and to hold a spider and to throw winkey out the window and to hang of the roof of the front porch.

Suds was also treated badly by his younger siblings. I know this because zipper-nose tickled his feet and his baby brother called him a wat, wat, wat.

Suds was also treated unfairly by judy bilings

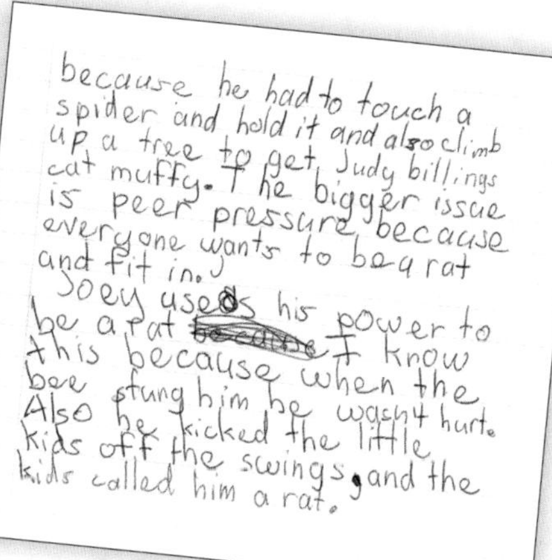

because he had to touch a spider and hold it and also climb up a tree to get Judy billings cat muffy. The bigger issue is peer pressure because everyone wants to be a rat and fit in.

Joey useds his power to be a rat. I know this because when the bee stung him he wasnt hurt. Also he kicked the little kids off the swings, and the kids called him a rat.

Who is this for?

LEVELS

P–Z+

GENRE / TEXT TYPE

any

SKILL

supporting ideas with reasons and text evidence

Hat Tip: *A Curricular Plan for the Writing Workshop, Grade 4* (Calkins and colleagues 2011d)

13.20 Writing to Question and Critique

Who is this for?

LEVELS

P–Z+

GENRE / TEXT TYPE

any

SKILLS

questioning, critiquing

Strategy Read actively, thinking about your own questions and critiques as you read. Think, "What about this text do I believe? What do I wonder more about? When do I think the author is wrong?" The kinds of responses you have are ones you should keep track of, on sticky notes or in a notebook, and plan to write more about when time allows.

Lesson Language *Many approach a book believing that all that's in there is truth, but in reality the reader plays a really important role. Janet Angelillo once wrote, "[Readers] don't have to accept everything that is written on the page . . . they have a responsibility as thinkers to question and make meaning from their reading" (2003, 6). That means that you, and you, and you each have an important job as you read. Not just to soak in the story or the information, but to also have ideas. To think, question, wonder, and maybe even critique what the author says.*

Prompts

- What are you agreeing with in this text?
- What do you disagree with?
- Do you think the author is wrong in any spots? Start writing there.
- Talk to me about your reactions to what the author is presenting here as fact.
- Now, what do you think you'll jot based on that reaction?

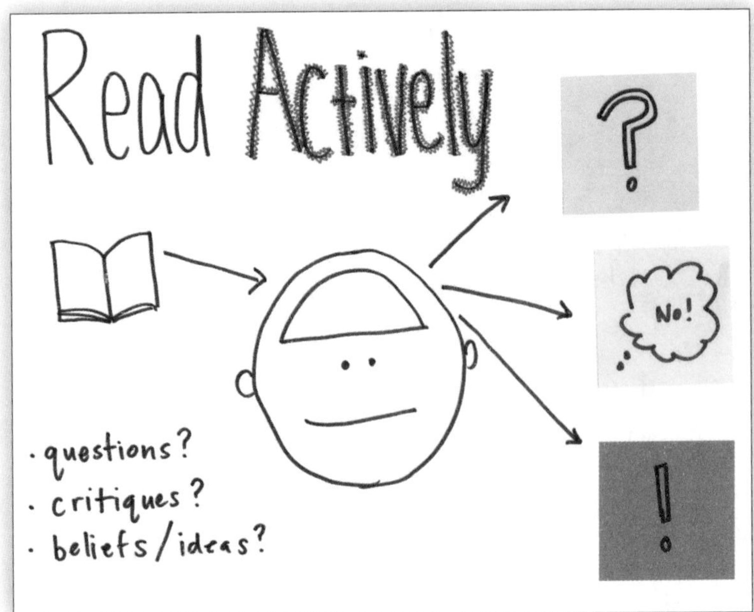

13.21 Write from Inside the Story

Strategy Instead of writing about the story, try to write from inside the story, as if you are there. Use every part of you to actually be in the story as you write about what's happening, what the characters are thinking and feeling. This will help you empathize with characters and come to new thoughts about the story.

Prompts

- Imagine yourself there. What do you see? Hear? Feel?
- If you were in the character's shoes now, what would you be experiencing?
- What is something you think happened there, even if the author didn't say it?
- Can you try it again, from a different perspective?
- Try to imagine being the character.
- What else do you picture?
- Describe what's happening, from her perspective.

Writing from Outside the Story

From "A Pet" in Every Living Thing (Rylant 1988):

I think it's really sad that Emmanuella's fish died. It's like her parents got her a fish that was old because they know it was going to die. She's really sad about it, because the fish was really her friend.

Writing from Inside the Story

From "A Pet" in Every Living Thing (Rylant 1988):

Emmanuella is holding the fish for the last time and she can feel the weight of the fish. It's cold and she realizes it doesn't have the life it used to. She is waiting, pausing, before she buries him. As she looks over her shoulder she sees her parents watching her from inside the house. She thinks about how she is always alone, they are always giving her space. To have this fish for even a short time meant she didn't have to feel alone. As she buries the fish, she puts his castle next to him, because she doesn't want him to feel totally alone, like her.

Who is this for?

LEVELS

R–Z+

GENRE / TEXT TYPE

fiction

SKILLS

visualizing, inferring

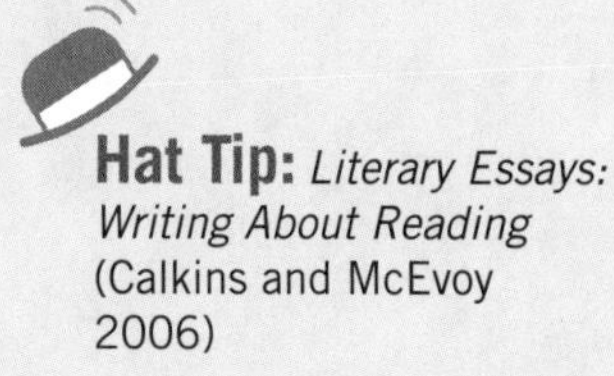

Hat Tip: *Literary Essays: Writing About Reading* (Calkins and McEvoy 2006)

13.22 Idea Connections

Who is this for?

LEVELS

R–Z+

GENRE / TEXT TYPE

any

SKILLS

synthesizing, interpreting, comparing and contrasting

Strategy Take several of your best ideas that you recorded on sticky notes as you read. Put them on an open page and look across them. Try to make connections between the ideas—either by putting them together, comparing the ideas, or contrasting the ideas.

Lesson Language *To take the thinking you do in the moment on a page and grow it into something larger, you can try to put ideas together. Sometimes you'll put them together and merge them into one greater idea. For example, if in one part of* Freedom Summer *(Wiles 2005) you noted "I think the spongy tar is a symbol" and in another place you noted "The narrator seems to admire John Henry," you might put those ideas together to grow an idea that incorporates both, such as "It takes a lot of courage to go against the grain, to not be stuck in what everyone expects or thinks of you." You might also put two ideas alongside each other and realize that you have something to say that brings about the differences in the idea. For example, if you said, "There is such disrespect in this place and time" and "The narrator seems to admire John Henry," you might see the difference here is between the children in the story, like John Henry and the adults, who are really the ones who perpetrate the negative stereotypes. The point of all of this is that by trying to see the relationships between your ideas, you'll hopefully develop new thinking.*

Prompts

- Is there a similarity between these ideas or do they express different things?
- Reread these two ideas. What are you thinking now?
- If you were to put these two ideas together and make a new statement, what would you say?
- Do these two ideas fit together under a common idea or theme?
- Who are these two ideas about? What are they about?
- When you look at this idea against a different idea, what do you notice?

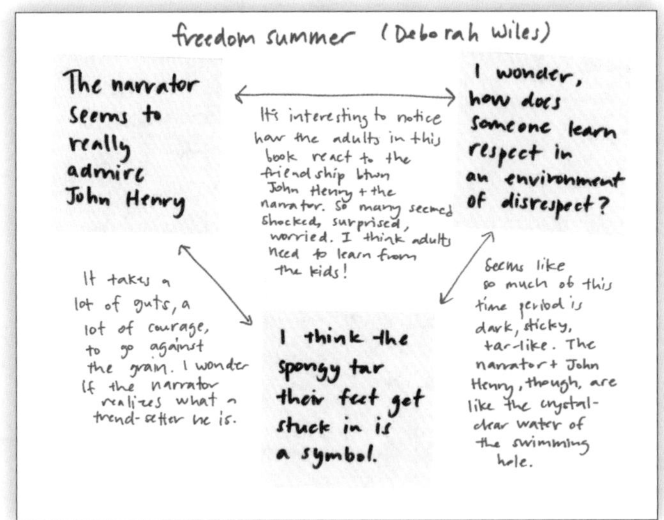

13.23 Pile It On

Strategy Collect all the jots that have to do with one idea. Look across them, to pile the ideas together. Write about a new idea that takes into account all the ideas on the sticky notes.

Teacher Tip: A similar strategy for helping students to synthesize ideas about character traits to form theories can be found in Chapter 6, page 186.

Lesson Language *Sometimes as we read and keep track of our thinking on sticky notes, we start to realize that we're tracking an idea over the course of the story. When we do, we can remove the sticky notes and lay them in a line, thinking about how we can pile one idea on top of the other. As we do, our idea may become clearer, more developed, or more complex. For example, if in one part of* The Other Side *(Woodson 2001) we say, "Her mom won't let her play. That's not fair." And then later notice the mother again and jot, "Her mother just wants to keep her safe." And then at the end say, "Now her mother is quiet. I think she sees she's safe." We might pile those ideas together to write about a new, more complex thought about the impact of the characters on one another, such as, "Sometimes parents worry too much and it takes their children to teach them to relax" or about a theme, "Segregation can cause people to fear the unknown."*

Prompts

- Look across your ideas. What do they have in common?
- Start writing, maybe a new idea will emerge.
- Start with, "So now I'm thinking . . ."
- What's a new idea you're having?
- It looks like you pushed your thinking and came up with a completely new idea!

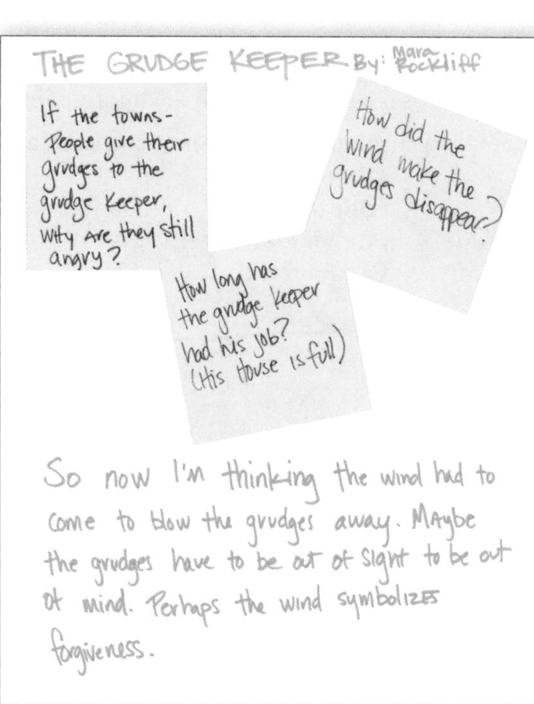

Who is this for?

LEVELS

R–Z+

GENRE / TEXT TYPE

fiction

SKILLS

synthesizing, interpreting, inferring

Hat Tip: Independent Reading Assessment: Fiction series (Serravallo 2012)

Appendix: Text Leveling Correlation Chart

Knowing text level characteristics coupled with knowing a reader's abilities can help us match students to texts, ensuring that their time spent reading is not a struggle, but rather an engaging time to explore books and work on goals. Levels also help us introduce the right strategies at the right time. Certain strategies simply won't work if they are too sophisticated for the sorts of texts the child is reading (for instance, I can't imagine I'd teach too many kindergarteners about tracking flashbacks and multiple plot lines). Other strategies are too simplistic and don't offer the student enough challenge (for instance, I wouldn't teach most eighth graders to get their mouth ready to say the first sound in a word.)

Once the first printings of this book were out in the world, I started to notice that some readers weren't always familiar with the leveling system I've chosen to use in this book, the Fountas and Pinnell Text Level Gradient™. For this reason, I'm including the following correlation chart to help you match the information in the margins to a more familiar leveling system if that's the case for you. Or, if you don't use any text leveling system, you can at least consider the typical range of levels associated with each grade.

The suggested correlations draw from a variety of sources including but not limited to: The Teachers College Reading and Writing Project's website, Common Core State Standards Appendix A, and Fountas and Pinnell's *Leveled Literacy Intervention* materials. There were slight variations in each of these sources, and an Internet search for "level correlation chart" easily yields a dozen more variations! What follows is a synthesis of all the information I collected and is simply a guide rather than an endorsement of these correlations.

Grade Level	Fountas and Pinnell Text Level Gradient™	Reading Recovery Level	DRA Level	Lexile Level
K	A–D	1–5/6	A–6	Up to 450
1	D–J	5/6–17	6–18	80–500
2	J–M	17–20	18–28	450–650
3	M–P	20–38	28–38	550–770
4	P–S	38–40	38–40	770–860
5	S–V	40–N/A	40–50	830–980
6	V–X	N/A	60	980–1030
7	X–Y	N/A	70	1030–1070
8	Y–Z+	N/A	80	1070–1155

Bibliography

Adler, David A. The Young Cam Jansen series. New York: Penguin Putnam Books for Young Readers.

_____. 1997. *A Picture Book of Jackie Robinson*. New York: Holiday House.

_____. 2004. *Cam Jansen: The Mystery of the Stolen Diamonds*. New York: Penguin Putnam Books for Young Readers.

Afflerbach, Peter P. 1990. "The Influence of Prior Knowledge on Expert Readers' Main Idea Construction Strategies." *Reading Research Quarterly* 25 (1): 31.

Afflerbach, Peter P., P. David Pearson, and Scott G. Paris. 2008. "Clarifying Differences Between Reading Skills and Reading Strategies." *The Reading Teacher* 61 (5): 364–73.

Akhavan, Nancy. 2014. *The Nonfiction Now Lesson Bank, Grades 4–8: Strategies and Routines for Higher-Level Comprehension in the Content Areas*. Thousand Oaks, CA: Corwin.

Allington, Richard L. 2011. *What Really Matters for Struggling Readers: Designing Research-Based Programs*. New York: Pearson.

Anderson, Richard C., Paul T. Wilson, and Linda G. Fielding. 1988. "Growth in Reading and How Children Spend Their Time Outside of School." *Reading Research Quarterly* 23 (3): 285–303.

Angelillo, Janet. 2003. *Writing About Reading: From Book Talk to Literary Essays, Grades 3–8*. Portsmouth, NH: Heinemann.

Applegate, Katherine. 2007. *Home of the Brave*. New York: Square Fish.

Archambault, John, and Bill Martin Jr. 2012. *Chicka Chicka Boom Boom*. New York: Little Simon.

Arlon, Penelope, and Tory Gordon-Harris. 2012a. *Farm*. New York: Scholastic.

_____. 2012b. *Penguins: Meet the Heroes of a Frozen World*. New York: Scholastic.

_____. 2012c. *See Me Grow*. New York: Scholastic.

Atwell, Nancie. 2007. *The Reading Zone: How to Help Kids Become Skilled, Passionate, Habitual, Critical Readers*. New York, NY: Scholastic.

_____. 2014. *In the Middle: A Lifetime of Learning About Writing, Reading, and Adolescents*, 3d ed. Portsmouth, NH: Heinemann.

Baglio, Ben M. 2002. *Dog at the Door*. New York: Scholastic

Barnhouse, Dorothy, and Vicki Vinton. 2012. *What Readers Really Do: Teaching the Process of Meaning Making*. Portsmouth, NH: Heinemann.

Barrows, Annie. 2007. *Ivy and Bean* (Book 1). San Francisco: Chronicle Books.

Baumann, James F., and Edward J. Kame'enui. 1991. "Research on Vocabulary Instruction: Ode to Voltaire." In *Handbook of Research on Teaching the English Language Arts*, edited by James Flood and Julie M. Jensen, 604–32. New York: Macmillan.

Baumann, James F., Edward J. Kame'enui, and Gwynne E. Ash. 2003. "Research on Vocabulary Instruction: Voltaire Redux." In *Handbook of Research on Teaching the English Language Arts*, edited by James Flood, Dianne Lapp, James R. Squire, and Julie M. Jensen, 752–85. Mahwah, NJ: Lawrence Erlbaum.

Bear, Donald, Marcia Invernizzi, Shane R. Templeton, and Francine A. Johnston. 2015. *Words Their Way*, 6th ed. New York: Pearson.

Beaver, Joetta, and Marc Carter. 2015. Developmental Reading Assessment, Grades 4–8, 2d ed. New York: Pearson.

Beck, Isabel L., Margaret G. McKeown, and Linda Kucan. 2013. *Bringing Words to Life: Robust Vocabulary Instruction,* 2d ed. New York: The Guilford Press.

Becker, Bonny. 2012. *A Visitor for Bear*. Somerville, MA: Candlewick Press.

Becker, Wesley C. 1977. "Teaching Reading and Language to the Disadvantaged—What We Have Learned from Field Research." *Harvard Educational Review* 47 (4): 518–43.

Beers, Kylene. 2002. *When Kids Can't Read—What Teachers Can Do: A Guide for Teachers 6–12.* Portsmouth, NH: Heinemann.

Beers, Kylene, and Robert Probst. 2012. *Notice and Note: Strategies for Close Reading.* Portsmouth, NH: Heinemann.

_____. 2016. *Reading Nonfiction: Notice & Note Stances, Signposts, and Questions*. Portsmouth, NH: Heinemann.

Benoit, Peter. 2011. *The Hindenburg Disaster*. New York: Scholastic.

Berger, Melvin. 1995. *Germs Make Me Sick!* New York: HarperCollins.

Betts, E. A. 1946. *Foundations of Reading Instruction, with Emphasis on Differentiated Guidance.* New York: American Book Company.

Bittman, Mark. 2008. *How to Cook Everything: 2,000 Simple Recipes for Great Food*, 10th ed. Hoboken, NJ: John Wiley & Sons.

Blume, Judy. 1970. *Are You There, God? It's Me, Margaret.* New York: Bantam Doubleday Dell Books for Young Readers.

_____. 2014. *Freckle Juice*. New York: Atheneum Books for Young Readers.

Boelts, Maribeth. 2009. *Those Shoes*. Somerville, MA: Candlewick Press.

Bomer, Randy, and Katherine Bomer. 2001. *For a Better World: Reading and Writing for Social Action*. Portsmouth, NH: Heinemann.

Boston, L. M. 2002. *An Enemy at Green Knowe*. Boston: HMH Books for Young Readers.

Boushey, Gail, and Joan Moser. 2014. *The Daily 5: Fostering Literacy in the Elementary Grades*, 2d ed. Portland, ME: Stenhouse Publishers.

Boyd, Candy Dawson. 1996. *Circle of Gold.* New York: Scholastic.

Boynton, Alice, and Wiley Blevins. 2007. *Navigating Nonfiction, Grade 3*. New York: Scholastic.

Brenner, Barbara. 1998. *If You Were There in 1492: Everyday Life in the Time of Columbus.* New York: Aladdin Paperbacks.

Brett, Jan. 2010. "Activities." http://janbrett.com/activities_pages.htm. Last accessed February 18, 2015.

Buckner, Aimee. 2009. *Notebook Connections: Strategies for the Reader's Notebook*. Portland, ME: Stenhouse Publishers.

Bunting, Eve. 1993. *Fly Away Home*. New York: Clarion Books.

_____. 2006. *One Green Apple.* New York: Clarion Books.

Burroway, Janet. 2006. *Imaginative Writing: The Elements of Craft*. New York: Longman.

Calkins, Lucy. 2000. *The Art of Teaching Reading*. New York: Pearson.

Calkins, Lucy, and colleagues. 2011a. *A Curricular Plan for the Reading Workshop, Grade K.* Portsmouth, NH: Heinemann.

_____. 2011b. *A Curricular Plan for the Reading Workshop, Grade 1.* Portsmouth, NH: Heinemann.

_____. 2011c. *A Curricular Plan for the Reading Workshop, Grade 4.* Portsmouth, NH: Heinemann.

_____. 2011d. *A Curricular Plan for the Writing Workshop, Grade 4.* Portsmouth, NH: Heinemann.

_____. 2013. The Units of Study in Opinion/Argument, Information, and Narrative Writing series. Portsmouth, NH: Heinemann.

Calkins, Lucy, and Madea McEvoy. 2006. *Literary Essays: Writing About Reading.* In *Units of Study for Teaching Writing, Grades 3–5* by Lucy Calkins and colleagues. Portsmouth, NH: Heinemann.

Calkins, Lucy, and Kathleen Tolan. 2010a. *Building a Reading Life: Stamina, Fluency, and Engagement.* In *Units of Student for Teaching Reading: A Curriculum for the Reading Workshop, Grades 3–5* by Lucy Calkins and colleagues. Portsmouth, NH: Heinemann.

_____. 2010b. *Following Characters into Meaning: Building Theories, Gathering Evidence.* In *Units of Study for Teaching Reading, Grades 3–5: A Curriculum for the Reading Workshop* by Lucy Calkins and colleagues. Portsmouth, NH: Heinemann.

_____. 2010c. *Navigating Nonfiction in Expository Text: Determining Importance and Synthesizing* (Volume 1). In *Units of Student for Teaching Reading, Grades 3–5: A Curriculum for the Reading Workshop* by Lucy Calkins and colleagues. Portsmouth, NH: Heinemann.

_____. 2010d. *Navigating Nonfiction in Narrative and Hybrid Text: Using Text Structures to Comprehend* (Volume 2). In *Units of Student for Teaching Reading, Grades 3–5: A Curriculum for the Reading Workshop* by Lucy Calkins and colleagues. Portsmouth, NH: Heinemann.

Cameron, Ann. 1987. *Julian's Glorious Summer.* New York: Yearling.

Carle, Eric. 1994. *The Very Hungry Caterpillar.* New York: Philomel Books.

Carver, Ronald P. 1994. "Percentage of Unknown Vocabulary Words in Text as a Function of the Relative Difficulty of the Text: Implications for Instruction." *Journal of Reading Behavior* 26 (4): 413–37.

Cazet, Denys. The Minnie and Moo series. New York: DK Children.

Cherry-Paul, Sonja, and Dana Johansen. 2014. *Teaching Interpretation: Using Text-Based Evidence to Construct Meaning.* Portsmouth, NH: Heinemann.

Clay, Marie. 1993. *Reading Recovery: A Guidebook for Teachers in Training.* Portsmouth, NH: Heinemann.

_____. 2000. *Running Records for Classroom Teachers.* Portsmouth, NH: Heinemann.

_____. 2001. *Change Over Time: In Children's Literacy Development.* Portsmouth, NH: Heinemann.

"Cleaning Up After Isaac." *Time for Kids.* September 2012.

Clements, Andrew. 2001. *Jake Drake, Bully Buster.* New York: Aladdin Paperbacks.

Cobb, Charlene, and Camille Blachowicz. 2014. *No More "Look Up the List" Vocabulary Instruction.* Portsmouth, NH: Heinemann.

Coerr, Eleanor. 2004. *Sadako and the Thousand Paper Cranes.* New York: Puffin Books.

Collins, Kathy. 2004. *Growing Readers: Units of Study in the Primary Classroom.* Portland, ME: Stenhouse Publishers.

_____. 2008. *Reading for Real: Teach Students to Read with Power, Intention, and Joy in K–3 Classrooms.* Portland, ME: Stenhouse Publishers.

Collins, Kathy, and Matt Glover. 2015. *I* Am *Reading: Nurturing Young Children's Meaning Making and Joyful Engagement with Any Book.* Portsmouth, NH: Heinemann.

"Coral Reefs in Trouble." *Time for Kids.* September 2012.

Creech, Sharon. 2005. *Granny Torrelli Makes Soup.* New York: HarperCollins.

Cristaldi, Kathryn. 1992. *Baseball Ballerina.* New York: Random House.

Csikszentmihalyi, Mihaly. 2008. *Flow: The Psychology of Optimal Experience.* New York, NY: Harper Perennial Modern Classics.

Cunningham, Patricia M. 1979. "A Compare/Contrast Theory of Mediated Word Identification." *The Reading Teacher* 7 (32): 774–78.

Cunningham, Patricia M., and Dorothy P. Hall. The Month-by-Month Phonics series. Greensboro, NC: Carson Dellosa Publishing.

Cunningham, Anna E., and Keith E. Stanovich. 1991. "Tracking the Unique Effects of Print Exposure in Children: Associations with Vocabulary, General Knowledge, and Spelling." *Journal of Educational Psychology* 83 (2): 264–74.

Curtis, Christopher. 1995. *The Watsons Go to Birmingham—1963*. New York: Delacorte Press.

Dahl, Roald. 1961. *James and the Giant Peach*. New York: Alfred A. Knopf, Inc.

_____. 1964. *Charlie and the Chocolate Factory*. New York: Alfred A. Knopf, Inc.

Daniels, Harvey. 1994. *Literature Circles: Voice and Choice in the Student-Centered Classroom*. Portland, ME: Stenhouse Publishers.

Danziger, Paula. 1995. *Amber Brown Is Not a Crayon*. New York: Scholastic.

Delpit, Lisa. 2006. *Other People's Children: Cultural Conflict in the Classroom*. New York: The New Press.

dePaola, Tomie. 1979. *Oliver Button Is a Sissy*. Boston: HMH Books for Young Readers.

DiCamillo, Kate. 2000. *Because of Winn-Dixie*. Somerville, MA: Candlewick Press.

_____. 2002. *The Tiger Rising*. Somerville, MA: Candlewick Press.

Dubowski, Cathy. 2009. *Shark Attack!* New York: DK Children.

Duke, Nell. 2014. *Inside Information: Developing Powerful Readers and Writers of Informational Text Through Project-Based Instruction*. New York: Scholastic.

Duke, Nell, and V. Susan Bennett-Armistead. 2003. *Reading & Writing Informational Text in the Primary Grades*. New York: Scholastic.

Dussling, Jennifer. 2011. *Bugs! Bugs! Bugs!* New York: DK Publishing.

Ehri, Linnea C., and Claudia Robbins. 1992. "Beginners Need Some Decoding Skills to Read Words by Analogy." *Reading Research Quarterly* 27: 12–27.

Falconer, Ian. 2004. *Olivia*. New York: Atheneum Books for Young Readers.

Feely, Jenny. 2012. *The Weather Today*. Temecula, CA: Okapi Educational Materials.

Fountas, Irene C., and Gay Su Pinnell. 2010a. *Benchmark Assessment System 1*, 2d ed. Portsmouth, NH: Heinemann.

_____. 2010b. *The Continuum of Literacy Learning, Grades PreK–8: A Guide to Teaching*, 2d ed. Portsmouth, NH: Heinemann.

Friedman, Mel. 2009. *Antarctica*. Danbury, CT: Children's Press.

Gantos, Jack. 2011. *Joey Pigza Swallowed the Key*. New York: Scholastic.

Gardiner, John Reynolds. *Stone Fox*. 2010. New York: HarperCollins.

Gibbons, Pauline. 1993. *Learning to Learn in a Second Language*. Portsmouth, NH: Heinemann.

_____. 2014. *Scaffolding Language, Scaffolding Learning: Teaching English Language Learners in the Mainstream Classroom*, 2d ed. Portsmouth, NH: Heinemann.

Goodman, Yetta M., Dorothy J. Watson, and Carolyn L. Burke. 2005. *Reading Miscue Inventory: From Evaluation to Instruction*. Katonah, NY: Richard C. Owens Publishers, Inc.

Guthrie, John T., Allan Wigfield, and Wei You. 2012. "Instructional Contexts for Engagement and Achievement in Reading." In *Handbook of Research on Student Engagement*, edited by Sandra L. Christenson, Amy L. Reschly, and Cathy Wylie, 601–34. New York: Springer Publishing Company.

Harris, Theodore Lester, and Richard E. Hodges, eds. 1995. *The Literacy Dictionary: The Vocabulary of Reading and Writing.* Newark, DE: The International Reading Association.

Harvey, Stephanie. 2014. "Thinking Intensive Learning: Close Reading Is Strategic Reading." Presentation at the annual meeting of the National Council of Teachers of English. Washington, DC.

Harvey, Stephanie, and Anne Goudvis. 2000. *Strategies That Work: Teaching Comprehension for Understanding and Engagement.* Portland, ME: Stenhouse Publishers.

_____. 2005. *The Comprehension Toolkit: Language and Lessons for Active Literacy, Grades 3–6.* Portsmouth, NH: Heinemann.

_____. 2007. *Strategies That Work: Teaching Comprehension for Understanding and Engagement,* 2d ed. Portland, ME: Stenhouse Publishers.

Harvey, Stephanie, Anne Goudvis, and Judy Wallis. 2010. *Comprehension Intervention: Small-Group Lessons for the Comprehension Toolkit, Grades 3–6.* Portsmouth, NH: Heinemann.

Hattie, John. 2009. *Visible Learning: A Synthesis of Over 800 Meta-Analyses Relating to Achievement.* New York: Routledge.

Heard, Georgia. 2014. *The Revision Toolbox: Teaching Techniques That Work,* 2d ed. Portsmouth, NH: Heinemann.

Henkes, Kevin. "For Teachers, Librarians and Parents." www.kevinhenkes.com/for-teachers-librarians-parents/. Last accessed February 18, 2015.

Hesse, Karen. 2009. *Out of the Dust.* New York: Scholastic.

Hjemboe, Karen. 2000. *My Horse.* New York: Lee & Low Books.

Howe, James. The Pinky and Rex series. New York: Simon Spotlight.

_____. 1996. *Pinky and Rex and the Bully.* New York: Simon Spotlight.

_____. 1998. *Pinky and Rex and the Perfect Pumpkin.* New York: Simon Spotlight.

Hoyt, Linda. 2008. *Revisit, Reflect, Retell: Time-Tested Strategies for Teaching Reading Comprehension.* Portsmouth, NH: Heinemann.

Hsueh-chao, Marcella Hu, and Paul Nation. 2000. "Unknown Vocabulary Density and Reading Comprehension." *Reading in a Foreign Language* 13 (1): 403–30.

Irvine, Sarah. 2007. *No Animals, No Plants: Species at Risk.* New York: Scholastic.

Ivey, Gay, and Peter H. Johnston. 2013. "Engagement with Young Adult Literature: Outcomes and Processes." *Reading Research Quarterly* 48 (3): 1–21.

Johnson, Dolores. 2002. *We Play Music.* New York: Lee & Low Books.

Johnston, Peter. 2004. *Choice Words.* Portland, ME: Stenhouse Publishers.

Jones, Stephanie. 2006. *Girls, Social Class, and Literacy: What Teachers Can Do to Make a Difference.* Portsmouth, NH: Heinemann.

Juzwik, Mary. 2009. *The Rhetoric of Teaching: Understanding the Dynamics of Holocaust Narratives in an English Classroom.* New York: Hampton Press.

Kalman, Bobbie. 1996. *Sea Otters.* New York: Crabtree Publishing.

_____. 1999. *What Is a Primate?* New York: Crabtree Publishing.

Keene, Ellin Oliver. 2006. *Assessing Comprehension Thinking Strategies.* Huntington Beach, CA: Shell Education.

_____. 2008. *To Understand: New Horizons in Reading Comprehension.* Portsmouth, NH: Heinemann.

_____. 2012. *Talk About Understanding: Rethinking Classroom Talk to Enhance Comprehension.* Portsmouth, NH: Heinemann.

Keene, Ellin Oliver, and Susan Zimmermann. 2007. *Mosaic of Thought: The Power of Comprehension Strategy Instruction*, 2d ed. Portsmouth, NH: Heinemann.

Kenney, Karen L. 2007. *Harsh or Heroic? The Middle Ages*. Danbury, CT: Children's Press.

Kent, Deborah. 1993. *The Titanic*. Danbury, CT: Children's Press.

Kline, Suzy. 1997. *Horrible Harry in Room 2B*. New York: Puffin Books.

Kramer, Sydelle. 1993. *To the Top! Climbing the World's Highest Mountain*. New York: Random House Books for Young Readers.

Krashen, Stephen. 2004. *The Power of Reading: Insights from the Research*, 2d ed. Englewood, CO: Libraries Unlimited.

Kuhn, Melanie R. 2008. *The Hows and Whys of Fluency Instruction*. New York: Pearson.

Landau, Elaine. 2003. *The Civil Rights Movement in America*. New York: Scholastic.

Laufer, Batia. 1988. "What Percentage of Text-Lexis Is Essential for Comprehension?" In *Special Language: From Humans Thinking to Thinking Machines*, edited by Christer Laurén and Marianne Nordman, 316–23. Clevedon, UK: Multilingual Matters.

Lehman, Chris, and Kate Roberts. 2014. *Falling in Love with Close Reading: Lessons for Analyzing Texts—and Life*. Portsmouth, NH: Heinemann.

L'Engle, Madeleine. 1962. *A Wrinkle in Time*. New York: Square Fish.

Lesesne, Teri. 2010. *Reading Ladders: Leading Students from Where They Are to Where We'd Like Them to Be*. Portsmouth, NH: Heinemann.

Levine, Ellin. 2007. *Henry's Freedom Box*. New York: Scholastic.

Lobel, Arnold. The Frog and Toad series. New York: HarperCollins.

_____. 1979. *Days with Frog and Toad*. New York: HarperCollins.

Lowry, Lois. 2009. *Crow Call*. New York: Scholastic.

Macken, JoAnn. 2005. *Bighorn Sheep*. Pleasantville, NY: Weekly Reader Early Learning.

Martin, Bill. 2010. *Brown Bear, Brown Bear, What Do You See?* New York: Henry Holt and Co.

Martinelli, Marjorie, and Kristine Mraz. 2012. *Smarter Charts, K–2: Optimizing an Instructional Staple to Create Independent Readers and Writers*. Portsmouth, NH: Heinemann.

_____. 2014. "Smarter Charts: Bringing Charting to Life." Heinemann Digital Campus Course. Portsmouth, NH: Heinemann.

Marzollo, Claudio. 1992. *Kenny and the Little Kickers*. New York: Cartwheel Books.

McDonald, Megan. 2001. *Judy Moody Gets Famous!* Somerville, MA: Candlewick Press.

_____. 2010. *Judy Moody Was in a Mood*. Somerville, MA: Candlewick Press.

Miller, Debbie. 2012. *Reading with Meaning: Teaching Comprehension in the Primary Grades*, 2d ed. Portland, ME: Stenhouse Publishers.

Miller, Donalyn. 2009. *The Book Whisperer: Awakening the Inner Reader in Every Child*. San Francisco: Jossey-Bass.

Miller, George A. 1999. "On Knowing a Word." *Annual Review of Psychology* 50: 1–19.

Monjo, F. N. 1970. *The Drinking Gourd: A Story of the Underground Railroad*. New York: HarperCollins.

Mraz, Kristine, and Marjorie Martinelli. "Chart Chums." chartchums.wordpress.com. Last accessed March 10, 2015.

_____. 2014. *Smarter Charts for Math, Science & Social Studies: Making Learning Visible in the Content Areas*. Portsmouth, NH: Heinemann.

Nagy, William E., Richard C. Anderson, and Patricia A. Herman. 1987. "Learning Word Meanings from Context During Normal Reading." *American Educational Research Journal* 24 (2): 237–70.

National Association of Independent Schools. 2010. "Sample Cultural Identifiers." www.nais.org /Articles/Pages/Sample-Cultural-Identifiers.aspx. Last accessed February 14, 2015.

National Reading Panel. 2000. *Teaching Children to Read: An Evidence-Based Assessment of the Scientific Research Literature on Reading and Its Implications for Reading Instruction.* Bethesda, MD: National Institutes of Health.

Nelson, Robin. 2009. *Life Cycles: Worms.* Minneapolis, MN: Lerner Publishing.

Newkirk, Barbara. 2000. *Bedtime Fun.* New York: Lee & Low Books.

Newkirk, Thomas. 2011. *The Art of Slow Reading: Six Time-Honored Practices for Engagement.* Portsmouth, NH: Heinemann.

Newman, Sandra. 2010. *Ancient Greece.* New York: Scholastic.

Nichols, Maria. 2006. *Comprehension Through Conversation: The Power of Purposeful Talk in the Reading Workshop.* Portsmouth, NH: Heinemann.

Nicklin, Flip, and Linda Nicklin. 2008. *Face to Face with Whales.* Washington, DC: National Geographic Children's Books.

Osborne, Mary Pope. The Magic Tree House series. New York: Random House.

Owocki, Gretchen. 2012. *The Common Core Lesson Book, K–5: Working with Increasingly Complex Literature, Informational Text, and Foundational Reading Skills.* Portsmouth, NH: Heinemann.

Oxenbury, Helen, and Michael Rosen. 1997. *We're Going on a Bear Hunt.* New York: Little Simon.

Palacio, R. J. 2012. *Wonder.* New York: Knopf Books for Young Readers.

Parkes, Brenda. 2000. *Read It Again! Revisiting Shared Reading.* Portland, ME: Stenhouse Publishers.

Parkes, Brenda, and Judith Smith. 1989. *The Little Red Hen.* Pelham, NY: Benchmark Education.

Parks, Deborah. 2003. *Getting Physical: The Science of Sports.* New York: Scholastic.

Parragon. 2012. *Horses and Ponies.* New York: Discovery Kids.

Paterson, Katherine. 1978. *The Great Gilly Hopkins.* New York: HarperCollins Children's Books.

Pearson, P. D., and M. C. Gallagher. 1983. "The Instruction of Reading Comprehension." *Contemporary Educational Psychology* 8: 317–44.

Peterson, John. 1978. *The Littles Go Exploring.* New York: Scholastic.

Peterson, Margareth E. and Leonard P. Haines. 1992. "Orthographic Analogy Training with Kindergarten Children: Effects of Analogy Use, Phonemic Segmentation, and Letter-Sound Knowledge." *Journal of Reading Behavior* 24: 109–127.

Pink, Daniel. 2009. *Drive: The Surprising Truth about What Motivates Us.* New York: Penguin Books.

Pinkney, Andrea. 2008. *Boycott Blues: How Rosa Parks Inspired a Nation.* New York: HarperCollins.

Podendorf, Illa. 1982. *Jungles.* Danbury, CT: Children's Press.

Polacco, Patricia. "Activity Ideas." http://patriciapolacco.com/participation/activity_ideas/index.html. Last accessed February 18, 2015.

Porcelli, Alison, and Cheryl Tyler. 2008. *A Quick Guide to Boosting English Acquisition in Choice Time, K–2.* Portsmouth, NH: Heinemann.

Pressley, Michael, R. Wharton-McDonald, R. Allington, C. Block, L. Morrow, D. Tracey, K. Baker, G. Brooks, J. Cronin, E. Nelson, and D. Woo. 2000. "A Study of Effective First-Grade Reading Instruction." *Scientific Studies of Reading* 5: 35–38.

Pressley, Michael, and Richard L. Allington. 2015. "Skills Emphasis, Meaning Emphasis, and Balanced Reading Instruction." In *Reading Instruction That Works*, 4th ed. New York: Guildford Press.

Purcell-Gates, Victoria, Nell Duke, and Joseph A. Martineau. 2007. "Learning to Read and Write Genre-Specific Text: Roles of Authentic Experience and Explicit Teaching." *Reading Research Quarterly* 42 (1): 8–45.

Rasinski, Timothy V. 2010. *The Fluent Reader: Oral and Silent Reading Strategies for Building Fluency, Word Recognition and Comprehension*, 2d ed. New York: Scholastic.

Ray, Katie W., and Matt Glover. 2008. *Already Ready: Nurturing Writers in Preschool and Kindergarten*. Portsmouth, NH: Heinemann.

Richardson, Jan, and Maria Walther. Next Step Guided Reading Assessment series. New York: Scholastic.

Robb, Laura. 2014. *Vocabulary Is Comprehension: Getting to the Root of Text Complexity*. Thousand Oaks, CA: Corwin.

Roberts, Kate, and Maggie Beattie Roberts. 2014. "Teaching Beyond the Main Idea: Nonfiction and Point of View (Part I)." kateandmaggie.com/2014/02/05/teaching-beyond-the-main-idea-nonfiction-and-point-of-view-part-i/. Last accessed February 18, 2015.

Roberts, Kate, and Katy Wischow. 2014. *The Literary Essay: Analyzing Craft and Theme*. In *Units of Study in Argument, Information, and Narrative Writing: A Common Core Workshop Curriculum* by Lucy Calkins and colleagues. Portsmouth, NH: Heinemann.

Rosenblatt, Louise. 1978. *The Reader, the Text, the Poem: The Transactional Theory of the Literary Work*. Carbondale, IL: Southern Illinois University Press.

Routman, Regie. 1994. *Invitations: Changing as Teachers and Learners K–12*. Portsmouth, NH: Heinemann.

Rowling, J. K. 1998. *Harry Potter and the Sorcerer's Stone*. New York: Scholastic.

Rupley, William H., John W. Logan, and William D. Nichols. 1998/1999. "Vocabulary Instruction in a Balanced Reading Program." *The Reading Teacher* 52 (4): 336-46.

Ryan, Pam Muñoz. 2000. *Esperanza Rising*. New York: Scholastic.

Rylant, Cynthia. The Henry and Mudge series. New York: Aladdin Paperbacks.

_____. The Poppleton series. New York: Scholastic.

_____. The Mr. Putter and Tabby series. Boston: HMH Books for Young Readers.

_____. 1988. *Every Living Thing*. Parsippany, NJ: Modern Curriculum Press.

_____. 1997. *Poppleton*. New York: Scholastic.

_____. 1998. *Poppleton Everyday*. New York: Scholastic.

Santman, Donna. 2005. *Shades of Meaning: Comprehension and Interpretation in Middle School*. Portsmouth, NH: Heinemann.

Serafini, Frank. 2001. *The Reading Workshop: Creating Space for Readers*. Portsmouth, NH: Heinemann.

Serravallo, Jennifer. 2010. *Teaching Reading in Small Groups: Differentiated Instruction for Building Strategic, Independent Readers*. Portsmouth, NH: Heinemann.

_____. 2012. Independent Reading Assessment: Fiction series. New York: Scholastic.

_____. 2013a. Independent Reading Assessment: Nonfiction series. New York: Scholastic.

_____. 2013b. *The Literacy Teacher's Playbook, Grades 3–6: Four Steps for Turning Assessment Data into Goal-Directed Instruction*. Portsmouth, NH: Heinemann.

______. 2013c. "Teaching Reading in Small Groups: Matching Methods to Purposes." Heinemann Digital Campus Course. Portsmouth, NH: Heinemann.

______. 2014. *The Literacy Teacher's Playbook, Grades K–2: Four Steps for Turning Assessment Data into Goal-Directed Instruction*. Portsmouth, NH: Heinemann.

Serravallo, Jennifer, and Gravity Goldberg. 2007. *Conferring with Readers: Supporting Each Student's Growth and Independence*. Portsmouth, NH: Heinemann.

Settel, Joanne. 1999. *Exploding Ants: Amazing Facts About How Animals Adapt.* New York: Atheneum Books for Young Readers.

Shanahan, Kerrie. 2012a. *Amazing Salamanders*. Temecula, CA: Okapi Educational Materials.

______. 2012b. *Animals That Store Food*. Temecula, CA: Okapi Educational Materials.

Sharmat, Marjorie W. 1982. *Nate the Great and the Missing Key*. New York: Bantam Doubleday Dell Books for Young Readers.

Simon, Seymour. 2003. *The Moon*. New York: Simon and Schuster.

______. 2006. *Sharks*. San Francisco, CA: Chronicle Books.

Sinatra, Gale M., Kathleen J. Brown, and Ralph E. Reynolds. 2002. "Implications of Cognitive Resource Allocation for Comprehension Strategies Instruction." In *Comprehension Instruction: Research-Based Best Practices*, edited by Cathy Collins Block and Michael Pressley, 62–76. New York: Guilford Press.

Slobodkina, Esphyr. 1987. *Caps for Sale: A Tale of a Peddler, Some Monkeys and Their Monkey Business*. New York: HarperCollins.

Smith, Michael, and Jeffrey Willhelm. 2010. *Fresh Takes on Teaching Literary Elements: How to Teach What Really Matters About Character, Setting, Point of View, and Theme*. New York: Scholastic.

Smith, Robert Kimmel. 2006. *Chocolate Fever*. New York: Puffin.

Snicket, Lemony. 1999. *A Series of Unfortunate Events, Book 1: The Bad Beginning*. New York: HarperCollins Children's Books.

Snowball, Diane, and Faye Bolton. 1999. *Spelling K–8: Planning and Teaching*. Portland, ME: Stenhouse Publishers.

Sonnenblick, Jordan. 2013. *Are You Experienced?* New York: Feiwel and Friends.

Spinelli, Jerry. 1993. *Fourth Grade Rats*. New York: Scholastic.

______. 2002. *Loser*. New York: HarperCollins Children's Books.

______. 2004. *Crash*. New York: Dell Laurel-Leaf.

Stahl, Steven A., and Patricia D. Miller. 1989. "Whole Language and Language Experience Approaches for Beginning Reading: A Quantitative Research Synthesis." *Review of Educational Research* 59 (1): 87–116.

Stanovich, Keith E. 1986. "Matthew Effects in Reading: Some Consequences of Individual Differences in the Acquisition of Literacy." *Reading Research Quarterly* 21 (4): 360–407.

Stanovich, Keith E., and Anna E. Cunningham. 1993. "Where Does Knowledge Come From? Specific Associations Between Print Exposure and Information Acquisition." *Journal of Educational Psychology* 85 (2): 211–29.

Steig, William. 1969. *Sylvester and the Magic Pebble*. New York: Aladdin Paperbacks.

______. 1971. *Amos and Boris*. New York: Ferrar, Straus and Giroux.

Stolberg, Tina. 2003. *Moving Day Surprise*. New York: Lee & Low Books.

Sulzby, Elizabeth. 1985. "Children's Emergent Reading of Favorite Storybooks: A Developmental Study." *Reading Research Quarterly* 20 (4): 458–81.

Sulzby, Elizabeth, and William Teale. 1991. "Emergent Literacy." In *Handbook of Reading Research*, Vol. 2, edited by R. Barr, M. L. Kamil, P. B. Mosenthan, and P. D. Pearson, 727–58. New York: Longman.

Taberski, Sharon. 2000. *On Solid Ground: Strategies for Teaching Reading, K–3.* Portsmouth, NH: Heinemann.

_____. 2011. *Comprehension from the Ground Up: Simplified, Sensible Instruction for the K–3 Reading Workshop*. Portsmouth, NH: Heinemann.

Taylor, Barbara M., Barbara J. Frye, and Geoffrey M. Maruyama. 1990. "Time Spent Reading and Reading Growth." *American Educational Research Journal* 27 (2): 351–62.

Teachers College Reading and Writing Project. 2014. "Resources." http://readingandwritingproject.org/resources. Last accessed February 18, 2015.

Thaler, Mike. 2010. *The Book Report from the Black Lagoon.* New York: Scholastic.

Tovani, Cris. 2004. *Do I Really Have to Teach Reading? Content Comprehension, Grades 6–12.* Portland, ME: Stenhouse Publishers.

Von Sprecken, Debra, Jiyoung Kim, and Stephen Krashen. 2000. "The Home Run Book: Can One Positive Reading Experience Create a Reader?" *California School Library Journal* 23 (2): 8–9.

White, E. B. 1952. *Charlotte's Web*. New York: Harper & Brothers.

"White House Turned 200!" *Scholastic News* 63 (5): 4, October 9, 2000.

White, Zoe Ryder. 2008. *Playing with Poems: Word Study Lessons for Shared Reading, K–2.* Portsmouth, NH: Heinemann.

Wiggins, Grant. 2013. "On So-Called 'Reading Strategies'—The Utter Mess That Is the Literature and Advice to Teachers." http://grantwiggins.wordpress.com/2013/03/04/on-so-called-reading-strategies-the-utter-mess-that-is-the-literature-and-advice-to-teachers/. Last accessed December 1, 2014.

Wilde, Sandra. 2000. *Miscue Analysis Made Easy: Building on Student Strengths.* Portsmouth, NH: Heinemann.

Wiles, Deborah. 2005. *Freedom Summer.* New York: Alladin.

Wilhelm, Jeffrey D., Tanya N. Baker, and Julie Dube. 2001. *Strategic Reading: Getting Students to Lifelong Literacy, 6–12.* Portsmouth, NH: Boynton/Cook Publishers, Inc.

Willems, Mo. 2004. *Knuffle Bunny: A Cautionary Tale*. New York: Hyperion Books for Children.

Woodson, Jacqueline. 2001. *The Other Side.* New York: Putnam Juvenile.

Woolley, Marilyn. 2012. *Amazing Sea Lizards.* Temecula, CA: Okapi Educational Materials.

Zion, Gene. 2006. *Harry the Dirty Dog.* New York: HarperCollins.